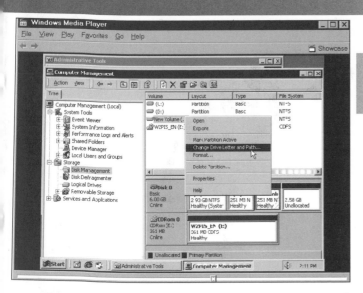

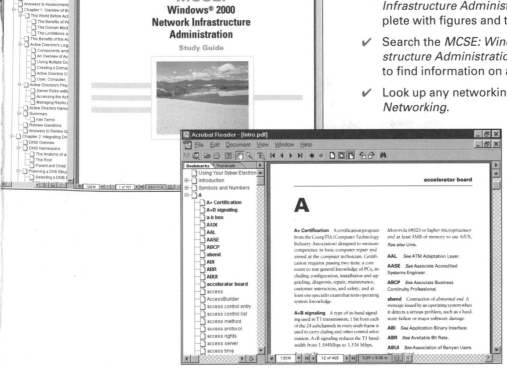

Prepare for Microsoft's tough simulation questions with the brand-new WinSim 2000 program!

✓ Use the simulators to guide you through real-world tasks step-by-step, or watch the movies to see the "invisible hand" perform the tasks for you.

Search through two complete books in PDF— MCSE: Windows 2000 Network Infrastructure Administration Study Guide *and the* Dictionary of Networking!

✓ Access the entire *MCSE: Windows 2000 Network Infrastructure Administration Study Guide*, complete with figures and tables, in electronic format.

✓ Search the *MCSE: Windows 2000 Network Infrastructure Administration Study Guide* chapters to find information on any topic in seconds.

✓ Look up any networking term in the *Dictionary of Networking*.

SYBEX

MCSE: Windows 2000 Network Infrastructure Administration Study Guide

Exam 70-216: Objectives

OBJECTIVE	PAGE
Installing, Configuring, Managing, Monitoring, and Troubleshooting DNS in a Windows 2000 Network Infrastructure	
Install, configure, and troubleshoot DNS.	
Install the DNS Server service; Configure a root name server; Configure zones; Configure a caching-only server; Configure a DNS client; Configure zones for dynamic updates; Test the DNS Server service; Implement a delegated zone for DNS; Manually create DNS resource records.	189, 191, 193, 197, 202, 204, 205, 207, 483
Manage and monitor DNS.	207
Installing, Configuring, Managing, Monitoring, and Troubleshooting DHCP in a Windows 2000 Network Infrastructure	
Install, configure, and troubleshoot DHCP.	
Install the DHCP Server service; Create and manage DHCP scopes, superscopes, and multicast scopes; Configure DHCP for DNS integration; Authorize a DHCP server in Active Directory.	150, 152, 153, 170
Manage and monitor DHCP.	173
Configuring, Managing, Monitoring, and Troubleshooting Remote Access in a Windows 2000 Network Infrastructure	
Configure and troubleshoot remote access.	
Configure inbound connections; Create a remote access policy; Configure a remote access profile; Configure a virtual private network (VPN); Configure multilink connections; Configure Routing and Remote Access for DHCP Integration.	348, 350, 358, 363, 382, 412, 502
Manage and monitor remote access.	375
Configure remote access security.	
Configure authentication protocols; Configure encryption protocols; Create a remote access policy.	368, 358, 371
Installing, Configuring, Managing, Monitoring, and Troubleshooting Network Protocols in a Windows 2000 Network Infrastructure	
Install, configure, and troubleshoot network protocols.	
Install and configure TCP/IP; Install the NWLink protocol; Configure network bindings.	113, 116, 124
Configure TCP/IP packet filters.	325

SYBEX

NOTE Exam objectives are subject to change at any time without prior notice and at Microsoft's sole discretion. Please visit Microsoft's Training & Certification Web site (www.microsoft.com/trainingandservices) for the most current listing of exam objectives.

SYBEX

MCSE:
Windows 2000
Network Infrastructure
Administration
Study Guide

MCSE:
Windows® 2000 Network Infrastructure Administration

Study Guide

Paul Robichaux

with James Chellis

San Francisco • Paris • Düsseldorf • Soest • London

SYBEX

Associate Publisher: Neil Edde
Contracts and Licensing Manager: Kristine O'Callaghan
Developmental Editor: Dann McDorman
Associate Developmental Editor: Benjamin Tomkins
Editor: Donna Crossman
Production Editors: Jennifer Campbell, Shannon Murphy
Technical Editors: Donald Fuller, Scott Warmbrand
Book Designer: Bill Gibson
Graphic Illustrator: Tony Jonick
Electronic Publishing Specialist: Bill Gibson
Proofreaders: Kimberly August, Erika Donald, Amey Garber, Jennifer Greiman, Camera Obscura, Nancy Riddiough
Indexer: Matthew Spence
CD Coordinator: Kara Eve Schwartz
CD Technician: Keith McNeil
Cover Design: Archer Design
Cover Photograph: Natural Selection

Library of Congress Card Number: 00-103813

ISBN: 0-7821-2755-X

SYBEX

To Our Valued Readers:

In recent years, Microsoft's MCSE program has established itself as the premier computer and networking industry certification. Nearly a quarter of a million IT professionals have attained MCSE status in the NT 4 track. Sybex is proud to have helped thousands of MCSE candidates prepare for their exams over these years, and we are excited about the opportunity to continue to provide people with the skills they'll need to succeed in the highly competitive IT industry.

For the Windows 2000 MCSE track, Microsoft has made it their mission to demand more of exam candidates. Exam developers have gone to great lengths to raise the bar in order to prevent a paper-certification syndrome, one in which individuals obtain a certification without a thorough understanding of the technology. Sybex welcomes this new philosophy as we have always advocated a comprehensive instructional approach to certification courseware. It has always been Sybex's mission to teach exam candidates how new technologies work in the real world, not to simply feed them answers to test questions. Sybex was founded on the premise of providing technical skills to IT professionals, and we have continued to build on that foundation, making significant improvements to our study guides based on feedback from readers, suggestions from instructors, and comments from industry leaders.

The depth and breadth of technical knowledge required to obtain Microsoft's new Windows 2000 MCSE is staggering. Sybex has assembled some of the most technically skilled instructors in the industry to write our study guides, and we're confident that our Windows 2000 MCSE study guides will meet and exceed the demanding standards both of Microsoft and you, the exam candidate.

Good luck in pursuit of your MCSE!

Neil Edde
Associate Publisher—Certification
Sybex, Inc.

SYBEX Inc. 1151 Marina Village Parkway, Alameda, CA 94501
Tel: 510/523-8233   Fax: 510/523-2373   HTTP://www.sybex.com

Acknowledgments

This book was an exciting project for a number of reasons. MCSE books are always especially demanding, since they have to accurately present the right information for you to pass the test, and what's "right" isn't always clear from the Microsoft exam objectives! In this case, I was fortunate to be aided by a great group of editors and production professionals at Sybex. My thanks to Dann McDorman, Ben Tomkins, Neil Edde, Skye McKay, Donna Crossman, Jennifer Campbell, and Shannon Murphy—and that's just on the editorial side! A number of unsung heroes handled the mind-numbing tasks of laying out the book, producing illustrations, and all the other drudge work required to turn a manuscript into a finished book. These heroes include Donald Fuller, Scott Warmbrand, Tony Jonick, Bill Gibson, Keith McNeil, Kara Schwartz, Brianne Agatep, Marilyn Smith, Jeff Gammon, Rebecca Rider, Julie Sakaue, Liz Paulus, Rachel Boyce, Malka Geffen, Rodda Leage, and Stacey Gerson.

My friends at StudioB Productions did their usual excellent job handling the business end of the project; my thanks to David Talbott, David Rogelberg, Sherry Rogelberg, and Kristin Pickens for their efforts.

Jerry Condon and Ned Studt of EntireNet were astonishingly patient as the schedule for this book made a train wreck of my work for them; I appreciate their understanding and patience.

Finally, I am blessed with a wonderful wife and two sons who understand that working at home isn't just an all-day pajama party. They make my life a daily joy, and I am thankful to them for their help, support, and love, and I am thankful to God for sending them to me.

—Paul Robichaux with James Chellis

Contents at a Glance

Contents

ICSE: Windows 2000 Network Infrastructure dministration Study Guide

am 70-216: Objectives

Exam objectives are subject to change at any time without prior notice and at Microsoft's sole discretion. Please visit Microsoft's Training & Certification Web site (www.microsoft.com/trainingandservices) for the most current listing of exam objectives.

SYBEX

Table of Exercises

Introduction

Microsoft's new Microsoft Certified Systems Engineer (MCSE) track for Windows 2000 is the premier certification for computer industry professionals. Covering the core technologies around which Microsoft's future will be built, the new MCSE certification is a powerful credential for career advancement.

This book has been developed, in cooperation with Microsoft Corporation, to give you the critical skills and knowledge you need to prepare for one of the core requirements of the new MCSE certification program for Windows 2000. You will find the information you need to acquire a solid understanding of Windows 2000's network tools and concepts, to prepare for Exam #70-216: Implementing and Administering a Microsoft® Windows® 2000 Network Infrastructure, and to progress toward MCSE certification.

Why Become Certified in Windows 2000?

As the computer network industry grows in both size and complexity, the need for *proven* ability is increasing. Companies rely on certifications to verify the skills of prospective employees and contractors.

Whether you are just getting started or are ready to move ahead in the computer industry, the knowledge, skills, and credentials you have are your most valuable assets. Microsoft has developed its Microsoft Certified Professional (MCP) program to give you credentials that verify your ability to work with Microsoft products effectively and professionally. The MCP credential for professionals who work with Microsoft Windows 2000 networks is the new MCSE certification.

Over the next few years, companies around the world will deploy millions of copies of Windows 2000 as the central operating system for their mission-critical networks. This will generate an enormous need for qualified consultants and personnel to design, deploy, and support Windows 2000 networks.

Windows 2000 is a huge product that requires professional skills of its administrators. Consider that Windows NT 4 has about 12 million lines of code, while Windows 2000 has more than 35 million! Much of this code is needed to deal with the wide range of functionality that Windows 2000 offers.

Windows 2000 actually consists of several different versions:

Windows 2000 Professional The client edition of Windows 2000, which is comparable to Windows NT 4 Workstation, but also includes the best features of Windows 98 and many new features.

Windows 2000 Server/Windows 2000 Advanced Server A server edition of Windows 2000 for small to mid-sized deployments. Advanced Server supports more memory and processors than Server does.

Windows 2000 Datacenter Server A server edition of Windows 2000 for large, wide-scale deployments and computer clusters. Datacenter Server supports the most memory and processors of the three versions.

With such an expansive operating system, companies need to be certain that you are the right person for the job being offered. The MCSE is designed to help prove that you are.

 As part of its promotion of Windows 2000, Microsoft has announced that MCSEs who have passed the Windows NT 4 core exams must upgrade their certifications to the new Windows 2000 track by December 31, 2001, to remain certified. The Sybex MCSE Study Guide series, published by Sybex, covers the full range of exams required for either obtaining or upgrading your certification. For more information, see the "Exam Requirements" section later in this Introduction.

Is This Book for You?

If you want to acquire a solid foundation in Windows 2000 network infrastructure management, this book is for you. You'll find clear explanations of the fundamental concepts you need to grasp.

If you want to become certified as an MCSE, this book is definitely for you. However, if you just want to attempt to pass the exam without really understanding Windows 2000, this book is *not* for you. This book is written for those who want to acquire hands-on skills and in-depth knowledge of Windows 2000.

If your goal is to prepare for the exam by learning how to use and manage the new operating system, this book is for you. It will help you to achieve the high level of professional competency you need to succeed in this field.

What Does This Book Cover?

This book contains detailed explanations, hands-on exercises, and review questions to test your knowledge.

Think of this book as your complete guide to Windows 2000's networking tools and services. It begins by covering the most basic concepts, such as the fundamentals underlying TCP/IP and what network services Windows 2000 offers. Each chapter teaches you how to perform important tasks, including the following:

- Configuring IP routing, remote access, and virtual private networking

- Configuring and managing a Domain Name Service (DNS) server

- Configuring a Windows 2000 certificate authority

- Configuring and managing Windows Internet Name Service (WINS) and Dynamic Host Configuration Protocol (DHCP)

You will also learn how to configure aspects of the operating system, tune your server's performance, work with applications, and troubleshoot your system.

Throughout the book, you will be guided through hands-on exercises, which give you practical experience for each exam objective. At the end of each chapter, you'll find a summary of the topics covered in the chapter, which also includes a list of the key terms used in that chapter. The key terms represent not only the terminology that you should recognize, but also the underlying concepts that you should understand to pass the exam. All of the key terms are defined in the glossary at the back of the study guide.

Finally, each chapter concludes with 20 review questions that test your knowledge of the information covered. You'll find an entire practice exam, with 50 additional questions, in Appendix A. Many more questions, as well as multimedia demonstrations of the hands-on exercises, are included on the CD that accompanies this book, as explained in the "What's on the CD?" section at the end of this Introduction.

The topics covered in this book map directly to Microsoft's official exam objectives. Each exam objective is covered completely.

How Do You Become an MCSE?

Attaining MCSE certification has always been a challenge. However, in the past, individuals could acquire detailed exam information—even most of the exam questions—from online "brain dumps" and third-party "cram" books or software products. For the new MCSE exams, this simply will not be the case.

To avoid the "paper-MCSE syndrome" (a devaluation of the MCSE certification because unqualified individuals manage to pass the exams), Microsoft has taken strong steps to protect the security and integrity of the new MCSE track. Prospective MSCEs will need to complete a course of study that provides not only detailed knowledge of a wide range of topics, but true skills derived from working with Windows 2000 and related software products.

In the new MCSE program, Microsoft is heavily emphasizing hands-on skills. Microsoft has stated that "Nearly half of the core required exams' content demands that the candidate have troubleshooting skills acquired through hands-on experience and working knowledge."

Fortunately, if you are willing to dedicate time and effort with Windows 2000, you can prepare for the exams by using the proper tools. If you work through this book and the other books in this series, you should successfully meet the exam requirements.

This book is a part of a complete series of MCSE Study Guides, published by Sybex, that covers the five core Windows 2000 requirements as well as the new Design electives you need to complete your MCSE track. Titles include the following:

- *MCSE: Windows 2000 Professional Study Guide*
- *MCSE: Windows 2000 Server Study Guide*
- *MCSE: Windows 2000 Network Infrastructure Administration Study Guide*
- *MCSE: Windows 2000 Directory Services Administration Study Guide*
- *MCSE: Windows 2000 Network Security Design Study Guide*
- *MCSE: Windows 2000 Network Infrastructure Design Study Guide*
- *MCSE: Windows 2000 Directory Services Design Study Guide*

There are also study guides available from Sybex on additional MCSE electives.

Exam Requirements

Successful candidates must pass a minimum set of exams that measure technical proficiency and expertise:

- Candidates for MCSE certification must pass seven exams, including four core operating system exams, one design exam, and two electives.

- Candidates who have already passed three Windows NT 4 exams (70-067, 70-068, and 70-073) may opt to take an "accelerated" exam plus one core design exam and two electives.

 If you do not pass the accelerated exam after one attempt, you must pass the five core requirements and two electives.

The following table shows the exams that a new certification candidate must pass.

All of these exams are required

Exam #	Topic	Requirement Met
70-216	Implementing and Administering a Microsoft® Windows® 2000 Network Infrastrucuture	Core (Operating System)
70-210	Installing, Configuring, and Administering Microsoft® Windows® 2000 Professional	Core (Operating System)
70-215	Installing, Configuring, and Administering Microsoft® Windows® 2000 Server	Core (Operating System)
70-217	Implementing and Administering a Microsoft® Windows® 2000 Directory Services Infrastructure	Core (Operating System)

One of these exams is required

Exam #	Topic	Requirement Met
70-219	Designing a Microsoft® Windows® 2000 Directory Services Infrastructure	Core (Design)
70-220	Designing Security for a Microsoft® Windows® 2000 Network	Core (Design)
70-221	Designing a Microsoft® Windows® 2000 Network Infrastructure	Core (Design)

Two of these exams are required

Exam #	Topic	Requirement Met
70-219	Designing a Microsoft® Windows® 2000 Directory Services Infrastructure	Elective
70-220	Designing Security for a Microsoft® Windows® 2000 Network	Elective
70-221	Designing a Microsoft® Windows® 2000 Network Infrastructure	Elective
Any current MCSE elective	Exams cover topics such as Exchange Server, SQL Server, Systems Management Server, Internet Explorer Administrators Kit, and Proxy Server (new exams are added regularly)	Elective

For a more detailed description of the Microsoft certification programs, including a list of current MCSE electives, check Microsoft's Training and Certification Web site at www.microsoft.com/trainingandservices.

The Windows 2000 Network Infrastructure Administration Exam

The Windows 2000 Network Infrastructure Administration exam covers concepts and skills required for administering Windows 2000 networking services. It emphasizes the following areas of Windows 2000:

- Standards and terminology

- Planning

- Implementation

- Troubleshooting

This exam can be quite specific regarding Windows 2000 networking requirements and operational settings, and it can be particular about how administrative tasks are performed in the operating system. It also focuses on fundamental concepts relating to Windows 2000 Server's operation as a network operating system. Careful study of this book, along with hands-on experience, will help you prepare for this exam.

Microsoft provides exam objectives to give you a very general overview of possible areas of coverage of the Microsoft exams. For your convenience, we have added in-text objectives listings at the points in the text where specific Microsoft exam objectives are covered. However, exam objectives are subject to change at any time without prior notice and at Microsoft's sole discretion. Please visit Microsoft's Training and Certification Web site (www.microsoft.com/trainingandservices) for the most current exam objectives listing.

Types of Exam Questions

In the previous tracks, the formats of the MCSE exams were fairly straightforward, consisting almost entirely of multiple-choice questions appearing in a few different sets. Prior to taking an exam, you knew how many questions you would see and what type of questions would appear. If you had purchased the right third-party exam preparation products, you could even be quite familiar with the pool of questions you might be asked. As mentioned earlier, all of this is changing.

In an effort to both refine the testing process and protect the quality of its certifications, Microsoft has introduced adaptive testing, as well as some new exam elements. You will not know in advance which type of format you will see on your exam. These innovations make the exams more challenging, and they make it much more difficult for someone to pass an exam after simply "cramming" for it.

Microsoft will be accomplishing its goal of protecting the exams by regularly adding and removing exam questions, limiting the number of questions that any individual sees in a beta exam, limiting the number of questions delivered to an individual by using adaptive testing, and adding new exam elements.

Exam questions may be in multiple-choice, select-and-place, simulation, or case study–based formats. You may also find yourself taking an adaptive format exam. Let's take a look at the exam question types and adaptive testing, so you can be prepared for all of the possibilities.

Multiple-Choice Questions

Multiple-choice questions include two main types of questions. One is a straightforward type that presents a question, followed by several possible answers, of which one or more is correct.

The other type of multiple-choice question is more complex. This type presents a set of desired results along with a proposed solution. You must then decide which results would be achieved by the proposed solution.

You will see many multiple-choice questions in this study guide and on the accompanying CD, as well as on your exam.

Select-and-Place Questions

Select-and-place exam questions involve graphical elements that you must manipulate in order to successfully answer a question. For example, a question could present a diagram of a computer network, as shown below.

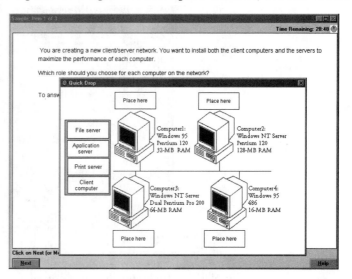

The diagram shows several computers next to boxes that contain the text "Place here." The labels represent different computer roles on network, such as print server and file server. Based on information given for each computer, you are asked to drag and drop each label to the correct box. You need to place *all* of the labels correctly. No credit is given if you correctly label only some of the boxes.

Simulations

Simulations are the kinds of questions that most closely represent and test the actual skills you use while working with Microsoft software interfaces. These types of exam questions include a mock interface on which you must perform certain actions according to a given scenario. The simulated interfaces look nearly identical to what you see in the actual product, as shown in the example below.

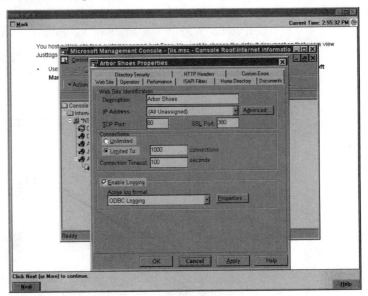

Simulations are by far the most complex element introduced into Microsoft exams to date. Because of the number of possible errors that can be made on simulations, it is worthwhile to consider the following recommendations from Microsoft:

- Do not change any simulation settings that don't pertain to the solution directly.

- Assume that the default settings are used when related information has not been provided.

- Make sure that your entries are spelled correctly.

- Close all of the simulation application windows after completing the set of tasks in the simulation.

The best way to prepare for the simulation questions is to spend time working with the graphical interface of the product on which you will be tested.

We recommend that you study with the Edge Test WinSim 2000 product, which is included on the CD that accompanies this study guide. By completing the exercises in this study guide and working with the WinSim 2000 software, you can greatly improve your level of preparation for simulation questions.

Case Study–Based Questions

Case study–based questions first appeared in the Microsoft Certified Solution Developer program (Microsoft's certification program for software programmers). Case study–based questions present a scenario with a range of requirements. Based on the information provided, you need to answer a series of multiple-choice and ranking questions. The interface for case study–based questions has a number of tabs that each contains information about the scenario. At present, this type of question appears only in the Design exams.

Adaptive Exam Format

Microsoft presents many of its exams in an *adaptive* format. This format is radically different from the conventional format previously used for Microsoft certification exams. Conventional tests are static, containing a fixed number of questions. Adaptive tests change, or "adapt," depending on your answers to the questions presented.

The number of questions presented in your adaptive test will depend on how long it takes the exam to ascertain your level of ability (according to the statistical measurements on which the exam questions are ranked). To determine a test-taker's level of ability, the exam presents questions in increasing or decreasing order of difficulty.

Unlike the previous test format, the adaptive format will *not* allow you to go back to see a question again. The exam only goes forward. Once you enter your answer, that's it—you cannot change it. Be very careful before entering your answer. There is no time limit for each individual question (only for the exam as a whole). Your exam may be shortened by correct answers (and lengthened by incorrect answers), so there is no advantage to rushing through questions.

How Adaptive Exams Determine Ability Levels

As an example of how adaptive testing works, suppose that you know three people who are taking the exam: Herman, Sally, and Rashad. Herman doesn't know much about the subject, Sally is moderately informed, and Rashad is an expert.

Herman answers his first question incorrectly, so the exam presents him with a second, easier question. He misses that, so the exam gives him a few more easy questions, all of which he misses. Shortly thereafter, the exam ends, and he receives his failure report.

Sally answers her first question correctly, so the exam gives her a more difficult question, which she answers correctly. She then receives an even more difficult question, which she answers incorrectly. Next, the exam gives her a somewhat easier question, as it tries to gauge her level of understanding. After numerous questions of varying levels of difficulty, Sally's exam ends, perhaps with a passing score, perhaps not. Her exam included far more questions than were in Herman's exam, because her level of understanding needed to be more carefully tested to determine whether or not it was at a passing level.

When Rashad takes his exam, he answers his first question correctly, so he is given a more difficult question, which he also answers correctly. Next, the exam presents an even more difficult question, which he also answers correctly. He then is given a few more very difficult questions, all of which he answers correctly. Shortly thereafter, his exam ends. He passes. His exam was short, about as long as Herman's test.

Benefits of Adaptive Testing

Microsoft has begun moving to adaptive testing for several reasons:

- It saves time by focusing only on the questions needed to determine a test-taker's abilities. An exam that might take an hour and a half in the conventional format could be completed in less than half that time when presented in adaptive format. The number of questions in an adaptive exam may be far fewer than the number required by a conventional exam.

- It protects the integrity of the exams. By exposing a fewer number of questions at any one time, it makes it more difficult for individuals to collect the questions in the exam pools with the intent of facilitating exam "cramming."

▪ It saves Microsoft and/or the test-delivery company money by reducing the amount of time it takes to deliver a test.

 We recommend that you try the Edge Test Adaptive Exam, which is included on the CD that accompanies this study guide.

Exam Question Development

Microsoft follows an exam-development process consisting of eight mandatory phases. The process takes an average of seven months and involves more than 150 specific steps. The MCP exam development consists of the following phases:

Phase 1: Job Analysis   Phase 1 is an analysis of all of the tasks that make up a specific job function, based on tasks performed by people who are currently performing that job function. This phase also identifies the knowledge, skills, and abilities that relate specifically to the performance area to be certified.

Phase 2: Objective Domain Definition   The results of the job analysis provide the framework used to develop objectives. The development of objectives involves translating the job-function tasks into a comprehensive set of more specific and measurable knowledge, skills, and abilities. The resulting list of objectives—the *objective domain*—is the basis for the development of both the certification exams and the training materials.

Phase 3: Blueprint Survey   The final objective domain is transformed into a blueprint survey in which contributors are asked to rate each objective. These contributors may be past MCP candidates, appropriately skilled exam development volunteers, or Microsoft employees. Based on the contributors' input, the objectives are prioritized and weighted. The actual exam items are written according to the prioritized objectives. Contributors are queried about how they spend their time on the job. If a contributor doesn't spend an adequate amount of time actually performing the specified job function, his or her data is eliminated from the analysis. The blueprint survey phase helps determine which objectives to measure, as well as the appropriate number and types of items to include on the exam.

Phase 4: Item Development   A pool of items is developed to measure the blueprinted objective domain. The number and types of items to be written are based on the results of the blueprint survey.

Phase 5: Alpha Review and Item Revision   During this phase, a panel of technical and job-function experts reviews each item for technical accuracy, then answers each item, reaching a consensus on all technical issues. Once the items have been verified as technically accurate, they are edited to ensure that they are expressed in the clearest language possible.

Phase 6: Beta Exam   The reviewed and edited items are collected into beta exams. Based on the responses of all beta participants, Microsoft performs a statistical analysis to verify the validity of the exam items and to determine which items will be used in the certification exam. Once the analysis has been completed, the items are distributed into multiple parallel forms, or *versions*, of the final certification exam.

Phase 7: Item Selection and Cut-Score Setting   The results of the beta exams are analyzed to determine which items should be included in the certification exam based on many factors, including item difficulty and relevance. During this phase, a panel of job-function experts determines the *cut score* (minimum passing score) for the exams. The cut score differs from exam to exam because it is based on an item-by-item determination of the percentage of candidates who answered the item correctly and who would be expected to answer the item correctly.

Phase 8: Live Exam   As the final phase, the exams are given to candidates. MCP exams are administered by Sylvan Prometric and Virtual University Enterprises (VUE).

Microsoft will regularly add and remove questions from the exams. This is called item *seeding*. It is part of the effort to make it more difficult for individuals to merely memorize exam questions passed along by previous test-takers.

Tips for Taking the Windows 2000 Network Infrastructure Administration Exam

Here are some general tips for taking the exam successfully:

- Arrive early at the exam center so you can relax and review your study materials. During your final review, you can look over tables and lists of exam-related information.

- Read the questions carefully. Don't be tempted to jump to an early conclusion. Make sure you know *exactly* what the question is asking.

- Answer all questions. Remember that the adaptive format will *not* allow you to return to a question. Be very careful before entering your answer. Because your exam may be shortened by correct answers (and lengthened by incorrect answers), there is no advantage to rushing through questions.

- On simulations, do not change settings that are not directly related to the question. Also, assume default settings if the question does not specify or imply which settings are used.

- Use a process of elimination to get rid of the obviously incorrect answers first on questions that you're not sure about. This method will improve your odds of selecting the correct answer if you need to make an educated guess.

Exam Registration

You may take the exams at any of more than 1,000 Authorized Prometric Testing Centers (APTCs) and VUE Testing Centers around the world. For the location of a testing center near you, call Sylvan Prometric at 800-755-EXAM (755-3926), or call VUE at 888-837-8616. Outside the United States and Canada, contact your local Sylvan Prometric or VUE registration center.

You should determine the number of the exam you want to take, and then register with the Sylvan Prometric or VUE registration center nearest to you. At this point, you will be asked for advance payment for the exam. The exams are $100 each. Exams must be taken within one year of payment. You can schedule exams up to six weeks in advance or as late as one working day prior to the date of the exam. You can cancel or reschedule your exam if you contact the center at least two working days prior to the exam. Same-day registration is available in some locations, subject to space availability. Where same-day registration is available, you must register a minimum of two hours before test time.

You may also register for your exams online at www.sylvanprometric.com or www.vue.com.

When you schedule the exam, you will be provided with instructions regarding appointment and cancellation procedures, ID requirements, and information about the testing center location. In addition, you will receive a registration and payment confirmation letter from Sylvan Prometric or VUE.

Microsoft requires certification candidates to accept the terms of a Non-Disclosure Agreement before taking certification exams.

What's on the CD?

With this new book in our best-selling MCSE study guide series, we are including quite an array of training resources. On the CD are numerous simulations, practice exams, and flashcards to help you study for the exam. Also included are the entire contents of the study guide. These resources are described in the following sections.

The Sybex Ebook for Windows 2000 Network Infrastructure Administration

Many people like the convenience of being able to carry their whole study guide on a CD. They also like being able to search the text to find specific information quickly and easily. For these reasons, we have included the entire contents of this study guide on a CD, in PDF format. We've also included Adobe Acrobat Reader, which provides the interface for the contents, as well as the search capabilities.

Sybex WinSim 2000

We developed WinSim 2000 to allow you to get some hands-on practice with the skills you need to know to pass the exam. The WinSim 2000 product provides both audio/video files and hands-on experience with key features of the Windows 2000 Server operating system. Built around the exercises in this study guide, WinSim 2000 can give you the knowledge and hands-on skills that are invaluable for understanding Windows 2000 (and passing the exam). A sample screen from WinSim 2000 is shown below.

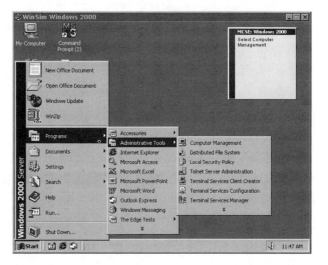

The Sybex MCSE Edge Tests

The Edge Tests are a collection of multiple-choice questions that can help you prepare for your exam. There are three sets of questions:

- Bonus questions specially prepared for this edition of the study guide, including 50 questions that appear only on the CD

- An adaptive test simulator that will give the feel for how adaptive testing works

- All of the questions from the study guide presented in a test engine for your review

A sample screen from the Sybex MCSE Edge Tests is shown below.

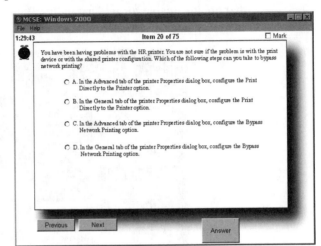

Sybex MCSE Flashcards for PCs and Palm Devices

The "flashcard" style of exam question offers an effective way to quickly and efficiently test your understanding of the fundamental concepts covered in the Windows 2000 Network Infrastructure Administration exam. The Sybex MCSE Flashcards set consists of 100–150 questions presented in a special engine developed specifically for this study guide series. The Sybex MCSE Flashcards interface is shown below.

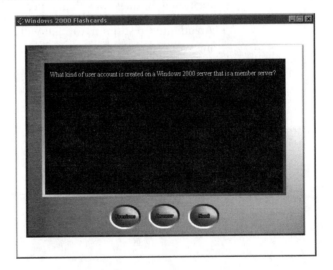

Because of the high demand for a product that will run on Palm devices, we have also developed, in conjunction with Land-J Technologies, a version of the flashcard questions that you can take with you on your Palm OS PDA (including the PalmPilot and Handspring's Visor).

How Do You Use This Book?

This book can provide a solid foundation for the serious effort of preparing for the Windows 2000 Network Infrastructure Administration exam. To best benefit from this book, you may wish to use the following study method:

1. Study each chapter carefully. Do your best to fully understand the information.

2. Complete all hands-on exercises in the chapter, referring back to the text as necessary so that you understand each step you take. If you do not have access to a lab environment in which you can complete the exercises, install and work with the exercises available in the WinSim 2000 software included with this study guide.

3. Answer the review questions at the end of each chapter. If you would prefer to answer the questions in a timed and graded format, install the Edge Tests from the CD that accompanies this book and answer the chapter questions there instead of in the book.

4. Note which questions you did not understand and study the corresponding sections of the book again.

5. Make sure you complete the entire book.

6. Before taking the exam, go through the training resources included on the CD that accompanies this book. Try the adaptive version that is included with the Sybex MCSE Edge Test. Review and sharpen your knowledge with the MCSE Flashcards.

In order to complete the exercises in this book, you'll need to have access to at least one machine running Windows 2000 Server and one running Windows 2000 Professional. Some exercises may require you to have administrative access, or to be part of an Active Directory domain.

To learn all of the material covered in this book, you will need to study regularly and with discipline. Try to set aside the same time every day to study and select a comfortable and quiet place in which to do it. If you work hard, you will be surprised at how quickly you learn this material. Good luck!

Contacts and Resources

To find out more about Microsoft Education and Certification materials and programs, to register with Sylvan Prometric or VUE, or to get other useful information, check the following resources.

Microsoft Certification Development Team
www.microsoft.com/trainingandservices/mcp/examinfo/certsd.htm

Contact the Microsoft Certification Development Team through their Web site to volunteer for one or more exam development phases or to report a problem with an exam. Address written correspondence to:

Certification Development Team
Microsoft Education and Certification
One Microsoft Way
Redmond, WA 98052

Microsoft TechNet Technical Information Network
www.microsoft.com/technet/subscription/about.htm

(800) 344-2121

Use this Web site or number to contact support professionals and system administrators. Outside the United States and Canada, contact your local Microsoft subsidiary for information.

Microsoft Training and Certification Home Page
www.microsoft.com/trainingandservices

This Web site provides information about the MCP program and exams. You can also order the latest Microsoft Roadmap to Education and Certification.

Palm Pilot Training Product Development: Land-J
www.land-j.com

(407) 359-2217

Land-J Technologies is a consulting and programming business currently specializing in application development for the 3Com PalmPilot Personal Digital Assistant. Land-J developed the Palm version of the Edge Tests, which is included on the CD that accompanies this study guide.

Sylvan Prometric
www.sylvanprometric.com

(800) 755-EXAM

Contact Sylvan Prometric to register to take an MCP exam at any of more than 800 Sylvan Prometric Testing Centers around the world.

Virtual University Enterprises (VUE)
www.vue.com

(888) 837-8616

Contact the VUE registration center to register to take an MCP exam at one of the VUE Testing Centers.

Assessment Test

1. The Time to Live (TTL) attached to a DNS record _____.

   A. Cannot be used by a resolver, only by servers making recursive queries

   B. Is used only by resolvers

   C. Is used to determine how long to cache retrieved results

   D. Is refreshed each time the record is modified

2. Which of the following settings *cannot* be adjusted when using RIP?

   A. The RIP version that can be used for incoming and outgoing traffic on each interface

   B. The set of peer routers from which routes will be accepted

   C. The default announcement interval

   D. The location where received RIP routes are stored

3. To convert an existing RRAS server into a VPN server, you must do which of the following? (Choose all that apply.)

   A. Enable remote access on the server's General Properties tab.

   B. Add L2TP or PPTP ports.

   C. Disable IP routing.

   D. Enable the DHCP relay agent.

4. Deploying Microsoft's Windows 2000 PKI implementation will allow you to do all of the following except one. Which is it?

   A. Issue new certificates.

   B. Revoke or cancel old certificates.

   C. Encrypt EFS using certificates.

   D. Monitor and control which certificates are doing what.

5. To enable DHCP-DNS integration, you must do which of the following?

    A. Configure the *scope only* to allow it to use Dynamic DNS

    B. Configure the *server only* to allow it to use Dynamic DNS

    C. Configure the scope *and* the server

    D. Configure the scope *or* the server

6. RRAS allows you to create which types of routing-related filters?

    A. Route filters only

    B. Peer filters only

    C. Route and peer filters

    D. Packet filters only

7. What is the IPSec Policy Agent?

    A. It is an optional component that's required when using IPSec *with* Active Directory.

    B. It is an optional component that's required when using IPSec *without* Active Directory.

    C. It is an optional component that's required when using IPSec with L2TP.

    D. It is a mandatory component that's required to use IPSec.

8. The seven layers of the OSI model do which of the following?

    A. Map exactly to Windows 2000 networking services and components

    B. Provide a useful conceptual framework for grouping similar services

    C. A and B

    D. None of the above

9. To test whether a DNS server is answering queries properly, you can use which of the following tools?

    A. The *ping* tool

    B. The *nslookup* tool

    C. The *tracert* tool

    D. The *ipconfig* tool

10. What are the three private address ranges?

    A. 10.0.0.0

    B. 168.192.x.y

    C. 172.16.x.y

    D. 192.168.x.y

11. WINS is normally used to resolve NetBIOS names _____.

    A. Only when DNS is disabled

    B. After broadcast requests failed

    C. Before broadcast resolution is attempted

    D. Only for clients that are already registered in the WINS database

12. WINS replication is necessary because of which of the following?

    A. On large networks, WINS queries will cross subnets unnecessarily.

    B. The WINS server software is still unreliable.

    C. Having multiple WINS servers provides load balancing.

    D. None of the above.

13. You have installed the DHCP Server service on a member server in your domain and have configured a scope, but clients cannot lease an address. What is the most likely cause of this problem?

    A. The scope is not activated.

    B. There are too many DHCP servers.

    C. The DHCP server is not authorized.

    D. The DHCP server is in another subnet.

14. Which of the following statements about Windows 2000 Dynamic DNS is true?

    A. DDNS requires a Microsoft DHCP server to work.

    B. The Windows 2000 DDNS server can interoperate with recent versions of BIND.

    C. DDNS clients may not register their own addresses.

    D. DDNS only works with Microsoft clients and servers.

15. VPN connections require which of the following? (Choose two.)

    A. The Windows 2000 VPN add-on

    B. The name or IP address of the VPN server

    C. The phone number of the VPN server

    D. An existing TCP/IP connection

16. In a replication partnership, the partner that sends a "new data available" message is called which of the following?

    A. WINS master

    B. Pull partner

    C. Push partner

    D. WINS secondary

17. To reject any incoming call from a client that can't use a specified level of encryption, you would do which of the following?

    A. Turn off the No Encryption check box on the Encryption tab of the remote access policy's profile

    B. Turn off the No Encryption check box on the Security tab of the server Properties dialog box

    C. Create a new remote access profile named "Require encryption"

    D. Check the Require Encryption check box in each user's user profile

18. Which of the following is *not* an OSI layer?

    A. Session

    B. Application

    C. Presentation

    D. Service

19. DHCP address range exclusions are assigned at which level?

    A. Server level

    B. Scope level

    C. Superscope level

    D. Multicast scope level

20. You have just attached your server to a dedicated connection between a satellite and your company's home office. The dedicated connection is providing you with three addresses. All clients must have direct access to a DOS-based database to enter and retrieve information. What is the best way to attach your 18 clients to the database?

    A. ICS

    B. Proxy DNS

    C. Proxy server

    D. NAT

21. IPSec _____.

    A. Can be used by itself

    B. Can be used only with L2TP

    C. Cannot be used with L2TP

    D. Requires third-party software for Windows 2000

22. Removing all of the EFS recovery keys on a local machine will do which of the following?

    A. It will turn off recovery on that local machine, and affect any recovery policies imposed by higher-level GPOs.

    B. It will turn off recovery on that local machine, but not affect any recovery policies imposed by higher-level GPOs.

    C. It will turn on recovery on that local machine, and affect any recovery policies imposed by higher-level GPOs.

    D. It will turn on recovery on that local machine, but not affect any recovery policies imposed by higher-level GPOs.

23. Which of the following are true of the routing table? (Choose all that apply.)

    A. It is automatically maintained by the routing protocols.

    B. It is normally not maintained across reboots.

    C. It may be manually edited from the command line.

    D. It is made up of multiple entries, each containing a network ID, a forwarding address, and a metric.

24. The DHCP relay agent serves which function on the network?

    A. It listens for DHCP messages on a network and forwards them to a DHCP server on another network.

    B. It accepts DHCP messages from multiple networks and consolidates them for a single DHCP server.

    C. It allows DHCP clients to use WINS services.

    D. It relays DHCP requests to a Dynamic DNS server.

25. Which of the following protocols is *not* required for an Active Directory installation?

   A. TCP/IP

   B. DNS

   C. LDAP

   D. NetBEUI

26. You can control VPN access through which of the following mechanisms? (Choose two.)

   A. Individual user account properties

   B. Remote access policies

   C. Remote access profiles

   D. Group policy objects

27. Which of the following is not a role type played by Microsoft Certificate Server?

   A. Enterprise root CA.

   B. Stand-alone root CA.

   C. Subordinate root CA.

   D. Enterprise subordinate CA.

28. What is a mirrored rule?

   A. It is a *single* rule that specifies the same source and destination for two different protocols.

   B. It is a *single* rule that specifies the same source and destination for inbound and outbound traffic.

   C. It is a *pair* of rules that specify the same source and destination for two different protocols.

   D. It is a pair of rules that specifies different source and destination addresses for the same protocol.

29. What is the replication of DNS data from one server to another called?

   A. Replication pass

   B. Zone transfer

   C. Replication transfer

   D. Zone replication

30. If settings on a local machine conflict with settings assigned by a DHCP server, which of the following statements are *not true*? Choose all that apply.

   A. None of the conflicting settings will apply.

   B. The DHCP-assigned settings override the locally-assigned settings.

   C. Whichever settings are applied first take effect.

   D. The locally assigned settings override the DHCP-assigned settings.

31. To enable dial-up users to get a fixed IP address, you must do which of the following?

   A. Define an address pool on the IP tab of the server's Properties dialog box

   B. Define an address pool in the remote access policy

   C. Add a DHCP address range for the dial-up users

   D. Disable the DHCP address allocator

Answers to Assessment Test

1. C. The TTL indicates how long the record may be safely cached; it may or may not be modified when the record is edited. See Chapter 2 for more information on TTL.

2. D. The RIP implementation in Windows 2000 allows you to mix RIP versions, control which peer routers can send you updates, and how often your router will broadcast updates to others. However, it does now allow you to change where the routing table data are stored. For more information, see Chapter 8.

3. A and B. RRAS includes the needed components to act as a VPN server, but you have to enable them, then create appropriate VPN ports. For more information, see Chapter 10.

4. C. A certificate authority, or CA, is a service that lets you issue new certificates, revoke or cancel old ones, and monitor and control certificates. It does not serve to encrypt files systems, such as EFS. See Chapter 14 for more information.

5. D. You can enable integration either on one scope only or on all scopes on a server. See Chapter 5 for more details.

6. C. Route filters let you accept or ignore individual routes; peer filters give you control over which other routers your router accepts routing information from. For more information, see Chapter 3.

7. D. The IPSec Policy Agent is the component that downloads IPSec policy settings from the local computer or Active Directory. Accordingly, presence is required for IPSec to function. See Chapter 11 for more details.

8. B. The OSI model is a stylized network model that can be used to compare and contrast implementations from different vendors. See Chapter 1 for more information on the OSI model.

9. B. *Nslookup* allows you to look up name and address information. For more details, see Chapter 6.

10. A, C, D. The private address ranges are 10.x.y.z, 172.16.x.y and 192.168.x.y. The private address ranges will not be forwarded by a router. For more information, see Chapter 13.

11. C. WINS normally is used to resolve names before the client makes a last-chance broadcast request. See Chapter 2 for more information.

12. A. Replicating WINS data allows local WINS servers on each subnet to answer queries instead of forcing the queries to cross subnets. See Chapter 7 for more details.

13. C. If the DHCP server isn't authorized, it will not answer lease requests; therefore, the client will end up with no address. For more information, see Chapter 4.

14. B. DDNS works with BIND 8.2 and later. See Chapter 2 for more information on DDNS.

15. B, C. VPN connections piggyback on top of regular dial-up or dedicated TCP/IP connections, and they require you to specify the name or address of the server you're calling. For more information, see Chapter 12.

16. B. There's no such thing as a WINS secondary or a WINS master; the push partner sends a "please send me new data" message. See Chapter 7 for more information.

17. A. The profile associated with each remote access policy controls whether that policy will require, allow, or disallow encryption. To force encryption, create a policy that disallows using No Encryption. See Chapter 9 for more details.

18. D. The session, application, and presentation layers are all part of the OSI model, but the service layer isn't. See Chapter 1 for more information on the OSI layers.

19. B. Scopes or ranges of addresses can be assigned only at the scope level. The scope range includes the exclusion range. See Chapter 5 for more details.

20. D. Because transparent access to a database is required, the best solution is NAT. ICS would change port addresses, which would be unacceptable in a database access. A proxy server is normally used for caching and single address access and is incompatible with non-ODBC-compliant databases. For more information, see Chapter 13.

21. A. IPSec is a stand-alone protocol included in Windows 2000 that can be used by itself or in conjunction with L2TP. For more information, see Chapter 3.

22. B. Deleting all of the EFS recovery keys will turn off EFS in that scope, but will not affect the policies of higher-level GPOs. See Chapter 14 for more details.

23. A, C, D. The routing engines maintain the contents of the routing table, although you may add or remove entries manually. Persistent routes, which are the default, are automatically maintained until you delete them manually. For more information, see Chapter 8.

24. A. The DHCP relay agent allows you to use a DHCP server that resides on one network with clients that live on a separate network. See Chapter 9 for more information.

25. D. NetBEUI is being deprecated, but the other three protocols are required for AD. For more information, see Chapter 4.

26. A and B. You can allow users to make VPN connections by modifying individual account properties; if you're using a native-mode Windows 2000 domain, you can also use remote access policies. For more information, see Chapter 10.

27. C. An MCS can be an enterprise root or subordinate CA, or a stand-alone root or subordinate CA. There is no such role as a "subordinate root CA." See Chapter 14 for more details.

28. B. A mirrored rule that maps a source address of A and a destination of B actually acts as two rules: source A/destination B for outbound traffic and source B/destination A for inbound traffic. See Chapter 11 for more details.

29. B. Zone transfer is the term used for the transfer of resource records from one zone to another. For more details, see Chapter 6.

30. A, B, C. Local settings always override settings specified by the DHCP server. For more information, see Chapter 12.

31. A. To assign static IP addresses to dial-up clients, you have to define a pool of addresses on the server; this pool is used instead of allowing DHCP assignments to clients. For more information, see Chapter 9.

Chapter

1

Understanding Windows 2000 Networking

Microsoft has put an immense amount of time and effort into building Windows 2000. While it's not fair to say that it's an entirely new product since it still retains a great deal of core code from Windows NT, the Internet Information Server, and Exchange Server, it *is* one of the largest and most complicated commercial software projects ever undertaken. Windows 2000 is a large, complicated, and very powerful operating system. To use it effectively, you have to understand how it works and how to make it do what you want it to do. Since this book is a study guide for the Implementing and Administering a Microsoft Windows 2000 Network Infrastructure exam, it makes sense to lead off with a discussion of the network protocols included in Windows 2000—what they're for, how they work, and what you can do with them.

Physicists talk a lot about *frames of reference*, because accurately expressing the velocity or position of some object is much easier when you have something to compare it to. In the same vein, having a good frame of reference helps when comparing network protocols. To establish such a frame, this chapter will begin with the *Open Systems Interconnection (OSI)* network model, a sort of idealized way to stack various protocols together. However, remember the old saw: in theory, there's no difference between theory and practice, but in practice there is.

Stacking Things Up with OSI

The International Organization for Standardization (ISO) began developing the Open Systems Interconnection (OSI) reference model in 1977. It has since become the most widely accepted model for understanding network communication; once you understand how the *OSI model* works, you can use it to compare network implementations on different systems.

When you want to communicate with another person, you need to have two things in common: a communications language and a communications medium. For example, if you don't speak Russian it wouldn't do you any good to call Moscow, even though your phone *could*. Computer networks are no different; for communication to take place on a network composed of a variety of different network devices, both the language and medium must be clearly defined. The OSI model (and networking models developed by other organizations) attempts to define rules that cover both the generalities and specifics of networks, including:

- How network devices contact each other and, if they have different languages, how they communicate with each other

- Methods by which a device on a network knows when to transmit data and when not to

- Methods to ensure that network transmissions are received correctly and by the right recipient

- How the physical transmission media are arranged and connected

- How to ensure that network devices maintain a proper rate of data flow

- How bits are represented on the network media

The OSI model isn't a product—you won't see vendors offering OSI version 4 for Windows 2000. It's just a conceptual framework you can use to better understand the complex interactions taking place among the various devices on a network. The OSI model doesn't do anything in the communication process; appropriate software and hardware do the actual work. The OSI model simply defines which tasks need to be done and which protocols will handle those tasks at each of the seven layers of the model. The seven *layers* are:

- Application (Layer 7)

- Presentation

- Session

- Transport

- Network

- Data link

- Physical (Layer 1)

You can remember the seven layers using a handy acronym like "All Pitchers Sometimes Take Naps During Preseason."

Each of the seven layers has a distinct function, which you'll explore in the remainder of this section.

Protocol Stacks

The OSI model splits communication tasks into smaller pieces called subtasks. Protocol implementations are computer processes that handle these subtasks. Specific protocols fulfill subtasks at specific layers of the OSI model. When these protocols are grouped together to complete a whole task, the assemblage of code is called a *protocol stack*. The stack is just a group of protocols, arranged in layered stacks like a wedding cake, that implements an entire communication process. Each layer of the OSI model has a different protocol associated with it. When more than one protocol is needed to complete a communication process, the protocols are grouped together in a stack. An example of a protocol stack is TCP/IP, which is widely used for Unix and the Internet—the TCP and IP protocols are implemented at different OSI layers.

Each layer in the protocol stack receives services from the layer below it and provides services to the layer above it. Novell explains the relationship like this: Layer N uses the services of the layer below it (layer N-1) and provides services to the layer above it (layer N+1).

For two computers to communicate, the same protocol stacks must be running on each computer. Each layer of the protocol stack on one computer communicates with its equivalent, or peer, on the other computer. The computers can have different operating systems and still be able to communicate if they are running the same protocol stacks. For example, a DOS machine running TCP/IP can communicate with a Macintosh machine running TCP/IP (see Figure 1.1).

FIGURE 1.1 Each layer communicates with its counterparts on other network hosts.

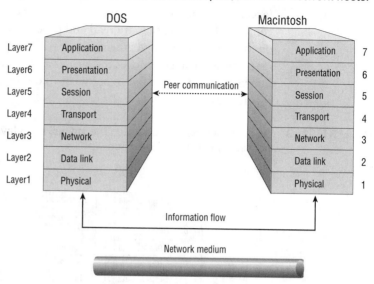

Communication between Stacks

When a message is sent from one machine to another, it travels down the layers on one machine and then up the layers on the other machine, as shown in Figure 1.2.

FIGURE 1.2 Traffic flows down through the stack on one computer, then up the stack on the other.

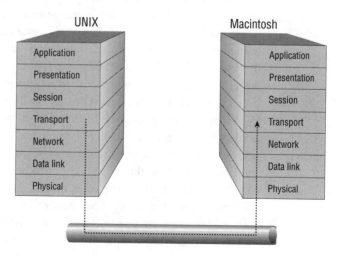

As the message travels down the first stack, each layer it passes through (except the data link layer) adds a header. These headers contain pieces of control information that are read and processed by the corresponding layer on the receiving stack. As the message travels up the stack of the other machine, each layer removes the header added by its peer layer and uses the information it finds to figure out what to do with the message contents (see Figure 1.3).

FIGURE 1.3 As packets flow up and down the stacks, each layer adds or removes necessary control information.

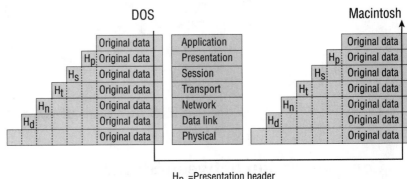

As an example, consider the network we're using while writing this book. It's a TCP/IP network containing several Windows 2000, Macintosh, and Windows NT machines, all connected using the TCP/IP protocol. When we mount a share from our Windows 2000 file server on the Mac desktop, at layer 7, the Mac Finder requests something from the W2K server. This request is sent to the Mac's layer 6, which receives the request as a data packet, adds its own header, and passes the packet down to layer 5. At layer 5, the process is repeated, and it continues until the packet makes it to the physical layer. The physical layer is responsible for actually moving some bits across the network wiring in the office, so it carries the request packet to a place where the Windows 2000 machine can "hear" it. At that point, the request packet begins its journey up the layers on the Windows 2000 file server. The header that was put on at the data link layer of the Mac OS is stripped off at the data link layer on the Windows 2000 machine. The Windows data link layer driver performs the tasks requested in the header and passes the requests to the next, higher layer. This process is repeated until the Windows 2000 file server receives the packet and interprets the request. The Windows 2000 server would then formulate an appropriate response and send it to the Mac.

The Physical Layer

The physical layer is responsible for sending bits from one computer to another. Physical layer components don't care what the bits *mean*; their job is to get the bits from point A to point B, using whatever kind of optical, electrical, or wireless connection the points are connected with. This level defines physical and electrical details, such as what will represent a 1 or a 0, how many pins a network connector will have, how data will be synchronized, and when the network adapter may or may not transmit the data (see Figure 1.4).

FIGURE 1.4 The physical layer makes a physical circuit with electrical, optical, or radio signals.

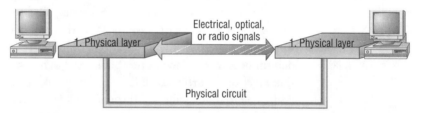

The physical layer addresses all the minutiae of the actual physical connection between the computer and the network medium, including the following:

- Network connection types, including multipoint and point-to-point connections.

- Physical topologies, or how the network is physically laid out (e.g., bus, star, or ring topologies).

- Which analog and digital signaling methods are used to encode data in the analog and digital signals.

- Bit synchronization, which deals with keeping the sender and receiver in synch as they read and write data.

- Multiplexing, or the process of combining several data channels into one.

- Termination, which prevents signals from reflecting back through the cable and causing signal and packets errors. It also indicates the last node in a network segment.

The Data Link Layer

The data link layer provides for the flow of data over a single physical link from one device to another. It accepts packets from the network layer and packages the information into data units called frames; these frames are presented to the physical layer for transmission. The data link layer adds control information, such as frame type, routing, and segmentation information, to the data being sent.

This layer also provides for the error-free transfer of frames from one computer to another. A *Cyclic Redundancy Check (CRC)* added to the data frame can detect damaged frames, and the data link layer in the receiving computer can request that the CRC information be present so that it can check incoming frames for errors. The data link layer can also detect when frames are lost and request that those frames be sent again.

In broadcast networks such as Ethernet, all devices on the LAN receive the data that any device transmits. [Whether a network is broadcast or point-to-point (where only the destination computer receives the information) is determined by the network protocols used to transmit data over it.] The data link layer on a particular device is responsible for recognizing frames addressed to that device and throwing the rest away, much as you might sort through your daily mail to separate good stuff from junk. Figure 1.5 shows how the data link layer establishes an error-free connection between two devices.

FIGURE 1.5 The data link layer establishes an error-free link between two devices.

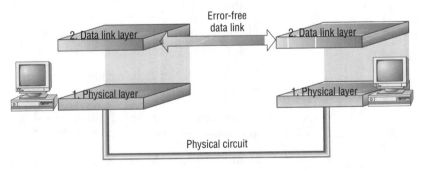

The Institute of Electrical and Electronic Engineers (IEEE) developed a protocol specification known as IEEE 802.X. (802.2 is the standard that divides this layer into two sublayers. The MAC layer varies for different network types and is described further in standards 802.3 through 802.5.) As part of that specification (which today we know as Ethernet), they split the data link layer into two sublayers:

- The *Logical Link Control (LLC)* layer establishes and maintains the logical communication links between the communicating devices.

- The *Media Access Control (MAC)* layer acts like an airport control tower, controlling the way multiple devices share the same media channel in the same way that a control tower regulates the flow of air traffic into and out of an airport.

Figure 1.6 illustrates the division of the data link layer into the LLC and MAC layers.

FIGURE 1.6   The IEEE split the ISO data link layer into the LLC sublayer and the MAC sublayer.

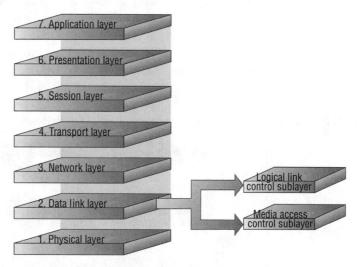

The LLC sublayer provides *Service Access Points (SAP)* that other computers can refer to and use to transfer information from the LLC sublayer to the upper OSI layers. This is defined in the 802.2 standard.

The MAC sublayer, the lower of the two sublayers, provides for shared access to the network adapter and communicates directly with network interface cards. Network interface cards have a unique 12-digit hexadecimal MAC address (frequently called the hardware Ethernet address) assigned before they leave the factory where they are made. The LLC sublayer uses MAC addresses to establish logical links between devices on the same LAN.

The Network Layer

The network layer handles moving packets between devices that are more than one link away from each other. It makes routing decisions and forwards packets as necessary to help them travel to their intended destination. In larger networks, there may be intermediate devices and subnetworks between any two-end systems. The network layer makes it possible for the transport layer (and layers above it) to send packets without being concerned with whether the end system is on the same piece of network cable or on the other end of a large wide-area network.

To do its job, the network layer translates logical network addresses into physical machine addresses (MAC addresses, which operate at the data link layer). The network layer also determines the quality of service (such as the priority of the message) and the route a message will take if there are several ways a message can get to its destination.

The network layer also may split large packets into smaller chunks if the packet is larger than the largest data frame the data link layer will accept. The network reassembles the chunks into packets at the receiving end.

Intermediate systems that perform only routing and relaying functions and do not provide an environment for executing user programs can implement just the first three OSI network layers. Figure 1.7 shows how the network layer moves packets across multiple links in a network.

FIGURE 1.7   The network layer moves packets across links to their destination.

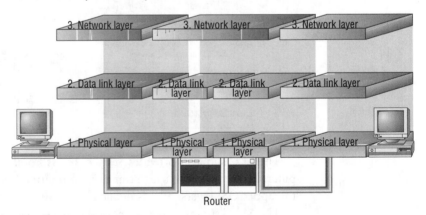

The network layer performs several important functions that enable data to arrive at its destination. The protocols at this layer may choose a specific route through an internetwork to avoid the excess traffic caused by sending data over networks and segments that don't need access to it. The network layer serves to support communications between logically separate networks. This layer is concerned with the following:

- Addressing, including logical network addresses and services addresses

- Circuit, message, and packet switching

- Route discovery and route selection

- Connection services, including network layer flow control, network layer error control, and packet sequence control

- Gateway services

In Windows 2000, the various routing services for TCP/IP, AppleTalk, and IPX/SPX perform network-layer services (see Chapter 8, "Managing IP Routing," for more on these services). In addition, the TCP/IP, AppleTalk, and IPX stacks provide routing capacity for those protocols.

The Transport Layer

The transport layer ensures that packets are delivered error-free, in sequence, and with no losses or duplications. This layer also breaks large messages from the session layer into smaller packets to be sent to the destination computer and reassembles packets into messages to be presented to the network layer. The transport layer typically sends an acknowledgment to the originator for messages received (as in Figure 1.8).

FIGURE 1.8 The transport layer provides end-to-end communication with integrity and performance guarantees.

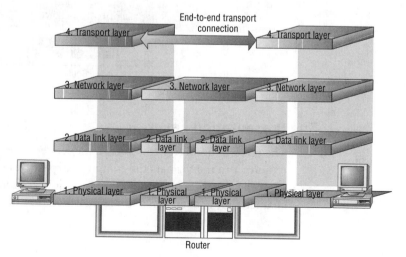

The Session Layer

The session layer allows applications on separate computers to share a connection called a session. This layer provides services, such as name lookup and security, to allow two programs to find each other and establish the communications link. The session layer also provides for data synchronization and checkpointing so that, in the event of a network failure, only the data sent after the point of failure would need to be re-sent. This layer also controls the dialog between two processes and determines who can transmit and who can receive at what point during the communication (see Figure 1.9).

FIGURE 1.9 The session layer allows applications to establish communication sessions with each other.

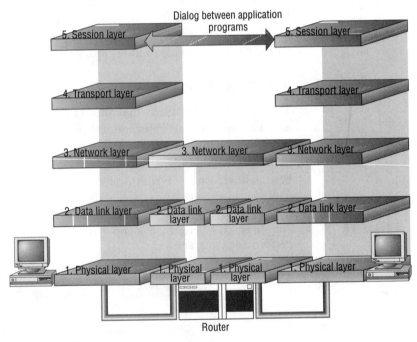

The Presentation Layer

The presentation layer translates data between the formats the network requires and the formats the computer expects. The presentation layer performs protocol conversion; data translation, compression, and encryption; character set conversion; and the interpretation of graphics commands.

The network redirector, long a part of Windows networking, operates at this level. The redirector is what makes the files on a file server visible to the client computer. The network redirector also makes remote printers act as though they are attached to the local computer. Figure 1.10 shows the presentation layer's role in the protocol stack.

FIGURE 1.10   The presentation layer allows applications to establish communication sessions with each other.

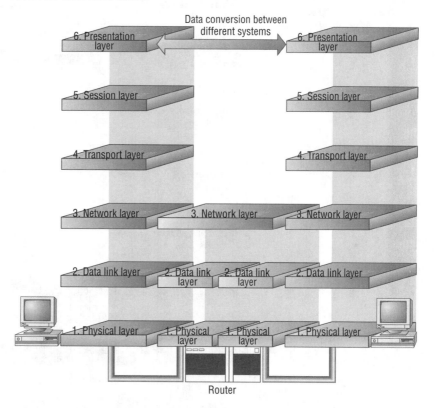

The Application Layer

The application layer is the topmost layer of the OSI model, and it provides services that directly support user applications, such as database access, e-mail, and file transfers. It also allows applications to communicate with applications on other computers as though they were on the same computer. When a programmer writes an application program that uses network services, this is the layer the application program will access. For example,

Internet Explorer uses the application layer to make its requests for files and Web pages; the application layer then passes those requests down the stack, with each succeeding layer doing its job (as in Figure 1.11).

FIGURE 1.11 The application layer is where the applications function, using lower levels to get their work done.

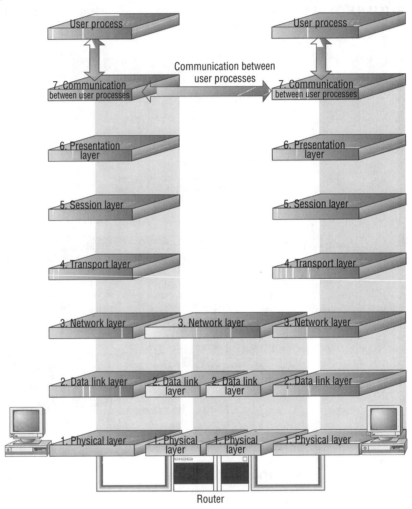

Microsoft's Network Components and the OSI Model

By this time, you may be ready to let loose with a hearty shout of "So what?" Because the OSI model is so abstract, it can be hard to tell how its concepts relate to the actual network software and hardware you use in the real world. This section will make the link clearer so you'll understand why you had to wade through all the OSI material.

Drivers

Every device in a computer requires a device driver to make it work. Some drivers—for instance, the driver for an IDE hard disk or for the keyboard—are built into the operating system. Other devices require that drivers be installed separately when the device is attached or installed in the computer. Network adapter cards are of the second type; driver software must be provided by the manufacturer and installed in the computer so that the computer will be able to access the network adapter card. Windows 2000 really blurs this distinction, since it includes drivers for several hundred different network cards as part of the distribution speed.

In the olden days (e.g., when Windows 3.1 was Microsoft's latest and greatest), network drivers were vendor-specific, both for the operating system and the card. If you wanted to put a 3Com Ethernet card and an IBM Token Ring card in the same server, good luck! Worse yet, most drivers could only be bound to a single protocol stack and a single card, so if you wanted to have, say, two cards using TCP/IP on one server, you couldn't.

A variety of vendors tried to solve this problem by developing driver interfaces that allowed multiple cards to be bound to multiple protocols. Apple and Novell developed the *Open Driver Interface (ODI)*, and Microsoft countered with the *Network Driver Interface Specification (NDIS)*. Microsoft's operating systems have supported NDIS ever since, making it possible to bind either multiple protocols to one card or the same protocol to multiple cards.

Drivers and the OSI Model

Network adapter cards and drivers provide the services corresponding to the data link layer in the OSI model. In the IEEE model, the data link layer is split into the Logical Link Control (LLC) sublayer, which corresponds to the software drivers, and the Media Access Control (MAC) sublayer, which corresponds to the network adapter. If you think of the drivers as intermediaries between the higher layers and the card hardware that handles the business of forming packets and stuffing them into a wire, then you've got the right idea.

The Basics of Network Protocols

Paul Revere's famous line, "One if by land, two if by sea," is one of the best-known communications protocols in existence. Protocols are nothing more than an agreed-upon way in which two objects (people, computers, home appliances, or whatever) can exchange information. There are protocols at various levels in the OSI model. In fact, it is the protocols at a particular level in the OSI model that provide that level's functionality. Protocols that work together to provide a layer or layers of the OSI model are known as a protocol stack or protocol suite.

How Protocols Work

A protocol is a set of basic steps that both parties (or computers) must perform in the right order. For instance, for one computer to send a message to another computer, the first computer must perform the steps given in the following general example:

1. Break the data into small sections called packets.

2. Add addressing information to the packets identifying the destination computer.

3. Deliver the data to the network card for transmission over the network.

The receiving computer must perform the same steps, but in reverse order:

1. Accept the data from the network adapter card.

2. Remove the transmitting information that was added by the transmitting computer.

3. Reassemble the packets of data into the original message.

Each computer needs to perform the same steps, in the same way and in the correct order, so that the data will arrive and be reassembled correctly. If one computer uses a protocol with different steps or even the same steps with different parameters (such as different sequencing, timing, or error correction), the two computers won't be able to communicate with each other.

Network Packets

Networks primarily send and receive small chunks of data called *packets*. Network protocols at various levels of the OSI model construct, modify, and disassemble packets as they move data down the sending stack, across the network, and back up the OSI stack of the receiving computer. Packets have the following components:

- A source address specifying the sending computer
- A destination address specifying where the packet is being sent
- Instructions that tell the computer how to pass the data along
- Reassembly information (if the packet is part of a longer message)
- The data to be transmitted to the remote computer (often called the *packet payload*)
- Error-checking information to ensure that the data arrives intact

These components are assembled into slightly larger chunks; each packet contains three distinct parts (listed below and seen in Figure 1.12), and each part contains some of the components listed above.

Header   A typical header includes an alert signal to indicate that the data is being transmitted, source and destination addresses, and clock information to synchronize the transmission.

Data   This is the actual data being sent. It can vary (depending on the network type) from 48 bytes to 4K.

Trailer   The contents of the trailer (or even the existence of a trailer) varies among network types, but it typically includes a CRC. The CRC helps the network determine whether or not a packet has been damaged in transmission.

FIGURE 1.12   A packet consists of a header, the data, and a trailer.

| Header | Data | Trailer |

Protocols and Binding

Many different protocol stacks can perform network functions, and many different types of network interface cards can be installed in a computer. A computer may have more than one card, and a computer may use more than one protocol stack at the same time.

The *binding* process is what links the protocol stack to the network device driver for the network interface adapter. Several protocols can be bound to the same card; for instance, both TCP/IP and AppleTalk can be bound to the same Ethernet adapter. In addition, one computer with several interface adapters—for instance, a server that must be able to communicate with both a local area network and a network backbone—can have the same protocol bound to two or more network cards.

The binding process can be used throughout the OSI layers to link one protocol stack to another. The device driver (which implements the data link layer) is bound to the network interface card (which implements the physical layer). TCP/IP can be bound to the device driver, and the NetBIOS session layer can be bound to TCP/IP.

Bindings are particularly important to Windows 2000, because you'll often want to change the bindings so that protocols you don't need on a particular network aren't bound to some network adapters. For example, it's very common to unbind the NetBIOS protocol from the network card connected to a Web server's Internet connection.

Are We Connecting Here?

There are two ways that communication between computers can be arranged: connectionless and connection-oriented. It's important to understand the differences between them since different Windows 2000 services use both types.

Connectionless Protocols

It might seem ridiculous to talk about a connectionless protocol for networks, but you use at least two of them just about every day: radio and television. Connectionless systems optimistically assume that all data will get through, so the protocol doesn't guarantee delivery or correct packet ordering. Think of shouting a message out of your window to someone walking by outside—there's no guarantee that they'll hear you, but it's quick and easy. These optimistic assumptions mean that there's no protocol overhead spent on these activities, so connectionless protocols tend to be fast. The *User Datagram Protocol (UDP)* (part of the TCP/IP protocol standard) is an example of a connectionless Internet transport protocol.

Connectionless systems normally work pretty well on lightly loaded networks like most local area networks. Unfortunately, they break down quickly in large or heavily loaded networks where packets can be dropped due to line noise or router congestion.

All is not lost for connectionless transports, however, since higher level protocols will know what data has not reached its destination after some time and request a retransmission. However, connectionless systems do not necessarily return data in sequential order, so the higher-level protocol must sort out the data packets.

Connection-Oriented Protocols

Connection-oriented systems work more like your telephone—you have to dial a number and establish a connection to the other end before you can send a message. Connection-oriented protocols pessimistically assume that some data will be lost or disordered in most transmissions. They guarantee that transmitted data will reach its destination in the proper sequence and that all data will get through. To accomplish this, connection-oriented protocols retain the transmitted data and negotiate for a retransmission when needed. Once all the needed data has arrived at the remote end, it can be reassembled into its proper sequence and passed to the higher-level protocols. This means that any application can depend upon a connection-oriented transport to reliably deliver data exactly as it was transmitted. *Transmission Control Protocol (TCP)* is an example of a connection-oriented Internet protocol.

For local area systems where data isn't likely to be dropped, it makes sense to push serialization and guaranteed delivery up to higher-level protocols that are less efficient since they won't be used often anyway. But in wide area networks like the Internet, it would simply take too much time for higher-level protocols to sort out what data had been sent and what was missing, so the transport protocol simply takes measures to guarantee that all the data gets through in order.

Network Protocols and Windows 2000

So far, you've been reading about a lot of abstract material that might not seem pertinent to Windows 2000. Now it's payoff time—you're about to get a tour of the network protocols included with Windows 2000 and learn how each of them fits into the models you've read about up to this point.

There are a number of protocol stacks afoot in the world's networks today. Besides NetWare, AppleTalk, NetBIOS, and TCP/IP, there are a bunch of entrenched specialty protocols like IBM's SNA, Digital's (now Compaq's) DECnet, and others besides. Even though these protocols actually work at different levels of the OSI model, they fall neatly into three distinct groups, as seen in the following list and in Figure 1.13:

- Application protocols provide for application-to-application interaction and data exchange.

- Transport protocols establish communication sessions between computers.

- Network protocols handle issues such as routing and addressing information, error checking, and retransmission requests.

FIGURE 1.13 The OSI protocol stack can be simplified by grouping its layers into three new categories.

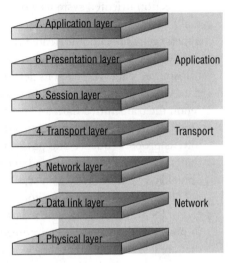

Microsoft networking products come with four network transports, and each is intended for networks of different sizes with different requirements. Each network transport has different strengths and weaknesses. In general, *NetBEUI* is intended for small, single-server networks. *NWLink* is intended for medium-sized networks (in a single facility, perhaps) or for networks that require access to Novell NetWare file servers. AppleTalk's primary use is interoperating with Macintosh computers (a topic which is too specialized to talk about further here). TCP/IP is a complex transport sufficient for globe-spanning networks such as the Internet, and Microsoft is doing everything possible to position TCP/IP as a one-size-fits-all network protocol. In Windows 2000, TCP/IP is required to use Active Directory and is the default protocol for Windows 2000.

NetBEUI

NetBEUI stands for NetBIOS Extended User Interface. (NetBIOS stands for Network Basic Input/Output System.) NetBEUI implements the NetBIOS Frame (NBF) transport protocol, which was developed by IBM in the mid-1980s to support LAN workgroups under OS/2 and LAN Manager.

When IBM developed NetBEUI, they didn't intend for it to allow networked PCs to have enterprise-wide connectivity. Instead, NetBEUI was developed for workgroups of 2 to 200 computers. NetBEUI traffic can't be routed between networks, so it's constrained to small local area networks consisting of relatively small numbers of clients and servers.

NetBEUI has a number of advantages including the following:

- It's fast on small networks, because it has very low overhead.

- It's easy to set up and implement.

- It's largely self-tuning.

You can think of NetBEUI like a small sports car (say, a Mazda Miata or an Alfa Romeo Spyder). It's not suitable for large loads or long trips, but it's fast. Like a sports car, NetBEUI has some drawbacks, too:

- NetBEUI cannot be routed between networks. This makes it totally unsuitable for large-scale networks.

- There are few management or maintenance tools for NetBEUI, which makes it difficult to troubleshoot.

- NetBEUI offers very little cross-platform support.

- Microsoft is trying to do away with NetBEUI in favor of TCP/IP.

Like a sports car, one of the disadvantages of NetBEUI is that it's not suitable for long trips; it can't be routed. Because it's not widely used, there is—outside the realm of Microsoft operating systems—very little software available to help you analyze NetBEUI problems. However, there's an alternate flavor of NetBEUI called *NBT* (which stands for NetBIOS over TCP/IP). NBT is routable and, because it uses TCP/IP as its transport, it gains all of the advantages of TCP/IP. However, Microsoft's trying to kill off NBT, too.

NWLink

NWLink is Microsoft's implementation of Novell's IPX/SPX protocol stack, which is used in Novell NetWare. In fact, it's fair to say that NWLink is nothing more than IPX for Windows NT. IPX is the protocol; NWLink is the networking component that implements it.

IPX is included with Windows 2000 primarily to allow Windows 2000 clients and servers to interconnect with Novell NetWare servers and clients. Microsoft clients and servers can then be added to existing network installations, over time easing the migration between platforms and obviating the need for a complete cut-over from one networking standard to another. (IPX is also a popular protocol for networked games, guaranteeing its appearance in future Microsoft operating systems for some years to come.)

The advantages of NWLink include the following:

- It's easy to set up and manage.
- It's routable.
- It's easy to connect to installed NetWare servers and clients.

Think of NWLink as the sedan of network protocols. NWLink provides a reasonable middle ground between the simple, nonroutable NetBEUI transport protocol and the complex, routable TCP/IP protocol. Like Net-BEUI, IPX has many self-tuning characteristics, and it does not require much administrative knowledge or skill to set up. However, NWLink has some disadvantages such as the following:

- It is difficult to exchange traffic with other organizations.
- It has limited support in Windows 2000.
- It doesn't support standard network management protocols.

Truly large networks (networks that connect many organizations) may find it difficult to work over IPX, because there is no effective central IPX addressing scheme—as there is with TCP/IP—to ensure that two networks don't use the same address numbers. IPX doesn't support the wide range of network management tools available for TCP/IP.

TCP/IP

TCP/IP is actually two sets of protocols bundled together: The *Transmission Control Protocol (TCP)* and the *Internet Protocol (IP)* go together like peanut butter and chocolate. TCP/IP, and a suite of related protocols, were developed by the Department of Defense's Advanced Projects Research Agency (ARPA, or later DARPA) beginning in 1969. Their original goal was to develop network protocols that were robust enough to route around damage caused by nuclear war. Happily, that design goal was never tested, but some aspects of that design have led to the redundant, distributed whole we call the Internet.

TCP/IP is by far the most widely used protocol for interconnecting computers, and it is the protocol of the Internet. This is because, while ARPA originally created TCP/IP to connect military networks together, it provided the protocol standards to government agencies and universities free of charge. The academic world leapt at the chance to use a robust protocol to interconnect their networks, and the Internet was born. Many organizations and individuals collaborated to create higher-level protocols for everything from news groups, mail transfer, file transfer, printing, remote booting, and even document browsing.

To support NetBIOS over TCP/IP, Microsoft has included NBT (NetBIOS over TCP/IP). If you're already using a TCP/IP network, supporting NBT allows older clients to use NetBIOS-based services without actually allowing any NetBEUI traffic across your network.

TCP/IP is currently the protocol king because of its rapid and widespread adoption. It also brings some significant advantages to the table, including the following:

- Broad connectivity among all types of computers and servers, including direct access to the Internet

- Strong support for routing, using a number of flexible routing protocols (see Chapter 8, "Managing IP Routing," for more on these protocols)

- Support for advanced name and address resolution services (which will be covered in more depth in the next chapter): the Domain Name Service (DNS), the Dynamic Host Configuration Protocol (DHCP), and the Windows Internet Name Service (WINS)

- Support for a wide variety of Internet-standard protocols, including protocols for mail transport, Web browsing, and file and print services

- Centralized network number and name assignment, which facilitates internetworking between organizations

If you have a network that spans more than one metropolitan area, or if you want to connect to (or over) the Internet, you'll need to use TCP/IP. Think of TCP/IP as the 18-wheeler of transport protocols. It's not fast or easy to use, but it can carry an immense amount of payload and it's mechanically very robust.

Like a truck, TCP/IP has some disadvantages:

- It's harder to set up than NetBEUI or IPX.

- Its routing and connectivity features impose relatively high overhead.

- It's slower than IPX and NetBEUI.

Even given these disadvantages, we'll all have to learn to live with TCP/IP, since it's the core protocol that Windows 2000 depends on for all of its network services.

Summary

In this chapter, you learned:

- How the OSI networking model is organized
- What each level of the OSI stack does
- Which network protocols are included with Windows 2000 and what they do

Key Terms

Before you take the exam, be sure you're familiar with the following terms:

Binding

Cyclic Redundancy Check (CRC)

Frames of reference

Internet Protocol (IP)

Layer

Logical Link Control (LLC)

Media Access Control (MAC)

NetBIOS over TCP/IP (NBT)

NetBEUI

Network Driver Interface Specification (NDIS)

NWLink

Open Driver Interface (ODI)

Open Systems Interconnection (OSI)

OSI model

Packet

Packet payload

Protocol stack

Service Access Points (SAP)

Transmission Control Protocol (TCP)

User Datagram Protocol (UDP)

Review Questions

1. The OSI model is _____.

   A. A network protocol you can install in Windows 2000

   B. An optional hardware component you add to your network

   C. A framework used for describing and comparing different network systems

   D. The designation used to specify network software that can be used on different physical media

2. The physical layer of the OSI model _____.

   A. Handles the details of physical data transmission between two devices

   B. Is required for higher-level protocols to work

   C. Guarantees the reliable delivery of data

   D. A and B

   E. A and C

3. Which of the following protocols *cannot* be routed?

   A. NetBEUI

   B. TCP

   C. IP

   D. NWLink

4. A connectionless protocol _____.

   A. Doesn't guarantee data delivery

   B. Keeps packets in the correct order

   C. Is suitable for use in heavily loaded networks

   D. Establishes an initial negotiation connection, then drops it to begin communications

5. Which of the following services is *not* provided by a component at the application layer of the OSI model?

   A. Web server

   B. E-mail server

   C. Guaranteed data delivery

   D. File transfer

6. The Transmission Control Protocol (TCP) is an example of which type of protocol?

   A. A connectionless protocol

   B. A connection-oriented protocol

   C. A nonroutable protocol

   D. A protocol not designed for use on wide-area networks

7. The presentation layer of the OSI model does which of the following?

   A. Translates data between the network and application formats

   B. Buffers data for use by the network interface card's driver

   C. Can be removed without affecting network services

   D. Allows applications on separate machines to establish a communication session

8. A network packet usually contains which of the following elements?

   A. A header, data, and a trailer

   B. A header, data, and a footer

   C. A header, a payload, and a footer

   D. A prologue, data, and an epilogue

9. The network layer of the OSI model usually includes which of the following?

   A. Addressing, routing, and flow control

   B. Addressing and routing only

   C. Flow control only

   D. None of the above

10. NWLink is primarily intended for which of the following?

   A. Playing multiplayer LAN games

   B. Connecting to the Internet

   C. Connecting to files and printers shared by Windows 9*x* clients

   D. Connecting to NetWare services

11. Which of the following statements about NetBIOS is *not* true?

   A. It's routable.

   B. It doesn't rely on a central name server.

   C. It's designed for small networks.

   D. It's primarily intended for peer-to-peer networks.

12. A network binding does which of the following?

   A. Associates a protocol with an application

   B. Associates a protocol with a network adapter

   C. Associates a network adapter with an application

   D. Associates two network adapters

13. Connectionless protocols trade off _____.

   A. Reduced overhead for reduced reliability

   B. Increased transmission speed for reduced reliability

   C. Smaller packet size for increased bandwidth

   D. Reliable delivery for automatic address allocation

14. Which of the following capacities does TCP/IP provide (choose two)?

   A. Routability

   B. Automatic configuration of small peer networks

   C. Support for NetWare clients

   D. Flexible name and address resolution

15. Translation between the logical and physical network addresses happens at which layer?

   A. Presentation layer

   B. Application layer

   C. Network layer

   D. Service layer

16. A packet trailer _____.

   A. Is pulled behind a packet truck

   B. Usually contains error-checking data

   C. Is only present in UDP packets

   D. Is required for all packets generated at the session layer

17. What are the two sublayers of the data link layer?

   A. Data link and network

   B. MAC and data link control

   C. Data link and LLC

   D. Link control and logical

18. The presentation layer of the OSI model _____.

   A. Is only used for mainframe-to-PC communications

   B. Is not supported in Windows 2000

   C. Handles format, protocol, and character set conversion

   D. Is implemented as part of the network driver

19. Which of the following is a critical function of the data link layer?

A. Filter out packets received by a device that is not addressed to it

B. Throw out malformed packets

C. Provide a way for two devices that use different character sets to communicate

D. Provide flow control

20. A MAC address _____.

A. Is guaranteed to be a unique hardware address for an Ethernet device

B. May be changed by the system administrator

C. Is not present on non-TCP/IP devices

D. Is used only at the physical layer

Answers to Review Questions

1. C. The OSI model is a framework used for describing and comparing different network systems.

2. D. The physical layer of the OSI model handles the details of physical data transmission between two devices and is required for higher-level protocols to work. The data link layer guarantees the reliable delivery of data.

3. A and B. Examples of routable protocols are TCP/IP, IPX/SPX (NWLink), and AppleTalk. The IP and IPX portions are routable; the TCP and SPX portions denote connections.

4. A. A connectionless protocol does not guarantee data delivery. Data delivery is the responsibility of the upper-layer protocols. Connection-oriented protocols keep packets in the correct order (sequenced) and are suitable for use in heavily loaded networks.

5. C. Guaranteed data delivery is a transport function, not something provided by the application.

6. B. TCP is connection-oriented; its sibling, UDP, is connectionless.

7. A. The presentation layer of the OSI model translates data between the network and application formats.

8. A. A network packet usually contains a header, data, and a trailer.

9. A. Addressing, routing, and flow control are all network layer functions.

10. D. NWLink is Microsoft's implementation of Novell's IPX/SPX protocol set.

11. A. NetBIOS isn't routable unless it's encapsulated.

12. B. Bindings tie a protocol to a particular NIC so you can use that protocol on the attached network.

13. A and B. Connectionless protocols have lower overhead than connection-oriented protocols and they are faster, but they don't guarantee sequencing or delivery.

14. A and D. NWLink supports NetWare clients, and NetBEUI provides self-configuration for small networks.

15. C. The network layer is responsible for translating between logical and physical network addresses.

16. B. Not all protocols include trailers; those that do typically use them for error correction and control.

17. B. The two sublayers of the data link layer are MAC (Media Access Control) and data link control.

18. C. The Windows 2000 network redirector operates at the presentation layer. It handles conversion between on-disk file systems and network requests.

19. A. The data link layer screens broadcast packets so that packets not addressed to the receiving device don't ascend its network stack.

20. A. The MAC address is a unique hardware-specific ID that's used at the data link layer. Any Ethernet device will have a MAC address, even if it's not using TCP/IP.

Chapter

2

Windows 2000 Network Naming Services

In Chapter 1, you learned the basic protocols that Windows 2000 uses to move data over the network. While TCP/IP, IPX, and NetBEUI are all useful, they act as transports for moving data from point A to point B; in that role, they're a necessary part of the network infrastructure, but they don't *do* anything themselves. Consider the U.S. interstate highway system: It has a set of protocols for signaling (big green signs), routing (loop highways, cloverleaf interchanges), and flow control. However, the existence of the interstate highway system doesn't give you a way to get from Houston to Hyannisport; for that, you need navigational information and some kind of vehicle.

Windows 2000 includes three *network naming* services that you need to understand to pass the exam: the Dynamic Host Configuration Protocol (DHCP), the Domain Name Service (DNS), and the Windows Internet Name Service (WINS). These services provide network name and address information to applications that request it.

One of the most interesting things about the three services in this chapter is that all three are open Internet standards, defined by documents called *Internet Requests for Comments (RFCs)*. RFCs are documents that outline the function and form of network protocols and services; they act as standards that any vendor can follow to implement a service that will (or at least should) interoperate with other vendors. Relevant RFCs will be highlighted in the discussion of each service; although they're highly technical and rather dry, they serve as the ultimate authority on how these services are designed to work.

If you want to read along with the RFCs cited in this chapter, you'll find them online at http://www.faqs.org/rfcs/.

By the time you finish this chapter, you'll have a solid understanding of how DNS, DHCP, and WINS work; that will prepare you to learn how to configure and manage these services in later chapters.

Dynamic Host Configuration Protocol

The Dynamic Host Configuration Protocol is designed to automate configuration of TCP/IP clients. In theory, you can put one or more DHCP servers on your network, program them with a range of network addresses and other configuration parameters, and let clients automatically obtain IP addressing information without manual intervention. While theory and practice often diverge (especially when software's involved), DHCP pretty much delivers on this promise. With appropriate DHCP configurations, your TCP/IP clients—running any OS that has DHCP support—can be configured with little or no manual intervention from you.

What DHCP Does

DHCP's job is to centralize the process of IP address and option assignment. What does this mean? Simply put, you can configure a DHCP server with a range of addresses, then sit back and let it assign IP parameters like addresses, default gateways, DNS server addresses, and so on. DHCP is defined by a series of RFCs, notably 1533, 1534, 1541, and 1542. In brief, the DHCP process goes like this: When TCP/IP starts up on a DHCP-enabled host, a special message is sent out requesting an IP address and a subnet mask from a DHCP server.

Any DHCP server that hears the request checks its internal database, then replies with a message containing the information the client requested. The contents of this message vary, depending on how the DHCP server is configured—there are numerous different pieces of information that you can specify to pass to the client on a Windows 2000 DHCP server. When the client accepts the IP offer, it is then extended to the client for a specified period of time called a *lease*. If the DHCP server has given out all the IP addresses in its range, it won't make an offer; if no other servers make an offer, the client's TCP/IP initialization will fail.

This lease procedure is surprisingly similar to what happens when you lease a car. After you negotiate acceptable terms with a car dealer, you sign a lease. This lease permits you the use of a certain car for a specific period of time. If the car dealership doesn't have the terms or vehicle you want, you don't drive off the lot with it.

Good Things about DHCP

DHCP seems like just the kind of helpful, unobtrusive tool we all want to use to simplify our network management tasks. It has some significant advantages such as the following:

- DHCP capability is bundled with Windows 2000, so adding it to your network doesn't cost anything extra.

- Once you enter the IP configuration information in one place—the server—it's automatically propagated to clients, eliminating the chance that a user will fat-finger some parameters and require you to fix it.

- Configuration problems are minimized, clearing up a labyrinth of possible situations that lead to big messes and obscure, hard-to-find problems.

- IP addresses are conserved, since DHCP only assigns them when a client requests one. A pool of 254 Class C addresses lasts a lot longer when they can be reused.

- IP configuration becomes almost completely Plug-and-Play. In most cases, you can unbox and plug in a new system (or move one), then watch as it magically receives a configuration from the server.

Bad Things about DHCP

Lest you think that DHCP is the best thing for network administrators since Diet Mountain Dew, let me point out a few actual and potential drawbacks of DHCP. These include the following:

- Not all DHCP client implementations work properly with Windows 2000's DHCP server. It's an open question of whether this is the fault of Microsoft or the other vendors, since the DHCP RFCs leave some areas open to interpretation.

- "Garbage in, garbage out" still rules. If you put incorrect information into your DHCP server, it will automatically be blasted onto all your DHCP clients, meaning you may have to clean up after yourself by visiting each machine and reconfiguring it—just what you were trying to avoid by using DHCP.

- If you're not careful, DHCP can become a single point of failure for your network. If you only have one DHCP server and it's not available, clients won't be able to request or renew leases.

- If you want to use DHCP on a multisegment network, you must either put a DHCP server on each segment or ensure that your router can forward BootP broadcasts.

DHCP and Windows 2000

The DHCP service in Windows 2000 is moderately different from the one included in Windows NT. For starters, you manage DHCP servers using the DHCP snap-in for the Microsoft Management Console (MMC). Chapter 5 covers the process of installing and configuring the snap-in, as well as using it to manage your DHCP servers. A larger, though less visible, change is that DHCP and the Domain Name Service (DNS) are now integrated so that DNS records can be updated whenever a DHCP-assigned address changes as the result of a lease issue or release.

Ideally, you'll integrate dynamic DNS and DHCP on your Windows 2000 networks. When a DHCP client receives an IP address, the DHCP server dictates how dynamic updates occur. By default, here's what happens:

1. The DHCP client computer updates the DNS record that identifies which IP address is associated with that computer's name.

2. The DHCP server updates the corresponding DNS resource record that identifies which name belongs with the newly issued IP address.

How DHCP Works

DHCP is a pretty simple process; at the end of the process (and if all goes well), the client will have an IP address and whatever other parameters the DHCP server owner wanted to supply. Since an IP address is required to communicate with other devices on a TCP/IP network, the DHCP negotiation happens very early in the Windows 2000 boot cycle.

Each network adapter in a system has its own IP address; if you have multiple NICs that are configured to use DHCP, you'll see below the process happening once for each DHCP-aware NIC.

Stage One: IP Discovery

The first step in the DHCP mating dance is the *discovery* stage. It's triggered the first time a client's DHCP-configured TCP/IP stack starts, or when you switch from using an assigned IP address to using DHCP. Just to complicate things further, it can also occur when a specific IP address is requested but unavailable or immediately after a formerly used IP address was released.

At the time of the lease request, the client doesn't know what its IP address is, nor does it know the IP address of the server. To work around this, the client uses 0.0.0.0 as its address and 255.255.255.255 for the server's address, then it sends out a broadcast *DHCP discover message* on UDP ports 67 and 68. The discover message contains the hardware MAC address and NetBIOS name of the client.

Once the first discover message is sent, the client waits one second for an offer. If no DHCP server responds within that time, the client repeats its request three more times at 9-, 13-, and 16-second intervals. If the client still doesn't hear an answer, it will continue to broadcast discover messages every five minutes until it gets an answer. If no DHCP server ever becomes available, no TCP/IP communications will be possible. The Windows 2000 client will automatically pick what it thinks is an unused address (from the 169.254.xy address block) at this point instead of waiting indefinitely for an answer. Even though a static address has been assigned, the DHCP client will continuously poll every five minutes for a DHCP server, then switch back to using a DHCP-assigned address when the server becomes available. For more information on the automatic assigning of private IP addresses, see Chapter 13.

Remember that the discover message broadcasts won't be heard outside the client's local subnet unless your routers support BootP forwarding.

Stage Two: IP Lease Offer

In the second phase of the DHCP process, any DHCP server that received the discover message broadcast and that has valid address information to offer responds with an *offer message*. (This feature allows you to configure multiple DHCP servers so that you're protected against a single-point failure.) The Windows 2000 DHCP server registers itself in Active Directory, and it won't begin offering leases until it successfully registers in the directory. (See Chapter 6 for more on DHCP server authorization.) The offer message is a proposal from the server to the client, and it contains an IP address, a subnet mask, a lease period (in hours), and the IP address of the DHCP server offering the proposal. The IP address being offered is temporarily reserved so that the server doesn't offer the same address to multiple clients. All offers are sent directly to the requesting client's hardware MAC address.

Stage Three: IP Lease Selection

Once the client has received at least one offer, the third phase of the DHCP process begins. In this phase, the client machine will select an offer from those it received. Windows 2000 always accepts the first offer that arrives; to signal acceptance, the client broadcasts an acceptance message containing the IP address of the server it selected. It has to be broadcast so that the servers whose offers weren't selected can un-reserve (pull back) the addresses they offered.

Stage Four: IP Lease Acknowledgment

Once the chosen DHCP server receives the acceptance message from the client, it marks the selected IP address as leased, then sends an acknowledgment message, called a *DHCPACK*, back to the client. It's also possible that the server might send a negative acknowledgment, or *DHCPNACK*, to the client; DHCPNACKs are most often generated when the client is attempting to renew a lease for its old IP address after that address has been reassigned elsewhere. Negative acceptance messages can also mean that the requesting client has an inaccurate IP address resulting from physically changing locations to an alternate subnet.

The DHCPACK message includes any DHCP options specified by the server, along with the IP address and subnet mask. When the client receives this message, it stuffs the parameters into the TCP/IP stack, which can then proceed just as though the user had manually given it new configuration parameters.

Manually configured entries on the client override any DHCP supplied entries.

This four-step process may seem overly complicated, but each step is necessary. The aggregate result of these steps is that one server assigns one address to one client. For example, if each server offering a lease immediately assigned an IP address to a requesting workstation, there would soon be no numbers left to assign. Likewise, if the DHCP client controlled whether it accepted or rejected the lease (instead of waiting for a DHCPACK or DHCP-NACK message), a slow client could cause the server to mark an assigned address as free, then assign it somewhere else—leaving two clients with the same offer.

DHCP Lease Renewal

Nothing lasts forever, not even DHCP leases. That raises the question of what happens when the lease expires or needs to be renewed. No matter how long the lease period is, the client will send a new lease request message to the DHCP server when the lease period is half over. If the server hears the request message, and there's no reason to reject it, it sends a DHCPACK to the client. This will reset the lease period, just like signing a renewal rider on a car lease.

If the DHCP server isn't available, something sends the client an "eviction notice" indicating that the lease can't be renewed. The client can then use the address for the rest of the lease period; once 87.5% of the lease period has elapsed, the client will send out another renewal request. At that point, any DHCP server that hears the renewal could respond to this *DHCP request message* with a DHCPACK and renew the lease.

Any time the client gets a DHCPNACK message, it must stop using its IP address immediately and start the leasing process over from the beginning by requesting a brand-new lease.

When a client initializes TCP/IP, it will always attempt to renew its old address. Just like any other renewal, if the client has time left on the lease, it will continue to use the lease until its end. If the client is unable to get a new lease by that time, all TCP/IP functions will stop until a new, valid address can be obtained.

DHCP Lease Release

Although leases can be renewed repeatedly, at some point they're likely to run out. Furthermore, the lease process is an "at will" process—the client or server can cancel the lease before it ends. In addition, if the client doesn't succeed in renewing the lease before it expires, out it goes! This release process is an important function that's useful for reclaiming extinct IP addresses formerly used by systems that have moved or switched to a non-DHCP address.

Domain Name Service

In the late '70s, there was only a handful of networked computers, and all of the computer name-to-address mappings were contained in a single file called HOSTS. This was stored at the Stanford Research Institute's Network Information Center (SRI-NIC). Whenever anybody wanted to update their HOSTS file, they would download the latest HOSTS file from Stanford. This actually worked for a while, until so many computers got on the network that managing the HOSTS file became too difficult. Since bandwidth was pretty limited back then, Stanford got overloaded with updates and queries. Another problem stemmed from the HOSTS file's structure. It was a flat name structure, requiring each computer across the whole Internet to have a unique name. The ARPANET was created to find the solution to this problem (among others), which led to DNS, a distributed database using a hierarchical naming structure.

The original design goal for DNS was to replace the cumbersome, centrally-administered HOSTS file system with a lightweight, fast, distributed database that would allow for a hierarchical name space, distributed administration, extensive data types, virtually unlimited database size, and reasonable performance.

The Domain Name System (DNS) is a set of protocols and services that allows users of the network to utilize hierarchical, user-friendly names instead of IP addresses when looking for network resources. This system is used extensively on the Internet and in many private enterprises today. If you've used a Web browser, Telnet application, FTP utility, or other similar TCP/IP utilities on the Internet, then you have probably used a DNS server.

The DNS protocol's best-known function is mapping user-friendly names to IP addresses. For example, suppose the FTP site at Microsoft had an IP address of 157.55.100.1. Most people would reach this computer by specifying **ftp.microsoft.com** instead of its alienating IP address. Besides being easier to remember, the name is more reliable. The numeric address could change for any number of reasons, but that name can remain in spite of the change. There's another lesser-known DNS function, though: It can turn addresses into names, a function often used to generate human-readable reports and logs of various types.

The primary specifications for DNS are defined in Requests for Comments (RFCs) 974, 1034, and 1035. The Windows 2000 DNS server supports the requirements found in RFCs 1033, 1034, 1035, 1101, 1123, 1183, 1536, and 2136.

What DNS Does

DNS's job is to translate between computer host names and IP addresses. DNS works at the application layer of the OSI reference model and uses TCP and UDP at the transport layer. The DNS model is pretty plain: Clients make requests ("what's the IP address for www.robichaux.net?") and get back answers ("209.155.222.222"). If a particular server can't answer a query, it can forward it to another, presumably better informed, server.

Think of DNS like a telephone book. When you want to call someone and you know their name, you can look them up in the book; in essence, the book maps human-readable names into (telephone) network addresses.

To really understand how DNS works, it's important to learn about some fundamental parts of the system.

Domain Naming Made Simple(r)

The Domain Name System is composed of a distributed database of names that establishes a logical tree structure called the domain name space. Each node, or domain, in that space has a unique name. Robichaux.com and robichaux.net are thus two different domains, and they can contain subdomains.

A domain name identifies the domain's position in the logical DNS hierarchy in relation to its parent domain by separating each branch of the tree with a period (.). Figure 2.1 shows a few of the top-level domains, where the Microsoft domain fits, and a host called Tigger within the microsoft.com domain. If someone wanted to contact that host, they would use the fully qualified domain name (FQDN): tigger.microsoft.com.

FIGURE 2.1   The DNS hierarchy

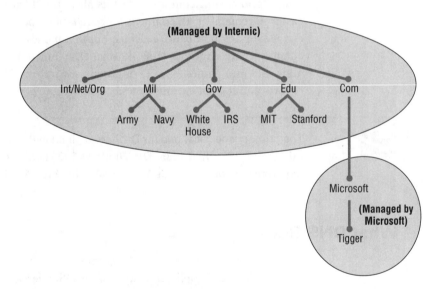

Each node in the DNS database tree, along with all the nodes below it, is called a domain. Domains can contain both hosts (computers) and other domains (subdomains). For example, the Microsoft domain microsoft.com could contain computers, like betanews.microsoft.com, and subdomains, like exchange.microsoft.com. These subdomains can, and usually do, contain hosts; the host adds its name to its domain, as in `dev1.exchange .microsoft.com`.

Each domain is associated with a DNS *name server*. In other words, for every domain registered in the DNS, there's some server that can give an authoritative answer to queries about that domain. For example, the `robichaux.net` domain is handled by a name server at an Internet provider. This means that any resolver or name server can go straight to the source if it can't resolve a query by looking in its own cache.

Domain names and host names must contain only characters a-z, A-Z, 0-9, and - (hyphen). Other common and useful characters, like the & (ampersand), / (slash), . (period), and _ (underscore), are forbidden. This is in conflict with NetBIOS's naming restrictions; however, you'll find that Windows 2000 is smart enough to take a NetBIOS name like Server_1 and turn it into a legal DNS name.

DNS and the Internet

You're undoubtedly familiar with how DNS works on the Internet; if you've ever sent or received Internet e-mail or browsed Web pages on the net, you've got first-hand experience using DNS. Internet DNS depends on a set of top-level domains that serve as the root of the DNS hierarchy. These top-level domains and their authoritative name servers are managed by the Internet Network Information Center (`http://www.internic.com`). The top-level domains are organized in two ways: by organization and by country. Table 2.1 shows some of the most common top-level domains.

TABLE 2.1 Common top-level DNS domains

Top-Level Domain Names	Type of Organization
com	Commercial (for example, `globalknowledge.com` for Global Knowledge Network).
edu	Educational (for example, `gatech.edu` for the Georgia Institute of Technology).
gov	Government (for example, `whitehouse.gov` for the White House in Washington, D.C.).
int	International organizations (for example, `nato.int` for NATO). This top-level domain is fairly rare.

TABLE 2.1   Common top-level DNS domains *(continued)*

Top-Level Domain Names	Type of Organization
mil	Military organizations (for example, usmc.mil for the Marine Corps). There is a separate set of root name servers for this domain.
net	Networking organizations and Internet providers (for example, hiwaay.net for HiWAAY Information Systems). Many commercial organizations have registered names under this domain, too.
org	Noncommercial organizations (for example, fido-net.org for FidoNet).
AU	Australia.
UK	United Kingdom.
CA	Canada.
NU	Niue (a tiny Pacific island).
US	United States.
JP	Japan.

Beneath each top-level domain, there can be additional subdomains. For example, commercial organizations in Japan will have .co.jp on the end of their domain names. My local police department has a server in the ci.athens.al.us domain: "ci" for city, "Athens" because the city's name is Athens, "al" for Alabama, and the top-level "US" domain.

DNS and Windows 2000

Windows 2000 relies on TCP/IP, and Active Directory requires DNS—even if you're not connected to the Internet! Naturally, Windows 2000 includes a DNS server that has all the functionality of the Windows NT 4.0 version. It also adds some neat features that (surprise!) are even interoperable with other DNS implementations.

Dynamic DNS

In Windows NT when you use DHCP to assign IP addresses to clients, you have no way to keep the corresponding DNS records up-to-date. For example, if I have a DNS entry for `minuteman.robichaux.net` pointing to 192.168.0.202, that's great until minuteman's DHCP lease is released and it gets a new address. At that point, you get the choice of either fixing the DNS record by hand or relying on NetBIOS and WINS for name resolution. You may have a similar problem if you use a dial-up ISP—every time you dial up, you get a different IP address.

The *Dynamic DNS (DDNS) standard*, described in RFC 2136, was designed to solve this exact problem. DDNS allows DNS *clients* (not resolvers) to update information in the DNS database files. For example, a Windows 2000 DHCP server can automatically tell a DDNS server which IP addresses it's assigned to, and to what machines. Windows 2000 DHCP clients can do this, too, but for security reasons it's better to let the DHCP server do it. The result: IP addresses and DNS records stay in synch so that you can use DNS and DHCP together seamlessly.

Because DDNS is a proposed Internet standard, you can even use Windows 2000's DDNS-aware parts with Unix-based DNS servers.

DNS and Active Directory

In the next section, "How DNS Works," you can expect to learn where the Windows 2000 DNS server stores all of its resource information. Actually, you'll learn about how those resource records are organized and how they're stored in a standard primary or secondary zone. However, there's another new Windows 2000 feature of interest in this section: You can store DNS data in Active Directory, or AD, instead of in regular disk files.

While it might seem odd to use AD to store information that AD will have to run, it makes sense. Consider a typical DNS zone data file on disk—it's plain text, easily editable. It's not replicated, it's probably not secured, and there's no way to delegate control over it. All of these limitations go away when you build what Microsoft calls an *Active Directory-Integrated (ADI) zone*. In an ADI zone, Active Directory stores all of the DNS zone data in AD, so it gains all of the benefits of AD—especially improved security and seamless replication. Note that there's no such thing as an ADI secondary zone.

How DNS Works

DNS is a widespread, highly distributed system that, for the most part, works remarkably well and with little fuss. Knowing how servers and resolvers communicate with each other, and what kind of queries are passed around, is critical to properly configuring your network. That knowledge begins with understanding what's actually in the DNS database itself.

What's in the DNS Database?

No matter where your *zone* information is stored, you can rest assured that it contains a bunch of different items—some of which are new for Windows 2000. While the DNS snap-in makes it unlikely that you'll ever need to edit these files by hand, it's good to know exactly what data are contained in there.

The first thing to understand is the fact that each zone file consists of a number of *resource records*. Each resource record, or RR, contains information about some resource on the network, such as its IP address. There are several types of resource records you need to know about to effectively manage your DNS servers.

Start of Authority (SOA) Records

The first record in any database file is the Start of Authority (SOA) Record, which looks like this:

```
@ IN SOA <source host> <contact e-mail> <ser. no.>
<refresh time>
<retry time> <expiration time> <TTL>
```

The SOA defines the general parameters for the DNS zone, including who the authoritative server is for the zone. Table 2.2 lists the attributes stored in the SOA record.

TABLE 2.2 The SOA record structure

Field	Meaning
source host	The host on which this file is maintained.
contact e-mail	The Internet e-mail address for the person responsible for this domain's database file.
serial number	The "version number" of this database file that should increase each time the database file is changed.

TABLE 2.2 The SOA record structure *(continued)*

Field	Meaning
refresh time	The elapsed time (in seconds) that a secondary server will wait between checks to its master server to see if the database file has changed, and a *zone transfer* should be requested.
retry time	The elapsed time (in seconds) that a secondary server will wait before retrying a failed zone transfer.
expiration time	The elapsed time (in seconds) that a secondary server will keep trying to download a zone. After this time limit expires, the old zone information will be discarded.
time to live	The elapsed time (in seconds) that a DNS server is allowed to cache any resource records from this database file. This is the value that is sent out with all query responses from this zone file when the individual resource record doesn't contain an overriding value.

Name Server (NS) Records

NS records list the name servers for a domain; this allows other name servers to look up names in your domain. A zone file may contain more than one name server record. The format of these records is simple:

```
<domain> @ IN NS <nameserver host >
```

"Domain" is the name of your domain, and "nameserver host" is the FQDN of a name server in that domain. There are a couple of interesting shortcuts that can be used in DNS records such as the following:

- In a zone file, the @ symbol represents the root domain of the zone. The "IN" in the records stands for Internet.

- Any domain name in the database file which is *not* terminated with a period will have the root domain appended to the end. For example, an entry that just has the name "sales" will be expanded by adding the root domain to the end, while "sales.robichaux.net." won't be expanded.

What do these records actually look like? Here's a small sample:

```
@ IN NS ns1.robichaux.net
@ IN NS ns2.robichaux.net
```

NS records play a key role in the referral process you'll be learning about later in the chapter.

The Host Record

A *host record* (also called an address or an A record) is used to statically associate a host's name to its IP addresses. The format is pretty simple. Here's an example from my DNS database:

```
minuteman IN A 192.168.0.204
titan IN A 192.168.3.144
```

The A record ties a host name (which is part, you'll recall, of a FQDN) to a specific IP address. This makes them suitable for use when you have devices with statically assigned IP addresses; in that case, you'd create these records manually using the DNS snap-in. As it turns out, if you enable DDNS your DHCP server can create these for you; that automatic creation is what enables DDNS to work.

The Pointer Record

A records are probably the most visible component of the DNS database, since Internet users depend on them to turn FQDNs like www.microsoft .com and www.delta-air.com into IP addresses so that browsers and other components can find them. However, the host record has a lesser-known but still important twin: the *pointer (PTR) record*. The A record maps a host name to an IP address, and the PTR record does just the opposite. Having both types of records makes it possible to do *reverse lookups*, where a resolver asks a DNS server to cough up the FQDN associated with a particular IP address. This is a useful function for, among other things, preventing people with made-up or illegal domain names from using services like e-mail or FTP servers.

The Alias Record

Almost every company on the Web has a URL of www.companyname.com. This is pretty much standard, but did you ever stop to consider whether all of those domains actually have machines named www? In fact, many (if not most) of them don't; they use DNS alias records (more properly known as canonical name, or CNAME, entries, which allow them to use more than one name to point to a single host). For example, one client I recently visited (call them `inTexas.com`, since that's where they are) had a machine whose "real" A record name was `kingkong.intexas.com`. The same machine had CNAME records that pointed the names `mail.intexas.com` and `ftp.intexas.com` to the same machine. A resolver that queried their DNS server for either *mail* or *ftp* would actually get the A record for *kingkong* back. Here's how they did it:

```
ftp IN CNAME kingkong
kingkong IN A 172.30.1.14
```

The Mail Exchange Record

The mail exchange, or MX, record tells us which servers can accept mail bound for this domain. Each MX record contains two parameters—a preference and a mailserver—as shown in the following example:

```
<domain> IN MX <preference> <mailserver host>
```

Why use MX records? As an example, consider the `robichaux.net` domain. Users in my organization have addresses of `someuser@robichaux.net`. To make sure that mail is delivered where I want it to go—my Exchange server—I have two MX records: one points to `hawk.robichaux.net`, and one points to my ISP's mail server. When someone on the Internet tries to send SMTP mail to any user whose address ends in `robichaux.net`, their mail server will look to see if that domain contains an MX record. If it does, the sending server will use the host specified in the MX record to deliver the mail.

Attentive readers will notice that I said my domain has *two* MX records. That's because MX records have preferences attached to them. If multiple MX records exist for a domain, the DNS server uses the mail server with the lowest preference, then tries the other mail servers when the most preferred host can't be contacted. The two records I use look like this:

```
Robichaux.net. IN MX 100 mail.pair.com
Robichaux.net. IN MX 10 mail.robichaux.net
```

Service Records

Windows 2000 depends on some (relatively) new services, like LDAP and Kerberos. These protocols postdate the DNS system by quite a while. Normally, clients use DNS to find the IP address of a machine whose name they already know. Microsoft wanted to extend this system by devising a way for a client to locate a particular *service* by making a DNS query. For example, a Windows 2000 client can query DNS servers for the location of a domain controller—this makes it much easier (both for the client and for the administrator) to manage and distribute logon traffic in large-scale networks. For this approach to work, Microsoft had to have some way to register the presence of a service (or, really, a TCP/IP protocol) in DNS, but none of the RR types you've read about so far offer any way to do so. Enter the *service record (SRV)*.

SRV records tie together the location of a service (like a domain controller) with information about how to contact the service. Think of a CNAME record: It ties a name to an IP address. The MX record extends the concept by adding another parameter, the preference. SRV records take it even further by providing seven items of information. Let's look at an example to help clarify this powerful concept:

```
ldap.tcp.robichaux.netSRV 10 100 389 hsv.robichaux.net
ldap.tcp.robichaux.netSRV 20 100 389 msy.robichaux.net
```

The first field, "ldap.tcp.robichaux.net," takes some explaining because it's actually a composite: It contains a service name ("ldap" for LDAP or "kerb" for Kerberos), a transport protocol (TCP or UDP), and the domain name for which the service is offered. Thus, "ldap.tcp.robichaux.net" indicates that this SRV record is advertising an LDAP server for the robichaux.net domain. The next field is just the record type—SRV in this case.

The two numbers following are the priority and the weight. The priority field specifies a preference, just like the preference field in an MX record. The SRV record with the lowest priority will be used first. The weight is a little different: Service records with equal priority will be chosen according to their weight. Consider the case of three SRV records of priority 0 and weight 100. That tells the DNS server to answer queries by picking one of the three at random since they have equal weight. If one record had a weight of 50 (instead of 100), it would be chosen half as often as either of the other records.

The next field is the port number on which the service is offered: 389 for LDAP or 88 for Kerberos. The final entry in the record defines the DNS name of the server which offers the service (in this case, hsv.robichaux.net and msy.robichaux.net). You'll read later how these service records are actually used in DNS queries; for now it's enough to understand that they exist.

You can define other types of service records; if your applications support them they can query DNS to find the services they need.

Where Are the Zone Databases?

Let's assume for a minute that you're not using an ADI zone. The only reason we make that assumption is to illustrate where the zone database files live on a non-ADI server, as well as to describe what's in them. As it turns out, you can specify names for some, but not all, of these files when you install DNS on your Windows 2000 server.

The Domain Name File

Each domain that has a forward lookup zone on your server will have its own database file. For example, when you create a new zone named robichaux .net on a Windows 2000 DNS server, you'll end up with a new file named robichaux.net.dns in the system's DNS directory (%systemroot%\ system32\DNS). The file is pretty much empty when you create the zone: It contains only an SOA record for the domain and one NS record listing the name of the server you just created. As you add new A records to the domain, they're stored in this file.

The Reverse Lookup File

This database file holds information on a single reverse lookup zone. These zones are usually named after the IP address range they cover; for example, a reverse lookup zone that can handle queries for the 172.30.1.* block will be named 1.30.172.in-addr.arpa. Remember that the reverse lookup database allows a resolver to provide an IP address and request a matching host name. It looks like the domain database file (e.g., it has SOA and name server records), but instead of A records it has one PTR record for each host designated in the reverse lookup zone.

DNS reverse lookup is frequently used as a sort of backdoor authentication method. For example, most modern mail servers can be configured to refuse incoming mail from servers whose IP address can't be resolved with a reverse lookup. This prevents people with real IP addresses but fake DNS names from using those mail servers. Who mixes real addresses with fake names? Spammers! Reverse lookups are also valuable for troubleshooting name resolution problems, since you can always find the IP address of a machine even if you're not sure what its domain name is supposed to be.

The Cache File

The cache file contains host information needed to resolve names outside the authoritative domains—in short, it holds a list of the names and addresses of root name servers. If your DNS server will be able to connect to the Internet, you can leave this file alone; if not, you can edit it so that it lists the authoritative roots for your private network.

The Boot File

Sometimes a de facto standard is a powerful thing. In the Unix world, the Berkeley Internet Name Daemon (BIND) is *the* de facto standard DNS server, and Microsoft wisely chose to copy some of its key features in their own DNS implementation. Boot files are one such feature.

Consider what a *primary DNS server* must do when it boots. Somehow, it has to figure out what zones it's supposed to be serving, decide whether it's authoritative for any of them, and link up with other servers in the zone, if any. You can choose the method by which Windows 2000 DNS servers get this information: from AD, from the registry, or from a BIND-style boot file. The boot file, which must be named %systemroot%\system32\dns\boot, controls the DNS server's startup behavior. Boot files only support four commands:

Directory The directory command specifies where the other files named in the boot file can be found. This is almost always the %systemroot%\system32\dns directory. You use the command along with a directory path, like this:

```
directory f:\winnt\system32\dns
```

Cache The cache command specifies the file of root hints used to help your DNS service contact name servers for the root domain. This command, *and* the file it refers to, *must* be present. For example: cache cache.dns points the DNS server at the default cache.dns file shipped with Windows 2000.

Primary The primary command specifies a domain for which this name server is authoritative, as well as a database file that contains the resource records for that domain. You can use multiple primary commands in a single boot file. For example:

```
primary robichaux.net          robichaux.net.dns
primary hsv.robichaux.net      hsv.robichaux.dns
```

Secondary   The secondary command designates a domain as being one that your server handles as a *secondary*. That means your server is authoritative, but it pulls DNS information from one (or more) of the specified master servers. The command also defines the name of the local file for caching this zone. Multiple secondary command records may exist in the boot file. The secondary command takes three parameters, like this:

```
secondary wuolukka.com      ns.pair.com      wuolukka.dns
secondary robichauxs.com    ns2.pair.com     robichauxs.dns
```

How DNS Resolves Names

There are three types of queries that a client can make to a DNS server: recursive, iterative, and inverse. Remember that the client of a DNS server can be a *resolver* (what you'd normally call a client) or another DNS server.

Iterative queries are the easiest to understand: A client asks the DNS server for an answer, and the client returns the best kind of answer it has. This type of query is typically sent by one DNS server to another, after the original server has received a recursive query from a resolver. The answer may be "I don't know; go ask the server at x.y.z.1," or it may be an actual RR.

Most resolvers, however, use recursive queries, which are different from iterative queries. In a recursive query, the client sends a query to one name server, asking it to respond either with the requested answer or with an error. The error states one of two things: that the server can't come up with the right answer, or that the domain name doesn't exist. The name server isn't allowed to just refer the querier to some other name server. In addition, if your DNS server uses a forwarder, the requests sent by your server to the forwarder will be recursive queries.

Figure 2.2 shows an example of both recursive and iterative queries. In this example, a client within the Microsoft Corporation is querying its DNS server for the IP address for www.whitehouse.gov. Here's what happens to resolve the request:

1. The resolver sends a recursive DNS query to its local DNS server asking for the IP address of www.whitehouse.gov. The local name server is responsible for resolving the name and cannot refer the resolver to another name server.

2. The local name server checks its zones and finds no zones corresponding to the requested domain name.

3. The root name server has authority for the root domain and will reply with the IP address of a name server for the GOV top-level domain.

4. The local name server sends an iterative query for www.whitehouse .gov to the GOV name server.

5. The GOV name server replies with the IP address of the name server servicing the `whitehouse.gov` domain.

6. The local name server sends an iterative query for `www.whitehouse.gov` to the `whitehouse.gov` name server.

7. The `whitehouse.gov` name server replies with the IP address corresponding to `www.whitehouse.gov`.

8. The local name server sends the IP address of `www.whitehouse.gov` back to the original resolver.

FIGURE 2.2   A sample DNS query

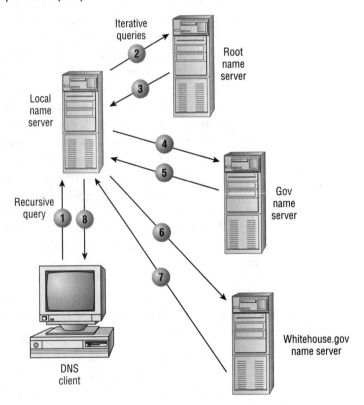

What about inverse queries? They use PTR records; instead of supplying a name and then asking for an IP address, the client first provides the IP address and then asks for the name. Since there's no direct correlation in the DNS name space between a domain name and its associated IP address, this search would be fruitless without use of a special trick: the `in-addr.arpa`

domain. Nodes in the `in-addr.arpa` domain are named after the numbers in the dotted-octet representation of IP addresses, but because IP addresses get more specific from left to right and domain names get less specific from left to right, the order of IP address octets must be reversed when building the `in-addr.arpa` tree. With this arrangement, administration of the lower limbs of the DNS `in-addr.arpa` tree can be given to companies as they are assigned their Class A, B, or C subnet address.

Once the domain tree is built into the DNS database, a special pointer record is added to associate the IP addresses to the corresponding host names. In other words, to find a host name for the IP address 206.131.234.1, the resolver would query the DNS server for a pointer record for 1.234.131.206 .in-addr.arpa. If this IP address was outside the local domain, the DNS server would start at the root and sequentially resolve the domain nodes until arriving at 234.131.206.in-addr.arpa, which would contain the PTR record for the desired host.

Caching and Time to Live

When a name server is processing a recursive query, it may be required to send out several queries to find the definitive answer. Name servers are allowed to cache all the received information during this process; each record contains something called a time to live, or TTL. Think of the expiration date on a carton of milk as a TTL: it specifies how long the milk will be good before you have to throw it out.

The name server owner sets the TTL for each RR on their server. If your data changes a lot, you can use smaller TTL values to help ensure that data about your domain is more consistent across that network. However, if you make the TTL too small, the load on your name server will go up. That's because once data is cached by a DNS server, the server begins decreasing the TTL from its original value; when it hits zero, the server flushes the RR from its cache. If a query comes in that can be satisfied by this cached data, the TTL that's returned with it equals the current amount of time left before flush time. Client resolvers also have data caches and honor the TTL value so that they, too, know when to flush.

Queries for Services

Windows 2000 uses some special domains (not unlike the `in-addr.arpa` domain you just read about) to make it possible for domain clients to look up services they need. It turns out that RFC 2052 ("A DNS RR for specifying the location of services (DNS SRV)") specifies how this mechanism should work. However, there's a Microsoft twist: the underscore (_) character isn't legal in domain names, so Microsoft uses it to mark its special domains and to keep them from colliding with RFC 2052-compliant domains. There are a total of five of these trick Windows 2000 domains, as listed below:

_msdcs   This domain contains a list of all the Windows 2000 domain controllers in a domain. Each domain controller, global catalog, and PDC emulator is listed here.

_sites   Each site has its own subdomain within the _sites domain. In AD parlance, a site is a group of connected network subnets that have high bandwidth between them.

_tcp   This domain lists service records for services that run on TCP: LDAP, Kerberos, the kpasswd password changer, and the global catalogs.

_udp   This domain lists services that run on UDP: Kerberos and the kpasswd service.

When any network client wants to find a service (say, a domain controller), it can query its DNS server for the appropriate SRV record. By making a recursive query, the client can force the local DNS server to poke around in the domain until it finds the desired information.

This is really an introduction to DNS; you'll learn more about DNS esoterica like zone transfers in Chapter 6.

Windows Internet Name Service

NetBIOS works by broadcasting tons of network resource information—which shares a server offers, where the domain master browser is, and so on—so that any client can hear what its peers have to offer. Broadcasts work OK for smaller networks, but they generate a lot of unnecessary and undesirable clutter in larger networks. Since NetBIOS packets aren't routable, the problem is even worse: Not only do all those broadcasts clutter the network, they don't even do any good since only machines on the local subnet can hear them!

Microsoft solved the routability problem by offering NetBIOS over TCP/IP, or NBT. However, NBT still sends out broadcasts. While NBT broadcasts do allow NetBIOS-style name resolution on TCP/IP networks, Microsoft's designers realized that it was possible to come up with a better solution, and the Windows Internet Name Service (WINS) was born.

WINS is documented in RFCs 1001 and 1002.

What WINS Does

WINS listens to NBT broadcasts and collates them in a central source. In this role, it effectively serves as a clearinghouse for NetBIOS naming information. When you consider how NBT works, this makes a lot of sense. A pure NetBIOS network can use NetBIOS addresses. When one machine wishes to communicate with another, it can use information broadcast by its local master browser to find the address of the target machine. That approach doesn't work as well in TCP/IP, since the source machine has to already know the target's IP address to be talking to it!

Think back to what you know about DNS. When a TCP/IP application needs an address, it calls the resolver, which uses the DNS query mechanism to obtain an IP address. The application then uses the address to open a communication channel. If you apply this same model to the crusty old NBT protocol, you'll see how WINS works: It provides a service that maps NetBIOS names to IP addresses. This service works in three simple steps:

1. Each time a WINS client (e.g., a machine that's been given the address of a WINS server) starts up, it registers its NetBIOS name and IP address with the WINS server.

2. When a WINS client wants to talk to another computer, the resulting NBT name query is sent directly to the WINS server instead of being broadcast all over the local network.

3. If the WINS server finds the destination host's NetBIOS name and IP address in its database, it returns this information directly to the WINS client. If it doesn't, the WINS server can then make a standard NBT broadcast (if necessary) to hunt down the necessary address.

Because the WINS server receives updates from each WINS client as it starts up, its database entries are always current. You can set up multiple WINS servers on a network so that queries and answers are distributed; the servers can replicate their database entries according to the method and schedule you specify.

WINS and Windows 2000

The WINS implementation in Windows 2000 is largely unchanged from what Microsoft shipped with Windows NT 4.0. The biggest difference is that Microsoft is pushing DNS and TCP/IP as the linchpins of Active Directory-based networks, so WINS is being shoved off to the side, sort of like campaign finance reform. However, there are some interesting Windows 2000 features to consider about WINS.

First, WINS is integrated with DNS. What that means is that DNS-capable clients such as Web browsers can transparently take advantage of WINS resolution (provided you've turned this integration on). That allows you to fetch a Web page, or other resource, from a machine when all you know is its NetBIOS name. Your application uses the resolver, which makes a DNS query; the DNS server can ask the WINS server for the address after it fails to find it in its local zone.

How WINS Works

When a WINS client starts, the client exchanges WINS messages with its designated WINS server. Each client can actually hold addresses for a *primary and a secondary WINS server*; the secondary will be used if the primary doesn't answer. The intent of these messages is to allow the client to register its address with the server, without allowing name or address duplication. This message exchange occurs in four phases, which I call the "Four Rs": *name registration*, *name renewal*, *name release*, and *name resolution*. Let's see what those steps entail.

Name Registration

When a client starts in a WINS network, they're required to register their name and IP address with their designated WINS server. When the WINS server gets a *name registration request*, it has to evaluate it by asking two questions:

Is the name unique?   Duplicate names are undesirable, since they make it impossible to tell which computer *really* has a particular name—sort of the computer equivalent of cloning. If the WINS server receives a request to register a name that it already has in its database, it'll send a challenge to the currently registered owner of the disputed name. The challenge message is repeated three times, at 500-millisecond (half-second) intervals—less if the server receives a reply. If the current owner of the name responds (saying, in effect, "Hey, that's still my name!"), the WINS server rejects the new request by sending a negative name request back to the machine attempting to claim the already-in-use NetBIOS name. If the currently registered owner *doesn't* reply, then the name is deleted from the database, and a positive acknowledgment is sent to the requesting machine.

When the client happens to be a multihomed system, the WINS server sends challenge and confirmation messages to each of the client's IP addresses in sequence, until the server either receives a reply or tries each address three times.

Is the name valid?   NetBIOS names have restrictions: They must be equal to or less than 15 characters long, and they can't contain certain characters. The WINS server will reject any registration request for an invalid name.

Assuming the WINS server gets a request for a unique, valid name, it registers the name in its database and returns a message confirming the registration. This confirmation includes a time-to-live (TTL) for the WINS record; this TTL functions exactly as the TTL on a DNS record.

What happens if the client sends a request to its primary WINS server and never gets an answer back? Simple: The client tries again. After three tries, the client will then make three attempts to contact the secondary WINS server, if one is configured. If that fails, too, the client will attempt to register its name the old-fashioned way: by sending out an NBT broadcast.

Name Renewal

Earlier in this chapter, you learned how DHCP leases are offered and renewed. Guess what? WINS clients have to renew their names with the server every so often. With WINS, the client has to notify the server that it wants to continue using its registered name so that the server will reset the TTL.

When the TTL has reached 50 percent of its original value, the WINS client sends a name renewal message to the primary WINS server. This message contains the client's name, the source, and the destination IP addresses for the client and the server. If there's no response, the message will be resent once more when one-eighth of the original TTL remains. If there's *still* no response from the primary server, the client will then attempt renewal through the secondary WINS server, if one is configured. If the effort is successful, the WINS client will attempt to register with the secondary server as though it was the first attempt. If, after three attempts, the WINS client fails to contact the secondary WINS server, it'll switch back to the primary one.

Once successful contact is made, either the primary or secondary WINS server will respond by sending the client a new TTL period. This process will continue as long as the client computer is powered on and as long as it remains a WINS client.

Name Release

A WINS client can relinquish ownership of its name at any time by sending a *name release* message, which contains its IP address and name. However, this is most often done when the client machine is cleanly shut down. When the server receives a name release message, it deletes the client's information from its database and returns a positive release message comprised of the released name and a new TTL of zero. At this point, the client will stop responding to its former NetBIOS name.

If the IP address and name sent by the client don't match the WINS database, the WINS server will return a negative release message. If the client doesn't get either a positive or negative release message, it will send up to three B-node broadcasts notifying all other systems, including non-WINS clients, to remove the now invalid name from their NetBIOS name caches.

Name Resolution

So far, you've learned about the communications only between a WINS-enabled computer and a WINS server. How do regular network clients get information from the WINS database? The basic idea is that the client should try to exhaust other methods of resolution before it resorts to blasting out network broadcasts (although, as you'll see, the process works a little differently in practice).

Here's how the process works, assuming you're trying to map a network drive on a server named TRIDENT:

1. You type **net use g: \\trident\public** into a command-line window.

2. NBT will check the system's local name cache to see if it already has an IP address on file for TRIDENT. If the name is found in the cache, the Address Resolution Protocol (ARP) will then be used to turn the name into a hardware address. This deftly avoids adding unnecessary traffic on the network.

3. If the name isn't in the local cache, the name query goes directly to the primary WINS server. If the primary server is up, and the name is

found in its database, the information is returned to the requestor, where it's added into the local cache. If the server fails to respond, the request is repeated twice before the client switches to the secondary WINS server and starts over.

4. If neither the primary nor secondary WINS servers can resolve the name, the client will revert to making a broadcast. If another system hears the broadcast and returns an address for the requested name, it goes into the local cache.

5. If the broadcast doesn't generate a useful answer, NBT will search the LMHOSTS file for an answer. If that fails, it will then check the HOSTS file and, finally, DNS. If none of these works, the command fails.

Summary

In this chapter, you learned:

- What the Dynamic Host Configuration Protocol (DHCP) is

- How DHCP issues TCP/IP configuration information to clients

- What the Domain Name Service (DNS) does

- How DNS clients and servers function

- What the Windows Internet Name Service (WINS) does and how it works

Key Terms

Before you take the exam, be sure you're familiar with the following terms:

Active Directory-Integrated (ADI) zone

DHCP discover message

DHCP offer message

DHCP request message

DHCPACK

DHCPNACK

Dynamic DNS (DDNS) standard

Host record

Lease

Name server

Network naming

Pointer record (PTR)

Primary DNS server

Requests for Comments (RFC)

Resolver

Resource records

Reverse lookups

Secondary DNS server

Service record (SRV)

WINS name registration

WINS name release

WINS name renewal

WINS name resolution

Zone transfer

Zones

Review Questions

1. WINS is primarily used for which of the following?

   A. Mapping NetBIOS names to IP addresses

   B. Mapping domain names to IP addresses

   C. Mapping IP addresses to domain names

   D. Mapping dynamic DNS entries to DHCP clients

2. DHCP is primarily designed for what purpose?

   A. Automatically delivering IP address information to clients

   B. Allowing clients to centrally register their configurations

   C. Automating DNS name registration

   D. Enabling routing of WINS traffic

3. Active Directory requires which of the following?

   A. TCP/IP and DHCP

   B. TCP/IP and DNS

   C. DNS and NetBIOS

   D. DNS and DHCP

4. A primary DNS server performs which of the following functions?

   A. It acts as an authority for the zones it hosts.

   B. It holds data that can be copied to a secondary DNS server.

   C. A and B.

   D. Neither A nor B.

5. Which of the following is *not* a part of the DHCP negotiation?

   A. Lease request

   B. Lease scavenging

   C. Lease offer

   D. Lease acknowledgment

6. Windows 2000 uses service (SRV) records for _____.

    A. Registering the IP address assigned to a particular host

    B. Registering the host name associated with an IP address

    C. Registering the NetBIOS name attached to an IP address

    D. Registering the information needed to contact resource services like LDAP and Kerberos servers

7. A time-to-live (TTL) on a WINS registration indicates which of the following?

    A. The elapsed time since the registration was issued

    B. The time remaining before the registration becomes invalid

    C. The date and time the registration was issued

    D. The elapsed time since the WINS database was last restarted

8. Which of the following is *not* true of an Active Directory-Integrated DNS zone?

    A. It can only exist on an Active Directory domain controller.

    B. It can only exist in a network with at least one Active Directory domain controller.

    C. It is replicated by AD instead of by the traditional primary/secondary model.

    D. It takes advantage of AD security policies.

9. Dynamic DNS exists to _____.

    A. Allow DNS registration of IP addresses assigned via WINS

    B. Eliminate duplicate A records

    C. Allow DNS registration of IP addresses assigned via DHCP

    D. A and B

    E. B and C

10. Reverse DNS lookups depend on which of the following?

    A. The presence of at least one WINS server

    B. A forward lookup zone and an A record for the IP address

    C. A reverse lookup zone and a PTR record for the IP address

    D. The existence of a proper SRV record

11. To enable DHCP on a multisegment network, you need which of the following?

    A. A DHCP server on each segment

    B. Two DHCP servers on any one segment

    C. Routers or software that can forward DHCP requests

    D. A or B

    E. B or C

    F. A or C

12. The DHCP discover message _____.

    A. Allows the server to find other DHCP servers

    B. Enables a client to find available DHCP servers

    C. Is sent directly to the last known DHCP server address

    D. Isn't sent until lease renewal time

13. If a DHCP server returns a DHCPNACK message, which of the following is *not* a possible cause?

    A. The server has assigned all of its available addresses.

    B. The client is trying to renew an address that it no longer owns.

    C. The client's current IP address doesn't belong in the server's scope.

    D. The client has an improper IP address or subnet mask.

14. A Start of Authority (SOA) record _____.

    A. Contains a list of all hosts in the domain

    B. Indicates whether or not zone transfers are permitted

    C. Specifies which server is authoritative for a particular domain

    D. Controls whether a server is a primary or secondary name server

15. If you have multiple DNS SRV records with the same priority, what will happen when a resolver asks for an SRV record?

    A. The weights of the records will be used to determine which one is returned.

    B. The records are always equally likely to be returned.

    C. A record is randomly chosen and returned.

    D. Nothing, because you can't have multiple SRV records for one service.

16. The primary difference between a recursive and an iterative DNS query is that _____.

    A. Recursive queries always return an answer.

    B. Iterative queries require the resolver to make multiple queries for an answer.

    C. Iterative queries don't take advantage of forwarding.

    D. Recursive queries must always use forwarding.

17. What will the server produce if a WINS client tries to register a name that's already in use?

    A. Successful registration

    B. Conflict message

    C. Registration failure

    D. Challenge message

18. The four DHCP steps are which of the following?

    A. Discovery, offer, request, acknowledge

    B. A forward lookup zone and an A record for the IP address

    C. A reverse lookup zone and a PTR record for the IP address

    D. The existence of a proper SRV record

19. A DNS zone transfer does which of the following?

    A. Copies information from a secondary server to a primary

    B. Copies information from a primary server to a secondary

    C. Copies information from a primary server to a client

    D. Copies information from a primary server to a root server

20. Windows 2000 supports which types of zone transfer?

    A. Partial and complete

    B. Complete only

    C. Incremental and authoritative

    D. Authoritative and partial

Answers to Review Questions

1. A. WINS is designed to allow DNS-style name resolution without requiring DNS.

2. A. DHCP's purpose is to automate client TCP/IP configuration.

3. B. DHCP isn't required for AD, but TCP/IP and DNS are.

4. C. The primary server is authoritative for its zone; it also holds the master copy of the zone data.

5. B. Scavenging, or the reclamation of expired lease data, isn't part of the DHCP negotiation.

6. D. Instead of using NetBIOS broadcasts, Windows 2000 machines use SRV records to find domain controllers and global catalog servers.

7. B. A WINS TTL indicates the length of time before that registration becomes stale.

8. A. Active Directory-Integrated zones can only be created on DNS servers that run the DNS dynamic update protocol.

9. E. Dynamic DNS doesn't work with WINS.

10. C. Reverse lookups use PTR records.

11. F. You can either put one DHCP server on each subnet or use a DHCP relay agent or proxy to forward requests.

12. B. The discover message is broadcast on the local subnet so that the client can find out which servers are available.

13. A. If the server runs out of addresses, it won't offer a lease in the first place.

14. C. The SOA record indicates which name server is authoritative and what time limits should be used for zone data.

15. A. If the priorities are equal, the DNS server will use the weights; if the weights are equal, records will be returned round-robin style.

16. B. Recursive queries put the burden on the server, while iterative queries put the workload on the resolver.

17. D. The server sends a challenge to the original registrant and records the new registration only if the original holder doesn't answer.

18. A. The four phases in order are discovery, offer, request, and acknowledge.

19. B. Zone transfers are normally used to load secondaries with their zone data.

20. C. Authoritative and incremental transfers (AXFR and IXFR) are the two transfer types defined in the DNS RFCs.

Chapter 3

Windows 2000 Connectivity & Security Services

In the preceding two chapters, you learned about a variety of
services included with Windows 2000 and about their fundamental underpinnings. There's one more significant group of services that you haven't
learned about yet: services that provide remote network connectivity and
security.

To see why these services are necessary, hark back to, say, 1985. Even if you
were lucky enough to have a computer on your desk, most companies weren't
using any kind of meaningful LAN, much less providing remote access. The
Internet was still restricted largely to the academic and government sectors,
with occasional islands of access at large technology companies. Fast-forward
to 2000: The Internet is a pervasive communications tool, companies have
embraced networks at all organizational levels, and workers often expect the
ability to get to their data remotely, no matter where they are.

Windows 2000 delivers several services that change these capabilities into
actualities, including the following:

- *Dial-Up Networking (DUN)* allows Windows 2000 machines to
  make or receive dial-up calls to other computers using a regular analog
  modem or ISDN line.

- *Multiprotocol routing*, or just routing, allows a Windows 2000 computer to accept packets from other computers on its local network,
  sort out the correct destination for each, and route them accordingly.
  The "multiprotocol" comes from the fact that Windows 2000
  includes routing services for IPX/SPX, TCP/IP, and AppleTalk, and it
  can be expanded to handle other protocols—all concurrently.

- *Virtual private networks (VPNs)* combine the utility and security of a
  dedicated private network with the flexibility and cost savings of the
  Internet. When you use a VPN, as far as your computer and the remote
  server can tell, you're directly connected, but your traffic is actually
  encrypted and passed over an insecure intermediate network, like the
  Internet.

- The *IP Security Extensions (IPSec)* add authentication and privacy to the Internet Protocol you've come to know and love. This makes it possible to transfer sensitive information to other hosts across the Internet without fear of compromise, just by putting IPSec-capable routers at each end of the connection.

- Digital certificates offer an easy-to-use way to provide strong authentication, access control, and privacy protection on your network. You've already used digital certificates if you've ever made a purchase from a Web site secured by the Secure Sockets Layer (SSL) protocol. Microsoft includes a Certificate Services module that allows you to issue, revoke, and manage digital certificates for users and computers on your network.

Dial-Up Networking

In science fiction books and movies, it seems like computers are both ubiquitous and wireless. How often do you see someone have to wait for a connection? Virtually never. However, we're not quite there yet. LANs provide relatively high-speed connectivity to attached machines, but where does that leave those of us who work from home, travel, or need to access data on a remote computer?

Until ubiquitous wireless access is available (and let's hope it's soon), we're stuck with the familiar concept of having one computer (usually referred to as the client) dial a remote server. Once the connection is established, a variety of protocols and services make it possible for us to view Web pages, transfer files and e-mail, and do pretty much anything we could do with a hardwired LAN connection, albeit at reduced speed.

What DUN Does

From reading Chapter 1, you already understand that Windows 2000 network protocols are actually implemented as drivers that live way down in the bowels of the operating system. These drivers normally work with hardware network interfaces to get packets from point A to point B. What about dial-up connections?

The answer is both simple and instructive. Think back to the OSI layer cake you saw in Figure 1.1. Each layer has a function, and each layer serves as an intermediary between the layer above it and the one below. By substituting one driver for another at some level in the stack, you can dramatically change how things work. That's exactly what Windows 2000's DUN subsystem does: It makes the dial-up connection appear to be just another network adapter. The DUN driver takes care of the work of making a slow asynchronous modem appear to work just like a fast LAN interface. Applications and services that use TCP/IP, NWLink, AppleTalk, or whatever protocols you're using on your DUN connection never know the difference. In fact, you can configure Windows 2000 to use your primary connection first, then pass traffic over a secondary connection (like a dial-up link) if the primary connection is down.

On the server side, DUN allows you to host one or more network users who dial into your Windows 2000 machine. Windows 2000 Professional allows one dial-up user; the Server and Advanced Server versions allow up to 255, though by the time you allow that many connections you'll probably be overloading your server. Depending on how you configure the DUN server, users who dial in can either see only resources on the server or the whole network; you also get to control who can log on, when they can log on, and what they can do once they've logged on. As far as Windows 2000 is concerned, a user connected via DUN is no different than one using resources over your LAN, so all the access controls and permissions you apply remain in force for DUN users.

DUN and Windows 2000

The Windows 2000 DUN client is largely unchanged from its Windows NT and Windows 98 predecessors, although the user interface is slightly different. Likewise, the server components are pretty much the same as they were in Windows NT (down to the ongoing use of the term Remote Access Service, or RAS, instead of the now-preferred DUN). However, the Windows 2000 Server DUN service is part of a component called *Routing and Remote Access Service (RRAS)*. RRAS provides multiprotocol routing (more on that in a bit) and dial-up access.

Probably the biggest change from NT 4.0 is that Windows 2000 finally allows you to apply remote access policies. With Windows NT, you could control whether or not individual users could dial in, but there was no way to set that permission for groups of users. The Windows 2000 Group Policy Object (GPO) mechanism provides a way to apply dial-up permission and capability settings to groups of users.

How DUN Works

There are a lot of pieces required to successfully complete a dial-up call from your computer to a server at another physical location. Understanding what these pieces are, how they work, and what they do for you is key to your ability to pass Microsoft's exams.

Infrastructure Stuff

Let's start with a look at the physical layer plumbing that underlies voice and data calls. Most of this stuff will be familiar to anyone who's ever used a modem before, but you may pick up a few useful nuggets along the way.

POTS

POTS stands for plain old telephone service. This seems like an awfully dismissive term when you consider how flexible and robust the actual POTS infrastructure really is. There was an editorial in a computer magazine called *80 Micro* (we hope that doesn't date us too much!) in 1982 or so. The writer, Wayne Green, asserted that we'd never get much better than 1200bps out of ordinary phone lines. Maybe if we were really lucky and if the phone company (remember, there was only one phone company in 1982) cooperated, then we could squeeze 4800bps or so across the wires, but that was all. Of course, the prevalent modem speed at the time was 300bps, so a sixteen-fold improvement sure seemed luxuriant at the time. Now, of course, we know better. Modems now offer a theoretical maximum speed of 56Kbps; in practice, many users routinely get connections at 51 or 52Kbps, a whopping more-than-tenfold increase over that original pessimistic prediction.

How is this possible? The word "modem" is actually an acronym for "modulator-demodulator"; the original Bell System modems took digital data and modulated it into screechy audio tones suitable for use on regular phone lines. Since phone lines are purposely designed to pass only the low end of the audible frequency range that most humans can hear, the amount of data that could be scrunched into those audio tones was limited. However, in the early 1990s some bright engineers discovered that you could communicate much faster if only the path between the sender and receiver was all-digital! An all-digital path doesn't have any signal loss–inducing analog components, so it preserves the original signal quality faithfully—which in turn makes it possible to put more information into the original signal. As it happens, phone companies nationwide were in the process (or had just completed) major upgrades to replace their aging analog equipment with newer, better digital equivalents. These upgrades made it possible for people in most areas to get almost-56Kbps speeds without changing any of the wiring in their houses or offices.

ISDN

The Integrated Services Digital Network, or ISDN, was supposed to be the Next Big Thing. Back in the mid-1970s when it was designed, no one had any idea that you'd be able to get 56Kbps speeds out of an ordinary phone line, so ISDN's speeds of up to 128Kbps over a single pair of copper wires seemed pretty revolutionary. In addition, ISDN had a lot of nifty features like call forwarding, caller ID, and multiple directory numbers (so you could have more than one number, perhaps with different ringing patterns, associated with a single line). So what happened? Why aren't we all using ISDN now?

It turns out that the major phone companies missed the boat. ISDN requires the same kind of all-digital signal path that 56Kbps modems do; it also requires special equipment on both ends of the connection. The phone companies were slow to promote ISDN as a faster alternative to regular dial-up service, so customers avoided it. This avoidance led the phone companies to think no one wanted ISDN. In some places, ISDN is so much more expensive than POTS service that it's cheaper to use multilink PPP with POTS lines instead of ISDN.

ISDN still has some advantages, though. Because it's all-digital, call setup times are much faster than they are for analog modems—it only takes about half a second to establish a new ISDN call. Modern ISDN adapters and ISDN-capable routers can seamlessly stitch together multiple ISDN channels to deliver bandwidth in 64Kbps increments. Since you can use ISDN lines for regular analog voice, data, and fax traffic, you can make a single ISDN act like two analog lines, a single 128Kbps data line, or a 64Kbps data line plus an analog line—quite a neat trick for one pair of wires!

Other Connection Methods

POTS and ISDN aren't available everywhere. For example, one client of ours has a Windows 2000 network installed on land and on ships that communicate with the land-based offices via a satellite-based connection. In theory, it's a dial-up connection like any other, but in actuality it uses a packet-based protocol called X.25. X.25 is pretty well entrenched in Western Europe and parts of the Pacific Rim; in general, it can be used to substitute for a regular dial-up connection in Windows 2000, assuming you have the right drivers and hardware.

Any other on-demand connection that's established using the *Point-to-Point Protocol (PPP)* can be thought of as a dial-up connection, and Windows 2000 doesn't make any distinction between POTS, ISDN, and other dial-ups—they're all treated identically.

PPP, Your Best Friend

The Point-to-Point Protocol, or PPP, might just as well be called the Peer-to-Peer Protocol, since it enables any two computers to establish a TCP/IP connection over a serial link. That normally means a dial-up modem connection, but it could just as easily be a direct serial cable connection, an infrared connection, or any other type of serial connection. When one Windows 2000 machine dials another, we call the machine that initiates the connection a "client," and the machine that receives the call is a "server"—even though the PPP itself makes no such distinction.

There are actually at least six distinct protocols that run on top of PPP. Understanding what they do helps make the actual PPP negotiation process clearer. These protocols include the following:

The Link Control Protocol (LCP) LCP handles the details of establishing the lowest-level PPP link; in that regard you can think of it almost as if it were part of the physical layer. When one PPP device calls another, they use LCP to agree that they want to establish a PPP connection.

The Challenge Handshake Authentication Protocol (CHAP) CHAP (and its siblings MS-CHAP, PAP, and SPAP, which will be covered in Chapter 12) allows the client to authenticate itself to the server. This authentication functions much like a normal network logon; once the client presents its logon credentials, the server can figure out what access to grant.

The Callback Control Protocol (CBCP) Once the client has authenticated itself, the server can decide whether it should hang up and call the client back. The client can also request a callback at a number it provides; although this isn't as secure as having the server place a call to a predetermined number, it provides some additional flexibility. No matter which end requests the callback, CBCP is used to negotiate whether a callback is required, whether it's permitted, and when it happens. If a callback occurs, the connection is re-established and re-authenticated, but the CBCP stage is skipped.

The Compression Control Protocol (CCP) CCP allows the two sides of the connection to determine what kind of compression, if any, they want to use on the network data. Since PPP traffic actually consists of wrapped-up IP datagrams, and since IP datagram headers tend to be fairly compressible, negotiating effective compression can significantly improve overall PPP throughput.

The IP Control Protocol (IPCP)   At this point in the call, the two sides have agreed to authentication, compression, and a callback. They haven't yet agreed on what IP parameters to use for the connection. These parameters, which include the maximum packet size to be sent over the link (the maximum transmission unit, or MTU), have a great impact on the overall link performance, so the client and server negotiate them based on the traffic they expect to be passed.

The Internet Protocol (IP)   Once the IPCP negotiation has been completed, each end has complete knowledge of how to communicate with its peer. That knowledge allows the two sides to begin exchanging IP datagrams over the link.

Figure 3.1 shows how these protocols work together to lead up to establishing the link. Remember this diagram, because you'll see it again (with more arrows on it) when you start reading about PPTP. Now you can see what happens after the link is established and traffic begins flowing.

FIGURE 3.1   The PPP negotiation dance

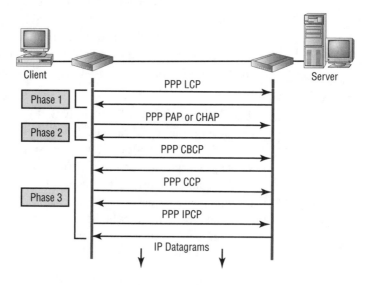

From Remote to Local

Normally when you hear about network communication, you hear about using TCP/IP, NetBEUI, AppleTalk, or IPX/SPX on a hardwired LAN. How do these protocols fit in with PPP? In the case of TCP/IP, that's an easy question to answer: The client routes all (or some) of its outgoing TCP/IP traffic to its PPP peer, which can then inspect the IP datagrams it gets back from the PPP stack to analyze and route them properly.

Windows 2000 doesn't just support TCP/IP, of course, so consider what has to happen when a client using NWLink comes calling. After the LCP negotiation completes, the server will know which protocols the client wishes to use. If the server doesn't want to use one or more of those protocols, it can drop the call or cause the client to warn its user (that's what Windows 2000 does). After the other PPP setup steps complete, the client and server can wrap other types of network traffic inside an IP datagram. This process, called *encapsulation*, is exactly like smuggling: The client takes a packet with some kind of "forbidden" content, wraps it inside an IP datagram, and sends it to the server. The server, in turn, processes the IP datagram, routing real datagrams normally and handling any encapsulated packets with the appropriate protocol. At that point, the client can communicate with the server without knowing that its non-TCP/IP packets are being encapsulated in any way—that troublesome detail is hidden deep in the bowels of the OSI model.

Routing

*R*outing is the process of delivering traffic to the correct destination. We use real-world routing concepts all the time: The U.S. interstate highway system, road construction detours, and postal letters marked with a forwarding address all use routing in a way we understand pretty well. Network routing is analogous, but not exactly identical, to these real-world routing systems.

 Although Windows 2000 supports routing IPX, AppleTalk, and IP, only IP routing will be covered in this section. It's the most widely used, and it's the one you're most likely to see on the test.

What Routing Does

In very simple networks, no routing is necessary. For example, my five-year-old son goes to a kindergarten where each child has a little cubbyhole with their name written on it. When it's time to drop off party invitations, Valentine cards, and the like, each child can make a direct connection with the desired cubbyhole, and no intermediate routing takes place.

More complex systems support, and even require, routing. Consider what happens when I get ready to mail this completed chapter. I'm in Alabama, and my editor is in California. If you look at a map of the physical topology of the Internet, you'll see that there are a large number of potential routes to get from here to there. Some may be better than others; for instance, one route would carry my packets east, across the Atlantic, through Europe, and across Russia and the Pacific Ocean to the West Coast of the U.S. That's a legal route, but it would be terribly inefficient.

Routing combines the idea that each packet on a network has a source and destination with the idea of associating routes with costs. Paradoxically, it's usually cheaper to fly from New York City to Los Angeles than it is to fly the shorter distance from L.A. to San Francisco. Following this principle, routing systems allow administrators to attach a *metric,* or cost, to each leg of a route. In a bit, you'll see how routing systems use this metric information to calculate the most efficient route for packets to take.

The actual way in which the metric information is used in calculations varies between RIP version 1, RIP version 2, and OSPF; the important point to remember is that all three protocols use metrics to figure out the "best" route in any situation.

Routing and Windows 2000

Windows 2000 includes, and improves on, the routing capabilities included with Windows NT 4.0. Each of the routable protocols Windows 2000 supports can be routed using the Routing and Remote Access Service (RRAS). In addition, AppleTalk can be routed if you install the Services for Macintosh (SFM) package. Windows NT supported simple IP routing, but it couldn't share routing information with dedicated routers. Since a router needs to know where its "neighbors" are to figure out what the network topology looks like, this was a critical omission. Windows 2000 fixes this problem, as well as a number of other limitations, by including a long laundry list of routing features:

- It supports versions 1 and 2 of the Routing Information Protocol (RIP), as well as the Open Shortest Path First (OSPF) protocol. Third-party vendors also sell add-on products that allow RRAS to handle the

Border Gateway Protocol (BGP), a complex protocol that is used in large routers that connect directly to the Internet backbone.

- It supports *unicast routing*, in which one machine sends directly to one destination address. It also supports *multicast routing*, where one machine sends to an entire network.

- It supports *network address translation (NAT)*, a service that allows multiple LAN clients to share a single public IP address and Internet connection. (See Chapter 13 for more on NAT.)

- It allows *demand-dial routing*. Demand-dial routes normally bring up only the associated link when outbound traffic is addressed to a network on those routes, although you can configure them to persist. Demand-dialing lets you effectively use impermanent connection methods, like analog modems or ISDN, to mimic a dedicated Internet connection.

How Routing Works

In this section, the discussion of routing theory and practice will be confined to IP routing, even though the same concepts apply to IPX/SPX and Apple-Talk routing. The basic underlying idea is that each packet on a network has a source address and a destination address, which means that any device that receives the packet can inspect its headers to determine where it came from and where it's going. If such a device also has some information about the network's design and implementation—like how long it takes packets to travel over a particular link—it can intelligently change the routing to minimize the total cost.

According to the OSI model, a gateway and a router are two different things. However, Microsoft uses the terms interchangeably, and so will we.

Figure 3.2 shows an imaginary network made up of six interconnected local networks. These networks, imaginatively named A through F, are connected by links of varying speeds and costs. This accurately mirrors what happens in the real world, where it's common for internal networks (or Internet providers) to have multiple ways to establish a link between two points.

FIGURE 3.2 An example network

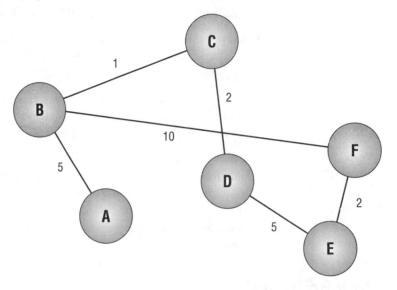

Imagine that a client machine on network B wants to send traffic to a machine on network E. The most obvious route would probably be B to F to E, but you could also use B to C to D to E. Notice the costs: B-F-E has a total cost of 12, while the seemingly longer B-C-D-E actually has a lower cost of 8! That doesn't appear to make sense, since the latter route has a longer path. When you consider what "cost" really means, though, things get better. Assigning link costs is entirely up to you. Normally, you assign costs that reflect your preference for how you want traffic to flow. An expensive or slow link would probably deserve a higher cost than a cheaper or faster link; by assigning your most expensive links (say, a metered ISDN connection) a high cost, you'd make them too expensive to use if there were less expensive links available.

Now, revisit Figure 3.2 with the assumption that each circle is really a router. After all, you can hide all of the complexity of the network behind a router, since only the router is in charge of moving packets. Call your client machine "X" and your server "Y." When X wants to send traffic to Y, it already knows the destination IP address of its target. X will build a packet, including its IP address as the source and Y's address as the destination. X will then use its default gateway setting to send that packet to router B.

Router B receives the packet and has both source and destination address information. By examining the IP addresses, it can determine that it doesn't "know" a direct route to the network where Y is located. However, there are two intermediate nodes that claim to know how to reach Y: C and F. Since C has the lowest link cost, the router at B will send the packet to C in a simple routing algorithm. When C receives it, it will go through the same process, forwarding the packet on to D, and so on. Eventually the packet gets where it's going.

Static Routing

Static routing systems don't make any attempt to discover other routers or systems on their networks. Instead, you tell the routing engine how to get data to other networks; specifically, you tell it what other networks are reachable from your network by specifying their network addresses and subnet masks, along with a metric for that network. This information goes into the system's routing table, a big list of known routes to other networks. When an outgoing packet arrives at the routing engine, the engine can examine the routing table to select the lowest-cost route to the destination. If there's no explicit entry in the routing table for that network, the packet goes to the default gateway, which is then entrusted with getting it where it needs to go.

Static routing is faster and more efficient than dynamic routing. Static routing works well when your network doesn't change much. You can identify the remote networks to which you want to route, then add static routes to them to reflect the costs and topology of your network. In Windows 2000, you maintain static routes with the route command, which allows you to either see the contents of the routing table or modify it by adding and removing static routes to individual networks.

Dynamic Routing

By contrast with static routing, dynamic routing doesn't depend on your adding fixed, unchangeable routes to remote networks. Instead, a *dynamic routing* engine can discover its surroundings by finding and communicating with other nearby routers in an internetwork.

This process, usually called router discovery, enables a newly added (or rebooted) router to configure itself. This is roughly equivalent to the process that happens when you move into a new neighborhood. Within a short time of your arrival, you'll probably meet most of the people who live close, either by them coming to you or you going to them. At that point, you have useful information about the surrounding environment that could only come from people who were already there.

The two major dynamic routing protocols in Windows 2000 are the Routing Information Protocol (RIP) and the Open Shortest Path First

(OSPF) protocol. Each has its advantages and disadvantages, but they share some common features and functionality. Each router (whether a hardware device, a Windows 2000 machine, or whatever) is connected to at least two separate physical networks. When the router starts, the only information it has is drawn from its internal routing table. Normally, that means it knows about all the attached networks plus whatever static routes have been previously defined. The router then receives configuration information that tells it about the state and topology of the network.

As time goes on, the network's physical topology can change. For example, take a look at the network in Figure 3.3. If network G suddenly dropped off the air, the routers in sites A, D, and E would need to readjust their routing tables since they can no longer route traffic directly to G. The process by which this adjustment happens is what makes routing dynamic, and it's also the largest area of difference between the two major dynamic routing protocols for IP.

FIGURE 3.3   A more complex dynamically routed network

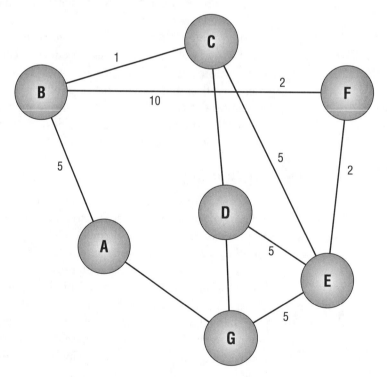

The Routing Information Protocol (RIP)

RIP is like NetBEUI: It's simple and easy to configure, but it has performance limitations that restrict its usefulness on medium-to-large networks. RIP routers begin with a basically empty routing table, but they immediately begin sending out announcements that they know will reach the networks to which they're connected. These announcements may be broadcast or multicast. Routers on other networks that hear these announcements can add those routes to their own routing tables. The process works both ways, of course; our hypothetical router will hear announcements from other routers, then add those routes to its list of places it knows how to reach.

In addition to sending and receiving announcements, RIP 2 routers have the ability to receive triggered updates. When you know that your network topology is changing (perhaps because you've added connectivity to another network), you can send out a trigger that contains information about the changes. This trigger forces all the RIP routers you own to assimilate the changes immediately. Triggered updates are also useful, since routers that detect a link or router failure can update their routing tables and announce the change, making their neighbors aware of it sooner rather than later.

Microsoft's RIP implementation supports both version 1 and version 2 of RIP. The primary difference between the two versions is the manner in which updates are sent: RIP 1 uses broadcasts every 30 seconds, and RIP 2 uses multicasts only when routes change. RIP 2 also supports simple (e.g., plain text) username/password authentication, which is handy to prevent unwanted changes from cluttering your routing tables.

Speaking of changes, you can use the RRAS snap-in to set up two kinds of filters that screen out some types of updates. *Route filters* allow you to pick and choose about which networks you want to admit knowing and for which you want to accept announcements. *Peer filters* give you control over which neighboring routers your router will listen to.

RIP also incorporates features that attempt to prevent route loops. In Figure 3.3 the network topology has the potential to cause a route loop. Why? Say that someone in E wants to send a packet to a machine in A, but the G to A and D to C links are down. E sends the packet to G, which recognizes that it can't reach A. G also knows that the route D-C-B-A will work, so it sends the packet to D. When the packet reaches D, D knows it can't talk to C, so it sends the packet to E because E-G-A is normally a valid route. Voilà, a routing loop! This might seem like a contrived example, but in real life, where internetwork links are often concentrated among a small number of physical links, it's a real problem. RIP offers several methods for resolving and preventing loops, including the split-horizon and poison reverse algorithms. Despite their cool names, it's not important to understand how they work to pass the exam—it's enough to know what they're for and that RIP implements them to protect against routing loops.

The Open Shortest Path First (OSPF) Protocol

RIP is designed for fairly small networks—as it turns out, it can only handle fifteen router-to-router hops. If you have a network that spans more than sixteen routers at any point, RIP won't be able to cache routes for it; some parts of the network will appear to be (or will be!) unreachable. The Open Shortest Path First (OSPF) protocol is designed for use on large or very large networks. It's much more efficient than RIP, but it also requires more knowledge and experience to set up and administer.

RIP routers continually exchange routing data with one another, which allows incorrect route entries to propagate. Instead of doing that, each OSPF router maintains a map of the state of the internetwork. This map, called a *link state map*, provides a continually updated reference to the state of each internetwork link. Neighboring routers group into an *adjacency* (think neighborhood); within an adjacency, routers synchronize any changes to the link state map. When the network topology changes, whichever router notices it first floods the internetwork with change notifications. Each router that receives the notification updates its copy of the link map, then recalculates its internal routing table.

The "SPF" in OSPF refers to the algorithm that OSPF systems use to calculate routes: Routes are calculated so that the shortest path (e.g., the one with the lowest cost) is used first. SPF-calculated routes are always free of loops, which is another nice advantage over RIP.

Microsoft's OSPF implementation supports (but doesn't require) the use of *route filters*, so any Windows 2000 OSPF router can choose to accept routing information either from other OSPF routers or other types of routers (e.g., those using RIP). In addition, a desirable feature not always found in OSPF routers is that you can change any of the OSPF settings discussed in Chapter 8, "Managing IP Routing," and have them take effect immediately without having to stop and restart the router.

IP Security Extensions

The original specifications for IP (Internet Protocol) made no provisions for any kind of security. That lack wasn't accidental; it stemmed from two completely different causes. One was the expectation that users and administrators would continue to behave fairly well and not make serious attempts to compromise other people's traffic. The other was that the cryptographic technology needed to provide adequate security wasn't widely available, or even widely known about. As the Internet expanded, it became clear that robust authentication and privacy protection were desirable, but version 4 of the IP specification (which is what most of us are using now) didn't include it. As the installed base of IP-capable devices grew, so too did the complexity of devising a security protocol that wouldn't screw up all those devices. Finally, though, in the late 1990s vendors began releasing products that incorporated the IP Security Extensions (better known as just IPSec) to IP version 4.

 A number of major vendors, including Microsoft, Cisco, Nortel, and RSA Security, are shipping IPSec products. However, the standard itself is still somewhat in flux; if you're thinking of implementing IPSec in a mixed-vendor network, make sure your devices can all talk to each other. Refer to RFC 1825 for additional information on IPSec.

What IPSec Does

IPSec has two separate features, but they go together: authentication and encryption. You can use them together or separately, and each feature has a number of options and parameters you can tweak to fine-tune security on your network.

Authentication Authentication protects your network, and the data it carries, from tampering. This tampering might take the form of a malicious attacker sitting between a client and a server, altering the contents of packets (the so-called "man in the middle" attack), or it might take the form of an attacker joining your network and impersonating either a client or a server. IPSec uses an *authentication header (AH)* to digitally sign the entire contents of each packet. This signature provides three separate benefits:

1. Protection against replay attacks. If an attacker can capture packets, save them until a later time, and send them again, then they can impersonate a machine after that machine's no longer on the network. This is called a replay attack; IPSec's authentication

mechanism prevents replay attacks by including the sender's signature on all packets.

2. Protection against tampering. IPSec's signatures provide data integrity, meaning that an interloper can't selectively change parts of packets to alter their meaning.

3. Protection against spoofing. Normally when you hear about authentication, it means the process of a client or server verifying another machine's identity. IPSec authentication headers provide authentication because each end of a connection can verify the other's identity.

Encryption   Authentication protects your data against tampering, but it doesn't do anything to keep people from seeing it. For that you need encryption, which actually obscures the payload contents so that a man in the middle can't read the traffic as it goes by. To accomplish this, IPSec provides the *Encapsulating Security Payload (ESP)*. ESP is used to encrypt the entire payload of an IPSec packet, rendering it undecipherable by anyone other than the intended recipient. ESP only provides confidentiality, but it can be combined with AH to gain maximum security.

IPSec and Windows 2000

Windows 2000 implements IPSec, which in and of itself is a big deal since it involves a large number of changes to the TCP/IP stack and its underpinnings. Microsoft's IPSec implementation is actually licensed from, and was written by, Cisco, which guarantees good compatibility with other standards-based IPSec clients.

There are some other nifty Windows 2000 features that make IPSec more useful. Imagine a large network of computers, some running IPSec. When two computers want to communicate, it would be ideal if they could automatically take advantage of IPSec and if both ends supported it. You'd also want to ensure that the security settings you wanted were applied to all IPSec-capable machines. With Windows NT, or with most other operating systems, that would mean hand-configuring each IPSec machine to use the settings you wanted.

The solution lies in the Windows 2000 Group Policy mechanism. First, you specify the IPSec settings you want to use on your network. Then, each Windows 2000 machine runs a service called the IPSec Policy Agent. When the system starts, the Policy Agent connects to an Active Directory server and fetches the IPSec policy and then passes it to the IPSec code. (You can read more about the guts of the Policy Agent in the next section.)

How IPSec Works

IPSec is a pretty complex protocol; in fact, what is referred to as "IPSec" is actually a collage of several protocols with different but interrelated functions. You'll begin by digging under the covers to see what those protocols are, then you'll see how they work together to deliver the capabilities discussed earlier in this chapter.

Parts of IPSec

IPSec appears to be a single unitary protocol, but it's implemented in three different protocols plus a number of Windows 2000 drivers and services.

The Internet Security Agreement/Key Management Protocol (ISAKMP) and Oakley

ISAKMP provides a way for two computers to agree on security settings and exchange a security key that they can use to communicate securely. In IPSec-speak, a *security association (SA)* provides all the information needed for two computers to communicate securely. The SA contains a policy agreement that controls which algorithms and key lengths the two machines will use ("Let's use 128-bit RC5 and SHA-1"), plus the actual security keys used to securely exchange information. Think of this agreement like a contract: It specifies what each party is, and is not, willing to do as part of the agreement.

There are two steps to this process. First, the two computers use the ISAKMP to establish a security agreement. This is called the ISAKMP SA. To establish the ISAKMP SA, the two computers must agree on the following three things:

1. Which encryption algorithm (DES, triple DES, 40-bit DES, or none) they'll use

2. Which algorithm they'll use for verifying message integrity (MD5 or SHA-1)

3. How connections will be authenticated: using a public-key certificate (see Chapter 14), a shared secret key, or Kerberos

Once the ISAKMP SA is in place, the two machines can use the Oakley protocol to securely agree on a shared master key. This key, called the ISAKMP master key, is used along with the algorithms negotiated in the ISAKMP SA to establish a secure connection. After the secure connection is brought up, the two machines start another round of negotiations. These negotiations cover the following:

- Whether the Authentication Header protocol will be used for this connection

- Whether the Encapsulating Security Payload protocol will be used for this connection

- Which encryption algorithm will be used for the ESP protocol

- Which authentication protocol will be used for the AH protocol

After *these* negotiations are finished, the two machines end up with *two* new SAs: one for inbound traffic and another for outbound traffic. These SAs are called *IPSec SAs* to distinguish them from the ISAKMP SA. At this point, Oakley is used again to generate a new set of session keys. The master ISAKMP key is used whenever new SAs are negotiated; once the SA negotiation finishes, though, the communications using that SA are protected using the SA-specific keys.

The Authentication Header (AH)

The AH protocol provides data integrity and authentication, but how? The answer lies in how the IPSec packet is actually constructed. Figure 3.4 shows a sample AH packet (note that this example shows a TCP packet, but AH works the same way for UDP). There are two features that lend AH its security. The first security feature is that the packet signature (which is contained in the AH itself) is computed on the entire packet: payload and headers. That means that an attacker can't modify any part of the packet, including the IP or TCP/UDP header. The second security booster is that the AH is placed between the IP header and the TCP or UDP header; this adds further tamper-proofing.

FIGURE 3.4 An AH packet

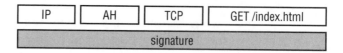

The Encapsulating Security Payload (ESP)

The ESP protocol is designed to deliver message confidentiality. Take a look at a sample ESP packet (Figure 3.5) to see how it accomplishes this. The first thing you'll probably notice is that this packet is more complex in construction than the AH packet, because ESP alone provides authentication, replay-proofing, and integrity checking. It does so by adding three separate components: an ESP header, an ESP trailer, and an ESP authentication block. Each of these components contains some of the data needed to provide the necessary authentication and integrity checking. To prevent tampering, an ESP client has to sign the ESP header, application data, and ESP trailer into one unit; of course, ESP is used to encrypt the application data and the ESP trailer to provide confidentiality. The combination of this overlapping signature and encryption operation provides good security.

FIGURE 3.5   An ESP packet

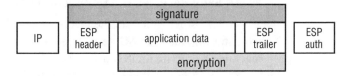

How Harry Meets Sally

Now it's time to tie all this protocol business together by showing you how it actually works in practice. As an example, say that Harry wants to establish a connection to a file server run by Sally. Harry and Sally are both members of the same Windows 2000 domain, so they can use the Windows 2000 default of Kerberos authentication. As you read over the steps involved, keep in mind that this entire process is utterly transparent to users on both machines, as well as to most intervening routers and network devices. The negotiation and agreement process is transparent to both the users and the applications they're using.

At Boot Time

When Harry's computer boots, the IPSec Policy Agent service starts. It connects to Active Directory and downloads the current IPSec policy for the domain. If this connection attempt fails, Harry's machine will keep trying until it successfully gets an IPSec policy, since without one the IPSec stack doesn't know what to do.

When the policy is retrieved, policy settings are passed to the ISAKMP/Oakley subsystem and to the actual IPSec drivers in the kernel.

When Harry Initiates a Connection

When Harry initially attempts to make a connection to any foreign machine, his computer's IPSec driver will check the active IPSec policy to see whether any IP filters are defined. These filters (which will be covered in more detail in Chapter 11, "Managing IP Security") specify destination networks, traffic types, or both; for the destination or traffic type, the filter also specifies whether IPSec is mandatory, optional, or forbidden.

After Harry's IPSec driver determines that it's allowed to use IPSec when talking to machines on Sally's subnet, it will use ISAKMP to establish an ISAKMP SA with Sally's server.

When Sally Receives the Connection Request

When Sally's machine sees the incoming ISAKMP request from Harry's workstation, her ISAKMP service replies to the request, and the two machines negotiate an ISAKMP SA as described earlier. This SA includes a shared secret key that can be used to establish connection-specific SAs.

The Dance Begins

Now that an ISAKMP SA has been established, the two machines have everything they need to establish a pair of IPSec SAs, so they do so. Once those negotiations are complete, each computer has two IPSec SAs in place: one for outbound traffic and one for inbound.

Harry's request (whatever it is) is processed by the IPSec stack on his computer. His IPSec code uses AH and/or ESP to protect the outbound packets, then transfers them to the lower-level parts of the IP stack for delivery to Sally's server. When her server gets the packets, it uses Sally's IPSec stack to decrypt them (if necessary), verify their authenticity, and pass them up the TCP/IP stack for further processing.

Virtual Private Networks

Most people think the Internet was the first true wide-area network. As it turns out, there are a number of others that could legitimately argue that they deserve the title. For example, ARINC, a joint venture among the major U.S. airlines, operates its own private network for transmitting airline data between airports, travel and reservation agents, airplanes in flight, and so on. Likewise, private networks used for credit-card authorization and time-sharing access to mainframes provided wide-area networking before the Internet took hold as a consumer technology.

Private networks offer superior security: Since you own the wires, you control what they're used for, who can use them, and what kind of data passes over them. However, they're not very flexible. Hark back to our sample routed network. If you imagine each of those networks is in a separate city, then that implies a requirement for leased lines to implement the internetwork connection, and leased lines are expensive. To make things worse, most private networks face a dilemma: Implementing enough capacity to handle peak loads almost guarantees that much of that capacity will sit idly much of the time, even though it still has to be paid for. (In fact, the old-school CompuServe service got started as a way to make a buck on excess network capacity that would ordinarily have been idle nights and weekends.)

One way to work around this problem is to maintain private dial-up services so that a field rep in Chicago can dial the home office in Boston (or wherever). Dial-ups are expensive, and they have the same excess capacity problem that truly private networks do. As an added detriment, users who need to dial in from long distances have to pay long distance charges unless they use toll-free numbers (in which case the remote access cost goes up dramatically).

Virtual private networks (VPNs) offer a solution: You get the security of a true private network with the flexibility, ubiquity, and low cost of the Internet. How does this magic work? Read on.

What VPNs Do

At any time, two parties can create a connection over the Internet. The idea behind a VPN is that you can use this property to let two parties establish an encrypted *tunnel* between them. Think of the tunnels that the North Koreans have dug in and around the Demilitarized Zone (DMZ)—they act as secure, private shortcuts between two different geographical points. VPNs do the same thing by establishing a tunnel, or virtual circuit, between a client and a server, using the Internet as a transportation medium. The VPN software on each end takes care of encrypting the VPN packets as they go; when they leave one end of the tunnel, their payloads are encrypted and encapsulated inside regular IP packets that cause them to be delivered to the remote machine. Figure 3.6 shows one way to conceptualize this process—imagine two tin cans and a string stretched all the way across the Internet and you've got the right idea.

As an example, let's say that we're in the field at a client site. As long as we're somewhere that our ISP serves, we can dial into their local point of presence and get connected to the Internet. At that point, we can open a VPN connection back to our servers at our office and do whatever we could do sitting in front of a normal desktop machine.

FIGURE 3.6   Drilling a tunnel through the Internet

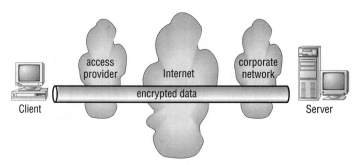

VPNs and Windows 2000

Windows NT included support for the *Point-to-Point Tunneling Protocol (PPTP)*, a Microsoft-specific VPN protocol, and Windows 2000 matches that and raises it by adding support for Cisco's Level 2 Tunneling Protocol (L2TP). L2TP provides a more generic tunneling mechanism than PPTP; when combined with IPSec, L2TP also allows you to establish VPNs using a wide range of non-Microsoft hardware and software products, including routers and access devices from companies like Cisco, Red Creek, and Nortel.

There are some other worthwhile enhancements in Windows 2000's VPN support, too, including the following:

- You can finally set up account lockout policies for dial-up and VPN users; this capacity has existed for network and console users for some time.

- The Extensible Authentication Protocol (EAP) allows Microsoft or third parties to write modules that implement new authentication methods and retrofit them to fielded servers. One example of EAP: the EAP-TLS module that implements smartcard/certificate-based access control for VPN and dial-up users.

- If you're using Active Directory in native mode, you can use remote access policies to apply and enforce consistent policies to all users in a site, domain, or organizational unit. These policies can include which encryption and authentication protocols users may, or must, use when talking to your servers.

How you enable VPN support on your Windows 2000 machine depends on whether you're using a server or a client. Client configuration is easy (as you'll see in Chapter 12, "Installing and Configuring Network Clients"): Just install the Dial-Up Networking service normally, then use the Make New Connection wizard to create a new VPN connection. On the server side, you'll need to install and configure the Routing and Remote Access Service, then enable it to accept incoming VPN connections. (See Chapter 10, "Managing Virtual Private Networking," for more on the specifics of how to do this.)

How VPNs Work

Dealing with the highest level first: How does a VPN client connect to a VPN server? This process assumes some things. First, it assumes that the VPN server is already connected to the Internet in some way (how doesn't really matter as long as the server has an IP address and the client knows what it is). Here's what happens:

1. The client establishes a connection to the Internet. This connection can use Dial-Up Networking or any other connection method; what matters is that the client is able to send packets out to the Internet.

2. The client sends a VPN connection request to the server. The exact format of the request varies, depending on whether the VPN is using PPTP or L2TP.

3. The client authenticates itself to the server. Again, the exact process varies according to the VPN protocol in use. If the client can't provide valid credentials, the buck stops here.

4. The client and server negotiate parameters for the VPN session. This negotiation allows the two ends to agree on an encryption algorithm and strength.

5. The client and server go through the PPP negotiation process described earlier in this chapter, because L2TP and PPTP both depend on the lower-level PPP protocols (for reasons that will be clearer in a short while).

Since the contents of data passed around in steps 2 and 3 vary according to the tunneling protocol in use, now would be a good time to examine the differences. First, though, you should understand encapsulation and how VPNs use it to wrap one kind of data inside another.

An Encapsulation Primer

In the beginning, most networks could only carry one kind of data. Each network vendor had its own protocol, and most of the time there was no way to intermingle data using different protocols on the same piece of wire. Over time and under customer pressure, vendors began to find ways to allow a single network to carry many different types of traffic, resulting in the current melting pot of traffic types found on most large networks. What about the Internet? You think of it as carrying exclusively TCP/IP, but what if there were a way to smuggle AppleTalk, IPX, or even NetBEUI traffic inside a TCP/IP packet? Actually, there is a way to do that, and it's called encapsulation.

Encapsulation works because software at each level of the OSI model has to see header information to figure out where a packet's coming from and where it's going, but the payload contents aren't important to most of those components. By fabricating the right kind of header and prepending it to whatever you want in the payload, you can route foreign traffic types through IP networks with no trouble.

VPNs depend on encapsulation, because their security depends on being able to keep the payload information encrypted. The following steps demonstrate what happens to a typical packet as it goes from being a regular IP datagram to a PPTP packet (see also Figure 3.7):

1. Some application creates a block of data bound for a remote host. In this case, it's a Web browser.

2. The client-side TCP/IP stack takes the application's data and turns it into a TCP/IP packet, first by adding a TCP header and then by adding an IP header. At this point, you can call the whole mess an *IP datagram*, since it contains all of the necessary addressing information to be delivered by IP.

3. Since the client's connected via PPP, it adds a PPP header to the IP datagram. This PPP + IP combination is called a PPP frame. If you were using PPP instead of a VPN protocol, the packet would go across the PPP link without further modification.

4. However, in this example you *are* using a VPN, so the next step is for the VPN to encrypt the PPP frame, turning it into gibberish.

5. A Generic Routing Encapsulation (GRE) header is combined with the encrypted payload. GRE really is generic; in this case, the protocol ID fields in the GRE header tell anyone who cares that this is an encapsulated PPTP packet.

6. Now that you have a tag to tell you what's in the payload, the PPTP stack can add an IP header (specifying the destination address of the VPN server, not the original host from step 2) and a PPP header.

7. The now innocent-looking packet can be sent out over your existing PPP connection. The IP header specifies that it should be routed to the VPN server, which can pick it apart and reverse steps 1 through 6 when the packet arrives.

FIGURE 3.7 Journey of a packet

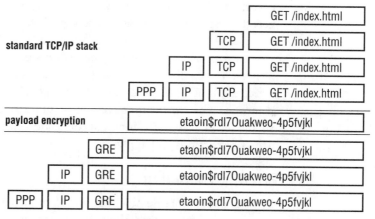

Encapsulation allows the use of VPN data inside of ordinary-looking IP datagrams, which is part of what makes VPNs so powerful—you don't have to change any of your applications, routers, or network components (unless they have to be configured to recognize and pass GRE packets). Everything "just works."

PPTP Tunneling

PPTP is a pretty straightforward protocol. Microsoft likes to call it a *de facto* industry standard, which is arguably true (based on the number of PPTP-capable clients and servers, anyway). However, it's mostly confined to sites that are all-Microsoft. There are PPTP clients for Mac OS and Linux, but most of the time PPTP-based networks are used primarily with Windows 95/98/NT/2000.

PPTP works by encapsulating packets using the mechanism just described. The encryption step is performed using Microsoft's Point-to-Point Encryption (MPPE) algorithm. The encryption keys used to encrypt the packets are generated dynamically for each connection; in fact, the keys can be changed periodically during the connection.

When the client and server have successfully established a PPTP tunnel, the authorization process begins. This process is basically an exchange of credentials with the object of allowing the server to decide whether the client is permitted to connect or not. The server sends a challenge message to the client, and the client answers with an encrypted response. When the server gets the response, it can check it to see whether the answer is right—this is the equivalent of asking your spouse "What was the name of the first movie we saw together?"—since presumably only one other person knows the answer. The challenge-response process allows the server to determine which account is trying to make a connection. Once it knows that, it can determine whether the user account is authorized to make a connection. If so, the server accepts the inbound connection; any access controls or remote access restrictions still apply.

L2TP/IPSec Tunneling

L2TP is much more flexible than PPTP, but it's also more complicated. It was designed to be a general-purpose tunneling protocol, not limited to VPN use. L2TP itself doesn't offer any kind of security. When you use L2TP, you're setting up an unencrypted, unauthenticated tunnel. Doing so over the Internet would be foolhardy, since anyone who wanted could read your allegedly private traffic. The fix: Use L2TP in conjunction with IPSec. The overall flow of an L2TP + IPSec tunnel session looks a little different from that of a PPTP session, since IPSec security is different. Here's what happens under the hood:

1. The client and server establish an IPSec security association, using the ISAKMP and Oakley protocols discussed in the previous section. At this point, the two machines have an encrypted channel between them.

2. The client builds a new L2TP tunnel to the server. Since this happens *after* the channel has been encrypted, there's no security risk.

3. The server sends an authentication challenge to the client.

4. The client encrypts its answer to the challenge and returns it to the server.

5. The server checks the challenge response to see whether or not it's valid; if so, the server can determine which account is connecting. Subject to whatever access policies you've put in place, at this point the server can accept the inbound connection.

Note that steps 3 through 5 mirror the steps described for PPTP tunneling. That's no accident, since the authorization process is a function of the remote access server, not the VPN stack. All the VPN does is provide a secure communications channel, and something else has to decide who gets to use it.

Certificate Services

If you have a driver's license, then you already know what a digital certificate is even if you don't know you know! Think of what your license actually does: It binds some attributes that describe you, like hair color, weight, and name, to a unique identifier, the license number. Anyone who trusts your state's Department of Motor Vehicles can trust that the attributes on the license (even the crappy picture!) match the real person who holds the license.

Digital certificates work the same way. They tie a set of attributes, like an e-mail address or logon name, to a unique identifier called a public key. For that reason, you'll sometimes hear them called public-key certificates. In Chapter 14, "Installing and Configuring Certificate Services," you'll read a lot more about the specifics of how public keys work; this section will be enough to whet your appetite for all the cool things you can do with them.

What Certificate Services Does

Microsoft's Certificate Services package provides a piece of software that security people call a *certificate authority (CA)*. If you think about what "authority" means in phrases like "Port Authority" or "Metropolitan Atlanta Rapid

Transit Authority," you'll get a correct sense of what a certificate authority does. Its job is to control the issuance and use of digital certificates for the users and computers in some group. You could set up a CA for a single organizational unit, a Windows 2000 domain, or an entire enterprise.

The CA actually has several distinct functions. Besides issuing certificates when it gets a legitimate request, it also allows administrators to revoke certificates once they're no longer needed. You can control what newly issued certificates may be used for; for example, you could apply a restriction that would permit anyone to request a certificate for secure e-mail but that wouldn't allow those certificates to be used for encrypting files.

These functions are all controlled by a robust set of permissions. For example, you can control who can request new certificates and which computers may be used to request them. As with almost any other setting in Active Directory's Group Policy Objects (GPOs), you can delegate control over these settings to whatever part of your organization needs to have it.

Microsoft's CA can stand alone, or it can act as part of a hierarchy of CAs. This hierarchy, known as a certification chain, can contain CAs from inside and outside a single organization. That allows you to have secure communications with business partners and suppliers without necessarily having to issue your certificates to them or generate a user account on your server.

Certificate Services and Windows 2000

Microsoft first introduced their Certificate Services package with Internet Information Server (IIS) 3.0. Having your own CA made it much easier to issue and manage digital certificates for use with Web-based applications that use SSL, and Microsoft wanted to encourage Web providers to use their tools instead of someone else's. That first CA was functional, if limited; besides working with IIS, it could be used with Exchange 5.0 to provide users with e-mail security.

When Microsoft shipped IIS 4.0, they updated the CA to make it more robust and flexible. The CA that is provided with Windows 2000 is an updated version of that product. It's now completely integrated into the operating system, so you manage it using the same familiar snap-in interface you use for managing practically everything else. It also takes full advantage of Active Directory for certificate storage.

The CA can stand alone, but you'll normally use it to generate machine certificates for IPSec and end-user certificates for smartcard logon or EAP-TLS authentication.

How Certificate Services Works

The actual process of issuing a digital certificate is something only a cryptographer could love, since it involves a lot of arcana made necessary by the demand for high security and assurance when doling out certificates. However, the overall flow of data between the client and the CA is fairly easy to understand. These steps show what happens, as does Figure 3.8:

1. The CA receives a certificate request ("please issue me a certificate") from a client. This request can be generated through a Web page offered by the CA, manually by the end user, or automatically by various system components.

2. The CA checks the incoming request to see that it is complete and correct (e.g., to see whether or not the requestor already has a certificate, to see whether or not the name on the certificate is a duplicate, and so on).

3. The CA checks whatever policies the group administrator has chosen to apply to make sure the request is in line with those policies. Sometimes this means that the CA must push the request off to a queue, where it sits and waits for human approval. If you configure the CA to do so, it can automatically approve requests that meet the specified policy.

4. The CA takes the attributes specified in the certificate request, adds in some of its own data (like the name of the CA and a copy of its own certificate), and asks a system cryptographic service to sign it. This signature, equivalent to the seal on a driver's license or a college diploma, serves as both protection against tampering and an assertion of validity. (Which cryptographic service actually does the signing is up to you, as you'll see in Chapter 14.)

5. The CA returns a copy of the new certificate to the requestor.

6. Optionally, it publishes the new certificate in Active Directory or in a shared folder. This allows other users, computers, and programs to look up certificates in a domain- or organization-wide directory.

FIGURE 3.8 The flow of certificate data between client and CA

1. The CA receives a certificate request ("please issue me a certificate") from a client. This request can be generated through a Web page offered by the CA, manually by the end user, or automatically by various system components.

2. The CA checks the incoming request to see that it is complete and correct (e.g., to see whether or not the requestor already has a certificate, to see whether or not the name on the certificate is a duplicate, and so on).

3. The CA checks whatever policies the group administrator has chosen to apply to make sure the request is in line with those policies. Sometimes this means that the CA must push the request off to a queue, where it sits and waits for human approval. If you configure the CA to do so, it can automatically approve requests that meet the specified policy.

4. The CA takes the attributes specified in the certificate request, adds in some of its own data (like the name of the CA and a copy of its own certificate), and signs it. This signature, equivalent to the seal on a driver's license or a college diploma, serves as both protection against tampering and an assertion of validity.

5. The CA returns a copy of the new certificate to the requestor.

6. Optionally, it publishes the new certificate in Active Directory or in a shared folder. This allows other users, computers, and programs to look up certificates in a domain- or organization-wide directory.

Summary

In this chapter, you learned:

- What dial-up networking and remote access services come with Windows 2000

- How multi-protocol network routing works in Windows 2000

- What IPSec is and how it works

- What virtual private network (VPN) services are available in Windows 2000

Key Terms

Before you take the exam, be sure you're familiar with the following terms:

Adjacency

Authentication header (AH)

Certificate authority (CA)

Demand-dial routing

Dial-Up Networking (DUN)

Dynamic routing

Encapsulating Security Payload (ESP)

Encapsulation

IP datagram

IP Security Extensions (IPSec)

IPSec SA

Link site map

Metric

Multicast routing

Multiprotocol routing

Network address translation (NAT)

Peer filters

Point-to-Point Protocol (PPP)

Point-to-Point Tunneling Protocol (PPTP)

Route filters

Routing

Routing and Remote Access Service (RRAS)

Security Association (SA)

Static routing

Tunnel

Unicast routing

Virtual private network (VPN)

Review Questions

1. IPSec provides which of the following?

    A. Confidentiality and authentication

    B. Confidentiality only

    C. Authentication only

    D. None of the above

2. Windows 2000 supports which of the following PPP authentication methods? (Choose all that apply.)

    A. CHAP

    B. MS-CHAP

    C. PAP

    D. NT LAN Manager

3. Before a VPN connection can be established, you must have which of the following?

    A. An existing LAN or dial-up connection

    B. An existing IPSec connection

    C. A set of VPN credentials

    D. Windows 2000 clients talking to Windows 2000 servers

4. Routing services store a source, a destination, and a _____ for each route.

    A. Cost, or metric

    B. Expiration time

    C. Set of packet filters

    D. Last-used timestamp

5. Windows 2000 includes support for routing which protocols?
(Choose all that apply.)

A. AppleTalk

B. IPX

C. IP

D. NetBEUI

6. What is the primary difference between static and dynamic routing?

A. Static routes aren't updated when routing topology changes.

B. Dynamic routing is faster and more efficient.

C. Static routing engines use router discovery protocols to find peer
routers.

D. Dynamic routing engines must be seeded with an initial set of
routes.

7. Microsoft's routing engine _____.

A. Supports RIP version 1 only

B. Supports RIP version 2 only

C. Supports RIP versions 1 and 2

D. Does not support RIP

8. Instead of a routing table, OSPF routers use which of the following?

A. A network neighborhood

B. A route list

C. A route database

D. A link state map (database)

9. Which two of the following statements are *not* true of OSPF routing?

   A. OSPF routers continually exchange routes with each other.

   B. OSPF routes are guaranteed to be loop-free.

   C. OSPF routers maintain a RIP-style routing table.

   D. OSPF is not as efficient as RIP.

10. Which of the following statements is true of OSPF route filters?

   A. They allow the router to selectively accept or reject routes from its peers.

   B. They can be used only to filter routes coming from OSPF peers.

   C. They can be used only to filter routes coming from RIP routers.

   D. They are required when you use OSPF.

11. IPSec provides authentication by adding what to packets?

   A. The authentication header (AH)

   B. The signature header (SH)

   C. The authorization header (AH)

   D. The digital signature header (DSH)

12. In Windows 2000, IPSec policy settings are _____.

   A. Distributed by Group Policy and retrieved by the IPSec Policy Agent

   B. Enforced by the IPSec Policy Agent

   C. Distributed by the IPSec Policy Agent

   D. Distributed and enforced by the Group Policy mechanism

13. IPSec negotiation involves which of the following?

   A. The ISAKMP security agreement only

   B. The ISAKMP SA plus a single IPSec SA

   C. The ISAKMP SA plus two IPSec SAs

   D. Two IPSec SAs only

14. The IPSec Encapsulating Security Payload (ESP) protocol _____.

   A. Provides message confidentiality only

   B. Provides authentication only

   C. Provides both message confidentiality and authentication

   D. Does not provide confidentiality or authentication

15. IPSec policy filters can specify _____.

   A. Whether IPSec connections are permitted or not

   B. Whether IPSec connections are mandatory or optional

   C. A and B

   D. None of the above

16. Virtual private networks _____.

   A. Transport private traffic across dedicated networks

   B. Encapsulate private traffic and transport it over a public network

   C. Cannot be used with Windows 2000 clients

   D. Can be used with L2TP or PPTP

17. The major differences between PPTP and L2TP are which of the following? (Select all that apply.)

   A. L2TP doesn't provide privacy, only tunneling.

   B. PPTP can be used only to tunnel TCP/IP.

   C. L2TP may be used with IPSec, while PPTP stands alone.

   D. PPTP is supported by major industry vendors, while L2TP is a proprietary Microsoft standard.

18. Which of the following is true of the Windows 2000 Certificate Services module? (Choose all that apply.)

    A. It issues and revokes digital certificates.

    B. It is required to use IPSec.

    C. It may be used to generate smartcard certificates.

    D. It interoperates with other X.509 version 3 CAs.

19. PPTP encrypts its packets with _____.

    A. Microsoft Point-to-Point Encryption (MPPE)

    B. IPSec ESP

    C. Triple DES

    D. The strongest cipher available from the operating system

20. Which of the following is true of demand-dial routes? (Choose all that apply.)

    A. They only come up when needed to move traffic to a remote destination.

    B. They can be configured to be permanent.

    C. They may not be used with OSPF or RIP.

    D. They are not supported by Windows 2000.

Answers to Review Questions

1. A. IPSec provides both confidentiality and authentication, although you get to choose which combination of these two you want to use.

2. A, B, C. NTLM isn't a PPP authentication method, although MS-CHAP can use NTLM credentials.

3. A. VPN connections just tunnel traffic across an existing connection.

4. A. The router needs to have cost, or metric, information so it can figure out the "best" route to a particular destination.

5. A, B, C. NetBEUI isn't routable.

6. A. Static routing is faster and more efficient, but it requires you to manually specify all the routes—there's no discovery.

7. C. RRAS can route using both version 1 and version 2 of RIP.

8. D. OSPF's link state map is more efficient, but it also requires somewhat more overhead to build and maintain.

9. A, C. OSPF routers don't exchange routing information per se, and they don't use a routing table. Instead, each router maintains its own link state map. RIP routers interchange routes; OSPF routers exchange link state data.

10. A. OSPF route filters are optional; when you use them, they give you control over which routers your OSPF router accepts or rejects.

11. A. The authentication header provides a keyed hash of the packet contents that the receiving end can use for verifying authenticity.

12. A. The IPSec Policy Agent fetches the policy from Group Policy when the system starts, then applies it locally.

13. C. The ISAKMP SA is used for initial negotiation. Each endpoint then needs its own IPSec SA.

14. C. ESP provides confidentiality by encrypting the packets, and it can also use an AH-style keyed hash to provide authentication.

15. C. Policy filters can specify whether IPSec connections are allowed and optional, allowed and mandatory, or not allowed at all.

16. B. VPNs take your traffic, protect it against eavesdropping and tampering, then ship it off using someone else's network.

17. A, B, C. PPTP is a Microsoft standard; L2TP (which is normally used with IPSec) was jointly developed by Microsoft and Cisco.

18. A, B, C, D. Certificate Services issue and revoke X.509v3 certificates. These certificates can be used for IPSec and smartcard logon, as well as secure e-mail and the Encrypting File System (EFS).

19. A. MPPE is the only protocol supported by PPTP.

20. A, B. You can use demand-dial routes to establish either permanent connections or connections that are established only when the RRAS machine has traffic that must transit that link.

Chapter 4

Installing and Configuring Basic Network Protocols

MICROSOFT EXAM OBJECTIVES COVERED IN THIS CHAPTER:

✓ **Install, configure, and troubleshoot network protocols.**

- Install the NWLink protocol.
- Install and configure TCP/IP.
- Configure network bindings.

Windows 2000 includes support for the same network protocols you're accustomed to in Windows NT 4.0. Some of these protocols, like TCP/IP, have assumed new importance. Others, like NetBIOS, are being quietly rolled out to pasture. However, the majority (including DLC and AppleTalk) survive relatively unchanged.

The Windows 2000 network infrastructure exam objectives require you to know how to install, configure, and troubleshoot network protocols. However, the exam itself focuses heavily on two protocols: TCP/IP and the NetWare-compatible *NWLink*. Accordingly, that's what this chapter will focus on. By the time you finish this chapter, you'll know how to install any network protocol Windows 2000 supports, and you'll know how to set basic configuration parameters for TCP/IP and NWLink. You'll also learn how to configure the bindings that attach protocols to particular NICs. Finally, you'll learn how to troubleshoot TCP/IP and NWLink problems.

Installing Network Protocols

Windows 2000 supports a wide range of network protocols, both in the set provided with Windows 2000 itself and from third-party vendors. In brief, any vendor who wants to write an NDIS-compatible driver can do so; in theory, any network protocol could potentially have a Windows 2000 version. In practice, Microsoft ships protocol stacks for TCP/IP, NetBEUI, Novell's IPX/SPX (which Microsoft calls NWLink), AppleTalk, and DLC. You install or remove all of these protocols using the same interface; once you actually install the protocol, you will still have to configure it. Since it's fairly simple, you will learn how to install NWLink first. Once that's done, you'll move on to the more complicated process of installing and configuring TCP/IP.

Installation Basics

You install network protocols through the Local Area Network Connection Properties dialog box, which lists all of the known protocols on your Windows 2000 machine. Protocols marked with a check indicate that they're bound to the adapter whose properties you're inspecting. Figure 4.1 shows an example of what this dialog box might look like on your machine.

FIGURE 4.1   The Local Area Connection Properties dialog box shows you which protocols are already installed.

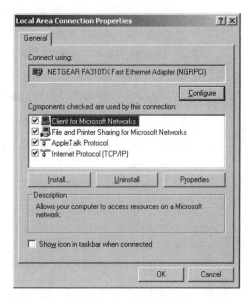

Installing and Configuring NWLink

Notice that NWLink isn't shown in Figure 4.1; that's OK because we're about to install it by following the instructions in Exercise 4.1.

Microsoft ✓ *Exam Objective*

Install, configure, and troubleshoot network protocols.

- Install the NWLink protocol.

EXERCISE 4.1

Installing NWLink

Follow these steps to install NWLink:

1. Open the Network and Dial-Up Connections folder (Start ≻ Settings ≻ Network and Dial-Up Connections).

2. Right-click the Local Area Connection icon and choose the Properties command. The Local Area Connection Properties dialog box appears, as shown earlier in Figure 4.1.

3. Click the Install... button. The Select Network Component Type dialog box appears. Select Protocol and click the Add... button.

4. The Select Network Protocol dialog box appears. Choose "NWLink IPX/SPX-Compatible Transport Protocol," then click the OK button.

5. If prompted, insert your Windows 2000 CD and click OK.

6. Click the Close button in the Local Area Connection Properties dialog box.

You may notice something missing from the above instructions: They don't say anything about rebooting. That's because one of the biggest improvements in Windows 2000 is that you can now install or remove network protocols usually without rebooting! That's good, because when you install NWLink you actually get two protocols: NWLink and NWLink NetBIOS. NWLink NetBIOS allows NWLink traffic to be encapsulated inside NetBIOS traffic. In other words, you can send NWLink traffic between machines running NetBIOS or between a Windows machine running NWLink and a NetWare server running Novell's NetBIOS implementation.

Configuring NWLink is very straightforward. Like NetBEUI, it's really not designed to be configured, so there aren't very many settings you can change. When you open the NWLink properties dialog box, you'll see the mostly empty dialog box shown in Figure 4.2. Its controls do the following:

- The Internal Network Number field lets you designate a network number (roughly equivalent to a TCP/IP network address) for this NIC. IPX and SPX use network numbers to route traffic for particular services directly to the machines that host them instead of depending on the Service Advertising Protocol (SAP).

- The Adapter group controls what types of network data frames your adapter recognizes as containing NWLink-compatible data. There are four separate and incompatible *frame types*: Ethernet 802.2, Ethernet 802.3, Ethernet II, and Ethernet SNAP. Normally you'll want to use the Auto frame type detection radio button, since it lets the NWLink stack decipher the frame types for you. Choosing the wrong frame type means that you won't be able to communicate with other machines. If necessary (for example, if Windows 2000 misidentifies the frame type), you can tell NWLink that a particular network number is using a particular frame type by selecting the Manual frame type detection radio button and using the Add button to specify the desired frame type and network number.

FIGURE 4.2 The NWLink Properties dialog box

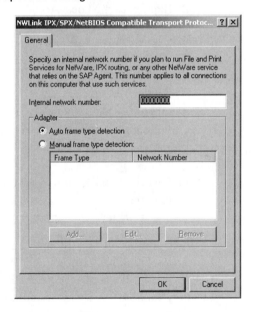

Installing and Configuring TCP/IP

TCP/IP is normally installed as part of the Windows 2000 setup process. This is no accident, since Microsoft would much rather have all its Windows 2000 customers use TCP/IP than NetBIOS. If you need to install TCP/IP manually, you still can. The process for installing it is very similar to the process required to install NWLink, as you can see in Exercise 4.2.

Microsoft ✓ ***Exam Objective***

Install, configure, and troubleshoot network protocols.

• Install and configure TCP/IP.

EXERCISE 4.2

Installing TCP/IP

Follow these steps to install the TCP/IP protocol:

1. Open the Network and Dial-Up Connections folder (Start ➤ Settings ➤ Network and Dial-Up Connections).

2. Right-click the Local Area Connection icon and choose the Properties command. The Local Area Connection Properties dialog box appears, as shown earlier in Figure 4.1.

3. Click the Install... button. The Select Network Component Type dialog box appears. Select Protocol and click the Add... button.

4. The Select Network Protocol dialog box appears. Choose Internet Protocol (TCP/IP), then click the OK button.

5. If prompted, insert your Windows 2000 CD and click OK.

6. Click the Close button in the Local Area Connection Properties dialog box.

When you install TCP/IP, it defaults to using DHCP for automatic configuration. Think back to Chapter 2 and the "Obtain an IP address automatically" button. If you want to use DHCP for automatic configuration you certainly can, but it's always useful to know how to manually configure a TCP/IP connection (especially since Microsoft will be asking you to prove you know how to as part of the exam!). Now you'll see what that configuration process entails.

Configuring Basic TCP/IP Settings

If you've bought into the rap that TCP/IP is convoluted and difficult to configure, Windows 2000's basic TCP/IP properties dialog box may surprise you. TCP/IP actually requires only two pieces of information to function: the IP address you want to use for this system and the subnet mask that corresponds to the network subnet the client is on. For example, in the Windows 2000 classes we teach we set up an in-classroom network that doesn't connect to any outside networks, including the Internet. We don't need a *default gateway* since that's used for routing, and we don't set up DNS until later in the class. With only these two parameters, machines can communicate with each other (although not having DNS is inconvenient, since it means we have to type IP addresses by hand).

Figure 4.3 shows the TCP/IP Properties dialog box. You get this dialog box by opening the Local Area Connection icon, selecting the Internet Protocol (TCP/IP) protocol, and clicking the Properties button. Of course, if you have multiple network adapters in a single computer, you can set independent TCP/IP properties for each adapter. Depending on what you want to do, you'll use either the automatic configuration buttons or the text fields.

FIGURE 4.3   The basic TCP/IP Properties dialog box

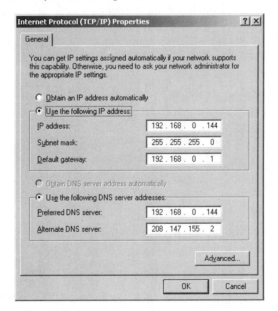

If You Want to Use DHCP

If you're configuring a Windows 2000 Professional machine, chances are probably pretty good that you're using DHCP with it. In that case, the default TCP/IP settings will work fine for you, since they configure the TCP/IP stack to get configuration parameters from any available *DHCP server* using the process outlined in Chapter 2. Remember that you can mix and match DHCP and non-DHCP machines; on a single client, you can use

DHCP to get everything except DNS server addresses if you want to. You have two basic choices:

- To configure a client to get its TCP/IP configuration information from a DHCP server, leave the "Obtain an IP address automatically" radio button selected.

- If you're using DHCP for basic IP addressing and you want to accept DNS server addresses from the DHCP server, leave the "Obtain DNS server address automatically" radio button selected.

If You Don't Want DHCP

We recommend against using DHCP on servers, since they're not nearly as dynamic as clients. Ideally you won't reboot servers unless they *need* it, and you won't be moving them around. Therefore, the "dynamic" in DHCP isn't really useful, and its other benefits are outweighed by the comfort that comes from knowing that your server has a correct and unchanging IP configuration. If you want to configure the TCP/IP settings yourself, start by selecting the "Use the following IP address" radio button, then fill in the other, following fields:

- In the IP address field, enter the IP address you want to use for this machine. Remember that Windows 2000 won't do any kind of sanity checking. The most common mistake people make with this field is to enter an address that doesn't match the address range they're using on their network.

- In the Subnet Mask field, enter the appropriate subnet mask for your network. (IP subnetting is a fairly complicated topic, and you don't need to know how to calculate subnets for the exam. If you're interested in learning more, see the Sybex book *TCP/IP 24seven* by Gary Govanus.)

- If you want this machine to be able to route packets to other networks, enter the gateway or router address you want it to use in the Default Gateway field. Again, remember that Windows 2000 will slavishly use whatever address you enter here, so make sure it's right.

- If you're using DNS on your network, enter the first DNS server you want this client to talk to in the Preferred DNS Server field. It's critical to get this right on a Windows 2000 network since DNS is required for Active Directory services. If you want to specify another server to use when the preferred server is unavailable or can't resolve a DNS query, enter it in the Alternate DNS Server field. (You can also specify additional servers, as you'll see in the following section on the Advanced TCP/IP Properties dialog box.)

Configuring Advanced TCP/IP Settings

The Advanced button in the TCP/IP Properties dialog box brings up something that looks more like you'd expect from TCP/IP. The Advanced TCP/IP Properties dialog box contains four tabs that let you extend and override the settings from the simpler dialog box shown in Figure 4.3.

Expanding the Basic Settings

The basic configuration dialog box you saw earlier lets you enter one IP address, one subnet mask, and one default gateway. For the majority of systems that's enough, but what if you want to configure a machine that can communicate on multiple IP addresses? For example, if you're setting up an IIS server, you may want it to answer to multiple IP addresses on a single physical network connection (such as the connection that links your server to the Internet). Adding multiple IP addresses in this manner is called *multihoming*. You may also want to specify multiple default gateways so that an outbound packet sent by your systems can be sent to whichever gateway is "cheapest" (more on what "cheap" means in a minute). The IP Settings tab of the Advanced TCP/IP Properties dialog box allows you to do both of these things. Figure 4.4 shows what it looks like.

FIGURE 4.4   The IP Settings tab of the Advanced TCP/IP Settings dialog box

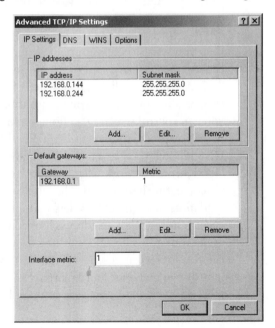

Your options on the IP Setting tab include the following:

- The IP Addresses control group lists the IP addresses currently defined for this network adapter. You can add new address bindings, edit existing bindings, or remove an additional address with the buttons at the bottom of the control group. Once you add an address here and close all open network properties dialog boxes (including the Local Area Connection dialog box), any changes you make here will become effective.

- The Default Gateways control group shows the routing gateways that are currently defined *for this computer only.* Each gateway has an IP address (to which the client sends outbound packets) and an associated metric, or cost. When deciding where to send packets bound for other networks, Windows 2000 will examine its internal TCP/IP routing table to see whether it already "knows" how to get packets to the destination network. If so, it uses that route. If not, it uses the default gateway. If you specify more than one default gateway, the system chooses a gateway by selecting the one that has the lowest cost. If that gateway is down, or if it can't get packets to the destination system, Windows 2000 will try the next-most-expensive gateway. This process repeats until the packets arrive at their destination or until the system runs out of gateways to try.

Expanding DNS and WINS Settings

If all you want to do is configure your clients to use two DNS servers, you can use the Preferred and Alternate Server Configuration fields in the basic TCP/IP Properties dialog box. The DNS tab of the Advanced TCP/IP Properties dialog box allows you to specify more than two servers; in addition, you can control which DNS domain names are appended to search queries when you don't specify a fully qualified domain name. Figure 4.5 shows the DNS tab, which is covered in more detail in Chapter 12, "Installing and Configuring Network Clients." However, we want to point out the most salient feature here as well: The DNS Server Addresses, In Order Of Use field (and its associated buttons) lets you specify multiple DNS servers. When the client resolver needs an address looked up, it will start by querying the server at the top of this list and working down the list until it finds an answer or runs out of servers to query. Adding servers to this list is a quick way to improve your clients' fault tolerance, since losing the preferred and alternate DNS servers will otherwise result in a loss of DNS service to the clients.

FIGURE 4.5 The DNS tab of the Advanced TCP/IP Properties dialog box

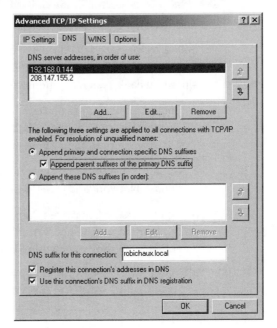

Likewise, the WINS tab (not shown here) allows you to specify multiple WINS servers. In fact, the only place where you can specify which WINS servers to use is in this tab (as you'll see in Chapter 12), because Microsoft is trying to move you away from using WINS (and NetBIOS!) to using pure TCP/IP and DNS. Finally, the Options tab lets you configure protocol-specific options, including whether or not the IP Security (IPSec) extensions are used and whether or not any type of packet filtering is enabled. Chapter 11 covers the settings available on this tab.

Before attempting exercise 4.3 on your network, be sure to choose an IP address *not* in use by any other host or device on your network!

EXERCISE 4.3

Configuring TCP/IP Settings

Follow these steps to add a second IP address to your existing NIC. Note that this exercise assumes that you're not using DHCP on that NIC, since you can't assign additional addresses to a DHCP-enabled NIC.

1. Choose an IP address on your network that's not currently in use by another device (e.g., 192.168.0.202). Make sure you know the correct subnet mask to use with that IP address (e.g., 255.255.255.0).

2. Open the Network and Dial-Up Connections folder (Start ➢ Settings ➢ Network and Dial-Up Connections).

3. Right-click the Local Area Connection icon and choose the Properties command. The Local Area Connection Properties dialog box appears, as shown earlier in Figure 4.1.

4. Select Internet Protocol (TCP/IP) in the Components list, and then click the Properties... button. The Internet Protocol (TCP/IP) Properties dialog box will appear.

5. Click the Advanced... button. The Advanced TCP/IP Properties dialog box will appear.

6. Click the Add... button in the IP Addresses control group. The TCP/IP Address dialog box will appear.

7. Type in the IP address and subnet mask you chose in Step 1.

8. Click the OK button in the Advanced TCP/IP Settings dialog box.

9. Click the OK button in the Internet Protocol (TCP/IP) Properties dialog box.

10. Click the OK button in the Local Area Connection Properties dialog box.

Installing NetBEUI

What about NetBEUI? Up to now, you've been reading that Microsoft is trying its darnedest to drive a pointed wooden stake through NetBEUI and replace it with TCP/IP. Although that's a lofty goal, there are still lots of NetBEUI networks and seats out there in the world, and it's important to know how to install NetBEUI in case you ever need it on a network. The good news is that there's virtually nothing new to learn by this point, because you install NetBEUI using steps that are almost identical to what you've already done while installing NWLink and TCP/IP. In this case, there are actually three separate pieces you may need to install to use NetBEUI:

- You need the NetBEUI protocol itself, which you install using the steps outlined in Exercise 4.1. Note that NetBEUI isn't installed by default on any version of Windows 2000.

- The Client for Microsoft Networks client allows your client machine to attach to shares and printers on other servers, no matter what transport protocol you're using. This is actually the Workstation service, which you may recognize from Windows NT 4.0.

- The File and Print Sharing for Microsoft Networks service allows your machine to act as a server, sharing resources with other machines just like the Server service in Windows NT 4.0.

NetBEUI is designed to be self-tuning, so there are no properties to set for it. However, do you remember the WINS tab on the Advanced TCP/IP Properties dialog box? As you'll see in Chapter 12, you can use a radio button there to turn off the use of NetBEUI over TCP/IP. As an alternative, you can remove the protocol or selectively unbind it from some or all of your network adapters. Speaking of adjusting bindings, next you'll learn how you do it!

Configuring Network Bindings

A *network binding* links a protocol to an adapter so that the adapter can carry traffic using that protocol. For example, if we say, "TCP/IP is bound to the onboard Ethernet port on our laptop," we're telling you a few things: TCP/IP is installed, our onboard Ethernet port has a driver that supports TCP/IP, and the adapter is configured to send and receive TCP/IP traffic. In Chapter 1, "Understanding Windows 2000 Networking," you read about the NDIS driver specification and its benefits. One of those benefits is the ability to bind more than one protocol to a NIC. That's how your Windows 2000 machine can run TCP/IP, NetBEUI, DLC, and AppleTalk at the same time, even if it has only one network card.

Install, configure, and troubleshoot network protocols.

• Configure network bindings.

Windows 2000 automatically creates bindings when you install a protocol or when you check or uncheck the check boxes in the Properties dialog box of a particular NIC. You can change these bindings manually; for example, it's commonly considered good practice to unbind NetBEUI and NWLink from adapters that are connected to, or visible from, the Internet. The Windows 2000 way of doing this is quite a bit different than the old-school Windows NT 4.0 scheme. You access the Windows 2000 binding list from within the Network and Dial-Up Connections folder. Select a local NIC (like the standard Local Area Connection item) and choose the Advanced ➤ Advanced Settings command. You'll see the Advanced Settings dialog box, as shown in Figure 4.6. This dialog box is divided into two distinct areas.

FIGURE 4.6 Adjusting bindings with the Advanced Settings dialog box

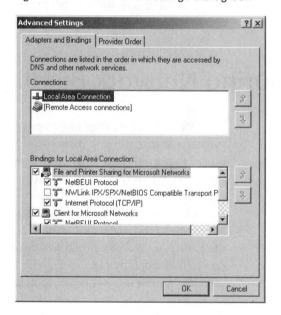

The Connections list, at the top of the dialog box, shows all the connections available on your computer. They're listed in the order that they'll be used for services. For example, in Figure 4.6 you can see that TCP/IP services (as well as everything else) will first use the LAN connection; if the requested action can't be taken there, the services will use a Remote Access connection instead. You can change the order in which connections are used by selecting a connection and using the up and down arrow buttons to the right of the list.

The Bindings list (in the bottom half of the dialog box) shows you which protocols and services are bound to the selected connection. For example, Figure 4.6 shows that the File and Printer Sharing for Microsoft Networks and Client for Microsoft Networks services are bound to the LAN adapter, and that the NetBEUI and TCP/IP protocols are bound to the File and Printer Sharing for Microsoft Networks service. What does this list actually tell you? Simple: It tells you which services are available on a connection. Beneath each service, you'll see a list of which protocols that service can use. Checking and unchecking services has the same effect as checking or unchecking items in the Adapter Properties dialog box.

There's a twist, though: You can turn individual protocols on or off on a per-service basis. For example, Exercise 4.4 walks you through the process of turning NWLink on for file and print sharing. In addition to turning protocols off and on, you can also control what order the protocols are used in. This is a valuable optimization, since many protocols have some sort of built-in retry behavior. Changing the bindings so that the most frequently used protocols are at the top of the list for each service means that the services never waste time trying the wrong protocol; instead, they'll try the most likely choice first, falling back to other protocols only if the first protocol fails.

EXERCISE 4.4

Editing Network Bindings

Follow these steps to bind IPX/SPX to the File and Printer Sharing service. You must complete Exercise 4.1 before doing this exercise.

1. Open the Network and Dial-Up Connections folder (Start ➢ Settings ➢ Network and Dial-Up Connections).

2. Select the Local Area Connection icon, then choose the Advanced ➢ Advanced Settings command. The Advanced Settings dialog box appears, as shown earlier in Figure 4.6.

3. Select Internet Protocol (TCP/IP) in the Components list, and then click the Properties... button. The Internet Protocol (TCP/IP) Properties dialog box will appear.

4. Click the Advanced... button. The Advanced TCP/IP Properties dialog box will appear.

5. In the Bindings for Local Area Connection list, find the File and Printer Sharing for Microsoft Networks item. Notice that each installed network protocol is listed below the service.

6. In the indented list, do two things: If NetBEUI is checked, uncheck it; and if NWLink is unchecked, check it.

7. Click the OK button in the Advanced Settings dialog box.

Troubleshooting Network Protocols

In a perfect world, troubleshooting would never be necessary. However, in the real world we troubleshoot things constantly to solve problems—such as, why the microwave isn't working (because lightning hit the power line last night), why one workstation can't see others on the network (its network cable was unplugged), and why fools fall in love (oops, we'll have to get back to you on that one).

Knowing how to effectively troubleshoot network problems is an essential part of managing even small networks, and Microsoft expects you to understand basic troubleshooting principles and how to apply them in Windows 2000 networking. Fortunately, you probably already know *what* to check; now you'll read about a set of tools that you can use to verify the proper functioning of your network. More importantly, you'll learn how to use those tools the right way at the right time.

What We Have Here Is a Failure to Communicate

When someone complains that their network is broken, your first impulse should be to ask "Well, what changed?" This might seem weird, but it's actually very practical. If a system is working and then it stops working, obviously something has changed somewhere—either as the result of an explicit change or by accident. Once you can identify what has, or has not, changed, you're ready to start looking for effects of the change and ways to fix whatever's gone wrong.

For example, one of the servers in our home office is a reliable old Intergraph TD-30. Even though it's been running Windows 2000 Advanced Server since very early in the beta cycle, it just keeps trucking along, never giving us any trouble. It happens to have a front-mounted power switch. When we can't contact it, our first suspicion is that it's been powered off. (With two sons under age 5, this is a reasonable suspicion, so it's always the first thing to check.)

The first sign of network trouble is usually pretty obvious, too: one machine can't talk to another. If you think back to the OSI networking model from Chapter 1, you'll remember that computers can communicate at several different layers. Using the above example, if we look at the back panel of *hawk*, our primary Windows 2000 server, we can see that its NIC has some LEDs that indicate network activity. Just because we see those lights blinking doesn't tell us anything about what kind of network data is being carried by the transport, application, session, or presentation layers—all it tells us is that the physical layer components are sending and receiving *something*.

First Things First

You can often save yourself a lot of unnecessary time and effort when troubleshooting a problem by doing something simple: stopping to think. It's hard to keep your wits about you when something's wrong with your network and end users are clamoring for your head on a stick, but if you can clearly identify the problem source you're well on your way to being able to effectively resolve it without any time-wasting detours.

What Kind of Problem Is It?

Sometimes this can be the most frustrating part of troubleshooting. Getting a phone call or a pager message that says, "The network is down" doesn't tell you much. Is it your connection to the Internet? your e-mail server? a file server somewhere on your LAN? Without knowing what specific service or connection is unavailable, you won't know what to start fixing.

Some types of problems immediately suggest a solution. For example, if a client calls us and says they get DNS errors when trying to connect to Web sites, our first two thoughts are that someone's changed their DNS settings or that their DNS servers are down. Likewise, if a user reports a problem reaching a particular share on a server, the problem may be on the client, the server, or the intervening network. If you can, arm yourself with as many details about how the problem is manifesting itself (including exact error messages), when it started, and whether or not it's consistent before you try to figure out what the problem is. Knowing these things beforehand can guide you to an easy, quick solution if it's a problem you've seen and fixed before–but only if you *know* you've seen it before!

Who's Having the Problem?

Knowing which users or computers are affected by a problem is very important, since that gives you insight into possible causes (including user mistakes) and helps you select a course of action.

If One User Reports a Problem

If one user on your network has a problem, our experience has been that more often than not the problem stems from some change the user made. Windows contains a lot of interrelated components, and it's not evident to most people that a simple change they made in component A may have unexpected side effects on component B. When troubleshooting an end user problem, your first question should always involve whether or not they've changed anything on the machine. This includes changing control panel settings, installing or removing software, rebooting, or any other action that might have directly or indirectly changed the state of the machine. If you can find out what's changed, that will give you a list of potential places to start looking.

For example, in a class we recently taught, one user complained that he could no longer see the network after doing one of the labs. As it turned out, he had turned his machine into a DHCP server while experimenting, which meant that his previously assigned DHCP address could no longer be used. He'd picked another IP address at random, which turned out not to work with our classroom network configuration. Knowing what changed let us pinpoint and fix the problem quickly.

If Several Users Report the Same Problem

Multiuser troubleshooting is, paradoxically, both easier and harder than single-user troubleshooting. Most of the time one user can't change anything that will affect other users on the network, so you generally don't have to worry about that variable. On the other hand, the kinds of changes that can accidentally affect connectivity for many users at once are more likely to be things *you've* changed. The first step in fixing this kind of problem is identifying its scope. Is everyone on the network affected? Are only people in one workgroup or on one floor of a building affected? Is the problem limited to the lack of one key service (like DNS), or is all network traffic hosed? Answering this type of question helps you isolate where the problem's occurring so you can concentrate your efforts on that area.

Here's an example: While on a consulting assignment in Texas, users at the site we were visiting began reporting that inbound Internet mail wasn't arriving as expected. We checked the Exchange server and found that it was OK. What else could have changed? It turned out that the DNS entry for the mail server had been improperly altered by someone at the company's ISP, so mail couldn't be delivered until things were fixed. Knowing that the problem affected *everyone* helped us find the right solution instead of assuming another cause.

Accentuate the Physical

Physical layer connectivity is absolutely critical. If you don't have a physical connection to the network you want to talk to, how can you send packets to it? This might seem like an obvious question to ask, but the number of times that we've seen people forget to ask it and look for a more complex—and ultimately nonexistent—problem would boggle your mind. So, when you first notice a network problem, be sure to verify that all of your network cables are correctly connected; that your hub, router, or switch has power; and so on. Take a look at the activity or "heartbeat" lights on your NIC, hub, or switch to see whether the physical layer is reporting any type of activity.

Knowing something about the scope of the outage helps, too—if all your users begin complaining at once that the network is down, it's unlikely to be the fault of one user's network cable. Contrariwise, if a single user is having trouble with the network it's unlikely that a router or switch is to blame. If you've properly identified exactly who's having trouble, that may suggest a cause based on your knowledge of the physical topology. When we worked at Intergraph, for example, we used wall-mounted routers that plugged into ordinary power outlets. Every so often, someone on the cleaning crew would unplug a router at night to plug in a floor polisher or vacuum cleaner, then forget to plug it back in. Result: No one in that area would have network access the next morning!

If you verify that all of the physical connections are OK, with power and cabling all in good order, and you *still* have no connectivity, that indicates that the problem probably resides within a higher layer.

Using *Ipconfig* to See What's What

Windows 2000 includes a useful tool called *ipconfig*. As its name implies, it's used to configure, and to see the configuration of, TCP/IP interfaces on your local machine. In Chapter 12, "Installing and Configuring Network Clients," you'll learn how to use *ipconfig* to release and renew DHCP configurations. There's also a more fundamental troubleshooting use that you should know about. Typing **ipconfig** into a Windows 2000 command prompt window will present you with a neat summary of your current IP configuration, including the local DNS name, the IP addresses, and the subnet masks configured for all adapters on the computer. Figure 4.7 shows an example of this output. You can use *ipconfig* in this mode to get a quick snapshot of its IP configuration, even if it's using DHCP. For example, if you see that the problem machine has no IP address assigned, even though there's a DNS server, it suggests the possibility that the DHCP server isn't authorized in Active Directory.

FIGURE 4.7   The output from ipconfig

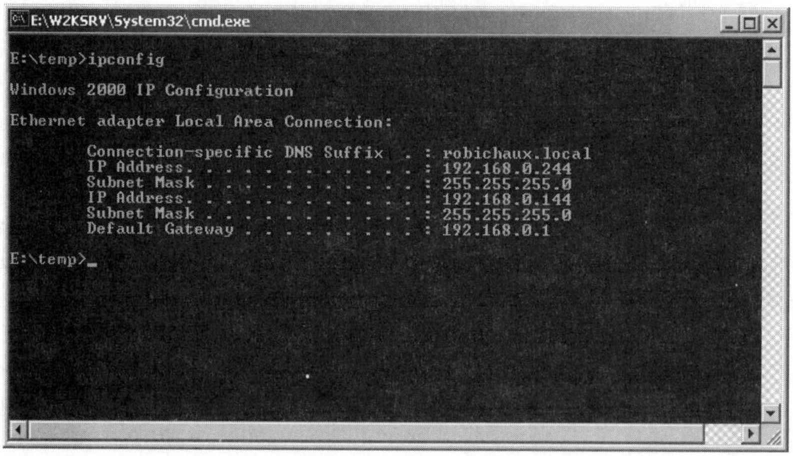

In addition to the DHCP-related switches that you'll see in Chapter 12, there's another switch of interest to troubleshooters: */all*. As you might expect, adding the */all* switch causes *ipconfig* to spill its guts and display everything it knows about the current IP configuration on all installed adapters. In addition to the DNS information and IP address that it ordinarily displays, you'll also get the MAC address of each NIC, the present WINS configuration (if any), and the IP addresses being used for the preferred and alternate DNS servers. Figure 4.8 shows an example of the *ipconfig /all* output.

FIGURE 4.8   The output from ipconfig /all

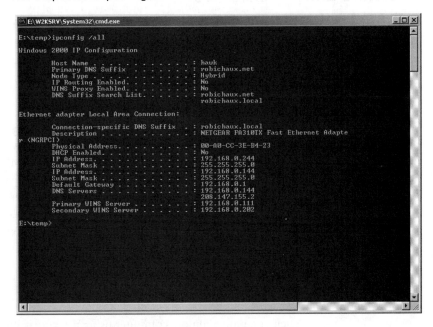

What can you do with all this information? It depends. If you're familiar enough with your network to know what IP address configurations should look like, often a quick check with *ipconfig* will tell you where the problem lies. For example, you might notice that an adapter that should be DHCP-enabled isn't, or vice versa. Even if you're not familiar with the details of your network, though, knowing how to find the IP addresses and subnet masks in use on your computers can be very valuable.

EXERCISE 4.5

Checking Configurations with *Ipconfig*

Follow these steps to run *ipconfig* and analyze its output:

1. Open a command window (Start ➢ Run, then enter **cmd** in the Run dialog box and click OK).

2. At the command prompt, type **ipconfig**. Notice that you see an abbreviated display containing the machine's connection-specific DNS suffix, its IP address, subnet mask, and default gateway.

3. Type **ipconfig /all**. Note that a great deal more information is displayed, including information on multiple adapters (if you have more than one).

Where'd My Packets Go?

The next step up from physical layer troubleshooting is tracing the route that packets take, or are attempting to take, between the source and destination. Once you've verified that all of the physical connections are in good shape, the next step is to see whether you can send *any* type of packet between points A and B.

TCP/IP includes a protocol called the *Internet Control Message Protocol (ICMP)*. ICMP is designed to pass control and status information between TCP/IP devices. One type of ICMP packet, popularly known as a *ping* packet, tells the receiving system to send back an ICMP response. This gives you confirmation of whether or not the ICMP ping packet reached the target, which in turn tells you whether or not you can get packets from place to place. Since name resolution and application services depend on lower-level protocols, this sort of "Is this thing on?" test is the next logical step after testing the underlying physical connection. The *ping* and *tracert* tools both use ICMP to help sniff out network problems.

The *Ping* Tool

When you ping a remote computer using the *ping* utility in its default mode, your computer will send out four ICMP ping packets and measure the time required before each packet's corresponding response arrives. When it finishes, *ping* gives you a helpful summary showing the number of packets sent and received; the minimum, maximum, and average round-trip times; and a percentage indicating how many ping packets got no response. The following is a sample session that pings the machine at IP address 206.151.234.1:

```
F:\Shared\abi-0.7.8>ping 206.151.234.1

Pinging 206.151.234.1 with 32 bytes of data:

Reply from 206.151.234.1: bytes=32 time=125ms TTL=250
Reply from 206.151.234.1: bytes=32 time=110ms TTL=250
Reply from 206.151.234.1: bytes=32 time=110ms TTL=250
Reply from 206.151.234.1: bytes=32 time=110ms TTL=250

Ping statistics for 206.151.234.1:
Packets: Sent = 4, Received = 4, Lost = 0 (0% loss),
Approximate round trip times in milli-seconds:
Minimum = 110ms, Maximum =  125ms, Average =  113ms
```

What does this tell you? First of all, you can see that all of the packets you sent arrived, and there are approximately five hops in between this machine and your target. You know the latter because the time to live, or TTL, value is 250. By default, the TTL on the packets that *ping* sends out is set to 255, and each routing device that routes the packets subtracts one from the TTL value. When a packet's TTL hits zero, it is dropped.

More importantly, this ping session shows that data is flowing normally between your machine and the target. Since all of the ping packets got there (notice the "0% loss" line near the bottom), you can comfortably say that any network problems on this link aren't because of a routing problem. Packets are flowing normally between here and there.

How would you identify a problem using this data? The most obvious way to tell is when *ping* times out without getting *any* packets back from the remote end. That's a big red flag indicating that either you typed the IP address wrong or that something is blocking traffic between the two ends of the connection. Likewise, high rates of packet loss signal that something may be wrong somewhere along the path between the machines.

The *Tracert* Tool

When your plumbing is stopped up, you can tell because your sink, toilet, or shower won't drain—but knowing that it won't drain doesn't tell you where the blockage is. Likewise, the *ping* utility can tell you whether or not packets are flowing, but it won't necessarily tell you where the problem is. Windows 2000 includes a tool called *tracert* (pronounced "traceroute" after the original Unix version) that takes advantage of the TTL in each IP packet to map out the path that the packets are taking as they flow to a remote system. Recall that each device that routes a packet decrements its TTL. *Tracert* begins by sending one ICMP ping packet with a TTL of 1. That means that the first router or gateway to encounter it will send an ICMP response, decrement the ping packet's TTL, notice that the TTL is now zero, and drop the packet. At that point, *tracert* sends a second packet with a TTL of 2. The first device responds and decrements the TTL, then routes the packet to the next hop. The next device in the chain responds to the *ping* , decrements the TTL, and drops the original packet. This process continues with *tracert* gradually incrementing the TTL until the packet finally reaches the desired destination host.

As it sends these packets, *tracert* keeps a running log of which hosts along the route have responded and which ones haven't. You can use this information to figure out where the stoppage is. For example, take a look at this *tracert* session:

```
F:\>tracert www.microsoft.com

Tracing route to microsoft.com [207.46.131.137]
over a maximum of 30 hops:

1   <10 ms   <10 ms   <10 ms   ELGRANDE [192.168.0.1]
2    *        *        *       Request timed out.
3    *        *        *       Request timed out.
4    *        *        *       Request timed out.
5    *        *        *       Request timed out.
```

You can clearly see that the problem lies at the first hop away from your machine, a machine named ELGRANDE running the Routing and Remote Access Services (RRAS) package. You know this because the trace shows no response from any machine "downstream" of ELGRANDE. (Just for fun, while writing this section we did a second *traceroute* on a Unix box outside our network at the same time and found that connectivity to Microsoft's Web site was blocked by a problem with an intermediate router in California!) In this case, it's easy to fix the problem on your end by restarting the RRAS service on ELGRANDE, but you wouldn't know that you need to do that unless you do a *tracert*.

What's Your Name Again?

Another thing that the tracert session shows you is that DNS resolution is working properly—after all, you'd typed in the DNS name for Microsoft's server, and your resolver was able to turn that into an IP address. Most of the time, you'll use troubleshooting tools like *ping* and *tracert* with IP addresses, since you frequently need to verify that packets can be moved at the IP level before trying to use higher-level services like DNS. Name resolution is important to Windows 2000 because of the way it uses DNS service records to locate network resources (see Chapter 2, "Windows 2000 Network Naming Services," if you need a refresher). In addition, users will want to type UNC paths by using easy-to-remember names like "minuteman," not IP addresses.

Part of troubleshooting network problems involves understanding how and when network name resolution is used, as well as how to test whether or not it's working properly. After reading Chapter 2, you already understand how DNS resolution works, and you understand the importance of making sure the DNS server addresses are set properly. Naturally, that should be the first thing you check when you notice that a client's getting DNS-related error messages. It's usually a good idea to check whether or not other clients are having related problems, too, since losing your DNS servers won't necessarily manifest itself at once. Windows 2000 DNS resolvers can maintain a cache of addresses, so if the DNS server dies after the address is stored in the cache the client won't have a problem until the cached record reaches its TTL and expires.

The *nslookup* tool allows you to query a DNS server to see what information it holds for a host record. You can query for a single piece of information from the command line, as in this example:

```
F:\>nslookup mail.robichaux.net
Server:  hawk.robichaux.net
Address:  192.168.0.144
Name:   mail.robichaux.net
Address:  209.68.1.225
```

Note that this session tells you what DNS server the query was made against, as well as what the answer is. If you run *nslookup* with no command-line arguments, it goes into interactive mode, in which you can make several queries in a row:

```
F:\>nslookup

Default Server:  hawk.robichaux.net

Address:  192.168.0.144

> www.naismith-engineering.com

Server:  hawk.robichaux.net

Address:  192.168.0.144

Non-authoritative answer:
Name:   www.hosting.swbell.net
Addresses:  216.100.99.6, 216.100.98.4, 216.100.98.6
Aliases:  www.naismith-engineering.com
```

```
> fly.hiwaay.net
Server:  hawk.robichaux.net
Address:  192.168.0.144

Non-authoritative answer:
Name:    fly.hiwaay.net
Address:  208.147.154.56

> www.apple.com
Server:  hawk.robichaux.net
Address:  192.168.0.144

Non-authoritative answer:
Name:    www.apple.com
Address:  17.254.0.91
```

You can use the *server ipAddress* command to switch resolution to the server at the specified IP address. That's very useful when your regular DNS server is down or can't seem to resolve a particular address. For example, look at this *nslookup* session, which begins when you switch to an (improperly configured) DNS server named "minuteman":

```
> server minuteman

Default Server:  minuteman.robichaux.net

Address:  192.168.0.201

> www.robichaux.net

Server:  minuteman.robichaux.net

Address:  192.168.0.201

DNS request timed out.

timeout was 2 seconds.

DNS request timed out.
```

```
timeout was 2 seconds.
*** Request to minuteman.robichaux.net timed-out
```

So, "minuteman" can't find the answer. No problem; switch to an alternate server named "hawk":

```
> server hawk
```

```
DNS request timed out.
```

```
timeout was 2 seconds.
*** Can't find address for server hawk: Timed out
```

Oops. Since "minuteman" is misconfigured, it can't find "hawk's" address. Try again with the IP address:

```
> server 192.168.0.144
```

```
DNS request timed out.
```

```
timeout was 2 seconds.
```

```
Default Server:  [192.168.0.144]
Address:  192.168.0.144
```

```
> www.robichaux.net
Server:  [192.168.0.144]
Address:  192.168.0.144
```

```
Name:    www.robichaux.net
Address:  209.68.1.225
```

Summary

In this chapter, you learned:

- How to install network protocols, including NetBEUI and TCP/IP
- How to configure network bindings
- How to troubleshoot network problems

Key Terms

Before you take the exam, be sure you're familiar with the following terms:

Default gateway

DHCP server

Frame types

Internet Control Message Protocol (ICMP)

NWLink

Ping

Ipconfig

Multihoming

Network binding

Nslookup

Tracert

Review Questions

1. The tool used to query a DNS server for address information is called which of the following?

    A. *Nslookup*

    B. *Ipconfig*

    C. *Tracert*

    D. *Ping*

    E. *Dcpromo*

2. To install and configure the TCP/IP protocol, you must _____.

    A. Have already installed NetBEUI

    B. Use DHCP

    C. Have a valid IP address and subnet mask

    D. A or B

    E. B or C

3. To add a new network protocol on a Windows 2000 computer, which of the following steps is *not* required?

    A. Opening the Properties dialog box for a network adapter

    B. Selecting the desired protocol and providing an installation disk if prompted

    C. Clicking the Install button in the adapter's Properties dialog box

    D. Editing the protocol's registry key under HKEY_LOCAL_MACHINE\SYSTEM\SERVICES

4. The *ipconfig/all* command shows you which of the following?

    A. The destination address of a remote host

    B. The MAC address of the nearest router

    C. Which domain the current console user is logged in to

    D. Local IP addresses and subnet masks

5. To change network bindings, you must _____.

   A. Use the Advanced Settings command in the Network and Dial-Up Connections window.

   B. Manually edit the Registry.

   C. Boot into the Windows 2000 recovery console.

   D. Remove and reinstall the affected protocols.

6. When manually configuring TCP/IP settings, which of the following is *not* required?

   A. A valid default gateway address

   B. A valid subnet mask

   C. A valid IP address

   D. A and B

   E. B and C

7. If you install NWLink but can't see any NetWare resources, one potential cause is which of the following?

   A. NetBEUI is conflicting with NWLink.

   B. NWLink is using an incorrect frame type.

   C. TCP/IP is encapsulating NWLink packets.

   D. Your NIC doesn't support NWLink packets.

8. Which of the following statements is *not* true?

   A. You can add multiple IP addresses to a single network adapter.

   B. If you have multiple adapters in a single computer, they must all use DHCP.

   C. NWLink and NetBEUI can both coexist with TCP/IP.

   D. NetBEUI is not installed by default.

9. One of your users reports that they can't reach a file server on the network. You find that the physical network and power cabling is OK. If you want to verify that basic network connectivity exists between the two machines, you'd probably use _____.

    A. The *nslookup* tool

    B. The *ipconfig* tool

    C. The *ping* tool

    D. The *nbtstat* tool

10. Changing the network bindings for one adapter _____.

    A. Changes the order in which protocols are used on that adapter only

    B. Changes which protocols may be used with that adapter only

    C. Changes which protocols may be used on all adapters

    D. Changes the order in which protocols are used on all adapters

    E. A and B

    F. C and D

11. To set up a Windows 2000 client that uses DHCP, you must do which of the following?

    A. Add the /mode:dhcpon switch to the boot.ini file.

    B. Select the Obtain An IP Address Automatically radio button in the TCP/IP Properties dialog box.

    C. Select the Use DHCP radio button in the TCP/IP Properties dialog box.

    D. Do nothing; DHCP support is automatic.

12. You need to add a second IP address to one of your NICs. Which of the following is *true* about IP address assignment?

A. You can't assign more than one IP address to an adapter.

B. You must use the Advanced button in the TCP/IP Properties dialog box.

C. You can assign multiple addresses to an adapter that's using DHCP.

D. You can only add a second IP address if you have a 100-Mbps NIC.

13. When you configure a TCP/IP client using the TCP/IP Properties dialog box, you can specify how many DNS servers for it to use when resolving name queries?

A. One

B. Two

C. Three

D. Four

14. You can determine whether or not a DNS server is responding to queries and whether or not it has a correct record for a host by using which of the following tools?

A. *Ping*

B. *Ipconfig*

C. *Nslookup*

D. *Tracert*

15. If you don't define a default gateway for a machine, the machine will be _____.

A. Unable to boot

B. Unable to send traffic anywhere except on its local subnet unless you add routes manually

C. Unable to use DHCP

D. Able to send and receive traffic to the Internet via the LAN

16. You configure which WINS servers the client uses by _____.

    A. Using the WINS tab of the Advanced TCP/IP Properties dialog box

    B. Using the registry

    C. Using DHCP

    D. Using the *ipconfig* command

17. When you're troubleshooting a network failure, the first common step is to check which of the following?

    A. The service pack level

    B. TCP/IP configuration

    C. DNS configuration

    D. Physical connectivity

18. The primary difference between *ping* and *tracert* is which of the following?

    A. *Tracert* can only be run by administrators.

    B. *Tracert* is only included with Windows 2000 Server.

    C. *Ping* does a single ping; *tracert* does a succession of pings to discover the network topology.

    D. *Tracert* does a single ping; *ping* does a succession of pings to discover the network topology.

19. Why might you want to reorder bindings on a NIC?

    A. To put most-used bindings last

    B. To remove unneeded bindings

    C. To put most-used bindings first

    D. To add new bindings by making room for old ones

20. Bindings are automatically created _____.

   A. When you install a protocol

   B. When you add or remove a protocol

   C. A and B

   D. None of the above

Answers to Review Questions

1. A. *Nslookup* is the DNS query tool provided with Windows 2000.

2. E. TCP/IP and NetBEUI are independent of each other.

3. D. You don't have to edit the registry manually to manage protocols.

4. D. *Ipconfig/all* shows the local IP addresses and subnet masks.

5. A. The Advanced Settings command is the only supported way to change network bindings in Windows 2000.

6. A. You only need to specify a default gateway if you want the computer to be able to send packets to a gateway for routing.

7. B. If NWLink guesses the wrong frame type, it won't be able to match the frame type in use on the network.

8. B. Any adapter can use either DHCP or manual addressing without reference to what the other adapters are using.

9. C. *Ping* tests for basic TCP/IP connectivity, *ipconfig* reports configuration information, *nbtstat* is for NBT, and *nslookup* is for DNS.

10. E. Modifying the bindings on one adapter has no effect on the others.

11. B. DHCP is turned on by default when you install W2000 Professional, but to manually enable it you need to use the Properties dialog box.

12. B. You use the Advanced button in the TCP/IP Properties dialog box to assign an IP address.

13. B. If you want to add more than two DNS servers, you must use the Advanced button in the TCP/IP Properties dialog box.

14. C. *Nslookup* determines whether or not a DNS server is responding to queries.

15. B. The default gateway specifies where packets that don't match any static routes are sent.

16. A. If you're using WINS on your network, you use the WINS tab to specify which servers to use.

17. D. A quick check of physical connectivity can keep you from wasting time looking for other nonexistent problems. The majority of networking problems occurs at the physical layer.

18. C. *Tracert* does successive pings, collating the responses it gets to develop a map of the topology.

19. C. Windows 2000 uses bindings in order of their appearance, so putting the most-used bindings first can boost performance.

20. C. Bindings are automatically created when you install, add, or remove a protocol.

Managing the Dynamic Host Configuration Protocol

MICROSOFT EXAM OBJECTIVES COVERED IN THIS CHAPTER:

✓ **Install, configure, and troubleshoot DHCP.**

- Install the DHCP Server service.
- Create and manage DHCP scopes, superscopes, and multicast scopes.
- Configure DHCP for DNS integration.
- Authorize a DHCP server in Active Directory.

✓ **Manage and monitor DHCP.**

n Chapter 2, "Windows 2000 Network Naming Services," you learned what the Dynamic Host Configuration Protocol (DHCP) is and what you use it for. Planning for and using DHCP in Windows 2000 is pretty straightforward, but there's a lot of semi-hidden lore you need to know to make sure your installation proceeds without trouble. In this chapter, you'll learn how to install and manage DHCP, including how to set up plain DHCP scopes, superscopes, and multicast scopes (these latter two are new in the Windows 2000 DHCP server). You'll also learn how to set up integration between Dynamic DNS and DHCP, as well as how to authorize a DHCP server to integrate with Active Directory.

DHCP Terminology, Yet Again

You already know what a DHCP lease is from Chapter 2. To properly learn how to configure your servers to hand out those leases, though, you need to have a bigger vocabulary. You can start with the concept of a *scope*, which is nothing more than a contiguous range of addresses. There's usually one scope per physical subnet, and a scope can cover a class A, class B, or class C network address. DHCP uses scopes as the basis for managing and assigning IP addressing information.

A *superscope* is an administrative convenience. It allows you to group two or more scopes together even though they're actually separate. In reality, a superscope is just a list of its child scopes. Microsoft's DHCP snap-in allows you to manage IP address assignment in the superscope, though you must still configure other scope options individually for each child scope.

Each scope has a set of parameters you can set. These parameters, or scope options, control what data are delivered to DHCP clients to complete the DHCP negotiation process with that particular server. For example, the DNS server name, default gateway, and default network time server are all separate options that can be assigned. More properly, these settings are called option types; you can use any of the types provided with Windows 2000, or you can roll your own. (Please note that there's another options buzzword, options class, that won't be discussed further here.)

What about IP addresses? Aren't they the *raison d'être* of DHCP? You bet. The scope defines what addresses could potentially be assigned, but you can influence the assignment process in two additional ways by specifying the following:

- Any IP addresses within the range that you *never* want automatically assigned. These addresses are called excluded addresses or just *exclusions*, and they're off-limits to DHCP. You'll typically use exclusions to tag any addresses that you never want the DHCP server to assign at all.

- Any IP addresses within the range for which you want a permanent DHCP lease. These addresses are known as *reservations*, since they essentially reserve a particular IP address for a particular device.

How do you know whether to use a reservation or an exclusion? The key is what you want to do with the addresses. Obviously you don't want them assigned to "ordinary" clients, but why not? If you have a range of addresses reserved for devices like routers, gateways, or printers, you'll normally exclude their addresses so that they don't participate in DHCP at all. Contrariwise, if you're using devices like laptops, and you want them to get DHCP settings without getting a new address each time they restart, you can use reservations.

The range of IP addresses that the DHCP server can actually assign is called its *address pool*. For example, say you set up a new DHCP scope covering the 192.168.0 subnet; that gives you 255 IP addresses in the pool. After adding an exclusion from 192.168.0.240 to 192.168.0.254, you're left with $255 - 14 = 241$ IP addresses in the pool. That means (in theory, at least) that you can service 241 unique clients at one time before you run out of IP addresses.

Installing DHCP

Installing DHCP is easy, since it uses the new Windows 2000 installation mechanism. Unlike some of the other services you'll see in this book, the actual installation installs just the service and its associated snap-in, starting it when it's done. At that point, it's not delivering any DHCP service, but you don't have to reboot or answer a bunch of intrusive wizard questions. Exercise 5.1 explains how to do the "installation."

Microsoft
✓ *Exam*
Objective

Install, configure, and troubleshoot DHCP.

- Install the DHCP Server service.

EXERCISE 5.1

Installing the DHCP Service

Follow these steps to install the DHCP server. Note that this exercise will only work on computers running Windows 2000 Server or Advanced Server.

1. Open the Windows Components wizard by opening the Add/Remove Programs in control panel (Start ➤ Settings ➤ Control Panels ➤ Add/Remove Programs).

2. Click the Add/Remove Windows Components icon. The Installation wizard will open and list all the components that it knows how to install or remove.

3. Select the Networking Services item from the component list, then click the Details... button.

4. When the Subcomponents of Network Services list appears, make sure that Dynamic Host Configuration Protocol (DHCP) is selected, then click the OK button.

5. If prompted, enter the path to the Windows 2000 distribution files.

When you install the DHCP server, you get the DHCP snap-in installed, too; you can open it by using the Start ➢ Programs ➢ Administrative Tools ➢ DHCP command. The snap-in is shown in Figure 5.1; as you can see, it follows the standard MMC model. The left-hand pane shows you which servers are available; you can connect to servers other than the one you're already talking to. Each server contains subordinate items grouped into folders. Each scope has a folder, which is named after the scope's IP address range. There's also a separate folder, Server Options, which holds options that are specific to a particular DHCP server. Within each scope, there are four subordinate views that show you interesting things about the scope such as the following:

- The Address Pool view shows you what the address pool looks like.

- The Address Lease view shows one entry for each current lease. Each lease shows the computer name to which the lease was issued, the corresponding IP address, and the current lease expiration time.

- The Reservations view shows you which IP addresses are reserved and which devices hold them.

- The Scope Options view lists the set of options you've defined for this scope. For example, Figure 5.1 shows three options: the default gateway (003 Router), the default DNS server (006 DNS Server), and the default DNS domain name (015 DNS Domain Name).

FIGURE 5.1   The DHCP snap-in

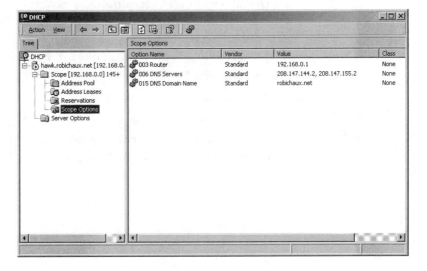

Authorizing DHCP for Active Directory

Once you've installed a server, your next step is to authorize the DHCP server in Active Directory. *Authorization*, which actually creates an Active Directory object representing the new server, helps keep unauthorized servers off your network. These renegade servers can cause two separate kinds of problems: They may hand out bogus leases, or they may fraudulently deny renewal requests from legitimate clients. How can you prevent this? You might start with threatening your end users with banishment back to Windows for Workgroups, then review how Active Directory can help.

Microsoft
✓ **Exam**
Objective

Install, configure, and troubleshoot DHCP.

- Authorize a DHCP server in Active Directory.

When you install a DHCP server using Windows 2000 and if Active Directory is present on your network, the server won't be allowed to provide DHCP services to clients until it's been authorized. If you install DHCP on a member server in an Active Directory domain or on a stand-alone server, you'll have to manually authorize the server. When you authorize a server, you're really adding its IP address to the Active Directory object that contains a list of the IP addresses of all authorized DHCP servers. At start time, each DHCP server queries the directory, looking for its IP address on the "authorized" list. If it can't find the list, or if it can't find its IP address on the list, the DHCP service fails to start. Instead, it logs an event log message indicating that it couldn't service client requests because it wasn't authorized. Exercise 5.2 shows you how this process works.

This mechanism only works with Windows 2000 DHCP servers; there's no way to monitor or restrict the presence of DHCP servers running under other operating systems, including Windows NT.

EXERCISE 5.2

Authorizing a DHCP Server

Follow these steps to authorize a DHCP server in Active Directory.

1. Open the DHCP snap-in (Start ➤ Programs ➤ Administrative Tools ➤ DHCP).

2. Right-click the server you want to authorize and choose the Authorize command.

3. Wait a short time (30–45 seconds) to allow the authorization to take place.

4. Right-click the server again. Verify that the Unauthorize command appears in the context menu; this indicates that the server is now authorized.

You can unauthorize a previously authorized server by right-clicking it and using the Unauthorize command.

Creating and Managing DHCP Scopes

In Chapter 2, we tantalized you by claiming that you can use any number of DHCP servers on a single physical network. This is possible if you divide the range of addresses you want assigned into multiple scopes. Each scope contains a number of useful pieces of data, but before you can find out what they are you need to have another DHCP vocabulary lesson.

Microsoft ✓ *Exam Objective*

Install, configure, and troubleshoot DHCP.

- Create and manage DHCP scopes, superscopes, and multicast scopes.

Creating a New Plain-Vanilla Scope

Like many other things in Windows 2000, the process of creating a new scope is driven by a wizard. In this case, the New Scope wizard does the dirty deed. The overall process is simple, as long as you know beforehand what the wizard is going to ask. If you think about what defines a scope, you'll be well prepared. You need to know the following:

- The IP address range for the scope you want to create

- Which IP addresses, if any, you want to exclude from the address pool

- Which IP addresses, if any, you want to reserve

- Values for the DHCP options you want to set, if any

This last item isn't strictly necessary for creating a scope, since the wizard doesn't ask for any options. However, to leave scopelessness behind and create a useful scope, you'll need to have *some* options to specify for the clients.

To create a scope, select a superscope or DHCP server in the DHCP snap-in, then use the Action ➤ New Scope command. That starts the New Scope wizard, whose operation will now be discussed in detail, with each wizard page in its own section.

The Boring Stuff

The first two wizard pages are pretty useless; the first page just tells you that you've launched the New Scope wizard, and the second allows you to enter a name and description for your scope. These tidbits will be displayed by the DHCP snap-in, so it's a good idea to pick a sensible name for your scopes so that other administrators will be able to figure out what the scope is *for*.

Defining the IP Address Range

The next wizard page, the IP Address Range page (Figure 5.2), is where you enter the start and end IP addresses for your range. The wizard does minimal checking on the addresses you enter, but it does automatically calculate the appropriate subnet mask for the address range you enter. You can modify the subnet mask if you know what you're doing.

FIGURE 5.2   The IP Address Range page of the New Scope wizard

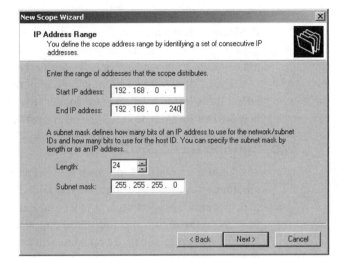

Adding Exclusions

The Add Exclusions page (Figure 5.3) allows you to create exclusion ranges as part of the scope creation process. To exclude one address, put it in the Start IP Address field; to exclude a range, fill in a starting and ending address. Remember that you can always add exclusions later, but it's best to include them when you create the scope so that no excluded addresses are ever passed out to clients.

FIGURE 5.3   The Add Exclusions page of the New Scope wizard

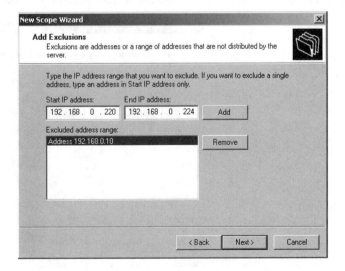

Setting a Lease Duration

The Lease Duration page (not shown) allows you to set the lease duration. By default, new leases start with a duration of eight days and zero hours. This isn't a bad default, but you may find that a shorter or longer duration makes sense for your network. If your network is highly dynamic, with lots of arrivals, departures, and moving computers, set the lease duration to be short; if it's less active, set it for longer. Remember that renewal attempts begin when half of the lease period is over, so don't set them *too* short.

Configuring Basic DHCP Options

The Configure DHCP Options page (not shown) allows you to choose whether you want to configure basic DHCP options (including the default gateway and DNS settings). If you choose to configure these options, you'll have to go through some additional pages, all of which are pretty simple. If you choose not to configure options, you can go back and do so later; if you choose to take that route, make sure you don't activate the scope until you've configured the options you want assigned.

Configuring a Router

The first Option Configuration page is the Router (Default Gateway) page (Figure 5.4), which allows you to enter the IP addresses of one or more routers that you want to use as gateways for outbound traffic. Type in the IP addresses of the routers you want to use, then use the Up and Down buttons to put the list in the order you want clients to use when attempting to send outgoing packets.

FIGURE 5.4 The Router (Default Gateway) page of the New Scope wizard

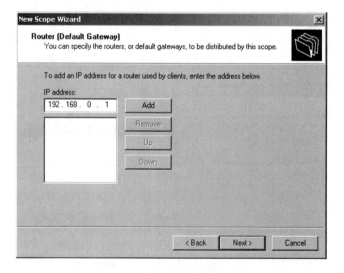

Providing DNS Settings

The Domain Name and DNS Servers page (Figure 5.5) lets you specify the set of DNS servers and the parent domain you want passed down to DHCP clients. Normally, you'll need to specify at least one DNS server by filling in its DNS name or IP address; you can also specify the domain you want Windows 2000 to use as its base domain for all connections that don't have their own connection-specific suffixes defined.

FIGURE 5.5   The Domain Name and DNS Servers page of the New Scope wizard

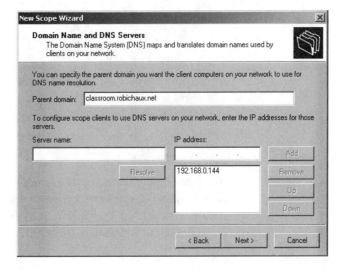

Providing WINS Settings

If you're still using WINS on your network, you can configure DHCP so that it passes WINS server addresses to your Windows clients (though if you want the Windows clients to honor it, you'll also need to define the WINS/NBT Node Type option for the scope). Like the DNS server page, on this page (Figure 5.6) you can enter the addresses of several servers, moving them into the order in which you want clients to try them. You may enter the DNS or NetBIOS name of each server, or you can enter an IP address.

FIGURE 5.6   The WINS Servers page of the New Scope wizard

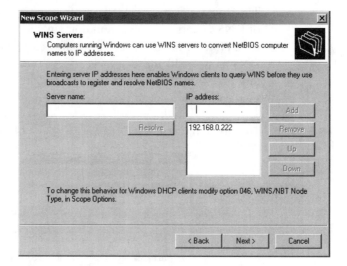

Activating the Scope

The final page allows you the option to activate the scope immediately after creating it. By default, the wizard will assume you want the scope activated unless you select the "No, I will active [sic] this scope later" radio button, in which case the scope will remain dormant until you manually activate it.

WARNING   Be sure to verify that there are no other DHCP servers assigned to the address range you choose!

EXERCISE 5.3

Creating a New Scope

Follow these steps to create a new scope for the 192.168.0 private class C network.

1. Open the DHCP snap-in (Start ➢ Programs ➢ Administrative Tools ➢ DHCP).

2. Right-click the server on which you want to create the new scope, and choose the New Scope command. The New Scope wizard will appear.

3. Click the OK button to dismiss the first (worthless) wizard page.

4. Enter a name and a description for your new scope, then click the Next button.

5. In the IP Address Range page, enter 192.168.0.1 as the start IP address for the scope and 192.168.0.254 as the end IP address. Leave the subnet mask controls alone (though when creating a scope on a production network you might need to change them). Click the Next button.

6. In the Add Exclusions page, click Next without adding any excluded addresses.

7. In the Lease Duration page, set the lease duration to three days, then click the Next button.

8. In the Configure DHCP Options page, click the Next button to indicate that you want to configure default options for this scope.

9. Enter a router IP address (e.g. 192.168.0.1) in the IP address field, then click the Add button. Once the address is added, click the Next button.

10. In the Domain Name and DNS Servers page, enter the IP address of a DNS server on your network in the IP address field, then click the Add button. When you're done, click the Next button.

11. On the WINS Servers page, click the Next button to leave the WINS options unset and display the Activate Scope page.

12. If your network is currently using the 192.168.0.x range, select the "No, I will active [sic] this scope later" radio button. Click the Next button. When the Wizard Summary page appears, click the Finish button to create the scope.

Changing Your Mind Later

Each scope has a set of properties associated with it. Except for the set of options assigned by the scope (more about this in the next section), these properties are exposed in the General tab of the Scope Properties dialog box

(Figure 5.7). Some of these properties, like the scope name and description, are self-explanatory. Others require a little more exposition:

- The Start IP Address and End IP Address fields allow you to set the size of the scope. The subnet mask is automatically calculated for you based on the IP addresses you enter.

- The controls in the Lease Duration For DHCP Clients group control how long leases in this scope will be valid. Your two choices are set by the Limited To and Unlimited radio buttons. If you choose to set lease duration limits, you use the Days, Hours, and Minutes controls to govern how long the leases will remain in use.

FIGURE 5.7 The General tab of the Scope Properties dialog box

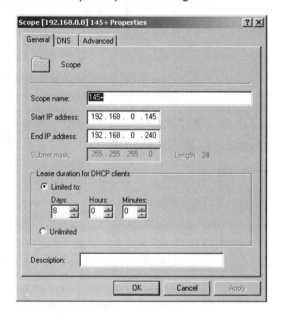

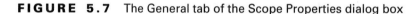

 Don't confuse the process of setting properties of the scope with setting the options associated with the scope—they're two entirely different operations.

When you make changes to these properties, bear in mind that they have no effect on existing leases. For example, say you create a scope from 172.30.1.1 to 172.30.1.199. You use that scope for a while, then edit its properties to reduce the range from 172.30.1.1 to 172.30.1.150. If a client

has, say, 172.30.1.180—an address legal under the scope before you changed it—the client will retain that address but will not be able to renew the address.

Managing Reservations and Exclusions

After defining the address pool, the next step is to create whatever reservations and exclusions you want used to reduce the size of the pool.

Adding and Removing Exclusions

When you want to exclude an entire range of IP addresses, you need to add that range as an exclusion. Normally, you'll want to do this before you enable a scope, since that prevents you from accidentally issuing any of the excluded IP addresses. In fact, you can't create an exclusion that includes a leased address—you have to get rid of the lease first.

Here's how to add an exclusion range:

1. Open the DHCP snap-in and find the scope to which you want to add an exclusion.

2. Expand the scope so you can see its Address Pool item.

3. Right-click Address Pool, then use the New Exclusion Range command. (You can use the Actions ➤ New Exclusion Range command instead.)

4. When the Add Exclusion dialog box appears (see Figure 5.8), use it to enter the IP addresses you want to exclude. To exclude a single address, type it into the Start IP address field; to exclude a range, put the ending address of the range into the End IP address field.

5. Click the Add button to add the exclusion.

FIGURE 5.8   The Add Exclusion dialog box

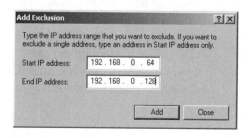

When you add exclusions, they appear in the Address Pool node under the scope where you add them. To remove an exclusion, just right-click it and use the Delete command. After confirming your command, the snap-in removes the excluded range and it becomes immediately available for issuance.

Adding and Removing Reservations

Adding reservations is simple, as long as you have the MAC address of the device for which you want to create a reservation. Since reservations belong to a single scope, you create and remove them within the Reservations node beneath each scope. You add reservations by right-clicking the scope and using the New Reservation command; that displays the New Reservation dialog shown in Figure 5.9.

FIGURE 5.9 The New Reservation dialog box

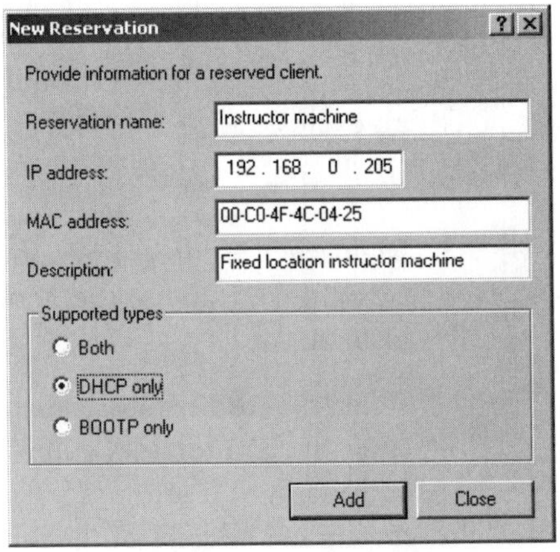

At a minimum, when you create a new reservation you must enter the IP address and MAC address for the reservation. If you like, you can also enter a name and description for the reservation. You can also choose whether the reservation will be made by DHCP only, BOOTP only (useful for remote-access devices that use BOOTP), or both.

To remove a reservation, right-click it and use the Delete command. This removes the reservation but does nothing to the client device (after all, it doesn't have a lease to revoke!).

There's no way to change a reservation once it's been created—you'll have to delete it and re-create it to change any of the associated settings.

Setting Options for Your Shiny New Scope

Once you've installed a server, authorized it in Active Directory, and fixed up the addresses pool, the next step is to set the options you want sent out to clients. You *must* configure the options you want sent out before you activate a scope; if you don't, clients may register in the scope without getting any options, rendering them useless.

Understanding Option Assignment

There are actually five different (and slightly overlapping) ways to control which DHCP options are doled out to clients.

Predefined Options

You predefine options so that they'll be available in the Server, Scope, or Client Options dialog boxes. Think of predefining options like the process of printing a restaurant menu—you have to pick the dishes you want to appear before diners can select from them.

Server Options

Server options are assigned to all scopes and clients of a particular server. That means if there's some setting you want *all* clients of a DHCP server to have, no matter what scope they're in, this is where you'd assign them. However, note that more specific options (like those that are set at the class, scope, or client level) will override server-level options. That gives you an escape valve; it's a better idea, though, to be careful about which options you assign if your server manages multiple scopes.

Scope Options

If you want a particular option value assigned only to those clients in a certain subnet, select that scope as the base for the option. For example, it's common to specify different routers for different physical subnets; if you have two scopes corresponding to different subnets, each scope would probably have a separate value for the router option.

Class Options

The idea behind class options is that you should be able to assign different options to clients in different classes. For example, Windows 2000 machines recognize a number of DHCP options that Windows 98 and Mac OS machines ignore. By defining a new Windows 2000 class, you could assign those options only to machines that report themselves as being in that class. The problem is that you need to have clients that are smart enough to do so, and most of them aren't.

Client Options

If you want to force certain options onto a specific client, you can do so—provided the client is using a DHCP reservation. You actually attach client options to a particular reservation; they'll override any scope, server, or class option. In fact, the only way to override a client option is to manually configure the client. The DHCP server manages client options.

Assigning Options

You can use the DHCP snap-in to assign options at the scope, server, reserved address, or class level (although we're now going to start pretending that the class options don't exist). The mechanism you use to assign these options is identical; the only difference is where you set the options. When you create an option assignment, remember that it applies to all the clients in the server or the scope *from that point forward*. Option assignments aren't retroactive, and they don't migrate from one scope to another.

To actually *create* a new option and have it assigned, select the scope or server where you want the option assigned, then select the corresponding Options node and use the Action ➤ Configure Options command. (To set options for a reserved client, right-click its entry in the Reservations node and use the Configure Options... command from there.) You'll then see the Configure Options dialog box (Figure 5.10), which lists all of the options you might potentially want to configure. To select an individual option, check the box next to it, then use the controls in the Data Entry control group to enter the value you want associated with the option. Continue to add options until you've specified all the ones you want attached to the server or scope, then click the OK button.

FIGURE 5.10   The Configure Options dialog box

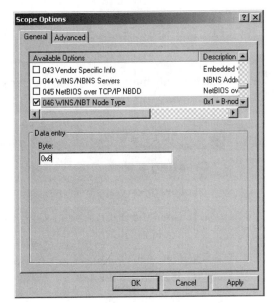

Activating and Deactivating Scopes

When you've completed the preceding steps and you're ready to unleash your new scope so that it can be used to make client assignments, the final required step is activating the scope. Activating a scope just tells the server that it's OK to start handing out addresses from that scope's address pool. As soon as you activate a scope, addresses from its pool may be assigned to clients. Of course, this is a necessary precondition to getting any use out of your scope.

If you later want to stop using a scope, you can, but beware: It's a permanent change. You turn off a scope by deactivating it, but when you do, DHCP tells all clients registered with the scope that they need to release their leases and renew them someplace else–the equivalent of a landlord who evicts his tenants when the building is condemned! Don't deactivate a scope unless you want clients to stop using it immediately.

Creating a Superscope

A superscope allows the DHCP server to provide multiple logical subnet addresses to DHCP clients on a single physical network. You create superscopes with the New Superscope command. It shouldn't surprise you to learn that this triggers the New Superscope wizard. However, this particular wizard is so simple that it didn't really need to be a wizard.

Creating a Superscope

To create a superscope, follow the steps in Exercise 5.4—the process is so easy that we've wrapped it up in an exercise for you to follow.

You can only have one superscope per server.

EXERCISE 5.4

Creating a New Superscope

Follow these steps to create a superscope.

1. Open the DHCP snap-in (Start ➤Programs ➤ Administrative Tools ➤ DHCP).

2. Follow the instructions in Exercise 5.3 to create two scopes: one for 192.168.0.1-192.168.0.127 and one for 192.168.0.128-192.168.0.240.

3. Right-click your DHCP server and choose the New Superscope... command. The New Superscope wizard appears. Dismiss the first wizard page by clicking the Next button.

4. In the Superscope Name page, name your superscope, then click the Next button.

5. The Select Scopes page will appear, showing a list of all scopes on the current server. Select the two scopes you created in step 2, then click the Next button.

6. The Wizard Summary page appears; click the Finish button to create your scope.

7. Verify that your new superscope appears in the DHCP snap-in.

You may notice that you can delete a superscope by right-clicking it and choosing the Delete command. Since a superscope is just an administrative fantasy, you can safely delete one at any time—it doesn't affect the "real" scopes that make up the superscope.

Adding and Removing Children

Adding a scope to an existing superscope is trivial—find the scope you want to add, then right-click it and use the Action ➤ Add to Superscope command. This causes the snap-in to show you a dialog box listing all of the superscopes known to this server; pick the one you want the current scope appended to and click the OK button.

If you later want to remove a scope from a superscope, open the superscope and right-click the target scope. The Context menu provides a Remove from Superscope command that will do the deed.

Activating and Deactivating Superscopes

Just as with regular scopes, you can activate and deactivate superscopes. The same restrictions and guidelines apply: To wit, you must activate a superscope before it can be used, and you must not deactivate it until you want all your clients to lose their existing leases and be forced to request new ones.

Creating Multicast Scopes

IP multicasting is becoming increasingly common as the amount of network bandwidth available on the average network increases. It's much more efficient to *multicast* a video or audio stream to multiple destinations than it is to broadcast it to the same number of clients, and the increased demand for multicast-friendly network hardware has resulted in some headscratching about how to automate the multicast configuration.

I'm MADCAP As Hell and I'm Not Going to Take It Anymore

DHCP is normally used to assign IP configuration information for *unicast* (or one-to-one) network communications. It turns out that there's a separate type of address space assigned just for multicasting: 224.0.0.0 -239.255 .255.255. However, multicast clients also need to have an "ordinary" IP address; clients can participate in a multicast just by knowing (and using) the multicast address for the content they want to receive.

How do they know what address to use? Ordinary DHCP won't help, since it's designed to assign IP addresses and option information to one client at a time. Realizing this, the IETF defined a new protocol, the *Multicast Address Dynamic Client Allocation Protocol (MADCAP)*. MADCAP provides an analog to DHCP, but for multicast use. A MADCAP server issues leases for multicast addresses only. MADCAP clients can request a multicast lease when they want to participate in a multicast.

There are some important differences between DHCP and MADCAP. First, you have to realize that the two are totally separate. A single server can be a DHCP server, a MADCAP server, or *both*; there's no implied or actual relation between the two. Likewise, clients can use DHCP and/or MADCAP at the same time—the only requirement is that every MADCAP client has to get a unicast IP address from *somewhere*.

Next, remember that DHCP can assign options as part of the lease process, but MADCAP cannot. The only thing MADCAP does is dynamically assign multicast addresses.

The Windows 2000 Server online help has a comprehensive checklist that covers how to set up IP multicasting, just in case you're interested.

Building Multicast Scopes

When you want to create a new multicast scope, right-click the server where you want the scope created and choose the New Multicast Scope option. Most of the steps you go through when creating a multicast scope are identical to those required for an ordinary unicast scope, so you'll see the differences highlighted in Exercise 5.5.

EXERCISE 5.5

Creating a New Multicast Scope

Follow these steps to create a new multicast scope.

1. Open the DHCP snap-in (Start ➤ Programs ➤ Administrative Tools ➤ DHCP).

2. Right-click your DHCP server and choose the New Multicast Scope... command. The New Multicast Scope wizard appears. Dismiss the first wizard page by clicking the Next button.

3. In the Multicast Scope Name page, name your multicast scope (and add a description if you'd like), then click the Next button.

4. The IP Address Range page will appear. Enter a start IP address of 224.0.0.0 and an end IP address of 224.255.0.0. Adjust the TTL to 1 to make sure that no multicast packets escape your local network segment. Click the Next button when you're done.

5. The Add Exclusions page will appear; click its Next button.

6. The Lease Duration page will appear. Normally you leave multicast scope assignments in place somewhat longer than their unicast brethren, hence the default lease length of 30 days. Click the Next button.

7. The wizard asks you if you want to activate the scope now. Click the No radio button, then the Next button.

8. The Wizard Summary page appears; click the Finish button to create your scope.

9. Verify that your new multicast scope appears in the DHCP snap-in. Delete it at your convenience.

Setting Multicast Scope Properties

Once you create a multicast scope, you can adjust its properties by selecting it and using the standard (and by now, very familiar) properties command. The Multicast Scope Properties dialog box has two tabs. The General tab allows you to change the scope's name, its start or end address, its TTL value, its lease duration, and its description—in essence, all of the settings you provided when you created it in the first place. The Lifetime tab (see Figure 5.11) allows you to limit how long your multicast scope will hang around. By default, a newly created multicast scope will live forever, but if you're creating a scope to provide MADCAP assignments for a single event (or a set of events that cover a limited duration), you can specify an expiration time for the scope. When that time is reached, the scope disappears from the server, but not before making all its clients give up their multicast address leases. This is a nice way to make sure the lease cleans up after itself when you're done with it.

FIGURE 5.11 The Lifetime tab of the Multicast Scope Properties dialog box

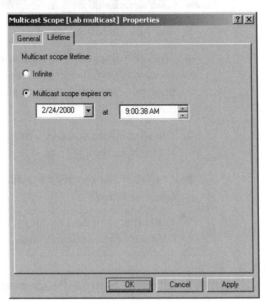

Integrating Dynamic DNS and DHCP

DHCP integration with Dynamic DNS is one of our favorite Windows 2000 features. It's simple in concept but powerful in action, since by setting up that integration you can pass out addresses to DHCP clients while still maintaining the integrity (and utility!) of your DNS services. There are actually two separate ways that the DNS server could potentially be updated. One way is for the DHCP client to tell the DNS server, "Hey, my address is now XYZ." This is easy to understand, but it's insecure since there's no way to trust the client to tell the truth. The default Windows 2000 method is better: The DHCP server tells the DNS server when it registers a new client. This relies on the likelihood that the DHCP server is more trustworthy than some random client.

Microsoft ✓ *Exam Objective*

Install, configure, and troubleshoot DHCP.

- Configure DHCP for DNS integration.

However, neither of these updates will take place unless you configure the DHCP server to use Dynamic DNS. There are actually two separate ways to make this change: If you change it at the scope level it will apply only to that scope, but if you change it at the server level it will apply to all scopes and superscopes served by the server. Whichever of these options you choose depends on how widely you want to support dynamic DNS; most of the sites we visit have enabled DNS updates at the server level, so that's what you'll learn about for the rest of the section.

Don't forget that you also have to instruct the DNS server to *accept* Dynamic DNS updates! For more on how to do so, see Chapter 6.

To actually update the settings at either the server or scope levels, you need to open the scope or server properties, which you do by right-clicking the appropriate object and choosing the Properties command. When you do, you'll see the General tab, which lets you adjust some general settings for the object you've just opened. Next to the General tab, though, is the DNS tab, which has the stuff you're interested in. Figure 5.12 shows the controls on the DNS tab.

FIGURE 5.12   The DNS tab of the Scope Properties dialog box

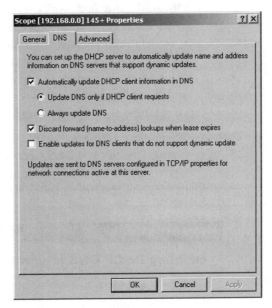

- The Automatically Update DHCP Client Information In DNS check box controls whether or not this DHCP server will attempt to register lease information with a DNS server. It must be checked to enable dynamic DNS.

    - The Update DNS Only If DHCP Client Requests radio button (which is on by default) tells the DHCP server to register the update only if the DHCP client asks for DNS registration. When this button is active, DHCP clients that aren't hip to DDNS won't have their DNS records updated. However, Windows 98 and Windows 2000 DHCP clients are smart enough to ask for the updates.

    - The Always Update DNS button forces the DHCP server to register *any* client to which it issues a lease. This setting may add DNS registrations for DHCP-enabled devices that don't really need them, like printer servers; however, it allows other clients (like Mac OS, Windows NT, and Linux machines) to have their DNS information automatically updated.

- The Discard Forward (Name-To-Address) Lookups When Lease Expires check box has a long name but a simple function. When a DHCP lease expires, what should happen to the DNS registration? Obviously, it would be nice if the DNS record associated with a lease vanished when the lease expired; when this check box is checked (as it is by default), that's exactly what happens. If you uncheck this box, your DNS will contain entries for expired leases that are no longer valid; when a particular IP address is reissued on a new lease, the DNS will be updated, but in between leases you'll have incorrect data in your DNS– always something to avoid.

- What about DNS servers that don't support Dynamic DNS? The Enable Updates For DNS Clients That Do Not Support Dynamic Update check box lets you handle these older clients graciously by making the updates using a separate mechanism.

EXERCISE 5.6

Enabling DHCP-DNS Integration

Follow these steps to enable a scope to participate in Dynamic DNS updates.

1. Open the DHCP snap-in (Start ➤ Programs ➤ Administrative Tools ➤ DHCP).

EXERCISE 5.6 *(continued)*

2. Right-click the DHCP server you configured in Exercise 5.1, and select the Properties command.

3. The Server Properties dialog box will appear. Click on the DNS tab.

4. Check the Automatically Update DHCP Client Information In DNS check box.

5. Check the Discard Forward (Name-To-Address) Lookups When Lease Expires check box.

6. Click the OK button to apply your changes and dismiss the Properties dialog box.

Monitoring & Troubleshooting DHCP

Unlike my dog, who gets grumpy if he's not fed by 6:00 A.M. or so, DHCP doesn't require a lot of ongoing care or feeding. However, it's useful to know how to monitor and troubleshoot it for those rare occasions when something does go wrong (apart from the fact that monitoring and troubleshooting are covered on the exam!).

Monitoring DHCP Leases

You monitor which DHCP leases have been assigned using the Address Lease view associated with a particular scope. When you open the scope and choose this view, you'll see an easy-to-read list of all the leases currently in force for that scope. This view will show you the client IP address, the client DNS name, the lease's duration, and the client's unique DHCP ID (if there is one).

Microsoft
✓ *Exam*
Objective

Manage and monitor DHCP.

Removing Client Leases

If you want to remove a client lease, you can do so by right-clicking it and using the Delete command. This actually removes the lease, but not before canceling it. Normally, it's better to let leases expire rather than manually canceling them, but sometimes circumstances dictate otherwise.

EXERCISE 5.7

Inspecting Leases

Follow these steps to create a tab-delimited text file containing information about all leases in a scope. You can use this file for analysis or recordkeeping.

1. Open the DHCP snap-in (Start ➤ Programs ➤ Administrative Tools ➤ DHCP).

2. Expand the target server's node in the MMC until you see the Address Leases node.

3. Right-click the Address Leases node and choose the Export List command.

4. When the Save As dialog box appears, select a location for the list file. Type a meaningful name in the Filename field and click the Save button.

5. Open the file you just created with Wordpad, Word, Excel, or any other tool that honors tab settings. Notice that the contents of the file mirror exactly what you saw in the DHCP snap-in.

Working with the DHCP Database Files

The following is true of DHCP database files:

- DHCP uses a set of database files to maintain its knowledge of scopes, superscopes, and client leases. These files, which live in `%systemroot%\system32\DHCP`, are always open when the DHCP service is running, and you shouldn't modify or alter them when the service is stopped. The primary database file is `dhcp.mdb`–it has all the goodies in it.

- `Dhcp.tmp` is a backup copy of the database file created during reindexing of the database. You normally won't see this file, but if the service fails during reindexing it may not remove the file when it should.

- J50.log (plus a number of files named J50*xxxxx*.log) is a log file that stores changes before they're written to the database. The DHCP database engine can recover some changes from these files when it restarts.
- J50.chk is a checkpoint file that tells the DHCP engine which log files it still needs to recover.

Removing the Database Files

If you're convinced that your database is corrupt because the lease information you see doesn't match what's on the network, the easiest repair mechanism is to remove the database files and start over with a clean slate. (On the other hand, if you're convinced that it's corrupt because the DHCP service fails at startup, you should check the event log.) To start over, stop the DHCP service and remove all of the files from %systemroot%\system32\ DHCP, then restart the service. Once you've done so, you can reconcile the scope (as described in the next section) to rebuild the database contents.

Changing the Database Backup Interval

By default, the DHCP service backs up its databases every 15 minutes. You can adjust this setting by editing the Backup Interval value under HKEY_ LOCAL_MACHINE\SYSTEM\CurrentControlet\Services\DHCPServer\ Parameters. This allows you to make backups either more frequently (if your database changes a lot, or if you seem to have ongoing corruption problems) or less often (if everything seems to be on an even keel).

Reconciling DHCP Scopes

As time passes, you may experience what we call DHCP drift, or when the contents of your DHCP database no longer reflect accurately what's on your network. Although Microsoft doesn't make any prominent mention of this fact in the DHCP documentation, the DHCP server actually records lease information in two places: the DHCP database *and* the server's Registry. When you reconcile a scope, the DHCP server will cross-check the database contents with the contents of the Registry, reporting (and fixing) any inconsistencies it finds. You can also reconcile scopes to recover from a corrupt DHCP database. You first remove the database files, then reconcile the server's scopes, and off you go.

Exercise 5.8 details the steps necessary to reconcile a single scope.

EXERCISE 5.8

Reconciling a Scope

Follow these steps to reconcile a single scope on your server.

1. Open the DHCP snap-in (Start ➤ Programs ➤ Administrative Tools ➤ DHCP).

2. Expand the target server's node in the MMC until you see the target scope.

3. Right-click the target scope and choose the Reconcile command.

4. The Reconcile dialog box appears, but it's empty. To start the reconciliation, click the Verify button.

5. If the database is consistent, you'll see a dialog box telling you so. If there are any inconsistencies, the dialog box will list them and allow you to repair them.

You can use a similar procedure to reconcile all scopes on a server. You just right-click the DHCP server and use the Reconcile All Scopes command instead of reconciling the individual scope. To recover a broken DHCP server the preferred way, you first remove the database files, then reconcile all scopes on the server to rebuild the database.

Summary

In this chapter, you learned:

- How to install and configure the DHCP service

- How to authorize DHCP servers in Active Directory

- How to manage and control client leases and options

Key Terms

Before you take the exam, be sure you're familiar with the following terms:

Address pool

DHCP authorization

DHCP integration

Exclusion

Multicast Address Dynamic Client Allocation Protocol (MADCAP)

Multicast scope

Reservation

Scope

Superscope

Unicast scope

Review Questions

1. When you install DHCP into an Active Directory domain, you will need to do which of the following?

   A. Authorize the server in Active Directory

   B. Delegate DHCP authority to the DHCP Admins global group

   C. Release all existing leases

   D. Give the server at least one superscope

2. What is a superscope?

   A. It is an administrative container that holds more than one scope.

   B. It is a way to assign multiple logical subnet addresses to DHCP clients on a single physical network.

   C. It's the same as a multicast scope.

   D. It's a scope that contains at least two sets of options.

3. What's the correct sequence of operations for creating a new scope?

   A. Create scope, assign options, activate scope

   B. Create scope, assign options, assign to superscope, activate superscope

   C. Create scope, authorize scope, activate scope

   D. Assign options, create scope, activate scope

4. To enable DHCP-DNS integration, you must do which of the following? (Choose all that apply.)

   A. Use Windows 2000 Professional clients

   B. Enable DNS updates on the DHCP server

   C. Enable dynamic updates on the DNS server

   D. Stop and restart the DHCP server

5. Which of the following is *not* true of a multicast scope?

    A. It may have a limited lifetime.

    B. It may assign leases of fixed or unlimited duration.

    C. It assigns options along with client leases.

    D. It cannot be part of a superscope.

6. What is the primary difference between an exclusion and a reservation?

    A. No difference; they're actually the same.

    B. Excluded addresses aren't bound to any particular MAC address; reserved addresses are managed by the DHCP server.

    C. Reserved addresses get DHCP options, but excluded addresses don't.

    D. Excluded addresses get DHCP options, but reserved addresses don't.

7. When you deactivate a scope, what happens to any current leases in the scope?

    A. Nothing; clients continue to use the leased addresses.

    B. Clients get an immediate lease revocation.

    C. Clients are automatically given new addresses from another active scope.

    D. You cannot deactivate a scope that has outstanding leases.

8. You assign two DNS server addresses as part of the options for a scope. Later you find a client workstation that is not using those addresses. What's the most likely cause?

    A. The client didn't get the option information as part of its lease.

    B. The client has been manually configured with a different set of DNS servers.

    C. The client has a reserved IP address in the address pool.

    D. There's a bug in the DHCP server service.

9. When you reconcile a DHCP scope, you're actually _____.

   A. Scanning the DHCP database for inconsistent lease information

   B. Asking each client to confirm its lease

   C. Releasing all client leases, then renewing them

   D. Testing the physical integrity of the database

10. Which of the following statements about client leases is/are true?

    A. Removing a lease has no effect on the client until renewal time.

    B. A single IP address can be leased to multiple clients.

    C. A reserved IP address may not be leased.

    D. An excluded IP address must be exclusively leased to a single client.

11. Client options are managed at the _____.

    A. DHCP server

    B. DHCP client

    C. DHCP scope

    D. DHCP superscope

12. Superscopes are used to _____.

    A. Allow one server to handle multiple logical subnets on one physical network

    B. Allow one server to handle multiple physical networks

    C. Allow one server to handle multiple logical subnets on multiple physical networks

    D. Allow multiple servers to service the same address ranges

13. A single server can support _____.

    A. One superscope

    B. One superscope per installed NIC

    C. Any number of superscopes

    D. One superscope, but only if Active Directory is available

14. What must you do in order to use a DHCP scope?

    A. Create it, authorize it, and activate it

    B. Create it and activate it

    C. Create it and authorize it

    D. Authorize it and activate it

15. When a DHCP client renews a lease, it gets which of the following?

    A. A complete set of options from the server.

    B. Only those options that changed since the lease was issued.

    C. No options; the lease is renewed by itself.

    D. Only the default gateway, IP address, and DNS server address.

16. Removing a child of a superscope has which of the following effects?

    A. It only deletes the scope from the server.

    B. It only deletes the scope from the superscope.

    C. It deletes the scope from the superscope and the server.

    D. It has no effect on the child scope.

17. MADCAP is used to do which of the following?

    A. Assign unicast addresses to clients

    B. Automate configuration for newly added DHCP servers

    C. Issue DHCP leases for multicast addresses

    D. Reset options to their default state

18. To integrate DHCP with dynamic DNS, you may _____.

    A. Enable integration at the scope level only

    B. Enable integration at the server level only

    C. Enable integration at the server and scope levels

    D. All of the above

19. You can change the DHCP database backup interval by doing which of the following?

A. Making a registry change

B. Reinstalling the DHCP service

C. Adjusting the Backup Interval field on the server's General Properties tab

D. Editing `DHCP.INI`

20. If you don't change the default lease duration for a scope, it will issue leases with which duration?

A. 24 hours

B. 7 days

C. 8 days

D. 30 days

Answers to Review Questions

1. A. The server must be authorized in Active Directory or it won't issue any leases.

2. B. A superscope is just a convenience for the administrator—it's a way to pass out a consistent group of options to multiple scopes.

3. A. You shouldn't activate the scope until you've assigned options; otherwise, clients who obtain leases before you finish won't get the complete set of options.

4. B, C. You must enable dynamic DNS support on the DNS server and on the DHCP server.

5. C. Multicast scopes don't assign options; they just assign multicast addresses.

6. B. Excluded addresses are just marked as excluded; the DHCP server doesn't maintain any information about them. Reserved addresses are marked as reserved.

7. A. Deactivating a scope has no effect on the client until it needs to renew the lease, at which point it has to find another server.

8. B. Manual settings override DHCP options.

9. A. Reconciling a server means that you're checking the lease information in the DHCP database against a backup copy saved in the Registry.

10. A. Removing a lease doesn't force the client to renegotiate it; it just removes the matching entry from the DHCP server database.

11. A. You assign options to clients at the server level, not at the scope or superscope.

12. A. The superscope groups multiple scopes into a single superscope for ease of management.

13. A. You may only create one superscope on a server.

14. A. Creating, authorizing, and activating the scope are all separate steps.

15. A. During lease renewal, the client gets all options offered by the server, not any subset.

16. B. If you want to stop using a scope altogether, you have to remove it from the superscope, then delete the scope itself.

17. C. MADCAP assigns multicast IP addresses to clients using a process similar to the "plain" DHCP lease process.

18. D. You can enable integration either on one scope only or on all scopes on a server.

19. A. The backup interval is controlled by the BackupInterval value under HKEY_LOCAL_MACHINE\SYSTEM\CurrentControlet\Services\ DHCPServer\Parameters.

20. C. The default lease expiration period is 8 days, though you can change it.

Chapter

6

Installing and Managing Domain Name Service (DNS)

MICROSOFT EXAM OBJECTIVES COVERED IN THIS CHAPTER:

✓ **Install, configure, and troubleshoot DNS.**

- Install the DNS Server service.
- Configure a root name server.
- Configure zones.
- Configure a caching-only server.
- Configure zones for dynamic updates.
- Test the DNS Server service.
- Implement a delegated zone for DNS.
- Manually create DNS resource records.

✓ **Manage and monitor DNS.**

The Domain Name Service (DNS) is mysterious to many Windows NT administrators largely because (as you learned in Chapter 2) DNS is usually considered to be part of the network plumbing. In many organizations, one group of people manages DNS and network services while a separate group manages file, print, and application servers. It's time to lift the cloud of mystery since DNS is a critical part of Windows 2000.

This chapter covers material related to installing and managing DNS for the "Install, configure, and troubleshoot DNS" and the "Manage and monitor DNS" exam objectives. "Configure a DNS client," another subobjective of this chapter's first objective, is covered in Chapter 12, "Installing and Configuring Network Clients."

Why is it so important? Active Directory depends absolutely on DNS, and many important system functions (including Kerberos authentication and finding domain controllers) are now handled through DNS lookups. Windows 2000 clients use DNS for name resolution, too, but they also use DNS to find Kerberos Key Distribution Centers (KDC), global catalog servers, and other services that may be registered in DNS.

In this chapter, you'll get a deeper understanding of how DNS works in general, plus an understanding of how to set up, configure, manage, and troubleshoot DNS in Windows 2000.

DNS Fundamentals

The Domain Name System is a hierarchically distributed database. That's a fancy way of saying that its layers are arranged in a definite order, and that its data are distributed across a wide range of machines. DNS is a standard set of protocols that defines the following:

- A mechanism for querying and updating address information in the database

- A mechanism for replicating the information in the database among servers

- A schema of the database

DNS began in the early days of the Internet when the Internet was a small network created by the Department of Defense for research purposes. Host names of computers were manually entered into a file located on a centrally administered server. Each site that needed to resolve host names had to download this file. As the number of computers on the Internet grew, so did the size of this HOSTS file as did the traffic generated by the downloading of this file. The need for a new system that would offer features such as scalability, decentralized administration, and support for various data types became more and more obvious. The Domain Name System (DNS), introduced in 1984, became this new system.

With DNS, the host names reside in a database that can be distributed among multiple servers, decreasing the load on any one server and providing the ability to administer this naming system on a per-partition basis. DNS supports hierarchical names and allows registration of various data types in addition to the host-name-to-IP-address mapping used in HOSTS files. By virtue of the DNS database being distributed, its size is unlimited and performance does not degrade much when adding more servers.

The latest version of the Windows 2000 operating system includes a new version of DNS. In addition to the features included in the Windows NT version of the DNS service, the Windows 2000 version adds support for a number of new features (described earlier in Chapter 2).

Servers, Clients, and Resolvers... Oh, My!

There are a few terms and concepts you will need to know before installing or managing a DNS server. Understanding these terms will make it easier to understand how the Windows 2000 DNS server works.

DNS Servers   Any computer providing domain name services is a *DNS server*. That being said, not all DNS servers are alike. Earlier implementations of DNS (for example, the popular Berkeley Internet Name Domain, or BIND) were originally developed for Unix, and they handled a fairly small and simple set of RFC requirements.

There is also the concept of primary and secondary DNS servers to consider. A *primary DNS server* is the "owner" of the zones defined in its database. The primary DNS server has the authority to make changes to the zones it owns. Secondary DNS servers receive a read-only copy of zones. The *secondary DNS server* can resolve queries from this read-only copy, but cannot make changes or updates. A single DNS server may contain multiple primary and secondary zones.

Any DNS server implementation supporting Service Location Resource Records (SRV RRs, as described in an Internet Draft: "A DNS RR for specifying the location of services [DNS SRV]") and Dynamic Update (RFC2136) is sufficient to provide the name service for Windows 2000–based computers. However, because Windows 2000 DNS is designed to fully take advantage of the Windows 2000 Active Directory service, it is the recommended DNS server for any networked organization with a significant investment in Windows or extranet partners with Windows-based systems.

Clients   A *DNS client* is any machine issuing queries to a DNS server. The client host name may or may not be registered in a name server (DNS) database. Clients issue DNS requests through processes called resolvers.

Resolvers   *Resolvers* handle the process of mapping a symbolic name to an actual network address. The resolver (which may reside on another machine) issues queries to name servers. When a resolver receives information from name servers, it caches that information locally in case the same information is requested again.

When a name server is unable to resolve a request, it may reply to the resolver with the name of another name server. The resolver must then address a message to this new name server in the hopes that the symbolic name will be resolved.

Queries   There are two types of queries that can be made to a DNS server: recursive and iterative (we'll discuss the difference shortly).

Root Servers   When a DNS server processes a recursive query and that query cannot be resolved from local zone files, the query must be escalated to a root DNS server. The *root server* is responsible for returning an authoritative answer for a particular domain *or* a referral to a server that can provide an authoritative answer. Since each DNS server is supposed to have a full set of root hints (which point to root servers for various top-level domains), your DNS server can refer queries recursively to other servers with the assistance of the root servers. You can also configure a DNS server to contain its own root zone; you might want to do so if you don't want your servers to be able to answer queries for names outside your network.

Installing and Configuring a DNS Server

DNS can be installed before, during, or after installing the Windows 2000 Active Directory service. If the Active Directory Installation Wizard cannot locate a DNS server, it will ask you if you would like the Active Directory Installation Wizard to install and configure a DNS server for you. Using this feature is the simplest method of installing a DNS server for your Windows 2000 Active Directory service. This section describes the steps to manually prepare a DNS server, and how to further configure Windows 2000 DNS to fully support your network infrastructure.

Installing a DNS Server

Installing the DNS server service is easy since you install it with the same tools you use to add other components. Exercise 6.1 leads you through the steps.

Microsoft ✓ *Exam* *Objective*

Install, configure, and troubleshoot DNS.

- Install the DNS Server service.

EXERCISE 6.1

Installing the DNS Service

Follow these steps to install the DNS server. Note that this exercise will work only on computers running Windows 2000 Server or Advanced Server. Microsoft strongly recommends that you configure your DNS servers to use static IP addresses, and we agree.

1. Open the Windows Components wizard by opening the Add/ Remove Programs in the Control Panel (Start ➤ Settings ➤ Control Panel ➤ Add/Remove Programs).

2. Click the Add/Remove Windows Components icon. The Installation wizard will open and list all the components it knows how to install or remove.

3. Select the Networking Services item from the Component list, and then click the Details... button.

EXERCISE 6.1 *(continued)*

4. When the Subcomponents of Network Services list appears, make sure that the Domain Name System (DNS) is selected, then click the OK button.

5. If prompted, enter the path to the Windows 2000 distribution files.

When you install the DNS server, you get the DNS snap-in installed, too; you can open it by using the Start ➢ Programs ➢ Administrative Tools ➢ DNS command. The snap-in is shown in Figure 6.1; as you can see, it follows the standard MMC model. The left-hand pane shows you which servers and zones are available; you can connect to servers in addition to the one you're already talking to. Each server contains subordinate items grouped into folders. Each zone has a folder, which is named after the zone itself. In the sample, you can see that the server NOTHOS has a root zone (the one labeled ".") with subordinate zones for "arpa" and "com," plus a forward lookup zone for `entirenet` `.com` and a reverse lookup zone for the 10.10.1.x Subnet that it serves. Under the `entirenet.com` domain, you can see the special _msdcs, _sites, _tcp, and _udp domains mentioned in Chapter 2. Notice that the right-hand pane shows the resource records defined for the selected zone; in this case, the records include a single SOA and NS record pair, plus several host RRs.

FIGURE 6.1   The DNS snap-in

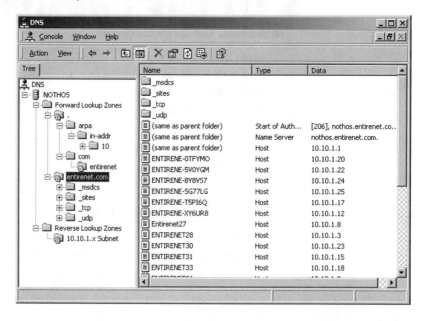

Configuring a DNS Server

Configuring a DNS server ranges from very easy to very difficult, depending on what you're trying to make it do. The simplest configuration is a caching-only server, in which you don't have to do anything except make sure the server's root hints are set correctly.

Microsoft ✓ ***Exam*** ***Objective***	**Install, configure, and troubleshoot DNS.** ▪ Configure a caching-only server.

Configuring a Caching-Only Server

Although all DNS name servers cache queries that they have resolved, caching-only servers are DNS name servers that only perform queries, cache the answers, and return the results. They are not authoritative for any domains, and the information that they contain is limited to what has been cached while resolving queries. Accordingly, they don't have any zone files, and they don't participate in zone transfers. When a caching-only server is first started, it has no information in its cache; the cache is gradually built over time.

Installing a caching-only server is so easy that it's almost not worth explaining again. Just in case you missed the earlier instructions, though, Exercise 6.2 explains the process.

EXERCISE 6.2

Installing a Caching DNS Server

Follow these steps to install a DNS server and configure it as a caching-only server. As with Exercise 6.1, this exercise will work only on computers running Windows 2000 Server or Advanced Server.

1. Install a DNS server as described in Exercise 6.1.

2. Open the DNS management snap-in (Start ➢ Programs ➢ Administrative Tools ➢ DNS).

3. Notice that the Forward and Reverse Lookup Zone folders are empty. You want them that way.

EXERCISE 6.2 *(continued)*

4. Right-click your DNS server and choose the Properties command. When the Properties dialog box appears, switch to the Root Hints tab (Figure 6.2). If your server is connected to the Internet, you should see a list of root hints for the root servers maintained by InterNIC. If not, use the Add button to add root hints as defined in the root.dns file.

5. Close the Properties dialog box by clicking OK.

FIGURE 6.2 The Root Hints tab of the DNS server Properties dialog box

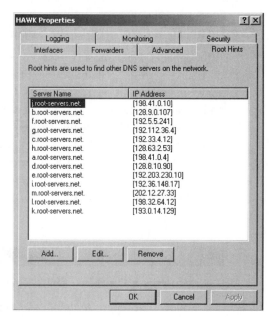

Configuring a Root Name Server

If your Windows 2000 servers aren't directly connected to the Internet, or if you want to prevent them from ever referring queries to the Internet, you can configure them to contain their own root zone. Remember that root zones are treated as the authoritative source of information for a top-level domain; by creating your own root zones, you can control exactly which domains your clients can resolve queries for. The process of doing this is pretty simple; you can use the Configure DNS Server wizard on a machine that you haven't previously configured (as you will in the exercise), or you can do it manually as in Exercise 6.3.

Microsoft ✓ *Exam* *Objective*

Install, configure, and troubleshoot DNS.

- Configure a root name server.

EXERCISE 6.3

Configuring a DNS Server as a Root Name Server

In this exercise will we configure the DNS server as a root server with one forward lookup zone. If you've already installed and configured a DNS server for the previous exercises, remove it and reinstall it.

1. Open the DNS management snap-in (Start ➢ Programs ➢ Administrative Tools ➢ DNS).

2. Click the DNS server to expand it, then right-click the server and select the Configure The Server command. When the Configure DNS Server wizard starts and begins guiding you through the process of setting up DNS, click Next.

3. Click the option "This is the first DNS server on this network." This option will make the server a root server. A root server can gain access to second-level domains on the Internet. Click Next.

4. Click the option "Yes, create a forward lookup zone," and then click Next. A *forward lookup zone* is a name-to-address database that helps computers translate DNS names into IP addresses and provides information about available resources.

5. Click the Standard Primary option, and then click Next. This will store a master copy of the new zone in a text file and facilitates the exchange of DNS data with other DNS servers that use text-based storage methods.

6. Type in *mycompany.com* (or whatever other name you want) as the name for your new zone, and then click Next.

7. Click the Create A New File With This Filename radio button, and then click the Next button. You can change the name of the zone file, but for this exercise leave it as is.

8. Click the No, Do Not Create A Reverse Lookup Zone radio button, then click Next.

9. Click Finish to complete the Configure DNS Server wizard.

Creating and Configuring Zones

You can use the New Zone wizard to create a new forward or *reverse lookup zone.* The process is substantially the same, even though the steps and wizard pages differ somewhat. In either case, you create a new zone first by right-clicking the server you want to host the zone and then by using the New Zone command; this kicks off the New Zone wizard.

Creating a New Forward Lookup Zone

Once you dismiss the initial, useless wizard page, the first choice you have to make is on the Zone Type page: What kind of zone do you want this to be? You can choose from Active Directory-integrated, standard primary, and standard secondary. Which option you'll use depends on what you're doing:

- If you want to store zone data in Active Directory, use an AD-integrated zone.

- If you need to manually transfer zone data to other DNS servers by moving the actual zone data, or if you're not using Active Directory, use the Standard Primary radio button.

- If you want to set up your server as a secondary zone server, choose the Standard Secondary radio button. Later in the process, you'll be prompted to specify which primary zone you want to transfer data from.

No matter which zone type you choose, the next step is to pick whether you want to create a forward or reverse lookup zone. At this point, we'll assume you want to create a forward zone (the steps for creating a reverse zone are covered in the next section).

Forward zones need to have names; you specify the name you want the zone to have using the Zone Name page of the wizard. For an AD-integrated or primary zone, you have to specify the name (including the suffix—*microsoft* isn't a valid name, but **microsoft.com** would be). If you're creating a secondary zone, there will be a Browse button you can use to locate the primary zone you want to copy.

If you're building a new AD-integrated zone, you're done once you specify the name. However, if you're setting up a standard primary zone you must specify where you want the zone data stored (Figure 6.3). The default file name will be the same as the zone name with .dns tacked on the end, but you can modify it freely. You can also combine more than one zone's data into a single zone file, though that makes it a little harder to sort out what's what.

FIGURE 6.3 The Zone File page of the New Zone wizard

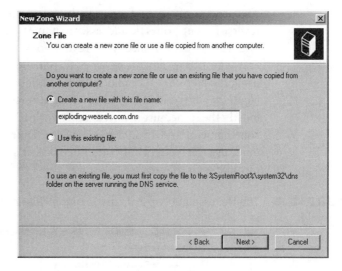

Since secondary zones have to transfer their zone data from somewhere else, you have to specify where exactly that comes from. Figure 6.4 shows the Master DNS Servers page of the New Zone wizard; use the controls here to specify which DNS servers your server will contact to request zone transfers. If you specify more than one server here, your server will try the servers in the order specified.

FIGURE 6.4 The Master DNS Servers page of the New Zone wizard

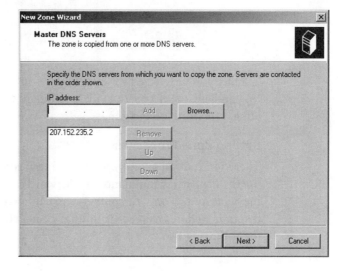

Creating a New Reverse Lookup Zone

The process of creating a reverse lookup zone is a little different, since reverse lookup zones tie addresses to names. The Reverse Lookup Zone page (Figure 6.5) lets you specify the reverse lookup zone's name in two ways. The easy way is to specify the network ID portion of the network the zone covers, using the Network ID radio button and field. The more complex, but equivalent, way is to fill in the name of the reverse zone itself. These two are mostly the same, just inverted: a network ID of 208.15.144 yields a reverse zone name of 144.15.208.in-addr.arpa. Unless you're a Unix stick-in-the-mud, use the Network ID radio button—it's less likely that you'll make a mistake with that route.

FIGURE 6.5 The Reverse Lookup Zone page of the New Zone wizard

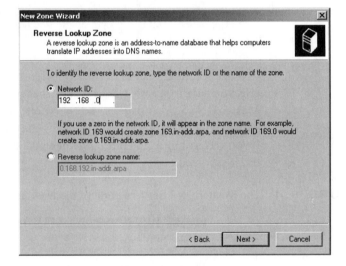

Once you've selected which network you want your reverse zone to point to, you have to select a zone file (see Figure 6.3), just as you did when creating a forward lookup zone.

Setting Zone Properties

There is a total of six tabs on the Properties dialog box you get when you use the Properties command on a forward or reverse lookup zone. You use the Security tab only to control who can change properties and make dynamic updates to records on that zone. The other tabs are discussed in the following list.

Microsoft
✓ **Exam**
Objective

Install, configure, and troubleshoot DNS.

- Configure zones.

 Secondary zones don't have a Security tab, and their SOA tab shows you the contents of the master SOA record, which you can't change.

The General Tab   Like General tabs everywhere in Windows 2000, the controls here (Figure 6.6) are pretty straightforward since they're mostly dedicated to settings that don't belong elsewhere. These settings include the following:

- The Status indicator (and the associated button) lets you see and control whether this zone can be used to answer queries. When the zone is running, the server can use it to answer client queries; when it's paused, the server won't answer any queries it gets for that particular zone.

- The Type indicator and button allow you to change the zone type between standard primary, standard secondary, and AD-integrated. As you change the type, the controls you see below the horizontal dividing line will change too. The most interesting controls are the ones you see for AD-integrated zones. For primary zones, you'll see a field that lets you select the zone filename; for secondary zones, you'll get controls that allow you to specify the IP addresses of the primary servers.

- The Allow Dynamic Updates field gives you a way to specify whether or not you want to support dynamic DNS updates from compatible DHCP servers. As you learned in Chapter 5, the DHCP server or DHCP client must know about and support dynamic DNS in order to use it, but the DNS server has to participate, too. You can turn dynamic updates on or off, or you can require that updates must be secured. By default, a standard primary zone won't accept dynamic updates, but an AD-integrated zone will. You can change these settings at will.

FIGURE 6.6 The General tab of the Zone Properties dialog box

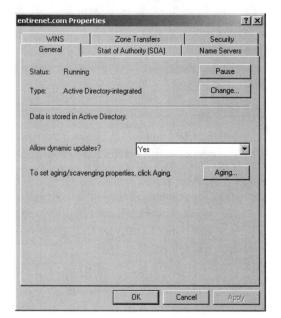

The Start of Authority (SOA) Tab The controls in the Start of Authority (SOA) tab (Figure 6.7) control the contents of the SOA record for this zone. The controls will make perfect sense if you think back to Chapter 2's description of what's in an SOA record. The following list describes these controls:

- The Serial Number field indicates which version of the SOA record the server currently holds; every time you change another field, you should increment the serial number so that other servers will notice the change and get a copy of the updated record.

- The Primary Server and Responsible Person fields indicate the location of the primary NS for this zone and the responsible administrator, respectively.

- The Refresh Interval field controls how often any secondary zones of this zone must contact the primary and get any changes that have been posted since the last update.

- The Retry Interval field controls how long secondary servers will wait after a zone transfer fails before they try again. They'll keep trying at the interval you specify (which should be shorter than the refresh interval) until they eventually succeed in transferring zone data.

- The Expires After field tells the secondary servers when to throw away zone data. The default of 24 hours means that a secondary that hasn't gotten an update in 24 hours will delete its local copy of the zone data.

- The Minimum (Default) TTL field sets the default TTL for all RRs created in the zone; you can still assign different TTLs to individual records if you want.

- The TTL For This Record field controls the TTL for the SOA record itself.

FIGURE 6.7   The Start of Authority tab of the Zone Properties dialog box

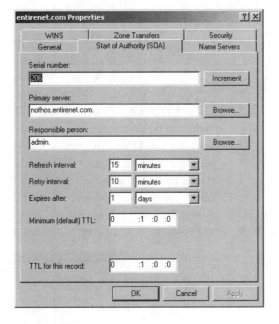

The Name Servers Tab   The NS record for a zone indicates which name servers are authoritative for a zone. That normally means the zone primary and any secondaries you've configured for the zone (remember, secondaries are authoritative read-only copies of the zone). You edit the NS record for a zone with the Name Servers tab (Figure 6.8). To be more specific, the tab shows you which servers are listed, and you use the Add, Edit, and Remove buttons to specify which name servers you want included in the zone's NS record.

FIGURE 6.8 The Name Servers tab of the Zone Properties dialog box

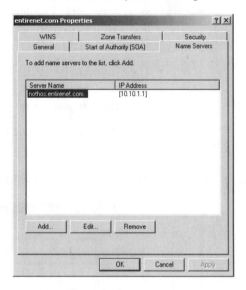

The WINS Tab The WINS tab (Figure 6.9) allows you to control whether this zone uses WINS forward lookups or not. These lookups pass queries that DNS can't resolve on to WINS for action; this is a useful setup if you're still stuck using WINS on your network. You must explicitly turn this option on with the Use WINS Forward Lookup check box in the WINS tab for a particular zone.

FIGURE 6.9 The WINS tab of the Zone Properties dialog box

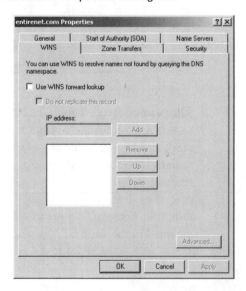

The Zone Transfers Tab   Zone transfers are necessary and useful since they're the mechanism used to propagate zone data between primary and secondary servers. For primary servers (whether AD-integrated or not), you can specify whether or not your servers will allow zone transfers and, if so, to whom. The Zone Transfers tab (Figure 6.10) lets you control these settings per zone by using the following controls:

- The Allow Zone Transfers check box controls whether or not the server will answer zone transfer requests for this zone at all—when it's off, no zone data will be transferred.

- Next, the three radio buttons control where zone transfer data will go when you have zone transfers enabled.

- The To Any Server button is the default; this setting allows any server, anywhere on the Internet, to request a copy of your zone data.

- The Only To Servers Listed On The Name Servers Tab button limits transfers to only those servers listed in the Name Servers tab for this zone. This is a more secure setting than the default, since it limits zone transfers to other servers for the same zone.

- The Only To The Following Servers button, along with its corresponding IP address controls, gives you even more control since you can specify exactly which servers are allowed to request zone transfers—this list can be larger, or smaller, than the list specified on the Name Servers tab.

- The Notify button lets you set up automatic notification triggers that are sent to secondary servers for this zone. Those triggers signal the secondary servers that changes have occurred on the primary; that way, the secondaries can request updates sooner than their normally scheduled interval.

Configuring Zones For Dynamic Updates

Dynamic update enables DNS client computers to register and dynamically update their resource records with a DNS server whenever changes occur. This reduces the need for manual administration of zone records. The DNS service allows dynamic update to be enabled or disabled on a per-zone basis at each server. There are some subtleties that you may not have thought of, though.

FIGURE 6.10   The Zone Transfers tab of the Zone Properties dialog box

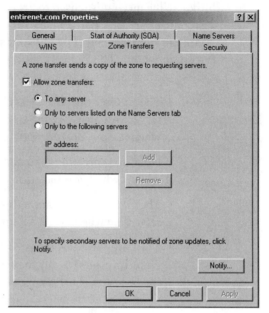

Microsoft
Exam
Objective

Install, configure, and troubleshoot DNS.

- Configure zones for dynamic updates.

A Windows 2000 client that has a statically assigned IP address will attempt to register its IP address with a dynamic DNS server when the IP address changes or when the machine reboots. DHCP clients will update DNS records whenever an IP address assignment changes (e.g., when a lease is renewed or issued). In both cases, the DHCP service on the client is responsible for sending the update for all IP addresses assigned to the machine, even those that aren't using DHCP.

What about secure updates? Turning on secure updates has no initial effect on clients, since they'll always try unsecured updates first. If an unsecured update fails, the client will try again with a secure update. If that fails, then the update fails.

What if you're not using Windows 2000 clients? The Windows 2000 DHCP server can register DNS data for machines to which it issues leases; in this role, it's called a *DNS proxy* since it's acting on behalf of another set of machines. While this gives all your computers access to dynamic DNS registrations, it opens some worrisome security issues because you must add the DHCP servers you want to act as proxies to the DnsProxyUpdate group in Active Directory. This tells the OS that you want those DHCP servers to be able to register clients, but it also means that any DHCP server running on an AD controller has full access to the DNS registration information—meaning that a malicious DHCP client could potentially poison your DNS information.

EXERCISE 6.4

Configuring Zones and Configuring Zones for Dynamic Updates

In this exercise, you will modify the properties of a forward lookup zone, configuring the zone to use WINS to resolve names not found by querying the DNS namespace. In addition, you'll configure the zone to allow dynamic updates.

1. Open the DNS management snap-in (Start ≻ Programs ≻ Administrative Tools ≻ DNS).

2. Click the DNS server to expand it, then expand the Forward Lookup Zones folder.

3. Right-click the zone you want to modify (which may be the one you created in the previous exercise), then choose the Properties command.

4. Switch to the WINS tab, then click the Use WINS Forward Lookup check box.

5. Enter the IP address of a valid WINS server on your network, click Add, and then click OK.

6. Notice that there's now a new WINS Lookup RR in your zone.

7. Repeat step 3 to reopen the Zone Properties dialog box; this time stay on the General tab.

8. Change the value of the Allow Dynamic Updates control to "Yes." Close the Properties dialog box.

Delegating Zones for DNS

DNS provides the ability to divide up the namespace into one or more zones, which can then be stored, distributed, and replicated to other DNS servers. When deciding whether to divide your DNS namespace to make additional zones, consider the following reasons to use additional zones:

- A need to delegate management of part of your DNS namespace to another location or department within your organization.

- A need to divide one large zone into smaller zones for distributing traffic loads among multiple servers, improve DNS name resolution performance, or create a more fault-tolerant DNS environment.

- A need to extend the namespace by adding numerous subdomains at once, such as to accommodate the opening of a new branch or site.

Microsoft ✓ *Exam* *Objective*

Install, configure, and troubleshoot DNS.

- Implement a delegated zone for DNS.

When delegating zones within your namespace, be aware that for each new zone you create, you will need delegation records in other zones that point to the authoritative DNS servers for the new zone. This is necessary both to transfer authority and to provide correct referral to other DNS servers and clients of the new servers being made authoritative for the new zone.

EXERCISE 6.5

Creating a Delegated DNS Zone

In this exercise, you'll create a delegated *subdomain* of the domain you created back in Exercise 6.3.

1. Open the DNS management snap-in (Start ➢ Programs ➢ Administrative Tools ➢ DNS).

2. Click the DNS server to expand it, then expand the Forward Lookup Zones folder.

3. Expand the DNS server, then locate the zone you created earlier.

4. Right-click the zone and choose the New Delegation command.

5. The New Delegation wizard will appear; click Next to get rid of the initial wizard page.

6. Enter **ns1** (or whatever other name you like) in the Delegated Domain field of the Delegated Domain Name page. This is the name of the domain for which you want to delegate authority to another DNS server. It should be a subdomain of the primary domain (e.g., to delegate authority for huntsville.robichaux.net, you'd enter **huntsville** in the Delegated Domain field).

7. When the Name Servers page appears, use the Add button to add the IP address(es) of the servers that will be hosting the newly delegated zone. For purposes of this exercise, it's OK to put in a fake IP address like **10.10.1.1**.

8. Click the Finish button. The delegation wizard will disappear, and you'll notice the new zone you just created appear beneath the zone you selected in step 4. The newly delegated zone's folder icon is drawn in gray to indicate that control of the zone is delegated.

Manually Creating DNS Records

From time to time you may find it necessary to manually add resource records to your Windows 2000 DNS servers. While dynamic DNS will free you from the need to fiddle with A and PTR records, other resource types (including MX records, required for the proper flow of SMTP e-mail) still have to be created manually. You can manually create A, PTR, MX, SRV, and 15 other record types. There are only two important things to remember: You must right-click the zone and use either the New Record command or the Other New Records command, and you must know how to fill in the fields of whatever record type you're using. For example, to create an MX record you need three pieces of information (the domain, the mail server, and the priority), but to create an SRV record you need several more.

Microsoft
✓ *Exam*
Objective

Install, configure, and troubleshoot DNS.

- Manually create DNS resource records.

EXERCISE 6.6

Manually Creating DNS RRs

It sometimes becomes necessary to manually create *resource records* in the DNS name server database. For example, a Microsoft Exchange mail server is installed on your network. To facilitate the exchange of mail, a resource record of the type MX must be created on your DNS server. In this exercise, we will manually create an MX record for the mailtest server in the domain you created back in Exercise 6.3.

1. In Control Panel, double-click Administrative Tools and then double-click DNS.

2. Expand your DNS server, then right-click its zone and use the New Mail Exchanger command.

3. Enter **mailtest** in the Mail Server field, and then click OK. Notice that the new record is already visible.

Next, create an alias (or CNAME) record to point to the mail server. (This assumes that you already have an A record for mailtest in your zone.)

1. Right-click the target zone and choose the Other New Records command. When the Resource Record Type dialog box appears, find Alias in the list and select it.

2. Click the Create Record button. The New Resource Record dialog box will appear.

3. Type **mail** into the Alias Name field.

4. Type **mailtest.*yourDomain*.com** into the Fully Qualified Name For Target Host field.

5. Click the OK button, and then click the Done button in the Resource Record Type dialog box.

Monitoring & Troubleshooting DNS

Now that your DNS name server has been set up, configured, and has some resource records created, you will want to confirm that your DNS name server is resolving and replying to client DNS requests. The simplest test is to use the *ping* command to make sure the server is alive, but where's the fun in that? A more exhaustive test would be to use *nslookup* to verify that you can actually resolve addresses for items on your DNS server. Before reading about troubleshooting, though, you should examine some basic monitoring and management issues.

Microsoft ✓ ***Exam Objective***   **Manage and monitor DNS.**

Monitoring DNS

You can use the DNS snap-in to do some basic server testing and monitoring. More importantly, you use the snap-in to monitor and set logging options. The Logging tab (Figure 6.11) lets you pick which events you want logged. The more of these options you turn on, the more log information you'll get. This is useful when you're trying to track what's happening with your servers, but it can result in a very, very large log file if you're not careful.

Microsoft ✓ ***Exam Objective***   **Install, configure, and troubleshoot DNS.**

▪ Test the DNS Server service.

FIGURE 6.11   The Logging tab of the Server Properties dialog box

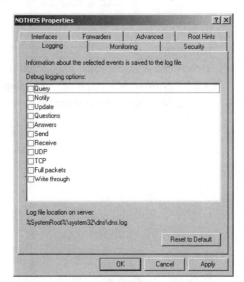

The Monitoring tab (Figure 6.12) gives you some simplistic testing tools. The "A simple query against this DNS server" test asks for a single record from the local DNS server; it's useful for verifying that the service is running and listening to queries, but not much else. The "A recursive query to other DNS servers" test is more sophisticated, using a recursive query to see whether forwarding is working OK. The Test Now button and the Perform Automatic Testing At The Following Interval control allow you to run these tests now or later, as you require.

FIGURE 6.12 The Monitoring tab of the Server Properties dialog box

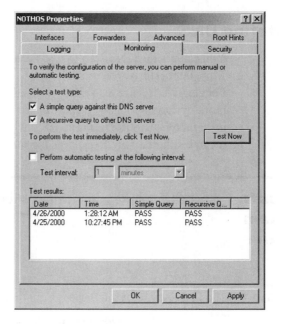

If the simple query fails, check that the local server contains the zone 1.0.0.127.in-addr.arpa. If the recursive query fails, check that your root hints are correct and that your root servers are running.

EXERCISE 6.7

Simple DNS Testing

In this exercise, you will enable logging, use the DNS MMC to test the DNS server, and view the contents of the DNS log.

1. In Control Panel, double-click Administrative Tools, and then double-click DNS.

2. Right-click the DNS server you want to test and use the Properties command.

3. Switch to the Logging tab, check all the Debug logging options, and then click the Apply button.

4. Switch to the Monitoring tab, check both "A simple query against this DNS server" and "A recursive query to other DNS servers."

5. Click the Test Now button several times, and then click OK.

6. Using Windows Explorer, navigate to the %windir%\System32\DNS folder, and use WordPad to view the contents of the dns.log file which is in Rich Text Format (RTF).

Troubleshooting DNS

When troubleshooting DNS problems, ask yourself the following basic questions:

- What application is failing? What works? What doesn't work?

- Is the problem basic IP connectivity, or is it name resolution? If the problem is name resolution, does the failing application use NetBIOS names, DNS names, or host names?

- How are the things that do and don't work related?

- Have the things that don't work ever worked on this computer or network?

- If so, what has changed since they last worked?

Troubleshooting Tools

Windows 2000 provides several useful tools that can help you diagnose and solve problems with DNS. This section discusses the following tools:

- You can use *nslookup* to perform DNS queries and to examine the contents of zone files on local and remote servers.

- You can use *ipconfig* to view DNS client settings, display and flush the resolver cache, and force a dynamic update client to register its DNS records.

- You can use Event Viewer to view DNS client and server error messages.

- The network redirector allows you to stop the DNS client and flush its cache by stopping and restarting it with the Net Stop and Net Start commands.

- You can configure the DNS server to monitor certain events and log them in the DNS log for your edification.

- You can perform test queries by using the Controls options on the Monitoring tab in the DNS console.

Nslookup

Nslookup is a standard command-line tool provided in most DNS server implementations, including Windows 2000. *Nslookup* offers the ability to perform query testing of DNS servers and to obtain detailed responses at the command prompt. This information can be useful for diagnosing and solving name resolution problems, for verifying that resource records are added or updated correctly in a zone, and for debugging other server-related problems. You can do a number of useful things with *nslookup*:

- Use *nslookup* in non-interactive mode to look up a single piece of data

- Enter interactive mode and use the debug feature

- From within interactive mode:

  - Set options for your query

  - Look up a name

  - Look up records in a zone

  - Perform zone transfers

  - Exit *nslookup*

When you are entering queries, it is generally a good idea to enter FQDNs so you can control what name is submitted to the server. However, if you want to know which suffixes are added to unqualified names before they are submitted to the server, you can enter *nslookup* in debug mode and then enter an unqualified name.

Let's start with using *nslookup* in plain old command-line mode:

```
nslookup <name> <server>
```

This code will look up a DNS name or address named *name*, using a server at an IP address specified by *server*. However, *nslookup* is a lot more useful in interactive mode since you can enter several commands in sequence. Running *nslookup* by itself (without specifying a query or server) puts it in interactive mode, where it will stay until you type **exit** and hit Return. Before that point, you can look up lots of useful stuff.

While in interactive mode, you can use the Set command to configure how the resolver will carry out queries. Table 6.1 shows a few of the options available with Set.

TABLE 6.1 Command-line options available with the Set command

Option	Purpose
set all	Shows all the options available with the set option.
set d2	Puts *nslookup* in debug mode so you can examine the query and response packets between the resolver and the sever.
set domain=<domain name>	Tells the resolver what domain name to append for unqualified queries.
set timeout=<time-out>	Tells the resolver which time-out to use. This option is useful for slow links where queries frequently time-out and the wait time must be lengthened.
set type=<record type>	Tells the resolver which type of resource records to search for (for example, A, PTR, or SRV). If you want the resolver to query for all types of resource records, type **set type=all**.

While in interactive mode, you can look up a name just by typing it: **<name>** [server]. In this example, *name* is the owner name for the record you are looking for, and *server* is the server that you want to query.

You can use the wildcard character (*) in your query. For example, if you want to look for all resource records that have K as the first letter, just type **k*** as your query.

If you want to query for a particular type of record (say, an MX record), use the Set Type command.

```
Set type=mx
```

This example tells *nslookup* that you're only interested in seeing MX records that meet your search criteria.

There are a couple of other cool tricks you can do with *nslookup*. First off, you can get a list of the contents of an entire domain with the Ls command. To find all the hosts in the apple.com domain, you'd type **Set type=a**, and then type **Ls -t apple.com**.

You can also simulate zone transfers by using the Ls command with the -d switch. This can help you determine whether or not the server you are querying allows zone transfers to your computer.

Type the following: **ls -d <domain name>**

Identifying What's Wrong

A successful *nslookup* response looks like this:

```
Server: <Name of DNS server>
Address: <IP address of DNS server>
<Response data>
```

Nslookup might also return an error. The following message means that the resolver did not locate a PTR resource record (containing the host name) for the server IP address. *Nslookup* can still query the DNS server, and the DNS server can still answer queries.

```
DNS request timed out.
Timeout was <x> seconds.
*** Can't find server name for address <IP Address>: Timed
out
*** Default servers are not available
Default Server: Unknown
Address: <IP address of DNS server>
```

The following message means that a request timed out. This might happen, for example, if the DNS service was not running on the DNS server that is authoritative for the name.

```
*** Request to <Server> timed-out
```

The following message means that the server is not receiving requests on UDP port 53.

```
*** <Server> can't find <Name or IP address queried for>:
No response from server
```

The following message means that this DNS server was not able to find the name or IP address in the authoritative domain. The authoritative domain might be on that DNS server or on another DNS server that this DNS server is able to reach.

```
*** <Server> can't find <Name or IP address queried for>:
Non-existent domain
```

The following message generally means that the DNS server is running but is not working properly. For example, it might include a corrupted packet, or the zone in which you are querying for a record might be paused. However, this message can also be returned if the client queries for a host in a domain for which the DNS server is not authoritative and the DNS server cannot contact its root servers, or it is not connected to the Internet, or it has no root hints.

```
*** <Server> can't find <Name or IP address queried for>:
Server failed.
```

Using *ipconfig*

You can use the command-line tool *ipconfig* to view your DNS client settings, to view and reset cached information used locally for resolving DNS name queries, and to register the resource records for a dynamic update client. If you use *ipconfig* with no parameters, it displays DNS information for each adapter, including the domain name and DNS servers used for that adapter. Table 6.2 shows some command-line options available with *ipconfig*.

TABLE 6.2 Command-line options available for the *ipconfig* command

Command	What It Does
Ipconfig /all	Displays additional information about DNS, including the FQDN and the DNS suffix search list.

TABLE 6.2 Command-line options available for the *ipconfig* command *(continued)*

Command	What It Does
Ipconfig /flushdns	Flushes and resets the DNS resolver cache. For more information about this option, see the section "Configuring a DNS Server" earlier in this chapter.
Ipconfig /displaydns	Displays the contents of the DNS resolver cache. For more information about this option, see "Configuring a DNS Server" earlier in this chapter.
Ipconfig /registerdns	Refreshes all DHCP leases and registers any related DNS names. This option is available only on Windows 2000–based computers that run the DHCP Client service. For more information about this option, see the section "Creating and Configuring Zones" earlier in this chapter.

DNS Log

You can configure the DNS server to create a log file that records the following types of events:

- Queries
- Notification messages from other servers
- Dynamic updates
- Content of the question section for DNS query message
- Content of the answer section for DNS query messages
- Number of queries this server sends
- Number of queries this server has received
- Number of DNS requests received over a UDP port
- Number of DNS requests received over a TCP port
- Number of full packets sent by the server
- Number of packets written through by the server and back to the zone

The DNS log appears in `%SystemRoot%\System32\dns\Dns.log`. Because the log is in RTF format, you must use WordPad to view it.

You can change the directory and file name in which the DNS log appears by adding the following entry to the registry with the REG_SZ data type:

```
HKEY_LOCAL_MACHINE\SYSTEM\CurrentControlSet\Services\DNS
\Parameters\LogFilePath
```

Set the value of LogFilePath equal to the file path and filename where you want to locate the DNS log.

By default, the maximum file size of `Dns.log` is 4 MB. If you want to change the size, add the following entry to the registry with the REG_DWORD data type:

```
HKEY_LOCAL_MACHINE\SYSTEM\CurrentControlSet\Services\DNS
\Parameters\LogFileMaxSize
```

Set the value of LogFileMaxSize equal to the desired file size in bytes. The minimum size is 64Kb.

Once the log file reaches the maximum size, Windows 2000 writes over the beginning of the file. If you make the value higher, data persists for a longer time, but the log file consumes more disk space. If you make the value smaller, the log file uses less disk space, but the data persists for a shorter time.

WARNING

Do not leave DNS logging turned on during normal operation because it sucks up both processing and hard disk resources. Enable it only when diagnosing and solving DNS problems.

EXERCISE 6.8

Simple DNS Troubleshooting

In this exercise, you'll get some hands-on practice with the *nslookup* tool, a simple but effective way to troubleshoot many types of DNS problems.

1. Open a Windows 2000 command prompt (Start ➤ Run, then enter **cmd.exe** in the Run dialog box).

2. When the command prompt window opens, type **nslookup** and hit the Return key. (For the rest of the exercise, use the Return key to terminate each command.)

EXERCISE 6.8

3. *Nslookup* will start, printing a message telling you the name and IP address of the default DNS server. Write these down; you'll need them later.

4. Try looking up a well-known address: type **http://www.microsoft .com**. Notice that the query returns several IP addresses (Microsoft load-balances Web traffic by using multiple servers in the same DNS record).

5. Try looking up a non-existent host: type **http://www.fubijar.com**. Notice that your server complains that it can't find the address. This is normal behavior.

6. Change the server to a non-existent host (try making up a private IP address that you know isn't a DNS server on your network, like 10.10.10.10). Do this by typing **server *ipAddress***. *Nslookup* will take a while to think about it, because it will try to turn the IP address into a host name. Eventually it will print a message telling you that the new default server is using the IP address you specified.

7. Try doing another lookup of a known DNS name. Type **mail.Robichaux.net**. Notice that *nslookup* is contacting the server you specified and that the lookup times out after a few seconds.

8. Reset your server to the original address you wrote down in step 3.

9. If doing so won't disrupt your network, unplug your computer from the network and repeat steps 4–8. Notice the difference in behavior.

Summary

In this chapter, you learned:

- How to install and configure the DNS service
- How to create, manage, and configure zones
- How to troubleshoot and monitor DNS services

Key Terms

Before you take the exam, be sure you're familiar with the following terms:

DNS client

DNS proxy

DNS server

Forward lookup zone

Primary DNS server

Resolvers

Resource record

Reverse lookup zone

Root server

Secondary DNS server

Subdomain

Review Questions

1. You have three DNS name servers on your network. Which features of Windows 2000 DNS might you use to improve fault tolerance while minimizing network traffic? (Choose all that apply.)

   A. Service resource location records

   B. Zone delegation

   C. Primary and secondary zones

   D. Incremental zone transfer

2. You have a router separating your internal network from the Internet. A DNS server on the internal side is able to answer simple queries, but it fails on recursive queries. What may be wrong?

   A. Name server is configured as a root server.

   B. The server does not support dynamic updates.

   C. The servers root hints are not configured or updated.

   D. The name server has only one network card.

3. DNS name resolution is very slow. What may be the cause?

   A. The name server database contains a large number of stale records.

   B. The name server is configured as a non-forwarding name server.

   C. The configured TTL for resource records is too short.

4. You have 3 DNS servers and see a high number of DNS zone transfer (SOA) records sent. What can you do to limit this traffic?

   A. Limit the number of zones.

   B. Increase the TTL for the SOA resource record type in all zones.

   C. Use incremental zone transfers.

   D. None of the above.

5. DNS queries are generating a lot of network traffic. What can you do to address this situation?

   A. Increase the TTL the resolver allows caching the resource records.

   B. Enable dynamic updates on all primary zones.

   C. Create hosts files on client computers.

   D. Install a secondary DNS server.

6. You create a new standard primary zone, then find that your DHCP clients aren't registering their IP addresses properly. This is probably due to which of the following?

   A. The zone is set to disallow dynamic updates.

   B. Standard zones require the client to update its IP address information manually.

   C. Primary zones can't accept dynamic updates.

   D. Standard zones don't support dynamic updates.

7. When using non–Windows 2000 clients, a Windows 2000 DHCP server can do which of the following for the clients?

   A. It can assign DNS server addresses.

   B. It can register WINS addresses.

   C. It can act as a dynamic DHCP proxy.

   D. It can remove stale resource records.

8. Jerry wants to configure a Windows 2000 DNS server so that it can answer queries for hosts on his intranet but not on the Internet. He can accomplish this by doing which of the following? (Choose two.)

   A. Installing the DNS server inside his company's firewall

   B. Configuring his server as a root server and leaving out root hints for the top-level domains

   C. Leaving forwarding turned off

   D. Disabling recursive lookups

9. To manually force a client to reregister itself with a dynamic DNS server, you would use which command?

    A. *Ipconfig* /renew

    B. *Ipconfig* /registerdns

    C. DNS /register

    D. DNS /dynamic /register

10. Blaise wants to load-balance his DNS servers. Which of the following will *not* reduce the load on his servers?

    A. Adding more secondary name servers

    B. Using AD-integrated zones

    C. Adding caching name servers

    D. Enabling the use of incremental zone transfers

11. Which of the following client operating systems support dynamic updates?

    A. Windows 95

    B. Windows 98

    C. Windows NT 4.0 Workstation

    D. Windows 2000 Professional

12. When using DHCP integrated dynamic updates, the client updates which record and the DHCP server updates which record?

    A. A, PTR

    B. PTR, A

    C. Host, A

    D. PTR, Reverse

13. You are not able to join a computer to your domain. After checking for the permission to join to a computer to the domain and checking the domain for functionality, what would you then check?

    A. DHCP server

    B. DNS server

    C. WINS server

    D. Dynamic Update Server

14. To promote a member server to a domain controller, what must the DNS server support?

    A. SRV Records

    B. The Dynamic Update Protocol

    C. Both SRV Records and the Dynamic Update Protocol

15. It took Bob approximately 5 minutes to log in to the domain this morning. When investigating the problem, you found out that only Bob's computer was experiencing the problem. What do you now suspect?

    A. The domain controller

    B. The DHCP server

    C. The DNS server

    D. Bob

16. What are the two primary DNS troubleshooting tools?

    A. *Ping*

    B. *Ipconfig*

    C. *Nslookup*

    D. *Set*

17. What is required for the *nslookup* utility to work?

   A. A forward lookup record

   B. A reverse lookup record

   C. Both a forward and a reverse record

   D. No lookup records at all

18. What are the two types of queries you can test from the Monitoring tab in DNS?

   A. DNS domain

   B. DNS subdomain

   C. Simple

   D. Recursive

19. You want to ensure that your DNS server can communicate with another DNS server. Which type of query would you run?

   A. Simple

   B. Nslookup

   C. Ping

   D. Recursive

20. When registering your domain name, you will be required to supply the addresses of how many DNS servers?

   A. 1

   B. 2

   C. 3

   D. None

Answers to Review Questions

1. C, D. By configuring primary and secondary zones, multiple servers will have copies of the zone files. Incremental zone transfers will minimize network traffic when zones are updated.

2. C. When a DNS server processes a recursive query and a query cannot be resolved from local zone files, the query must be escalated to a root DNS server. Each standards-based implementation of DNS includes a cache file (or root server hints) that contains entries for root servers of the Internet domains.

3. A. Having many stale resource records presents a few different problems. Stale resource records take up space on the server, and a server might use a stale resource record to answer a query. As a result, DNS server performance suffers. Enable Scavenging in your site to address this behavior.

4. C. TTL for the cache can be set on the DNS database (per individual RR by specifying the TTL field of the record and per zone through the minimum TTL field of the SOA record) as well as on the resolver side by specifying the maximum TTL the resolver allows to cache the resource records.

5. A. TTL for the cache can be set on the DNS database (per individual RR by specifying the TTL field of the record and per zone through the minimum TTL field of the SOA record) as well as on the resolver side by specifying the maximum TTL the resolver allows to cache the resource records.

6. A. Standard primary zones don't support dynamic updates by default; if you want dynamic updates, you'll have to turn them on in the General tab of the Zone Properties dialog box.

7. A, C. The Windows 2000 DHCP server always assigns DNS server addresses if you assign them; if you put the servers into the DnsUpdateProxy group, they can also act as proxy servers that register DNS information for DHCP clients that can't do so themselves.

8. B, C. Configuring his server as a root server and leaving forwarding off means that the server will either answer a query (for addresses it knows) or return a failure (for addresses it doesn't).

9. B. *Ipconfig* /registerdns forces the client to update its registration information. *Ipconfig* /renew refreshes a DHCP lease; the other two commands don't exist.

10. B. Adding more secondary or caching name servers will distribute the load across Blaise's servers. Using incremental zone transfers will reduce the overall load, but using AD-integrated zones may not have any effect—it depends on the AD architecture.

11. D. Windows 2000 is currently the only Microsoft OS that supports sending dynamic updates to a dynamic DNS server.

12. A. When DHCP is integrated with DNS, the client always updates the A (Host) record and the DHCP server updates the PTR (Reverse) record.

13. A. To join a computer to a domain you must have the right to join a computer to the domain, the correct domain name, a DNS Server and the domain controller must be operational.

14. A. To promote a member server to a domain controller, the DNS server must support SRV records. The Dynamic Update Protocol is optional.

15. C. A failed domain controller or DHCP server would affect more than one computer. A bad or incorrect DNS host record can cause a 5- to 10-minute delay in logging in to a domain. To fix the problem, delete the suspected DNS record and login again.

16. A, C. To troubleshoot DNS you could ping the domain name or use the *nslookup* utility.

17. C. For the *nslookup* utility to work properly, you require both a forward and a reverse lookup record. If only a forward record exists, the utility will fail every time.

18. C, D. The two types of queries you can test from the Monitoring tab are simple and recursive.

19. D. A recursive query tests the ability of your DNS server to communicate with another DNS server. A simple query tests the ability of a client to communicate with its DNS server.

20. B. When registering your domain name, you will be required to supply the address to the primary DNS server and the secondary DNS server. This provides fault tolerance for your new domain name.

Chapter 7

Managing the Windows Internet Name Service

MICROSOFT EXAM OBJECTIVES COVERED IN THIS CHAPTER:

- ✓ Install, configure, and troubleshoot WINS.
- ✓ Configure WINS replication.
- ✓ Configure NetBIOS name resolution.
- ✓ Manage and monitor WINS.

In Chapter 2, "Windows 2000 Network Naming Services," you learned how the WINS protocol works and what services it provides. Now it's time to learn how you install, configure, and manage WINS services under Windows 2000. It turns out that the WINS service is largely unchanged from its Windows NT predecessor, although it sports a spiffy new Microsoft Management Console (MMC)–based interface.

In this chapter, you'll learn how to install and configure the WINS service using the snap-in; you'll also learn how to plan effectively and troubleshoot WINS installations. Don't assume that you can neglect this material because Microsoft would like to see WINS disappear—it's still an important part of the exam objectives.

WINS and Replication

Microsoft expects you to know how to configure and control replication traffic between WINS servers. First, though, you'll probably find it helpful to understand what gets replicated and why. In Chapter 2 we discussed how WINS works, but we purposely didn't talk about how WINS replication functions because it's independent of the WINS protocol itself. Replication is a service that makes the WINS data stored on your servers more useful by making it available across subnets. Consider a network with two subnets and one WINS server on each. Normally, each WINS server will collect name resolution information about the hosts on its subnet; with proper use of the WINS proxy agent, each subnet can query the other subnet's WINS server for names on that subnet. However, that's an inefficient solution since all queries from one subnet for hosts on the other have to travel to the other subnet. Replicating WINS registrations from one server to another provides a way around this problem. Because the registrations are duplicated on both servers, a host on one subnet can get the IP address for a host on the other subnet without having to actually send a resolution request to the other subnet.

For replication to work properly, a couple of additional subtleties have to be considered that you haven't learned about yet. First is the concept of *convergence time*. If you think back to the meaning of "convergence" for IP routing—the state in which every router knows about all of its peers—you'll have a good idea how it applies to WINS. In a network with more than one WINS server, the convergence time for that network is the time it takes a change from any server to propagate to all other servers. You might think that a very short convergence time would be desirable, but it's actually the opposite. Short convergence times mean that every little change is replicated everywhere. WINS registrations, though, tend to be ephemeral since machines release their reservations when they shut down or reboot. Longer convergence times therefore reduce overall replication loads by not replicating changes—like name releases—that will just be rendered obsolete before the convergence interval has been reached.

WINS releases aren't always guaranteed to happen, either—since they happen at normal shutdown, an abnormal shutdown will leave a dangling registration. Eventually, the server will purge this record, but a WINS registration doesn't carry the same authority as, say, a DNS or DHCP record.

Pushing and Pulling

The relationship between two servers that replicate data back and forth is usually described as a partnership, and the servers are called *replication partners*. A single server can be involved with any number of replication partners; in fact, in large networks it's common for a single server to replicate to most of its peers.

WINS servers use two different types of replication partners: *pull partners* and *push partners*. Both provide the same result: Data from one server is copied to another. They're always paired, so that in any partnership one server pulls while the other pushes. However, the method of initiating the replication differs, and you can set different values for the parameters that govern when and how replication works for each set of partners.

Push Partners   If your spouse has ever had to nag you to complete some task around the house, you already know what push replication is, though perhaps not by that name. A push replication partner sends its partner a notice that says, "I have new data, so ask me if you want it." This exchange happens when the WINS server starts, and you can configure it to take place when a registered client's IP address changes or when a certain number of replicated changes have arrived from other partners.

This "I have new data" message is called a *push replication trigger*, and it signals the receiving server to request the changed data.

Pull Partners   A pull partner sends its partner a request for new data by sending a record number and asking for any records that are newer. This message is called a *pull replication trigger*, and it's not unlike stopping by the neighborhood watering hole and asking the bartender if anything is new. When the partner receives this request, it sends back the requested data. A pull trigger can be sent either on its own or in response to a push trigger received from a partner.

Pull requests are sent to a server's partners when the server starts and when the specified replication interval expires. You can also manually send a pull replication trigger to a partner at any time, as you'll see in a bit.

To further muddy the waters, Microsoft's WINS implementation allows a single pair of servers to be each other's push and pull partners. For servers A and B, that means A can push or pull to B, and vice versa. These *push/pull partnerships* are often used when you want to pair up servers in even groups across a high-speed LAN connection.

Who and What

How do you pair up servers? One way is to use automatic partner configuration, a new-for-Windows-2000 feature that allows one server to seek out and link up with other WINS servers on the network. This semi-magic feature works because each WINS server announces itself via periodic multicasts. When an unattached server hears a multicast mating call from another server, it adds the IP address of the announcing server to its list of replication partners, adding it both as a push and a pull partner of itself. It then configures pull replication at two-hour intervals. While this process is nifty, it's also ephemeral; automatic partnerships dissolve when either server in the pair is restarted.

You can also manually establish partnerships, which is the norm. Once you link two servers as replication partners, they stick together like Mulder and Scully until you break the partnership up.

What Gets Replicated

WINS data is replicated at the record level; that means that as individual records are updated they can be replicated, but the entire database won't be replicated. Each change to a record held by a server causes that server to increment an internal record called a *version ID*. When a replication partner asks, "What's new?" it's really asking whether the partner's version ID is higher than the one it already has.

How do servers know which version IDs belong to which servers? Each server maintains a table called the *owner-version mapping table* that keeps track of which WINS server owns (or holds) a particular registration, along with the highest version ID received from that server. When one server sends another a replication trigger, the sending server includes a copy of its owner-version mapping table; this allows the receiving server to determine what the sending server "knows" about the state of the WINS databases.

Installing WINS

As it was in Windows NT, WINS remains a stand-alone service that you manage and install like any other network service. In this case, you use the Windows Components wizard to actually install the service, and it begins running immediately after you install it. Exercise 7.1 covers the necessary steps.

Microsoft ✓ *Exam Objective*   **Install, configure, and troubleshoot WINS.**

EXERCISE 7.1

Installing the WINS Service

Follow these steps to install a WINS server:

1. Open the Add/Remove Programs in Control Panel (Start ➢ Settings ➢ Control Panels ➢ Add/Remove Programs).

2. When the Add/Remove Control Panel window appears, click the Add/Remove Windows Components icon. This starts the Windows Components wizard.

3. In the Components list, scroll down until the Networking Services item is visible. Select it and click the Details button.

4. The Networking Services window appears. Scroll down the Networking Services list until you see Windows Internet Name Service (WINS), and then select its check box. Click the OK button.

5. The Windows Components window reappears. Click the Next button.

Once you've installed WINS, you can start its snap-in from the Start menu (Start ➤ Programs ➤ Administrative Tools ➤ Windows Internet Name Service).

Using the WINS Snap-In

WINS as a service is pretty simple. As you learned in Chapter 2, its job is to listen for "here I am" broadcasts from NBT clients, then answer queries for NetBIOS-to-IP mappings so that clients can get address data without resorting to those bad old network broadcasts. As befits a simple service, the WINS snap-in is pretty simple; its functionality is mostly tucked into the Properties dialog boxes for the server and its databases. However, there's some other stuff you need to know to manage WINS effectively. You have to be able to manage data replication between WINS servers, because the most efficient way to implement WINS is to use several servers that share data so that broadcasts and requests never have to cross from one TCP/IP subnet to another.

Microsoft
✓ *Exam*
Objective

Configure NetBIOS name resolution.

Setting Server Properties

Each individual WINS server has its own group of settings, including settings that govern when the service replicates its data and how often it backs up its database. You control these settings by selecting a server in the WINS snap-in, then opening its associated Properties dialog box. For controlling these settings, the Properties dialog box has four separate tabs: the General tab, the Intervals tab, the Database Verification tab, and the Advanced tab.

The General Tab

The General tab (Figure 7.1) controls some useful but generally unremarkable server properties:

- The Automatically Update Statistics Every check box and the associated time controls let you govern how often your WINS server parses its logs and databases to gather statistical information, e.g., how many registration attempts have succeeded or failed. While useful in the aggregate, this statistical information isn't generally critical to the success or failure of your WINS implementation, and the default interval of 10 minutes is plenty frequent enough.

- The Database Backup control group lets you specify where you want your WINS database files backed up. The Windows NT WINS server had an unfortunate propensity to corrupt its databases, which is why these backup options are present. The generally accepted best practice is to keep a backup of your WINS databases on a separate physical volume on the same computer (you can't back up databases to a network drive). It's a good idea to keep a database backup, although WINS data can always be reloaded from a replication partner if it becomes necessary.

- The Back Up Database During Server Shutdown check box is another nice safety feature: It requests that the server make an additional backup of the database when the WINS server service is shutdown. This is in addition to the backup that takes place at scheduled intervals.

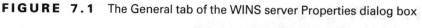

FIGURE 7.1 The General tab of the WINS server Properties dialog box

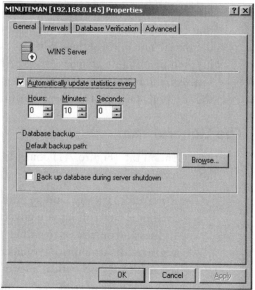

The Intervals Tab

Speaking of intervals, the server Properties dialog box also has an Intervals tab (see Figure 7.2). Unfortunately, it has nothing to do with database backups; instead, it controls the intervals at which the WINS server performs maintenance tasks on its databases. Unlike DNS, where records never expire, or DHCP, where the server handles database maintenance on its own, the WINS server allows you some measure of control over these tasks, at least to the extent of controlling how often they happen. There are four sets of controls in the dialog box; each one controls a separate maintenance activity:

- The *Renew interval* controls how often a WINS client has to renew its registration. The default value of six days is OK for most networks. Shorter values increase the load on the WINS server and network, but they also reduce convergence time.

 The Renew interval influences the values of the other intervals.

- The *Extinction interval* (four days by default) controls how long a released WINS record will remain marked as "released" before it's marked as "extinct."

- The *Extinction timeout*, set to six days by default, controls how long an extinct record may remain in the database before it's removed.

- The *Verification interval* regulates how long a stale record owned by another server can remain in the database before it's verified to see whether or not the registration is still valid. The standard value is 24 hours. Note that the Database Verification tab controls the actual settings that perform the verification.

Finally, the Restore Defaults button returns these control values to their original factory values.

FIGURE 7.2   The Intervals tab of the WINS server Properties dialog box

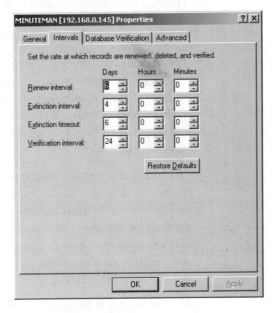

The Database Verification Tab

An inconsistent WINS database is bad. Because clients may depend on WINS for all their name resolution, it's desirable to have some way to cross-check database entries for correctness. However, that raises the question of what you check and what it gets checked against. After all, comparing two different copies of the same wrong data wouldn't do much good. Microsoft has implemented a mechanism that correlates WINS registrations between multiple servers so that conflicts or incorrect entries can be identified and flagged. Resolving conflicts or problems is still up to you, but at least you can find out where they are.

The *Database Verification* tab (Figure 7.3) allows you to adjust the interval at which database consistency and integrity are verified. In fact, these controls let you specify whether or not consistency checking is done at all. Here's what you can control:

- The Verify Database Consistency Every check box controls whether verification is turned on or not. When you turn it on (as it is by default), the interval you enter here will match the same interval in the Intervals tab—changing it in one place changes it in the other. If you want to you can turn off verification altogether, though we don't recommend doing so unless you have a very small network.

- The Begin Verifying At control allows you to specify when the verification pass begins. Normally, it begins two hours after the server starts, and the interval actually starts only after that initial pass completes.

- The Maximum Number Of Records Verified Each Period control gives you a limited way to throttle back verification. A 30,000-record WINS database is still pretty large, though, and since verification always involves network chatter between the two servers involved, you may benefit from turning this down somewhat if your WINS database has more than 1,000 or so records.

- The Verify Against radio button group is probably the most interesting item in this tab. When comparing two sets of data to see which version is correct, the choice of source is pretty important. You have two verification choices. The first is to verify registrations with the server that issued them. Think of this as verifying a driver's license by calling the issuing state's license bureau. It gives you complete verification, but it may involve calling lots of different places.

  The alternative is for you to verify data by checking it against a replication partner. If your server has only a single partner, this might not be very useful. However, since many WINS implementations use several partners, this option picks a partner at random and cross-checks the subject record against it. Using the same partner all the time might lead to a failure to spot a problem record, so the WINS verifier will automatically pick a new partner for each record it verifies.

FIGURE 7.3   The Database Verification tab of the WINS server Properties dialog box

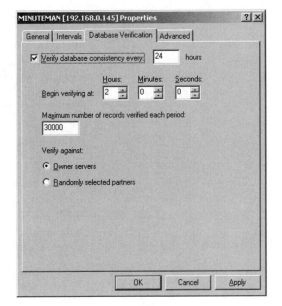

    You can also verify the database manually by right-clicking it and using the Verify Database Consistency command.

The Advanced Tab

By now, you're probably starting to figure out that the Advanced tab of a Microsoft Properties dialog box is usually one of two things. It can be either a dumping ground for settings that don't belong on other pages in the dialog box or a potentially dangerous group of things you shouldn't touch without a good reason. The Advanced tab of the WINS Properties dialog box (Figure 7.4) is a little of both.

FIGURE 7.4 The Advanced tab of the WINS server Properties dialog box

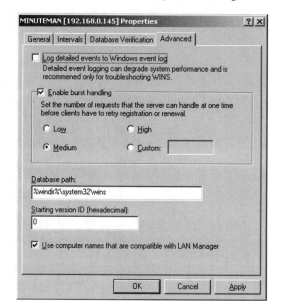

The following list describes what's in this dialog box:

- The Log Detailed Events To Windows Event Log check box allows you to turn on more detailed logging. Once you check this box, expect your event log to fill up pretty quickly, since the WINS service will begin logging each registration and renewal request as well as information about the request's success or failure.

- The Enable Burst Handling check box and control group give you gross (as opposed to fine) control over how many simultaneous requests your WINS server can accept. When you fly on a commercial airplane, there are only a limited number of restrooms; if they're all occupied you have to wait your turn. The same is true of WINS servers: If the server is busy, any client that attempts a registration or renewal has to wait until the server can handle it.

  Normally, burst handling is turned on. If you turn it off, you'll limit your server to processing a single request at a time—and that can cause a bottleneck. At the same time, you may not want your WINS server to accept lots of requests at once, so you can adjust its acceptance with the radio buttons in the control group. Selecting the Custom radio button and providing a number in the attached field will specify a firm limit on how many concurrent requests the server will accept.

- Normally, WINS databases are stored in the system's directory. Microsoft uses %windir% as shorthand for the directory where Windows 2000 is installed, so the default path for the WINS database appears in the Database path field as %windir%\system32\wins. You're free to change the path, preferably to someplace where it gets backed up regularly.

- WINS servers use a version ID in their database. This ID, which is incremented when changes occur, can be used to identify which server in a replication partnership has the more recent version of a registration. By changing the value in the Starting Version ID (Hexadecimal) field, you can twiddle the version ID of your database. Normally, you'd only do this if you wanted your database to appear to be newer than the version on its partner's database (perhaps because it had already replicated some incorrect data).

- The Use Computer Names That Are Compatible With LAN Manager check box instructs the WINS server to allow only the registration of names that are usable with older computers still stuck with LAN Manager. In practice, that means names that are less than 14 characters and contain only letters, numbers, and the underscore (_) character.

EXERCISE 7.2

Configuring NetBIOS Name Resolution

Follow these steps:

1. Install the WINS server as directed in Exercise 7.1.

2. Configure a WINS client to point to the WINS server you just installed.

Controlling WINS Replication

You control WINS replication at two levels. At the highest level, you can assign settings that apply to all replication partnerships in which the target server participates. While this is useful, it's equally useful to be able to control replication settings for individual partnerships, and you can do that, too.

Microsoft
Exam
Objective

Configure WINS replication.

Setting Properties for All Replication Partners

When you right-click the Replication Partners node in the WINS snap-in and choose the Properties command, the Replication Partners Properties dialog box appears. This dialog box has four tabs: the General tab, the Push Replication tab, the Pull Replication tab, and the Advanced tab. The defaults you set here will apply to all partners of the current server that don't have their own overriding settings in place; these settings will also apply to all newly added partners.

The General Tab

The General tab (Figure 7.5) has only two settings, and one of them is very simple. The other one, however, takes some explaining. The simple setting, the Replicate Only With Partners check box, controls whether or not this server will chastely confine its replication traffic to its defined partners. When the box is unchecked, the server will happily replicate with any server that asks it to, not unlike my dog Lightning.

The other check box has a pretty impressive name: Overwrite Unique Static Mappings At This Server (Migrate On). Remember that a WINS administrator can add static NetBIOS-to-IP mappings; these mappings stay in the database, as opposed to normal dynamic WINS records. They're normally used to provide WINS resolution for machines that aren't using NetBIOS, like Macintoshes and UNIX boxes. These static records normally work fine, but the check box is included to handle the case where the same name has both a static and a dynamic mapping attached to it. This can happen as you migrate from systems not using WINS to those that do—when the check box is on, a dynamic WINS registration request (which can only be generated by a real, live WINS client) will always trump a static mapping for the same name.

FIGURE 7.5 The General tab of the Replication Partner Properties dialog box

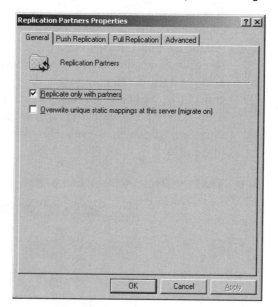

The Push Replication Tab

The Push Replication tab (Figure 7.6) lets you control how replication works for push partners of the current server. A push trigger request tells the partner that it needs to send a pull trigger. Because this is its sole function, the controls here are all pretty easy to understand:

- The two Start Push Replication check boxes let you control when this server will send push replication triggers. You can send push triggers when the WINS service starts or when a client registers a new or changed IP address with the server.

- The Number Of Changes In Version ID Before Replication control gives you a further measure of control since it allows you to specify how much drift in the owner-version mapping table you're willing to accept. For example, if you set this value to 50, you're telling your server to wait until it's accumulated 50 changes before sending out a push trigger to its partners. These changes may be changes to registrations owned by the server, or they may be changes received from other replication partners.

The Use Persistent Connections For Push Replication Partners check box is perhaps the exception to the rule that these controls are simple to understand. Normally, WINS servers will bring up new connections each time they initiate a replication, then tear the connection down when they're done. On some networks, this can waste bandwidth unnecessarily since the connection setup and teardown may have to be done several times in fairly rapid succession. To work around this, you can specify that you want a partner connection to be persistent, meaning that the two partners will maintain an open communication session even when they're not actively replicating data back and forth.

FIGURE 7.6 The Push Replication tab of the Replication Partner Properties dialog box

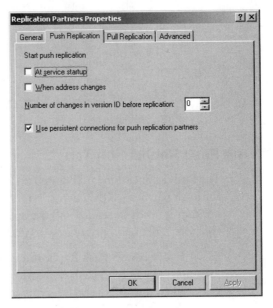

The Pull Replication Tab

You get a separate, and different, set of properties to control for pull partners, as you can see from Figure 7.7. Since pull partners actually reach out to their partners to seek updates, you have more options to configure when using them:

- The Start Time controls let you regulate when replication starts.

- The Replication Interval controls govern how often the pull partner sends pull triggers to its partners.

- The Number Of Retries field specifies how many times you want a pull partner to send pull triggers before it skips a particular partner.

- The Start Pull Replication At Service Startup check box, turned on by default, gives you a way to control when the first pull trigger is sent by the service.

- The Use Persistent Connections For Pull Replication Partners check box does the same thing as its counterpart on the Push Replication tab.

FIGURE 7.7 The Pull Replication tab of the Replication Partner Properties dialog box

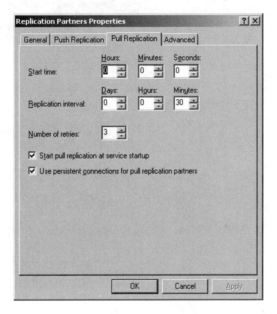

The Advanced Tab

The Advanced tab (Figure 7.8) of the Replication Partners Properties dialog box has two primary functions; it just so happens that they're not related to each other in any way.

The first function allows you to block the replication of records from certain owners. This allows your servers to remain willfully (and blissfully) ignorant of replicated data from the owners of those IP addresses specified in the Block Records For These Owners list. This is an easy way to screen out WINS records offered by rogue servers, or by servers in a test lab, that you don't want polluting your "real" WINS database.

Automatic partner configuration is the reason for the remaining controls on this tab. The Enable Automatic Partner Configuration check box controls whether or not this server will attempt to buddy up automatically with other servers on the network. When this box is checked, you can use the multicast interval and TTL controls to configure automatic multicast announcements from this WINS server (half of the mating call described earlier). Automatic partners are configured as both push and pull partners.

FIGURE 7.8 The Advanced tab of the Replication Partner Properties dialog box

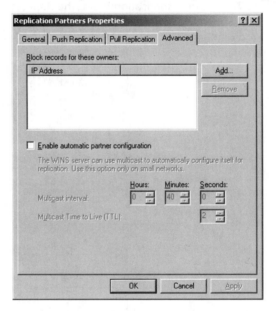

EXERCISE 7.3

Configuring WINS Replication

Follow these steps:

1. Open the WINS snap-in (Start ➢ Administrative Tools ➢ WINS).

2. Choose the WINS server you want to manage, and then expand it so you can see its Replication Partners node.

3. Right-click the Replication Partners node and choose the Properties command. The Replication Partners Properties dialog box appears.

EXERCISE 7.3 *(continued)*

4. Make sure the Replicate Only With Partners check box is marked.

5. Switch to the Push Replication tab, and then check both Start Push Replication check boxes.

6. Switch to the Pull Replication tab and check the Start Pull Replication At Service Startup check box.

7. Click the OK button in the Properties dialog box.

Choosing Your Partners

Once you've configured the settings you want applied to all replication partners of a server, you're ready to select the partners themselves. You do this from the Replication Partners node of the server.

Changing partnership status for a server requires you to have administrative access to both servers.

Turning On Automatic Partner Configuration

If you want your server to participate in automatic partner configuration with other like servers, use the controls described in the preceding section about the Advanced tab of the Replication Partners node in the snap-in.

Manually Linking Partners

Adding a partner manually is trivial: Navigate to the server you want to partner up and right-click its Replication Partners node. When the context menu appears, select the New Replication Partner command, and then specify the IP address or name of the server with which you want to partner. This adds the new server as a push/pull partner, but you can change the replication type to match your needs after the partnership is created.

Removing a Partnership

If you want to remove a replication partner from a server, open the server's Replication Partners node, then right-click the server you want to whack, and choose the Delete command. After the confirmation dialog appears, click the Yes button and—voilà!—it disappears.

Controlling Replication for an Individual Partner

Each individual partner listed in the Replication Partners node has its own list of server settings, all of which you can change. For example, you can change from a pull partner to a push partner, or vice versa, and you can set a few of the settings you just explored at the all-servers level.

When you open the Properties dialog box for a specific replication partner, the General tab doesn't show you anything except the NetBIOS name and IP address of the partner server. The Advanced tab, though (Figure 7.9), is considerably more interesting, because it allows you to change the server's replication partner type from the pull-down menu. This is a fairly innocuous change, since it only affects how the server you're managing sends requests to the partner server—it doesn't actually change anything on the partner server.

FIGURE 7.9 The Advanced tab of the server Properties dialog box

Before changing the replication type, you might want to force a replication with the target partner to ensure that you get an up-to-date replication.

In addition, there are two additional control groups that give you some control over pull and push replication with this particular partner. The controls in the Pull Replication group are a subset of the ones in the Pull Replication tab of the Replication Partner Properties dialog box; you can specify the start time and Replication interval, as well as whether or not you want to use persistent connections. Likewise, the Push Replication control group has a pair of controls that match the Push Replication tab on the All-Partners dialog box. In both cases, the primary difference is that you can't use the individual server's Properties dialog box to control what happens when the service starts.

Forcing Replication

By right-clicking a replication partner, you can send a replication trigger request directly to that partner. This allows you to force replication at any time, not just at the scheduled intervals.

Monitoring & Troubleshooting WINS

WINS is pretty trouble-free in most circumstances, with the possible exception of a corrupt database. From time to time you may find registration problems, most of which are easy to isolate and fix.

Microsoft ✓ *Exam Objective* | **Manage and monitor WINS.**

Using WINS Statistics

The WINS snap-in maintains a database of statistical information that you may find useful, or at least interesting. They include the number of successful and failed registrations, itself a good measure for how busy your WINS servers are, as well as more esoteric stuff like the number of successful and failed WINS queries.

By default, these statistics are hidden, but you can reveal them by selecting a WINS server in the snap-in and using the Show Server Statistics command (either from the Action menu or the Context menu). This pops up a floating window that displays the pertinent statistics.

If you want to clear the statistics, perhaps because you've restarted the server or have made some other change and want a clean start, use the Show Server Statistics command, but click Reset instead of OK.

If you want to control how often the statistics are updated, check out the General tab of the Server Properties dialog box (jump back to Figure 7.1).

Viewing WINS Records

It's often useful to peek at the WINS records in your database, particularly if you know or suspect that something's wrong with a particular record. However, for any but a very small WINS database, sifting through the records manually will be prohibitively time-consuming. You can actually search the database in two separate ways, both of which are available by choosing the server of interest, right-clicking its Active Registrations node, and choosing the appropriate command from the following:

- The Find By Name command lets you query the database for WINS records that start with or contain a particular string of characters. For example, you can search for all records that start with "SALES" or all that start with "SA" for that matter. You'll typically use this command to find out whether or not there's a registration for a known name, usually as part of troubleshooting.

- The Find By Owner command lets you search for all of the WINS registrations held by a particular owner. This is the fastest way to see which records any given server owns, and you can use the filtering options in the search dialog box (Figure 7.10) to screen out records you're not interested in. The Record Types tab (Figure 7.11) allows you to search or filter records for a particular type of server, e.g., a domain controller or RAS server.

FIGURE   7.10   The Owners tab of the Find By Owner search dialog box

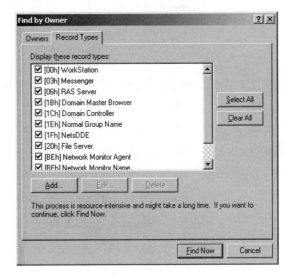

FIGURE   7.11   The Record Types tab of the Find By Owner search dialog box

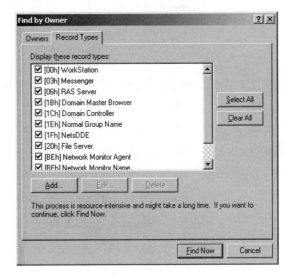

Compacting the Database

The WINS server will periodically go through its database and clean it up, deleting records that are no longer needed. This process, called *online compaction*, works fine, but it can't reclaim space that's no longer used—it just removes unused records without reclaiming the space they used to take up. To really purge your WINS database, you need to compact it while the WINS service is stopped. The jetpack.exe utility allows you to do this. Jetpack takes two parameters: the name of the database file (normally the name is either dhcp.mdb or wins.mdb) you want to compact and the name of the temporary file you want it to use. Take a look at the following example: Jetpack wins.mdb junk.mdb. This code will compact the WINS database into a file named junk.mdb; when the compaction succeeds, junk.mdb will be renamed to wins.mdb and you can safely restart the WINS service. Exercise 7.4 walks you through the necessary steps.

EXERCISE 7.4

Compacting the WINS Database with Jetpack

Follow these steps:

1. Log on to the console of your WINS server.

2. Open the WINS snap-in (Start ➢ Administrative Tools ➢ WINS).

3. Right-click the WINS server you're on, then choose the All Tasks ➢ Stop command.

4. Open a command prompt (Start ➢ Run ➢ cmd.exe).

5. Change to the WINS database directory (by default, it's winnt\ system32\wins).

6. Type **"dir *.mdb"** and note the size of the wins.mdb file.

7. Type **jetpack wins.mdb temp.mdb**. Let Jetpack do its thing.

8. Type **"dir *.mdb"** and note the size of the wins.mdb file. Did the size change?

9. Switch back to the WINS MMC console, right-click the server, and use the All Tasks ➢ Start command.

Troubleshooting WINS

Troubleshooting WINS problems is usually pretty easy since neither the protocol nor the service is as complicated as something like DNS. When you have a name resolution problem, the first step is to determine where it's occurring; this is most likely at the client side, and you'll most often hear about it when a client can't resolve a particular network name. In that case, you need to begin by asking the client the following questions:

- Is the TCP/IP configuration correct? In particular, does the client have a WINS server configured?

- Can you use the ping command to ping the IP address of the WINS server? If not, that indicates an underlying network connectivity problem that you'll need to fix.

- Is the client using DNS or WINS to resolve the name? Whichever protocol they're using, does the desired name exist on the server?

- Is the WINS server running and accepting requests?

If you identify that the problem isn't with the client, there are some common causes of server misbehavior that you'll want to check. First, verify that the WINS server is running and accepting requests. Once you double-check and find that everything is OK, the next step is normally to search the database to see if the name requested by the client exists in the database or not. If it doesn't, there's the problem! Of course, you now have to decide if the problem is that the name isn't registered or if the *real* problem is that the name is registered by its owning server but that the record hasn't been replicated.

If the desired name does show up in the database, the problem may be that the server is returning bogus data because there's an old static mapping in place (in which case, you should remove it) or because there's a problem with the database. If the database is, or appears to be, corrupt or damaged, you can either run a consistency check on it or you can just stop the service and remove the database files. When you restart the service after doing so, the server will use its replication partners to get back the data it formerly owned, as well as any updates from other partners on the network.

Summary

In this chapter, you learned:

- How WINS servers replicate their data
- How to install and configure the WINS service
- How to control WINS replication

Key Terms

Before you take the exam, be sure you're familiar with the following terms:

Convergence time

Database verification

Extinction interval

Extinction timeout

Online compaction

Owner-version mapping table

Pull partner

Pull replication trigger

Push partner

Push replication trigger

Push/pull partnerships

Renewal interval

Replication partners

Verification interval

Version ID

Review Questions

1. The owner-version mapping table does which of the following?

    A. It describes which MAC addresses own which IP addresses.

    B. It describes which software versions different WINS servers are using.

    C. It specifies the last known update held by a server.

    D. It maps WINS server IP addresses to reservations.

2. Performing which of the following functions can repair a corrupt WINS database?

    A. Stopping the WINS service, removing the old database files, and restarting the service

    B. Removing the old database files

    C. Stopping and restarting the WINS service

    D. Restarting the server in directory service restore mode

3. A pull partner sends its partners what kind of triggers?

    A. Triggers that indicate that it has changes for them to replicate.

    B. Triggers that ask whether the partner has any new data.

    C. Triggers that ask the partner to send a trigger if the replication timer has expired.

    D. Pull partners never send triggers; they're only sent by push partners.

4. A single WINS server can be _____.

    A. A push or pull server only

    B. A push server only

    C. A pull server only

    D. A push, pull, or push/pull server

5. When two servers replicate WINS data, which of the following happens?

   A. Push partners get no updates until the pull partner has been updated.

   B. The entire database is replicated.

   C. Only changed records are replicated.

   D. No data is exchanged until the two servers have authenticated.

6. Which of the following statements about automatic partner configuration is *not* true?

   A. It uses IP multicasts to identify partner servers.

   B. Automatic partnerships cannot be configured as pull or push partners.

   C. Automatic partners use a two-hour replication interval.

   D. Automatic partnerships end when either partner is rebooted or shut down.

7. When a WINS record is released, it will be marked as extinct when which of the following happens?

   A. The release interval is reached.

   B. The extinction interval is reached.

   C. The extinction timeout is reached.

   D. The tombstone timeout is reached.

8. If a static mapping and a dynamic mapping both exist, and you want the dynamic mapping to overwrite the static mapping, you should set which of the following functions?

   A. The Overwrite Unique Static Mappings At This Server (Migrate On) check box on the Replication Partners node's Advanced tab

   B. The Prefer Dynamic Mappings Over Static Mappings check box on the Replication Partners node's General tab

   C. The Overwrite Unique Static Mappings At This Server (Migrate On) check box on the Replication Partners node's General tab

   D. The Overwrite Conflicting Static Mappings radio button on the server's General tab

9. When a client can't resolve a WINS name, what should you check first?

   A. You should check for corruption in the WINS database.

   B. You should check to see whether the specified name is in the WINS database.

   C. You should check the WINS server status.

   D. You should check the client's TCP/IP and WINS configuration.

10. You can configure pull replication to run _____.

   A. At intervals, when triggered, or at service startup

   B. Only when triggered

   C. Only at service startup

   D. Only at intervals

11. WINS users on one subnet can't resolve the names of computers on another subnet, but local resolution works fine. This is probably because of which of the following?

   A. There is no available WINS server for that subnet.

   B. There is no available WINS server on the local subnet.

   C. A router or firewall is blocking WINS traffic.

   D. Replication is turned off.

12. Joanne wants to configure her WINS server to replicate changes after 15 changes have been made to the server. To accomplish this, she should do which of the following?

   A. Set the "Number of changes in version ID field before replication" field on the Push Partners tab of the Replication Partner Properties dialog box to 15

   B. Set the "Number of changes in version ID field before replication" field on the Pull Partners tab of the Replication Partner Properties dialog box to 15

   C. Create a new replication partnership for each server her server talks to, specifying a change interval of 15

   D. Rebuild the WINS database on her server to force an update after each 15 changes

13. Rick notices that his WINS server is failing to answer queries for machines on its local subnet. He determines that the WINS database is corrupt. What is the easiest way to fix this?

A. Delete the WINS database files and reboot all the WINS clients

B. Compact the WINS database

C. Delete the WINS database files and let the server rebuild its database from its replication partners

D. Run a consistency check on the WINS database

14. To back up a WINS server's database file, you should use which of the following methods?

A. Copy the files from their default directory

B. Set the database backup path in the General tab of the server Properties dialog box

C. Change the database backup path in the registry

D. Stop the WINS service, then copy the files using Windows 2000 Backup

15. Malachi has a network containing three subnets (A, B, and C), each with its own WINS server (WINS-A, WINS-B, and WINS-C). Lately, clients of WINS-A haven't been able to resolve names on subnet C. What are the possible causes of this problem? (Select all that apply.)

A. WINS-A and WINS-C aren't replication partners, or their replication partnership is misconfigured.

B. WINS-A and WINS-C are running different operating systems.

C. A router or other network device is blocking connectivity between WINS-A and WINS-C, so replication fails.

D. WINS-A has a corrupted database.

16. One of the scheduled maintenance tasks required for Danielle's network servers is compacting the WINS database. How must she do this?

A. She must stop the WINS service, use Jetpack to compact the database, and restart the WINS service.

B. She must right-click the server and use the Compact Database command.

C. She must use Jetpack to compact the database.

D. She must stop the WINS service, use the Compact Database command, and restart the WINS service.

17. You can view WINS records by searching which of the following?

A. The server name that registered them

B. The name of the record itself

C. A and B

D. Neither A nor B

18. What does the Intervals tab of the server Properties dialog control?

A. It controls when the WINS database is backed up.

B. It controls when the server will send notifications to its partners.

C. It controls when client records are renewed, marked as extinct, or verified.

D. It controls when duplicate records are purged.

19. How can you verify database consistency? (Choose all that apply.)

A. Manually, by right-clicking a server and using the Verify Database Consistency command

B. Automatically, by relying on the settings in the Database Verification tab

C. Manually, by using the Jetpack utility

D. Automatically, by stopping and restarting the WINS service

20. To filter out WINS records owned by an undesirable server, you should do which of the following?

   A. Configure your router to block WINS traffic from the offending machine

   B. Shut down the WINS service on the offending machine

   C. Use the Advanced tab of the Replication Partner Properties dialog box

   D. Remove any replication partnerships with the offending machine

Answers to Review Questions

1. C. The owner-version mapping table links the IP address of a WINS server with its last known update version.

2. A. Deleting a WINS database forces the server to re-replicate the original contents from other hosts.

3. B. Pull partners send "so what's new" triggers; push partners send triggers that indicate that they have new data available.

4. D. A single server can act as a push, pull, or push/pull server with any number of partners.

5. C. WINS doesn't use authentication, and only changed records are replicated.

6. B. Partners in an automatic partnership are configured as both pull and push partners when you enable the partnership.

7. B. When the extinction interval is reached on a record, it's marked as extinct and can be purged when the extinction timeout is reached.

8. C. The others are all made up.

9. D. Most of the time, resolution problems can be traced back to improper client configuration.

10. A. The WINS service provides three different ways to trigger pull replication: when the WINS service starts, when a trigger arrives, or when the specified interval elapses.

11. A. If the local WINS server isn't available, the client won't get any answer. Since it can't resolve remote subnet names, the most likely problem is that there's no WINS server on the remote subnet.

12. A. Push partners send change notifications, so the answers involving pull partner configuration are bogus. You don't specify a change interval, and rebuilding the WINS database won't force replication.

13. C. A will work fine; B and D won't repair corruption. The easiest solution is to remove the files and let the partners backfill the necessary data.

14. B. The WINS server's automatic backup utility is the easiest way to complete backups; just specify the path and interval and let it do the rest. The service holds the files open, so A won't work. C has no effect on the actual backup, and D will work but requires you to shut down the service.

15. A, C. The Windows NT and Windows 2000 WINS servers are interoperable and can replicate with each other, provided that there are replication partnerships. If there's no partnership, or if there's no clear network path between WINS-A and WINS-C, replication will fail.

16. A. There is no Compact Database command, and you can only use Jetpack when the service is stopped.

17. C. The Find By Name and Find By Owner commands let you search for WINS records by a substring or by which server owns them.

18. C. The Intervals tab controls when the database scavenging routines move records from one state (like "stale" to "extinct"). It has no impact on backup intervals or replication.

19. A, B. Jetpack compacts databases, so using that won't help. Stopping and restarting the service will only work if you've configured the service to verify that database at startup. You can always verify the database manually or automatically by using methods A or B.

20. C. Since records can replicate between multiple machines (e.g., WINS-A replicates to WINS-B, which replicates records for both WINS-A and WINS-B to WINS-C), the only way to screen out undesirable records is to use the Block Records For These Owners list in the Advanced tab of the Replication Partner Properties dialog box.

Chapter

8

Managing IP Routing

MICROSOFT EXAM OBJECTIVES COVERED IN THIS CHAPTER:

✓ **Install, configure, and troubleshoot IP routing protocols.**

- Update a Windows 2000-based routing table by means of static routes.
- Implement Demand-Dial Routing.

✓ **Manage and Monitor IP routing.**

- Manage and monitor border routing.
- Manage and monitor internal routing.
- Manage and monitor IP routing protocols.

✓ **Configure TCP/IP packet filters.**

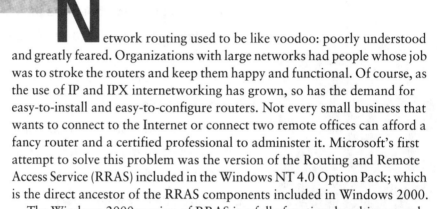

etwork routing used to be like voodoo: poorly understood and greatly feared. Organizations with large networks had people whose job was to stroke the routers and keep them happy and functional. Of course, as the use of IP and IPX internetworking has grown, so has the demand for easy-to-install and easy-to-configure routers. Not every small business that wants to connect to the Internet or connect two remote offices can afford a fancy router and a certified professional to administer it. Microsoft's first attempt to solve this problem was the version of the Routing and Remote Access Service (RRAS) included in the Windows NT 4.0 Option Pack; which is the direct ancestor of the RRAS components included in Windows 2000.

The Windows 2000 version of RRAS is a fully functional multi-protocol router. It can handle routing IP, IPX, and AppleTalk traffic, and it can be extended by third parties to add additional network protocols or routing methods. The idea behind using RRAS for routing is that you can just slap RRAS on a Windows 2000 machine and use it as a router in addition to whatever else you have it doing. For example, you could use a Windows 2000 Server computer with RRAS for routing, IIS for SMTP mail and Web service, and two NICs to serve as a combination firewall, router, and Internet server.

Although RRAS supports routing for IPX and AppleTalk networks, this chapter will stick with IP routing since that's what Microsoft emphasizes on the exam.

Understanding IP Addressing

Understanding IP addressing is critical to understanding how IP routing works. An IP address is a numeric identifier assigned to each machine on an IP network. It designates the location of the device it is assigned to on the network. As mentioned earlier, this type of address is a software address, not a hardware address, which is hard-coded in the machine or network interface card.

We're going to assume you're comfortable with binary notation and math for the remainder of this section.

The Hierarchical IP Addressing Scheme

An IP address is made up of 32 bits of information. These bits are divided into four sections (sometimes called octets or quads) containing one byte (8 bits) each. There are three methods for specifying an IP address:

- Dotted-decimal, as in 130.57.30.56

- Binary, as in 10000010.00111001.00011110.00111000

- Hexadecimal, as in 82 39 1E 38

All of these examples represent the same IP address.

The 32-bit IP address is a structured or *hierarchical address*, as opposed to a flat or nonhierarchical one. Although IP could have used either flat or hierarchical addressing, its designers chose hierarchical addressing—for a very good reason, as it turns out.

What's the difference between these two types of addressing? A good example of a flat addressing scheme is a driver's license number. There's no partitioning to it; the range of legal numbers isn't broken up in any meaningful way (say, by county of residence or date of issuance). If this method had been used for IP addressing, every machine on the Internet would have needed a totally unique address, just as each social security number is unique. The good news about flat addressing is that it can handle a large number of addresses, namely 4.3 billion (a 32-bit address space with two possible values for each position—either zero or one—giving you 2^{32}, which equals approximately 4.3 billion). The bad news—and the reason why flat addressing isn't used in IP—relates to routing. If every address were totally unique, every router on the Internet would need to store the address of each and every *other* machine on the Internet. It would be fair to say that this would make efficient routing impossible, even if only a fraction of the possible addresses were used.

The solution to this dilemma is to use a hierarchical addressing scheme that breaks the address space up into ordered chunks. Telephone numbers are a great example of this type of addressing. The first section of a telephone number, the area code, designates a very large area; the area code is followed by the prefix, which narrows the scope to a local calling area. The final segment, the customer number, zooms in on the specific connection.

By looking at a number like 256-233-xxxx, you can quickly determine that the number is located in the northern part of Alabama (area code 256) in the Athens/East Limestone area (the 233 exchange).

IP addressing works the same way. Instead of treating the entire 32 bits as a unique identifier, one part of the IP address is designated as the *network address*, and the other part as a *node address*, giving it a layered, hierarchical structure.

The Network Address   The network address uniquely identifies each network. Every machine on the same network shares that network address as part of its IP address. In the IP address 130.57.30.56, for example, the *130.57* is the network address.

The Node Address   The node address is assigned to, and uniquely identifies, each machine on a network. This part of the address must be unique because it identifies a particular machine—an individual, as opposed to a network that is a group. This number can also be referred to as a host address. In the sample IP address 130.57.30.56, the *.30.56* is the node address.

The designers of the Internet decided to create classes of networks based on network size. For the small number of networks possessing a very large number of nodes, they created the Class A network. At the other extreme is the Class C network, reserved for the numerous networks with a small number of nodes. The class distinction for networks in between very large and very small is predictably called a Class B network. How you would subdivide an IP address into a network and node address is determined by the class designation of your network. Table 8.1 provides a summary of the three classes of networks, which will be described in more detail in the following sections.

TABLE 8.1   Network Address Classes

Class	Format	Leading Bit Pattern	Decimal Range of First Byte of Network Address	Maximum # of Networks	Maximum Nodes per Network
A	Node	0	1—127	127	16,777,214
B	Node	10	128—191	16,384	65,534
C	Node	110	192—223	2,097,152	254

To ensure efficient routing, Internet designers defined a mandate for the leading bits section of the address for each different network class. For example, since a router knows that a Class A network address always starts with a zero, the router might be able to speed a packet on its way after reading only the first bit of its address. Table 8.1 illustrates how the leading bits of a network address are defined.

Some IP addresses are reserved for special purposes and shouldn't be assigned to nodes by network administrators. Table 8.2 lists the members of this exclusive little club, along with their reason for being included in it.

TABLE 8.2   Special Network Addresses

Address	Function
Network address of all zeros	Interpreted to mean "this network."
Network address of all ones	Interpreted to mean "all networks."
Network address 127	Reserved for loopback tests. Designates the local node and allows that node to send a test packet to itself without generating network traffic.
Node address of all zeros	Interpreted to mean "this node."
Node address of all ones	Interpreted to mean "all nodes" on the specified network; for example, 128.2.255.255 means "all nodes" on network 128.2 (Class B address).
Entire IP address set to all zeros	Used by the RIP protocol to designate the default route.
Entire IP address set to all ones (same as 255.255.255.255)	Broadcast to all nodes on the current network; sometimes called an "all ones broadcast."

Class A Networks

In a Class A network, the first byte is the network address, and the three remaining bytes are used for the node addresses. The Class A format is: `Network.Node.Node.Node`.

For example, in the IP address 49.22.102.70, *49* is the network address, and *22.102.70* is the node address. Every machine on this particular network would have the distinctive network address of *49*; within that network, though, you could have a whopping number of machines.

With the length of a Class A network address being a byte, and with the first bit of that byte reserved, seven bits in the first byte remain for manipulation. That means that the maximum number of Class A networks that could be created is 128. Why? Each of the seven bit positions can be either a zero or a one; this gives you a total of 2^7 positions: a total of 128. To complicate things further, it was also decided that the network address of all zeros (0000 0000) would be reserved. This means the actual number of usable Class A network addresses is 128 minus 1, or 127. There's actually another reserved Class A address, too—127—which consists of a network address of all ones (111 1111). Since you start with 128 addresses, and two are reserved, you're left with 126 possible Class A network addresses.

Each Class A network has three bytes (24 bit positions) for the node address of a machine, which means that there are 2^{24}—or 16,777,216—unique combinations. Therefore, there are precisely that many possible unique node addresses for each Class A network. Because addresses with the two patterns of all zeros and all ones are reserved, the actual maximum usable number of nodes for a Class A network is 2^{24} minus 2, which equals 16,777,214.

Class B Networks

In a Class B network, the first two bytes are assigned to the network address, and the remaining two bytes are used for node addresses. The format is: `Network.Network.Node.Node`.

For example, in the IP address 130.57.30.56, the network address is *130.57*, and the node address is *30.56*.

With the network address being two bytes, there would be 2^{16} unique combinations. But the Internet designers decided that all Class B networks should start with the binary digits 1 and 0. This leaves 14 bit positions to manipulate; therefore, there are 16,384 (or 2^{14}) unique Class B networks.

This gives you an easy way to recognize Class B addresses. If the first two bits of the first byte can only be 10, that gives us a decimal range from 128 up to 191. Remember that you can always easily recognize a Class B network by looking at its first byte—even though there are 16,384 different Class B networks. If the first number in the address falls between 128 and 191, it is a Class B network.

A Class B network has two bytes to use for node addresses. This is 2^{16} minus the two patterns in the reserved-exclusive club (all zeros and all ones), for a total of 65,534 possible node addresses for each Class B network.

Class C Networks

The first three bytes of a Class C network are dedicated to the network portion of the address, with only one measly byte remaining for the node address. The format is: `Network.Network.Network.Node`.

In the example IP address 198.21.74.102, the network address is *198.21.74*, and the node address is *102*.

In a Class C network, the first three bit positions are always binary 110. The calculation is such: Three bytes, or 24 bits, minus three reserved positions leaves 21 positions. There are therefore 2^{21} or 2,097,152 possible Class C networks, each of which has 254 possible node addresses (remember, all zeroes and all ones are special addresses: 256 - 2 = 254).

The lead bit pattern of 110 equates to decimal 192 and runs through 223. Remembering our handy easy-recognition method, this means that (although there are a total of 2,097,152 possible Class C networks) you can always spot a Class C address if the first byte is between 192 and 223.

Each unique Class C network has one byte to use for node addresses. This leads to 2^8, or 256, minus the two special club patterns of all zeros and all ones, for a total of 254 node addresses for each Class C network.

Class D networks, used for multicasting only, use the address range 224.0.0.0 to 239.255.255.255. Class E networks (reserved for future use at this point) cover 240.0.0.0-255.255.255.255.

Subnetting a Network

If an organization is large and has a whole bunch of computers, or if its computers are geographically dispersed, it makes good sense to divide its colossal network into smaller ones connected together by routers. These smaller nets are called *subnets*. The benefits to using subnets include the following:

- Reduced network traffic: We all appreciate less traffic of any kind, and so do networks. Without routers, packet traffic could choke the entire network. With routers, most traffic will stay on the local network—

only packets destined for other networks will pass through the router and over to another subnet. This traffic reduction also improves overall performance.

- Simplified management: It's easier to identify and isolate network problems in a group of smaller networks connected together than within one gigantic one.

As the saying goes, "Where there is no vision, the people perish." The original designers of the IP protocol envisioned a teensy Internet with only mere tens of networks and hundreds of hosts. Their addressing scheme used a network address for each physical network. As you can imagine, this scheme and the unforeseen growth of the Internet created a few problems.

To name one, a single network address can be used to refer to multiple physical networks. An organization can request individual network addresses for each one of its physical networks. If these requests were granted, there wouldn't be enough addresses to go around. Another problem relates to routers—if each router on the Internet needed to know about every physical network, routing tables would be impossibly huge. There would be an overwhelming amount of administrative overhead to maintain those tables, and the resulting physical overhead on the routers would be massive (CPU cycles, memory, disk space, and so on). Because routers exchange routing information with each other, an additional, related consequence is that a terrific overabundance of network traffic would result.

Although there's more than one way to approach this tangle, the principal solution is the one that will be covered in this book—subnetting. As you might guess, subnetting is the process of carving a single IP network into smaller logical subnetworks. This trick is achieved by subdividing the host portion of an IP address to create something called a *subnet address*. The actual subdivision is accomplished through the use of a *subnet mask*—more on that later.

Implementing Subnetting

Before you can implement subnetting, you need to determine your current requirements and plan on how best to implement your subnet scheme. Follow these guidelines:

- Determine the number of required network IDs: one for each subnet and one for each WAN connection.

- Determine the number of required host IDs per subnet: one for each TCP/IP computer and one for each router interface.

Based on these two data points, create:

- One subnet mask for your entire network.

- A unique subnet ID for each physical segment.

- A range of host IDs for each subnet.

An organization with a single network address can have a subnet address for each individual physical network. It's important to remember that each subnet is still part of the shared network address, but it also has an additional identifier denoting its individual subnetwork number. This identifier is called a subnet address. For example, take a parent who has two kids. The children inherit the same last name as their parent. People make further distinctions when referring to someone's individual children as in, "Kelly, the Jones's oldest who moved into their guest house, and Jamie, the Jones's youngest who now has Kelly's old room." Those further distinctions are like subnet addresses for people.

Subnetting solves several addressing problems. First, if an organization has several physical networks but only one IP network address, it can handle the situation by creating subnets. Next, because subnetting allows many physical networks to be grouped together, fewer entries in a routing table are required, notably reducing network overhead. Finally, these things combine to collectively yield greatly enhanced network efficiency.

Information Hiding

As an example, suppose that the Internet refers to Widget Inc. only by its single network address, 130.57. Suppose as well that Widget Inc. has several divisions, and each is an independent business unit. Because Widget's network administrators have implemented subnetting, the Widget routers use the subnet addresses to route the packets to the correct internal subnet when packets come into its network. Thus, the complexity of Widget Inc.'s network can be hidden from the rest of the Internet. This is called *information hiding*. Routers on the Internet see only one external address for the Widget network.

Information hiding also benefits the routers inside the Widget network. Without subnets, each Widget router would need to know the address of each machine on the entire Widget network—causing additional overhead and poor routing performance. The subnet scheme eliminates the need for each router to know about every machine on the entire Widget network; their routers need only the following two types of information:

- The addresses of each machine on subnets to which they are attached

- The other subnet addresses

How to Implement Subnetting

Subnetting is implemented by assigning a subnet address to each machine on a given physical network. For example, in Figure 8.1, each machine on Subnet 1 has a subnet address of 1.

FIGURE 8.1 A sample subnet

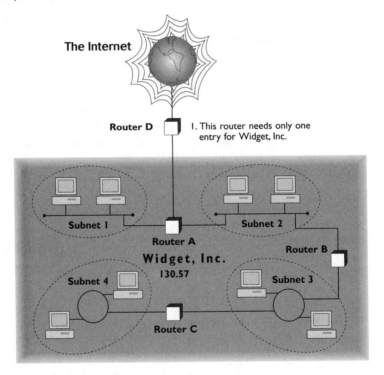

Next, you'll see how a subnet address is incorporated into the rest of the IP address.

The network portion of an IP address can't be altered. Every machine on a particular network must share the same network address. In Figure 8.1, you can see that all of Widget Inc.'s machines have a network address of 130.57. That principle is constant. In subnetting, it's the host address that's manipulated; the network address doesn't change. The subnet address scheme takes a part of the host address and recycles it as a subnet address. Bit positions are stolen from the host address to be used for the subnet identifier. Figure 8.2 shows how an IP address can be given a subnet address.

FIGURE 8.2   Network vs. host addresses

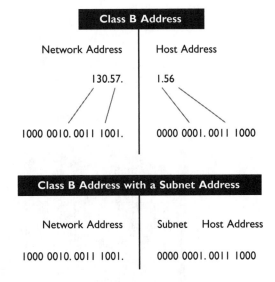

Since the Widget Inc. network is a Class B, the first two bytes specify the network address and are shared by all machines on the network—regardless of their particular subnet. Here, every machine's address on the subnet must have its third byte read 0000 0001. The fourth byte, the host address, is the unique number that identifies the actual host. Figure 8.3 illustrates how a network address and a subnet address can be used together.

Subnet Masks

For the subnet address scheme to work, every machine on the network must know which part of the host address will be used as the subnet address. This is accomplished by assigning each machine a subnet mask.

The network administrator creates a 32-bit subnet mask comprised of ones and zeros. The ones in the subnet mask represent the positions that refer to the network or subnet addresses. The zeros represent the positions that refer to the host part of the address. This combination is illustrated in Figure 8.4.

FIGURE 8.3 The network address and its subnet

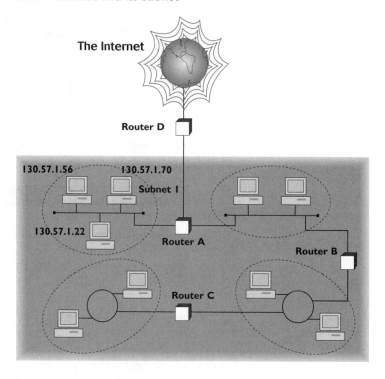

FIGURE 8.4 The subnet mask revealed

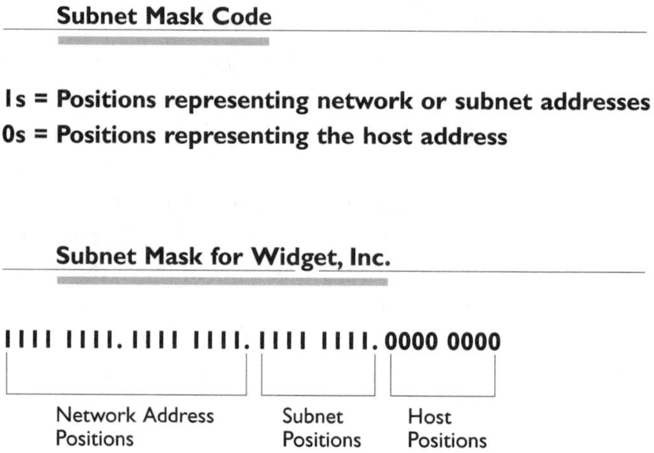

Subnet Mask Code

1s = Positions representing network or subnet addresses
0s = Positions representing the host address

Subnet Mask for Widget, Inc.

Network Address Positions	Subnet Positions	Host Positions

In our Widget Inc. example, the first two bytes of the subnet mask are ones because Widget's network address is a Class B address, formatted as Net.Net.Node.Node. The third byte, normally assigned as part of the host address, is now used to represent the subnet address. Hence, those bit positions are represented with ones in the subnet mask. The fourth byte is the only part in our example that represents the unique host address.

The subnet mask can also be expressed using the decimal equivalents of the binary patterns. The binary pattern of 1111 1111 is the same as decimal 255. Consequently, the subnet mask in our example can be denoted in two ways, as shown in Figure 8.5.

FIGURE 8.5   Different ways to represent the same mask

Subnet Mask in Binary: 1111 1111. 1111 1111. 1111 1111. 0000 0000

Subnet Mask in Decimal: 255 .   255 .   255 .   0

(The spaces in the above example are only for illustrative purposes. The subnet mask in decimal would actually appear as 255.255.255.0.)

Not all networks need to have subnets, and therefore don't need to use subnet masks. In this event, they are said to have a *default subnet mask*. This is basically the same as saying they don't have a subnet address. The default subnet masks for the different classes of networks are shown in Table 8.3. (Now you know where the familiar "255.255.255.0" comes from!)

TABLE 8.3   Special Network Addresses

Class	Format	Default Subnet Mask
A	Net.Node.Node.Node	255.0.0.0
B	Net.Net.Node.Node	255.255.0.0
C	Net.Net.Net.Node	255.255.255.0

Once the network administrator has created the subnet mask and assigned it to each machine, the IP software applies the subnet mask to the IP address to determine its subnet address. The word "mask" carries the implied meaning of "lens" in this case—the IP software looks at its IP address through the lens of its subnet mask to see its subnet address. An illustration of an IP address being viewed through a subnet mask is shown in Figure 8.6.

FIGURE 8.6 Applying the subnet mask

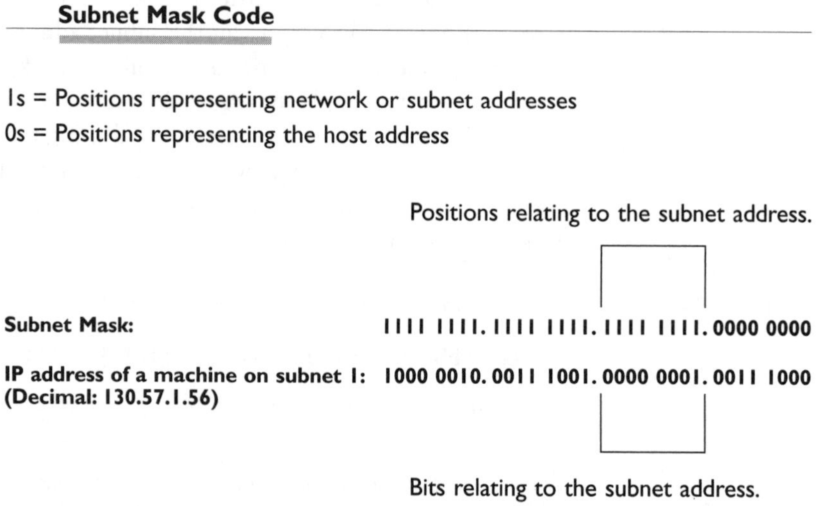

Subnet Mask Code

1s = Positions representing network or subnet addresses
0s = Positions representing the host address

Positions relating to the subnet address.

Subnet Mask: 1111 1111. 1111 1111. 1111 1111. 0000 0000

IP address of a machine on subnet 1: 1000 0010. 0011 1001. 0000 0001. 0011 1000
(Decimal: 130.57.1.56)

Bits relating to the subnet address.

In this example, the IP software learns through the subnet mask that, instead of being part of the host address, the third byte of its IP address is now going to be used as a subnet address. The IP software then looks at the bit positions in its IP address that correspond to the mask, which are 0000 0001.

The final step is for the subnet bit values to be matched up with the binary numbering convention and converted to decimal. In the Widget Inc. example, the binary-to-decimal conversion is simple, as illustrated in Figure 8.7.

FIGURE 8.7 Converting the subnet mask to decimal

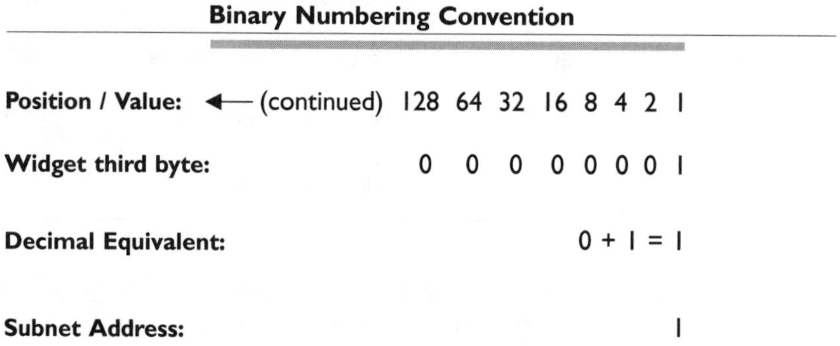

Binary Numbering Convention

	128	64	32	16	8	4	2	1
Position / Value: ◄— (continued)	128	64	32	16	8	4	2	1
Widget third byte:	0	0	0	0	0	0	0	1
Decimal Equivalent:							0 + 1	= 1
Subnet Address:								1

By using the entire third byte of a Class B address as the subnet address, it is easy to set and determine the subnet address. For example, if Widget Inc. wants to have a Subnet 6, the third byte of all machines on that subnet will be 0000 0110 (decimal 6 in binary).

Using the entire third byte of a Class B network address for the subnet allows for a fair number of available subnet addresses. One byte dedicated to the subnet provides eight bit positions. Each position can be either a one or a zero, so the calculation is 2^8, or 256. Because you cannot use the two patterns of all zeros and all ones, you must subtract two for a total of 254. Thus, our Widget Inc. can have up to 254 total subnetworks, each with 254 hosts.

Although the official IP specification limits the use of zero as a subnet address, some products actually permit this usage. Microsoft's TCP/IP stack allows it, as does the software in most routers (provided you enable this feature). This gives you one additional subnet. However, you should not use a subnet of zero (all zeros) unless all of the software on your network recognizes this convention.

Calculating the Number of Subnets

The formulas for calculating the maximum number of subnets and the maximum number of hosts per subnet are:

- 2^x number of masked bits in subnet mask - 2 = maximum number of subnets

- 2^x number of unmasked bits in subnet mask - 2 = maximum number of hosts per subnet

In the formulas, masked refers to bit positions of 1, and unmasked refers to positions of 0. The downside to using an entire byte of a node address as your subnet address is that you reduce the possible number of node addresses on each subnet. As explained earlier, without a subnet a Class B address has 65,534 unique combinations of ones and zeros that can be used for node addresses.

If you use an entire byte of the node address for a subnet, you then have only one byte for the host addresses, leaving only 254 possible host addresses. If any of your subnets will be populated with more than 254 machines, you have a problem. To solve it, you would then need to shorten the subnet mask, thereby lengthening the host address; this gives you more available host addresses on each subnet. A side effect of this solution is that it shrinks the number of possible subnets.

Figure 8.8 shows an example of using a smaller subnet address. A company called Acme Inc. expects to need a maximum of 14 subnets. In this case,

Acme does not need to take an entire byte from the host address for the subnet address. To get its 14 different subnet addresses, it only needs to snatch four bits from the host address ($2^4 - 2 = 14$). The host portion of the address has 12 usable bits remaining ($2^{12} - 2 = 4094$). Each of Acme's 14 subnets could then potentially have a total of 4094 host addresses; 4094 machines on each subnet should be plenty.

FIGURE 8.8 An example of a smaller subnet address

Acme, Inc.

Network Address:	132.8 (Class B; net.net.host.host)
Example IP Address:	1000 0100. 0000 1000. 0001 0010. 0011 1100
Decimal:	132 . 8 . 18 . 60

Subnet Mask Code

1s = Positions representing network or subnet addresses
0s = Positions representing the host address

Subnet Mask:

Binary:	1111 1111. 1111 1111. 1111 0000. 0000 0000
Decimal:	255 . 255 . 240 . 0

(The decimal '240' is equal to the binary '1111 0000.'
Refer to Table 3.3: Decimal to Binary Chart.)

Positions relating to the subnet address.

Subnet Mask: 1111 1111. 1111 1111. 1111 0000. 0000 0000

IP address of a Acme machine: 1000 0100. 0000 1000. 0001 0010. 0011 1100
(Decimal: 132.8.18.60)

Bits relating to the subnet address.

Binary to Decimal Conversion for Subnet Address

Subnet Mask Positions:	1	1	1	1	0	0	0	0
Position / Value: ← (continue)	128	64	32	16	8	4	2	1
Third Byte of IP address:	0	0	0	1	0	0	1	0
Decimal Equivalent:				0 + 16 = 16				
Subnet Address for this IP address:				16				

Putting Subnets to Work

Wait a minute, this is confusing! All those numbers—how can you ever remember them? You can step back a minute and take a look at the primary classes of networks and how to subnet each one. You'd start with Class C because it uses only 8 bits for the node address, so it's the easiest to calculate.

Class C

As you know, a Class C network uses the first three bytes (24 bits) to define the network address. This leaves you one byte (8 bits) with which to address hosts. So, if you want to create subnets, your options are limited because of the small number of bits left available.

If you break down your subnets into chunks smaller than the default Class C, then figuring out the subnet mask, network number, broadcast address, and router address can be kind of confusing. Table 8.4 summarizes how you can break a Class C network down into one, two, four, or eight smaller subnets, with the subnet masks, network numbers, broadcast addresses, and router addresses. The first three bytes have simply been designated x.y.z. (Note that the table assumes you can use the all-zero subnet, too.)

TABLE 8.4 Class C Subnets

Number of Desired Subnets	Subnet Mask	Network Number	Router Address	Broadcast Address	Remaining Number of IP Addresses
1	255.255.255.0	x.y.z.0	x.y.z.1	x.y.z.255	253
2	255.255.255.128	x.y.z.0	x.y.z.1	x.y.z.127	125
	255.255.255.128	x.y.z.128	x.y.z.129	x.y.z.255	125
4	255.255.255.192	x.y.z.0	x.y.z.1	x.y.z.63	61
	255.255.255.192	x.y.z.64	x.y.z.65	x.y.z.127	61
	255.255.255.192	x.y.z.128	x.y.z.129	x.y.z.191	61
	255.255.255.192	x.y.z.192	x.y.z.193	x.y.z.255	61
8	255.255.255.224	x.y.z.0	x.y.z.1	x.y.z.31	29
	255.255.255.224	x.y.z.32	x.y.z.33	x.y.z.63	29

TABLE 8.4 Class C Subnets *(continued)*

Number of Desired Subnets	Subnet Mask	Network Number	Router Address	Broadcast Address	Remaining Number of IP Addresses
	255.255.255.224	x.y.z.64	x.y.z.65	x.y.z.95	29
	255.255.255.224	x.y.z.96	x.y.z.97	x.y.z.127	29
	255.255.255.224	x.y.z.128	x.y.z.129	x.y.z.159	29
	255.255.255.224	x.y.z.160	x.y.z.161	x.y.z.191	29
	255.255.255.224	x.y.z.192	x.y.z.193	x.y.z.223	29
	255.255.255.224	x.y.z.224	x.y.z.225	x.y.z.255	29

For example, suppose you want to chop up a Class C network, 200.211.192.x, into two subnets. As you can see in the table, you'd use a subnet mask of 255.255.255.128 for each subnet. The first subnet would have network number 200.211.192.0, router address 200.211.192.1, and broadcast address 200.211.192.127. You could assign IP addresses 200.211.192.2 through 200.211.192.126—that's 125 different IP addresses. (Notice that heavily subnetting a network results in the loss of a progressively greater percentage of addresses to the network number, broadcast address, and router address.) The second subnet would have network number 200.211.192.128, router address 200.211.192.129, and broadcast address 200.211.192.255.

Now, you may be wondering how you can subnet a Class C network as in the table above. If you use the $2^x - 2$ calculation, the subnet 128 in the table doesn't make sense! It turns out that there's a legitimate reason to do it this way:

1. Remember that using subnet zero is a no-no according to the RFCs, but by using it you can subnet your Class C network with a subnet mask of 128. This uses only one bit, and according to your trusty calculator, $2^1 - 2 = 0$, giving you zero subnets.

2. By using a router that supports subnet zero, you can assign 1–127 for hosts and 129–254 as stated in the table. This saves a bunch of addresses! If you were to stick to the method defined by RFC standards, the best you could gain is a subnet mask of 192 (two bits), which allows you only two subnets ($2^2 - 2 = 2$).

To figure out how many valid subnets exist, subtract the subnet mask from 256. Our example yields the following equation: 256 - 192 = 64. So 64 is your first subnet.

To determine a second subnet number, add the first subnet number to itself. To determine a third subnet number, add the first subnet number to the second subnet number. To determine a fourth subnet number, add the first subnet number to the third subnet number. Keep adding the first subnet number in this fashion until you reach the actual subnet number. For example, 64 plus 64 equals 128, so your second subnet is 128. 128 plus 64 is 192. Because 192 is the subnet mask, you cannot use it as an actual subnet. This means your valid subnets are 64 and 128.

The numbers between the subnets are your valid hosts. For example, the valid hosts in a Class C network with a subnet mask of 192 are:

- Subnet 64: 65 – 126 which gives you 62 hosts per subnet (using 127 as a host would mean your host bits would be all ones). That's not allowed because the all ones format is reserved as the broadcast address for that subnet.

- Subnet 128: 129 – 190. Huh? What happened to 191–254? The subnet mask is 192, which you cannot use, and 191 would be all ones and used as the broadcast address for this subnet. Anything above 192 is also invalid for this subnet because these are automatically lost through the subnetting process.

As you can see, this solution wastes a lot of precious addresses: 130 to be exact! In a Class C network, this would certainly be hard to justify—the 128 subnet is a much better solution if you only need two subnets.

Okay…so what happens if you need four subnets in your Class C network?

Well, by using the calculation of 2^x *number of masked bits* - 2, you would need three bits to get six subnets (2^3 - 2 = 6). What are the valid subnets and what are the valid hosts of each subnet? Let's figure it out.

11100000 is 224 in binary and would be our subnet mask. This must be the same on all workstations.

NOTE   You're likely to see test questions that ask you to identify the problem with a given configuration. If a workstation has the wrong subnet mask, the router could "think" the workstation is on a different subnet than it actually is. When that happens, the misguided router won't forward packets to the workstation in question. Similarly, if the mask is incorrectly specified in the workstation's configuration, that workstation will observe the mask and send packets to the default gateway when it shouldn't.

To figure out the valid subnets, subtract the subnet mask from 256. 256 - 224 = 32, so 32 is your first subnet. The other subnets would be 64, 96, 128, 160, and 192. The valid hosts are the numbers between the subnet numbers except the numbers that equal all ones. These numbers would be 63, 95, 127, 159, 191, and 223. Remember that using all ones is reserved for the broadcast address of each subnet.

Subnet	Hosts
32	33–62
64	65–94
96	97–126
128	129–158
160	161–190
192	193–222

Are you getting all this? You can add one more bit to the subnet mask just for fun. You were using 3 bits, which gave you 224. By adding the next bit, the mask now becomes 240 (11110000).

By using 4 bits for the subnet mask you get 14 subnets because $2^4 - 2 = 14$. This subnet mask also gives you only 4 bits for the host addresses or 14 hosts per subnet. As you can see, the amount of hosts per subnet gets reduced rather quickly when subnetting a Class C network.

The first valid subnet for subnet 240 is 16 (256 - 240 = 16). Your subnets are then 16, 32, 48, 64, 80, 96, 112, 128, 144, 160, 176, 192, 208, and 224. Remember that you cannot use the actual subnet number as a valid subnet, so 240 is invalid as a subnet number. The valid hosts are the numbers between the subnets, except for the numbers that are all ones—the broadcast address for the subnet.

So your valid subnets and hosts are:

Subnet	Hosts
16	17–30
32	33–46
48	49–62
64	65–78
80	81–94
96	97–110

Subnet	Hosts
112	113–126
128	129–142
144	145–158
160	161–174
176	177–190
192	193–206
208	209–222
224	225–238

Now that you've made it through that, you can do it all again for a Class B network.

Class B

Because a Class B network has 16 bits for host addresses, you have plenty of available bits to play with when figuring out a subnet mask. Remember that you have to start with the leftmost bit and work towards the right. For example, a Class B network would look like X.Y.0.0, with the default mask of 255.255.0.0. Using the default mask would give you one network with 16,384 hosts.

The default mask in binary is 11111111.11111111.00000000 .00000000. The ones represent the network, and the zeros represent the hosts. So when creating a subnet mask, the leftmost bit(s) will be borrowed from the host bits (zeros, not ones) to become the subnet mask. You use the 16 bits available for hosts.

If you use only one bit, you have a mask of 255.255.128.0. This mask will be somewhat harder to subnet than the Class C 128 subnet mask. With 16 bits, you typically don't need to worry about a shortage of host IDs, so using 128 just isn't worth the trouble. The first mask you should use is 255.255.192.0, or 11111111.11111111.11000000.00000000.

You now have three parts of the IP address: the network address, the subnet address, and the host address. A 192 mask is figured out the same way as a Class C network address 192 address, but this time you'll end up with a lot more hosts.

There are two subnets because $2^2 - 2 = 2$. The valid subnets are 64 and 128 (256 - 192 = 64, and 64 + 64 = 128). However, there are 14 bits (zeros) left over for host addressing. This gives you 16,382 hosts per subnet ($2^{14} - 2 = 16382$).

Subnet	Hosts
64	X.Y.64.1 through X.Y.127.254
128	X.Y.128.1 through X.Y. 191.254

You can add another bit to our subnet mask, making it 11111111.11111111. 11100000.00000000 or 255.255.224.0. There are six subnets ($2^3 - 2 = 6$). The valid subnets are 32, 64, 96, 128,160, and 192 (256 - 224 = 32). The valid hosts are listed below:

Subnet	Hosts
32	X.Y.32.1 through 63.254
64	X.Y.64.1 through 95.254
96	X.Y.96.1 through 127.254
128	X.Y.128.1 through 159.254
160	X.Y.160.1 through 191.254
192	X.Y.192.1 through 223.254

So, if you use a 255.255.224.0 subnet mask, you can create six subnets, each with 8192 hosts.

You can add a few more bits to the subnet mask and see what happens. If you use 9 bits for the mask, it gives you 510 subnets ($2^9 - 2 = 510$). With only seven bits for hosts you have 126 hosts per subnet ($2^7 - 2 = 126$). The mask looks like this:

11111111.11111111.11111111.10000000 or 255.255.255.128

You could add even more bits and see what you get. If you use 14 bits for the subnet mask you get 16,382 subnets ($2^{14} - 2 = 16382$), but this gives us only two hosts per subnet ($2^2 - 2 = 2$). The subnet mask looks like this:

11111111.11111111.11111111.11111100 or 255.255.255.252

Why would you ever use a 14-bit subnet mask with a Class B address? Well, believe it or not, this approach is actually very common. Think about having a Class B network and using a subnet mask of 255.255.255.0. You'd have 254 subnets and 254 hosts per subnet, right? Imagine also that you have a network with many WAN links. Typically, you'd have a direct connection between each site. Each of these links must be on its own subnet or network.

There will be two hosts on these subnets—one address for each router port. If you used the mask as described above (255.255.255.0), you would waste 252 host addresses per subnet. By using the 255.255.255.252 subnet mask, you have many, many subnets available—each with only two hosts.

You can use this approach only if you are running a routing algorithm like OSPF (which we will talk about more later in the chapter). These routing protocols allow what is called variable length subnet masks (VLSM). VLSM allows you to run the 255.255.255.252 subnet mask on your interface to the WANs, and run 255.255.255.0 on your router interfaces in your LAN. It works because the routing protocols like EIGRP and OSPF transmit the subnet mask information in the update packets that it sends to other routers. RIP doesn't support this feature.

Class A

Class A networks have a ton of bits available. A default Class A network subnet mask is only 8 bits or 255.0.0.0, giving you a whopping 24 bits to play with.

If you use a mask of 11111111.1111111.00000000.00000000, or 255.255.0.0, you'll have eight bits for subnets or 254 subnets (2^8 - 2 = 254). This leaves 16 bits for hosts, or 65,534 hosts per subnet (2^{16} - 2 = 65534). Instead, you could split the 24 bits evenly between subnets and hosts, giving each one 12 bits. The mask would look like this: 11111111.11111111 .11110000.00000000 or 255.255.240.0. Please take the time to figure out your valid subnets and hosts. (We'll wait!)

The answer is 4094 subnets each with 4094 hosts (2^{12} - 2 = 4094). Knowing which hosts and subnets are valid is a lot more complicated than it was for either class B or C networks.

The second octet will be somewhere between 1 and 254. However, the third octet you will need to figure out. Because the third octet has a 240 mask, you'll get 16 (256 - 240 = 16) as your base subnet number. The third octet must start with 16 and will be the first subnet, the second subnet will be 32, and so on. This means that your valid subnets are:

X.1-254.16.1 through X.1-254.31.254.

X.1-254.32.1 through X.1-254.47.254

X.1-254.48.1 through X.1-254.63.254

And so on for the remaining bits.

New to Microsoft, but old to Cisco, is the way that address ranges are written. For example, an address of 131.107.2.0 with a subnet address of 255.255.255.0 is listed as 131.107.2.0/24 since the subnet mask contains 24 ones. An address listed as 141.10.32.0/19 would have a subnet mask of 255.255.224.0, or 19 ones (default subnet mask for a class B plus 3 bits). This is the new nomenclature used in all Microsoft exams.

Understanding IP Routing

IP routing is simple to understand at the most basic level: Packets have addresses, and the process of routing involves getting a packet from its source to its destination. The mechanics of how that happens are a little more complicated, though. To fully understand the rest of this chapter, you should have already read the routing-related parts of Chapter 3, you need to understand the basic ideas behind routing, and you need to know the differences between OSPF and RIP1/RIP2.

The "R" in RRAS

RRAS provides a multiprotocol router—that's a fancy way of saying that the RRAS routing engine can handle multiple network protocols and multiple routing methods on multiple NICs, all without breaking a sweat. When you consider that a Motorola 68030 running at 25MHz is what powers most of the T1-speed routers out there on the net right now, you can see why a machine big enough to handle Windows 2000 shouldn't have any trouble with routing!

RRAS provides some specific features that are of interest when the conversation turns to network routing. These features include the following:

- It can bring up connections to specific networks when the router receives packets addressed to those networks. This is *demand-dial routing*, and it allows you to use on-demand links instead of nailed-up connections. This is especially nice for ISDN, which combines per-minute fees in most places with really fast call setup times. PPTP connections can be demand-dialed, too, or you can use demand-dial interfaces to make long-distance connections only when they're needed.

- You can establish *static routes* that specify where packets bound for certain networks should go. The most common use of this feature is to link a remote network with your LAN; the remote network gets one static route that basically says, "Any traffic leaving my subnet should be sent to the router," then RRAS handles it from there.

- It provides *dynamic routing* using versions 1 and 2 of the Routing Information Protocol (RIP) and the Open Shortest Path First (OSPF) protocol. These protocols, which you should remember from Chapter 3, provide two different ways for your router to share routing information with other routers "near" it in network space.

- It provides *packet filtering* to screen out undesirable packets in both directions. For example, you can create a packet filter to keep out FTP traffic, or you can add a filter to a demand-dial interface so that it will be brought up only for Web or mail traffic. Other traffic types will pass if the link is up, but they won't cause RRAS to open the link if it's not already open. (See the section "Configuring TCP/IP Packet Filters" later in the chapter for more details.)

Some RRAS Buzzwords

You might not have realized it, but most of the material in the preceding chapters of this book just built on your existing knowledge of Windows applications and network protocols. Routing is different, though, because at bottom it has nothing to do with Windows 2000—so there's a whole new vocabulary to learn.

What's an Internetwork?

An internetwork is just a network of networks. For example, Figure 8.9 shows a sample internetwork that actually contains five distinct networks: Atlanta, Boston, Orlando, Portland, and San Diego. The internetwork is the collection of all of these networks, any of which could ordinarily stand alone. (Don't confuse "an internetwork" with "the Internet"; the Internet we all use is actually just a really large, really complex internetwork.)

FIGURE 8.9 Our sample internetwork

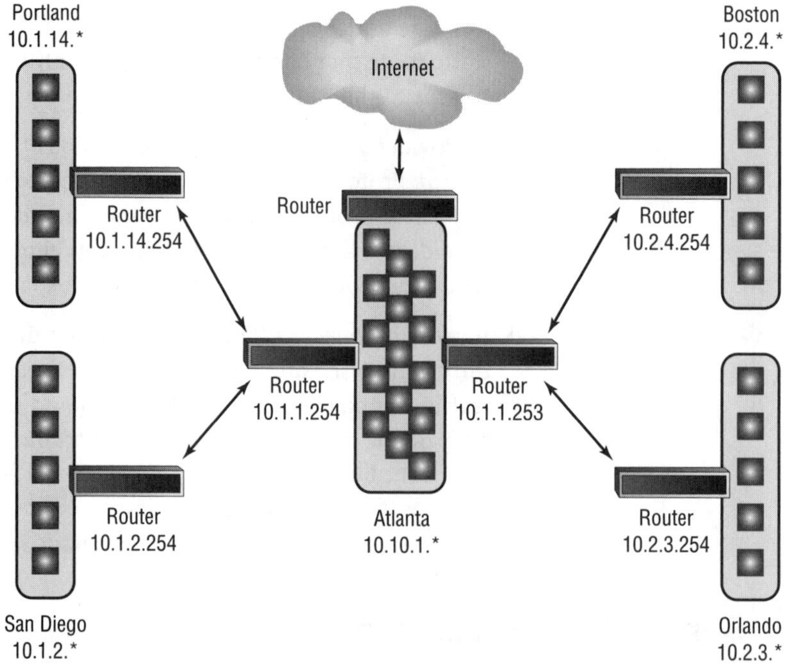

Our sample internetwork uses routers to connect the four satellite networks with headquarters in Atlanta. Throughout the rest of the chapter, you'll examine different configuration choices for the routers and how these choices affect the overall performance and reliability of the internetwork.

Routing Tables

A routing table is a database that stores route information. Think of it like a road map for the internetwork—the routing table lists which routes exist between networks, so the router or host can look up the necessary information when it encounters a packet bound for a foreign network. Each entry in the routing table contains the following four pieces of information:

- The network address of the remote host or network

- The forwarding address to which traffic for the remote network should be sent

- The network interface that should be used to send to the forwarding address

- A cost, or *metric*, that indicates what relative priority should be assigned to this route

For example, you could write the San Diego-Atlanta route as `10.1.1.0:10.10.1.254:ATL:1`, assuming that the interface name was "ATL" and that you wanted to use a metric of 1. The actual format of how these entries are stored isn't important (in fact, it's not visible in RRAS); what's important for you to know is that every routing table entry contains that information.

Routing tables actually can contain these three different kinds of routes:

- *Network routes* provide a route to an entire network. For example, the San Diego-to-Atlanta route is a network route since it can be used to route traffic from any host in San Diego to any host in Atlanta.

- *Host routes* provide a route to a single system. Think of them as short-cuts—they provide a slightly more efficient way for a router to "know" how to get traffic to a remote machine, so they're normally used when you want to direct traffic to remote networks through a particular machine.

- The *default route* is where packets go when there's no explicit route for them. This is similar to the default gateway you're used to config-uring for TCP/IP clients. Any time a router encounters a packet bound for some remote network, it will first search the routing table; if it can't find a network or host route, it will use the default route instead. This saves you from having to configure a network or host route for every network you might ever want to talk to.

Static Routing

Static routes specify how to get packets to a specific network. For example, the simplest way to configure our sample internetwork is to configure each router in a remote office with a single static route entry that routes all pack-ets for foreign addresses over the link to Atlanta. For example, say someone in San Diego wants to access a resource on the Boston network. The packet goes from the client machine to the San Diego router, which examines its routing table and finds no network route for the Boston network. The default route kicks in, and the packet goes to Atlanta, which *does* have a net-work route for Boston.

If you instead defined a static route for the San Diego-Boston hop, what would it look like? The remote network address is 10.2.4.0, and the corre-sponding forwarding address is 10.1.1.254—this combination effectively says, "All packets going to Boston should be sent to Atlanta" (sort of as Delta Air Lines does it). The interface and metric will vary according to how you set up the route.

Border Routing

Border routing is what happens when packets leave your internetwork and go to another one someplace else. Consider what happens when you use your home computer to browse a Web site. TCP/IP packets from your machine go to your ISP (probably via PPP, over an analog, cable, DSL, or ISDN connection). The ISP examines the destination address of the packets and determines that they should go to some other network that it doesn't have a direct connection to.

As an example, consider what happens when you want to fetch a Web page from Microsoft's Web site. You're dialed into a local ISP (such as `hiwaay.net`), which is connected to several upper-tier providers, including Sprint and Cable & Wireless. Microsoft uses so much bandwidth that it acts as its own ISP, but its Web server farm is located on yet another network.

Figure 8.10 shows this internetwork with a dashed border area around each piece of the internetwork: one for HiWAAY, one for Cable & Wireless, one for `msft.net`, and one for Microsoft proper. The thick black lines between borders indicate *backbone* links that join border areas together.

FIGURE 8.10 Networks are divided into border areas linked by backbones.

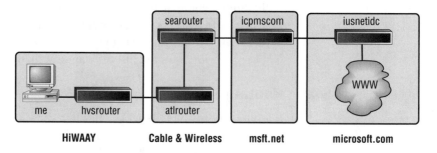

So, what does this have to do with border routing? Everything! In a border routing network, some routers are responsible for handling packets inside the area (more on that in a minute), while others manage network communication with other areas. These border routers are responsible for storing routes to other borders that they can reach over the backbone. Because this represents a huge number of potential routes, border routing normally uses dynamic routing protocols like OSPF and RIP 2 to allow a border router at HiWAAY to discover routes in the adjacent Cable & Wireless border area.

Internal Routing

Internal routing is a generic term that refers to the process of moving packets around on your own internetwork. This might seem like a bogus distinction, but it makes sense when you think about border routing. Border routers act like the ticket agents at an international airport; they can help you get from Huntsville to Hong Kong, but they're not much use if you want driving directions from the airport to the nearest Waffle House. Internal routers can use static or dynamic routing techniques to build the routing table for their local areas.

Roto-Routing

This is when a big truck comes to your house and uses bizarre flexible metal devices to clean out your sewer and septic system piping.

More on RIP and OSPF

Both RIP and OSPF are dynamic router configuration protocols, but there are some subtle—and blatant—differences.

RIP   A RIP-capable router periodically sends out announcements—"Here are the networks I know how to route to"—while simultaneously receiving announcements from its peers. This exchange of routing information makes each router able to learn what routers exist on the network and which destination networks each of them knows how to reach. Each route has an associated cost; the cost is the *sum* of the costs for each router in the route. RIP attempts to do least-cost routing by searching its routing table to find the lowest-cost route that will reach a particular destination. (If you really want lots of hard-core details on the RIP protocol itself, see RFC2453, the authoritative source for how RIP works.)

RIP has two operation modes. In *periodic update mode*, a RIP router sends out its list of known routes at periodic intervals (which you define). The router marks any routes it learns from other routers as RIP routes, which means they remain active only while the router is running. If the router is stopped, the routes vanish. This mode is the default for RIP on LAN interfaces, but it's not suitable for demand-dial connections because you don't want your router bringing up a connection just to announce its presence.

In *auto-static mode*, the RRAS router only broadcasts the contents of its routing table when a remote router asks for it. Better still, the routes that the RRAS router learns from its RIP neighbors are marked as static routes in the routing table, and they persist until you manually delete them—even if the router is stopped and restarted or if RIP is disabled for that interface. Auto-static mode is the default for demand-dial interfaces. (The opposite of auto-static mode is periodic mode, in which the router sends out updates when it has something to share.)

OSPF Like RIP, OSPF is designed to allow routers to dynamically share routing data. However, the actual process of how those routes are discovered and shared is dramatically different (though too complex to go into here). OSPF networks are broken down into areas; an area is a collection of interconnected networks. Think of an area as a subsection of an inter-network. Areas are interconnected by backbones. Each OSPF router keeps a link state database only for the areas it's connected to. Special OSPF routers called *area border routers* interlink areas. Figure 8.11 shows how this looks.

FIGURE 8.11   A simple OSPF network

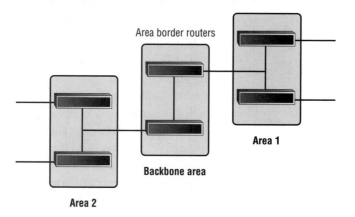

Installing RRAS

The RRAS components are installed on computers running Windows 2000 Server and Advanced Server, whether or not you choose to activate them. Before your server will be able to route IP packets (or do any of the other things RRAS can do, as discussed in Chapters 9, 10, and 13), you have to activate and configure RRAS. This process is normally handled through the RRAS Server Setup wizard. Exercise 8.1 leads you through the process of installing the Routing and Remote Access Service.

Microsoft
✓ *Exam*
Objective

Manage and monitor IP routing.

- Manage and monitor IP routing protocols.

EXERCISE 8.1

Installing the Routing and Remote Access Service for IP Routing

Follow these steps to install a RRAS remote access server:

1. Open the RRAS MMC console (Start ➤ Programs ➤ Administrative Tools ➤ Routing and Remote Access).

2. Select the server you want to configure in the left pane of the MMC. Right-click the server and choose the Configure and Enable Routing and Remote Access command. The RRAS Setup wizard will appear. Click the Next button.

3. In the Common Configurations page of the wizard, make sure the Network Router radio button is selected, and then click the Next button.

4. The Remote Client Protocols page then appears, listing the protocols currently installed on your RRAS server. If this list contains all of the protocols you want to route, leave the "Yes, all of the required protocols are on the list" button selected. If you need to add or remove protocols, click the "No, I need to add protocols" button. Click the Next button. If you specified that you need to tweak the protocol list, the wizard will stop at this point.

5. The Demand-Dial Connections page appears. It's only there to ask if you want to use demand-dialed connections or not; you still have to set the connections up (either manually or using the Demand-Dial wizard) after you complete the RRAS Setup wizard. When you choose to use demand-dial connections, the wizard will automatically set up your RRAS installation so that it can take incoming demand-dial calls as well. In that case, congratulations! You've just built a remote access server!

EXERCISE 8.1 *(continued)*

If you chose *not* to use demand-dial connections, click the Next button and you'll see the wizard summary page. The remaining steps only appear if you indicate that you want to use demand-dial interfaces. Go ahead and complete them so that you'll be ready to create demand-dial interfaces in the exercises later in the chapter.

6. If you chose to use demand-dial connections, the next page you'll see is the IP Address Assignment page, which controls how RRAS assigns IP addresses to incoming demand-dial calls. If you want to use DHCP (either a DHCP server on your network or the built-in address allocator), leave the Automatically radio button selected. If you want to pick out an address range, select the From A Specified Range Of Addresses button. Click the Next button.

7. If you chose to manually pass out IP addresses, the next page that appears is the Address Range Assignment page (Figure 8.12). You use this page to specify which IP address ranges you want handed out to incoming calls (whether demand-dial or from remote access users). Use the New, Edit, and Delete buttons to specify the address ranges you want to use, then click the Next button.

FIGURE 8.12 The Address Range Assignment page

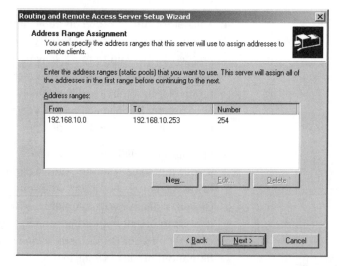

Configuring IP Routing

When the summary page of the RRAS Setup wizard appears, it's going to remind you to do either two or three of the following things:

- Add demand-dial interfaces if you want to support demand dialing.

- Give each routable interface a network address for each protocol it carries. For example, if you're using TCP/IP and IPX on a computer with three NICs, each NIC that participates in routing needs to have distinct TCP/IP and IPX addresses.

- Install and configure the routing protocols (e.g., OSPF or RIP for IP in this case) on the interfaces that should support them.

These three steps form the core of what you must do to make your RRAS server into an IP router. You begin by examining how RRAS treats interfaces.

Setting IP Routing Properties

The IP Routing node in the RRAS console has several subnodes, including the blandly named General node. When you select the General node and give the Properties command, you'll find that there are settings you can change that apply to all installed IP routing protocols on the server. These settings in and of themselves aren't earth-shattering, but they do give you some additional control over how routing works.

The General Tab

First up is the General tab, which should probably be called the Logging tab because that's all it contains. There are four radio buttons that you use to control what information the IP routing components of RRAS log. These buttons include the following:

- The Log Errors Only radio button instructs the server to log IP routing-related errors and nothing else. This gives you adequate indication of problems *after* they happen, but it doesn't point out potential problems noted by warning messages.

- The Log Errors And Warnings radio button is the default choice; this instructs RRAS to log error and warning messages to the event log without adding any informational messages. If you get in the habit of carefully reviewing your event logs, these warning messages may give you welcome forewarning of incipient problems.

- The Log The Maximum Amount Of Information radio button causes the IP routing stack to log messages about almost everything it does. This gives you a lot of useful fodder when you're troubleshooting, but it can flood your logs with minutiae if you're not careful—don't turn it on unless you're trying to isolate and fix a problem.

- The Disable Event Logging radio button turns off all IP routing event logging. *Don't* use this option since it will keep you from being able to review the service's logs in case of a problem.

The Preference Levels Tab

The Preference Levels tab (Figure 8.13) gives you a way to tweak the router's behavior by telling it what class of routes to prefer. In the earlier discussion of routing, you read that the router selects routes based on cost metric information. That's true, but there's another factor that comes into play: the preference level of the routing source. The default configuration for RRAS causes it to prefer local and static routes to dynamically discovered routes. What does that mean? As an example, say there are two routing table entries indicating routes to 216.80.*—one that you've entered as a static route and one that your router has discovered via a RIP peer. In this example, the router will always try to use the static route first; if it can't, it will try to use the RIP-generated route. You can change the router's class preference by selecting the class you want to tweak and using the Move Up and Move Down buttons.

FIGURE 8.13 The Preference Levels tab

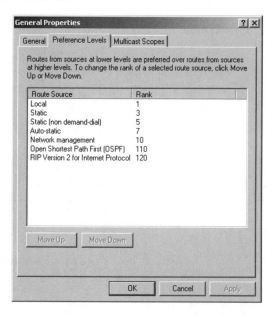

The Multicast Scopes tab is for setting and managing multicast scopes, which will not be covered further in this chapter.

Managing Routing Protocols

Routing protocols typically don't take a lot of management; once you install RIP or OSPF, the protocol engine takes care of exchanging routes with remote routers. Unlike what you may be accustomed to with dedicated routers using a router OS like Cisco's IOS, there's no way to directly edit the contents of the routing table generated by dynamic routing protocols. That means your management of these protocols is pretty much limited to installing them, configuring them to meet your needs, and watching them as they run.

Microsoft
✓ Exam
Objective

Manage and monitor IP Routing.

- Manage and monitor border routing.

Installing RIP and OSPF

You add routing protocols from the General subnode beneath the IP Routing node in RRAS. This is quite different from the way you manage network protocols in Windows NT, but it makes sense—there's no reason to install RIP or OSPF unless you're using RRAS, so it's logical that you would install it from there. Exercise 8.2 explains how to install the RIP and OSPF protocols; you'll need them installed for the later exercises in the chapter.

EXERCISE 8.2

Installing the RIP and OSPF Protocols

Follow these steps to install a RRAS remote access server:

1. Open the RRAS MMC console (Start ➢ Programs ➢ Administrative Tools ➢ Routing and Remote Access).

2. Select the server you want to configure in the left pane of the MMC. Expand it until you see the General node beneath IP Routing.

3. Right-click the General node and select the New Routing Protocol command. The New Routing Protocol dialog box will appear.

4. Select the routing protocol you want to install (in this case, choose RIP Version 2 for Internet Protocol), then click the OK button.

5. The RRAS console refreshes its display, revealing a new node labeled RIP under the IP Routing node.

6. Right-click the General node and select the New Routing Protocol command. This time when the New Routing Protocol dialog box appears, select Open Shortest Path First (OSPF) and click the OK button.

Setting RIP Properties

The RIP protocol is pretty much self-tuning. Once you configure an RRAS router to use the RIP protocol, it will quietly go off, look for peer routers, and exchange routing information without a whole lot of effort on your part. There is a small group of settings you can change through the RIP Properties dialog box (which you open by selecting the RIP node under IP Routing in the RRAS console, and then selecting the Action ➤ Properties command).

The General Tab

The General tab (Figure 8.14) has the same logging controls you saw on the IP Routing Properties dialog box General tab. That's not too surprising (hint: guess what's on the corresponding tab of the OSPF Properties dialog box?), but there's an additional control you can use. The Maximum Delay (Seconds) control governs how long the router will wait to send an update notification to its peers. (You'll learn more about these updates when you read about the specifics of triggered updates in a bit.)

The Security Tab

The Security tab (Figure 8.15) lets you control what router announcements your router will accept. By default, the RRAS RIP implementation will happily ingest routes supplied by any other router; you can restrict this behavior by supplying either a list of routers to trust or a list of routers whose routes you want to reject.

FIGURE 8.14   The General tab of the RIP Properties dialog box

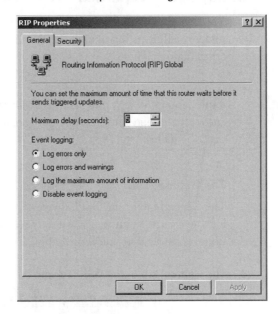

FIGURE 8.15   The Security tab of the RIP Properties dialog box

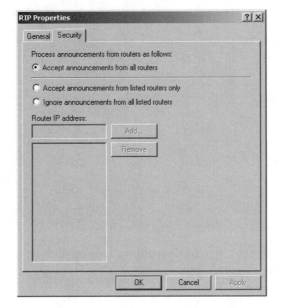

Setting OSPF Properties

You can also set some OSPF-specific properties by selecting the OSPF node under the IP Routing item in the RRAS console and opening the OSPF Properties dialog box.

If the descriptions in this section seem cursory, it's because you need to know what these settings do, not necessarily how the guts of OSPF work, to pass the exam.

The General Tab

The General tab of the OSPF Properties dialog box (Figure 8.16) contains the logging controls that you've already seen twice in this chapter, plus two additional controls that you'll probably have occasion to use.

FIGURE 8.16   The General tab of the OSPF Properties dialog box

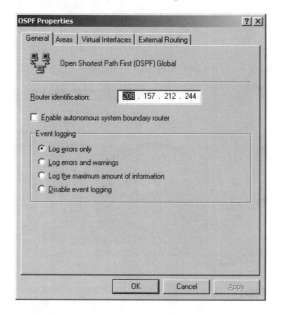

These controls include the following:

- The Router Identification field allows you to enter an IP address that your router uses to identify itself. While it's not a good idea to assign a bogus IP address as your router's identifier, you may want to choose the public IP address, even for internal interfaces.

- The Enable Autonomous System Boundary Router check box controls whether or not your OSPF router will advertise routes it finds from other sources (including its static routes and routes it learns via RIP) to the outside world. The External Routing tab won't be enabled unless you check this box; check it only if you want this particular RRAS router to try to exchange OSPF routing information with its peers.

The Areas Tab

The Areas tab lists the OSPF areas that your router knows about. You can add, edit, or remove areas from the list using the corresponding buttons below the list box.

The Virtual Interfaces Tab

Recall that OSPF conceptually divides networks into areas, some of which may be part of the backbone and some of which aren't. Since a non-backbone router won't be connected to the backbone, there has to be some other way to allow backbone and non-backbone routers to share routing information. There is—the virtual link. A virtual link connects a backbone area border router and a non-backbone area border router. Once the link is created, the two routers can share routing information just as though they were connected to the same physical network. You use the Virtual Interfaces tab to create and edit these virtual links.

The External Routing Tab

OSPF isn't the only potential source for routing information—your router can acquire routes from a number of other sources. You might not want all of those routes to be accepted and used, though. When you use OSPF, you can control which additional routing sources the OSPF components will use by checking the appropriate boxes on the External Routing tab (Figure 8.17). The two radio buttons at the top, Accept Routes From All Route Sources Except Those Selected and Ignore Routes From All Route Sources Except Those Selected, let you control the meaning of the check boxes in the Route sources list. By default, OSPF will accept all routes from all sources. To turn off individual route sources (say, static routes), check the appropriate box. If you want to reject all route sources *except* for a particular group, use the Ignore Routes radio button, and then check the route sources you do want to use.

This tab will be active only if you check the Enable Autonomous System Boundary Router check box on the General tab.

FIGURE 8.17 The External Routing tab of the OSPF Properties dialog box

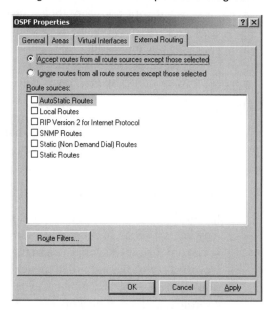

The Route Filters button allows you to either ignore or accept individual routes. This is a handy way to screen out particular routes that you don't want without disallowing entire classes of route source information.

Managing Static Routes

When you use static routes, there's some good news and some bad news. The good news is that they're simple to manage and configure since they don't participate in any kind of automatic discover process. Static routes are conceptually very simple—they combine a destination network address with a subnet mask to provide a list of potential destinations. (For more on TCP/IP subnetting, see the Sybex book *TCP/IP: 24Seven.*) The destination addresses are reached through a particular interface on your router, and they're sent to a specified gateway (normally another router, either on your end or on some remote network). Finally, there's a metric associated with the static route.

Microsoft
✓ ***Exam***
Objective

Install, configure, and troubleshoot IP routing protocols.

• Update a Windows 2000-based routing table by means of static routes.

You create new static routes in two ways: by using the *route add* command from the command line or by right-clicking the Static Routes node in the RRAS console and using the New Static Route command. The next sections will take a look at how those methods work.

Using *route add*

The *route add* command allows you to add new static routes; you can choose whether these routes remain in the routing table after the system reboots. Routes that stick around in this manner are called persistent routes. The command itself is simple:

```
route add destination mask netMask gateWay metric interface
```

You specify the destination, net mask, gateway, metric, and interface name on the command line. These parameters are all required, and *route add* does some basic sanity checking to make sure that the net mask and destination match and that you haven't left anything out. One speed bump: You have to specify the interface as a number, not as a name. However, the *route print* command (which will be covered a little later) lists its interfaces and the associated numbers.

Using RRAS

When you create a new static route using the RRAS console, all you have to do is choose the New Static Route command, and you'll see the Static Route dialog box (Figure 8.18). You have to provide the same parameters as with the *route add* command—the interface you want to use to connect, the destination and network mask, the gateway for the outbound packets, and a metric. If you're creating a route that's not bound to a LAN interface, you can also use the Use This Route To Initiate Demand-Dial Connections check box to specify that the route should bring up a new demand-dial connection on the specified interface.

FIGURE 8.18 Use the Static Route dialog box to create new static routes

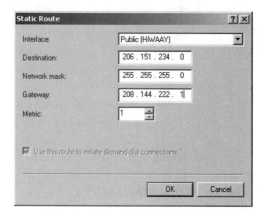

EXERCISE 8.3

Adding and Removing Static Routes

Follow these steps to add, then remove, a static route (you remove it only to make sure it doesn't interfere with any other machines on your network):

1. Open the RRAS MMC console (Start ➤ Programs ➤ Administrative Tools ➤ Routing and Remote Access).

2. Select the server you want to configure in the left pane of the MMC. Expand it until you see the Static Routes node beneath IP Routing.

3. Right-click the Static Routes node and select the New Static Route command. The Static Route dialog box will appear (as seen previously in Figure 8.18).

4. Select the interface you want to use from the Interface pull-down list; you can use the internal interface or any other interface you've already defined.

5. Enter the destination address (try 216.92.80.0) and a net mask of 255.255.255.0.

6. For the gateway address, enter the IP address of your RRAS server.

7. Click the OK button. The RRAS console will reappear.

8. Right-click the Static Routes item and choose the Show IP Routing Table command. The IP Routing Table window will appear. Verify that your newly added static route is present in the table.

9. Select the Static Routes item. Note that the right pane of the MMC changes to list all static routes that you've defined. Compare the list with the contents of the IP Routing Table window.

10. Right-click the static route you added and use the Delete command to remove it.

Creating and Managing Interfaces

The Routing Interfaces node in the RRAS snap-in shows you a summary of the routable interfaces available on your machine for *all* protocols. It lists all of the LAN and demand-dial interfaces, plus two special interfaces maintained by RRAS: Loopback and Internal. Each of the interfaces displayed has a type, a status (either enabled or disabled), and a connection status associated with it. For example, one of the machines in our test lab has two LAN interfaces—"Public (HiWAAY)" and "Private (192.168.0.x)" shown. Each of those interfaces represents a potential destination for routed packets.

For each of the interfaces, you can right-click it to get a context menu with some useful commands, including Disable, Enable, and the ever-popular Unreachability Reason (that command tells you why an interface is marked as "unreachable"). There are some commands specific to demand-dial interfaces, which will be covered in the following sections.

What "Unreachable" Really Means

A demand-dial interface can have several different states. First off, the enabled and disabled states that appear in the Status column indicate whether the link is administratively available—that is, whether you're allowing people to use it or not. The Connection State column shows you whether the connection is *working* or not, which makes it more useful. The default state for a demand-dial connection is Disconnected, which is perfectly reasonable. When RRAS tries to establish a connection, the state changes to Connected—also eminently logical. In both the connected and disconnected states, any static routes tied to the demand-dial interface are available.

When RRAS tries to dial a number and fails to connect, it will continue to try again until it reaches the redial limit set in the Dialing tab of the interface's Properties dialog box. If the redial limit is reached, the interface will be marked as Unreachable for a timeout period. As long as the interface is unreachable, any static routes pointing to it will be unavailable—they'll actually disappear from the routing table. After the timeout period, RRAS will try again to dial; if it fails this time, it tacks another ten minutes onto the timeout and tries again. The timeout starts at ten minutes and works up from there; if it reaches six hours, it will stop incrementing the counter so the timeout will stay there until a successful connection is made or until you restart the RRAS service.

Fortunately, you can adjust both the minimum and maximum values for this timeout from their defaults (ten minutes and six hours, respectively). You make this change by adding two REG_DWORD values to HKLM\System\ CurrentControlSet\Services\Router\Interfaces\InterfaceName (where *InterfaceName* matches the name of the interface for which you want to change the time). The MinUnreachabilityInterval value controls both the minimum retry interval *and* how much the retry interval is incremented after each failure; the MaxUnreachabilityInterval sets the upper limit. Both of these values must be expressed in seconds.

Managing LAN Interfaces

Each LAN interface has properties of its own; these interfaces, which appear when you select the General node under the IP Routing node in RRAS, correspond to the LAN interfaces you've defined in RRAS. These interfaces allow you to set general properties for the interface; once you add specific routing protocols to the interface, you can configure those protocols individually (as you'll see in a short while). To see the properties for an interface, just select the General node in the console, pick the interface of interest from the right-hand pane, and use the Action ➢ Properties command.

The General Tab

The General tab (Figure 8.19) allows you to set some useful parameters for the entire interface, including whether or not this interface will send out router discovery advertisements so that other routers on your network can find it.

FIGURE 8.19 The General tab

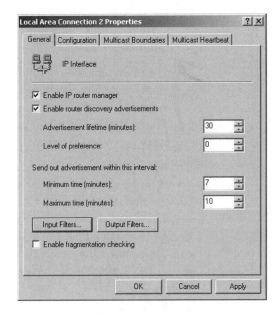

The controls on the General tab do the following:

- The Enable IP Router Manager check box controls whether this interface allows IP routing at all. When checked, the administrative status of this interface will appear as "Up," indicating that it's available for routing traffic. When unchecked, the interface will be marked as "Down," and it won't route any packets nor will other routers be able to communicate with it.

- The Enable Router Discovery Advertisements check box controls whether or not this router will broadcast *router discovery messages*. These messages allow clients to find a "nearby" (in network terms) router without any manual configuration on your part. When this check box is enabled, the other controls below it become active so you can set the following fields:

  - How long advertisements are valid, as in the Advertisement Lifetime (Minutes) field. Clients will ignore any advertisement they receive after its lifetime has expired.

- What preference level is assigned to the use of this particular router. Clients use routers with higher preferences first; if there's more than one router with equal preference levels, the client can randomly select one.

- The minimum and maximum time intervals for sending advertisements. RRAS will send out advertisements at a randomly chosen interval that falls between the minimum and maximum; with the default settings, that means RRAS will send an advertisement every seven to ten minutes.

- The Input Filters and Output Filters buttons allow you to selectively accept or reject packets on the specified interface. You can accept all packets that don't trigger a filter, or accept only those packets that match filter criteria. Each type of filter can use the source or destination IP address and net mask as filter criteria. For example, you can construct a filter that rejects all packets from 206.151.234.0 with a net mask of 255.255.255.0; that effectively screens out any traffic from that subnet.

- The Enable Fragmentation Checking check box tells your router to reject any fragmented IP packets instead of accepting them for processing. Since flooding a router with fragmented IP packets is a popular denial-of-service attack, you may want to check this box.

The Configuration Tab

The Configuration tab (Figure 8.20) may seem out of place in the Interface Properties dialog box, since it essentially duplicates what you see when you edit the properties of a LAN interface from the Network and Dial-Up Connections folder. You use this tab to set the IP address, subnet mask, and default gateway for an interface if you want it to use a different set of parameters than the ones defined for the interface. The Advanced button allows you to specify multiple IP addresses and default gateways, just as the TCP/IP Properties dialog box does.

There are two other tabs in the Interface Properties dialog box but they're related to multicasting, which is beyond the scope of this exam.

FIGURE 8.20   The Configuration tab

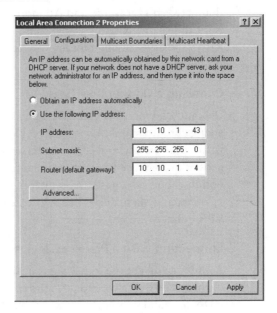

Setting Up Demand-Dial Interfaces

When you install RRAS, it will automatically create an interface for each LAN connection it can find. You're on your own, however, if you want to create new demand-dial interfaces. Fortunately, there's an easy way to do this with the Demand Dial Interface wizard, which you activate with the New Demand-Dial Interface command (available when you right-click the Routing Interfaces node in the RRAS console).

Microsoft
✓ *Exam*
Objective

Install, configure, and troubleshoot IP routing protocols.

- Implement demand-dial routing.

Naming the Interface

The first step in the wizard is the Interface Name page, where you specify the name you want the new interface to have. This is the name you'll see in the RRAS console, so you should choose some name that identifies the source and destination of the connection (for example, "HSV-ATL" for a connection between Huntsville and Atlanta). This is particularly useful when you want to use one RRAS console somewhere on a network to manage many RRAS servers—having an easy way to see which link you're working with can be very valuable.

Choosing a Connection Type

Demand-dial interfaces can use a physical device (like a modem or an ISDN adapter) or a virtual private networking (VPN) connection. For example, you can have a demand-dial connection that opens a VPN tunnel to a remote network when it sees traffic destined for that network. Depending on which option you choose here, the remaining wizard pages will differ. (Skip to "Connecting via a VPN" below if you want to establish a demand-dialed VPN connection.)

Connecting with a Physical Device

Assuming you choose to use a physical device as the basis for your network, the next step in the wizard prompts you to choose a device (like a modem or ISDN terminal adapter) to use for this demand-dial interface. If the device you want to use doesn't already exist, you'll need to add it; for that reason, you're probably best off adding and configuring modems and so on before setting up RRAS.

Connecting via a VPN

If you specify that you want to use a VPN connection, the next step is to specify what type of VPN connection to use. You do this through the VPN Type page, which offers you the following three choices:

- The Automatic radio button tells RRAS to figure out the connection type when negotiating with the remote server. This is the most flexible choice, so it's selected by default.

- The Point-to-Point Tunneling Protocol (PPTP) radio button tells RRAS that this connection will always use PPTP.

- Likewise, the Layer 2 Tunneling Protocol (L2TP) radio button indicates that you want this connection to always use L2TP.

Who You Gonna Call?

The next step is the same for both VPN and physical connections, even though the wizard page is labeled differently. For VPNs you'll see a page titled Network Address, while for ordinary dial-up connections the page is labeled Phone Number. In either case, you should enter the phone number or IP address (whichever is appropriate) of the remote router.

Setting Routing and Security Options

The next step for both types of router connection is the Protocols and Security page (Figure 8.21), which contains five configuration check boxes. They are the following:

- The Route IP Packets On This Interface and Route IPX Packets On This Interface check boxes control whether this interface will handle the specified packet types or not. By default, IP routing is enabled but IPX routing isn't.

- If you want to add a user account so that a remote router (running RRAS or not) can dial in, check the Add A User Account So A Remote Router Can Dial In check box. When this check box is active, you can also choose to require that the remote router authenticates itself (using the same credentials) when you call it—just check the Authenticate Remote Router When Dialing Out check box.

- Some routers can handle PAP, CHAP, or MS-CHAP authentication, but others can only handle PAP. If your remote partner falls into this latter group, make sure that Send A Plain-Text Password If That Is The Only Way To Connect is checked.

- If the system that your RRAS server is calling isn't running RRAS, it may expect you to manually interact with it, perhaps through a terminal window. This is what the last check box, Use Scripting To Complete The Connection With The Remote Router, is for—check it and you'll get a terminal window after the modem connects so you can provide whatever commands or authenticators you need.

FIGURE 8.21 The Protocols and Security page

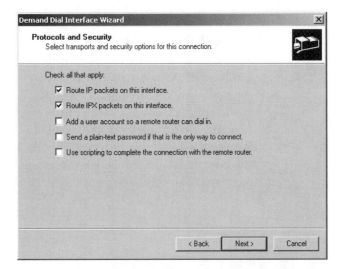

Setting Dial-In Credentials

If you choose to allow remote routers to dial in to the RRAS machine you're setting up, you'll have to create a user account with appropriate permissions. The Demand Dial Interface wizard handles the account creation process for you, assuming you fill out the Dial-In Credentials page (Figure 8.22). Microsoft recommends that you pick a username that makes evident which routers use the link; in this case, "HSV-MCO" tells you right away that this account is used for the Huntsville-Orlando link. You can use ICAO airport identifiers, city names, or whatever else you like, so long as you can figure out what's what.

FIGURE 8.22   The Dial-In Credentials page

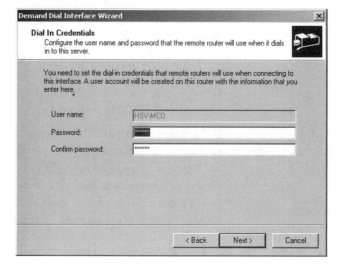

Setting Dial-Out Credentials

If you want your router to initiate calls to another router, you'll need to tell your local RRAS installation what credentials to use when it makes an outgoing call. Unlike the Dial-In Credentials page (Figure 8.23), RRAS makes no attempt to do anything with the credentials you provide on this page. (Actually, it does check the two password fields to make sure you've typed the same password into each one, but that's it.) The credentials you provide here must match the credentials the remote router expects to see, or your router won't be able to authenticate itself to the remote end.

FIGURE 8.23   The Dial-Out Credentials page

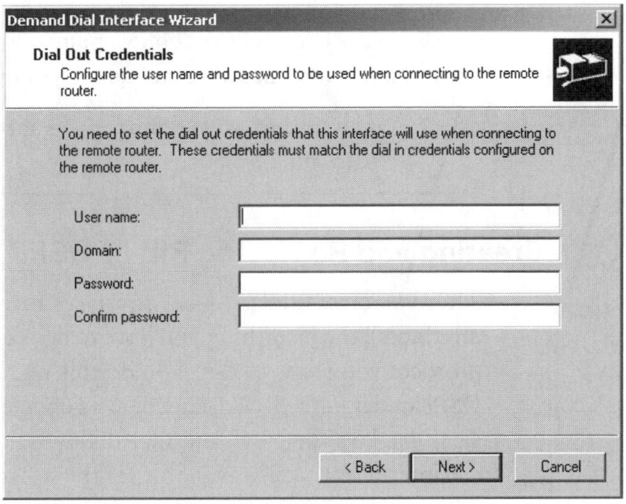

EXERCISE 8.4

Creating a Demand-Dial Interface

In this exercise, you'll create a simple demand-dial interface. This requires you to have the phone number, user name, and password for the remote end (your ISP or whomever you're calling).

1. Open the RRAS MMC console, select the server you want to create the interface on, and select its Routing Interfaces node.

2. Right-click the Routing Interfaces node and select the New Demand Dial Interface command. This starts the Demand Dial Interface wizard. Click the Next button on the first wizard page (and after each of the subsequent steps).

3. Specify a name for the interface on the Interface Name page.

4. Select the Connect Using A Modem, ISDN Adapter, Or Other Physical Device radio button on the Connection Type page.

5. On the Protocols and Security page, make sure the Route IP Packets On This Interface check box is the only one selected.

6. In the Dial Out Credentials page, fill in the username, domain (if any), and password needed to connect to the remote network.

7. When the wizard summary page appears, click the Finish button to create the interface.

Creating and Removing RIP or OSPF Interfaces

After you create the physical interfaces (using either demand-dial or LAN interfaces), the next thing you have to do is create an interface for the routing protocol you want to use. You do this by right-clicking either the RIP or OSPF nodes in the RRAS console and choosing the New Interface command. That displays the New Interface dialog box, which simply lists all the physical interfaces that are available for the selected protocol. For example, if you have two NICs in a computer and have already bound RIP to both of them, you can add OSPF to either or both, but when you try to add another RIP interface you'll get an error message.

Once you select the interface you want to use and if RRAS can create the interface, it adds the interface to the appropriate item in the console and opens the corresponding properties dialog box.

You can remove a RIP or OSPF interface by selecting it in the appropriate folder and pressing the Delete key, by using the Action ➤ Delete command, or by using the Delete command on the context menu.

Setting RIP Interface Properties

RIP interfaces have their own properties, all of which are specific to the RIP protocol. You adjust these settings by selecting the RIP interface and using the familiar Properties command from the Context or Action menus.

The General Tab

The General tab of the RIP Interface Properties dialog box (Figure 8.24) lets you control the router's operational mode, which protocols it uses to send and accept packets, and a couple of other useful things.

FIGURE 8.24   The General tab of the RIP Interface Properties dialog box

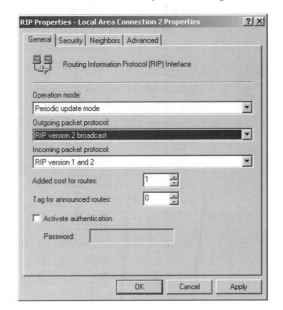

Here's what you can do with the General tab:

- The Operation Mode pull-down list controls the router's mode. By default, demand-dial interfaces will be set to auto-static update mode, while LAN interfaces will be set to use periodic update mode.

- The Outgoing Packet Protocol pull-down list controls what kind of RIP packets this router sends out. If your network has all RIP version 2 routers, choose RIP Version 2 Multicast to make RRAS send out efficient RIP multicasts; if you have a version 1 or a mix of version 1 and version 2, there are selections for those, too. The fourth choice, Silent RIP, is useful when you want your RRAS router to listen to other routers' routes but not advertise any of its own. Typically, you'll use Silent RIP when you're using RRAS to connect a small network (like a branch office) that doesn't have any other routers to a larger network—the small network doesn't have any routes to advertise because it's only connected to one remote network.

- Use the Incoming Packet Protocol pull-down list to specify what kinds of RIP packets this interface will accept. You can choose to accept only RIP version 1 packets, only RIP version 2 packets, both version 1 and version 2 packets, or none at all. The default setting is to accept both version 1 and version 2 packets.

- The Added Cost For Routes field lets you control how much this router will increase the route cost. Normally, it's best to leave this as 1 since setting it too high may increase the interface's cost so much that no one uses it (unless, of course, that's what you *want* to happen!).

- The Tag For Announced Routes field gives you a way to supply a tag included in all RIP packets sent by this router. RRAS doesn't use RIP tags, but other routers can use them.

- The Activate Authentication check box and Password field give you an identification tool for use with your routers. If you turn on authentication, all incoming and outgoing RIP packets must contain the specified password. Therefore, all of this router's neighbors need to use the same password. The password is transmitted as clear text, so this option doesn't provide you with any security.

The Security Tab

The Security tab (see Figure 8.25) helps you regulate which routes your RIP interface will accept from and broadcast to its peers. There are good reasons to be careful about which routes you accept into your routing table since a malicious attacker can simply flood your router with bogus routes and watch, laughing, as your routers send traffic off on a wild goose chase. Likewise, you may not want to advertise every route in your routing table, particularly if the same routers handle both Internet and intranet traffic. You can use the controls on this tab to discard routes that fall within a particular range of addresses, or you can accept only those routes that fall within a particular range.

FIGURE 8.25   The Security tab of the RIP Interface Properties dialog box

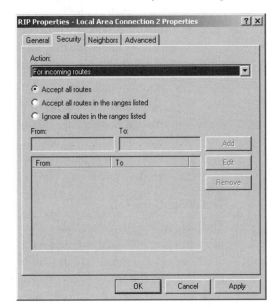

The default setting is to accept all routes, but you can change it using these controls:

- The Action pull-down list lets you choose whether you want to impose settings on incoming routes that your router hears from its peers or on outgoing routes that it announces. Depending on which of these options you choose, the wording of the three radio buttons below the pull-down will change.

- The From and To fields, the Add, Edit, and Remove buttons, and the address range list are all used to specify which set of addresses you want to use with the restriction radio buttons.

- The restriction radio buttons in the center of the dialog box control the action applied to incoming or outgoing routes:

  - The default setting, "Announce all routes" (outgoing) or "Process all routes" (incoming) does just that—all routes are accepted or announced, no matter the source.

- Selecting "Announce all routes in the ranges listed" (outgoing) or "Accept all routes in the range listed" (incoming) causes RRAS to silently ignore any routes that fall outside of the specified ranges. You normally use this option when you want to limit the scope of routes that your router can exchange traffic over.

- The "Do not announce all routes in the range listed" (outgoing) and "Ignore all routes in the ranges listed" (incoming) settings tells RRAS to silently ignore any routes that fall within the specified ranges. This is useful for filtering out routes that you don't want to make available, or those you don't want to use to reach remote systems.

The Neighbors Tab

The Neighbors tab (Figure 8.26) gives you a finer degree of control over how this particular interface interacts with its peer RIP routers. By specifying a list of trusted neighbor routers (an OSPF concept that Microsoft's mixed in to its RIP implementation), you can choose to use neighboring routers' routes in addition to, or instead of, broadcast and multicast RIP announcements.

FIGURE 8.26 The Neighbors tab of the RIP Interface Properties dialog box

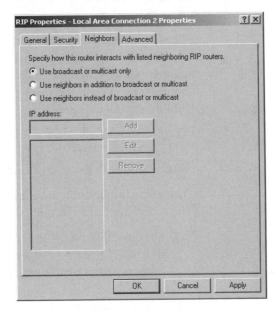

You will see the following radio buttons on the Neighbors tab:

- The Use Broadcast Or Multicast Only radio button tells RRAS to ignore any RIP neighbors. This is the default setting. It means that any router that can successfully broadcast or multicast routes to you can load its routes into your routing table.

- The Use Neighbors In Addition To Broadcast Or Multicast radio button tells RRAS to accept routes from RIP peers as well as from the neighbors you've specified.

- The Use Neighbors Instead Of Broadcast Or Multicast radio button indicates that you don't trust RIP announcements that your router picks up from the net; instead, you're telling RRAS to trust only those neighbors that are defined in the neighbor list.

Speaking of the neighbor list, you manage the list of trusted neighbor routers using the IP address field, the Add, Edit, and Remove buttons, and the list itself. These controls are enabled when you specify that you want to use neighbor-supplied routing information; once the controls are activated, you can add router IP addresses to the neighbor list.

The Advanced Tab

The Advanced tab (Figure 8.27) contains twelve controls that govern some fairly esoteric RIP behavior. Though it may be esoteric, you still need to know what these controls do and how they work for the exam, so read on.

FIGURE 8.27   The Advanced tab of the RIP Interface Properties dialog box

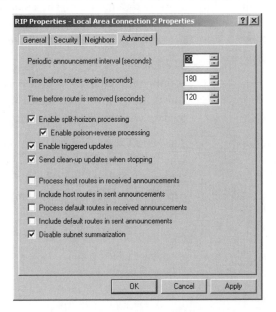

The first three controls are only active when you turn on periodic update mode on the General tab:

- The Periodic Announcement Interval (Seconds) field controls the interval at which periodic router announcements are made.

- The Time Before Routes Expire (Seconds) field controls how long the route may stay in the routing table before it's considered to be expired. The arrival of a new RIP announcement for the route resets the timer—it will be marked as invalid only if it reaches the expiration timer without being renewed through a new announcement.

- The Time Before Route Is Removed (Seconds) field controls the interval that may pass between the time a route expires and the time it's removed.

The next group of check boxes controls update processing and loop detection:

- The Enable Split-Horizon Processing check box turns on split-horizon processing, in which a route learned by a RIP router on a network is not rebroadcast to that network. Split-horizon processing helps prevent routing loops, so it's on by default.

  The Enable Poison-Reverse Processing check box (which is only active when the Enable Split-Horizon Processing check box is on) modifies the way split-horizon processing works. When poison-reverse is turned on, routes learned from a network are rebroadcast to the network with a metric of 16, a special value that tells other routers that the route is unreachable. It also prevents routing loops while still keeping the routing tables up to date.

- The Enable Triggered Updates check box indicates whether you want routing table changes to be immediately sent out when they're noticed (the default) or not. Triggered updates help keep the routing table up-to-date with minimum latency.

- The Send Clean-Up Updates When Stopping check box controls whether or not RRAS will send out announcements that mark the routes it was handling as unavailable. This immediately lets its RIP peers know that the routes it was servicing are no longer usable.

The last set of controls governs what happens with host and default routes (remember them from earlier in the chapter?):

- By default, RRAS ignores any host routes it sees in RIP announcements. Turn on the Process Host Routes In Received Announcements check box if you want it to honor those routes instead of ignoring them.

- The Include Host Routes In Sent Announcements check box directs RRAS to send host route information as part of its RIP announcements; normally it won't do this.

- The Process Default Routes In Received Announcements and Include Default Routes In Sent Announcements check box have the same function as their host-route counterparts.

- The Disable Subnet Summarization check box is active only if you have RIP version 2 specified as the outbound packet type for the router. When subnet summarization is turned off, RIP won't advertise subnets to routers that are on other subnets.

Setting OSPF Interface Properties

OSPF has its own set of properties that you can set on OSPF-enabled interfaces. These properties are both simpler and more complex than RIP—there aren't as many of them since OSPF is largely self-tuning, but the properties you *can* set tend to be somewhat more abstruse.

Microsoft ✓ *Exam Objective*

Manage and monitor IP routing.

- Manage and monitor border routing.

The General Tab

The General tab (Figure 8.28) of the OSPF Properties dialog box controls, among other things, whether or not OSPF is enabled on a particular interface address.

FIGURE 8.28 The General tab of the OSPF Properties dialog box

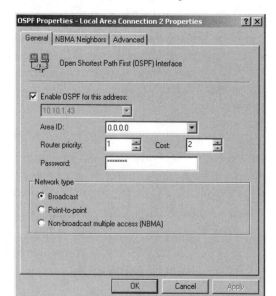

Here's what you can do with the controls on the General tab:

- The Enable OSPF For This Address check box, combined with the address pull-down, specify whether OSPF is active or not on the *selected* address. Since a single interface can have multiple IP addresses, you use this check box and pull-down to specify which IP addresses are OSPF-capable. The settings you make in the OSPF Properties dialog box apply to the IP address you select here.

- The Area ID pull-down allows you to select which OSPF area this interface is a part of. There's a simple rule: One IP address can be in one area. However, if you have multiple IP addresses defined, each one can be in a separate area.

- The Router Priority field controls the priority of this interface, relative to other OSPF routers in the same area. OSPF supports the concept of a designated router in an area; that router serves as the default router for the area it's in. The router with the highest priority will become the designated router unless there's an existing designated router when this router joins the party.

- The Cost field controls the metric attached to this router's routes in the link state database.

- The Password field works just like it does for RIP—all routers within an area can share a common plaintext password for identification. This does nothing for access control (especially since the default password is an easy-to-guess "12345678").

The Network Type controls influence how this router interacts with its peers, but to understand what its controls do you have to know some more buzzwords. A *broadcast router* is one that can talk to any number of other routers—like a typical LAN router, which can see any number of other routers on the LAN. A *point-to-point router* is one that has only one peer. For example, a typical DSL installation will have one router on your end and one on the ISP end—that's a point-to-point configuration. The third option, *non-broadcast multiple access (NBMA)*, is a little harder to define. An NBMA router is one where a single router can talk to multiple peers without using a broadcast, as in an ATM or X.25 network. You use these radio buttons to specify what kind of network your router is participating in. If you set the router to NBMA mode, you can use the NBMA Neighbors tab to specify which routers your NBMA router should talk to.

The NBMA Neighbors Tab

If you think back to the description of RIP neighbors, you learned that Microsoft had recycled an OSPF concept for use in RIP. The NBMA Neighbors tab (see Figure 8.29), then, should look like the RIP Neighbors tab; as it happens, the two are very similar. The pull-down at the top of the tab lets you pick the IP address whose neighbors you're configuring. Once you've picked an IP address, you can use the remaining controls in the tab to specify the IP addresses and priorities of the NBMA neighbors you want this router interface to talk to.

FIGURE 8.29 The NBMA Neighbors tab of the OSPF Properties dialog box

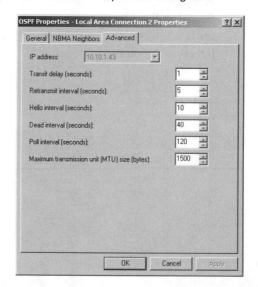

The Advanced Tab

The Advanced tab (shown in Figure 8.30) contains a bunch of parameters that didn't fit anywhere else in the OSPF configuration user interface. The first thing you'll probably notice is that you can choose which IP address you're configuring. Past that point, you'll need to use the six fields that give you access to some inner OSPF workings.

FIGURE 8.30 The Advanced tab of the OSPF Properties dialog box

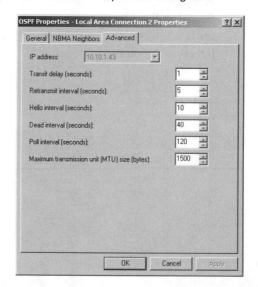

The six fields of the Advanced tab include the following:

- The Transit Delay (Seconds) field specifies how long you think it will take for a link state update to propagate outward from this router; this value is used by the OSPF engine to decide how stale route information is when it arrives.

- The Retransmit Interval (Seconds) is for your best estimate of the round-trip delay required for two routers to communicate—if it takes longer than this interval for a packet to arrive, it will be retransmitted.

- The Hello Interval (Seconds) field controls how often OSPF routers send out "here I am" packets to discover other routers. This value must be the same for all routers on the same network; lowering the interval will speed up the discovery of topology changes at the expense of generating more OSPF traffic.

- The Dead Interval (Seconds) field controls the interval after which a router is marked as "dead" by its peers. Microsoft recommends using an integral multiple of the hello interval for the dead interval; for example, if your hello interval is set to the default of 10 seconds, the default dead interval of 40 seconds will work fine.

- The Poll Interval (Seconds) field controls how long an NBMA router will wait before attempting to contact an apparently dead router to see whether it's really dead or not. This interval should be set to at least twice the dead interval.

- The Maximum Transmission Unit (MTU) Size (Bytes) field regulates how big an OSPF IP packet can be. Your best bet is to leave this value alone.

Managing IP Routing

Managing IP routing is fairly simple: if you understand how the options described earlier in this chapter work, you know about 75 percent of what you need to know to keep IP routing working smoothly. All of the remaining skills you need center around monitoring your routers to make sure traffic is flowing smoothly and troubleshooting the occasional problem.

Microsoft
✓ *Exam*
Objective

Manage and monitor IP routing.

- Manage and monitor border routing.
- Manage and monitor internal routing.

Monitoring IP Routing Status

There are a number of status displays built into the RRAS console. Knowing that they exist, and what they display, makes it much easier to see all of the various health and status data that RRAS maintains. Each of these commands shows you something different.

The General ➤ Show TCP/IP Information Command As you would expect, this display shows a broad general selection of IP routing data, including the number of routes in the route table, the number of IP and UDP datagrams received and forwarded, and the number of connection attempts. You can use the Select Columns command (right-click in the TCP/IP Information window) to customize what you see in this view.

The Static Routes ➤ Show IP Routing Table Command This command shows you the entire contents of the routing table, including the destination, net mask, and gateway for each route. This version of the routing table doesn't show you where the route came from (e.g., whether it was learned by RIP or OSPF).

RIP ➤ Show Neighbors This command shows you which RIP neighbors exist; for each router, you can see how many bad packets and bad routes that neighbor has tried to foist off on your router.

OSPF ➤ Show Areas This command shows you a list of all the defined areas (keep in mind there will only be one area per interface). For each area, you can see whether that area is up or not, as well as the number of shortest-path computations performed on the link.

OSPF ➤ Show Link-state Database This command presents a view of the entire contents of the link-state database, which is far outside the scope of this book. If you want to know more about the format of the link-state database and what its fields mean, see *CCNP: Advanced Cisco Router Configuration Study Guide* by Todd Lammle, Kevin Hales, and Donald Porter (Sybex, 1999).

OSPF ➤ Show Neighbors This command shows you everything RRAS knows about the OSPF neighbors of this router, including the type of neighbor (point-to-point, broadcast, or NBMA), the neighbor's state, and its router ID.

OSPF ➤ Show Virtual Interfaces   This command shows you a list of virtual interfaces for this OSPF router. Unless you have a fairly complicated OSPF network, this is likely to be blank.

EXERCISE 8.5

Monitoring Routing Status

Follow these steps:

1. Open the RRAS MMC console (Start ➤ Programs ➤ Administrative Tools ➤ Routing and Remote Access).

2. Select the server whose status you want to monitor in the left pane of the MMC. Expand it until you see the IP Routing node.

3. Select the Routing Interfaces node. Note that the right pane of the MMC now lists all known interfaces along with their status and connection state.

4. Select the General node beneath IP Routing. Note that the right pane of the MMC updates to show the IP routing interfaces, their IP addresses, their administrative and operational states, and whether or not IP filtering is enabled on each interface.

5. Right-click the General node and choose the Show TCP/IP Information command. Check the number of IP routes shown.

6. Right-click the Static Routes node and choose the Show IP Routing Table command. Note that the number of routes listed corresponds to the route count in the TCP/IP Information window, and that some of the routes listed are automatically generated.

Using the *route print* Command

You already learned how to use the *route add* command to add a new static route from the command line. However, the *route print* command can show you all or part of the routing table from the command line. Just typing *route print* into a command window will give you a complete dump of the entire routing table; adding a wildcard IP address (for example: Route print 206.151.*) will display only routes that match 206.151.

Troubleshooting

A comprehensive overview of IP routing troubleshooting could easily fill a book this length—or two. Microsoft's online help is pretty good at suggesting probable causes and solutions for most routing problems, and you have to know only the most blatant problems (and their solutions) for the exam. To wit, when you suspect that your RRAS server isn't routing traffic properly, begin by verifying the following:

- The RRAS service is running and configured to act as an IP router.

- The router's TCP/IP configuration is correct (including a static IP address).

- You have IP routing protocols attached to each interface where you need them.

Next, you need to verify the following routing-specific settings and behaviors:

- If you're using OSPF, make sure that the Enable OSPF On This Interface check box is turned on in the interface's OSPF Properties dialog box.

- Check to be sure that your router is receiving routes from its peers. Do this by opening the routing table and looking at the Protocol column. Seeing entries marked as OSPF or RIP tells you that at least some peers are getting routing information through. If you don't see any RIP or OSPF routes, that's a bad sign.

- You need to have a static default route enabled if your router hasn't received any default routes. To do this, add a new static route with a destination of 0.0.0.0, a net mask of 0.0.0.0, and either a demand-dial or LAN interface appropriate for your network setup.

Configuring TCP/IP Packet Filters

One of the most useful and least appreciated features in RRAS is its ability to selectively filter TCP/IP packets in both directions. You can construct filters that allow or deny traffic into or out of your network, based on rules that specify source and destination addresses and ports. The basic idea behind packet filtering is simple: You specify filter rules, and incoming packets are measured against those rules. You have two choices: Accept all packets except those prohibited by a rule, or drop all packets except those permitted by a rule.

Microsoft ✔ **Exam** *Objective*

Configure TCP/IP packet filters.

Filters are normally used to block out undesirable traffic. Of course, the definition of "undesirable" varies, but in general the idea is to keep out packets that your machines shouldn't see. For example, you could configure a packet filter that would block all packets to a Web server except those on TCP ports 80 and 443. On the other hand, you could just as easily create a filter that blocks all outgoing packets on the ports used by the MSN and AOL instant messaging tools. Another example (and one that is more helpful for the exam) is the use of filters for a PPTP or L2TP server; these filters screen out everything except VPN traffic so that you can expose a Windows 2000 VPN server without fear of compromise.

Filters are associated with a particular interface; the filters assigned to one interface are totally independent of those on all other interfaces, and inbound and outbound filters are likewise separate. You create and remove filters by using the Input Packet Filters and Output Packet Filters buttons on the General tab of the interface's Properties dialog box (flip back to Figure 8.19 for a look at the tab). The mechanics of working with the filters are identical; just remember that you create inbound filters to screen traffic coming to the interface and outbound filters to screen traffic going back out through that interface.

To create a filter, find the interface on which you want the filter, then open its Properties dialog box. Click the appropriate packet filter button and you'll see a dialog box like the Input Filter dialog box (Figure 8.31).

FIGURE 8.31 The Input Filters dialog box

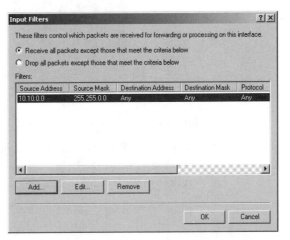

This dialog box has the following six salient parts:

- The Receive All Packets Except Those That Meet The Criteria Below and the Drop All Packets Except Those That Meet The Criteria Below radio buttons control what this filter does. To make a filter that excludes only those packets you specify, select the Receive All Packets... button. To do the opposite, and accept only those packets that meet your rule, select the Drop All Packets... button. Note that these buttons will be inactive until you create a filter rule.

- The Filters list, which is initially empty, shows you which filters are defined on this interface. Each filter's entry in the list shows you the source address and mask, the destination address and mask, and the protocol, port, and traffic type specified in the rule.

- The Add, Edit, and Remove buttons do what you'd expect.

Creating a filter is straightforward: click the Add button and you'll see the Add IP Filter dialog box (Figure 8.32). The conditions you specify here must *all* be true to trigger the rule. For example, if you specify both the source and destination addresses, only traffic from the defined source to the defined destination will be filtered.

FIGURE 8.32   The Add IP Filter dialog box

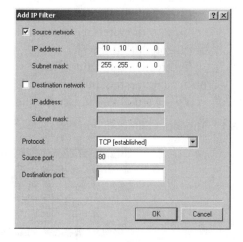

Follow these steps to fill out the Add IP Filter dialog box:

- To create a filter that blocks packets by their origin or source address, check the Source Network check box and supply the IP address and subnet mask for the source you want to block.

- To create a filter that blocks according to destination, check the destination network and fill in the appropriate address and subnet mask.

- To filter by protocol, choose the protocol you want to block: Any (which blocks everything), TCP, established TCP, IP, UDP, ICMP, or Other. For each of these protocols, you'll have to enter some additional information; for example, if you select TCP you have to specify the source or destination port numbers (or both), while for Other you'll have to enter a protocol number (more on that in Exercise 8.6).

Once you've specified the filter you want, click the OK button and you'll see it in the filter list. Filters go into effect as soon as you close the interface's Properties dialog box; you can always go back and add, edit, or remove filters at any time.

Configuring VPN Packet Filters

Packet filters provide a useful security mechanism for blocking unwanted traffic on particular machines. It's a good idea to use packet filters to keep non-VPN traffic out of your VPN servers. The rules for doing this are fairly straightforward.

PPTP Packet Filters

You need at least two filters to adequately screen out non-PPTP traffic. The first filter allows traffic with a protocol ID of 47 (the Generic Routing Encapsulation, or GRE, protocol you'll meet again in Chapter 11) to pass to the destination address of the PPTP interface. The second filter allows inbound traffic bound for TCP port 1723 (the PPTP port) to come to the PPTP interface.

You can add a third filter if the PPTP server also works as a PPTP client; in that case, the third filter needs the interface's destination address, a protocol type of TCP (established), and a source port of 1723.

Once you've created these filters, select the Drop All Packets Except Those That Meet The Criteria Below radio button in the Input Filters dialog box and close it. That's not quite all you have to do, though! You have to repeat the process on the output side, creating two or three corresponding output filters that screen out any traffic not originating from the VPN interface and using the correct protocols. (See Exercise 8.6 to get the step-by-step process.)

EXERCISE 8.6

Configure PPTP Packet Filters

In this exercise (which you shouldn't attempt on your production VPN server until you've been successful in trying it on another, less critical machine), you'll set up RRAS IP packet filters that block everything except PPTP traffic on the specified interface.

1. Open the RRAS console and expand the server and IP Routing nodes to expose the General node of the server you're working on. Select the General node.

2. Right-click the appropriate interface, then choose the Properties command.

3. In the General tab of the interface Properties dialog box, click the Input Filters button. The Input Filters dialog box will appear.

4. Click the Add button and the Add IP Filter dialog box will appear.

5. Fill out the Add IP Filter dialog box as follows:

   a. Check the Destination Network check box.

   b. Fill in the destination IP address field with the IP address of the VPN interface.

   c. Supply a destination subnet mask of 255.255.255.255.

   d. Select a protocol type of TCP, and then specify a source port of 0 and a destination port of 1723.

   e. Click the OK button.

6. The Input Filters dialog box reappears, listing the new filter you created in step 5. Repeat step 5, but this time specify Other in the Protocol field and fill in a protocol ID of 47. When you're done, click the OK button and you'll go back to the Input Filter dialog box.

7. In the Input Filter dialog box, click the Drop All Packets Except Those That Meet The Criteria radio button, then click the OK button.

8. Repeat steps 3-7, but this time create output filters. Make sure to specify the IP address of the VPN adapter as the source, not the destination!

9. Close the interface Properties dialog box.

L2TP Packet Filters

To use L2TP packet filters, you have to go through the same basic process, but the filters you need are slightly different. There are a total of four filters required—two input filters and two output filters:

- An input filter with a destination of the VPN interface address and a net mask of 255.255.255.255, filtering UDP with a source and destination port of 500

- An input filter with a destination of the VPN interface address and a net mask of 255.255.255.255, filtering UDP with a source and destination port of 1701

- An output filter with a source of the VPN interface address and a net mask of 255.255.255.255, filtering UDP with a source and destination port of 500

- An output filter with a source of the VPN interface address and a net mask of 255.255.255.255, filtering UDP with a source and destination port of 1701

Summary

In this chapter, you learned:

- How IP routing works

- How to create and manage interfaces for IP routing

- How to set OSPF and RIP routing parameters

- How to manage demand-dial routing

Key Terms

Before you take the exam, be sure you're familiar with the following terms:

Area border routers

Auto-static mode

Backbone

Border routing

Broadcast router

Default route

Default subnet mask

Demand-dial routing

Dynamic routing

Hierarchical address

Host routes

Information hiding

Internal routing

Metric

Network address

Network routes

Node address

Non-broadcast multiple access (NBMA)

Packet filtering

Periodic update mode

Point-to-point router

Router discovery messages

Static routes

Subnets

Subnet address

Subnet mask

Review Questions

1. An RRAS connection that brings up a link when it's needed to pass traffic is called which of the following?

   A. Demand-dial interface

   B. Nonpersistent connection

   C. Traffic demand interface

   D. Transient interface

2. What is an internetwork?

   A. The Internet

   B. A collection of individual networks

   C. A linked collection of individual networks

   D. Networks linked with at least 128Kb/sec of bandwidth

3. Routing table entries usually contain which of the following? (Choose all that apply.)

   A. The destination address for a remote network

   B. A metric for the route

   C. The date and time when the route was created

   D. The forwarding address where remote traffic should be sent

4. Static routes _____.

   A. Can be generated by OSPF or RIP

   B. Usually change frequently

   C. Are manually generated and stay in the routing table until removed

   D. Are not supported by RRAS

5. When creating a demand-dial interface, what must you do if you want to allow incoming calls to your router?

   A. You must create a suitable user account for the remote router to use.

   B. The Demand-Dial wizard will use the system account to configure the dial-in credentials.

   C. You can accept incoming calls without authentication.

   D. You can require the use of callback on incoming calls.

6. RIP routers can operate in which mode(s)?

   A. Periodic update or auto-static modes

   B. Periodic update or triggered update modes

   C. Auto-static or manual static modes

   D. Periodic update or automatic update modes

7. Leigh is setting up an RRAS router at a remote site so that it can connect back to the corporate LAN. Leigh will need which of the following interfaces?

   A. A demand-dial interface for connecting the remote and LAN routers

   B. RIP or OSPF for routing discovery

   C. A and B

   D. None of the above

8. Which of the following is true of a border router?

   A. It acts as a gateway between routing areas.

   B. It routes traffic internal to an area.

   C. It cannot be used with RRAS.

   D. None of the above

9. What is the function of the OSPF Properties dialog box's External Routing tab?

   A. It provides control over external routing to and from OSPF peers.

   B. It controls how OSPF interacts with RIP.

   C. It gives you control over which route sources the OSPF engine will use in addition to OSPF-delivered routes.

   D. It allows you to turn off static routing.

10. Which of the following two statements are true of the auto-static mode of RRAS?

    A. It cannot be used with RIP.

    B. It is normally used with demand-dial connections.

    C. It combines RIP discovery with static routes by marking RIP peer routes as static so they persist when the peer isn't available.

    D. It must be used with OSPF.

11. Which of the following is/are true of the RIP and OSPF protocols? (Choose all that apply.)

    A. They can coexist on a single RRAS server.

    B. They can coexist on a single RRAS server, provided it has at least two NICs.

    C. They can share routing data in the same routing table.

    D. They may be used to interoperate with non-Windows 2000 routers.

12. How do you control router discovery messages?

    A. Through the General tab of the Properties dialog box for a LAN interface

    B. Through the Discovery tab of an OSPF or RIP interface

    C. Through the General tab of an OSPF or RIP interface

    D. By adding an input filter that rejects them

13. If you're using OSPF routers with a DSL or T1 connection, how should your RRAS router be configured?

   A. It should be configured as a point-to-point router.

   B. It should be configured as an NBMA router.

   C. It should be configured as a broadcast router.

   D. None of the above

14. You can configure a single LAN interface with multiple IP addresses. If you do, which of the following statements is *not* true?

   A. You can configure OSPF independently on each of the IP addresses.

   B. Each IP address can participate in the same OSPF area.

   C. One IP address may not be another's RIP or OSPF neighbor.

   D. You may not have only one of the IP addresses participating in RIP.

15. To create a new demand-dial interface, you need _____.

   A. To use the Demand-Dial wizard

   B. The correct credentials for the remote router you want to call

   C. A and B

   D. None of the above

16. When you configure RIP on an interface, you can filter routes based on what?

   A. Based on the originating router or network ID

   B. Based on the origin network ID only

   C. Based on the originating router only

   D. Based on the route source

17. RIP and OSPF authentication _____.

    A. Is for identification only

    B. Provides identification and connection security

    C. Provides connection security only

    D. Is not supported by RRAS

18. RIP supports loop detection by using which check box(es)?

    A. The Enable Poison-Reverse Processing and Enable Split-Horizon Processing check boxes on the Advanced tab of the RIP interface Properties dialog box

    B. The Enable Loop Detection check box on the Advanced tab of the RIP interface Properties dialog box

    C. The Enable Poison-Reverse Processing and Enable Split-Horizon Processing check boxes on the Advanced tab of the RIP Properties dialog box

    D. The Prevent Routing Loop check box on the Advanced tab of the RIP Properties dialog box

19. If you can send packets to an RRAS router but the packets aren't routed, what should you check?

    A. The RRAS service status

    B. The RRAS routing configuration

    C. The RRAS server's TCP/IP configuration

    D. All of the above

20. Joe set up a new RRAS router that seems to be functioning properly, but it isn't routing traffic. He's already verified that RRAS is running and properly configured. Which of the following are possible causes of the problem? (Choose all that apply.)

    A. No routes are being learned from peer routers.

    B. There's no static default route.

    C. There are no RIP neighbors defined.

    D. The router's authentication credentials are wrong.

Answers to Review Questions

1. A. Demand-dial interfaces come up when there's traffic to pass over the link.

2. C. The term "internetwork" refers to a group of networks linked in some way; the Internet is the best-known internetwork, but there are lots of others.

3. A, B, D. Routing table entries contain destinations, metrics, and the forwarding address for that particular destination.

4. C. Static routes stay in the routing table until you remove them; they're not dynamic in any way.

5. A. You have to either create the account yourself or use the Add A User Account So A Remote Router Can Dial In check box in the Demand-Dial wizard.

6. A. RIP routers support both periodic (or timed) updates and a mode in which updated entries are sent around as they arrive.

7. A. RIP and OSPF are optional; you can use static routes on a remote dial-up router to avoid fooling with dynamic routing protocols.

8. A. Border routers connect adjacent routing areas; they don't route anything "inside" an area.

9. C. The OSPF routing engine can use routes that it hears from non-OSPF sources. You use this tab to control which of those sources the OSPF router will listen to.

10. B, C. Auto-static mode marks RIP-provided routes as static, making it suited for demand-dial use.

11. A, C, D. RIP and OSPF can happily coexist on a single machine with one NIC, and they can exchange data with any standards-compliant RIP or OSPF router.

12. A. You can control whether the router supports discovery messages with the Enable Router Discovery Advertisements check box on the General tab of the interface Properties dialog box.

13. A. Point-to-point routers are used on dedicated two-ended links; broadcast and NBMA routers are used on LAN/WANs or packet-switching networks, respectively.

14. B. A single interface can only take part in one OSPF area.

15. C. When you use the wizard to create an interface, you still need an authorized username and password for the router you're dialing into.

16. A. RIP routes can be filtered based on the network they cover or on the router that's offering them.

17. A. The plaintext authentication included with RIP and OSPF is only useful for allowing routers to recognize each other, not for any real security.

18. A. Poison-reverse processing and split-horizon processing are the two loop detection algorithms that RIP can use; you enable them on each of the desired interfaces.

19. D. Any of these factors could prevent traffic from flowing and should be checked.

20. A, B. RIP neighbors are optional. If no routes are arriving or if there's no static default route, the router may not be able to route traffic.

Managing Remote Access Services

MICROSOFT EXAM OBJECTIVES COVERED IN THIS CHAPTER:

✓ **Configure and troubleshoot remote access.**

- Configure inbound connections.
- Create a remote access policy.
- Configure a remote access profile.
- Configure multilink connections.
- Configure Routing and Remote Access for DHCP integration.

✓ **Manage and monitor remote access.**

✓ **Configure remote access security.**

- Configure authentication protocols.
- Configure encryption protocols.
- Create a remote access policy.

✓ **Manage and monitor network traffic.**

Some Windows 2000 features are only thinly disguised retreads from Windows NT and its various service and option packs. Others are wholly new. The remote access service component of the Routing and Remote Access Service (RRAS) falls somewhere in between—RRAS itself dates back to the NT 4 Option Pack, but the Windows 2000 implementation of remote access adds a ton of new features not present in the older version.

> **NOTE** One of the objectives in this chapter—the "Configure and troubleshoot remote access" objective—has one more subobjective, which is not covered in this chapter. You can find this subobjective, "Configure a virtual private network (VPN)," in both Chapter 10 ("Managing Virtual Private Networking") and Chapter 12 ("Installing and Configuring Network Clients").

Before you can get into the details of what these features do and how you configure them to provide remote access for your network, you need to understand some of the terms and concepts specific to RRAS remote access. That's where you'll begin, and then you'll move on to reviewing the features and configuration settings that you need to understand to meet the exam objectives.

Learning More Remote Access Buzzwords

In Chapter 3, "Windows 2000 Connectivity and Security Services," you learned about the basic concepts that underlie remote access. At bottom, remote access services provide another way to carry the network protocols you're already using. In the case of RRAS, they also provide some security services necessary to effectively provide remote access. For example, you'll probably want to have the ability to restrict user dial-up access by group membership, time of day, or other factors, and you'll need a way to specify the various callback, authentication, and encryption options that the protocols support.

Security Goodies

In the bad old days, remote access was seldom a part of most networks. It was too hard to implement, too hard to manage, and too hard to secure. It's reasonably easy to secure your networks from unauthorized physical access, but doing so for remote access was perceived (rightly or wrongly) as being much harder. There are a number of security policies, protocols, and technologies that have been developed to ease this problem.

User Authentication

One of the first steps in establishing a remote access connection involves allowing the user to present some credentials to the server. This is like showing your invitation to the doorkeeper at a fancy party; some parties have more elaborate authentication mechanisms than others. The same is true of remote access; you can use any or all of the following five authentication protocols that Windows 2000 supports.

Password Authentication Protocol (PAP)   *PAP* is the simplest—and least secure—authentication protocol. It transmits all authentication information in clear text with no encryption, which makes it vulnerable to snooping. In addition, it has no way for a client and server to authenticate each other. Since other protocols offer better security, PAP is falling out of favor, and Microsoft recommends turning it off unless you have clients that cannot use a more secure protocol.

Shiva Password Authentication Protocol (SPAP)   SPAP is a slightly more secure version of PAP that's primarily intended for talking to remote-access hardware devices made by Shiva (which is now owned by Intel). It's included for backward compatibility, but isn't in wide use.

Challenge Handshake Authentication Protocol (CHAP)   *CHAP* (sometimes called MD5-CHAP because it uses the RSA MD5 hash algorithm) has a major security advantage over PAP: It doesn't transmit password information in the clear. Instead, the server sends a challenge encrypted with the DES algorithm to the client, which must decrypt it and return the correct response. This allows the server to verify the user's credentials without sending those credentials across an insecure link.

Although NT's RAS client can use MD5-CHAP when dialing into a third-party device, an unmodified NT RAS server will not support MD5-CHAP clients. This is because MD5-CHAP requires that the server store passwords in clear text. For security purposes, the SAM database stores NT passwords as a hash, never in clear text.

Microsoft CHAP (MS-CHAP)   Microsoft has extended the CHAP protocol to allow the use of Windows authentication information (among other things, that's what the Log On With Dial-Up Networking check box in the Windows 2000 logon dialog box does). There are actually two separate versions of MS-CHAP. Version 2 is much more secure than version 1, and all Microsoft operating systems support version 2. Some other OSes support MS-CHAP version 1 as well.

Extensible Authentication Protocol (EAP)   *EAP* is pretty nifty. Instead of hardwiring any one authentication protocol, a client-server pair that understands EAP can negotiate an authentication method. The computer that asks for authentication is called the authenticator. The authenticator is free to ask for several difference pieces of information, making a separate query for each one. This allows the use of almost any authentication method, including secure access tokens like SecurID, one-time password systems like S/Key, or ordinary username/password systems.

Each authentication scheme supported in EAP is called an *EAP type*. Each EAP type, in turn, is implemented as a plug-in module. Windows 2000 can support any number of EAP types at once; the RRAS server can use any EAP type to authenticate if a) you've allowed that module to be used, and b) the client has the module in question. Windows 2000 actually comes with the following two EAP types:

- EAP MD5-CHAP implements the version of CHAP that uses the MD5 hash algorithm. The EAP version of CHAP is identical to the regular version, but the challenges and responses are packaged and sent as EAP messages. This means that if you turn EAP MD5-CHAP on and disable regular CHAP on the server, plain CHAP clients won't be able to authenticate.

- EAP Transport Level Security (TLS) allows you to use public-key certificates as an authenticator. TLS (which you may recall from Chapter 3), is very similar to the familiar Secure Sockets Layer (SSL) protocol used for Web browsers. When EAP TLS is turned on, the client and server send TLS-encrypted messages back and forth. EAP TLS is the strongest authentication method you can use; as a bonus, it supports smartcards. However, EAP TLS requires your RRAS server to be part of a Windows 2000 domain.

There's a third EAP authentication method included with Windows 2000, but it's not really an EAP type. EAP-RADIUS is a fake EAP type that passes any incoming message to a RADIUS server for authentication. (*RADIUS* stands for *Remote Authentication for Dial-In User Service.*)

Connection Security

There are some additional features you can use to provide connection-level security for your remote access clients. You've already learned about one in Chapter 3: The Callback Control Protocol, or CBCP, allows your RRAS servers or clients to negotiate a callback with the other end. When CBCP is enabled, either the client or the server can ask the server to call the client back at a number supplied by the client or a prearranged number stored on the server.

Another nifty option is that the RRAS server can be programmed to accept or reject calls based on the Caller ID or Automatic Number Identification (ANI) information transmitted by the phone company. For example, you can instruct your primary RRAS server to accept calls from only your home analog line; while this keeps you from calling it when you're on the road, it also keeps the server from talking to strangers.

Finally, you can specify various levels of encryption to protect your connection from interception or tampering; the exact type and kind of encryption used will vary according to the options you specify.

Access Control

Apart from the connection-level tricks you can use to prohibit outside callers from talking to your servers, you can restrict which users can make remote connections in a number of ways. First of all, you can allow or disallow remote access from individual user accounts. This is the same limited control you have in Windows NT, but it's just the start for Windows 2000.

Besides turning dial-in access on or off for a single user, you can use *remote access policies* to control whether users can get access or not. Like group policies, remote access policies give you an easy way to apply a consistent set of policies to groups of users. However, the policy mechanism is a little different: You create rules that include or exclude the users you want in the policy. Unlike group policies, remote access policies are only available in native Windows 2000 domains (that is, in domains where there are no Windows NT domain controllers present). That means that you may not have the option to use remote access policies until your Windows 2000 deployment is further along.

What Multilink Is All About

Many parts of the world don't have high-speed broadband access yet. In fact, many places don't have ISDN or even phone lines that support 56K modems. Wouldn't it be nice if there were some way to aggregate multiple analog or ISDN lines to make them act like one faster connection? In fact, there is. The multilink extensions to the Point-to-Point Protocol (PPP) provide a way to gang up several independent PPP connections so that they act as a single connection. For example, if I use two phone lines and modems to place a two-line multilink call to my ISP, instead of getting the usual 48Kbps connection I end up with an apparent bandwidth of 96Kbps. The multilink PPP software on my Windows 2000 machine and on the ISP's router takes care of stringing all of the packets together to make this process seamless.

Windows 2000's RRAS service supports multilink PPP for inbound and outbound calls; as you'll see in Chapter 12, "Installing and Configuring Network Clients," the Dial-Up Networking client supports it, too. The primary drawback to multilink calls: They take up more than one phone line apiece.

Installing Remote Access

In Chapter 8, "Installing IP Routing," you learned how to install and configure RRAS for use as an IP router. As it turns out, some of the steps required to install and configure an RRAS server for remote access are similar, while others are different. The overall process is still driven by the Routing and Remote Access Server Setup wizard; the primary difference in this case is that you'll use the wizard to set up a dial-up server, not an IP router. Exercise 9.1 will lead you through the process of configuring an RRAS server using the wizard.

EXERCISE 9.1

Installing the Routing and Remote Access Service

Follow these steps to install an RRAS remote access server:

1. Open the RRAS MMC console (Start ➢ Programs ➢ Administrative Tools ➢ Routing and Remote Access).

2. Select the server you want to configure in the left pane of the MMC. Right-click the server and choose the Configure and Enable Routing and Remote Access command. The RRAS Setup wizard will appear. Click the Next button.

3. In the Common Configurations page of the wizard, select the Remote Access Server radio button, and then click the Next button.

4. The Remote Client Protocols page (Figure 9.1) appears, listing the protocols available for remote access clients. If you need to add another protocol to the list, click the No, I Need To Add Protocols button; if all the protocols you want to use are on the list, leave the Yes, All Of The Required Protocols Are On The List button selected. Click the Next button.

5. If you indicated that you need to add additional protocols, the wizard will stop. If the protocols you need are already present, it will continue.

6. The Macintosh Guest Authentication page appears. The Mac OS allows anonymous remote access. If you want your RRAS server to imitate this behavior, click the Allow Unauthenticated Access For All Remote Clients button. Click the Next button. (Please note that this will occur only if Macintosh File and Print services are loaded.)

7. The IP Address Assignment page appears. If you want to use DHCP (either a DHCP server on your network or the built-in address allocator), leave the Automatically radio button selected. If you want to pick out an address range, select the From A Specified Range Of Addresses button. Click the Next button.

   If you choose to use static addressing, at this point the wizard will give you the opportunity to define one or more address ranges to be assigned to remote clients.

8. The Managing Multiple Remote Access Servers page appears. You use this page to configure your RRAS server to work with other RADIUS-capable servers on your network. In this case, you don't want to use RADIUS, so leave the No, I Don't Want To Set Up This Server To Use RADIUS Now button selected, and then click the Next button.

9. The Wizard Summary page appears. Click the Finish button to start the RRAS service and prepare your server to be configured. If the RRAS service is running on the same server as a DHCP server, you'll see a message indicating that you need to configure the DHCP relay agent (more on that later).

FIGURE 9.1   The Remote Client Protocols page

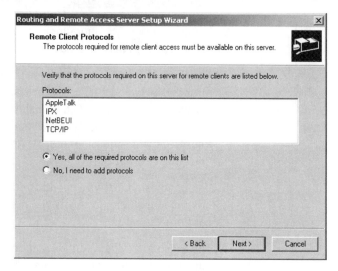

Configuring Your Remote Access Server

Most of the configuration necessary for a remote access server happens at the server level. In particular, you use the server's Properties dialog box to control whether the server allows remote connections at all, what protocols and options it supports, and so forth. You also have to configure settings for your users, which you'll read about in the next section.

To open the RRAS server's Properties dialog box, pick the server you're interested in and use the Action ➢ Properties command (or the Properties command on the Context menu).

Setting General Configuration Options

The General tab of the server Properties dialog box (Figure 9.2) has only one check box of interest for remote access configurations: When checked, the check box that says Remote Access Server allows the RRAS service to act as a remote access server. You need to know this so that you can switch remote access capability on and off without deactivating and reactivating the RRAS service, which causes the service to erase its settings.

FIGURE 9.2 The General tab of the RRAS server Properties dialog box

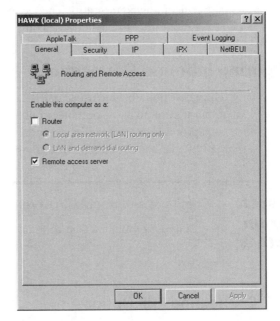

The other tabs in this dialog box control specific settings for different protocols. Note that the tabs you see will depend on which protocols you have installed; for example, on a server that doesn't have IPX installed, you won't have the IPX tab. The other tabs available from this dialog box include the following:

- The Security tab lets you specify what authentication providers and settings you want the server to use. The controls on this tab are covered in the "Configuring Security" section later in the chapter.

- The next four tabs—IP, IPX, NetBEUI, and AppleTalk—control the specific settings applied to each protocol you have installed. In particular, these tabs govern whether or not the associated protocol can be used for remote access clients as well as whether remote clients can reach the entire network or only the remote access server itself. The next section, "Configuring Inbound Connections," discusses each of these tabs independently.

- The PPP tab controls which PPP protocols—including multilink—the clients on this server are allowed to use. The section "Configuring PPP Options" discusses these settings in detail.

- The Event Logging tab controls what level of log detail is kept for incoming connections. The section on monitoring your RRAS servers more fully discusses these controls.

Configuring Inbound Connections

The whole point behind using an RRAS server is to allow remote clients to call it, but it's not an all-or-nothing proposition. You can set separate options for each protocol that the server supports; since all of those protocols are carried via PPP, there are some generic PPP options you can set as well.

Microsoft ✓ *Exam Objective*

Configure and troubleshoot remote access.

- Configure multilink connections.

Configuring PPP Options

The PPP tab (Figure 9.3) of the RRAS server Properties dialog box lets you control the PPP-layer options available to clients that call in. The settings you specify here control whether or not the related PPP options are available to clients; remote access policies can be used to control whether individual connections make use of them or not. There are a total of four check boxes on this tab:

- The Multilink Connections check box, which is on by default, controls whether or not the server will allow clients to establish multilink connections when they call in.

- The Bandwidth Allocation Protocol (BAP) and Bandwidth Allocation Control Protocol (BACP) allow a client and server to dynamically add or remove links during a multilink session. This is handy because it lets you throttle the amount of available bandwidth up or down on demand—provided you have the Dynamic Bandwidth Control Using BAP Or BACP check box turned on. It's only available when you have the Multilink Connections check box on.

- The PPP Link Control Protocol (LCP) is used to establish a PPP link and negotiate its settings. There are a variety of LCP extensions defined in various RFCs; these extensions allow a client and server to dynamically agree on exactly which protocols are being passed back and forth, among other things. The Link Control Protocol (LCP) Extensions check box controls whether or not these extensions are available. Windows 9x, NT, and 2000 clients depend on the LCP extensions, so you should leave this check box marked.

- The Software Compression check box controls whether RRAS will allow a remote client to use the Compression Control Protocol (CCP) to compress PPP traffic. In some cases, hardware compression at the modem level is more efficient, but not everyone has a compression-capable modem. Leave this check box turned on as well.

FIGURE 9.3 The PPP tab of the RRAS server Properties dialog box

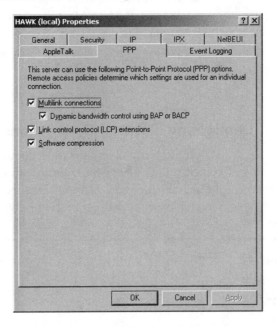

EXERCISE 9.2

Controlling Multilink for Incoming Calls

It doesn't make sense to enable multilink connections if you have only one phone line; in addition, you may want to turn them off to keep a small number of users from hogging all your lines. To control whether multilink is on or off, follow these steps:

1. Open the RRAS MMC console (Start ➤ Programs ➤ Administrative Tools ➤ Routing and Remote Access).

EXERCISE 9.2 *(continued)*

2. Right-click the server you want to configure in the left pane of the MMC, then choose the Properties command. The server Properties dialog box will appear.

3. Switch to the PPP tab by clicking it.

4. To turn multilink capability off, make sure the Multilink Connections check box is turned off. To turn it back on, simply check the appropriate check box.

5. If you decide to turn multilink capability on, you should also enable the use of BAP/BACP to make it easier for your server to adjust to the load placed on it. To do so, make sure the Dynamic Bandwidth Control Using BAP Or BACP check box is marked.

6. Click the OK button.

Configuring IP-Based Connections

TCP/IP is far and away the most commonly used remote access protocol; coincidentally, it's also the most configurable of the protocols that Windows 2000 supports. Both of these facts are reflected in the IP tab of the server Properties dialog box (Figure 9.4).

Microsoft
Exam
Objective

Configure and troubleshoot remote access.

- Configure inbound connections.

FIGURE 9.4   The IP tab of the RRAS server Properties dialog box

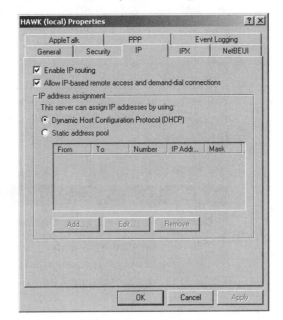

The controls on the tab do the following:

- The Enable IP Routing check box controls whether or not RRAS will route IP packets between the remote client and other interfaces on your RRAS server. When this box is checked, as it is by default, remote clients' packets can go to the RRAS server or to any other host to which the RRAS server has a route. To limit clients to only accessing resources on the RRAS server itself, uncheck this box.

- The Allow IP-Based Remote Access And Demand-Dial Connections check box controls whether clients may use IP over PPP. It might seem odd to have this choice since the overwhelming majority of PPP connections use IP, but if you want to limit your server to NetBEUI, IPX, or AppleTalk remote clients, you can do so by making sure this box is unchecked.

- The IP Address Assignment control group lets you specify how you want remote clients to get their IP addresses. The default setting here will vary, depending on what you told the RRAS wizard during setup. If you want to use a DHCP server on your network as the source of IP addresses for remote clients, select the DHCP radio button (making sure, of course, that you've got the DHCP relay agent installed and running). If you'd rather use static address allocation, select the Static Address Pool button, then use the controls beneath the address list to specify which IP address ranges you want issued to clients.

If you choose to use static addressing, be sure that you don't use any address ranges that are part of a DHCP server's address pool. Better still, you can add the ranges you want reserved for remote access as excluded ranges in the DHCP snap-in.

EXERCISE 9.3

Configuring Incoming Connections

For this exercise, you're going to configure your RRAS server so that it only accepts inbound calls that use the IP protocol. You may have to skip some steps (as noted) if you don't have all four network protocols loaded.

1. Open the RRAS MMC console (Start ➤ Programs ➤ Administrative Tools ➤ Routing and Remote Access).

2. Right-click the server you want to configure in the left pane of the MMC, then choose the Properties command. The server Properties dialog box will appear.

3. Switch to the IP tab by clicking it. Verify that both the Enable IP Routing and the Allow IP-Based Remote Access And Demand-Dial Connections check boxes are marked.

4. Switch to the IPX tab if you have one. Uncheck the Allow IPX-Based Remote Access And Demand-Dial Connections check box.

5. If your Properties dialog box has a NetBEUI tab, switch to it, then uncheck the Allow NetBEUI-Based Remote Access Clients To Access check box.

6. If your Properties dialog box has an AppleTalk tab, switch to it, then uncheck the Enable AppleTalk Remote Access check box.

7. Click the OK button. After a brief pause, the Properties dialog box will disappear, and your changes will become effective.

Configuring IPX-Based Connections

You may recall from Chapter 2, "Windows 2000 Network Naming Services," that IP and IPX are very similar in many respects. Even though the particulars differ, they both involve addresses that must be assigned to every device on the network. Accordingly, the IP and IPX tabs of the server Properties dialog box aren't as different as you might expect. The IPX tab (Figure 9.5) includes two controls that give you power over whether this server speaks IPX or not.

FIGURE 9.5   The IPX tab of the RRAS server Properties dialog box

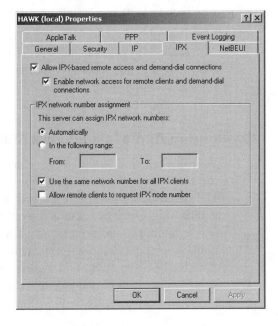

The IPX tabs include the following:

- The Allow IPX-Based Remote Access And Demand-Dial Connections check box controls whether this server will accept IPX connections or not.

- The Enable Network Access For Remote Clients And Demand-Dial Connections check box controls whether IPX clients can reach only this server or other IPX-capable servers on your network.

Notice that each protocol tab has a check box like this but that each one is labeled differently. Make sure you get their names straight for the exam.

In addition, the IPX Network Number Assignment control group gives you a way to have this server automatically assign IPX network numbers to dial-up clients. Your best bet will be to leave the Automatically radio button selected, which tells the server to pass out numbers as it sees fit. If necessary, you can manually assign numbers in a specified range. The two other check boxes give you some additional control:

- The Use The Same Network Number For All IPX Clients check box, on by default, indicates whether you want all IPX clients to get the same network number or not. Normally, you'll want this to be on so that all your IPX resources will be immediately visible to clients.

- The Allow Remote Clients To Request IPX Node Number check box is normally off by default, because it's a potential security hole. When this check box is on, clients can request a particular IPX node number; in theory, this could allow a malicious remote client to impersonate another IPX device. Leave this box unchecked.

Configuring AppleTalk and NetBEUI Connections

The AppleTalk and NetBEUI tabs control whether or not your server will accept remote connections using those protocols. Since AppleTalk and Net-BEUI are both pretty simple, there aren't really any configuration options on the tabs—just check boxes that you use to specify whether your server will allow incoming connections or not. The AppleTalk check box is labeled Enable AppleTalk Remote Access, while its NetBEUI counterpart reads Allow NetBEUI-Based Remote Access Clients To Access. The NetBEUI version also has an associated pair of radio buttons that regulate whether Net-BEUI clients can see only the RRAS server or the entire network.

Configuring User Access

Now that you've set up the server to accept incoming calls, it's time to determine who can actually *use* it. You do this in two ways: by setting up *remote access profiles* on individual accounts, and by creating and managing *remote access policies* that apply to groups of users. This distinction is subtle but important, because you manage and apply profiles and policies in different places.

Using User Profiles

Windows 2000 stores a ton of information for each user account. Collectively, this information is known as the account's profile, and it's normally stored in Active Directory. Some settings in the user's profile are available through the two user-management snap-ins—Active Directory Users and Computers, or Local Users and Groups—depending on whether or not your RRAS server is part of an Active Directory domain. In either case, the interesting part of the profile is the Dial-In tab of the user's properties dialog box (Figure 9.6). It turns out that this tab has a number of interesting controls that regulate how the user account may be used for dial-in access.

FIGURE 9.6   The Dial-In tab of the user's Properties dialog box

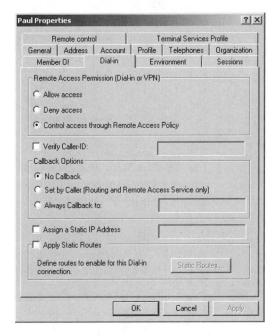

These controls include the following:

The Remote Access Permission (Dial-in or VPN) Control Group   The first, and probably most familiar, controls on this tab are in the Remote Access Permission control group; they control whether this account has dial-in permission or not. They're similar to the controls you may remember from the Windows NT User Manager; however, Windows 2000 has a new wrinkle. In addition to explicitly allowing or denying access (with the Allow access and Deny access radio buttons, of course), you can leave the access decision up to a remote access policy, provided you're using Windows 2000 in native mode.

The Verify Caller-ID Check Box   If you like, you can force RRAS to verify the user's Caller ID information and use the results of that verification to decide whether the user gets access or not. When you check the Verify Caller-ID check box and enter a phone number in the field, you're explicitly telling RRAS to reject a call from anyone who provides that username and password but whose Caller ID information doesn't match what you enter. That means you need to be careful to get the number right!

The Callback Options Control Group   The Callback Options control group gives you three choices for regulating callback. The first (and default setting) is the No Callback radio button. When selected, the server will never honor callback requests from this account. If you choose the Set By Caller radio button instead, the calling system can specify a number where it wants to be called, and the RRAS server will call the client back at that number. The final choice, Always Callback To, allows you to enter a number that the server will call back no matter where the client's actually calling from. This is less flexible, but more secure, than the second option.

The Assign a Static IP Check Box   If you want one particular user to always get the same static IP address, you can arrange it by checking the Assign A Static IP Address check box and then entering the desired IP address. This allows you to set up non-dynamic DNS records for individual users, guaranteeing that their machines will always have a usable DNS entry. On the other hand, this is much more error-prone than the dynamic DNS-DHCP combination you *could* be using instead.

The Apply Static Routes Control Group   In an ordinary LAN, you don't have to do anything special to clients to enable them to route packets—just configure them with a default gateway, and the gateway handles the rest. For dial-up connections, though, you may want to define a list of static routes that will enable the remote client to reach hosts on your network, or elsewhere, without requiring that packets be sent to a gateway in between. If you want to define a set of static routes on the client, you'll have to do it manually. If you want to assign static routes on the server, check the Apply Static Routes check box, then use the Static Routes button to add and remove routes as necessary.

Remember that these settings apply to individual users, so you can assign different routes, caller ID, or callback settings to each user.

You might not want to do this on your production systems since it may reduce your ability to dial in and fix problems.

Using Remote Access Policies and Profiles

Windows 2000 includes support for two additional configuration systems: remote access policies and remote access profiles. Policies determine who may and may not connect; you define rules with conditions that the system evaluates to see whether a particular user can connect or not. Profiles contain settings that determine what happens during call setup and completion. (Don't confuse remote access profiles with the dial-in settings associated with a user profile.)

You can have any number of policies in a native Windows 2000 domain; each policy may have exactly one profile associated with it.

Settings in an individual user's profile override settings in a remote access policy.

You manage remote access policies through the Remote Access Policies folder in the RRAS snap-in. By default, there's only one policy listed there: "Allow access if dial-in permission is enabled." That should give you a clue as to how policies work: They contain conditions that you pick from a list. When a caller connects, the policy's conditions are evaluated, one by one, to see whether the caller gets in or not. *All* of the conditions in the policy must match for the user to gain access. If there are multiple policies, they're evaluated according to an order you specify.

Creating a New Policy

To create a policy, just right-click the Remote Access Policies folder or in the list of policies and use the New Remote Access Policy command. This command starts the Add Remote Access Policy wizard, which uses a series of steps to help you define the policy. First stop: the Policy Name page (Figure 9.7), in which you define a friendly name for the policy. This is the name that appears in the snap-in's policy list.

Microsoft ✓ **Exam Objective**

Configure and troubleshoot remote access.

- Create a remote access policy.

Microsoft ✓ **Exam Objective**

Configure remote access security.

- Create a remote access policy.

FIGURE 9.7 The Policy Name page of the Add Remote Access Policy wizard

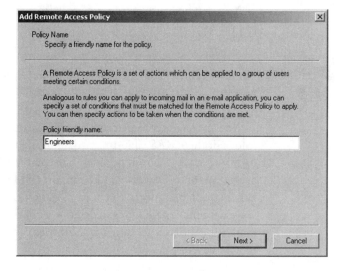

Next, you'll see a page listing the conditions for this policy (Figure 9.8). Since you're just defining the policy, this page will initially be blank. Since this isn't very helpful, you'll need to use the Add button to create a condition for the policy. Clicking the Add button displays the Select Attribute dialog box, which is much more interesting.

FIGURE 9.8   The Conditions page of the Add Remote Access Policy wizard

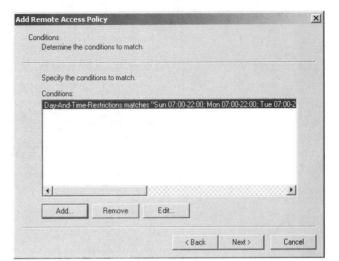

The Select Attribute dialog box (Figure 9.9) lists all of the attributes that you can evaluate in a policy (see Table 9.1; attributes marked as "IAS only" work only with the Internet Authentication Service, which will not be discussed here). These attributes are drawn from the RADIUS standards, so you can (and in some cases, should) intermix your Windows 2000 RRAS servers with RADIUS servers. Once you choose an attribute and click the Add button another dialog box appears, which you use for editing the value of the attribute. For example, when selected the Day-and-Time-Restrictions attribute pops up a calendar grid that lets you select which days and times are available for logging on. Each attribute has its own unique editor, which makes sense when you consider the wide range of attribute values. After you select an attribute and give it a value, you can add more attributes or move on to the next wizard step by clicking the Next button.

If you want to restrict dial-in access based on an account's group membership, check out the Windows Groups attribute.

FIGURE 9.9 The Select Attribute dialog box

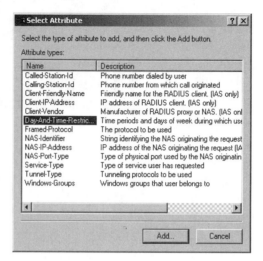

TABLE 9.1 Remote Access Policy Attributes

Attribute Name	What It Specifies
Called-Station-ID	Phone number of remote access port called by the caller
Calling-Station-ID	Caller's phone number
Client-Friendly-Name	(IAS only) Name of the RADIUS server that's attempting to validate the connection
Client-IP-Address	(IAS only) IP address of the RADIUS server that's attempting to validate the connection
Client-Vendor	(IAS only) Vendor of remote access server that originally accepted the connection; used to set different policies for different hardware
Day-and-Time-Restriction	Weekdays and times when connection attempts are accepted or rejected
Framed-Protocol	Protocol to be used for framing incoming packets (e.g., PPP, SLIP, etc.)

TABLE 9.1 Remote Access Policy Attributes *(continued)*

Attribute Name	What It Specifies
NAS-Identifier	(IAS only) Friendly name of the remote access server that originally accepted the connection
NAS-IP-Address	(IAS only) IP address of the remote access server that originally accepted the connection
NAS-Port-Type	Physical connection (e.g., ISDN, POTS) used by the caller
Service-Type	Framed (for PPP) or login (telnet)
Tunnel-Type	Which tunneling protocol should be used (L2TP or PPTP)
Windows-Groups	List of groups that the caller is in

The Permissions page of the wizard has only two radio buttons, but they're important because they specify whether the policy you create allows or prevents users from connecting. The two buttons, Grant Remote Access Permissions and Deny Remote Access Permissions, do what their names imply. Once you choose a permission and click the Next button, the User Profile page appears. Its primary characteristic is the Edit Profile button, which you use to edit the user profile attached to the policy. You don't have to edit the profile when you create the policy; you can always come back to it later. Once you create the policy, it will appear in the snap-in and you can manage it independently of the other policies.

EXERCISE 9.4

Creating a Remote Access Policy

In this exercise, you'll create an adjunct policy that adds time and day restrictions to the default policy. This exercise requires you to be in a native-mode Windows 2000 domain.

1. Open the RRAS MMC snap-in (Start ➢ Programs ➢ Administrative Tools ➢ Routing and Remote Access).

2. Expand the server you want to configure in the left pane of the MMC.

EXERCISE 9.4 *(continued)*

3. Select the Remote Access Policies folder. The right pane of the MMC will display a single policy, "Allow access if dial-in permission is enabled."

4. Select the Action ➤ New Remote Access Policy command. The Add Remote Access Policy wizard will start.

5. In the Policy Name page, type **Working hours restrictions**, and then click the Next button.

6. In the Conditions page, click the Add button. The Select Attributes dialog box will appear.

7. Select the Day-and-Time-Restrictions attribute, and then click the Add button.

8. The Time Of Day Constraints dialog box will appear. Use the calendar controls to allow remote access Monday-Saturday from 7am to 7pm, then click the OK button.

9. The Conditions page reappears, this time with the new condition listed. Click the Next button.

10. The User Profile page appears. Click the Finish button (you'll edit the profile in the next exercise).

Working with Existing Policies

After you complete Exercise 9.4, you'll be better equipped to see a couple of additional policy-management features. To begin, you can reorder policies by right-clicking a policy in the MMC window and using the Move Up and Move Down commands. Since policies are evaluated in the order of their appearance in the snap-in and since all conditions of all policies must match for a user to get access, this is a good way to establish a set of policies that filter out some users. For example, you could create one policy that only allows members of the marketing department to dial in between 8am and 5pm, then add another that allows engineers free rein to dial in anytime.

In addition, when you open the policy's Properties dialog box (Figure 9.10), you can add and remove conditions to the policy, change the policy's name, or control whether a user whose connection matches the policy's conditions will be granted or denied access.

FIGURE 9.10   The policy's Properties dialog box

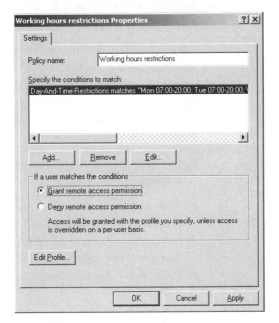

Of course, you can always delete a policy you no longer need by right-clicking it and using the Delete command; the snap-in will prompt you for confirmation before it removes the policy.

Using Remote Access Profiles

Remote access profiles are an integral part of remote access policies. Each policy has a profile associated with it; the profile determines what settings will be applied to connections that meet the conditions stated in the policy. You can create one profile for each policy, either when you create the policy or later (by using the Edit Profile button in the policy's Properties dialog box). The profile contains settings that fit into six distinct areas; each area has its own tab in the profile Properties dialog box. These tabs include the Dial-In Constraints tab, the IP tab, the Multilink tab, the Authentication tab, the Encryption tab, and the Advanced tab.

Microsoft ✓ *Exam Objective*

Configure and troubleshoot remote access.

- Configure a remote access profile.

EXERCISE 9.5

Configuring a User Profile for Dial-In Access

For security reasons, it's usually a good idea to limit access to the administrative accounts on your network. In particular, I usually tell clients to restrict remote access for the Administrator account; that way, the potential exposure from a dial-up compromise is somewhat reduced. Here's how to configure the Administrator account's user profile to restrict dial-up access:

1. Log on to your computer using an account that has administrative privileges.

2. Open the Active Directory Users and Computers snap-in (Start ➤ Programs ➤ Administrative Tools ➤ Active Directory Users and Computers) if you're using an RRAS server that's part of an AD domain. If not, open the Local Users and Groups snap-in (Start ➤ Programs ➤ Administrative Tools ➤ Local Users and Groups) instead.

3. Expand the Users folder. Right-click the Administrator account in the right-hand pane, then choose the Properties command. The Administrator Properties dialog box will appear.

4. Switch to the Dial-In tab by clicking it. On machines that participate in Active Directory, the Permission group should have the Control Access Through Remote Access Policy radio button set.

5. Click the Deny Access radio button to prevent the use of this account over a dial-in connection.

6. Click the OK button.

The Dial-In Constraints Tab

The Dial-in Constraints tab (Figure 9.11) has most of the settings that you think of when you consider dial-in access controls. The controls here allow you to adjust how long the connection may be idle before it gets dropped, how long it can be up, what dates and times the connection may be established, and what dial-in port and medium can be used to connect.

FIGURE 9.11   The Dial-In Constraints tab of the Edit Dial-In Profile Properties dialog box

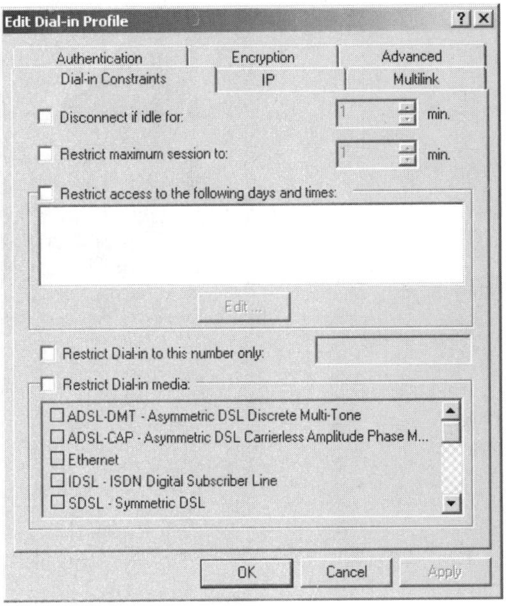

The IP Tab

The IP tab (Figure 9.12) gives you control over the IP-related settings associated with an incoming call. If you think back to the server-specific settings covered earlier in the chapter, you'll remember that the server preferences include settings for other protocols besides IP; this is not so in the remote access profile. In the remote access profile, you can specify where the client gets its IP address. As a bonus, you can define IP packet filters that screen out particular types of traffic to and from the client.

The Multilink Tab

The profile mechanism also gives you a degree of control over how the server handles multilink calls; you exert this control through the Multilink tab (Figure 9.13) of the profile Properties dialog box. Your first choice is to decide whether to allow them at all and, if so, how many ports you want to allow a single client to use at once. Normally, this setting is configured so that the server-specific settings take precedence, but you can override them.

FIGURE 9.12   The IP tab of the Edit Dial-In Profile Properties dialog box

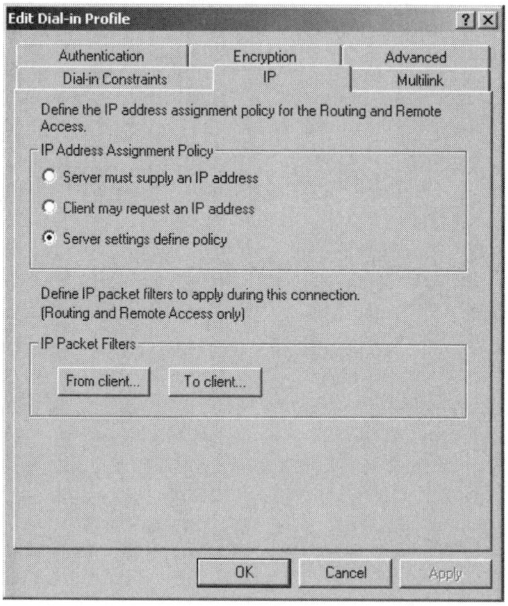

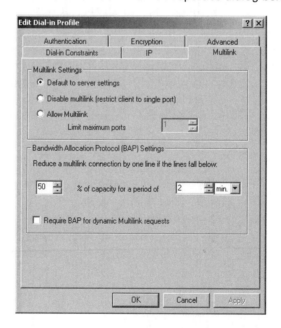

FIGURE 9.13   The Multilink tab of the Edit Dial-In Profile Properties dialog box

The Bandwidth Allocation Protocol (BAP) Settings control group gives you a way to control what happens during a multilink call when the bandwidth usage drops below a certain threshold. For example, why tie up three analog lines to provide 120Kbps of bandwidth when the connection is only using 85Kbps? You can tweak the capacity and time thresholds; by default, a multilink call will drop one line every time the bandwidth usage falls below 50 percent of the available bandwidth and stays there for two minutes. The Require BAP For Dynamic Multilink Requests check box allows you to refuse calls from clients that don't support BAP; this is an easy way to make sure that no client can hog your multilink bandwidth.

The settings you specify on the Multilink tab will be ignored unless you have multilink and BAP/BACP enabled on the server.

The Authentication Tab

The Authentication tab (Figure 9.14) allows you to specify which authentication methods you're willing to allow on this specific policy. Note that these settings, like the other policy settings, will only be useful if the server's settings match. For example, if you turn EAP authentication off in the server Properties dialog box, turning it on in the Authentication tab of the profile Properties dialog box will have no effect.

Speaking of EAP authentication (as well as CHAP, MS-CHAP, and PAP/SPAP), each authentication method has a check box. Check the appropriate boxes to control the protocols that you want this profile to use. If you enable EAP, you can also choose which specific EAP type you want the profile to support. You can also choose to allow totally unauthenticated access; thankfully, this option is off by default.

FIGURE 9.14   The Authentication tab of the Edit Dial-In Profile Properties dialog box

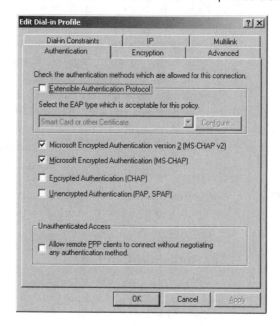

The Encryption Tab

The Encryption tab (Figure 9.15) controls what type of encryption you want your remote users to have access to.

Microsoft ✓ *Exam* *Objective*	**Configure remote access security.** ▪ Configure encryption protocols.

Unfortunately, instead of labeling the tab's check boxes with algorithm names and key lengths, Microsoft labels them with the following adjectives:

▪ The No Encryption check box means what it says. When this box is checked, users can connect using no encryption at all; when it's unchecked, a remote connection must be encrypted or it'll be rejected.

▪ The Basic check box means single DES for IPSec or 40-bit Microsoft Point-to-Point Encryption (MPPE) for PPTP.

- The Strong check box means 56-bit encryption (single DES for IPSec; 56-bit MPPE for PPTP).

- The Strongest check box means triple DES for IPSec or 128-bit MPPE for PPTP connections. This option will only be available on Windows 2000 installations that use the full-strength High Encryption Pack.

FIGURE 9.15 The Encryption tab of the profile Properties dialog box

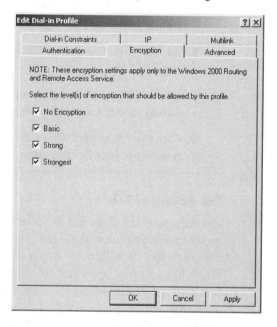

EXERCISE 9.6

Configuring Encryption

In this exercise, you'll force all connections to your server to use encryption. Any client that can't use encryption will be dropped; accordingly, don't do this on your production RRAS server unless you're sure that all of your clients are encryption-capable.

1. Open the RRAS snap-in (Start ➤ Programs ➤ Administrative Tools ➤ Routing and Remote Access).

2. Expand the server you want to configure in the left pane of the MMC.

EXERCISE 9.6 *(continued)*

3. Select the Remote Access Policies folder. The right pane of the MMC will display the policies defined for this server. Select the "Allow access if dial-in permission is enabled" policy.

4. Use the Action ➢ Properties command. The policy Properties dialog box will appear.

5. Click the Edit Profile button. The Edit Dial-in Profile dialog box will appear (refer back to Figure 9.11).

6. Switch to the Encryption tab (see Figure 9.15 from earlier in this chapter).

7. Uncheck the No Encryption check box. Make sure that the Basic, Strong, and Strongest (if present) check boxes are all marked.

8. Click the OK button. When the policy Properties dialog box reappears, click its OK button.

The Advanced Tab

The Advanced tab (Figure 9.16) is primarily useful if you want your RRAS server to interoperate with RADIUS equipment from other vendors. You use the tab to specify additional attributes you want incorporated into the profile. When you first open the tab, you'll see only two attributes specified: a Service-Type of Framed and a Framed-Protocol of PPP. That combination allows the RRAS server to tell its peers that it's handling a framed PPP connection. There are several dozen additional attributes available through the Add... button; some are defined in the RADIUS standard, while others are specific to particular vendors. It's not necessary to know what attributes are on this list, only that you use the Advanced tab to add additional attributes when combining RRAS with third-party RADIUS-based solutions.

FIGURE 9.16   The Advanced tab of the profile Properties dialog box

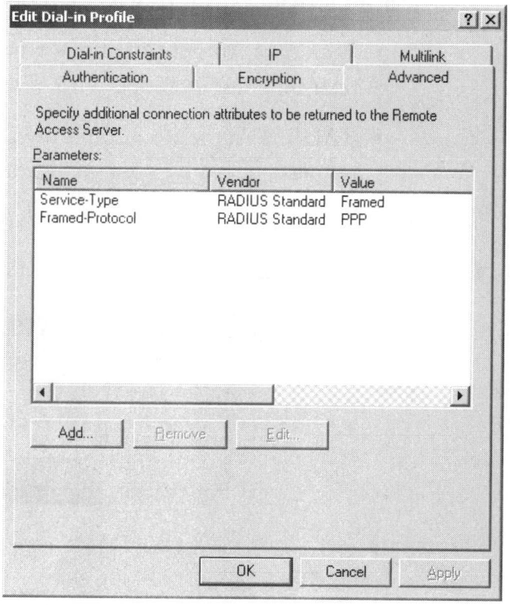

Configuring Security

Remote access security is a touchy topic in some quarters, probably because no one wants to admit not having it. There are several different aspects involved with remote access security configuration, the most fundamental of which involves configuring the types of authentication and encryption the server will use when accepting client requests.

Controlling Server Security

The Security tab of the server's Properties dialog box (Figure 9.17) allows you to specify which authentication and accounting methods RRAS uses.

Microsoft
Exam
Objective

Configure remote access security.

- Configure authentication protocols.

You can choose one of two authentication providers by using the Authentication Provider drop-down list. Your choices include the following:

- Windows Authentication is what Microsoft calls the built-in authentication suite included with Windows 2000.

- RADIUS Authentication allows you to send all authentication requests heard by your server on to a RADIUS server for approval or denial.

FIGURE 9.17 The Security tab of the RRAS server Properties dialog box

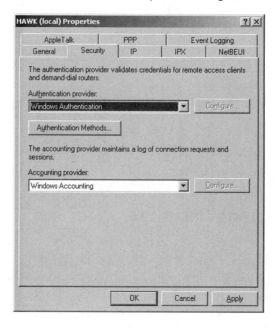

As a bonus, you can use the Accounting Provider drop-down list on the Security tab to choose between Microsoft-style accounting, in which connection requests are maintained in the event log, and RADIUS accounting, in which all accounting events are sent to a RADIUS server for action.

What if you want to change the set of authentication methods that a particular server will allow? You might think that you'd do it with the Configure… button next to the Authentication Provider drop-down list, but that's actually used to set up communications with RADIUS servers when using RADIUS authentication. To configure the server by telling it which authentication methods you want it to use, you have to use the Authentication Methods… button, which displays the Authentication Methods dialog box

(Figure 9.18). If you look back over the list of authentication protocols earlier in the chapter, you'll find that each one has a corresponding check box here: EAP, MS-CHAP v2, MS-CHAP, CHAP, SPAP, and PAP are all represented. If you're feeling *really* adventurous, you can turn on totally unauthenticated access by checking the Allow Remote Systems To Connect Without Authentication check box, but that's a really, really bad idea since it allows literally anyone to connect to, and use, your server (and thus by extension your network)!

FIGURE 9.18 The Authentication Methods dialog box

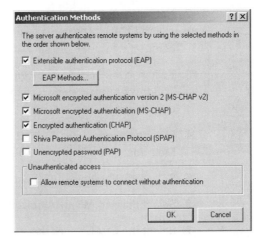

There's actually a special set of requirements for using CHAP since it requires access to each user's encrypted password. Windows 2000 normally doesn't store user passwords in a format that CHAP can use, so you have to take some additional steps if you want to use CHAP. First, enable CHAP at the server and policy levels. Next, you need to edit the default domain GPO's Password Policy object to turn on the "Store password using reversible encryption for all users" policy setting. After you've done that, each user's password must be either reset or changed, which forces Windows 2000 to store the password in reversibly-encrypted form. After these steps are completed for an account, that account can be used with CHAP. These steps aren't required for MS-CHAP or MS-CHAP v2; for those protocols, you just enable the desired version of MS-CHAP at the server and policy levels.

EXERCISE 9.7

Configuring Authentication Protocols

For this exercise, you're going to configure your RRAS server so that it only accepts inbound calls that use the IP protocol. You may have to skip some steps (as noted) if you don't have all of the four network protocols loaded.

1. Open the RRAS MMC snap-in (Start ➢ Programs ➢ Administrative Tools ➢ Routing and Remote Access).

2. Navigate to the server whose authentication support you want to change. Select the server, and then use the Action ➢ Properties command to open the server Properties dialog box.

3. Switch to the Security tab (refer back to Figure 9.17). Make sure that Windows Authentication is selected in the Authentication Provider drop-down.

4. Click the Authentication Methods button. The Authentication Methods dialog box will appear.

5. Select the Extensible Authentication Protocol (EAP) check box.

6. Select the two MS-CHAP check boxes.

7. Select the CHAP check box.

8. Clear the SPAP and PAP check boxes.

9. Clear the Allow Remote Systems To Connect Without Authentication check box.

10. Click the OK button; when the server Properties dialog box reappears, click its OK button.

Controlling Security at the Policy Level

You can apply authentication restrictions at the policy level, too. As you saw in the preceding sections, policy-level settings don't exactly override the server settings. For example, you could configure your server to allow CHAP, MS-CHAP, and MS-CHAP v2, then set up a policy that would prevent some users from using CHAP. On the other hand, if you disable CHAP at the server level you can't build a policy that will magically allow it.

Having said that, the trick to remember is to configure your server with the *sum* of the authentication methods you want to be able to use, then create specific policies that limit which authentication methods (and other settings, particularly dial-in constraints) individuals or groups can use on that server.

Managing Your Remote Access Server

RRAS server management is generally pretty easy since in most cases there's not much to manage. You set up the server, it answers calls, and life is good. You'll probably find it necessary to monitor the server's ongoing activity, and you may find it necessary to log activity for accounting or security purposes.

Seeing What's Going On

You can monitor your server's activity in a number of ways, including having the server keep local copies of its logs or having it send logging data to a remote RADIUS server. In addition, you can always monitor the current status of any of the ports on your system. Microsoft's documentation distinguishes between event logging, which records significant things that happen like startup and shutdown of the RRAS service, and authentication and accounting logging, which tracks things like when user X logged on and logged off. The settings for both types of logging are intermingled in the RRAS snap-in.

Microsoft ✓
Exam
Objective

Manage and monitor remote access.

Monitoring Overall Activity

The Server Status node in the RRAS snap-in shows you a summary of all the RRAS servers known to the system. Depending on whether or not you use the features discussed in Chapter 8 to manage multiple RRAS servers from one console, you may only see the local server's information here. When you select the Server Status item, the right-hand pane of the MMC will list each known RRAS server; each entry in the list tells you whether the server is up or not, what kind of server it is, how many ports it has, how many ports are currently in use, and how long the server's been up. You can right-click any Windows 2000 RRAS server in this view to start, stop, restart, pause, or resume its RRAS service, disable RRAS on the server, or remove the server's advertisement from Active Directory (provided, of course, that you're using AD).

Controlling Remote Access Logging

A vanilla RRAS installation will always log *some* data locally, but that's pretty worthless unless you know what gets logged and where it goes. Each RRAS server on your network has its own set of logs, which you manage through the Remote Access Logging folder. Within that folder, you'll normally see a single item labeled Local File, which is the log file stored on that particular server.

If you don't have Windows accounting or Windows authentication turned on, you won't have a local log file. Depending on whether or not you're using RADIUS accounting and logging, you may see additional entries. However, the rest of this section will stick with local file logging.

Setting Server Logging Properties

The first place where you can control server logging is at the server level—you use the Event Logging tab (Figure 9.19) to control what level of detail you want in the server's event log. Bear in mind that these controls regulate *all* logging by RRAS, not just remote access log entries. You have four choices for the level of logged detail:

- The Log Errors Only radio button instructs the server to log errors and nothing else. This gives you adequate indication of problems *after* they happen, but it doesn't point out potential problems noted by warning messages.

- The Log Errors And Warnings radio button is the default choice. This forces the server to log error and warning messages to the event log, giving you a nice balance between information content and log volume.

- The Log The Maximum Amount Of Information radio button causes the RRAS service to log mass quantities of messages, covering literally everything the server does. While this voluminous output is useful for troubleshooting (or even for getting a better understanding of how remote access works), it's overkill for everyday use.

- The Disable Event Logging radio button turns off all event logging for RRAS. *Don't use this option*. It will disallow you from reviewing the service's logs in case of a problem.

FIGURE 9.19   The Event Logging tab of the server Properties dialog box

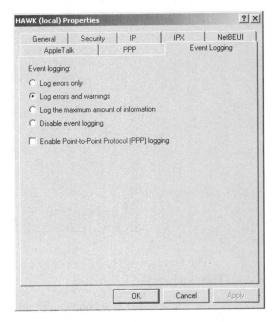

The Enable Point-to-Point Protocol (PPP) Logging check box allows you to turn on logging of all PPP negotiations and connections. This can provide valuable information when you're trying to figure out what's wrong, but it adds a lot of unnecessary bulk to your log files. Don't turn it on unless you're trying to pin down a problem.

Setting Log File Properties

You can select an individual log file in the snap-in to control what that log file contains. More precisely, you can control what events should be logged in that file from the time of the change forward. You make these changes by selecting the log file and using the Action ➤ Properties command (or one of its equivalents) to open the log file Properties dialog box. This dialog box has two tabs: The Settings tab (Figure 9.20) controls what gets logged in the file, and the Local File tab controls the format of the file itself.

FIGURE 9.20 The Settings tab of the Local File Properties dialog box

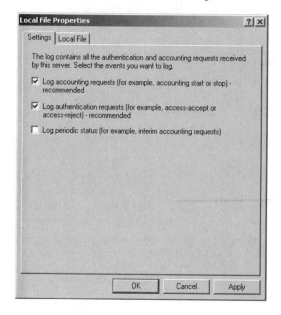

The Settings tab has three check boxes that control what gets logged. They include the following:

- The first, Log Accounting Requests, should always be checked since it governs whether events related to the accounting service itself will be logged (as well as accounting data).

- The second, Log Authentication Requests, should also remain checked—it adjusts whether successful and failed logon requests are logged or not.

- The third check box, Log Periodic Status, should normally remain off; it controls whether or not interim accounting packets are permanently stored on disk.

FIGURE 9.21   The Local File tab of the Local File Properties dialog box

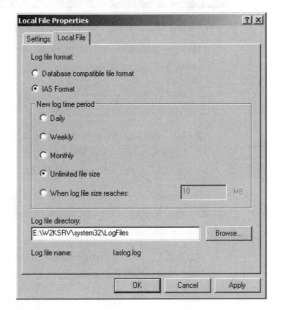

The Local File tab (Figure 9.21) controls how the log file is written to disk. You use this tab to designate three things:

- The Log File Format field determines the format of the log file. By default, RRAS will use the old-school Internet Authentication Service (IAS) format, which was originally used by the IAS component included as part of the Windows NT Option Pack. You can instead choose to use the database-compatible file format, which is available only in Windows 2000. This format makes it easy for you to take log data and store it in a database, enabling more sophisticated post-processing for things like billing and chargebacks.

- The New Log Time Period field controls how often new log files are created. For example, some administrators prefer to get a new log file each week or each month, while others are content to let the log file grow without end. You can choose to have RRAS start new log files each day, each week, each month, or when the log file reaches a certain size.

- The Log File Directory field shows where the log file's stored. By default, each server logs its data in `%systemroot%\system32\LogFiles\iasLog.log`. By using the Log File Directory field, you can change this location to wherever you want.

EXERCISE 9.8

Changing Remote Access Logging Settings

Having correct accounting and authorization data is critical to maintaining a good level of security.

1. Open the RRAS MMC snap-in (Start ➤ Programs ➤ Administrative Tools ➤ Routing and Remote Access).

2. Navigate to the server whose logging settings you want to change. Expand the target server, then select the Remote Access Logging node. The right-hand MMC pane will list the log files on that server.

3. Locate the log file named "Local log file," and then open its Properties dialog box by right-clicking it and choosing the Properties command.

4. The Local File Properties dialog box appears. Make sure the Log Accounting Requests and Log Authentication Requests check boxes are marked.

5. Switch to the Local File tab. Select an appropriate time period for log rollover by choosing one of the radio buttons in the New Log Time Period control group.

6. Click the OK button.

Reviewing the Remote Access Event Log

You use the Local File tab to find out exactly where the log file lives, but what do you do with it then? Windows 2000 online help has an exhaustive list of all the fields logged for each connection attempt and accounting record; you don't need to have all those fields memorized, and you don't have to know how to make sense of the log entries. The Windows 2000 Resource Kit includes a handy utility called *iasparse* that will digest an RRAS log in IAS or database formats and then produce a readable summary.

Why bother reviewing the logs? One nice feature is that each entry in the authentication log indicates which remote access policy applied (either to accept or reject the connection). This is a good way to identify problems with policies since sometimes multiple policies can combine to have an effect you didn't expect. Furthermore, if it's desirable in your environment you can use the logged data to generate accounting reports to tell you things like the average utilization of your dial-in ports, the top ten users of dial-in connect time, or how much online time accounts in a certain Windows group used. Unfortunately, though, you're on your own when it comes to building tools to generate reports that will tell you whatever it is you want to know—there aren't any reporting tools included with Windows 2000.

Monitoring Ports & Port Activity

You can monitor port status and activity from the RRAS snap-in, too. The Ports folder under the server contains one entry for each defined port; when you select the Ports folder, then, you'll see a list of the ports and their current status. The list indicates whether each port is a dial-in or VPN port and whether or not it's active, so you can get a quick summary of your server's workload at any time.

Double-clicking an individual port displays the Port Status dialog box (Figure 9.22). This dialog box shows you pretty much everything you'd care to know about an individual port, including its line speed, the amount of transmitted and received data, and the network addresses for each protocol being carried on the port. This is a useful tool for verifying whether a port is in active use or not, and the Errors control group gives you a count of the number of transmission and reception errors on the port.

FIGURE 9.22   The Port Status dialog box

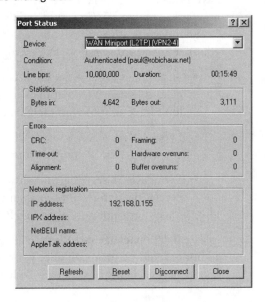

Integrating RRAS with DHCP

If you want your RRAS clients to use a DHCP server on your network, you may need to do a little fancy dancing to get things working properly. By design, the DHCP protocol is intended to allow clients and servers on the same IP network to communicate. RFC 1542 sets out how the BOOTP protocol (on which DHCP is based) should work in circumstances where the client and server are on different IP networks. If there's no DHCP server available on the network where the client's located, you can use a *DHCP relay agent* to forward DHCP messages from the client to the DHCP server's network. The relay agent acts like a radio repeater, listening for DHCP client requests and retransmitting them on the server's network.

Microsoft ✓ *Exam* *Objective*

Configure and troubleshoot remote access.

• Configure Routing and Remote Access for DHCP integration.

The bottom line is that each network that has a DHCP client on it must have either a DHCP server or a DHCP relay agent. Otherwise, the client has no way to reach a DHCP server and get a lease.

What does this mean for your remote access deployment? It depends on your network configuration, as described by the following:

• On a small or simple network, you may choose to use static IP addressing and assign each dial-in client a fixed IP address. In this case, you don't have to fool with DHCP at all.

• If your RRAS server is also a DHCP server, you're OK since dial-in clients will get an IP address from that server's address pool.

• If your RRAS server is on a different IP network from your DHCP servers, or if you want to assign client addresses out of an address range that's not part of any DHCP scope, you need a relay agent.

The RRAS package includes a DHCP relay agent that you install as an additional routing protocol; once you install and configure it, it can tie your remote access clients to whatever DHCP infrastructure you want to use.

Installing the DHCP Relay Agent

First, a couple of caveats: You can't install the relay agent on a computer that's already acting as a DHCP server, nor can you install it on a system running Network Address Translation (NAT) with the addressing component installed. (See Chapter 13, "Managing Network Address Translation," for more on NAT and automatic addressing.) As long as you meet these requirements, the actual installation process is easy (see Exercise 9.9). Once you have the agent installed, you're ready to configure it to forward requests when and where you want them to be relayed.

Configuring the DHCP Relay Agent

As is typical of other RRAS components, you actually configure the DHCP relay agent in two places: from the Relay Agent Properties dialog box and again on each individual interface. The configuration settings required for each of these two places are different.

Setting DHCP Relay Agent Properties

When you select the DHCP Relay Agent item under the IP Routing node and open its Properties dialog box, you'll see the contents of Figure 9.23. The only thing you can do here is specify to which DHCP servers you want *this particular* DHCP relay agent to forward requests. The only restriction is that the RRAS server that's running the DHCP relay agent must be able to route IP packets to the destination network. The servers you specify here apply to all network interfaces to which you attach the relay agent; there's no way to configure independent forwarding addresses for individual network interfaces.

FIGURE 9.23 The DHCP Relay Agent Properties dialog box

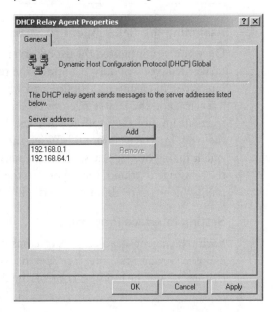

Installing the DHCP Relay Agent on an RRAS Server

Follow these steps to install the DHCP relay agent on an RRAS server:

1. Open the Routing and Remote Access snap-in (Start ➢ Programs ➢ Administrative Tools ➢ Routing and Remote Access).

2. Locate the server on which you want to install the DHCP relay agent.

3. Expand the server's configuration until you see the General node (*serverName* ➢ IP Routing ➢ General).

4. Right-click the General node and choose the New Routing Protocol command. The New Routing Protocol dialog box will appear.

5. Select DHCP Relay Agent from the list of routing protocols, and then click the OK button.

6. The IP Routing node will now have a child node named DHCP Relay Agent. Select it and use the Properties command to open its Properties dialog box.

7. In the DHCP Relay Agent Global Properties dialog box, add the IP addresses of the DHCP servers you want DHCP requests forwarded to, and then click the OK button.

Assigning the Relay Agent to Specific Interfaces

Once you've configured the list of servers to which you want DHCP requests forwarded, you still have to attach the relay agent to particular network interfaces. In Chapter 8, you learned what it means to create an interface for a service, and the DHCP agent is no different. You use the same mechanism to create an interface, too: Right-click the DHCP Relay Agent item and use the New Interface command. When the New Interface for DHCP Relay Agent dialog box appears, select the network interface to which you want the relay agent bound. Once you do, the interface-specific properties dialog box (which you're about to meet) will appear.

Setting Interface Properties

Each relay agent–enabled interface has its own set of properties, which are exposed through the interface-specific Relay Agent Properties dialog box (Figure 9.24). The topmost control, the Relay DHCP Packets check box, lets you control whether DHCP relaying is active on this interface or not—you can turn it on or off without restarting the RRAS service.

The other two controls affect how long relayed DHCP requests will bounce around your network. The hop count controls the number of intervening routers between the client and the DHCP server that the DHCP traffic can traverse, and the boot threshold controls how long the relay agent waits before forwarding any DHCP messages it hears. If you want to give a local DHCP server first crack at incoming requests, adjust the boot threshold up so that the local server has a chance to respond before the message is forwarded.

FIGURE 9.24 The interface-specific DHCP Relay Agent Properties dialog box

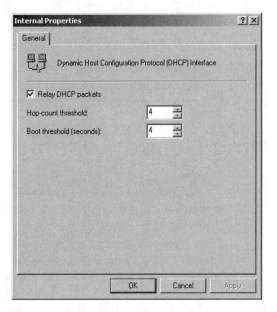

EXERCISE 9.10

Configuring the DHCP Relay Agent on a Network Interface

In this exercise, you'll add a new DHCP Relay Agent interface for your LAN connection, then specify configuration parameters for it. In practice, you'd need to add the DHCP Relay Agent to whichever interface remote clients use, but since I can't assume anything about the configuration of your lab machine, this lab is simplified somewhat.

EXERCISE 9.10 *(continued)*

1. Install the DHCP Relay Agent on your server according to the instructions in Exercise 9.9.

2. Right-click the DHCP Relay Agent item and choose the New Interface command.

3. The New Interface for DHCP Relay Agent dialog box appears, listing each of the interfaces to which you could attach the relay agent. Select Local Area Connection and click the OK button.

4. The interface-specific Properties dialog box (Figure 9.24) appears. If you have a DHCP server on your local network, increase the boot threshold to 5 seconds; if you don't, decrease it to 0.

5. Click the OK button. Note that the list of DHCP Relay Agent interfaces has been updated to reflect the new interface.

Monitoring Network Traffic

Sometimes the best way to see what's happening on your network is to watch the traffic as it passes. Since you'd have a really hard time doing that by looking at the lights on your Ethernet hub, Microsoft includes a tool called Network Monitor on the Windows 2000 Server and Advanced Server CDs. This tool is a direct descendant of the Windows NT Network Monitor, which in turn is based on the same-named tool provided with the Systems Management Server (SMS) product. Network Monitor is an example of a type of program called a network analyzer (or "sniffer" after the Network General Sniffer toolset). Network analyzers capture raw traffic from the network, then decode it just as the protocol stack would. Because they don't depend on a protocol stack, you can use an analyzer to monitor traffic for protocol types you don't actually have installed; for example, you might use Network Monitor to capture and decode AppleTalk packets while troubleshooting a Mac connectivity problem, even without having AppleTalk on your workstation.

Microsoft ✓ *Exam Objective*

Manage and monitor network traffic.

Network Monitor comes in two pieces: the application, which you install on Windows 2000 Server or Advanced Server; and the driver, which you install on any Windows 2000 machine. To monitor traffic on a machine, it must have the driver installed (it's automatically installed when you install the application). The driver is required because it puts the network card into *promiscuous mode*, in which the card will accept packets not addressed to it—obviously a requirement to monitor overall network traffic.

Before you install and use Network Monitor, there are a couple of caveats you need to know about. First, the Windows 2000 Network Monitor only works with Windows 2000 clients—if you want to use it to monitor Windows NT, 95, or 98 clients you need the Network Monitor drivers from the SMS product CD. More importantly, the Windows 2000 version of Network Monitor allows you to watch traffic to and from only the server that it's installed on; the SMS version of Network Monitor supports watching traffic anywhere on your network.

What Network Monitor Does

Network Monitor basically allocates a big chunk of RAM to use as a *capture buffer*. When you tell it to start capturing network packets, it copies every packet it sees on a particular NIC to the buffer, gathering statistical data as it goes. When you stop the capture process, you can analyze the buffered data in a variety of ways, including by applying *capture filters* that screen out packets you're not interested in.

Installing the Network Monitor Driver

If you want to use the Network Monitor to capture packets from a machine that doesn't already have Network Monitor on it, you need to install the Network Monitor driver on the target machine. Exercise 9.11 explains this process, which is basically just another application of something you learned back in Chapter 4.

EXERCISE 9.11

Installing the Network Monitor Driver

In this exercise, you'll install the Network Monitor driver. Be forewarned that many organizations watch their network very closely for signs of network analyzer use, so completing this exercise may bring you a visit from the Men In Black. You may be prompted for the Windows 2000 CD, too, so have it handy.

1. Open the Network and Dial-Up Connections folder (Start ➤ Settings ➤ Network and Dial-up Connections).

2. Find the LAN interface you want to enable Network Monitor to monitor, right-click it, and choose the Properties command.

3. When the Properties dialog box appears, click the Install button. The Select Network Component Type dialog box will appear; click Protocol in the Component list and click the Add button.

4. The Select Network Protocol dialog box appears. Select Network Monitor Driver and click the OK button.

5. Once the driver's installed, the Properties dialog box will reappear; then click the Close button.

Installing the Network Monitor Application

Once you've installed the Network Monitor driver on at least one other machine, you can install the Network Monitor application itself and start monitoring. To actually install Network Monitor, use the Add/Remove Programs Control Panel. Switch to the Add/Remove Windows Components icon, then select the Management and Monitoring Tools item and click the Details button. When the Management and Monitoring Tools dialog box appears, make sure Network Monitor Tools is checked, then click the OK button. Once the installation finishes, you'll find Network Monitor at the bottom of the Administrative Tools group in the Start menu's Program Files group.

A Whirlwind Tour of Network Monitor

There's no way to sugarcoat the fact that Network Monitor is a complicated tool; it's made for complicated tasks and its interface reflects that. This section isn't going to teach you how to troubleshoot subtle network problems with Network Monitor, but it will explain how to use Network Monitor to do some simple tasks that will give you a good head start on learning to use it well enough to pass the exam (and, it is hoped, to solve the occasional problem, too).

Forget about right-clicking since Network Monitor doesn't support it. (It's beginning to show its age!)

When you first start Network Monitor, it will ask you to choose a network to monitor. The list of networks you see will depend on the number of NICs you have installed; if you only have one NIC, Network Monitor will automatically select the correct network for you. Once you've done that, you'll see the Network Monitor window (Figure 9.25). While it may seem overwhelming, there's logic to what you see.

FIGURE 9.25 The rather daunting main Network Monitor window

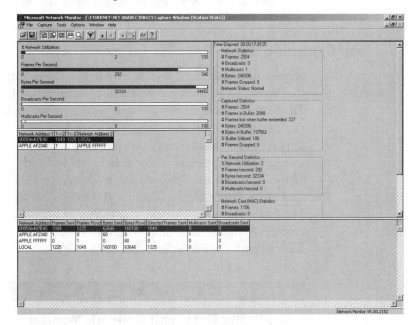

The following list explains what you'll see in the main Network Monitor window (you can turn specific panes on and off with the Window menu):

- The pane in the upper-left corner displays bar graphs of current network utilization (which explains why it's called the Graph pane), including the number of frames, bytes, broadcasts, and multicasts per second. This pane updates only when a capture is in progress.

- The pane in the middle of the left side shows information about connections captured during the current session (the Session Stats pane). This information includes the source and destination network addresses and how many packets have gone in each direction between the two endpoints.

- The entire right side of the window contains the Total Stats pane, which lists a variety of interesting statistics (including the total number of unicast, broadcast, and multicast frames, plus the amount of data currently in the capture buffer). Like the Session Stats pane, this pane's contents are continuously updated during a capture.

- The bottom portion of the window contains the Station Stats frame, which tells you what's been happening on the machine you're running Network Monitor on.

Capturing Data

When you capture data, you're just filling up a big buffer with the packets as they arrive; Network Monitor doesn't attempt to analyze them at that point. To control capture activity, you can use either the toolbar buttons (the ones that use the standard start, stop, and pause symbols) or the commands in the Capture menu: Start, Stop, Stop and View, Pause, and Continue. Starting and stopping capture is pretty straightforward, although you may need to adjust the buffer size upward from its default of 1Mb. You do this using the Capture ➢ Buffer Settings command. Once you start the capture, Network Monitor will continue working until you've filled the buffer or stopped the capture. At that point, you can view the data or save it to a disk file for later analysis with the File ➢ Save As command.

EXERCISE 9.12

Capturing Data with Network Monitor

In this exercise, you'll use Network Monitor to gather a full capture buffer so you can experiment with display filters in the next exercise.

1. Install Network Monitor as described in Exercise 9.11.

2. Use the Capture ➢ Buffer Settings command to increase the capture buffer size to 2Mb. This gives you room for 4096 frames of data.

3. Start a capture with the Capture ➢ Start command. While the capture is going, use a Web browser to request a Web page from the machine you're running Network Monitor on. (This step is necessary for the next exercise.)

4. Let it run until the buffer is full; you can tell by watching the "# Frames in Buffer" line in the Total Stats pane.

5. Save the capture buffer to disk with the File ≻ Save As command. You'll need it for the next exercise.

Viewing Data

After you stop a capture, you can view the accumulated data with the Capture ≻ View Captured Data command. This opens a new kind of window: the Frame Viewer (see Figure 9.26). This window lists every captured frame, summarizing its source and destination address, the time at which it was captured (relative to the start of the capture operation), the network type, and the protocol in use. While the display of all this data is certainly interesting, it's hard to pick out much useful detail unless you have *impeccable* timing. It's more likely that you'll need to use Network Monitor's filtering functions to pick out just the data you want.

FIGURE 9.26   The Frame Viewer window

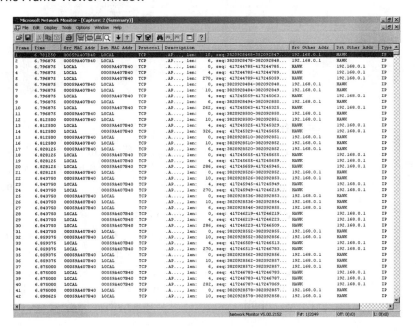

If you want to see the full contents of an individual frame, just double-click it. This causes two new panes to appear in the Frame Viewer window: The Detail pane is in the middle, and the Hex pane is at the bottom (see Figure 9.27). This gives you an easy way to inspect, bit by bit, the contents of any captured frame in the buffer.

FIGURE 9.27 The Frame Viewer window with the Detail and Hex panes visible

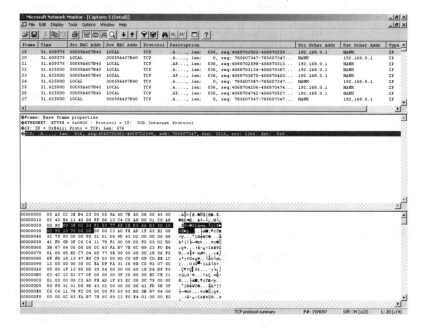

Using Filters

You can create two types of filters in Network Monitor: Capture filters screen out unwanted packets before they're recorded to the capture buffer, and display filters display some packets but not others.

Working with Capture Filters

You create and manage capture filters using the Capture ➤ Filters command, available from the standard Network Monitor window. This displays the Capture Filter dialog box (Figure 9.28). Don't let the appearance of this dialog box intimidate you; if you understand the following rule, you can build as complex a group of filters as you like.

FIGURE 9.28   The Capture Filter dialog box

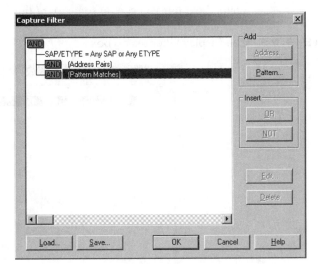

The rule to remember is that filters are grouped in a tree. The default filter says that any SAP/ETYPE (Service Access Point or Ethernet Type—both of these tags mark packets with the protocol they're using) will be captured. This is because the three conditions under the root of the tree all use the *and* modifier. While you can use *and*, *or*, and *not* for your own filters, you can't remove the original tree branches.

Say, for example, that you want to create a filter that captures traffic going to port 80 on a particular machine. Capture filters don't care about ports, but you could create a filter based on the address by selecting the SAP/ETYPE branch and using the Edit button to capture only IP packets. Next, edit the (Address Pairs) item so that you've specified the proper destination address. If you were looking for packets with a particular payload, you could specify a pattern to capture that traffic with the (Pattern Matches) branch, too. (Unfortunately, that's about all you can do with capture filters in the Windows 2000 version of Network Monitor; there are a bunch of additional features that only work in the SMS version.)

Working with Display Filters

Once you've captured some data, you can create display filters that give you much finer control over what you see. This is handy since it's difficult to pick out the few frames you're looking for from a full capture buffer. You create display filters while you're looking at the Frame Viewer window; use the Display ➤ Filter command to bring up the Display Filter dialog box (Figure 9.29).

The mechanics of this dialog box work just like they do in the Capture Filter dialog box, but you can do some extra things.

FIGURE 9.29   The Display Filter dialog box

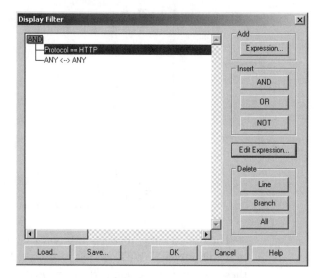

Now revisit the earlier example: You want to create a filter that only displays traffic to the Web server on a specific machine. This is easy to do, as you'll see in Exercise 9.13.

EXERCISE 9.13

Creating a Display Filter

Using the capture buffer from Exercise 9.12, you can create a display filter to limit what appears in the Frame Viewer.

1. If you have quit Network Monitor since the previous exercise, reopen the capture buffer you saved by using the File ≻ Open command.

2. When the Frame Viewer window appears, use the Display ≻Filters command to open the Display Filter dialog box.

3. Select the Protocol = Any line, and click the Edit Expression button. You'll see the Protocol tab of the Expression dialog box (Figure 9.30).

EXERCISE 9.13 *(continued)*

4. Click the Disable All button to remove all the protocols. Any protocol that's disabled will be screened out by the filter.

5. Select HTTP in the Disabled Protocols list and click the Enable button; now HTTP should be the only enabled protocol. Click the OK button.

6. Optionally, select the ANY <--> ANY filter and use the Edit Expression button to add an address rule to the filter. Normally you don't need to do this because the Windows 2000 version of Network Monitor monitors only traffic between your computer and one other at a time.

7. Click the OK button in the Display Filter dialog when you're done. The Frame Viewer window will reappear, but notice that the frame numbers (in the leftmost column) are no longer consecutive—the filter is screening out any traffic that doesn't match its criteria.

8. Double-click a frame to see its contents. Since you're looking at unencrypted HTTP packets, you can clearly see the requests and responses.

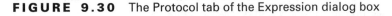

FIGURE 9.30 The Protocol tab of the Expression dialog box

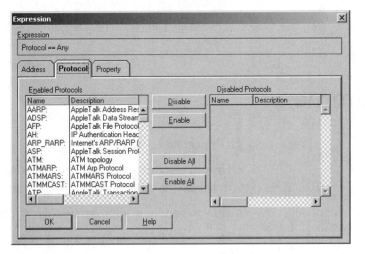

The Tools Menu

The Tools menu has four commands in it that are of varying degrees of usefulness. They include the following:

- The Identify Network Monitor Users command scans the network looking for other NICs in promiscuous mode. This is a dead giveaway that someone is doing *something* they're not supposed to, since apart from running a network analyzer there's no reason why an ordinary user should have their NIC in that mode. When Network Monitor finishes its scan, it displays a dialog box listing all instances of Network Monitor it finds on the network.

Remember this command, since it's one of the things Microsoft *really* wants you to know how to do.

- The Find Routers command doesn't do anything unless you have the version of Network Monitor that comes with SMS; in that case, it does a *tracert*-like repetitive ping to find routers on the network.

- The Resolve Addresses From Name command does the equivalent of a reverse lookup for non-DNS names. At least, that's what it does if you have the SMS version of Network Monitor; if you don't, it does nothing.

- The Performance Monitor command opens the System Performance snap-in.

Summary

In this chapter, you learned:

- How to install and configure the Routing and Remote Access Service to handle dial-in connections

- How to configure appropriate encryption and security settings

- How to configure and use remote access policies and profiles

Key Terms

Before you take the exam, be sure you're familiar with the following terms:

Capture buffer

Capture filters

Challenge Handshake Authentication Protocol (CHAP)

DHCP relay agent

EAP type

Extensible Authentication Protocol (EAP)

Iasparse

Password Authentication Protocol (PAP)

Promiscuous mode

Remote access policies

Remote access profiles

Remote Authentication for Dial-In User Service (RADIUS)

Review Questions

1. If you want to allow your RRAS server to interoperate with your existing DHCP servers, you need to use which of the following?

   A. The DHCP relay agent

   B. A Microsoft DHCP server

   C. Dynamic DNS

   D. The WINS proxy agent

2. You want to support smartcard authentication for your remote access users. This requires you to use which of the following?

   A. MS-CHAP v3

   B. MS-CHAP v2

   C. EAP with the EAP-TLS type

   D. EAP with any EAP type

3. Joanna wants her remote users to use encryption on their dial-in connections. To accomplish this, she must _____.

   A. Create a new group policy object that specifies which encryption method to use.

   B. Create a remote access policy and edit its profile to turn off the No Encryption option.

   C. Require everyone to use IPSec on their dial-in connections.

   D. Buy a third-party network access server.

4. You have a local DHCP server for your dial-in clients, but you also want to use the DHCP relay agent to forward requests to a remote DHCP server if the local server doesn't answer a request. To do this, you must do which of the following?

A. Add a static route to the remote server.

B. Adjust the boot threshold on the DHCP Relay Agent interface for the remote network so that the local server has enough time to respond.

C. Adjust the DHCP Forwarding Time parameter in the registry.

D. Adjust the forwarding time in the DHCP Relay Agent Global Properties dialog box.

5. Which of the following steps is *not required* to enable the use of CHAP with RRAS?

A. Enabling reversible password encryption for all users

B. Resetting or changing passwords for all users who want to use CHAP

C. Disabling support for MS-CHAP v1 and MS-CHAP v2

D. Enable CHAP as a supported authentication protocol

6. You can choose to grant users dial-in access by doing which of the following? (Choose two.)

A. Creating a remote access policy that allows the desired users access

B. Setting the remote access settings on the user's dial-in profile to "Allow access"

C. Adding the user accounts to the Dial-In Users group

D. Modifying the group policy for the users' container

7. Remote access policies require which of the following?

A. Active Directory must be running in native mode.

B. The RRAS server must be a member of an Active Directory domain.

C. You must use Windows 2000 Advanced Server.

D. You must use third-party software.

8. When applying a remote access policy, the user will be granted access under which of the following conditions?

   A. Only if the policy specifies that access should be granted

   B. Only if the policy does not specify that access should be denied

   C. Only if the policy specifies that access should be granted and all the policy's conditions are met

   D. Only if all the policy's conditions are met

9. Kelly is trying to dial in to your Windows 2000 remote access server. She is unable to make a connection. This may be because of which two of the following conditions?

   A. Her client is unable to negotiate a compatible authentication protocol with the server.

   B. There is a remote access policy that prohibits her from connecting.

   C. She is not using Windows 2000 Professional.

   D. Encryption is disabled on the server.

10. The DHCP relay agent _____.

    A. Is always required on RRAS servers

    B. Is required on RRAS servers that use static addressing for clients

    C. May not be used on servers running NAT or DHCP

    D. Can only be run on non-RRAS servers

11. Donna Jo set up an RRAS server for her company's sales force. Since some users are using handheld devices that don't support MS-CHAP, she enabled CHAP on the server. However, users report that they can't connect using those devices. What does Donna Jo need to do to fix the problem? (Choose all that apply.)

    A. Enable reversible password encryption

    B. Enable CHAP in the filter set

    C. Disable support for MS-CHAPv1 and MS-CHAPv2

    D. Change or reset the password for the handheld device users

12. Rick's company is switching over to using smartcards for authentication with Windows 2000. What does Rick have to do to enable smartcard support for dial-in users? (Choose all that apply.)

A. He must enable EAP-MD5 CHAP on the server.

B. He must enable EAP-TLS support in the policies that apply to smartcard users.

C. He must enable EAP-TLS support on the server.

D. He must enable EAP-TLS support on each individual user account.

13. Thèrese needs to set up RRAS callbacks for a single group of users who work from home. She could accomplish this by enabling callbacks for each individual user in that user's Properties dialog box or by doing which of the following?

A. Creating a Windows 2000 security group, then configuring a remote access policy for the group

B. Creating a remote access profile for the group

C. Moving the users to a server that has callbacks enabled

D. Enabling callbacks on the server

14. Hannah's management has asked her to configure a remote access server so that it restricts what times of day users can dial in. She creates a remote access policy that contains time-of-day restrictions, but it doesn't work. What is the most likely cause?

A. The time-of-day policy hasn't been replicated throughout the domain.

B. The time-of-day policy doesn't have a high enough priority.

C. The time-of-day policy has a priority that's too high.

D. The time-of-day policy is not linked to an active remote access profile.

15. To get maximum security for VPN connections, you should use the
_____ tab of the _____ dialog box to
enable the _____ method.

   A. Encryption; selected profile's Properties; Strongest

   B. Security; selected profile's Properties; Maximum

   C. Security; server Properties; 3DES/MPPE-128

   D. Encryption; server Properties; Strongest

16. Which of the following authentication methods is *not* available in the
Authentication Methods dialog box?

   A. MS-CHAPv2

   B. MS-CHAPv1

   C. EAP-Fortezza

   D. PAP/SPAP

17. João's employer wants to implement billing and chargebacks for
remote access across all of its sites. What is the easiest way for him to
accomplish this?

   A. He can configure his RRAS servers to use the Windows Accounting
provider, then write a custom set of scripts to extract the log data.

   B. He can configure his RRAS servers to use RADIUS as the accounting provider, plus a third-party accounting package.

   C. He can configure his RRAS server to use RADIUS as the accounting provider; no external package is necessary.

   D. He can configure his RRAS servers to use the Windows Accounting provider with the Windows 2000 License Manager.

18. Which of the following is true of the RRAS snap-in's Server Status item?

A. It is useless because it only shows one server at a time.

B. It allows you to see all known RRAS servers and their current status.

C. It does not allow you to start, stop, restart, or pause RRAS on a server.

D. It can only view servers that are published in Active Directory.

19. Users in the state where Sarah's company is located can get inexpensive ISDN lines. Sarah wants to enable remote users to get high-bandwidth connections. To accomplish this she should do which of the following? (Choose all that apply.)

A. Enable multilink connections in the PPP tab of the server Properties dialog box

B. Configure a remote access policy with the desired multilink settings

C. Enable dynamic bandwidth control

D. Disable dynamic bandwidth control

20. Susan wants to know if anyone else on her network is using Network Monitor, since she's the only person with permission to do so. To accomplish this, she should do which of the following?

A. Perform a port scan on her network for port 2112

B. Use the Tools ➤ Identify Network Monitor Users command in Network Monitor

C. Use the Computer Management snap-in to look for instances of the Network Monitor service

D. Use the Network Monitoring snap-in to look for instances of the Network Monitor application

Answers to Review Questions

1. A. The DHCP relay agent allows DHCP broadcasts to bridge routers, which is usually what you'll need to make RRAS work with an external DHCP server.

2. C. EAP requires you to use the EAP-TLS type for any kind of certificate-based authentication; EAP-TLS is the only authentication method that supports certificates at all.

3. B. Windows 2000 includes support for encryption. To meet her requirements, Joanna needs to create a policy that allows the desired users to connect, then set its profile to disallow unencrypted calls.

4. B. The boot threshold for an interface controls how long the relay agent will wait before forwarding DHCP requests it hears on that interface.

5. C. CHAP requires that passwords must be stored with reversible encryption, and each user who wants to use CHAP must reset or change their passwords.

6. A, B. You can enable individual user accounts for dial-in by editing their profiles, or you can use remote access policies to allow or deny access to groups.

7. A. You can only use remote access policies in a native-mode AD domain.

8. C. Policies must explicitly grant access if you want them to be used to grant access, and for the policy to take effect all its conditions must match.

9. A, B. If the client can't negotiate an authentication method, the call will be dropped. Likewise, if there's a policy that explicitly or implicitly denies Kelly access her call attempt will fail.

10. C. The DHCP relay agent can be added to any interface on any RRAS server unless the RRAS server is running NAT with address allocation or DHCP. Normally, the agent will be added on an RRAS server that's using a DHCP server elsewhere on the network.

11. A, D. Turning on CHAP just tells the server to accept it; you must also turn on reversible password encryption *and* reset or change the password for each user you want to use CHAP—this forces the system to store the password in reversible form.

12. B, C. You can only enable or disable authentication methods.

13. A. Remote access policies allow you to create policies that target specific groups (provided you're in Windows 2000 native mode).

14. B. Policies are evaluated in order, so if the time-of-day restrictions have too low a priority, another policy may allow the connection to proceed instead of stopping it.

15. A. The Encryption tab of the remote access profile Properties dialog box lets you choose which algorithm sets you want to support. "Strongest" means triple DES for IPSec or 128-bit RC4 for MPPE.

16. C. Fortezza is a U.S. Department of Defense standard not supported by Windows 2000; the other methods are all supported.

17. B. This answer may be a matter of opinion; however, RADIUS is designed to support centralized accounting for large sites, and a third-party package would be required to analyze the RADIUS logs and generate bills from them.

18. B. The RRAS snap-in gives you a quick summary of the server status; you can start, stop, restart, or pause the RRAS service if you need to by right-clicking the server in question.

19. A, B C. Multilink is on by default, but Sarah will have to turn it back on if it's off. Using a policy gives Sarah maximum control over what clients can do. The clients must also be configured with the correct set of phone numbers. Using BAP or BACP for dynamic bandwidth control gives maximum efficiency.

20. B. Port 2112 has nothing to do with Network Monitor, and the Network Monitor service will be present on machines being monitored, not just those running the service. There is no Network Monitoring snap-in. The correct answer is to use the built-in function for spotting Network Monitor on the network—the Tools ➤ Identify Network Monitor Users command.

Chapter

10

Managing Virtual Private Networking

MICROSOFT EXAM OBJECTIVE COVERED IN THIS CHAPTER:

✓ **Configure and troubleshoot remote access.**

    ▪ Configure a virtual private network (VPN).

*V*irtual private networks (VPNs) are increasingly popular because they essentially give you something for nothing. If you have users outside your network boundary (whether they're telecommuting, traveling, or permanently located somewhere where they can't reach your network), VPNs give you an easy-to-implement, easy-to-manage solution to the problem of how you allow these remote users access.

The objective listed above has other subobjectives, which are covered in Chapter 9, "Managing Remote Access Services."

Conventional dial-up access still works fine, but (as you saw in Chapter 3) it can be expensive to implement, painful to manage, and vulnerable to attack. VPNs offer a way around these problems by offering low initial and ongoing cost, easy management, and excellent security. Windows 2000's Routing and Remote Access Service (RRAS) component includes two complete VPN implementations: one using Microsoft's *Point-to-Point Tunneling Protocol (PPTP)* and one using a combination of the Internet-standard IPSec and *Layer 2 Tunneling Protocol (L2TP)* protocols.

In this chapter, you'll learn how to set up and configure RRAS as a VPN server using PPTP and L2TP + IPSec (which we'll lump together and call L2TP from now on). This chapter assumes that you've already read through Chapters 8 and 9 (which cover IP routing and RRAS, respectively).

In this chapter, we'll be talking about deploying VPNs for remote access, not for internetworking.

Comparing PPTP & L2TP

Since you can choose between two different VPN protocols, how do you know which one is the proper choice in a given situation? If you know the differences and similarities between the two, you'll be better prepared to make the right choice. To make it easier, the following list summarizes the most important points of interest:

- PPTP and L2TP both depend on the PPP protocol to move data (note that this doesn't mean that either requires a dial-up PPP connection, though).

- PPTP requires an IP connection. L2TP can use PPP over IP, frame relay, X.25, or ATM.

- L2TP supports header compression; PPTP doesn't.

- L2TP connections can be encrypted and authenticated, but PPTP connections are only encrypted.

- L2TP must be used with IPSec (though IPSec can be used alone). PPTP always uses Microsoft Point-to-Point Encryption (MPPE).

Installing a VPN

The basic process of setting up a VPN is simple, but there are some things to think through before plunging ahead. Getting the VPN installation right may require small hardware or networking changes, plus proper configuration of the VPN service itself.

Setting Up Your Server

Stop for a minute and think about what a VPN server does. As Figure 10.1 illustrates, it sits between your internal network and the Internet, accepting connections from clients in the outside world. In the figure, Clients 1 and 2 are using two different ISPs (probably because they're at two different physical locations). A packet from Client 1, for example, goes from her computer to her ISP, then through some route, unknown to us, that eventually delivers it to the VPN server, which transforms it into a packet suitable for use on the internal network.

FIGURE 10.1 VPN, the Internet, and you

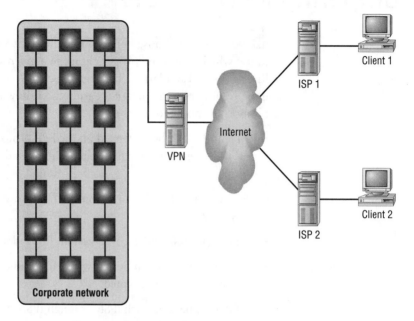

Imagine a line around the internal network. If you think of it as a security boundary, you've got the right idea. In general, you'll want your VPN server to be outside any firewalls or network security measures you have in place. The most common configuration is to use two NICs: One connects to the Internet, and the other connects either to the private network or to an intermediate network that itself connects to the private network. Of course, you can use any type of Internet connection you wish for the VPN server: cable modems, DSL, T-1, ISDN, or whatever.

The point behind giving the VPN its own network adapter is that your VPN clients need a public IP address to connect to, and you probably don't want them calling directly into your internal network. That also means that things will be easiest for your VPN users if the IP address for your VPN server's external interface is statically assigned, so it won't be changing on them when they least expect it.

Avoiding Some Subtle L2TP Pitfalls

As you learned in Chapter 3, "Windows 2000 Connectivity & Security Services," IPSec uses a fairly complex process to negotiate security agreements (SAs) between two endpoints of a secure connection. Part of this process involves the use of what Microsoft calls *machine certificates*. These are nothing more than digital certificates issued to machines instead of people. These certificates allow both ends of the connection to authenticate the computers involved, not just the people. In fact, machine-level authentication is a prerequisite step—on an L2TP VPN, the machine endpoints are authenticated before the VPN client ever sends an authentication request.

In most cases, these certificates will be issued automatically. That, of course, assumes that you've configured your certificate authority to issue certificates automatically to machines when they join a Windows 2000 domain. If you haven't already made this change, you can manually enroll machines by using the certificate authority tools to request a computer certificate for each machine that needs one; you can also force the CA to issue a certificate to the VPN server by restarting the VPN server or refreshing the local security policy.

For more on the Windows 2000 certificate authority, see Chapter 14, "Installing and Configuring Certificate Services."

It also assumes that your remote machines are able to join the domain in the first place. Let's say you want to allow employees to use VPN from home—but you don't want those machines joining your domain. In that case, you might be able to issue certificates manually to those users who are running Windows 2000, but your best bet will probably be to turn on PPTP instead until the L2TP infrastructure catches up.

Installing RRAS as a VPN Server

To get any use from your VPN, you need two pieces: a VPN client (discussed at length in Chapter 12, "Installing and Configuring Network Clients") and a VPN server. In Windows 2000's case, having a VPN server means that you're very likely to be using RRAS. Since Chapters 8 and 9 have already explained how to install RRAS, this chapter will give a bare-bones explanation just as a refresher.

Starting from Scratch

If you don't have RRAS installed at all, you'll need to install it, activate it, and configure it as a VPN server. The easiest way to do this is with the RRAS Setup wizard. You may remember that the wizard gives you a page with several radio buttons that you use to select the kind of server you want to set up. What you may not know is that if you followed the instructions in Exercise 9.1 ("Installing the Routing and Remote Access Service"), you actually already *have* a VPN server—when you install RRAS as a remote access server, the wizard automatically sets up VPN ports for you. Just in case you didn't follow the exercise steps, though, let's go through them again from the standpoint of how things look when you explicitly choose to build a VPN server.

Microsoft
✓ *Exam*
Objective

Configure and troubleshoot remote access.

• Configure a virtual private network (VPN).

EXERCISE 10.1

Installing the Routing and Remote Access Service as a VPN Server

Follow these steps to install a RRAS remote access server:

1. Open the RRAS MMC console (Start ➤ Programs ➤ Administrative Tools ➤ Routing and Remote Access).

2. Select the server you want to configure in the left pane of the MMC. Right-click the server and choose the Configure and Enable Routing and Remote Access command. The RRAS Setup wizard will appear. Click the Next button.

3. In the Common Configurations page of the wizard, make sure that the Virtual Private Network (VPN) Server radio button is selected, and then click the Next button.

4. The Remote Client Protocols page will appear, listing the protocols available for remote access clients. If you need to add another protocol to the list, click the No, I Need To Add Protocols button; if all the protocols you want to use are on the list, leave the Yes, All Of The Required Protocols Are On The List button selected. Click the Next button.

5. If you indicate that you need to add additional protocols, the wizard will stop. If the protocols you need are already present, it will continue.

6. The Internet Connections page appears next. This page lists all of the demand-dial and permanent network interfaces known to RRAS; you have to choose an interface to serve as the incoming "phone number" for VPN connections. Pick an interface, then click the Next button.

7. The IP Address Assignment page appears. If you want to use DHCP (either a DHCP server on your network or the built-in address allocator), leave the Automatically radio button selected. If you want to pick out an address range, select the From A Specified Range Of Addresses" button. Click the Next button.

   If you choose to use static addressing, at this point the wizard will give you the opportunity to define one or more address ranges to be assigned to remote clients.

8. The Managing Multiple Remote Access Servers page appears. You use this page to configure your RRAS server to work with other RADIUS-capable servers on your network. In this case, you still don't want to use RADIUS, so leave the No, I Don't Want To Set Up This Server To Use RADIUS Now button selected, then click the Next button.

9. The wizard summary page appears. Click the Finish button to start the RRAS service and prepare your server to be configured. If the RRAS service is running on the same server as a DHCP server, you'll see a message indicating that you need to configure the DHCP relay agent (more on that later).

Once you've completed this exercise, you'll have a complete, ready-to-go VPN server that will start accepting connections immediately (try it if you don't believe it!). However, you may want to configure the available ports to meet your VPN needs; you'll get to that in a minute.

If You're Already Using RRAS

If you're already using RRAS for IP routing or remote access, you can enable it as a VPN server without reinstalling. (Of course, if you want to start from scratch you can always right-click the server and use the Disable Routing and Remote Access command to wipe out the server's configuration.)

Recall from Chapters 8 and 9 that the General tab of the Server Properties dialog box contains controls that you use to specify whether your RRAS server is a router, a remote access server, or both. The first step in converting your existing RRAS server to handle VPN traffic is to make sure the Remote Access Server check box is marked on this tab. Making this change requires you to stop and restart the RRAS service, but that's OK because the snap-in will do it for you. (There are some additional configuration steps you can take; to find out what they are, read on!)

Configuring a VPN

VPN configuration is extremely simple, at least for PPTP. Either a server can accept VPN calls or it can't. If it can, it will have a certain number of VPN ports, all of which are configured identically. There's very little that you *have* to change or tweak to get a VPN server set up, but there are a few things you can adjust as you like.

Configuring VPN Ports

The biggest opportunity to configure your VPN server is to adjust the number and kind of VPN ports available for clients to use. The initial release of Windows 2000 supports up to 1000 simultaneous connections, though this may be more than your hardware can handle. In addition, you can enable or disable either PPTP or L2TP, depending on what you want your remote users to have access to. You accomplish this magic through the Ports Properties dialog box (Figure 10.2).

For conventional remote access servers, this dialog box shows you a long list of hardware ports, but for servers that support VPN connections there are some extra goodies: two WAN Miniport devices, one for PPTP and one for L2TP. These aren't really devices, of course. They're actually virtual ports maintained by RRAS for accepting VPN connections. You configure these ports with the Configure button, which displays the Configure Device dialog box (Figure 10.3). This is where the VPN rubber actually meets the road.

FIGURE 10.2   The Ports Properties dialog box

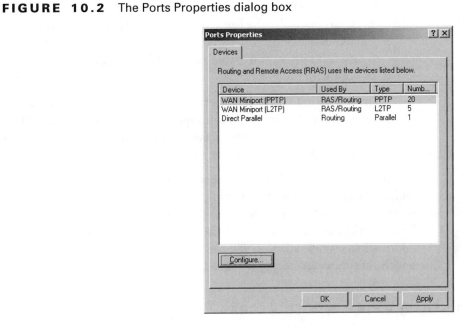

FIGURE 10.3   The Configure Device dialog box

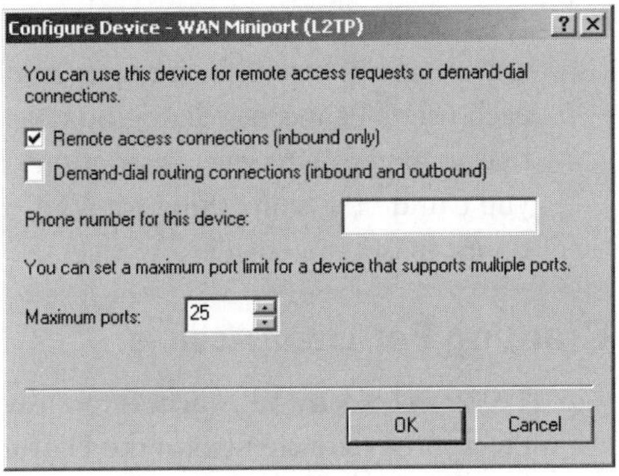

The three controls pertinent to a VPN configuration include the following:

- The Remote Access Connections (Inbound Only) check box must be activated in order to accept VPN connections with this port type. To disable a VPN type (say, if you wanted to turn off L2TP), uncheck this box in the corresponding device's Configure Device dialog box.

- The Demand-Dial Routing Connections (Inbound and Outbound) check box controls whether or not this VPN type can be used for demand-dial connections. By default, this box is checked; you'll need to turn it off if you don't want to use VPN connections to link your network with other networks.

- The Maximum Ports control lets you set the number of inbound connections that this port type will support. By default, you get 5 PPTP and 5 L2TP ports when you install RRAS; you can use from 0 to 1000 ports of each type by adjusting the number here.

You can also use the Phone Number For This Device field to enter the IP address of the public interface to which VPN clients connect. You might want to do this if your remote access policies accept or reject connections based on the number called by the client. Since you can assign multiple IP addresses to a single adapter, you can control VPN traffic by throttling which clients can connect to which addresses through a policy.

Setting Up a VPN Remote Access Policy

In Chapter 9, "Managing Remote Access Services," you learned how to use the remote access policy mechanism on a Windows 2000 native-mode domain. Now it's time to apply what you've learned to the VPN world. Recall that there are two ways to control which specific users can access a remote access server: You can grant dial-up permission to individual users in each user's Properties dialog box, or you can create a remote access policy that embodies whatever restrictions you want to impose. It turns out that you can do the same thing for VPN connections, but there are a few additional twists to consider.

Granting Per-User Access

To grant or deny VPN access to individual users, all you have to do is make the appropriate change on the Dial-in tab of each user's Properties dialog box. While this is the easiest method to understand, it gets tedious quickly if you need to change VPN permissions for more than a few users. Furthermore, there's no way to distinguish between dial-in and VPN permission.

Creating a Remote Access Policy for VPNs

You may find it helpful to create remote access policies that enforce the permissions you want end users to have. There are a number of ways to accomplish this result; which one you use will depend on your overall use of remote access policies. The simplest way is to create a policy that allows all of your users to use a VPN. In Chapter 9, you learned how to create remote access policies and specify settings for them; one thing you may have noticed was that there's a NAS-Port-Type attribute that you can use in the policy's conditions. That attribute is the cornerstone of building a policy that allows or denies remote access via VPN, since you use it to accept or reject connections arriving over a particular type of VPN connection. For best results, you'll use Tunnel-Type in conjunction with the NAS-Port-Type attribute, as described in Exercise 10.2.

Remember that you can only use remote access policies if you're in a native-mode Windows 2000 domain.

EXERCISE 10.2

Creating a VPN Remote Access Policy

Follow these steps to create a remote access policy that governs VPN use:

1. Open the RRAS MMC console (Start ➤ Programs ➤ Administrative Tools ➤ Routing and Remote Access).

2. Navigate to the server on which you want to create the policy, then expand the server node until you see the Remote Access Policies node.

3. Right-click the Remote Access Policies folder and choose the New Remote Access Policy command. This starts the Add Remote Access Policy wizard.

4. Name the policy "VPN Access" or something else that clearly indicates what it's for, and then click the Next button.

5. When the Conditions page of the wizard appears, use the Add button to add this condition: NAS-Port-Type attribute set to "Virtual (VPN)."

   If you want to restrict VPN users to either PPTP or L2TP, add this other condition: Tunnel-Type attribute set to the appropriate protocol.

EXERCISE 10.2 *(continued)*

6. In the Permissions page of the wizard, make sure the Grant Remote Access Permission radio button is selected (unless you're trying to *prevent* VPN users from connecting). Click the Next button when done.

7. The User Profile page appears next. If you want to create a specific profile (perhaps to restrict which authentication types VPN clients may use), use the Edit Profile... button to specify them. At a minimum, you should clear the No Encryption option on the Encryption tab of the remote access profile. When you're done tweaking the profile, click the Finish button to create and activate the policy.

If you don't want to grant VPN access to everyone, there are some changes you can make to the above process to fine-tune it. When you add the policy described in the exercise, it will end up after the default Allow Access If Dial-In Permission Is Enabled policy. This means that the default policy will take effect before the VPN-specific policy, so you'll probably want to move the VPN policy to the top of the list.

Let's say you want to allow everyone dial-up access, but you also want VPN capability to be reserved for a smaller group. The easiest way to accomplish this is to create an Active Directory group and put your VPN users in it. You can then create a policy using the two conditions outlined in the exercise *plus* a condition that uses the Windows-Groups attribute to specify the new group. As with the ordinary VPN policy in the exercise, if you create a policy using the Windows-Groups attribute, make sure to put it ahead of the default policy.

You can also delete the default remote access policy if you don't need it for dial-in users.

Troubleshooting VPNs

The two primary VPN problems are the inability to establish a connection at all and the inability to reach some needed resource once connected. There's a lot of common ground between the process of troubleshooting a VPN connection and an ordinary remote access connection.

Verifying the Simple Stuff

"Is it plugged in?" That's one of the first questions that support techs at mass-market vendors like Gateway and Packard Bell ask customers who call to report a dead computer. In the same vein, there are some extremely simple—but sometimes overlooked—things to check when your VPN clients can't connect.

This list presupposes that your client can make the underlying connection to their ISP; if not, see the troubleshooting steps in Chapter 12.

Check the following things:

- Is the RRAS server installed and configured on the server?

  - Is the server configured to allow remote access? (Check the General tab of the server Properties dialog box).

  - Is the server configured to allow VPN traffic? Check the Ports Properties dialog box to make sure that the appropriate VPN protocol is enabled and that the number of ports for that protocol is greater than zero.

  - Are there any available VPN ports? If you have only ten L2TP ports allocated, caller #11 will be out of luck.

- Do the client and server match?

  - Is the VPN protocol used by the client enabled on the server? Windows 2000 clients will try L2TP first and switch to PPTP as a second choice; however, clients on other OSes (including Windows NT) can normally expect either L2TP or PPTP.

  - Are the network protocols for all clients enabled on the server? This is particularly good to check if you have some IPX-using clients lurking in the woodpile.

- What about authentication?

  - Here's a favorite: Are the username and password correct? If not, don't expect to get a VPN connection.

  - Does the user account in question have remote access permissions, either directly on the account or through a policy?

  - Speaking of policy, do the authentication settings in the server's policies (if any) match the supported set of authentication protocols?

The Slightly More Esoteric

If you check all the simple stuff and find nothing wrong, it's time to move on to some slightly more sophisticated problems. These tend to affect more than one user, as opposed to the simple (and generally user-specific) issues outlined above. The problems include the following:

Policy Problems   If you're using a native-mode Windows 2000 domain, and you're using policies, those policies may have some subtle problems that show up under some circumstances.

- Are there any policies whose Allow or Deny settings conflict with each other? Remember that all conditions of all policies must match to gain user access; if any condition of any policy fails, or if there are any policies that deny access, it's "game over" for that connection.

- Does the user match all of the necessary conditions that are in place, such as Time and Date?

Network Stuff   If you're using static IP addressing, are there any addresses left in the pool? If the VPN server can't assign an address, it won't accept the connection.

If you're using IPX, be sure that the client and server settings that control whether or not the client can ask for its own node number match; if the server disallows it, the client won't be able to connect unless it already has an assigned number.

Domain Stuff   Windows 2000 RRAS servers can coexist with Windows NT RRAS servers, and both of them can interoperate with RADIUS servers from Microsoft and other vendors. Sometimes, though, this interoperation doesn't work exactly as you'd expect.

- Is the RRAS server's domain membership correct? Your RRAS servers don't have to be domain members unless you want to use native-mode features like remote access policies.

- If you're in a domain, are the server's group memberships correct? The server account must be a member of the RAS and IAS Servers security group.

Summary

In this chapter, you learned:

- How to install RRAS to provide VPN service
- How to configure VPN services on the server
- How to troubleshoot common VPN problems

Key Terms

Before you take the exam, be sure you're familiar with the following terms:

Layer 2 Tunneling Protocol (L2TP)

Machine certificates

Point-to-Point Tunneling Protocol (PPTP)

Virtual Private Network (VPN)

Review Questions

1. Windows 2000 includes native support for which of the following VPN-related protocols?

   A. The Point-to-Point Tunneling Protocol

   B. The Layer 2 Tunneling Protocol

   C. The Generic Tunneling Protocol

   D. A and B

   E. A and C

2. To use L2TP as a VPN protocol, it must _____.

   A. Be used instead of PPTP

   B. Be combined with IPSec

   C. Be used in a Windows 2000 native-mode domain

   D. Be used with dedicated VPN access devices

3. The VPN protocols in Windows 2000 can be used for which of the following?

   A. Remote access by network clients

   B. Linking networks at different physical sites

   C. A and B

   D. None of the above

4. How are VPN servers commonly configured?

   A. With a single network interface and two IP addresses

   B. With a Windows 2000 VPN Server

   C. By using RADIUS

   D. With separate public and private network interfaces

5. Monica wants to set up VPN access for her users, who are spread all over North America. There is no central Windows 2000 domain for her users. The most appropriate VPN solution in this case is which of the following?

    A. L2TP + IPSec

    B. PPTP

    C. Either A or B

    D. None of the above

6. Which two of the following benefits does L2TP + IPSec provide that PPTP does not?

    A. Complete end-to-end encryption

    B. Strong user authentication

    C. Machine authentication on both ends

    D. Data link encryption

7. How do you set the number of simultaneous VPN connections your server can support?

    A. By making a Registry change

    B. By selecting the appropriate number of ports during RRAS setup

    C. By using the Ports Properties dialog box

    D. By using a setting in the default domain policy GPO

8. To disable a specific VPN protocol, you would _____. (Choose all that apply.)

    A. Set the number of available ports for that protocol to zero.

    B. Uncheck the Remote Access Connections (Inbound Only) check box for that protocol.

    C. Delete the protocol from the IP Routing node in the RRAS console.

    D. Delete the protocol from the VPN Protocols node in the RRAS console.

9. What happens when a caller attempts to connect and there are no free VPN ports?

    A. The connection is refused.

    B. The connection is held in a pending state until there's a free port.

    C. A new port is automatically allocated.

    D. The caller gets a warning that the connection may be unusually slow.

10. To deny remote access requests from non-VPN users, you would probably do which of the following?

    A. Create a remote access policy that requires a Windows-Group attribute value of "VPN Users."

    B. Remove the user's dial-in permission on their Account Properties dialog box.

    C. Create a remote access policy that requires a NAS-Port-Type attribute value of "Virtual (VPN)."

    D. Add the users to the "No VPN Permissions" policy.

11. Which of the following must be true in order for a user to successfully connect via one of the VPN protocols? (Choose all that apply.)

    A. The user must have dial-in permission.

    B. The user must be using compatible authentication and VPN protocols.

    C. The user account must match all conditions in at least one remote access policy.

    D. The user must supply correct credentials.

12. What is the most likely result if authentication settings at the server and profile levels don't match?

    A. The RRAS service will fail to start.

    B. Incoming callers won't be able to authenticate.

    C. Incoming callers will be able to access network resources only on the RRAS server.

    D. The RRAS service will log event ID 1005 in the event log.

13. A VPN server *must* be which of the following?

    A. Part of an Active Directory domain

    B. Part of a Windows NT domain

    C. On a stand-alone server

    D. None of the above

14. A VPN server that uses remote access policies *must* be_____
_____.

    A. In a native-mode Active Directory domain

    B. In a mixed-mode Active Directory domain

    C. In a mixed or native-mode Active Directory domain

    D. On a stand-alone server

15. L2TP + IPSec VPN connections require _____.

    A. EAP-TLS authentication

    B. Machine certificates for the client and server computers

    C. IPSec-capable routers and switches

    D. EAP-RADIUS authentication

16. What provides the initial connection for L2TP?

    A. PPTP

    B. L2TP

    C. PPP

    D. IP

17. What type of encryption does PPTP use?

    A. L2TP

    B. IPSec

    C. RC3

    D. MPPE

18. Which of the following statements is *not* true?

   A. PPTP connections cannot be authenticated.

   B. L2TP connections can be authenticated, encrypted, or authenticated and encrypted.

   C. PPTP requires IPSec.

   D. PPTP works only on IP connections.

19. L2TP provides a secure tunnel by using which of the following?

   A. PPTP

   B. L2TP

   C. PPP

   D. IPSec

20. Bob tried to dial into his company Saturday at 9 AM but was denied access. Upon checking his remote access policy, you noticed that his group's conditions were set for 8 AM to 5 PM, Monday through Friday. What was the reason this problem occurred?

   A. The policy was not active.

   B. Bob must meet all conditions to be granted access.

   C. Bob must meet only one condition.

   D. The policy was in force.

Answers to Review Questions

1. D. PPTP and L2TP are the two protocols included with Windows 2000.

2. B. Using L2TP alone provides an unencrypted, insecure tunnel.

3. C. You can actually use PPTP and L2TP + IPSec to connect remote networks or to allow a client to dial in to a network; the protocols don't care which.

4. D. RADIUS is an authentication protocol. There's no such product as Windows 2000 VPN Server. Using separate private and public interfaces is the norm.

5. B. IPSec requires machine certificates, which means that Monica will have to set up and maintain a CA and public-key infrastructure. PPTP will be much easier to implement given these constraints.

6. A and C. IPSec authenticates machines, and it offers end-to-end security. PPTP and IPSec both authenticate users, and they both provide link encryption.

7. C. The number of simultaneous connections that a server can handle is limited by the number of available ports. You increase or reduce the number of ports to change the server's capacity.

8. A and B. Turning off the protocol doesn't prevent someone from turning it back on later; you can remove the protocol altogether to reduce overhead and prevent the protocol from being resurrected.

9. A. When there are no free ports, no new connections will be accepted.

10. C. Option A won't do anything unless you put users into that group, option B prevents the users from connecting using RRAS at all, and option D is nonexistent.

11. A, B, C, and D. All four of those conditions must be met for the connection to be accepted.

12. B. If the available authentication methods don't match, no one can be authenticated.

13. D. A VPN server can stand alone, or it can be part of a domain.

14. A. Remote access policies are only available in Active Directory's native mode.

15. B. IPSec requires machine certificates to negotiate a security association.

16. C. L2TP depends on a PPP connection, which can be established over IP, frame relay, X.25, or ATM.

17. D. PPTP is a Microsoft protocol, and it uses Microsoft's proprietary protocol, Microsoft Point-to-Point Encryption.

18. C. L2TP requires IPSec; PPTP has no connection with IPSec.

19. D. IPSec is used to secure L2TP connections; although L2TP can be used with no security, this is not recommended.

20. B. Since Bob's account didn't match all the policy conditions that allow him access, he was denied access. The policy doesn't allow access on Saturday, so Bob didn't match that particular condition.

Chapter

11

Managing IP Security

MICROSOFT EXAM OBJECTIVES COVERED IN THIS CHAPTER

✓ **Configure and troubleshoot network protocol security.**

✓ **Configure and troubleshoot IPSec.**

- Enable IPSec.
- Configure IPSec for transport mode.
- Configure IPSec for tunnel mode.
- Customize IPSec policies and rules.
- Manage and monitor IPSec.

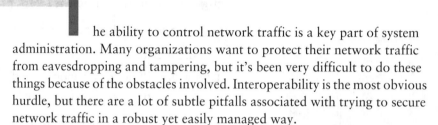

he ability to control network traffic is a key part of system administration. Many organizations want to protect their network traffic from eavesdropping and tampering, but it's been very difficult to do these things because of the obstacles involved. Interoperability is the most obvious hurdle, but there are a lot of subtle pitfalls associated with trying to secure network traffic in a robust yet easily managed way.

The Internet Engineering Task Force (IETF) attacked this problem some time ago, and the result was the Internet Protocol Security Extensions (IPSec). As the name suggests, IPSec is a set of extensions to the basic Internet Protocol (IP) that we all know and love. The word "extension" suggests that IPSec capability is layered on top of, and cannot be used without, IP, and that's certainly true in this case.

In this chapter, you'll learn how to install and configure IPSec and how to use the default security policies. You'll also learn how to define your own security policies and filters to customize the level of protection available to computers on your network.

Understanding How IPSec Works

In Chapter 3, you learned the fundamentals of how IPSec uses the Authentication Header (AH) and Encapsulating Security Payload (ESP) protocols to protect your network communications from tampering or spying. Now it's time to delve a little deeper into the mysterious world of IPSec so that you'll better understand how to manage it.

What IPSec Is For

The whole idea behind IPSec is that it operates at the network layer, and that users and applications never need to be aware of whether their traffic is being carried over a secure connection or not. In IPSec parlance, there are clients and servers, but this terminology is a little misleading. Any Windows 2000 machine may be an IPSec client or server—an *IPSec client* is the computer that attempts to establish a connection to another machine, and an *IPSec server* is the target of that connection. By choosing appropriate client and server settings, you can fine-tune which computers will use IPSec to talk to each other.

IPSec primarily provides two services: a way for computers to decide if they trust each other (*authentication*) and a way to keep network data private (*encryption*). The IPSec process calls for two computers to authenticate each other before beginning an encrypted connection. At that point, the two machines can use the Internet Key Exchange (IKE) protocol to agree on a secret key to use for encrypting the traffic between them. This process takes place in the context of IPSec *security associations (SAs)*, which was discussed back in Chapter 3.

If you're really interested in the guts of IKE, check out RFC 2409.

As if that weren't enough, the Windows 2000 implementation of IPSec explicitly supports the idea of policy-based security. Instead of running around changing security settings on every machine in a domain, you can set policies (specifics in a minute) that configure individual machines, groups of machines within an organizational unit or domain, or every Windows 2000 machine on your network.

When you use IPSec to encrypt or authenticate connections between two machines, that's called *end-to-end mode* because network traffic is protected before it leaves the originating machine, and it remains secured until the receiving machine gets it and decrypts it. (It's also called *transport mode.*) There's a second application, though: using IPSec to secure traffic that's being passed over someone else's wires. This use of IPSec is usually called *tunnel mode*, since it's used to encrypt traffic to pass over (or through) a tunnel, either one established by L2TP or an imaginary one established over someone else's network circuits.

In this chapter, and on the exam, when you see "IPSec tunnel mode" assume that it means IPSec for tunneling, not for VPN traffic. When you see L2TP mentioned, you can safely assume that it really means "L2TP + IPSec." See Chapter 10 for more details on the differences.

Learning Some New Vocabulary

In Chapter 3, you learned the basic set of IPSec buzzwords. Now it's time to build on that basis by adding some specific terms you'll encounter while setting up IPSec.

Security Filters   A security filter ties security protocols to a particular network address. The filter contains the source and destination addresses involved (either for specific hosts or networks, using a netmask), the protocol used, and the source and destination ports allowed for TCP and UDP traffic. For example, you can define a filter that specifies exactly what kind of IPSec negotiations you're willing to allow when a machine in your domain contacts a machine in the microsoft.com domain. As you might remember from Chapter 3, IPSec connections have two sides, inbound and outbound. That means that for each connection you need to have two filters: one inbound and one outbound. The inbound filter is applied when a remote machine requests security on a connection, and the outbound filter is applied before sending traffic to a remote machine.

Let's say that you want to create a rule to allow any machine in the robichaux.net domain to use IPSec when talking to any computer in the microsoft.com domain. For this to work, you need the following four filters:

- A filter for the robichaux.net domain for outbound packets with a source of *.robichaux.net and a destination of *.microsoft.com. (Yes, you can use DNS names and wildcards in filters.)

- A filter for the robichaux.net domain for inbound packets, this time with a source of *.microsoft.com and a destination of *.robichaux.net.

- An inbound filter in the microsoft.com domain that specifies a source of *.robichaux.net and a destination of *.microsoft.com.

- An outbound filter in the microsoft.com domain that specifies a source of *.microsoft.com and a destination of *.robichaux.net.

If any of these filters are missing or misconfigured, the IPSec negotiation process will fail and IPSec won't be used. If they're all there, though, when you try to establish an FTP connection from `hawk.robichaux.net` to `exchange.microsoft.com`, the outbound filter on your domain will fire, and it will trigger IPSec to request a security negotiation with Microsoft's machine (using the process described in Chapter 3). Assuming everything goes well and that the filters are OK, you'll end up with two IPSec SAs on your machine and the connection will be secured.

You normally group filters into *filter lists* for ease of management. Since you can stuff any number of individual filters into a filter list, you can easily build rules that enforce complicated behavior, then distribute those rules throughout your network as necessary.

Security Methods   Each IPSec connection uses a *security method*. That's a fancy way of saying that each connection uses a pre-specified encryption algorithm with a negotiated key length and key lifetime. You can use one of the two predefined security methods (High or Medium), or you can roll your own by specifying which security protocols (AH or ESP), encryption algorithms, and key lifetimes you want to use for a particular connection. When your computer is negotiating with a remote IPSec peer, the ISAKMP service works its way down the list of methods you've specified, trying to use the most secure method first. As soon as your ISAKMP and the one on the other end agree on a method, it's used.

Security Filter Actions   Filters specify a source and destination, but they also have to specify what action should take place when the criteria specified in the filter match. You can use the following five separate actions in each filter (though you can't combine them in the same filter):

- The "Permit" action tells the IPSec filter to take no action. It neither accepts nor rejects the connection based on security rules, meaning that it adds zero security. This action is sometimes called the *passthrough action*, since it allows traffic to pass through without modification. In general, you'll use it for applications like WINS servers, where there's no security-sensitive data involved.

- The "Block" action causes the filter to reject communications from the remote system. This prevents the remote system from making any type of connection, with or without IPSec.

- The "Accept unsecured" and "Allow unsecured" actions allow you to interoperate with computers that don't speak IPSec. The "Accept unsecured communication, but always respond using IPSec" policy says that it's OK to accept unsecured connections but that your machines will always ask for an IPSec connection before accepting the unsecured request. This policy allows you to handle both unsecured and secured traffic, with a preference for IPSec when it's available. The "Allow unsecured communication with non-IPSec aware computers" action allows your machines to accept insecure connections without attempting to use IPSec; as such, we recommend that you not use it in favor of the "Accept unsecured" action.

- The "Use these security settings" option lets you specify which security methods you want used on connections that trigger this filter. This option allows you to specify custom settings for either individual computers or remote networks.

The upcoming section, "Managing Rules with the Rules Tab," discusses an additional filter action, as well as a little more about when to use, or not use, each of these actions.

Security Policies   A security policy is a set of rules and filters that provide some level of security. Microsoft includes a number of pre-built policies, and you can roll your own. (In fact, you'll have to create your own policies for things like DHCP and remote access servers.) There are three included policies:

- "Client (Respond Only)" specifies that a Windows 2000 IPSec client will negotiate IPSec security with any peer that supports it but that it won't attempt to initiate security. Don't let the word "client" fool you in this context—we're talking about IPSec clients. Let's say you apply this policy to a Windows 2000 Server computer. When it initiates outbound network connections, it won't attempt to use IPSec. When someone opens a connection to it, though, it will accept IPSec if the remote end asks for it.

- "Secure Server (Require Security)" specifies that *all* IP communication to, or from, the policy target *must* use IPSec. In this case, all really does mean all: DNS, WINS, Web requests, and everything else that flows over an IP connection either has to be secured with IPSec or will be blocked. This may not be what you want unless you go all-IPSec on your network.

- "Server (Request Security)" is a mix of the two other policies. In this case, the machine will always attempt to use IPSec by requesting it when it connects to a remote machine and by allowing it when an incoming connection requests it. This policy provides the best general balance between security and interoperability.

You assign policies to computers in a number of ways. The easiest way is to store the policy in Active Directory and let the *IPSec Policy Agent* take care of applying it to the applicable machines. Once an IPSec policy is assigned to a machine through Active Directory, it remains assigned—even after the machine leaves the site, domain, or organizational unit (OU) that gave it the original policy—until another policy is provided. You can also assign policies directly to individual machines. In either case, you can manually unassign policies when you no longer want a policy in place on a specific machine.

Understanding IPSec Authentication

IPSec supports three separate authentication methods. Which ones you'll use will depend on what kind of network you have (e.g., with or without Active Directory) and who you're talking to. Since the first thing an IPSec client and server want to do is authenticate each other (sort of like two dogs who have just met for the first time), they need some way to agree on a set of credentials to use. The Windows 2000 version of IPSec supports three different authentication methods; they're used only during the initial authentication phase of building the SAs, not to generate encryption keys. The methods supported are:

- *Kerberos*, which is the authentication system used by Windows 2000 clients and servers in lieu of the older, and less secure, NT LAN Manager authentication scheme. Kerberos is a widely supported open standard that offers good security and a great deal of flexibility. Because it's natively supported in Windows 2000, it's the default authentication method; many third-party IPSec products include Kerberos support.

- *Certificates*, which use public-key certificates (see Chapter 14) for authentication. When you use certificate-based authentication, each end of the connection can use the other's public certificate to verify a digitally signed message. This provides great security, with some added overhead and infrastructure requirements. As you add machines to a domain in Windows 2000, they're automatically issued *machine certificates* that can be used for authentication; if you want to allow users and computers from other domains or organizations to connect to your IPSec machines, you'll need to explore certificate solutions that allow cross-organization certification.

- *Pre-shared keys*, which are basically just reusable passwords. The pre-shared key itself is just a word, code, or phrase that both computers know. The two machines use this password to establish a trust, but they don't send the plain-text phrase over the network. However, the unencrypted key is stored in Active Directory, so Microsoft recommends against using it in production. (since anyone who can snarf the key can impersonate you or the remote computer). However, most of the time you use this mode only when you need to talk to a third-party IPSec product that doesn't yet support certificate or Kerberos authentication.

Installing IPSec

The components necessary for a Windows 2000 machine to act as an IPSec client are already installed by default when you install Windows 2000 Professional, Server, or Advanced Server. However—also by default— there's no policy that requires the use of IPSec, so the default behavior for Windows 2000 machines is not to use it. The good news is that you don't really have to "install" IPSec; you just have to install the tool you use to manage it, then start assigning policies and filters to get the desired effect.

The IP Security Policy Management Snap-In

IPSec is managed through the IP Security Policy Management snap-in. (That's a mouthful, so we'll just call it the IPSec snap-in from now on.) Interestingly, there's no pre-built MMC console that includes this snap-in, so you have to create one by opening a console and adding the snap-in to it. One thing about this snap-in is slightly different from the normal routine: When you install it, you must choose whether you want to use it to manage a local IPSec policy, the default policy for the domain your computer is in, the default policy for another domain, or the local policy on another computer. This gives you an effective way to delegate control over IPSec policies, should you choose to do so. Exercise 11.1 leads you through the process of installing the snap-in for managing a local policy, then activating IPSec on the local computer.

Microsoft ✓ *Exam* *Objective*

Configure and troubleshoot IPSec.

- Enable IPSec.

Microsoft ✓ *Exam* *Objective*

Configure and troubleshoot network protocol security.

EXERCISE 11.1

Network Protocol Security and Enabling IPSec on the Local Computer

Follow these steps to install the IPSec snap-in for managing the local computer's IPSec policy:

1. Use the taskbar's Run command (Start ➤ Run) to launch MMC.exe. An empty MMC console window will appear.

2. Select the Console ➤ Add/Remove Snap-In command. When the Add/Remove Snap-In dialog box appears, click the Add button.

3. In the Add Standalone Snap-In dialog box, scroll through the snap-in list until you see the one marked "IP Security Policy Management." Select it and click the Add button.

4. The Select Computer dialog box (Figure 11.1) appears. Select the Local Computer (default setting) radio button, then click the Finish button.

5. Click the Close button in the Add Standalone Snap-In dialog box.

6. Click the OK button in the Add/Remove Snap-In dialog box.

7. Select the IP Security Policies on Local Machine node in the MMC. Note that the right pane of the MMC lists the three predefined policies discussed earlier in the chapter.

8. Right-click the "Server (Request Security)" policy and choose the Assign command.

9. Verify that the entry in the Policy Assigned column for the selected policy has changed to Yes.

This process in and of itself doesn't do much to improve your security posture, since all it does is enable your local computer to accept IPSec connections from other computers. The real payoff comes when you start applying IPSec policies in Active Directory, which you're about to do.

FIGURE 11.1 The Select Computer dialog box

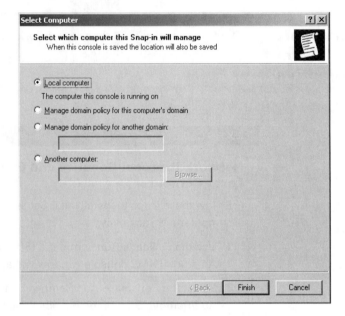

Configuring IPSec

You can configure IPSec by modifying the default policies, creating your own policies that embody the rules and filters you want to use, and by controlling how policies get applied to computers in your management scope. Because Group Policy management is outside the range of this book, the following sections will instead focus on how you customize and control the IPSec settings themselves.

Managing Policies

You manage policies at a variety of levels, depending on where you want them applied. However, you always use the IPSec snap-in to manage them, and the tools you use to create new policies or edit existing ones are the same whether you're using local or Active Directory policy storage.

Creating a New Policy

You create new policies by right-clicking the IP Security Policies folder in the snap-in and choosing the New IP Security Policy command. That activates the IP Security Policy wizard, which allows you to create a new policy. In fact, that's *all* the wizard does—you still have to manually edit the policy settings after it's created. The first two pages of the wizard are pretty innocuous; the first page tells you what the wizard does, and the second page allows you to enter a name and description for the policy. After that, things get slightly more interesting.

Setting the Default Response Rule

The next wizard page (Figure 11.2) asks you whether you want to use the *default response rule* or not. Since we haven't talked about this rule before now, now would be a good time to explain it. The default rule is what governs security when no other filter rule applies. For example, let's say you've set up security filters to accept secure connections from *.microsoft.com, *.cisco.com, and *.apple.com. When your server gets an incoming IPSec request from hawk.robichaux.net, you'd probably expect IPSec to reject the connection—and it will, unless you leave the default response rule turned on. That rule basically says, "Accept anyone who requests a secure connection." Paradoxically, for maximum security you might want to turn it off so that you only accept IPSec connections from known hosts. However, you can customize the settings associated with the default rule; that's the wizard's primary purpose.

If you choose not to use the default response rule, the wizard will skip the steps described below and take you directly to the completion page.

FIGURE 11.2   The Requests For Secure Communications page

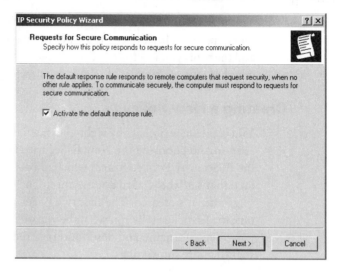

Choosing an Authentication Method for the Default Response Rule

If you choose to use the default response rule, you still have to configure an authentication method for it. To do so, you use the Default Response Rule Authentication Method page (Figure 11.3) You can choose one of the three authentication methods mentioned earlier; by default, Kerberos is selected, but you can choose a certificate authority or a pre-shared key instead. (If you choose to use a pre-shared key, make sure that you enter the same key on both ends of the connection.)

FIGURE 11.3   The Default Response Rule Authentication Method page

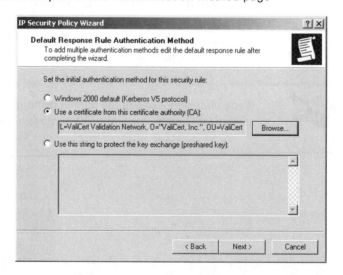

Finishing the Policy Wizard

When you complete the IP Security Policy wizard, the completion page contain s a check box labeled Edit Properties. This is the most interesting part of the wizard since it gives you access to the actual settings embedded within the policy.

Storing Policies in Active Directory

So far, you've read only about managing policies that apply to the local computer. You can also use the IPSec snap-in to create and manage policies that are stored in Active Directory, from which they can be applied to any computer or group of computers in the domain. You actually accomplish this application by completing these three separate, but related, steps:

1. You target the IPSec snap-in at Active Directory, then open it while logged in with a privileged account.

2. You edit or create the policy you want to apply using the tools in the snap-in.

3. You use the Group Policy snap-in to attach the policy to a site, domain, or organizational unit.

The first two steps are discussed throughout this chapter, but you should first take a minute to read about the third step. Since you can assign group policies to any site, domain, or organizational unit, you have the ability to fine-tune IPSec policy throughout your entire organization by using an appropriately targeted policy. For example, in Active Directory Users and Computers, you can create an organizational unit, then create a new group policy object that applies only to that OU. Finally, you can change the settings in that GPO so they enforce the IPSec policy you want applied to computers in that OU.

You may be asking, "But *how* do I do all that?" You don't actually use the IPSec snap-in to assign policies; you use it to configure them and to create policies that live in Active Directory. When you want to actually apply a policy to some group in the directory, you use the group policy snap-in itself. Exercise 11.2 explains how to assign an existing policy as the default policy for a domain.

Microsoft
✓ ***Exam***
Objective

Configure and troubleshoot IPSec.

- Enable IPSec.

> **EXERCISE 11.2**
>
> ### Enabling IPSec for an Entire Domain
>
> Follow these steps to configure a default IPSec policy for all domain computers. You must have administrative access to the domain for this to work.
>
> 1. Use the taskbar's Run command (Start ➤ Run) to launch MMC.exe. An empty MMC console window will appear.
>
> 2. Select the Console ➤ Add/Remove Snap-In command. When the Add/Remove Snap-In dialog box appears, click the Add button.
>
> 3. In the Add Standalone Snap-In dialog box, scroll through the snap-in list until you see the one marked Group Policy. Select it and click the Add button.
>
> 4. The Select Group Policy Object dialog appears. Click the Browse button to bring up the Browse For A Group Policy Object dialog box (Figure 11.4).
>
> 5. Select Default Domain Policy and click the OK button.
>
> 6. Click the Finish button in the Select Group Policy Object dialog box.
>
> 7. Click the Close button in the Add Standalone Snap-In dialog box, and then click the OK button in the Add/Remove Snap-In dialog box.
>
> 8. Expand the Default Domain Policy node until you find the IPSec settings (Default Domain Policy ➤ Computer Configuration ➤ Windows Settings ➤ Security Settings ➤ IP Security Policies on Active Directory).
>
> 9. Select the IP Security Policies on Active Directory item. The right side of the MMC window will list the available policies, including the three predefined policies and any new ones you've added using the IPSec snap-in.
>
> 10. Right-click the "Server (Request Security)" policy and select the Assign command. Notice that the Policy Assigned column for that policy now reads "Yes."

FIGURE 11.4   The Browse For A Group Policy Object dialog box

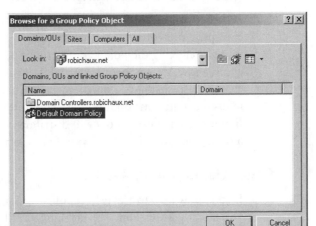

Useful Rules to Live By

IPSec policies are subject to the same rules that other objects assigned by group policy are subject to. Even though this book isn't about group policy objects, it's useful to understand those rules so you'll know how IPSec policy assignment really works.

The first rule is simple: A policy applied at the domain level will always trump a policy assigned to the local computer. The second rule is equally simple: A policy applied to an organizational unit always takes precedence over domain-level policies. That means that if you have conflicting policies at the domain and OU levels, the settings in the OU policy will be used.

The third rule is a little more complex: If you have a hierarchy of OUs set up in Active Directory, the policy for the lowest-level OU overrides the others. For example, let's say you have an OU named Sales, with subordinate OUs for North America and South America. If you assign two different IPSec policies to the Sales and North America OUs, the North America settings will triumph.

The fourth rule is subtle but important: If you assign an IPSec policy through Group Policy and then remove the Group Policy Object that assigned the policy, *the policy remains in effect*. When the IPSec Policy Agent goes looking for the policy while the GPO is missing, the agent assumes that the GPO server is temporarily unavailable. It then uses a cached copy of the policy, which means that you have to unassign the policy before removing the GPO that assigns it.

Assigning and Unassigning Policies

Whether you're defining policies that affect one computer or a multinational enterprise network, you assign and unassign IPSec policies the same way—by right-clicking the policy in question and using the Assign and Un-assign commands. Assigning a policy makes it take effect the next time IPSec policies are refreshed—you may remember that the IPSec Policy Agent downloads the policy information for a computer when the computer is restarted. If you're using Group Policy to distribute your IPSec settings, you can force a policy update using the Group Policy snap-in.

Other Useful Policy Tricks

If you know how to create new policies, assign them, and set their properties, you already know almost everything you'll need to know to manage IPSec (though we haven't covered the mechanics of changing policy settings just yet). There are a few additional tricks that you may find useful in your IPSec implementation.

Forcing a Policy Update

If you want to force one machine to update its IPSec policy, just stop and restart the IPSec Policy Agent service on that machine. When the service starts, it attempts to retrieve the newest available policy from Active Directory or the local policy store. Once the policy has been loaded, it's immediately applied. Restarting the policy agent forces it to refetch and reapply the correct policy—this can be useful when you're trying to troubleshoot a policy problem, or when you want to be sure that the desired policy has been applied. By default, the IPSec Policy Agent will refetch policies every 180 minutes anyway, although you can change that setting (as we'll see in a bit).

Policy Wrangling with the Context Menu

You can do some other nifty things with your IPSec policies by right-clicking them; the context menu that appears allows you to rename them, delete them, or import and export them. These latter commands might seem unnecessary, but they occasionally come in handy if you're not using Active Directory. For example, let's say you have a small network of computers using Windows 2000 Professional. You can create local IPSec policies on one machine, then export them and import them on the remaining machines. Doing so ensures a consistent set of IPSec policies without requiring that you have an Active Directory domain controller present.

Configuring IPSec Policies

Once you create a new policy using the IP Security Policy wizard, you still have to customize it to make it do anything useful. You do this with the policy Properties dialog box, from which you can add, remove, and manage rules, filter lists, and security actions. There are two separate tabs in the Properties dialog box: The General tab covers general policy-related settings like the policy name, and the Rules tab gives you a way to edit the rules associated with the policy.

Microsoft ✓ ***Exam Objective***

Configure and troubleshoot IPSec.

- Customize IPSec policies and rules.
- Configure IPSec for transport mode.

Setting General Properties

The General tab of the Properties dialog box (Figure 11.5) allows you to change the policy name and description, which appear in the IPSec snap-in. It's a good idea to use meaningful names for your policies so that you'll remember what each one is supposed to be doing. The Check For Policy Changes Every X Minutes field lets you change the interval at which clients who use this policy will check for updates. The default value of 180 minutes is OK for most applications since you're unlikely to be changing the policies *that* frequently.

FIGURE 11.5 The General tab of the IPSec Properties dialog box

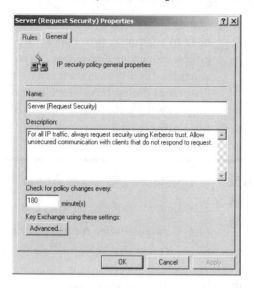

The Advanced button allows you to change the key exchange settings used by this particular policy, via the Key Exchange Settings dialog box (Figure 11.6). You can use the controls in this dialog box to control how often the policy requires generation of new keys, either after a certain amount of time (8 hours by default) or a certain number of sessions. The Methods...button displays a list of security methods that will be used to protect the key exchange; the method list included when you create a new policy always tries the highest-level security first, then drops down to less secure methods if the remote end can't handle them.

FIGURE 11.6 The Key Exchange Settings dialog box

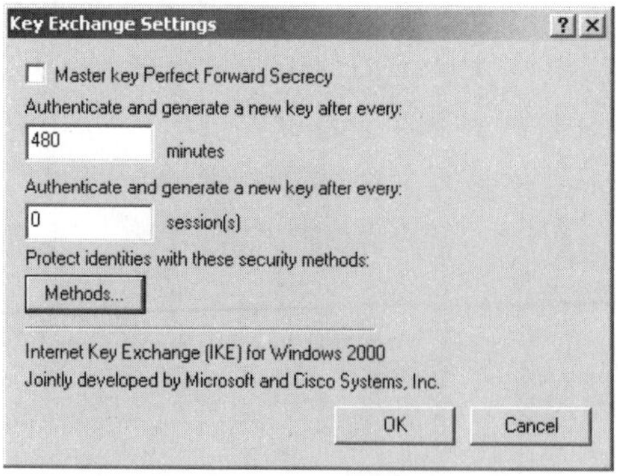

Managing Rules with the Rules Tab

The Rules tab of the policy Properties dialog box is probably more interesting than the General tab. That's because it allows you to change the rules included with the IPSec policy. Take a look at Figure 11.7 and you'll see what the rule set for the Server (Request Security) policy looks like.

FIGURE 11.7   The Rules tab of the Server (Request Security) Properties dialog box

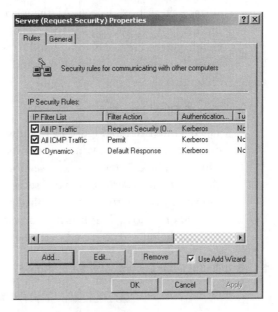

Here are the most important things to recognize on this tab:

- There are three rules, each of which ties a filter list to a *filter action* and authentication method. A single policy can contain an arbitrary number of rules; it's common to have a number of rules that are applied in different situations. It's also common to have many different policies defined in a single Active Directory domain or local policy store.

- Each rule has a check box next to it that controls whether or not the rule is actually applied. You can use these check boxes to turn individual rules on or off within a policy.

- The Add, Edit, and Remove buttons let you manipulate the list of rules. Note that rules aren't evaluated in any particular order, so there's no way to reorder them.

- The Use Add Wizard check box controls whether or not the Security Rule wizard is used to add a new rule (by default, this box is checked). When it's unchecked, you'll get dumped into the rule's Properties dialog box to set things up by hand.

There are five different tabs in the Edit Rule Properties dialog box, which is associated with each rule. You'll see this dialog box when you select a rule and click the Edit button, or when you create a new rule with the Use Add Wizard check box cleared. All the wizard does is ask you questions and fill out the tabs for you, so knowing what settings belong with each rule will enable you to create them by hand or with the wizard's help. Therefore, instead of going through each step of the wizard, you should know what's on each tab.

The IP Filter List Tab

The IP Filter List tab (Figure 11.8) shows which filter lists are associated with this rule. You manage which filter lists exist using a separate set of tools, which will be covered in a later section. For now, it's enough to know that all the filter lists defined on your server will appear in the filter list; you can choose any *one* of them to be applied as a result of this rule. If you like, you can add or remove filter lists here or in the Manage IP Filter Lists And Filter Actions dialog box, covered in the next section.

FIGURE 11.8 The IP Filter List tab of the Edit Rule Properties dialog box

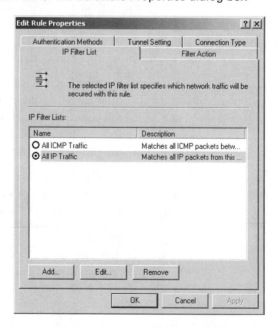

The Filter Action Tab

The Filter Action tab (see Figure 11.9) shows all of the filter actions defined in the policy; you can apply any filter action to the rule. Remember that you combine one filter list with one filter action to make a single rule, but you can group any number of rules into one policy. The Add, Edit, and Remove buttons do what you'd expect; the Use Add Wizard check box controls whether adding a new filter action fires up the corresponding wizard (which you'll get to in the next section) or dumps you into the Properties dialog box.

FIGURE 11.9   The Filter Action tab of the Edit Rule Properties dialog box

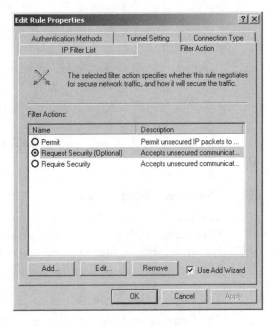

The Authentication Methods Tab

The Authentication Methods tab (Figure 11.10) allows you to define one or more authentication methods that you want a particular rule to use. You can have multiple methods listed; if so, IPSec will attempt to use them in the order of their appearance in the list (thus the Move Up and Move Down buttons). You have the same three choices mentioned earlier: Kerberos, certificates, or pre-shared keys.

FIGURE 11.10   The Authentication Methods tab of the Edit Rule Properties dialog box

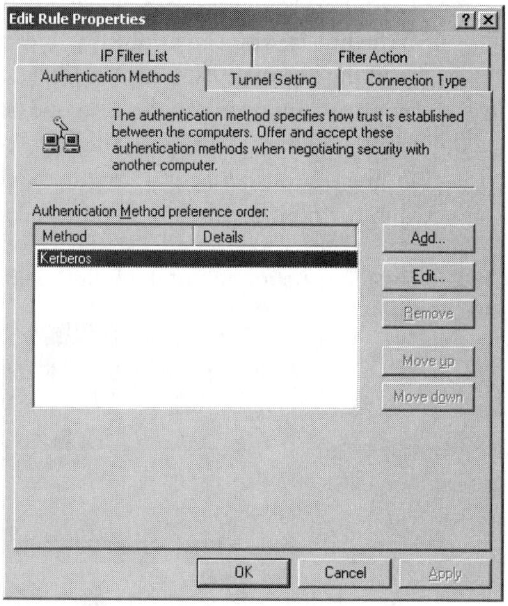

The Tunnel Setting Tab

The Tunnel Setting tab is what you use to specify that this rule forms an IPSec tunnel with another system (or *tunnel endpoint*). Accordingly, you'll read more about it in the section on configuring IPSec in tunnel mode, later in this chapter (see the section "Configuring IPSec for Tunnel Mode").

The Connection Type Tab

The Connection Type tab (Figure 11.11) allows you to specify what kind of connections this IPSec rule applies to. For example, you might want to specify different rules for dial-up and LAN connections depending on who your users are, where they're connecting from, and what they do while connected. Your basic choice is simple: There are three radio buttons that you use to select what type of connections this rule applies to. The All Network Connections button is selected by default, so when you create a new rule it'll apply to both LAN and remote access connections. If you only want the rule to cover LAN or RAS connections, just select the corresponding radio button.

FIGURE 11.11   The Connection Type tab of the Edit Rule Properties dialog box

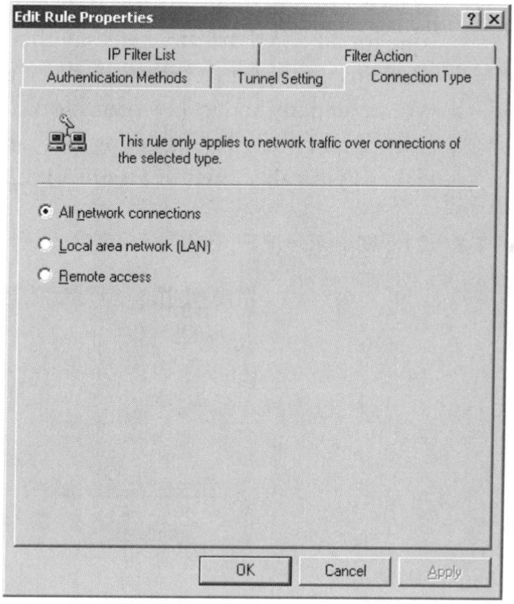

Managing Filter Lists and Actions

Although you can manage IP filter lists and filter actions from the Edit Rule Properties dialog box, it makes more sense to use the management tools provided in the snap-in. Why? Because the filter lists and actions live with the policy, not inside individual rules, the filter lists and actions you create in one policy scope (say, the default domain policy) are available to all policies within that scope.

You can manage filter lists and filter actions using the corresponding tabs in the Edit Rule Properties dialog box, but that obscures the fact that these items are available to any policy. You can instead use the Manage IP Filter Lists And Filter Actions command from the Context menu (right-click the IP Security Policies item or anywhere in the right-hand pane of the IPSec snap-in). This command displays the Manage IP Filter Lists And Filter Actions dialog box, which has a grand total of two tabs. Most of the items on these tabs are self-explanatory since they closely resemble the controls you've already seen. In particular, the function of the Add, Edit, and Remove buttons (as well as the Use Add Wizard check box) should be evident by this point. Instead of rehashing the controls, let's take a look at the process of defining a new filter list and an action to go with it.

Adding IP Filter Lists and Individual Filters

You get two IP filters for free with Windows 2000: one for all IP traffic, and one for all ICMP traffic. Let's say that you're a little more selective, though. Perhaps you want to create an IPSec policy to secure Web traffic between your company and its law firm. You'd first have to open the Manage IP Filter Lists And Filter Actions dialog box, at which point you'd see the Manage IP Filter Lists tab shown in Figure 11.12.

FIGURE 11.12 The Manage IP Filter Lists tab

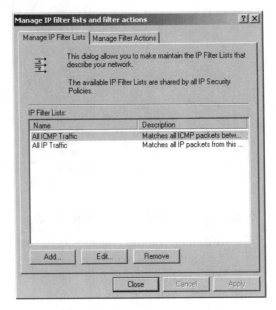

Since filter lists aren't used in order, there's no way to reorder items in the list, though you can add, edit, and remove them using the familiar controls beneath the list. When you edit or add a filter list, you'll see the IP Filter List dialog box (Figure 11.13). This dialog box allows you to name and describe the filter list, then add, remove, or edit the individual filters that make up the list.

FIGURE 11.13   The IP Filter List dialog box

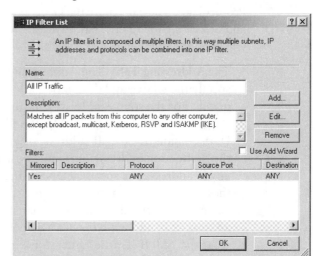

When you edit or add an individual filter, there are five pieces of information you need to know:

- The source and destination addresses you want the filter to use. These can be single IP addresses, single DNS names (at any level, so that `hawk.robichaux.net`, `robichaux.net`, and `net` are all valid), or IP subnet. There are also special "my" and "any" addresses (e.g., "My IP Address," "Any IP Address") that you can use to indicate the source and destination.

- Whether you want the filter to be *mirrored*. A mirrored filter automatically filters its opposite—if you set up a filter from your IP address to a remote address and configure it to allow only port 80, with mirroring you'll also get a filter that allows traffic *from* the remote end back to you on port 80.

- What protocols and ports you want the filter to apply to. You can choose any protocol type (including TCP, UDP, ICMP, and raw), and you can either select individual source and destination ports or use the "any port" buttons you'll meet in a minute.

How do you get these factoids into a filter? With the Filter Properties dialog box, naturally. When you use the Add or Edit buttons in the IP Filter List dialog box, you'll see the properties dialog for the appropriate filter (the new one or whichever one you'd selected before clicking the Edit button). This dialog box has three tabs in it: the General tab, the Addressing tab, and the Protocol tab. You can ignore the General tab since it's only used for naming and describing the filter. That leaves the Addressing and Protocol tabs, which do the following:

The Addressing Tab The Addressing tab (Figure 11.14) is where you specify the source and destination addresses you want this filter to match. For the source address, you can choose to use the IP address assigned to the IPSec server ("My IP Address"), any IP address, a specific DNS domain name or IP address, or a specific IP subnet. Likewise for the destination address, you can choose the IPSec computer's address, any IP address, or a specified DNS name, subnet, or IP address. You use these in combination to specify how you want the filter to trigger. For example, you could create a rule that says, "Match any traffic from my address to IP address *a.b.c.d*". You could also create a rule that does what the "All IP Traffic" filter does: match any traffic from your IP address (on any port) to any destination.

You can also use the Mirrored check box to specify a reciprocal rule. For example, the mirrored rule of the "All IP Traffic" rule matches traffic coming from any IP address on any port back to your IP address. Mirroring makes it easy to set up filters that cover both inbound and outbound traffic.

The Protocol Tab The Protocol tab (Figure 11.15) lets you match traffic coming from or sent to a particular port, using a specified protocol. This is useful, since UDP source port 80 and TCP destination port 80 are entirely different. You use the Select A Protocol Type pull-down menu and the Set The IP Protocol Port control group to specify the protocols and ports you want this filter to match.

FIGURE 11.14   The Addressing tab of the Filter Properties dialog box

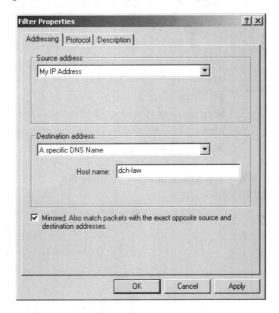

FIGURE 11.15   The Protocol tab of the Filter Properties dialog box

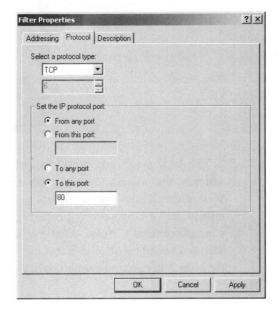

Adding a New Filter Action

The Manage Filter Actions tab (Figure 11.16) shows you which filter actions are defined in the current group of IPSec policies; you can add, edit, or remove filter actions to meet your needs. As part of Windows 2000, you get three filter actions—Permit, Request Security (Optional), and Require Security—that will probably meet most of your needs, but it's still a good idea to know how to create policies yourself instead of depending on Microsoft to do it for you.

FIGURE 11.16   The Manage Filter Actions tab

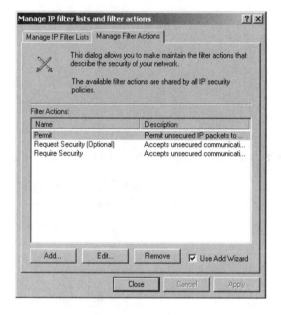

The Add button is the most interesting control in the batch since it lets you add new filter actions that can be used in any policy you define. The Use Add Wizard check box is normally on, so by default you'll get the rule wizard; instead, let's go through the property pages associated with a filter action so you can see what's in one. When you click the Add button with the Use Add Wizard check box off, the first thing you see is the Security Methods tab of the New Filter Action Properties dialog box (Figure 11.17).

FIGURE 11.17 The Security Methods tab of the New Filter Action Properties dialog box

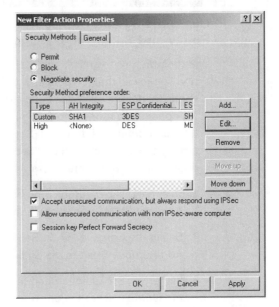

You use this tab to select which methods you want this filter action to use. In addition to the Permit and Block methods, you can use the Negotiate Security button to build your own custom security methods, choosing whatever AH and ESP algorithms meet your needs. The two check boxes at the bottom of the security methods list control what this IPSec computer will do when confronted with a connection request from a machine that doesn't speak IPSec. The options include the following:

- The "Accept unsecured communication, but always respond using IPSec" check box configures this action so that incoming connection requests will always be answered with an IPSec negotiation message. If the other end doesn't *habla* IPSec, the computer is allowed to accept the incoming request without any security in place.

- The "Allow unsecured communication with non IPSec-aware computer" check box configures the action to allow any computer—IPSec-capable or not—to communicate. Any machine that can't handle IPSec will get a normal, insecure connection. By default, this box isn't checked; if you check it, you must be certain that your IPSec policies are set up properly. If they're not, some computers that you *think* are using IPSec may connect without security.

Customizing and Configuring the Local Computer IPSec Policy and Rules for Transport Mode

In the previous exercise, you assigned the "Server (Request Security)" policy so that it would always be used. Now it's time to tweak it some. By default, all IPSec policies you create will be transport-mode (as opposed to tunnel-mode) policies. This is also true of the default local computer and domain IPSec policies. In this exercise, you'll modify the local computer's "Server (Request Security)" policy settings to improve its interoperability.

1. Use the Taskbar's Run command (Start ⟩ Run) to launch MMC.exe. An empty MMC console window will appear.

2. Select the Console ⟩ Add/Remove Snap-In command. When the Add/Remove Snap-In dialog box appears, click the Add button.

3. In the Add Standalone Snap-In dialog box, scroll through the snap-in list until you see the one marked IP Security Policy Management. Select it and click the Add button.

4. The Select Computer dialog box appears. Select the Local Computer radio button, then click the Finish button.

5. Click the Close button in the Add Standalone Snap-In dialog box, and then click the OK button in the Add/Remove Snap-In dialog box.

6. Select the IP Security Policies on Local Machine node in the MMC. In the right-hand pane of the MMC, right-click the "Server (Request Security)" policy and choose the Properties command. The Server (Request Security) Properties dialog box will appear.

7. Select the All IP Traffic rule, and then click the Edit button. The Edit Rule Properties dialog box will appear. Read the Description. Click OK.

8. Switch to the Filter Action tab. Select the Request Security (Optional) filter action, and then click the Edit button. The filter action's Properties dialog box will appear.

9. Click the Add button. When the New Security Method dialog box appears, click the Custom radio button, and then click the Settings button.

EXERCISE 11.3 *(continued)*

10. In the Custom Security Method Settings dialog box, check the data and address integrity without encryption (AH), in the drop-down list, select SHA1. Using the drop-down lists under (ESP), set Integrity to SHA1 and Encryption to 3DES.

11. First check the Generate A New Key Every check box and set the key generation interval to 24,000 Kbytes. (Kbytes must be in the range 20,480 – 2,147,483,647 Kb.) Then click the Generate A New Key Every check box and specify a key generation interval of 1800 seconds.

12. Click the OK button in the Custom Security Method Settings dialog box, and then click OK in the New Security Method dialog box.

13. When the Filter Properties dialog box resurfaces, use the Move Up button to move the custom filter you just defined to the top of the list.

14. Click the OK button in the Filter Properties dialog box.

15. Click the Close button in the Edit Rule Properties dialog box, then click the Close button in the Server (Request Security) Properties dialog box.

Configuring IPSec for Tunnel Mode

You can use IPSec tunnels to do a number of useful and interesting things. For example, you can establish a tunnel between two subnets—effectively linking them into an internetwork—without having to have a private connection between them. IPSec tunneling isn't intended as a way for clients to establish remote access VPN connections; instead, it's what you'd use to connect your Windows 2000 network to a remote device (say, a Cisco PIX) that doesn't support L2TP+IPSec or PPTP. You can also build a tunnel that directly connects two IP addresses.

Either way, you establish the tunnel by building a filter that matches the source and destination IP addresses, just as you would for an ordinary transport mode. You can use ESP and AH on the tunnel to give you an authenticated tunnel (AH only), an encrypted tunnel (ESP only), or a combination of the two. You control this behavior by specifying a filter action and security method. However, when you build a tunnel, you can't filter by port or protocol; the Windows 2000 IPSec stack doesn't support it.

Configure and troubleshoot IPSec.

- Configure IPSec for tunnel mode.

To properly construct a tunnel, you actually need two rules on each end: one for inbound traffic, and one for outbound traffic. Microsoft warns against using mirroring on tunnel rules; instead, if you want to link two networks (let's say Atlanta and Seattle), you'd need to specify settings as shown in Figure 11.18. Each side's rule has two filter lists. The Atlanta filter lists specify a filter for outgoing traffic that has the Seattle router as a tunnel endpoint, then another filter for incoming traffic from any IP subnet that points back to the Atlanta tunnel endpoint. In conjunction with these filter lists, of course, you'd specify a filter action that provided whatever type of security was appropriate for the connection.

FIGURE 11.18 Filter lists for a simple tunnel

Filter list 1:
    Filter from any IP address to specific IP subnet 10.3.*
    Tunnel endpoint of 10.3.1.254
    Authentication and security methods to taste
Filter list 2:
    Filter from specific IP subnet 10.3.* to any IP address
    Tunnel endpoint of 10.1.1.254
    Authentication and security methods to taste

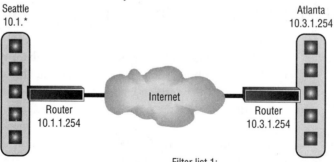

Seattle
10.1.*

Router
10.1.1.254

Internet

Atlanta
10.3.1.254

Router
10.3.1.254

Filter list 1:
    Filter from any IP address to specific IP subnet 10.1.*
    Tunnel endpoint of 10.1.1.254
    Authentication and security methods to taste
Filter list 2:
    Filter from specific IP subnet 10.1.* to any IP address
    Tunnel endpoint of 10.3.1.254
    Authentication and security methods to taste

You specify whether a connection is tunneled or not on a per-rule basis using the Tunnel Settings tab of the Edit Rule Properties dialog box (Figure 11.19). The two radio buttons specify whether this rule establishes a tunnel or not. The default button, "This rule does not specify an IPSec tunnel," is self-explanatory. To enable tunneling with this rule, select the other button, "The tunnel endpoint is specified by this IP address," then fill in the IP address of the remote endpoint.

FIGURE 11.19   The Tunnel Setting tab of the Edit Rule Properties dialog box

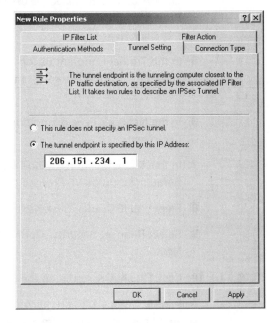

EXERCISE 11.4

Configuring a Policy for IPSec Tunnel Mode

This lab requires you to use two separate machines to which you have administrator access. Let's call them machine A and machine B. Before you start, you'll need their IP addresses, and you'll need to have their local IPSec policies open in an MMC console.

To configure machine A:

1. Right-click the IP Security Policies on Local Machine node, then choose the Create IP Security Policy command. The IP Security Policy wizard will appear. Click Next.

EXERCISE 11.4 *(continued)*

2. In the first wizard page, name your policy "Tunnel to B," then click the Next button.

3. On the Requests For Secure Communication page, turn off the Activate Default Response Rule check box, then click the Next button.

4. When the summary page for the wizard appears, make sure the Edit Properties check box is on, then click Finish. The Tunnel To B Properties dialog box will appear. Click the Add button on the Rules tab. Click Next.

5. In the Tunnel Endpoint dialog box, select "The tunnel endpoint is specified by this IP address" and enter the IP address of Machine B. Click Next.

6. In the Network Type dialog box, select Local Area Network (LAN). Click Next.

7. In the Authentication Method dialog box, select Windows 2000 Default (Kerberos V5 Protocol). Click Next.

8. Select All IP Traffic. Click Next.

9. Select Request Security (Optional) on the Filter Action page. Click Next.

10. Click Finish, OK, and then the Close button.

Now repeat steps 1-10 on machine B, creating rules using the appropriate IP addresses and names (e.g., Tunnel to A) in steps 2-5.

Managing and Monitoring IPSec

Now that you know how to configure IPSec, it's time to learn how to manage and monitor it. The management aspects of IPSec are pretty simple since about 90 percent of your workload will be building filter lists, rules, and filter actions that correctly specify the traffic and hosts you want protected. The other 10 percent falls under the general rubric of "watch it and fix it if it breaks."

Monitoring IPSec

How can you monitor IPSec traffic on your computers? There are a number of ways, but the two most useful methods are viewing the security associations and traffic flowing between specific computers and checking the event log for IPSec-related events.

Microsoft
Exam
Objective

Configure and troubleshoot IPSec.

- Manage and monitor IPSec.

Using the IP Security Monitor Tool

Microsoft was thoughtful enough to include a monitoring tool specific to IPSec. This may not seem like a big deal until you consider that encrypted IPSec traffic is awfully hard to read with a conventional network-monitoring tool. The ipsecmon.exe tool (Figure 11.20) provides an easy-to-understand summary of the current state of your computer's IPSec connections.

FIGURE 11.20   The IP Security Monitor in action

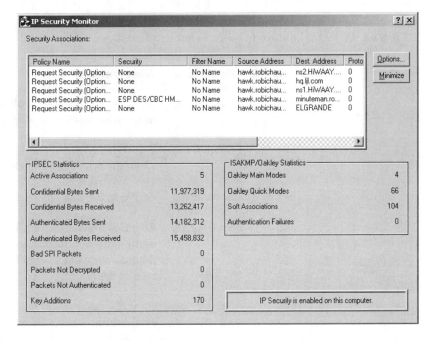

The list at the top of the *ipsecmon* window lists each policy currently in use, along with any filters applied, the source and destination addresses, and the protocols and ports in the filter. When you use a policy that makes IPSec optional, it's normal to see a mix of secure and insecure connections since not every machine you talk to will be able to speak IPSec. The IPSec Statistics and ISAKMP/Oakley Statistics areas will also give you some interesting data, including the number of bytes sent and received using the AH and ESP protocols (these totals will match if your policies specify that both should be used together).

The only option you have in *ipsecmon* is to change its refresh interval; clicking the Options button lets you adjust it from its 15-second default to whatever value is appropriate. Oddly, there's no manual refresh command, so you're at the mercy of the update interval.

Using Event Logging

If you turn on auditing for logon events and object access, you'll get a wealth of logged information that can be very useful when you're trying to troubleshoot a problem. In particular, IPSec logs events when it establishes a security association. Those event messages tell you what policy, filter, and filter actions were used, plus which security methods were active on the connection. Table 11.1 lists the most common event log messages you'll see and describes what they mean.

TABLE 11.1 Interesting IPSec Event Log Messages

Event ID	Appears in	What it means
279	System log	Generated by the IPSec Policy Agent; shows which policy was installed and where it came from.
284	System log	Generated by the IPSec Policy Agent; appears when the agent can't fetch a policy.
541	Security log	An IPSec SA was established.
542	Security log	An IPSec SA was closed. This happens when you terminate a connection to a remote machine. (May also appear as event 543, depending on the type of SA.)
547	Security log	IPSec SA negotiation failed, so no SA could be established.

EXERCISE 11.5

Monitoring IPSec Logon Activity

In this exercise, you'll turn on auditing for logon events and object access. In order to see anything in the log, you'll need at least two IPSec-capable machines that can talk to each other. It doesn't matter which one you use to do this exercise, provided that you have administrative access to it.

1. Use the Taskbar's Run command (Start ➢ Run) to launch MMC.exe. An empty MMC console window will appear.

2. Select the Console ➢ Add/Remove Snap-In command. When the Add/Remove Snap-In dialog box appears, click the Add button.

3. In the Add Standalone Snap-In dialog box, scroll through the snap-in list until you see the one marked Group Policy. Select it and click the Add button.

4. The Select Group Policy Object dialog box appears. Leave "Local Computer" set as the focus, then click the Finish button.

5. Click the Close button in the Add Standalone Snap-In dialog box, then click the OK button in the Add/Remove Snap-In dialog box.

6. Find and select the Audit Policy folder (Local Computer Policy ➢ Computer Configuration ➢ Windows Settings➢ Security Settings ➢ Local Policies ➢ Audit Policy).

7. Double-click the "Audit logon events" entry. When the Local Security Policy Setting dialog box appears, check the Success and Failure check boxes, then the OK button.

8. Double-click the "Audit object access" entry. When the Local Security Policy Setting dialog box appears, check the Success and Failure check boxes, then the OK button.

9. Establish an IPSec connection from the *other* machine to the one whose local security policy you just modified.

10. Examine the event log and ascertain whether the IPSec negotiation succeeded or failed.

Troubleshooting

Troubleshooting IPSec can be tricky. Microsoft's online help does a good job of explaining the various ins and outs, but the basic principles aren't that hard to understand. First, of course, you need to verify that you have basic, unsecured TCP/IP connectivity to the remote system. Since IPSec operates atop IP and UDP, if you can't get regular IP datagrams to the destination you won't be able to get IPSec packets there either. That means you need to perform all the standard connectivity and name resolution tests (including making sure the network cable's plugged in!) before you dive into IPSec troubleshooting.

Testing Policy Integrity

You can check policy integrity at any time by right-clicking a policy folder (like the "IP Security Policies on Local Machine" item), then choosing the All Tasks ➤ Check Policy Integrity command. The integrity checker makes sure that there are no errors or missing pieces in the policies, their filter lists, or their filter actions. It reports any errors it finds; normally, though, you'll only see a dialog box that displays "Integrity verified" when the test is complete.

Verifying That the Right Policy Is Assigned

If you don't have an IPSec policy assigned, or if you have the wrong one in place, your communication efforts may fail. There are several ways to check the policy to see whether it's the right one or not. These checks include the following:

- Use *ipsecmon*, since it tells you which policy is being used for the association with each machine.

- Check the event log for event ID 279; that's the IPSec Policy Agent's way of telling you what policy it has applied.

- Look on the Options tab of the Advanced TCP/IP Settings dialog box, which you get to from the TCP/IP Properties dialog box. The Options tab has a list of features that includes IPSec; select it, then click the Properties button to see the dialog box seen in Figure 11.21.

- Look in the appropriate group policy object (including the local computer policy) to see whether an IPSec policy is assigned. The IPSec snap-in will warn you that a group policy-based IPSec policy is assigned when you try to edit local policies on a computer.

You can also test to see which policy is in effect by using the *ping* command to send packets to the target computer. By watching the *ipsecmon* window, you can see whether a hard or soft SA is established when you connect, as well as what policy is in use for that SA.

FIGURE 11.21   The IP Security dialog box

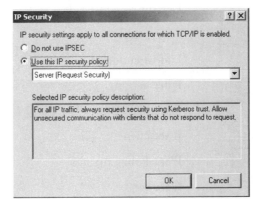

Checking for Policy Mismatches

If you have policies applied on each end, but you still can't establish a connection, it's possible that the policies don't match. To verify whether or not this is the case, review the event log and look for event ID 547. If you find any, read the descriptive text carefully since it can give you great clues. Make sure that the authentication and security methods used in the two policies have at least one setting in common.

Summary

In this chapter, you learned:

- How IPSec provides increased network security
- How to install the IPSec management snap-in
- How to use the built-in security policies
- How to build your own custom security policies and filters
- How to monitor IPSec traffic using *ipsecmon*

Key Terms

Before you take the exam, be sure you're familiar with the following terms:

Authentication

Certificates

Default response rule

Encryption

End-to-end mode

Filter action

Filter list

IPSec client

IPSec Policy Agent

IPSec server

Kerberos

Machine certificates

Mirrored

Passthrough action

Pre-shared keys

Security association (SA)

Security method

Transport mode

Tunnel endpoint

Tunnel mode

Review Questions

1. Joanne wants to change the interval at which her default domain IPSec policy is refreshed from the standard 3 hours to 24 hours. To implement this change, she should do which of the following?

    A. Right-click the policy and use the Change Refresh Time command.

    B. Open the General tab of the policy's Properties dialog box and adjust the "Check for policy changes" value.

    C. Open the Schedule tab of the policy's Properties dialog box and adjust the "Check for policy changes" value.

    D. Use a scheduled job to stop and restart the IPSec Policy Agent service.

2. The IPSec Policy Agent does which of the following? (Select all that apply.)

    A. It downloads IPSec policy information from the local machine.

    B. It downloads IPSec policy from Active Directory (if present).

    C. It clears any existing security associations.

    D. It restarts the IPSec driver.

3. Which of the following is *not* an IPSec authentication method?

    A. Kerberos

    B. Pre-shared keys

    C. NTLM authentication

    D. Certificates

4. You can assign _____ filter action(s) and _____ IP filter list(s) to a single policy rule.

    A. One; one

    B. Any number; any number

    C. One; any number

    D. Any number; one

5. Which of the following is true of IPSec tunnel mode? (Choose all that apply.)

    A. It establishes an encrypted or authenticated tunnel across an insecure network.

    B. It can only link two individual IP addresses.

    C. It is not designed for use as a VPN method.

    D. It requires you to use Group Policy for IPSec distribution.

6. A filter action specifies which of the following?

    A. Which security methods to use for traffic that matches the associated filter

    B. Whether to accept or reject traffic that matches the associated filter

    C. A and B

    D. None of the above

7. What order are IPSec policies applied in?

    A. First local, then domain, then OU

    B. First OU, then domain, then local

    C. First domain, then local, then OU

    D. First domain, then OU, then local

8. To force immediate reloading of the IPSec policy, you should do which of the following?

    A. Reboot the computer.

    B. Stop and restart the IPSec Policy Agent.

    C. Use the Refresh command in the IPSec snap-in.

    D. You can't.

9. Dianne wants to verify that IPSec is in use on her computer. She can do this using which of the following?

   A. The *ipconfig* tool

   B. The *tracert* tool

   C. The *ipsecmon* tool

   D. The IP Security Properties dialog box

10. The IPSec "Client (Respond Only)" policy is best suited for what use?

    A. When you want to make IPSec mandatory

    B. When you want to make IPSec optional

    C. When you want to prohibit the use of IPSec

11. When configuring a policy for IPSec tunneling, you shouldn't do which of the following?

    A. Use mirroring

    B. Use the "My IP Address" filter for the destination address

    C. Use the "Any IP Address" filter for the source address

    D. Use the Permit filter action

12. How does the Server (Request Security) policy handle security?

    A. It will provide security only when a client requests it.

    B. It will request security after initial contact from any client.

    C. It will provide security only when another server requests it.

    D. It will request security after initial contact from any server.

13. Malik has been assigned the task of building an IPSec rule that will secure all HTTP traffic sent to a particular external site. The best way to accomplish this is to do which of the following? (Choose all that apply.)

    A. Create a new policy that specifies the external site as a destination and uses the All IP Traffic IP filter list and the Require Security action.

    B. Enable the "Request Security (Optional)" policy.

    C. Enable the "Require Security" policy.

    D. Create a new policy that specifies the external site as a destination and uses a custom filter list for source and destination port 80 on the TCP protocol.

14. A filter can specify a match based on which of the following?

    A. Source and destination addresses

    B. Source and destination ports

    C. Network protocol

    D. A and B

    E. B and C

    F. A, B, and C

15. The IP filter list contains IP filters that specify which of the following?

    A. IP filters that specify whether to block or accept traffic.

    B. IP filters that specify protocols, ports, and addresses.

    C. IP filters that specify a destination address only.

    D. IP filters that specify whether to block or accept traffic, plus the protocols, ports, and addresses to match.

16. Configuring IPSec policies to use pre-shared authentication keys _____. (Choose all that apply.)

A. Can make you go blind

B. Can allow an attacker to steal the authentication key from Active Directory

C. Is usually required only if you're talking to older IPSec equipment

D. Cannot be used in conjunction with Kerberos authentication

17. To enable IPSec on a local computer, you must do what?

A. Assign an IPSec policy

B. Create an IPSec policy

C. Join the computer to a domain

D. Install the IPSec Policy Agent

18. How do you specify whether or not an IPSec rule can be used on a LAN?

A. You adjust the setting on the Connection Type tab of the Edit Rule Properties dialog box.

B. You delete the rule and recreate it with the Create LAN Rule context menu command.

C. You change the rule type in the registry.

D. You cannot specify where a rule may be used.

19. The "Allow unsecured communication with non-IPSec-aware computer" check box has which of the following effects when set?

A. It allows any computer to connect without using IPSec.

B. It allows any computer not using IPSec to connect normally while requiring IPSec for computers that support it.

C. It depends on the setting of the Permit, Block , and Negotiate Security radio buttons.

D. It depends on the setting of the "Accept unsecured communication, but always respond using IPSec" check box.

20. Marie is trying to isolate an IPSec negotiation failure on an otherwise working network. She checks the event log and finds event ID 547, recording the negotiation failure. From this log, Marie can establish which probable cause?

A. Negotiation has failed because there is a policy mismatch between the two computers.

B. Negotiation has failed because one endpoint has the wrong key material.

C. Negotiation has failed because one side has an incorrect tunnel endpoint.

D. Negotiation has failed for an unknown reason.

Answers to Review Questions

1. B. The "Check for policy changes" value specifies how often the IPSec Policy Agent should look for and re-download policy settings.

2. A, B, C, D. The IPSec Policy agent tries to download policy information from Active Directory; failing that, it will pull policy information from the local registry. Stopping the policy agent forces it to clear any extant SAs, and restarting it again restarts the IPSec driver as well.

3. C. NTLM authentication can't be used with IPSec.

4. A. You can define multiple rules in a policy but only one filter list and one filter action per rule.

5. A, C. Tunnel mode can link IP addresses or subnets, and it doesn't require Group Policy. If you need VPN service, use PPTP or L2TP + IPSec.

6. C. Filter actions specify whether to accept or reject traffic that matches the filter in question; if the traffic is accepted, the specified action also controls what security methods are used.

7. A. Domain policies take precedence over local policies, and the lowest-level OU policy wins.

8. B. Rebooting will work, but stopping and restarting the policy agent is an easier way to do the same task.

9. C. A and B have nothing to do with IPSec, and D doesn't exist.

10. B. The "Client (Respond Only)" policy tells an IPSec computer to answer with IPSec when another computer offers it but never to initiate an IPSec negotiation.

11. A. You can specify any source or destination IP address or filter action, but you must establish two separate rules instead of using mirroring.

12. B. This policy attempts to request security after initial contact from any *TCP/IP client*.

13. D. Method A will secure other types of traffic. Method B may fail to establish a secure connection to the target site. Method C will shut down all non-IPSec communication to all destinations.

14. F. You can specify filter matches based on the source or destination address, source or destination port, or the protocol used—and you can combine all five to build complicated filters.

15. B. The filter is just a matching criteria, so it describes a port, a protocol, a source address, and a destination address. The action determines whether traffic that matches a filter is permitted or blocked.

16. B, C. Because the pre-shared key is stored as a directory attribute, anyone with read access to the AD may be able to recover the key.

17. A. The default Windows 2000 install includes the policy agent and three policies. Domain membership isn't required; all you have to do is assign a policy using the IPSec snap-in.

18. A. The Connection Type tab lets you control where the rule can be applied.

19. A. This particular check box tells the IPSec stack to allow non-IPSec computers to connect at will—probably not exactly what you'd want.

20. A. The presence of event ID 547 indicates that negotiation failed.

Chapter 12

Installing and Configuring Network Clients

MICROSOFT EXAM OBJECTIVES COVERED IN THIS CHAPTER:

✓ **Install, configure, and troubleshoot DNS.**

- Configure a DNS client.

✓ **Install, configure, and troubleshoot WINS.**

✓ **Configure and troubleshoot remote access.**

- Configure a virtual private network (VPN).

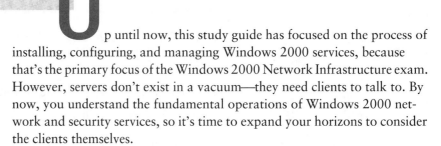

p until now, this study guide has focused on the process of installing, configuring, and managing Windows 2000 services, because that's the primary focus of the Windows 2000 Network Infrastructure exam. However, servers don't exist in a vacuum—they need clients to talk to. By now, you understand the fundamental operations of Windows 2000 network and security services, so it's time to expand your horizons to consider the clients themselves.

In this chapter, you'll first learn the details of configuring Windows 2000 network clients to use the DNS, DHCP, and WINS protocols. Then you'll find out how to configure a Windows 2000 Professional machine so that it can dial into and use a Windows 2000 Routing and Remote Access Service (RRAS) server. Finally, you'll learn how to configure Windows 2000 clients to use PPTP-based *Virtual Private Networks (VPNs)*.

Throughout this chapter you'll be reading about configuring clients, but don't let that term fool you—you can use these same procedures for configuring any Windows 2000 machine, no matter whether it's running Professional, Server, Advanced Server, or Datacenter Server.

Configuring DHCP Clients

As far as we're concerned, the Dynamic Host Configuration Protocol (DHCP) is the best thing for network administrators since the invention of Diet Coke. DHCP greatly eases the process of assigning and managing IP addresses and configuration information; with a properly setup and maintained DHCP infrastructure, you never have to worry about IP address conflicts, mistyped gateway addresses, and other staples of the "let the user configure it" school of administration. By default, new Windows 2000 installations rely on DHCP for their TCP/IP configuration; that offers you the tempting possibility of being able to unbox a new PC, install Windows 2000 on it, and not have to adjust any network settings on it at all. However, it's useful to know how to turn DHCP on and off on the client end.

Before You Turn On DHCP

The biggest thing to be aware of before enabling any DHCP clients is that you need a DHCP server for them to talk to. Windows 2000 (and Windows 98, but not any other version of Windows) has a "feature" built into it that can cause unintended consequences when you enable DHCP on the client without a server being present. The *Internet Connection Sharing (ICS)* and *Network Address Translation (NAT)* services offer an automatic configuration function that lets clients obtain IP addresses without a DHCP server. In practice, that means that if you switch a client into DHCP mode, it will pick an address in the 169. 254.x. y Class B address space—and unless that address space is already in use on your network, your client will have difficulty talking to other computers on the network! More precisely, all the clients that can't reach the DHCP server will have addresses in the same range, and they'll be able to see each other. Each time a client fails to contact a DHCP server, it picks an address from the 169.254 range and broadcasts it; if no other client answers the broadcast, the client uses the address as if it were manually assigned. However, the client "knows" that this isn't a real DHCP address, so it keeps attempting to renew its lease. Once it succeeds, it transparently switches to the DHCP address.

If you *do* have DHCP servers, you should verify that at least one of them is authorized for your clients when you enable DHCP for the first time. As you learned back in Chapter 2, "Windows 2000 Network Naming Services," the client sends out a mating call for DHCP servers, and if it can't find one it won't be able to obtain an IP address. In Windows 2000, the end result is the same one you see when there are no DHCP servers—the dreaded 169.254.x.y address.

One caveat that's mentioned in Microsoft's documentation: A Windows 2000 machine running the DHCP server service *must* have a static IP address. Don't expect to be able to use the DHCP client on your servers if you're running DHCP or DNS services on them.

Activating and Deactivating DHCP Clients

Microsoft never comes out and uses the acronym DHCP in the TCP/IP properties interface; instead, they use the more obvious, if less precise, phrase "Obtain an IP address automatically" throughout the Windows NT, Windows 9*x*, and Windows 2000 user interface. Once you know the IP address, the rest of what you need to know is pretty straightforward.

To adjust the DHCP status of a Windows 2000 client machine from the Internet Protocol (TCP/IP) Properties dialog box, which in turn appears when you open the Local Area Connection Properties dialog box, select Internet Protocol (TCP/IP) in the protocol list, and click Properties. The dialog box itself is shown in Figure 12.1. The salient controls are related to the ones explained in Chapter 4, "Installing and Configuring Basic Network Protocols," during the discussion of configuring the TCP/IP client stack with the information it needs to communicate over the network.

FIGURE 12.1 The Internet Protocol (TCP/IP) Properties dialog box

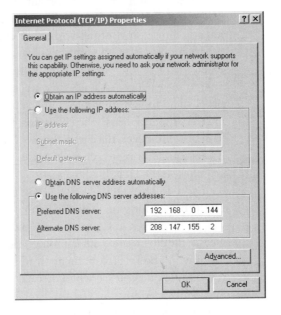

Controls in the Internet Protocol (TCP/IP) Properties dialog box include the following:

- The Obtain An IP Address Automatically and Use The Following IP Address controls are mutually exclusive ways to tell Windows 2000 how you want IP addresses handed out. To turn on DHCP, make sure that the Obtain An IP Address Automatically button is selected. To turn it off again, select Use The Following IP Address. Note that once you switch on DHCP, Windows 2000 forgets all about the prior contents of the three IP addressing fields.

- When you use DHCP, you may or may not want to receive DNS server configuration information as part of the DHCP payload. The Obtain DNS Server Address Automatically radio button instructs the Windows 2000 network stack to honor the DNS server information sent as part of the DHCP configuration; the Use The Following DNS Server Addresses radio button does the opposite, using instead the addresses you provide in the fields.

EXERCISE 12.1

Configuring a Windows 2000 Client to Use DHCP

Follow these steps:

1. Choose Start ➤ Settings ➤ Network and Dial-Up Connections.

2. Right-click the Local Area Connection icon and choose the Properties command. If you have more than one LAN adapter, choose the one you want to configure.

3. The Local Area Connection Properties dialog box will appear. Select Internet Protocol (TCP/IP) from the Components Checked Are Used By This Connection list.

4. Click the Properties button. The Internet Protocol (TCP/IP) Properties dialog box will appear, as shown earlier in Figure 12.1.

5. To turn on DHCP, click the Obtain An IP Address Automatically radio button.

6. To enable your client to get DNS server information from the DHCP server, select the Obtain DNS Server Address Automatically radio button.

7. Click OK to close the Internet Protocol (TCP/IP) Properties dialog box.

8. Click OK to close the Local Area Connection Properties dialog box.

Ipconfig Strikes Back

You may remember the *ipconfig tool* that was first mentioned in Chapter 4, "Installing and Configuring Basic Network Protocols." In particular, if you were paying close attention you'll remember that ipconfig has some options that make it particularly handy for DHCP clients: the */renew* and */release* switches. These switches allow you to request renewal of, or give up, your machine's existing address lease. This might not seem that useful since you can essentially do the same thing by toggling the Obtain An IP Address Automatically button, but it is—especially when you're setting up a new network.

For example, we spend about a third of our time teaching Windows 2000 classes for Global Knowledge (`http://am.globalknowledge.com`), usually in temporary classrooms set up at conferences, hotels, and so on. These classes use laptops, with one brawny laptop set up as a DNS/DHCP/DC server. Occasionally, a balky client will lose its DHCP lease (or not get one, perhaps because a cable has come loose or something), and the quickest way to fix it is to pop open a command-line window and quickly type **ipconfig /renew**. As if you couldn't guess by now, the switches do the following:

ipconfig /renew   Instructs the DHCP client to request a lease renewal. If it already has a lease, it requests a renewal from the server, which issued the current lease. This is exactly equivalent to what happens when the client reaches the half-life of its lease, as described in more detail in the section "How DHCP Works" in Chapter 2. If the client *doesn't* currently have a lease, the process is identical to what happens when you boot a DHCP client for the first time: It initiates the DHCP mating dance, listens for lease offers, and chooses one it likes.

ipconfig /release   Forces the client to immediately give up its lease by sending the server a DHCP release notification. The server updates its status information and marks the client's old IP address as "available," leaving the client with no address bound to its network interface. When you use this command, most of the time it will be immediately followed by ipconfig /renew; the combination releases the existing lease and gets a new one, probably with a different address. (It's also a handy way to force your client to get a new set of settings from the server before lease expiration time.)

If you have multiple network adapters in a single machine, you can provide the name of the adapter (or adapters) you want the command to work on, including the "*" character as a wildcard. For example, one of our servers has two network cards: one's an Intel EtherExpress, and one's a generic 100Mbps card from Best Buy. If we want to renew DHCP settings for both adapters, we can type **ipconfig /renew ***; if we just want to renew the generic card, we can type **ipconfig /renew ELNK1**.

Configuring DNS Clients

DNS configuration seems easy: After all, the only thing you have to do is click one radio button and fill in one (maybe two, if you're feeling energetic) IP addresses. There are some subtleties to the process, though, brought on by the presence of a DNS tab in the Advanced TCP/IP Settings dialog box. Some of the other tabs in that dialog box were discussed back in Chapter 4; now it's time to find out what the settings on the DNS tab do. First, though, you should start with the fundamentals of DNS client configuration: using the controls in the standard Internet Protocol (TCP/IP) Properties dialog box.

Microsoft ✓ *Exam* *Objective*

Install, configure, and troubleshoot DNS.

- Configure a DNS client.

Basic DNS Configuration

Figure 12.1 shows you pretty much everything you need to know about DNS configuration. As you learned earlier in this chapter, the Obtain DNS Server Information Automatically and the Use The Following DNS Server Addresses radio buttons control whether your client will pick up DNS information from the DHCP server or from the following two IP address fields:

- When you select the Obtain DNS Server Information Automatically button (which you can only do when DHCP is enabled), whatever DNS addresses you've put into your DHCP server configuration—or none, if you don't provide any—will be used by the client, with no way for you to override them. This button can only be selected when you've selected the Obtain An IP Address Automatically radio button.

- When you use the Use The Following DNS Server Addresses button, you must enter an address in the Preferred DNS Server field. You may optionally enter the address of another server in the Alternate DNS Server field; if you want to specify more than two servers, it'll cost you a trip to the Advanced button.

In a welcome departure from previous versions of Windows, you can change DNS modes and server addresses without having to reboot.

You can find the rest of the subobjectives for the exam objective "Install, configure, and troubleshoot DNS" in Chapter 6, "Installing and Managing Domain Name Service."

EXERCISE 12.2

Configuring a Windows 2000 Client to Use DNS

To configure basic DNS name resolution on a client machine, follow these steps:

1. Choose Start ➤ Settings ➤ Network and Dial-Up Connections.

2. Right-click the Local Area Connection icon and choose the Properties command. If you have more than one LAN adapter, choose the one you want to configure.

3. The Local Area Connection Properties dialog box will appear. Select Internet Protocol (TCP/IP) from the Components Checked Are Used By This Connection list.

4. Click the Properties button. The Internet Protocol (TCP/IP) Properties dialog box will appear, as shown earlier in Figure 12.1.

5. Select the Use The Following DNS Server Addresses radio button.

6. Enter an IP address (e.g., 207.69.188.185) in the Preferred DNS server field.

7. (Optional) Enter a different IP address (e.g., 207.69.188.186) in the Alternate DNS Server field.

8. Click OK to close the Internet Protocol (TCP/IP) Properties dialog box.

9. Click OK to close the Local Area Connection Properties dialog box.

Advanced DNS Configuration

Back in Chapter 4, you learned about some of the functions tucked away behind the Advanced button in the Internet Protocol (TCP/IP) Properties dialog box. Now it's time to examine one function—the DNS tab—in more detail. The tab itself is shown in Figure 12.2. It seems pretty busy, but the controls on it are all reasonably easy to understand.

FIGURE 12.2 The DNS tab of the Advanced TCP/IP Settings dialog

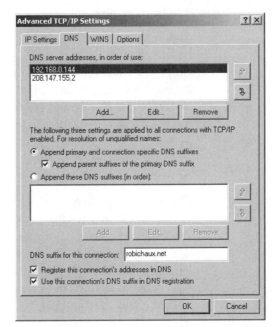

First you should understand the following settings of the DNS server list itself:

- The DNS Server Addresses, In Order Of Use list shows all the DNS servers currently defined for this client. Any DNS query is sent to the first server; if that server doesn't produce an answer, the query goes to the next one in the list. This process continues until a server returns a valid answer or until all the servers have been tried.

  You can add, edit, and remove servers with the buttons below the list, and you can change the order of a server in the list by selecting it and using the up and down arrows to the right of the list.

The DNS server list is used only for the network interface you're configuring. This allows you to use different DNS servers for NICs that are connected to different networks.

The remaining settings pertain only to this connection (or network adapter to be more precise):

- The Append Primary And Connection Specific DNS Suffixes radio button controls whether the DNS resolver will automatically append the *primary DNS suffix* and any connection-specific suffixes when it makes DNS requests. For example, say your primary DNS suffix is hsv.robichaux.net and your connection-specific suffix is eng.hsv.robichaux.net. When this radio button is active, and you initiate a DNS query for a machine named "hawk," the resolver will first look for hawk.hsv.robichaux.net, then for hawk.eng.hsv.robichaux.net.

- The Append Parent Suffixes Of The Primary DNS Suffix check box (which is only active when Append Primary And Connection Specific DNS Suffixes is selected) forces the resolver to tack on parent suffixes of the primary suffix. To recycle the example from the preceding bullet, if you couldn't find "hawk" in either eng.hsv.robichaux.net or hsv.robichaux.net, this check box would force the resolver to look in robichaux.net and plain old .net.

- The Append These DNS Suffixes (In Order) radio button and its associated controls allow you to provide a canned list of suffixes for the resolver. These are used in place of the primary and connection-specific suffixes, and they override any suffixes passed by the DHCP servers.

- The DNS Suffix For This Connection field specifies the default connection suffix you want to append to DNS queries. This overrides any suffix that may be specified by the DHCP server.

- The Register This Connection's Address In DNS check box, which is on by default, tells the DHCP client to register its name and IP address with the nearest dynamic DNS (DDNS) server. (See Chapter 6, "Installing and Managing Domain Name Service" for more information on dynamic DNS.)

- The Use This Connection's DNS Suffix In DNS Registration check box controls whether the primary or *connection-specific DNS suffix* is used when your client registers itself with the DDNS service.

Configuring WINS Clients

WINS gets a lot of bad press, only some of which it deserves. True, it's not as flexible or open as the DNS protocol, and that's why Microsoft is trying to move away from it. At the same time, though, WINS is deeply entrenched in many networks, and it will be for a long time to come. (See Chapter 7, "Managing the Windows Internet Name Service," to learn more about configuring and managing the Windows 2000 WINS server.) Unlike Windows NT, the WINS client configuration options in Windows 2000 are buried in the Advanced TCP/IP Settings dialog box. The WINS tab (see Figure 12.3) offers you a small group of controls for configuring how (if at all) your client uses WINS for name resolution.

Microsoft ✓ ***Exam Objective***   **Install, configure, and troubleshoot WINS.**

FIGURE 12.3   The WINS tab of the Advanced TCP/IP Settings dialog box

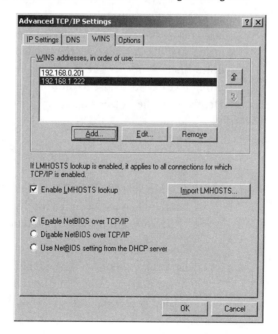

First, the WINS Addresses, In Order Of Use list and its related controls show you which WINS servers you have defined for this client. By default, this list will be empty, so you have to manually add WINS servers to it if you want to use WINS.

As with DNS, the WINS code will send WINS resolution requests to the servers on this list in the order of their appearance. You add, remove, and change server addresses with the buttons below the list, and you change the ordering of the servers by selecting a server and using the up and down arrow buttons along the list's right side.

The next group, which falls immediately below the WINS address list group, controls whether or not the old-style *LMHOSTS file* is used as a source for address resolution information. The Enable LMHOSTS Lookup check box controls whether or not Windows 2000 will use the IP-to-host-name mappings in the LMHOSTS file before querying a WINS server. When you check this box, LMHOSTS lookups are enabled for all connections that are using TCP/IP, not just the one whose properties you're editing. The Import LMHOSTS... button allows you to read the contents of a file into the WINS name cache, which is handy if you want to load a set of name mappings without keeping a file around on disk.

The final controls are the three radio buttons at the bottom of the dialog box. They control whether NetBIOS over TCP/IP is active at all. In the olden days of Microsoft networking, NetBEUI was the only transport that could carry NetBIOS traffic, but it wasn't routable and had poor performance on large networks. Microsoft devised a scheme for encapsulating NetBIOS inside TCP/IP (for a while, they called it NBT), and it's been a part of Windows since Windows NT 3.5 or so. In Windows 2000, NBT lives on, even though we expect its use to diminish as networks move toward pure TCP/IP. Here's what the buttons do:

- The Enable NetBIOS Over TCP/IP button is selected by default. It allows this client to exchange NetBIOS traffic with servers using TCP/IP as a transport.

- The Disable NetBIOS Over TCP/IP button turns off NBT, which is handy when you want to totally rid your network of all NetBIOS traffic, even when it's encapsulated.

- The Use NetBIOS Setting From The DHCP Server button forces this particular client to use the DHCP server's setting instead of either one of the two preceding buttons. If this button is *not* selected, whatever setting is in force will override the DHCP server's setting.

EXERCISE 12.3

Configuring a Windows 2000 Client to Use WINS

Follow these steps to enable WINS resolution on a Windows 2000 client.

1. Choose Start ≻ Settings ≻ Network and Dial-Up Connections.

2. Right-click the Local Area Connection icon and choose the Properties command. If you have more than one LAN adapter, choose the one you want to configure.

3. The Local Area Connection Properties dialog box will appear. Select Internet Protocol (TCP/IP) from the Components Checked Are Used By This Connection list.

4. Click the Properties button. The Internet Protocol (TCP/IP) Properties dialog box will appear, as shown earlier in Figure 12.1.

5. Click the Advanced… button. The Advanced TCP/IP Settings dialog box will appear.

6. Click the WINS tab.

7. Click the Add… button. When the TCP/IP WINS Server dialog box appears, enter the IP address for your WINS server and click the Add button.

8. (Optional) Enter additional WINS server addresses and reorder the servers as necessary.

9. Click OK to close the Advanced TCP/IP Settings dialog box.

10. Click OK to close the Internet Protocol (TCP/IP) Properties dialog box.

11. Click OK to close the Local Area Connection Properties dialog box.

Configuring Dial-Up Networking Clients

The process of making and changing dial-up connections in Windows 2000 is quite a bit different from what you're probably used to in Windows NT or Windows 98. The Network and Dial-Up Connections folder is now home base for *all* network connections, whether they're made through the *Dial-Up Networking (DUN)* subsystem or directly through some kind of network adapter. However, most of the settings you can apply to dial-up connections are similar (if not identical) to their forebears.

Creating New Connections

Like Windows 95, Windows 98, and Windows NT, Windows 2000 creates separate files for each connection you create; this helps keep related settings together. To create a new connection, you use the Make New Connection icon in the Network and Dial-Up Connections folder. This activates the Network Connection wizard, yet another of the seemingly hundreds of wizards tucked away at various points in Windows 2000. This particular wizard leads you through the process of setting up a new network connection, beginning with a meaningless introductory page (not shown here). The first "real" page of the wizard gives you five radio-button choices (as shown in Figure 12.4).

FIGURE 12.4   The Network Connection Type page of the Network Connection wizard

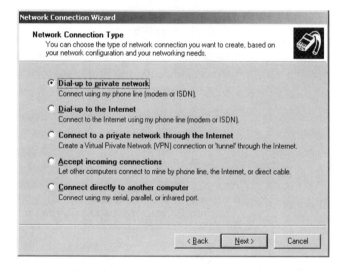

The following list includes all five radio-button choices, but only the first three will be covered in this chapter:

- **Dial-Up To Private Network** allows you to establish a dial-up connection to a host somewhere on someone else's network.

- **Dial-Up To The Internet** establishes vanilla dial-up connections to a host that speaks the *Point-to-Point Protocol (PPP)*.

- **Connect To A Private Network Through The Internet** allows you to create a virtual private network (VPN) connection on top of an established PPP session. You'll see more about VPNs at the end of this chapter.

- **Accept Incoming Connections** allows you to set up your system to accept incoming connections; you saw this button earlier in Chapters 9 and 10.

- **Connect Directly To Another Computer** makes it possible to establish a direct peer-to-peer connection to another Windows 2000 machine using a serial, parallel, or infrared connection.

The first step toward creating a new connection on a Windows 2000 client machine is to pick one of the first two radio buttons. Creating an Internet connection requires you to use the Internet Connection wizard, and that's not part of the test objectives.) Instead of describing that wizard, the next section will explain what happens when you select the first button, Dial-Up To Private Network.

Since the connections are files, you can copy them from Explorer. The fastest way to create several connections is to create one, copy it, and modify the copy's properties.

Specifying the Phone Number

Once you click Next on the Network Connection Type page, the next thing you'll see is the Phone Number To Dial page (see Figure 12.5). You use this page to specify the area code, phone number, and country code of the network you're dialing into. The fields are all self-explanatory, except for the Area Code field. It's disabled by default, unless you check the Use Dialing Rules check box to indicate that you want to use the *dialing rules* set up in the Modem control panel. These rules allow you to tell DUN what country and region you're in so that it knows to add the appropriate long-distance codes, area codes, and calling card numbers when it's dialing. Click Next once you've entered the calling information you want to use for this connection.

FIGURE 12.5 The Phone Number To Dial page of the Network Connection wizard

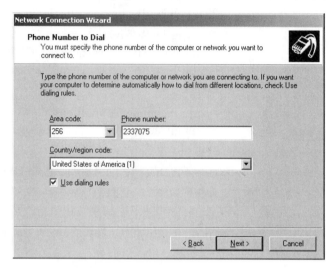

To Share or to Hoard?

The next page of the Network Connection wizard is where you specify whether this particular connection should be available to all users on the machine or just to you. This is a handy way for administrators to quickly set up a connection that any user on a particular client machine can use—selecting the For All Users button makes the connection available, while the Only For Myself button restricts its availability to the currently logged-on user.

The next page you'll encounter (see Figure 12.6) gives you two more sharing-related options. The first is a check box labeled Enable Internet Connection Sharing For This Connection. As you might suspect from its label, this check box turns on Internet Connection Sharing, or ICS, for this dial-up connection. ICS is really just a watered-down version of Network Address Translation (NAT), and it's covered as part of the discussion of NAT in Chapter 13, "Managing Network Address Translation." For this chapter, all you need to know about ICS is that the second check box, Enable On-Demand Dialing, tells the ICS code that it's allowed to bring up the connection when another network user wants to send some packets out to the Internet.

You'll be able to use ICS on Windows 2000 Server, not just on Professional. NAT, however, is only available on the Server products.

FIGURE 12.6   The Internet Connection Sharing page of the Network Connection wizard

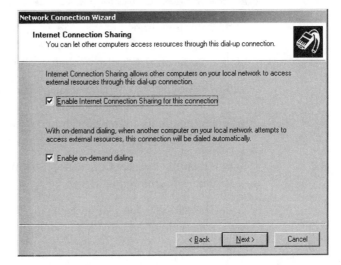

Naming Your Connection

The completion page of the Network Connection wizard asks you to identify this connection by giving it a name. The name you supply will be used to identify the connection in the Network and Dial-Up Connections folder, so make sure you give it a name that will help you remember what the connection's for! When you click the Finish button the connection information is stored on disk, and the connection dialog appears so you can test the new connection.

EXERCISE 12.4

Configuring a Windows Professional Client for Dial-Up Networking

Follow these steps:

1. Choose Start ➢ Settings ➢ Network and Dial-Up Connections.

2. Double-click the Make New Connection icon. The Network Connection wizard appears. Click the Next button.

3. Choose the Dial-Up To Private Network button and click Next.

4. Enter the phone number you want this connection to dial. Optionally, check the Use Dialing Rules box and enter a country code and/or area code. Click Next when you're done.

5. The Connection Availability page appears. If you want to make this connection available to all users, choose the For All Users radio button. If this connection should only be available to you, choose Only For Myself. Click the Next button when done.

6. When the Internet Connection Sharing page appears, click Next without turning on ICS.

7. The wizard's completion page appears. Type a name for this connection into the provided field, then click Finish.

8. The Connect dialog box appears. Enter a username and password; if necessary, adjust the phone number and click the Dial button to connect.

Setting Connection Properties

Once you've created a connection, you can change its properties at any time by opening its Properties dialog box. The Dial-Up Connection Properties dialog box has a total of five tabs that let you adjust all the pertinent settings for each individual connection. Don't confuse these settings with the ones present in the Local Area Connection Properties dialog box; they're entirely different.

The General Tab

The General tab of the Dial-Up Connection Properties dialog box (Figure 12.7) is where you specify the modem and phone number to use with this particular connection. In this tab, as with the other tabs in this dialog box, you may recognize the filled-in fields when you use the Network Connection wizard.

FIGURE 12.7 The General tab of the Dial-Up Connection Properties dialog box

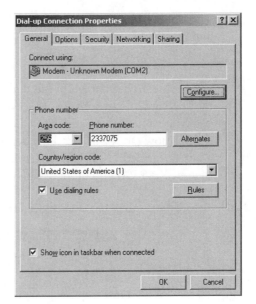

In this dialog box, you can do the following:

- Change the modem this connection uses, or settings for the modem you already have, with the Configure button. Note that you can also use the Phone and Modem Options control panel to adjust a broader range of modem settings.

- Change the phone number, area code, or country code used to dial this number.

- Change whether or not dialing rules (e.g., "I am now in area code 770") are used when DUN decides how to dial the number for this connection. When the Use Dialing Rules check box is on, the Rules button becomes active, allowing you to define new locations and edit the dialing rules attached to each.

- Change whether or not the connection shows a status/progress icon in the system tray whenever the connection is active. By default, dial-up connections have the Show Icon In Taskbar When Connected check box turned on.

The Options Tab

The Options tab (see Figure 12.8) holds settings that control how DUN dials and redials the connection. If the General tab is like the listing in a phone book, the Options tab is the equivalent of teaching your babysitter how to use the PBX in your house. (What do you mean, you don't have a PBX in your house?) The controls in this dialog box are segregated into two groups: the Dialing Options group holds controls that govern DUN's interface behavior while dialing, and the Redialing Options group controls whether or not and how DUN will redial if it doesn't immediately connect. (There's also a button labeled "X.25"; not surprisingly, you use it to change the settings of your X.25 PAD if you're using one.)

FIGURE 12.8   The Options tab of the Dial-Up Connection Properties dialog box

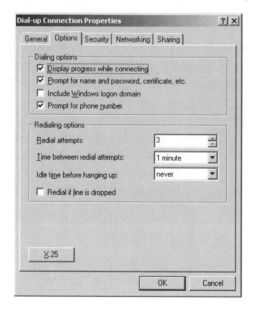

Dialing Options

There are four separate dialing options available in the Dialing Options group:

- The Display Progress While Connecting check box (on by default) instructs DUN to keep you updated on its progress as it attempts to raise the connection.

- The Prompt For Name And Password, Certificate, Etc. check box is also on by default. When it's on, Windows 2000 will prompt you for any credentials it needs to authenticate your connection to the remote server. This may be a username, a password, a public-key certificate, or some combination of the three, depending on what the remote end requires.

- The Include Windows Logon Domain check box is off by default; it forces DUN to include the domain name of the domain you're logged on to as part of the authentication credential. Leave this turned off unless you're dialing into a Windows NT/2000 network that has a trust relationship with your logon domain.

- The Prompt For Phone Number check box (normally on) tells DUN to display the phone number in the connection dialog box. This gives you a chance to edit it before dialing; you may want to uncheck it if you (or your users) are prone to accidental changes.

Redialing Options

The settings in the Redialing Options group control how DUN will attempt to redial the specified number if the remote end is busy or doesn't answer with a recognizable carrier tone. These settings include the following:

- The Redial Attempts field controls how many attempts DUN will make to raise the other end before giving up. The default value is 3, but you can set any value from 0 (meaning that DUN won't attempt to redial) to the ridiculous value of 999,999,999.

- The Time Between Redial Attempts pull-down menu controls how long DUN will wait after each failed call before it tries again. Values in the pull-down menu range from 1 second all the way to 10 minutes, with various increments in between.

- The Idle Time Before Hanging Up pull-down menu lets you specify an inactivity timer. If your connection is idle for longer than the specified period, your client will terminate the call. Note that the remote end may drop the call sooner than your client, depending on how it's configured. By default, this pull-down menu is set to "never," meaning that your client will never drop a call. If you want an inactivity timer, you can pick values ranging from 1 minute to 24 hours.

- The Redial If Line Is Dropped check box is a welcome Windows 2000 feature if you frequently have to use flaky telephone lines or service providers. Our experience has been that hotels in the U.S. have worse phone lines, on average, than anyplace else.

The Security Tab

How useful you find the Security tab to be will depend on whom you're calling. The default settings it provides will work fine with most Internet service providers and corporate dial-up facilities, but Windows 2000 has a broad range of security settings you can change if you need to. Figure 12.9 shows the Security tab itself; the Security Options group contains controls that directly affect the security of your connection, while the Interactive Logon And Scripting tab controls what canned script (if any) your client uses when connecting.

FIGURE 12.9   The Security tab of the Dial-Up Connection Properties dialog box

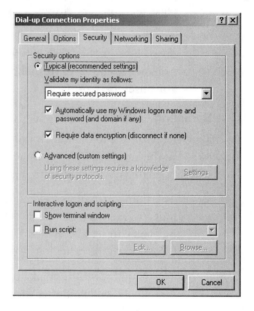

Security Options

The security options themselves are pretty straightforward; Microsoft has done a good job of labeling them clearly so that non-security weenies can understand what they mean. Here's the scoop: The security settings in effect for this connection are governed by your choice between the Typical (Recommended Settings) and Advanced (Custom Settings) radio buttons. Normally, your best bet is to stick with the typical settings and use its subordinate controls to pick a canned setting that matches your needs. These subordinate controls include the following:

- The Validate My Identity As Follows pull-down menu lets you choose between unsecured passwords (the default, and the only type of authentication that most networks support), secured passwords, and smartcard authentication (useful only when calling another Windows 2000 network).

- If you choose to require a secured password, the Automatically Use My Windows Logon Name And Password check box instructs DUN to offer the logon credentials you used to log on to the computer or domain to the remote end. Obviously this is only useful if you're dialing into a network that has access to your domain authentication information.

- If you require a secured password or smartcard authentication, the Require Data Encryption check box allows you to have either an encrypted connection or none at all. If you check this box, your client and the remote server will attempt to negotiate a common encryption method. If they can't (perhaps because the remote end doesn't offer encryption), your client will hang up.

Advanced Security Settings

If you select the Advanced (Custom Settings) radio button and then click the Settings button, you'll see the Advanced Security Settings dialog box shown in Figure 12.10. Its controls are more complex than the ones on the Security tab, so they bear a little more explanation.

FIGURE 12.10 The Advanced Security Settings dialog box

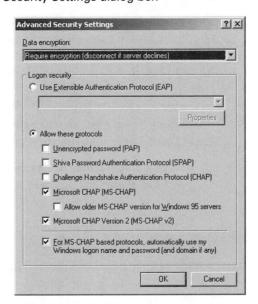

The first field is the Data Encryption pull-down menu. Windows 2000 offers you the opportunity to encrypt both sides of network connections using IPSec (see Chapter 11, "Configuring and Managing IPSec," for more IPSec goodies). This capability extends to dial-up connections, too. The pull-down menu gives you the following four choices:

- "No encryption allowed" means that the server will drop your call if it requires encryption, since you can't provide it.

- "Optional encryption" tells the client to request encryption but to continue the call if it's not available.

- "Require encryption" tells the client to request encryption and to refuse to communicate with servers that don't support it.

- "Maximum strength encryption" tells the client to only communicate with servers that offer the same strength encryption it does. For example, with this setting in force a North American Windows 2000 machine with the High Encryption pack won't talk to a French Windows 2000 machine, since the French machine uses the weaker exportable encryption routines.

The Logon Security group controls which authentication protocols this client is willing to admit it knows. The default setting, Use Extensible Authentication Protocol (EAP), is what you use if you want to use standard Windows 2000 authentication (using the MD5-Challenge method) or certificate-based authentication (using the "Smart card or other certificate" choice in the pull-down). Certificate-based authentication is fascinating but not on the MCSE exam, so it will not be discussed further in this book.

The other radio button, Allow These Protocols, is followed by a laundry list of authentication protocols. While the specifics of how they work are different, the basic idea behind each of these protocols is the same: Provide a secure way for a client to prove its identity to a server. By selecting the appropriate check boxes, you can make your client speak the same protocols as the remote end. These authentication protocols include the following:

- *PAP* is like English: It's spoken practically everywhere, even though it's not always the best way to communicate. Since PAP doesn't encrypt the client's password, it's falling out of favor.

- *SPAP* is a modified version of PAP spoken by some vendors' remote-access devices (notably those from Shiva, now a division of Intel).

- *CHAP* is a big improvement over PAP and SPAP, since it doesn't pass your passwords around in clear text. Almost all remote access vendors (and Unix vendors, for that matter) support CHAP authentication.

- Microsoft has its own versions of CHAP: *MS-CHAP* version 1 and version 2. Version 2 is much more secure, but only Windows NT and Windows 2000 servers support it. Some other systems (including Linux) offer support for one version but not the other.

Which protocols should you pick? We generally recommend avoiding PAP and SPAP unless you *must* talk to some elderly device that doesn't speak CHAP or MS-CHAP. If possible, allow only CHAP and MS-CHAP version 2 on your clients and servers. By default, when you turn on the Allow These Protocols button CHAP, MS-CHAP, and MS-CHAP version 2 will be enabled. This gives you the best mix of flexibility and security.

The Networking Tab

You use the Networking tab (see Figure 12.11) to control which protocols your client will attempt to use when communicating with other servers. With power comes responsibility, though—you have to tell DUN what kind of server it's calling in the first place, using the Type Of Dial-Up Server I Am Calling field. Your choices are PPP or SLIP (the Serial Line Internet Protocol, now relegated to ancient Unix boxes and dialup hardware). By default, PPP will be selected, and it's unlikely that you'll need to change it.

FIGURE 12.11 The Networking tab of the Dial-Up Connection Properties dialog box

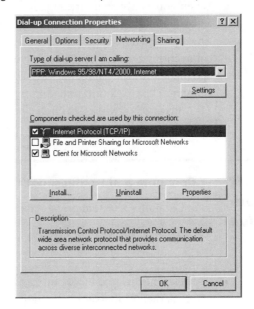

The list box in the middle of the tab shows the network protocols installed on the client. Protocols marked with a check are available for use with this connection. Normally, you'll see TCP/IP and Client for Microsoft Networks marked, which indicates that those two protocols can be used over the connection. The Install, Uninstall, and Properties buttons work just as they do in the Local Area Connection Properties dialog—by using them you can control which protocols live on your machine and what their settings are.

It's worth mentioning that selecting Internet Protocol (TCP/IP) in the protocols list and opening its properties dialog box gives you access to a set of properties that are completely distinct from any TCP/IP settings that may apply to your LAN interfaces. Normally, the dial-up TCP/IP settings are configured to obtain an IP address and DNS information from the remote server, although if you need to you can override these settings.

The Sharing Tab

The Sharing tab only contains two controls, and as it happens, they're the same ones you saw earlier in Figure 12.6: Enable Internet Connection Sharing For This Connection and Enable On-Demand Dialing.

Configuring a VPN Client

When you establish a virtual private network (VPN) connection, you're actually building an encrypted tunnel between you and some other machine. The tunneled data is carried over an insecure network, like the Internet. VPN connections are easy to set up and use, especially since you create and manage them with the same Network Connection wizard from earlier in this chapter. The first noticeable difference here is that you choose the Connect To A Private Network Through The Internet button at the beginning of the wizard; after that, things get even more different.

Microsoft ✓ *Exam* *Objective*

Configure and troubleshoot remote access.

- Configure a virtual private network (VPN).

After you click the Next button on the first page, the next difference you'll notice is the Public Network page, which allows you to tell DUN whether you want it to automatically dial the underlying connection for you or not.

By default, the Automatically Dial This Initial Connection radio button will be selected, so you can use the associated pull-down menu to choose which connection you want dialed. This is a terrific feature, since it largely automates the process of establishing VPN connections. Of course, if you only want VPN connectivity when you're already dialed up, you can select the Do Not Dial The Initial Connection button instead.

You can find more about this objective and VPN in Chapter 10, "Managing Virtual Private Networking."

Clicking the Next button again brings you to the Destination Address page. This page is so simple it's not worth an illustration; the only thing you do here is fill in the IP address (or DNS name) of the host you want to talk to over your tunnel. In other words, this is the address of the VPN server you're talking to. Enter the address or name, and then click Next. You'll then be presented with the same two sharing pages talked about earlier (see the section "To Share or to Hoard?"), followed by the summary page where you name the new connection. Once you click Finish, you can bring up the connection right then, or you can adjust its properties by opening the connection's properties dialog box.

Setting VPN Connection Properties

Surprisingly perhaps, most of the properties you set for a plain dial-up connection work the same way for VPN connections. In particular, the Options, Security, and Sharing tabs of the properties dialog boxes are identical across the two connection types. However, there are some minor differences on the other tabs, which include the following:

The General Tab   The VPN version of the General tab has a field where you enter the VPN server address or hostname instead of a phone number. In addition, the First Connect group lets you specify which dial-up connection, if any, you want brought up before the VPN connection is established.

The Networking Tab   The VPN Networking tab uses the top drop-down menu to let you indicate what kind of VPN call you're making. Automatic is the default setting, but you can explicitly ask for a *PPTP* or L2TP connection if you prefer.

EXERCISE 12.5

Configuring a Windows Client as a VPN Client

Follow these steps after you've completed Exercise 12.4:

1. Choose Start ➢ Settings ➢ Network and Dial-Up Connections.

2. Double-click the Make New Connection icon. The Network Connection wizard appears. Click the Next button.

3. Choose the Connect To A Private Network Through The Internet button and click Next.

4. Choose the dial-up connection you built in Exercise 12.4, then click the Next button.

5. Enter the IP address or DNS name of your VPN server (example: 192.168.0.25). Click Next when you're done.

6. The Connection Availability page appears. If you want to make this connection available to all users, choose the For All Users radio button. If this connection should only be available to you, choose Only For Myself. Click the Next button when done.

7. When the Internet Connection Sharing page appears, click Next without turning on ICS.

8. The wizard's completion page appears. Type a name for this connection into the provided field, then click Finish.

9. A confirmation dialog box labeled Initial Connection appears, notifying you that the dial-up connection you picked in step 4 will have to be brought up first. Click "Yes" to bring up the connection dialog box; once the connection goes through, log on to the VPN server using the correct credential information.

Summary

In this chapter, you learned:

- How to configure client machines to use the DNS, WINS, and DHCP services offered by Windows 2000 servers

- How to set up and configure Windows 2000 Professional as a remote access client

- How to configure Windows 2000 Professional as a VPN client

Key Terms

Before you take the exam, be sure you're familiar with the following terms:

Challenge Handshake Authentication Protocol (CHAP)

Connection-specific DNS suffix

Dialing rules

Dial-Up Networking (DUN)

Internet Connection Sharing (ICS)

Ipconfig tool

LMHOSTS file

Microsoft CHAP (MS-CHAP)

Network Address Translation (NAT)

Point-to-Point Protocol (PPP)

Point-to-Point Tunneling Protocol (PPTP)

Primary DNS suffix

/release

/renew

Virtual Private Network (VPN)

Review Questions

1. Joe sets up a new Windows 2000 Professional machine on his LAN. During installation, he specifies that he wants it to use DHCP to obtain address information. When the system boots, no other computers are visible on the network. Which of the following is the most likely cause of the problem?

   A. The computer couldn't contact a DHCP server on the network, so it used an address in the 169.254.x.x block.

   B. The DHCP service failed to start on Joe's computer.

   C. A group policy object prevents Joe's computer from using DHCP.

   D. The NIC is misconfigured.

2. To configure a Windows 2000 machine as a WINS client, you need which of the following?

   A. At least one WINS server on the network

   B. To configure the WINS tab of the Advanced TCP/IP Settings dialog

   C. Both A and B

   D. None of the above

3. To enable a Windows 2000 client to request Dynamic DNS updates, you must do which of the following?

   A. Turn on the Register This Connection's Address In DNS check box on the DNS tab of the Advanced TCP/IP Properties dialog

   B. Turn on the Use Dynamic DNS check box in the Internet Protocol (TCP/IP) Properties dialog box

   C. Disable DHCP on the client machine

   D. Make sure the correct connection-specific DNS suffix is provided in the DNS tab of the Advanced TCP/IP Properties dialog box

4. If settings on a local machine conflict with settings assigned by a DHCP server, which of the following statements is true?

   A. None of the conflicting settings will apply.

   B. The DHCP-assigned settings override the locally-assigned settings.

   C. Whichever settings are applied first take effect.

   D. The locally assigned settings override the DHCP-assigned settings.

5. To add maximum security to a Dial-Up Networking (DUN) call, you should do which of the following?

   A. Allow callbacks

   B. Turn on the Optional Encryption radio button

   C. Turn on the Require Encryption radio button

   D. Turn on the Require Encryption radio button and the Maximum Strength Encryption check box

6. The *ipconfig /release* command does which of the following?

   A. Releases, then renews, an expired DHCP lease

   B. Releases a WINS reservation

   C. Releases an existing DHCP lease

   D. Releases a dynamic DNS A record

7. You can control the protocols that are used on a dial-up connection by which *two* of the following?

   A. Editing the bindings for the dial-up connection

   B. Setting the desired protocols in the Networking tab of the Dial-Up Connection properties dialog box

   C. Reinstalling the DUN software with the correct set of protocols

   D. Checking the Allow Remote Server To Select Protocols check box on the General tab of the Dial-Up Connection properties dialog box.

8. Before a VPN connection can be established, which of the following must be true?

   A. The remote VPN server must be running Windows 2000 Server.

   B. The user must not be logged on using a smartcard.

   C. There must be a TCP/IP connection of some type between the client and server.

   D. The user must have logged in with a VPN-enabled account.

9. When creating a new Point-to-Point Tunneling Protocol (PPTP) connection, what must you enter?

   A. The IP address of the remote server

   B. The NetBIOS name of the remote server

   C. The phone number of the remote server

   D. The administrator password of the remote server

10. Marcia has to set up a Windows 2000 client to dial into an old remote access device. When she first installs the Dial-Up Networking client, she cannot authenticate to the remote server. Which of the following items might be to blame?

    A. The remote device doesn't support Windows 2000.

    B. The remote device is assigning an illegal TCP/IP address.

    C. Marcia's client is requiring CHAP or MS-CHAP authentication, and the device can't provide them.

    D. Multilink PPP must be enabled.

11. Which of the following is true of connection-specific DNS suffixes?

    A. They are optional.

    B. They are mandatory.

    C. They are automatically assigned.

    D. They automatically append the appropriate suffix for only one connection.

12. On a Windows 2000 client, you can control the use of NetBIOS in which of the following ways? (Choose all that apply.)

    A. You can completely disable NetBIOS over TCP/IP.

    B. You can enable NetBIOS over TCP/IP.

    C. You can accept the DHCP server setting that indicates whether or not NetBIOS will be used.

    D. You can enable NetBIOS over NetBEUI.

13. Jill wants to enable her Windows 2000 Professional client to use smartcard authentication when calling her company's RAS server. What must she do?

    A. Turn on smartcard authentication in the Security tab of the connection Properties dialog box.

    B. Ask her administrator to change her remote access profile.

    C. Log on with the smartcard installed; Windows will automatically ask her whether or not she wants to use it.

    D. Turn on smartcard authentication in the Computer Management snap-in.

14. Which of the following is true when you choose to get DNS server information from a DHCP server?

    A. The server settings apply in addition to whatever DNS servers you specify manually.

    B. You can override the server settings by making a Registry change.

    C. The server settings will only apply if you haven't manually configured a DNS server.

    D. You can't override the server settings.

15. To create several related DUN connections, the fastest approach is to do which of the following?

A. Create each connection using the Network Connection wizard

B. Create one connection using the Network Connection wizard and copy it, modifying the copy's properties

C. Create each connection manually

D. Create one connection manually, then copy it and modify the copy's properties

16. Which of the following is true if you specify more than one DNS server in the TCP/IP Properties dialog box?

A. A randomly chosen server is used for each query.

B. The server with the fastest response time will be used.

C. Servers are used in the order they're specified.

D. Servers will be used in the order specified by the DHCP server.

17. How many DNS servers can you include in the list Windows 2000 uses to resolve names?

A. One

B. Two

C. Three

D. More than three

18. How is Dynamic DNS registration controlled?

A. Per computer, in the System Properties dialog box

B. Per connection, in the General tab of the connection Properties dialog box

C. Per computer, in the TCP/IP Properties dialog box

D. Per connection, on the DNS tab of the Advanced TCP/IP Properties dialog box

19. Which of the following is *not true* about Internet Connection Sharing?

   A. It works with dial-up or LAN connections.

   B. It's controlled per connection.

   C. It's only available on Windows 2000 Professional.

   D. It's off by default when you create a new connection.

20. Bill wants to have his ISDN dial-up connection hang up automatically after ten minutes of inactivity. How can he accomplish this?

   A. By programming his ISDN adapter to drop idle connections

   B. By configuring the remote server to drop his connection after the specified idle period

   C. By using the Idle Time Before Hanging Up control in the Options tab of the connection he's using

   D. By using the Hang Up After control in the Connection tab of the connection he's using

Answers to Review Questions

1. D. When Joe's computer fails to connect to a DHCP server, it gets assigned an address in the 169.254 block. It will then be able to see any other machines that had a similar problem; if Joe can't see anyone else at all, it's probably a NIC problem.

2. C. WINS requires at least one WINS server, and you have to configure the client to use it.

3. A. DNS registration must be on to make dynamic DNS work; you control the registration settings from the DNS tab of the Advanced TCP/IP Properties dialog box.

4. D. Local settings always override settings received from a DHCP server.

5. D. You'll get maximum security from turning on encryption and enabling DUN to use the strongest encryption available from the OS.

6. C. *Ipconfig /release* forces a client to give up its lease.

7. A, B. You control protocol binding by editing the protocols or selecting the protocols you want to use from the Networking tab.

8. C. VPN connections piggyback on top of existing IP connections; they don't create the connections themselves.

9. A. PPTP connections require you to specify the DNS name or IP address of the remote machine.

10. C. If the local and remote sides don't have any authentication protocols in common, authentication will fail.

11. D. The connection-specific suffixes are used only with the corresponding connection; they're completely optional and must be manually configured.

12. A, B, C. The WINS configuration tab allows you to turn NBT on or off, or to honor the setting sent by the DHCP server.

13. A. Smartcard authentication for dial-up calls is controlled through the Security tab of an individual connection's Properties dialog box.

14. D. When you turn on the Obtain DNS Server Information Automatically button, you're stuck with whatever the server sends you.

15. D. Once you know what you're doing, the wizard slows down the process of creating connections, especially since the Microsoft defaults are good for most connections.

16. C. DNS servers are always used in the order you specify.

17. D. You can specify two in the General tab of the TCP/IP Properties dialog box; however, you can specify as many as you like in the DNS tab of the Advanced TCP/IP Properties dialog box.

18. D. Dynamic DNS registration is on by default. However, it's controlled on a per-connection basis.

19. C. ICS is available on all Windows 2000 products; it's off by default, but can be turned on through any LAN or dial-up connection.

20. C. By default, the idle period is set to "never" so Windows 2000 will keep the connection up indefinitely. To force it to use a particular timeout value, specify it on the Options tab.

Chapter

13

Managing Network Address Translation

MICROSOFT EXAM OBJECTIVES COVERED IN THIS CHAPTER:

- ✓ Install Internet Connection Sharing.
- ✓ Install NAT.
- ✓ Configure NAT properties.
- ✓ Configure NAT interfaces.

Until recently, Microsoft didn't offer a way for more than one person to share a single connection to the Internet. Linux and Mac OS users have been able to do this for a while, and a number of third parties have shipped products like WinGate. As part of Windows 98 Second Edition, Microsoft included a feature called *Internet Connection Sharing*, or *ICS*. The idea behind ICS is simple: If you have more than one computer and they're networked together, one computer can act as a gateway to the Internet. This is conceptually simple, but there's some behind-the-scenes magic that has to happen to implement it.

ICS actually implements a service called *Network Address Translation (NAT)*. Since every IP packet contains address information, you can probably guess how NAT got its name: It's a service that translates between your own network's addresses and addresses usable on the Internet. With either ICS or NAT, your entire network uses only a single IP address on the Internet. All outgoing traffic passes through the NAT machine on its way out. All inbound traffic is likewise addressed to the NAT machine, which is responsible for passing it back to the proper computer on your local network.

In this chapter, you'll get a deeper understanding of how NAT works in general, plus an understanding of how to set up, configure, and manage both NAT and ICS in Windows 2000.

NAT Fundamentals

The job of a NAT server seems simple enough at first glance: Allow a bunch of computers to masquerade behind a single IP address. (In fact, NAT is sometimes called "IP masquerading" in the Unix world.) However, there are some subtleties that make it more complex than a first glance would indicate. You can start exploring the process by looking at a simple representation of a network using NAT to connect to the Internet (Figure 13.1). In this network, there are six workstations and a NAT server, each with addresses in the 10.10.1.*x* range. Notice that the only machine connected to the Internet is the NAT server and that it actually has a second IP address assigned—those are both small but very important details, as you'll see shortly.

In the rest of this chapter, we'll use NAT to refer to the protocol used both by the ICS and NAT services in Windows 2000, but we'll call those components by their correct names.

FIGURE 13.1   A small NAT network

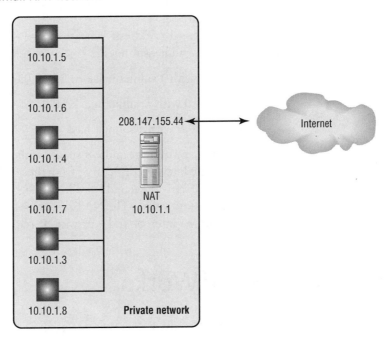

Private Addressing Made Simple

In the early days of the Internet, it must have seemed that the IP addressing scheme we've all come to recognize would provide a large enough address space for the foreseeable future. The problem, however, lies in the definition of "foreseeable"; it's pretty clear that the designers of IP addressing never expected the explosive growth of the Internet. Each device directly connected to the Internet normally needs its own address, and addresses have become scarce. When Mark Twain said, "Buy land; they're not makin any more of it," he might just as well have been talking about IP addresses.

As a workaround, the Internet Network Information Center (InterNIC), in conjunction with the Internet Assigned Numbers Authority (IANA), designated some address ranges as *private addresses*. These addresses cannot receive traffic from or send traffic to the Internet. In every other respect, though, they're just ordinary IP addresses. The idea behind private addresses is that you can use them to configure a network that's not connected to the Internet. That seems like a useful idea, until you want to hook your network up to the Internet. That's where NAT comes in: It translates between public and private addresses.

RFC 1597 (titled "Address Allocation for Private Internets") designates the three private address ranges:

- 10.0.0.0 with a subnet mask of 255.0.0.0

- 172.16.0.0 with a subnet mask of 255.240.0.0

- 192.168.0.0 with a subnet mask of 255.255.0.0

You can use any of these address spaces with impunity, since no router is allowed to route Internet traffic to or from those addresses. If you remember that Figure 13.1 shows a second IP address assigned to the computer running NAT, now you know why: The NAT server uses a public IP address to communicate with the Internet and a private IP address for the local network.

How NAT *Really* Works

For NAT to work, the NAT server must be able to do a number of things:

- Maintain two interfaces, one with a private IP address and one with a public IP address, and route packets between them.

- Determine where outbound packets are going, then edit their address data so that replies come back to the NAT box (after all, Internet servers can't send data back to the original clients).

- Receive replies sent in response to outbound packets, then readdress them to the correct client on the private network.

You can follow each of these steps to see what really happens when a client makes a request for some data on an Internet server. For this exercise, you can say that a client with a private IP address of 10.10.1.5 is trying to fetch a Web page from www.robichaux.net (216.92.40.80). The NAT router has two IP addresses: 10.10.1.1 on the private side and 208.170.118.207 on the Internet.

Maintaining Multiple Interfaces

Windows 2000 already understands how to route data between multiple IP addresses on the same computer—it just uses the same static routing code included with Windows NT. As you learned in Chapter 8, "Managing IP Routing," static routing just moves packets among multiple interfaces that you define yourself. In reality, though, you have to install and configure the Routing and Remote Access Service (RRAS) to use NAT on a Windows 2000 server (more on that a little later). ICS, though, doesn't require RRAS, even though it does the same kind of routing.

Deciding Where Outbound Packets Are Going

Take a look at Figure 13.2 to see what happens to the outbound packet. Here's the scoop:

1. The client generates its request and sends it to its default gateway—the NAT server. The packet's addressed to port 80 at IP address 216.92.40.80, the machine you're trying to reach.

2. The NAT server receives the packet and examines it to determine where it's bound. It creates an entry in its NAT table that ties the real destination address and port number to its origin and to a substitute port number it chooses at random. It also replaces the original source address of the packet with its own address, so that replies from the target machine will come back to the NAT machine.

3. The NAT server sends the rewritten packet over its external interface to the Internet, where it's routed and handled normally. At this point, there's essentially no way to tell that the request came from a computer behind the NAT server, since all the network's Internet traffic originates from, and is returned to, the NAT machine.

The NAT table is the key to this whole process, since it associates the original source address and port with the destination address and port. That way, when an incoming packet arrives, the NAT software can scan the table to identify the original source for the packet.

FIGURE 13.2 An outbound packet's journey through NAT

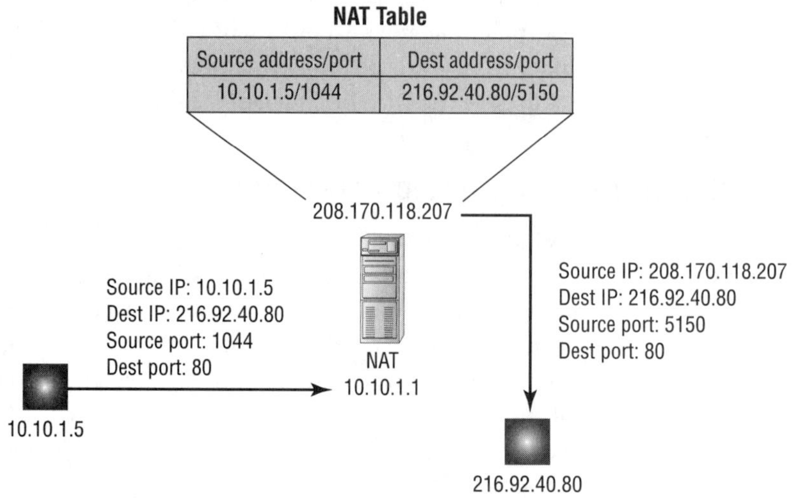

NAT Table

Source address/port	Dest address/port
10.10.1.5/1044	216.92.40.80/5150

208.170.118.207

Source IP: 10.10.1.5
Dest IP: 216.92.40.80
Source port: 1044
Dest port: 80

NAT
10.10.1.1

Source IP: 208.170.118.207
Dest IP: 216.92.40.80
Source port: 5150
Dest port: 80

10.10.1.5

216.92.40.80

Accepting and Distributing Inbound Packets

So far, you've seen the outgoing packet get rewritten so that it appears to be a request from port 5150 on a machine at 208.170.118.207 to port 80 on the machine at 216.92.40.80. You can assume that the packet reaches the destination machine without incident and that it's able to generate a reply packet containing the requested data. This packet is addressed to 208.170.118.207, port 5150. What happens when the packet reaches the NAT machine?

Figure 13.3 holds the answer. The Web server sends a packet back to the source address of the original request, which happens to be the address of the NAT server. When the NAT server receives the packet, it uses its table of port and address mappings to determine that the incoming packet is arriving in response to an outgoing packet sent from a particular address. In this case, the table tells the NAT software that an incoming packet addressed to port 5150 at 208.170.118.207 was sent in response to an outbound packet that reached the NAT server from 10.1.1.5's port 1044. In other words, the NAT table maps the original client address and source port to the destination address plus the source port that NAT used when it rewrote the packet.

FIGURE 13.3   An inbound packet's journey through NAT

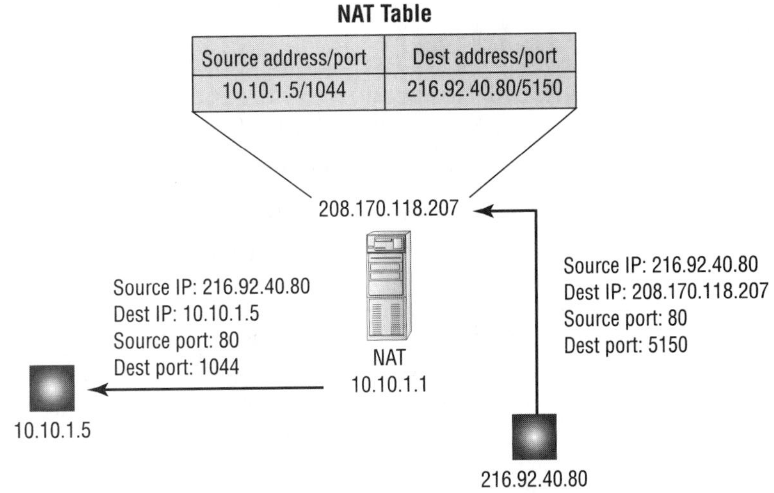

The NAT server can use this information to readdress the packet to the original source address (10.1.1.5) and port (1044). When that machine receives the packet, it appears to have come directly from the requested host. As far as the client and remote server can tell, NAT never even happened.

NAT Editors

The approach described above works fine for data where the IP address information is all in the packet headers, but it falls down for protocols that embed addressing information in the packet payload. For example, the File Transfer Protocol (FTP) embeds IP address data in the payload, as do NetBIOS over TCP/IP and the Point-to-Point Tunneling Protocol. The approved solution is for the NAT machine to inspect the packet payloads and change any addressing data it finds. However, this only works with certain data types; a special component called a *NAT editor* is responsible for changing data in the protocols it supports. Windows 2000 includes NAT editors for FTP, PPTP, NBT, and the Internet Control Message Protocol (ICMP). It also includes a similar capability called *NAT proxying* for videoconferencing (the H.323 protocol) and the Windows Remote Procedure Call (RPC) interprocess communications tool.

What's the Difference between ICS and NAT?

Up to this point, we've treated ICS and NAT as though they are identical. That's because they're extremely similar: They both implement NAT but with differing levels of bells and whistles. Microsoft expects you to know the differences between the two, including the following:

- What they run on: NAT requires Windows 2000 Server or Advanced Server, while ICS is available on Professional, Server, and Advanced Server.

- How you configure them: Checking one check box on the Sharing tab of a network adapter configures ICS. NAT requires you to use the Routing and Remote Access snap-in, and there are lots more configuration options available.

- How many public IP addresses they can use: With ICS, you expose a single public IP address (e.g., the address that your ISP assigns you). NAT can expose a number of public IP addresses, which is useful if you want to tie specific public IP addresses to individual machines on your LAN.

- How many networks they can link: ICS links one LAN to one public IP address, but NAT can link many LANs (provided they each have their own interfaces) to many public IP addresses.

Using Internet Connection Sharing

ICS is simple to install and use, provided you make the right decisions during installation. It's easy to configure, too; this ease of use and management comes at the expense of some functionality, though.

Installing ICS

Unlike almost every other service you've seen in this book, you don't install ICS using the Windows Components wizard. All you do is check one box on a Properties dialog tab, and the installation process is invisible after that—save for the changes ICS makes to your existing TCP/IP configuration.

Microsoft ✓ *Exam Objective*

Install Internet Connection Sharing.

Who Should Install ICS

ICS is primarily intended for connecting small office/home office (SOHO) networks to the Internet. In particular, it's designed for small networks that don't already have a full network infrastructure and that have a single connection to the Internet. Because ICS installs its own DHCP server (more on that in a minute) and it requires you to use the 192.168.* address block, it's not suitable for networks that already have their own DHCP server, that use static IP addresses, or that run DNS servers or Windows 2000 domain controllers.

Assuming you still want to install it, you must have administrative privileges on the target machine to do so.

What Happens When You Install ICS

Now that you understand how the underlying protocol works, you might be curious to see what happens on a machine when you install Internet Connection Sharing. ICS is a NAT implementation all right, but it leaves out some of the more powerful features included in the full-blown NAT version.

As an example, say you have a Windows 2000 Professional machine that's connected to your cable modem via an Ethernet NIC. You decide to install ICS so that you can add network connections for two other machines in your house, so you buy the necessary supplies and hardware to construct a LAN for your house. As part of that process, you add a second NIC to your Windows 2000 machine so it can run ICS. While this isn't strictly required, ICS *does* require you to have two independent network interfaces. One can be a modem or a NIC; the other must be a NIC.

When you install ICS, you attach it to one of the adapters—the one that's connected to the Internet. When you do so, some things change in your machine and adapter configurations:

- The *other* adapter (e.g., the one connected to your LAN) gets a new IP address of 192.168.0.1 and a subnet mask of 255.255.255.0.

- The Internet Connection Sharing service is started and set to run automatically at boot time.

- The DHCP address allocator service is enabled. The allocator gives out IP addresses in the range 192.168.0.1–192.168.0.254, using the standard 255.255.255.0 subnet mask. Think of it like a baby DHCP server, since there's no way to configure any of the options you learned about in Chapter 5 ("Managing the Dynamic Host Configuration Protocol").

- If you're using a dial-up connection on the Internet-connected adapter, automatic dialing is enabled.

These changes don't do anything special to the clients on your network; you must manually configure each of them to use DHCP so they can get the necessary settings from the *DHCP allocator*. ICS also doesn't make any changes to the adapter connected to the Internet. If you need to make changes (for example, because your ISP wants you to use DHCP with your cable modem), make them to the Internet adapter, *not* the LAN adapter.

Installing ICS

Installing ICS is easy: It's literally a one–check box operation. When you open the Network and Dial-Up Connections window, you'll see one icon for each adapter (whether real or dial-up) that you have installed. Find the adapter that you normally connect to the Internet with and right-click it, choosing the Properties command from the Context menu. When the Properties dialog box opens, click the Sharing tab, and you'll see the controls shown in Figure 13.4.

To enable ICS, just click the check box labeled Enable Internet Connection Sharing For This Connection, and that's it! If you want Internet traffic from other computers on your LAN to automatically bring up the connection (as you normally will), make sure the Enable On-Demand Dialing check box is on, too. That's all you have to do to set up a basic ICS configuration, apart from configuring each client to use DHCP.

Installing ICS interrupts any TCP/IP connection you have set up, so don't do it in the middle of any operations you don't want interrupted.

FIGURE 13.4   The Sharing tab

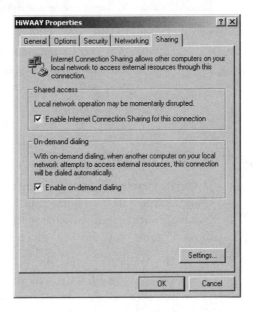

EXERCISE 13.1

Installing Internet Connection Sharing

Follow these steps to install ICS. Note that you can do this on Windows 2000 Professional, Server, or Advanced Server.

1. Open the Network and Dial-Up Connections window (Start ➢ Settings ➢ Network and Dial-up Connections).

2. Right-click the icon for the adapter that's connected to the Internet (bearing in mind that you can share a dial-up or VPN connection, too), and then choose the Properties command.

3. The adapter's Properties dialog box will appear. Click the Sharing tab. If you don't see the tab, it's probably because you're trying to share an unshareable connection, like the Local Area Connection, or because you're not logged on as an administrator.

4. On the Sharing tab, make sure the Enable Internet Connection Sharing For This Connection check box is on. If you want demand dialing turned on, make sure the Enable On-Demand Dialing check box is on as well.

5. Click the OK button.

Configuring ICS Options

Once you enable ICS, you'll have access to the Settings button at the bottom of the Sharing tab. This button allows you to configure two separate, but related, groups of settings that have to do with what entries are preloaded into the NAT table on your ICS computer. These settings include the following:

- The Applications tab controls *outbound port mapping*. Changing the settings here allows you to add entries to the NAT table so that computers on your network can make connections to remote services out on the Internet.

- The Services tab controls *inbound port mappings*; by adjusting settings here, you can control where requests from outside your network should be routed.

The Applications Tab

The Applications tab (Figure 13.5) allows you to create predefined routings for Internet services that you want your users to be able to access. For example, you might want to let users on your network access streaming audio and video sent from servers using Apple's QuickTime. QuickTime implements the Internet-standard Real Time Streaming Protocol (RTSP, defined in RFC 2326), but you have to make some adjustments to your NAT server to allow RTSP traffic to come inside. RTSP uses TCP port 554 and UDP ports 6970 through 6999. To make this work, you use the Add button on the Applications tab, which then displays the Internet Connection Sharing Application dialog box shown in Figure 13.6.

FIGURE 13.5 The Applications tab

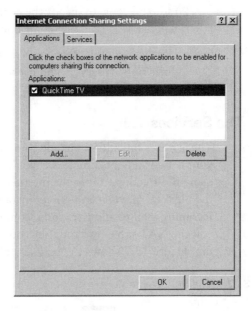

FIGURE 13.6 Adding a new application using the Internet Connection Sharing Application dialog box

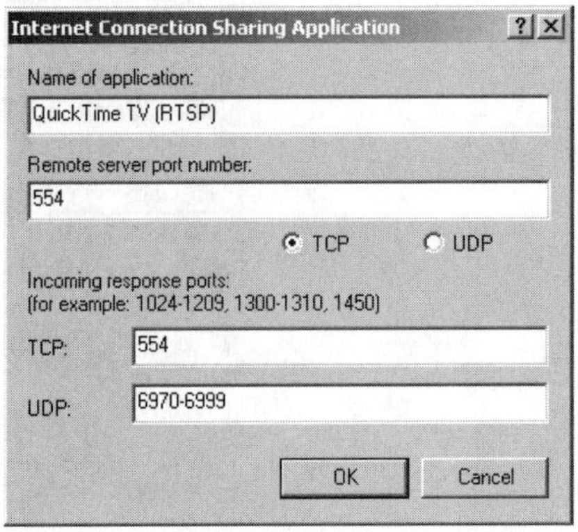

Fill out the dialog box like this:

- Use the Name Of Application field to specify some meaningful name that you'll recognize later.

- Use the Remote Server Port Number field (and the TCP and UDP radio buttons) to specify the port number and type that your machines will use when making connections to the outside world.

- Use the Incoming Response Ports fields to specify which TCP and UDP ports outside servers will use when sending data back to a client on your network.

The Services Tab

The Services tab allows outside computers to access some of the services on your network. For example, say you've set up a small home office and you're using ICS to connect it to the Internet. By making the appropriate entries in the NAT table, you can redirect incoming Web requests to one machine, incoming mail to another, and incoming FTP requests to a third. You can't edit the NAT table by hand, but you can achieve the same effect with this tab. Figure 13.7 shows the Services tab.

FIGURE 13.7   The Services tab

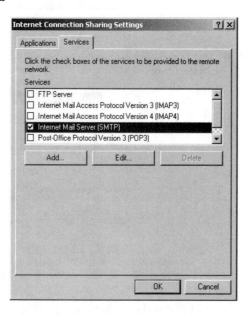

Microsoft helpfully added the six most common services: FTP for file transfer; telnet for remote administration; IMAP3, IMAP4, and POP3 for remote mail access; and SMTP for sending and receiving mail. Since these services all use well-known port numbers, you must first check the box next

Using Internet Connection Sharing

to the services you want to enable. That in and of itself probably won't be sufficient since checking the boxes doesn't specify which computer on your LAN should get the traffic. To do that, you need to use the Edit button, which displays the dialog shown in Figure 13.8. By specifying the local DNS name (e.g., **exchange**, not **exchange.robichaux.net**) or its IP address, you're instructing the NAT software to route incoming packets for that port to the server you specify.

FIGURE 13.8 Editing a predefined service

You can also add new services. For example, say you're using Exchange 5.5 as a Network News Transfer Protocol (NNTP) server, and you want outside hosts to be able to reach it. NNTP uses TCP port 119, so you'd click the Add button and fill out the resulting dialog box as shown in Figure 13.9.

FIGURE 13.9 Adding a new service

Using Network Address Translation

It's fair to describe ICS as "NAT Lite" since it offers many of the same features in a pretty, not-so-filling package. Earlier on, we saw that the primary differences between the ICS and NAT implementations in Windows 2000 are related to scale and scope. The good news is that the actual configuration isn't that much more difficult; there's just more of it.

Installing NAT

"Installing" NAT is a little bit of a misnomer because NAT is actually treated as another routing protocol you install under the aegis of the Routing and Remote Access Service (RRAS). In that light, when you install NAT what you're really doing is activating some components that provide services within the RRAS framework. Of course, you must install and run RRAS before you install NAT (but more on that in a minute).

Microsoft
✓ *Exam*
Objective

Install NAT.

What You Get When You Install NAT

Microsoft's documentation discusses three separate, but related, components that contribute to the NAT implementation. It's important to understand these components so that you'll understand the buzzwords used in their docs and on the exams. They include the following:

The Translation Component   No, it's not those little hand-held gizmos you see in old *Star Trek* episodes. The translation component handles the NAT functions themselves, including maintaining the NAT table for inbound and outbound connections.

The Addressing Component   This is what Microsoft calls the "DHCP address allocator" in its ICS documentation. Like the DHCP allocator, the *addressing component* is just a stripped-down DHCP server that assigns an IP address, a subnet mask, a default gateway, and the IP address of a DNS server.

The Name Resolution Component   When you install and configure NAT, it begins to act as a DNS server for the other machines on the local network. That service is provided by the *name resolution component*; when a client resolver makes a DNS query, it goes to the name resolution component on the NAT server, which forwards it to the DNS server defined on the Internet-connected adapter and returns the reply. Think of this like a proxy for DNS.

Of course, just because you install these components doesn't mean you'll have to use them all. You always need the translation component since it actually implements the NAT functionality. If you're running a DHCP server *or* the DHCP relay agent on your private LAN, you can't concurrently use the NAT addressing component. Likewise, if you're running an internal DNS server, you may not use the name resolution component. Don't worry; you'll see how to turn these off in a bit.

The Overall NAT Process

ICS hides a lot of the necessary gory details from you, but Microsoft assumes if you're macho enough to run NAT that you can take a little extra time to do some of the things ICS does for you. Most of these steps will be familiar to you from the material in Chapter 8 ("Managing IP Routing"), but some of it is specific to NAT configuration. Here's what you need to do:

1. Install RRAS and enable it. If you use the RRAS wizard (described in the next section), this is your last step. The wizard will take care of the other steps for you. If not (e.g., if you're installing NAT on an existing RRAS box, or if you just like to know what the wizard is doing behind your back), read on.

2. If you're not using a permanent connection (that is, not something that's always up like a dedicated analog line, ISDN line, DSL, or cable modem connection), you need to configure your dial-up connection to reach your ISP using these steps:

   a. Create a demand-dial interface to reach your ISP using the Demand Dial wizard.

   b. Use RRAS to make the dial-up port routable, as you did in Chapter 8.

3. Configure the local network adapter properly. This means that you need to give it an appropriate private IP address and network mask, and you need to make sure there's no default gateway specified.

4. Add a static IP route on the adapter that's connected to the Internet. The destination address must be 0.0.0.0, and the subnet mask should also be 0.0.0.0. This forces RRAS to send all traffic across that interface, which is what you want for Internet connectivity.

5. Add NAT as a routing protocol inside RRAS.

6. Add two NAT interfaces: one for your Internet adapter and one for the local network adapter.

7. If you want to use the addressing or name resolution components, you have to configure them.

Activating RRAS

As it turns out, RRAS is installed by default with Windows 2000 Server and Advanced Server, but it's not activated. Therefore, if you haven't already turned it on according to the directions in Chapter 8, you'll need to do so. There are two ways to set up NAT: You can use the Routing and Remote Access Service wizard to lead you through the process, or you can start up a bare-bones RRAS server and add NAT manually.

In either case, here's what you need to do:

1. Open the Routing and Remote Access Service snap-in (Start ➤ Programs ➤ Administrative Tools ➤ Routing and Remote Access).

2. When the RRAS snap-in opens, navigate to the server you want to manage. If you see a little red spot on the computer icon, that means RRAS is inactive on that machine.

3. Right-click the inactive machine, and then choose the Configure and Enable Routing and Remote Access command. This command starts the Routing and Remote Access Service wizard, which you first met back in Chapter 8.

4. Dismiss the first page of the wizard by clicking the Next button.

5. On the Common Configurations page of the wizard, you'll see radio buttons that let you choose what role you want this server to play. If you want to manually configure the server later, choose the Manually Configured Server radio button. If you want the wizard to lead you through the process, make sure the Internet Connection Server radio button is selected, and then click Next.

At this point, you've moved into *terra incognita*, since Chapter 8 doesn't talk about the setup process for NAT or ICS. Instead, you'll learn about it now.

Step 1: Choosing ICS or NAT

Once you complete the previous five steps, the next question is simple: the Internet Connection Server Setup page asks you to specify whether you want to set up ICS or NAT. If you select the ICS radio button, a snippy little dialog box tells you to set it up using the Network and Dial-Up Connections folder (but you already knew that, since you've read this far). To set up NAT properly, then, you must make sure that the Set Up A Router With The Network Address Translation (NAT) Routing Protocol radio button is selected. Then click the Next button.

Step 2: Selecting a Connection to Share

The next step in the wizard requires you to pick the connection that you want to share. As you can see in Figure 13.10, you can choose how you want the connection to be made. Your two choices are to use an existing Internet connection or to create a new demand-dial connection.

FIGURE 13.10   The Internet Connection page of the Routing and Remote Access Server Setup Wizard

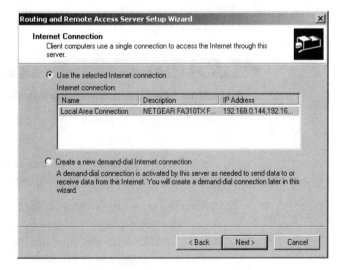

Here's what those options *really* mean:

- The Use The Selected Internet Connection radio button and the corresponding list of adapters that Windows 2000 thinks are connected to the Internet allow you to choose an adapter to share. Choosing this radio button and selecting an adapter is roughly equivalent to picking an adapter in the Network and Dial-Up Connections folder, opening its Properties dialog box, and clicking the ICS box on its Sharing tab. Notice that it will display dial-up connections even though the dialog says "adapter." Therefore, this is the button to use if you want to press an existing VPN or dial-up connection into service.

- The Create A New Demand-Dial Internet Connection button tells the wizard that you want to create a brand-new, demand-dial connection to use as your Internet pipeline. When you choose this option, it triggers the Demand Dial Interface wizard that you met in Chapter 8. Once you complete the wizard, the wizard will automatically add a NAT interface for the new demand-dial connection (but you'll see in a minute how to do so manually).

Installing NAT When RRAS Is Already Running

If you've already configured RRAS to handle IP or IPX routing, you'll probably want to know how to configure NAT without deactivating RRAS (which wipes out its configuration information) and reactivating it to start the wizard. The steps required to do this are described in Exercise 13.2; note that this only covers the installation and not the process of adding a NAT interface and configuring it.

EXERCISE 13.2

Installing NAT on a Running RRAS Server

Follow these steps to install NAT on a previously installed RRAS server:

1. Open the Routing and Remote Access snap-in (Start ➤ Programs ➤ Administrative Tools ➤   Routing and Remote Access).

2. Locate the server on which you want to enable NAT. If its icon has a little red down-pointing arrow, right-click it and choose the Enable and Configure Routing and Remote Access Service command, then proceed with the RRAS wizard as described in the preceding section.

3. Expand the server's configuration until you see the General node (*serverName* ➤ IP Routing ➤ General).

4. Right-click the General node and choose the New Routing Protocol command. The New Routing Protocol dialog box will appear.

5. Select Network Address Translation from the list of routing protocols, and then click the OK button.

6. The IP Routing node will now have a child node named Network Address Translation.

Adding a NAT Interface

You know from your previous exploration of RRAS in Chapter 8 that you have to add an interface in RRAS before it can do anything with packets bound to or from that interface. NAT is no different; before you can use NAT on your local network, you must add a *NAT interface* by using the RRAS interface. The actual process of adding a new NAT interface is fairly simple provided you know which adapter to put the interface on.

Microsoft ✔ *Exam Objective*

Configure NAT interfaces.

Adding a NAT Interface

Just like with ICS, you have to distinguish between adapters that are connected to your local network and those connected (or that can connect) to the Internet. NAT links these two interfaces, so you actually need to create both of them. ICS is smart enough to automatically create both interfaces for you, but RRAS requires you to do it yourself. There's a simple rule to follow:

- Create an interface for your local network adapter first, specifying it as such.

- Create the Internet adapter interface second. If you're using a dial-up connection, you need to also add some routing information.

EXERCISE 13.3

Adding and Configuring Public NAT Interface

Follow these steps to add a NAT interface:

1. Open the Routing and Remote Access snap-in (Start ➤ Programs ➤ Administrative Tools ➤ Routing and Remote Access).

EXERCISE 13.3 *(continued)*

2. Expand the RRAS tree until you see the Network Address Translation node (RRAS ➤ *serverName* ➤ IP Routing ➤ Network Address Translation).

3. Right-click Network Address Translation and choose the New Interface... command.

4. The New Interface for Network Address Translation dialog box will appear. Select the adapter you want to use and click OK.

5. The NAT Properties dialog box (covered later; see Figure 13.11 below) appears. Select "Public interface connected to the Internet" and click the OK button.

6. (Optional) If you want to specify an address pool for NAT clients, switch to the Address Pool tab and click the Add button. In the Add Address Pool dialog box, specify the starting address and subnet mask to be used for the pool, then click the OK button.

7. (Optional) If you want to create port mapping entries (as described later in the chapter), switch to the Special Ports tab and use the Add button to create them.

Removing NAT Interfaces

As it turns out, you can easily remove any NAT interface—just select it and use the Action ➤ Delete command (or the corresponding command on the Context menu). RRAS will ask you to confirm that you want to remove the interface. If you remove an interface that has active connections they'll be immediately closed, so don't do this if you (or your network users) are in the middle of something you don't want interrupted.

Setting NAT Interface Properties

Each NAT interface has its own set of properties. Unsurprisingly, you can edit these properties by right-clicking an interface and choosing the Properties command on the Context menu; this works just like it does for the other interface types you saw in Chapter 8.

The General Tab

The General tab lets you designate what kind of NAT interface this is. Normally, you'll need to add a pair of NAT interfaces: one for the adapter that's connected to the Internet and the other for your local adapter. That means you'll have reason to use both of the radio buttons on the General tab (Figure 13.11). These buttons include the following:

- The Private Interface Connected To Private Network button is what you use to specify that this interface is bound to the adapter on your local network.

- The Public Interface Connected To The Internet button specifies that this adapter is connected to the Internet. That means (duh!) that you use it only on the adapter that you use to connect to the Internet, whatever type of adapter it is.

The Translate TCP/UDP Headers radio button controls whether the built-in NAT editors do their thing on IP address data in the packet headers. If you turn this off, other clients on your local network won't be able to exchange data with Internet hosts. This should always be turned on for a public interface.

FIGURE 13.11   The General tab

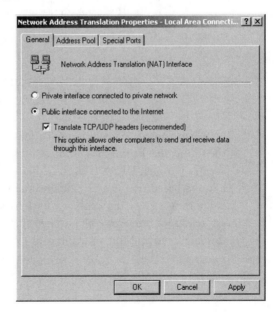

The Address Pool Tab

Remember from earlier in this chapter that the number of supported IP addresses is one of the differences between NAT and ICS? The Address Pool tab is where you inform NAT of which IP addresses it should expect traffic to come from. You can assign *address pool* information as a range or as a collection of individual addresses. No matter how deep the pool is, you manage it from this dialog box (see Figure 13.12) by using the list of addresses (or ranges) and the Add, Edit, Remove, and Reservations buttons.

FIGURE 13.12   The Address Pool tab

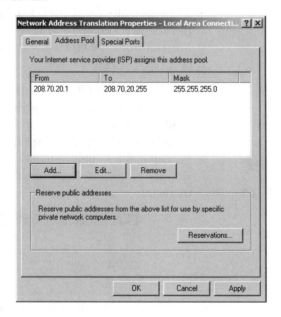

When you add a new range of addresses, you specify the starting address, the subnet mask, and the ending address. If you're using a single address, just specify it alone. RRAS tries to be helpful and calculate the correct ending address based on the start address and subnet mask you specify. When you edit a range, you can tweak any of these settings; removing a range from the address pool removes it as part of the public IP address set that can be used to reach machines on your internal LAN.

WARNING   Removing an address from the address pool *does not* prevent outside hosts from reaching your NAT server; it just prevents the NAT server from routing packets any further on your LAN.

The Reservations button allows you to reserve individual IP addresses from the public range and add static mappings in the NAT table that point to particular hosts on the inside of your network. This adds a degree of efficiency to the NAT process. For example, let's say that you have a Web server whose private IP address is 192.168.0.146. By adding a reserved address that maps that private IP to a single external public IP (say, 208.70.14.212, if that were in your address pool), you could register a DNS record for www.robichaux.net (or whatever other name you wanted it to have). The NAT table would contain a predefined entry that would map any traffic bound for 208.70.14.212 to 192.168.0.146. The only tricky part of adding a reservation is getting the matching addresses into the Add Reservation dialog box (Figure 13.13). You need to specify a single public IP address that maps to a single private IP address. If you want incoming traffic to reach through the NAT box and to the target machine, you must also check the Allow Incoming Sessions To This Address check box.

FIGURE 13.13   The Add Reservations dialog box

The Special Ports Tab

You can also edit the NAT table in a second way: You can specify which ports inbound traffic should be mapped to. This allows you to take traffic coming to any port on any of your public IP addresses and direct it to the port you wish on any machine on your private network. For example, you could channel any incoming Web requests to a single machine by mapping port 80 on the public interface to port 80 on your internal Web server. Of

course, you could do the same with SMTP or any other TCP or UDP protocol if you wish. All of this flexibility is yours for the asking, thanks to the Special Ports tab (Figure 13.14). In the example here, the Secure Sockets Layer
(SSL) port is mapped to 192.168.0.240 so that any SSL connection attempt
from the outside world will automatically be channeled to a single machine
on the private network. The *Special Ports tab* lists the *port mappings* you
have in effect, and you can add, edit, and remove them using the buttons at
the bottom of the tab.

FIGURE 13.14 The Special Ports tab

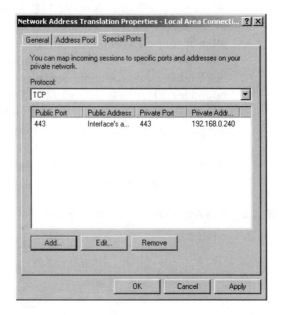

When you add or edit a special port, you'll see a dialog box like the one
shown in Figure 13.15. You use the controls in this dialog box to set up the
special port mapping you want to take effect:

- The Public Address group lets you specify what public address can
  receive traffic for this specific port. The On This Interface radio button
  (the default choice) accepts traffic on the specified port for all public
  IP addresses in the address pool. If you instead select the On This
  Address Pool Entry radio button, the public IP address you provide is
  the only one for which this port mapping will be active.

- Specify the port number the outside world will be using in the Incoming Port field.

- Use the Private Address field to specify the private address to which incoming traffic on the magic port will go.

- Use the Outgoing Port field to select the port that will be used for outbound traffic generated by hosts on your local network.

FIGURE 13.15   The Edit Special Port dialog box

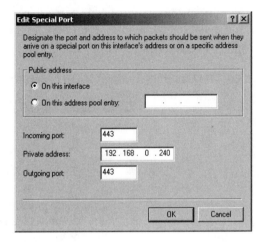

Configuring NAT Properties

Totally apart from configuring the interfaces themselves, there are some properties that pertain to all NAT interfaces and connections on your RRAS NAT server. You modify these settings through the NAT Properties dialog box, which you get by right-clicking the Network Address Translation node in the RRAS console and using the Properties command. The Properties dialog box has four tabs: the General tab, the Translation tab, the Address Assignment tab, and the Name Resolution tab.

Microsoft
✔ *Exam*
Objective

Configure NAT properties.

The General Tab

The General tab (Figure 13.16) is pretty uninteresting; it simply allows you to change the amount of event logging information that the NAT software writes to the system event log. The default is set to log errors only, but you can choose from three other levels: no logging at all, logging of errors and warnings, and logging of *everything*. The more detailed log information is useful when you're trying to troubleshoot a problem, but it can bulk up your event log quickly, so don't turn up logging unless you're trying to find and fix a problem.

FIGURE 13.16 The General tab of the NAT Properties dialog box

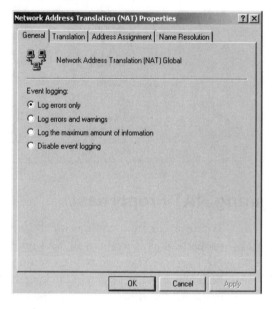

The Translation Tab

The Translation tab (Figure 13.17) is a little more interesting. It allows you to set scavenging times for port mappings, and it gives you access to an application mapping dialog very much like the one you saw earlier in Figure 13.6. The controls in the Translation tab do the following:

- The Remove TCP Mapping After and Remove UDP Mapping After fields allow you to control how long entries remain in the NAT table after their last use. The default behavior is to keep TCP mappings for 24 hours and UDP mappings for 1 minute.

- The Applications button allows you to open the Applications dialog box so you can add, remove, or edit application mappings. Any mappings you create with ICS are preserved for NAT and vice versa. This helps smooth the way if you start off with ICS and later migrate to a more sophisticated NAT implementation.

FIGURE 13.17   The Translation tab of the NAT Properties dialog box

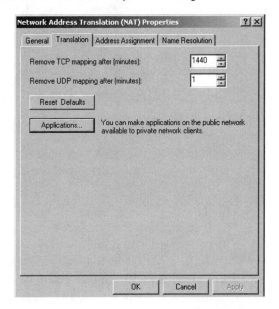

The Address Assignment Tab

The Address Assignment tab (Figure 13.18) controls whether the NAT addressing component is used or not. Recall that the NAT addressing component is just a baby DHCP server; it's not necessary to use it if you already have a DHCP server on your private network, but you can use it if you want to streamline the number and kind of services you have installed. The controls in this dialog box are simple: The Automatically Assign IP Addresses By Using DHCP check box controls whether the addressing component is active or not. If it is, the IP Address and Mask fields control the address range that's handed out. There's no way to change the default gateway address (it's always the private IP address of the NAT machine), default DNS server, or any of the other DHCP options.

FIGURE 13.18 The Address Assignment tab of the NAT Properties dialog box

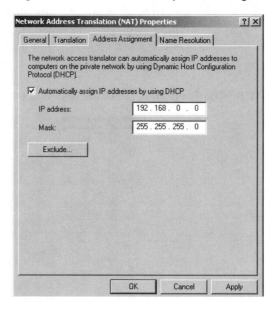

You can, however, exclude IP addresses that you don't want assigned by the allocator. You do this with the Exclude... button on the Address Assignment tab, which displays the Exclude Reserved Addresses dialog box (Figure 13.19). In this dialog box, you'll see a list of any reserved IP addresses, and you can modify the list contents with the ever-present Add, Edit, and Remove buttons. This is functionally equivalent to creating an exclusion range in the DHCP snap-in when you're using the "real" DHCP server.

To allow inbound connections from the Internet, you need to exclude the IP address of the target machine here, then assign that IP address statically to the target. Once you've done so, you'll be able to configure a special port pointing to the target.

FIGURE 13.19   The Exclude Reserved Addresses dialog box

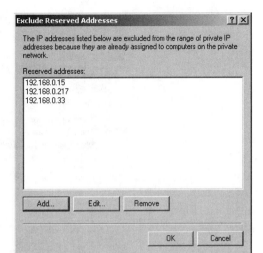

The Name Resolution Tab

You can choose to use the NAT name resolution component, or not, with the Name Resolution tab. When you turn on the component, its address is passed out by the addressing component, and client computers send all their DNS queries to the NAT computer that acts as a DNS proxy. You can still configure each individual client with the IP address of an external DNS server, but then you may not be able to resolve the names of hosts on your private LAN.

The Name Resolution tab (Figure 13.20) has two check boxes that control how resolution works. The first, Clients Using Domain Name System (DNS), is normally checked—a good thing since it controls whether the name resolution component is active or not. The second check box, Connect To The Public Network When A Name Needs To Be Resolved, specifies whether or not you want the Internet connection brought up just for DNS queries. The Demand-Dial Interface pull-down list lets you select which demand-dial interface, if any, you want brought up when a DNS query requires bringing the link up.

FIGURE 13.20 The Name Resolution tab of the NAT Properties dialog box

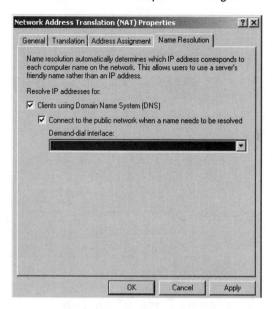

EXERCISE 13.4

Configuring NAT Properties

In this exercise, you'll set the logging level for the NAT components to a more reasonable value. You'll also turn on client name resolution. To configure NAT properties on a server, do the following:

1. Open the Routing and Remote Access snap-in (Start ➢ Programs ➢ Administrative Tools ➢ Routing and Remote Access).

2. Expand the RRAS tree until you see the Network Address Translation node (RRAS ➢ *serverName* ➢ IP Routing ➢ Network Address Translation).

3. Right-click Network Address Translation and choose the Properties command.

4. In the General tab, change the logging setting by selecting the Log Errors And Warnings radio button.

EXERCISE 13.4 *(continued)*

5. Switch to the Name Resolution tab, then check the Clients Using Domain Name System (DNS) check box.

6. Click the OK button.

Summary

In this chapter, you learned:

- The differences between Internet Connection Sharing and the Network Address Translation service

- How to install and configure ICS

- How to install and configure NAT

Key Terms

Before you take the exam, be sure you're familiar with the following terms:

Address pool

Addressing component

DHCP allocator

Inbound port mapping

Internet Connection Sharing (ICS)

Name resolution component

NAT editor

NAT interface

NAT proxying

Network Address Translation (NAT)

Outbound port mapping

Port mappings

Private addresses

Special Ports tab

Review Questions

1. ICS allows a network of computers to share which of the following?

   A. A routed TCP/IP subnet

   B. Multiple Internet connections

   C. Files and printers

   D. A single Internet connection on a single computer

2. The NAT component requires which of the following?

   A. Windows 2000 Server or Advanced Server

   B. Windows 2000 Professional

   C. A permanent Internet connection

   D. That all network clients be running Windows 2000

3. You control whether or not the NAT addressing component is enabled with the _____.

   A. General tab of the NAT Interface Properties dialog box

   B. Translation tab of the NAT Properties dialog box

   C. Address Assignment tab of the NAT Properties dialog box

   D. Name Resolution tab of the NAT Properties dialog box

4. For NAT to work properly, you must create _____.

   A. One NAT interface for the adapter connected to the public network

   B. One NAT interface for the adapter connected to the private network

   C. Two NAT interfaces: one for the public adapter, one for the private adapter

   D. One NAT interface for either the public or private adapters

5. A private address is one that _____.

    A. Has no zeroes in it

    B. Does not use the 192.192.* address space

    C. Cannot be used to exchange data with Internet addresses

    D. Is reserved for use by Internet service providers

6. NAT software must maintain a mapping that links which of the following?

    A. The source port and address with the destination port and address

    B. The source port and address with the destination port and address of the NAT server

    C. The source port and NAT server address with the destination port and address

    D. The source port and address with the destination address and NAT server port

7. Which of the following are differences between Internet Connection Sharing and NAT? (Choose two.)

    A. ICS only runs on Windows 2000 Professional.

    B. ICS can only share a single public IP address.

    C. NAT has more flexible configuration options.

    D. NAT requires a DSL or cable modem connection.

8. When you install ICS, which of the following will it *not* do?

    A. Reset the local network adapter's IP address

    B. Turn on the DHCP address allocator

    C. Automatically configure an Internet connection

    D. Interrupt any existing TCP/IP connections

9. To allow inbound data to reach a particular target machine, you must do which of the following?

   A. Make the target machine a NAT server.

   B. Create a special port.

   C. Disable the addressing component.

   D. Add a static route to the target machine.

10. You cannot use ICS on your network if _____.

    A. Your clients are using static IP addresses.

    B. You have a Windows 2000 domain controller.

    C. You are not using Windows 2000 DNS.

    D. You do not have a WINS server.

11. NAT can change the contents of packets so that they're properly addressed. This process is performed by which components?

    A. NAT proxy address generators

    B. NAT editors

    C. NAT packet filters

    D. NAT filters

12. Which of the following statements about the NAT address pool are true? (Choose all that apply.)

    A. Removing an address from the pool makes it inaccessible from the public network.

    B. The address pool can contain no more than eight addresses.

    C. The address pool must not overlap with any DHCP ranges.

    D. Each public address in the pool must map to a single private address.

13. Which two of the following statements are true of adding a reservation in the NAT address pool?

    A. It reserves an IP address from the public range.

    B. It reserves an IP address from the private range.

    C. It maps the reserved IP address to a specific public host.

    D. It maps the reserved IP address to a specific private host.

14. To define a NAT special port, you need to specify which of the following parameters?

    A. Which public address receives traffic for the port

    B. Which port numbers are used for inbound and outbound traffic

    C. Which private IP address receives traffic on the special port

    D. Which subnet mask is used for the port

15. When you create an interface and enable the Private Interface Connected To Private Network button on the General tab of the interface Properties dialog box, what are you doing?

    A. Creating a new mapping between a private and public interface

    B. Creating a new interface bound to the "outside," or public, adapter in your NAT server

    C. Creating a new interface bound to the "inside," or private, adapter in your NAT server

    D. Creating a new mapping for a specific protocol (e.g., HTTP, FTP, SMTP)

16. Arlene wants to set up NAT so that the public IP address A.B.C.D points to a machine on her LAN with private address 192.168.15.212. To do this, she must do which of the following?

    A. Create a special port

    B. Create a reserved address

    C. Install a packet filter

    D. Turn off the NAT addressing component

17. Andy wants to map incoming Web traffic sent to a single external address to a private server. To do this, he should do which of the following?

    A. Use ICS

    B. Use NAT with a reserved address

    C. Use NAT with a special port

    D. Give the private server a public address

18. Frank needs to configure his ICS machine so that other users on his LAN can access RealAudio traffic. To do this, Frank needs to add port mappings to the NAT mapping table. He can do this by doing which of the following?

    A. Switching from ICS to NAT

    B. Using the Applications tab of the ICS Properties dialog box

    C. Using the Port Mappings tab of the ICS Properties dialog box

    D. Manually configuring each client

19. What is the Translation tab of the NAT Properties dialog box is used to do?

    A. It creates application-specific port mappings.

    B. It specifies which NAT editors should be used.

    C. It creates port mappings for individual machines.

    D. It specifies which port filters should be applied.

20. Jerry configured NAT on his network. Users are now complaining that they can't use MSN Instant Messenger. Assuming that Jerry wants to fix this problem, what should he do?

    A. Open the necessary ports at the firewall

    B. Add an outbound NAT mapping for the required ports

    C. Add an inbound NAT mapping for the required ports

    D. Set up a proxy server

Answers to Review Questions

1. D. ICS is designed to allow a small office/home office network to share a single Internet connection.

2. A. NAT runs on the Windows 2000 Server family; it works with dial-up or permanent connections and any TCP/IP-capable client.

3. C. You control NAT addressing per server, not per interface, so you have to use the Address Assignment tab in the NAT Properties dialog box.

4. C. NAT depends on having one interface for each of the two adapters so it can transfer traffic between them.

5. C. Internet hosts aren't allowed to send or receive traffic to addresses that fall in the private range.

6. D. The NAT table ties the source port and address with the destination address and the fake port generated by the NAT server; that way, traffic sent from the destination back to that particular port can be returned to the original host on the private network.

7. B, C. ICS runs on all Windows 2000 family members, but NAT is available only on Windows 2000 Server and Advanced Server. ICS shares only one public IP address; NAT has many more configuration settings that you can change. ICS and NAT both work on dial-up, DSL, cable modems, or any other medium you can use to connect to the Internet.

8. C. ICS requires you to already have your Internet adapter set up.

9. B. A special port ties a source port to the private address of one of the machines on your network.

10. B. ICS requires you to use dynamic IP addressing, but it doesn't require DNS or WINS.

11. B. NAT editors modify the address-related data in packets as they flow through the NAT server.

12. A, C. The pool governs which addresses outside clients can use to reach specific internal machines. Many public addresses can map to a single private address. However, the address pool cannot contain any private addresses, meaning that it can't overlap any DHCP ranges on your network.

13. A, D. The reservations table ties a public IP address to an internal host, effectively making the private host visible on a public IP address.

14. A, B, C. Ports don't have subnet masks; the other parameters are all required.

15. C. Creating a private interface builds a new interface for the "inside," or private, NIC—the one connected to your internal network.

16. B. Creating a reserved address binds a public IP address to a specific internal machine.

17. C. ICS can't do port mapping; the correct way to funnel all traffic sent to one port to a private machine is to use a special port.

18. B. ICS allows you to configure port mappings with its Applications tab.

19. A. You create port mappings for applications, not for individual machines.

20. B. Outbound NAT mappings allow outbound traffic to be answered back to the original client machines.

Chapter 14

Installing and Configuring Microsoft Certificate Server

MICROSOFT EXAM OBJECTIVES COVERED IN THIS CHAPTER:

- ✓ Install and configure Certificate Authority (CA).
- ✓ Create certificates.
- ✓ Issue certificates.
- ✓ Revoke certificates.
- ✓ Remove the Encrypting File System (EFS) recovery keys.

Some security services require a way to authenticate users or protect data in transit. Just to name one instance, secure e-commerce depends on having some way to obscure credit card numbers and expiration dates in transit, so they can't be easily stolen. For example, IPSec connections can be set to require that each end of the connection authenticate itself; the Secure Sockets Layer, used to protect and secure Web traffic, is another example. Authentication and confidentiality can be implemented in several different ways, ranging from simple password exchanges to elaborate hardware-assisted security systems. One way is to use *digital certificates*, since they can provide both authentication and confidentiality. In fact, certificates are used throughout Windows 2000—IPSec, Kerberos authentication, Internet Information Server, and the Encrypting File System (EFS) all use them.

A *certificate authority*, or CA, is a service that lets you issue new certificates, revoke or cancel old ones, and monitor and control which certificates are doing what. Microsoft's CA implementation, Microsoft Certificate Server (MCS), began life as part of IIS; the Windows 2000 version is a fully functional CA that you can use to issue certificates inside or outside of your organization.

This chapter will explore the basic terms and concepts that underlie MCS. It will explain why encryption is important and how it's used to meet everyday business needs. It will also explain the terminology you need to understand to grasp what MCS is and what it does.

The chapter will next describe how to install MCS and the accompanying Certificates and Certificate Authority snap-ins (wizards make the installation procedures pretty easy). Then it will talk about the specifics of configuring MCS to issue certificates; finally, the chapter will close with a discussion of how you request, revoke, and manage certificates from the Certificates snap-in.

Understanding the Security Plumbing

Knowing how to configure MCS depends on your understanding of what it does and how it works. If this were a security book, we'd go into pages and pages and pages of detail on the cryptographic algorithms and nit-picky details of MCS. But since this is a study guide designed to prepare you for the Windows 2000 Network Infrastructure exam, we'll focus on what you need to understand about the plumbing that underlies MCS and how it interacts with other parts of the system.

Some Useful Buzzwords

If the first step toward learning to use MCS is understanding the fundamentals of how digital certificates work, then the first step towards *that* is learning the right vocabulary to use when talking about certificates and CA operations in MCS. As anyone who's ever visited a doctor or attorney knows, being equipped with the right buzzwords makes a big difference in your understanding of key concepts.

Everything You Ever Wanted to Know about Encryption (and Then Some)

When most people hear the words "encryption" or "cryptography," they immediately think of secret-key cryptography. In a secret-key system, two people who want to communicate use a single shared key that must be kept secret. The same key is used to encrypt and decrypt data, so if a user loses the secret key or if it's stolen, the data it encrypts becomes vulnerable. Secret-key systems tend to be fast and flexible, but their dependence on a single key makes them better suited for applications where you can change the key frequently—like IPSec. In addition, secret-key systems can only be used for encryption, not authentication (more about that in a second).

Instead of the single secret key used in a secret-key system, public-key systems use *two* keys, combined into a single keypair:

- A *public key*, which is designed to be spread freely around

- A *private key* (also called a secret key) which must be held only by its owner and should never be publicly disclosed

These keys complement each other; for example, if you encrypt something with your public key, it can only be decrypted with the corresponding private key (which only you hold), and vice versa. The security of these keys depends on the mathematical relationship between the public and private keys. You can't derive one from the other, so passing out the public key doesn't introduce any risk of compromising the private key.

What You Can Do with a Public Key

There are two fundamental operations associated with public key cryptography: encryption and signing.

- *Encryption* hides data so that only the intended party can read it. In public-key cryptography, for example, if Alice wants to send her boss Bob some private data, she uses Bob's public key to encrypt it, and then she sends it to him. Upon receiving the encrypted data, Bob uses his private key to decrypt it. The important concept here is that Bob can freely distribute his public key so that anyone in the world can send him encrypted data. If Alice and an attacker (let's call her Marlene) both have copies of Bob's public key, and Marlene intercepts an encrypted message from Alice to Bob, she won't be able to decrypt it. Only Bob's private key can do that, and he's the only person who holds it.

- *Signing* uses encryption to prove the origin and authenticity of some piece of data. If Alice wants the world to know that she is the author of a message, she signs it by encrypting it with her private key. She can then post the message publicly. This obviously doesn't provide any privacy, because anyone can decrypt the data using her public key. However, the fact that it can be decrypted using Alice's public key means that it must have been encrypted using Alice's *private* key, which only she holds—so it must have come from Alice.

In combination, signatures and encryption can be used to provide three features that customers demand, particularly for business-to-business e-commerce (one of the target markets for Windows 2000). These features include the following:

Privacy   Properly encrypted data can't be read by anyone except the intended recipients. Because public keys can be posted freely, complete strangers can communicate privately just by retrieving each other's public keys and using them to exchange encrypted messages.

Authentication   Transactions and communications involve two parties. Much of the time, it's desirable for one end or the other (or maybe both!) to verify the other's identity. For example, secure Web sites allow users to verify that the server's identity is as claimed. One way to implement authentication uses public keys: the client can encrypt a challenge message using the server's public key, then send it to the server. If the server can decrypt it and answer correctly, it demonstrates that the server has the proper private key thus proving its identity.

Authentication also allows you to verify that a piece of data wasn't tampered with after it was sent. This kind of authentication is usually implemented as a digital signature, using the public-key signing operations mentioned earlier. Let's say that you want to digitally sign e-mail messages you send out announcing new revisions of your book. To do that, you use software built into your Eudora e-mail client that does the following:

1. It examines the message content you provide and passes it through a special type of algorithm called a hash algorithm. Hash algorithms generate a unique "fingerprint" (or hash) for any block of data; it's practically impossible to produce two different messages that have an identical hash.

2. It encrypts the message and the fingerprint using your private key.

Anyone who wants to verify that the message is from you can do the same steps in reverse: First your software decrypts the message using your public key, then it computes a hash for the message. If the new hash and the decrypted version match, it proves that a) you sent the message, and b) the message hasn't been modified.

Non-repudiation   Non-repudiation is one aspect of "conventional" business often overlooked by e-commerce users. For example, if we sign a paper contract and give you a copy, it's pretty hard for us to later say, "Hey, we didn't sign that." Digital signatures can provide the same legal binding for electronic transmissions, and they're being used to do so increasingly more often.

What about Certificates?

Think of a digital certificate as a carrying case for a public key. A certificate contains the public key and a set of attributes, like the key holder's name and e-mail address. These attributes specify something about the holder: their identity, what they're allowed to do with the certificate, and so on. The attributes and the public key are bound together because the certificate is digitally signed by the entity that issued it. Anyone who wants to verify the certificate's contents can verify the issuer's signature.

For a real-world analogy, look in your wallet. If you have a driver's license, you have the equivalent of a digital certificate. Your license contains a unique key (your license number) and some attributes (an expiration date, your name, address, hair color, and so on). It's issued by a trusted agency and laminated to prevent it from being tampered with. Anyone who trusts the agency that issued your license and verifies that the lamination is intact can rely on its authenticity. At that point, though, the analogy breaks down—in the real world, only the government can issue a driver's license, so everyone knows that a license issued by Paul's Really Good DMV isn't valid. How do you make the same determination with a digital certificate? Read on to find the answer!

Infrastructure? Sounds Complicated!

Certificates are one part of what security experts call a public-key infrastructure (PKI). This sounds more complicated than it actually is. We use infrastructure components every day, even if we don't think about them. For example, highways, the U.S. Postal Service, the sewer lines in your house, and the Internet backbone your ISP connects to are all infrastructure components of various kinds. A PKI just provides a fundamental set of services that application programmers can use to deliver privacy, authentication, and non-repudiation in their applications. Basically, the PKI has to be able to do the following three things:

Manage Keys   A PKI makes it easy to issue new keys, review or revoke existing keys, and manage the trust level attached to keys from different issuers.

Publish Keys   A PKI offers a way for clients to find and fetch public keys and information about whether a specific key is valid or not. Without the ability to retrieve keys and know that they are valid, your users can't make use of public key services.

Use Keys   A PKI provides an easy-to-use way for users to use keys—not just by moving keys around where they're needed, but also by providing easy-to-use applications that perform public-key cryptographic operations for securing e-mail, network traffic, and other types of communication.

As you might imagine, these services don't just appear out of thin air; they're provided by different components that together make up PKI. Scott Culp, one of Microsoft's security gurus, likes to point out that a PKI is a set of capabilities, not a single tangible thing or object. What components do you need to make a usable PKI?

What's in a PKI?

The plumbing infrastructure in your house or apartment has a large number of different components: sinks, toilets, supply pipes, municipal pumping stations, and so on. Likewise, a PKI has several different components that you can mix and match to achieve the desired results. Microsoft's Windows 2000 PKI implementation offers the following functions:

- **Certificate authorities** issue certificates, revoke certificates they've issued, and publish certificates for their clients. Big CAs like Thawte and Verisign may do this for millions of users; with MCS, you can set up your own CA for each department or workgroup in your organization if you want to. Each CA is responsible for choosing what attributes it will include in a certificate and what mechanism it will use to verify those attributes before issuing the certificate. CAs also build and maintain lists of revoked certificates (known as *certificate revocation lists*, or *CRLs*.)

- **Certificate publishers** make certificates and CRLs publicly available, inside or outside an organization. This allows widespread availability of the critical material needed to support the entire PKI. In particular, a good certificate publisher will allow clients to automatically get the certificates they need. Microsoft's CA and clients support certificate publishers that use the Lightweight Directory Access Protocol (LDAP).

- **Management tools** allow you, as an administrator, to keep track of which certificates were issued, when a given certificate expires, and so on. The Certificate Services snap-in (more on that later) allows you to do these things, and more, for MCS.

- **PKI-savvy applications** allow you and your users to do useful things with certificates, like encrypt e-mail or network connections. Ideally, the user shouldn't have to know (or even necessarily be aware) of what the application is doing—everything should work seamlessly and automatically. The best-known examples of PKI-savvy applications are Web browsers like Internet Explorer and Netscape Navigator and e-mail applications like Outlook and Outlook Express. Windows 2000 includes the Encrypting File System (EFS), a PKI-aware file system that can automatically encrypt and decrypt files for you.

These components all work together to provide a full set of PKI services. However, this chapter will cover mostly the CA, the publisher, and the management tools.

Why EFS Is Your Friend

EFS is a little-talked-about Windows 2000 feature that's actually very cool. It encrypts files and folders transparently to you and your applications so that when you're logged in, everything in an EFS-encrypted folder looks like a normal document. To everyone else, of course, it's unreadable gibberish (Windows 2000 actually produces an "access denied" message when you try to open someone else's EFS files).

EFS files are always encrypted on disk. This happens because EFS is actually a filesystem driver that sits between the standard disk drivers and the applications. When Word (for example) requests a block of data from an EFS-protected file, EFS reads an encrypted block from disk, decrypts it in memory, and passes it back to Word without ever storing the unencrypted text on disk.

If you think that's cool, just wait! There's more. EFS supports recovery so that you always have a way to recover access to files that have been encrypted. It does this by encrypting the key used to protect the file twice: once for the owner, and once for the Administrator account (or whoever else has recovery authority). By default, administrators can act as recovery agents, but you can customize recovery access as much as you want, up to and including removing it completely.

Got a Question? Ask an Authority

How can you determine whether a certificate is valid or not? The answer lies in the concept of a *certificate hierarchy*. In a hierarchy, as shown in Figure 14.1, each certificate authority signs the certificates it issues using its own private key. Each CA actually has its own certificate, which contains the CA's public key. This CA certificate is itself signed by a higher-level CA. You can stack up any number of CAs in a hierarchy, with each CA certifying the authenticity of the certificates it has issued. Eventually, though, there must be a top-level CA, called a *root certificate authority*. Since there's nobody above the root CA in the hierarchy, there's nobody to vouch for its certificate. Instead, the root CA signs its own certificate, asserting that it is the root.

FIGURE 14.1 A simple certificate hierarchy

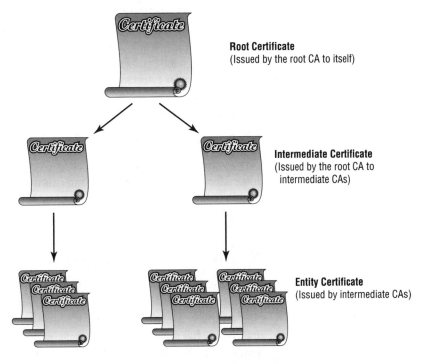

Root Certificate
(Issued by the root CA to itself)

Intermediate Certificate
(Issued by the root CA to
intermediate CAs)

Entity Certificate
(Issued by intermediate CAs)

The root CA is the CA at the top of the hierarchy; CAs lower in the hierarchy are variously called intermediate or subordinate CAs.

There's More Than One Way to Skin a Cat

Until now, you've been reading about only one type of CA. However, MCS supports two different *types* of CAs, and each type can operate in one of several different *roles*. The difference between types and roles is simple to understand. Cars and trucks are different types of vehicles. A single car or truck can be used in different roles: to carpool, to race, to put up on blocks as a lawn decoration, and so on.

Which type of CA you install determines whom you can issue certificates to and what they can be used for, so it's important to understand the distinctions between them. The only real configuration difference between the two is which set of policies it enforces, but the operational differences between them are important.

The Enterprise CA

The enterprise CA acts as part of the PKI for an enterprise. It issues and revokes certificates for end users *and* intermediate CAs according to the policy and security settings that you apply to the CA. As you'd expect from something labeled "enterprise," enterprise CAs require Active Directory access, though they don't necessarily have to be installed on an AD domain controller.

MCS machines acting as enterprise CAs have these five special attributes:

- All users and computers in their domains always trust them.

- Certificates issued by an enterprise CA can be used to log on to Windows 2000 domains if you're using smartcards (those little credit-card-looking things that actually pack an embedded microprocessor and cryptographic software).

- Enterprise CAs publish certificates and CRL information to Active Directory, from which any client in the enterprise can get them.

- Enterprise CAs use certificate *types* and *templates* to construct the content of newly issued certificates. You'll read about types and templates more in a later section, but for now it's important to understand that they deliver some useful capabilities. First, enterprise CAs can use templates to automatically fill in new certificates with the right set of attributes. Second, enterprise CAs can automatically fill in the holder's name for new certificates by looking it up in Active Directory.

- Enterprise CAs will always either reject or approve a certificate request. They'll never mark a request as pending and save it for human inspection. The CA makes this decision based on the security permissions on the security template and on permissions and group memberships in Active Directory.

The Stand-Alone CA

Stand-alone CAs don't require Active Directory access, because they're designed to do nothing but issue certificates for external use. In other words, a stand-alone CA is made to issue certificates to people who aren't part of your organization, like Internet users or business partners. Stand-alone CAs are very similar to enterprise CAs in most respects, with a few differences:

- Stand-alone CAs automatically mark incoming certificate requests as "pending," because the CA doesn't have access to Active Directory information to verify them.

- Certificates issued by a stand-alone CA can't be used for smartcard logons (though you may store them on a smartcard).

- Certificates and CRLs generated by the stand-alone CA aren't published anywhere—you must manually distribute them.

> You *can* install a stand-alone CA on a server that participates in an Active Directory organization. If you do, the CA will be able to publish certificate information if its server is a member of the Certificate Publishers group.

Some Windows 2000–Specific Terms to Know

Besides knowing the general terms used to talk about PKI components and their capabilities, you also have to know some specific terms that Microsoft uses in their products and on their exams. Most, but not all, of these terms are the same as those used by other PKI vendors.

Cryptographic Service Providers

Microsoft ships a set of cryptographic libraries with every copy of Windows NT, Windows 95/98, and Windows 2000. These libraries implement basic, low-level crypto operations, including both *secret-* and *public-key encryption*. They expose a set of application programming interfaces that Microsoft calls the CryptoAPI. Applications, and the operating systems themselves, make CryptoAPI calls when they need some cryptographic work done.

The libraries themselves are known as cryptographic service providers, or CSPs. Any system can have any number of CSPs installed on it, and MCS can use any CSP you've installed to sign certificates it issues. (Actually, that's not 100% correct—MCS can use any CSP that has signature capability to issue certificates, but it can't use encryption-only CSPs.)

Policy and Exit Modules

MCS supports using predefined sets of instructions that tell the CA what to do with incoming requests and how to proceed after a request is approved. The rules that govern how the CA handles an incoming request are built into *policy modules*, and rules that specify where and how a newly issued certificate is published are built into *exit modules*. While you can write your own policy and exit modules, it's much more likely that you'll use the ones Microsoft provides with Windows 2000.

A policy module is a set of instructions that tells the CA what to do with incoming certificate requests. A policy module can automatically approve or reject a request, based on any rules built into the module. It can also mark a request as "pending" and leave it for a human operator to approve or reject. Policy modules can also change the attributes listed in a certificate, adding or removing them according to its design. Microsoft's standard policy module does these three things:

- It processes each incoming request or marks it as pending, depending on whether you're operating an enterprise or a stand-alone CA.

- It adds an attribute to the certificate that specifies where the issuing CA's certificate may be obtained. This allows clients who want to verify the new certificate to get the issuer's certificate at the same time.

- It adds an attribute that specifies where the issuing CA's CRLs are available to clients.

An exit module allows the CA to do something with a certificate after it's been issued. For example, Microsoft's standard exit module can publish new certificates to Active Directory, store them in a shared folder, or e-mail them back to the requestor. It also publishes CRLs for the issuing CA, if you enable that feature.

Certificate Trust Lists

The *Certificate Trust List*, or CTL, is a way for PKI administrators to decide whom they trust. When you put a CA certificate on the CTL for your domain, you're explicitly telling your users' PKI clients that it's OK to trust certificates issued by that CA. The CTL actually lives in Active Directory, and as an administrator you can control who may (and may not) make changes to the CTL for a site, domain, or organizational unit.

Certificate Attributes

Each certificate has some combination of attributes in it. The X.509 standard defines which attributes are mandatory and which are optional (the standard calls optional attributes extensions, and so does Microsoft). MCS follows the standard closely—any certificate it generates is guaranteed to contain all of the mandatory attributes. There are nine significant attributes used by MCS, as shown in Table 14.1. The exact combination and contents of these attributes in a certificate are determined by the certificate template used when the certificate was generated—more on that in a minute.

TABLE 14.1   Interesting Certificate Attributes

Attribute Name	What It Specifies
Basic constraints	Specifies whether this certificate can be used to sign other certificates. If so, it also specifies how many levels deep the resulting hierarchy can be.
Default CSP list	Provides a list of CSPs that can be used with this type of certificate. For example, EFS requires certificates generated with the Microsoft RSA CSP.
Display name	Displays the name when someone views the certificate's information; this is a "friendly" name that's less complex than the certificate's distinguished name (DN).
E-mail name	Specifies the e-mail address associated with the holder of this certificate.
Extended key usage	Specifies a list of extended functions (including signing a CTL, encrypting e-mail, and establishing secure network connections) for which this certificate can be used. The extended key usage information coexists with, but doesn't override, the standard key usage fields.
Key usage	Specifies what combination of basic operations (digital signatures, encryption, and key exchange) this certificate can be used for.
Machine certificate template	Specifies whether certificates that use this template are intended for use by people or by computers.
Security permissions	Specifies who can request a particular kind of certificate. For example, the default permissions for the Administrator template allow only users with administrative access to request administrator-level certificates.

Certificate Templates

Earlier in the chapter we alluded to the fact that you can use certificate templates to help the CA know what items to add to a newly created certificate.

These templates act like rubber stamps: By specifying a particular template as the model you want to use for a newly issued certificate, you're actually telling the CA which optional attributes to add to the certificate, as well as implicitly telling it how to fill some of the mandatory attributes. Templates greatly simplify the process of issuing certificates since they keep you from having to memorize the names of all the attributes you might potentially want to put in a certificate.

Windows 2000 includes 22 different certificate templates. This might seem like a lot, and it is, but there's no supported way for you to build your own templates. The most useful certificate templates (e.g., the ones you're most likely to be using) are listed in Table 14.2.

TABLE 14.2 Some of the Supported Certificate Templates in Windows 2000

Template Name	What Certificates Based on the Template May Do	Who Gets Certificates Issued Using this Template
Administrator	Sign code; sign CTLs; secure e-mail and EFS file systems; authenticate clients	Domain administrators
Authenticated Session	Signature-only operations for authenticating clients	Network clients
Basic EFS	Encrypt EFS intermediate keys and files	Users who have access to EFS volumes
Code Signing	Sign executable code to assert its trustworthiness	Users who have authorization to sign executable objects
Computer	Authenticate computers to servers and vice versa	Computers in a domain
Domain Controller	Authenticate clients to servers and vice versa	Active Directory domain controllers
EFS Recovery Agent	Recover encrypted files when the original key material is unavailable	Users who have EFS recovery privileges

TABLE 14.2   Some of the Supported Certificate Templates in Windows 2000 *(continued)*

Template Name	What Certificates Based on the Template May Do	Who Gets Certificates Issued Using this Template
Enrollment Agent	Request certificates for users or computers	Users who are authorized to request certificates
Exchange Enrollment Agent (Offline request)	Generate offline certificate requests for Exchange mailbox owners	Users who can request new certificates for Exchange users
Exchange Signature Only	Signature-only certificate for Exchange users	Exchange users
Exchange User	Signature- and encryption-capable certificate	Exchange users
Smartcard Logon	Authenticate a client to a logon server	Smartcard holders who use smartcards to log on; cannot be used for secure e-mail or EFS security
Smartcard User	Client authentication and e-mail security	Smartcard holders who have permission to use their smartcards to log on *and* secure e-mail and EFS files
Subordinate Certification Authority	Issue and revoke certificates while acting as a subordinate CA	Computers acting as subordinate CAs
Trust List Signing	Sign the certificate trust list	Administrators who have authorization to modify the CTL
User	Authenticate client-to-server; sign and encrypt email; encrypt EFS data	Ordinary, unprivileged users
User Signature Only	Sign e-mail; sign client-to-server authentication messages	Users whom you don't want to have encryption capability

CA Roles

Whether your MCS servers are acting as enterprise or stand-alone CAs, they can assume one of four distinct roles. These roles govern the conditions under which the CA will issue certificates, as well as what those certificates can be used for once issued. In addition, the role your CA will play has some bearing on the questions you have to answer when you're installing the CAs in your network. Here are the role types:

- **Enterprise root CAs** sit at the top of a certificate hierarchy. While they can issue certificates to end users or subordinate CAs, the enterprise root normally is used only to issue certificates to subordinate CAs. That's because delegating issuance powers to the subordinates gives you maximum flexibility in setting permissions and choosing which templates to use.

- **Enterprise subordinate CAs** live in an enterprise CA hierarchy below the root. They typically issue certificates to computers and users, not to other subordinate CAs. By setting appropriate permissions at the enterprise subordinate CA level, you get fine-grained control over who can request and revoke certificates.

- **Stand-alone root CAs** stand alone, just like the name implies. They don't necessarily take part in your network at all, although they can be physically connected. They may or may not be part of your Active Directory infrastructure. Because stand-alone roots can be physically and logically disconnected from the network, they can be made pretty much impervious to network attacks, making them well-suited for use in issuing your most valuable certificate types.

- **Stand-alone subordinate CAs** normally issue certificates to people. They usually don't take part in Active Directory, although they can. Their lot in life is pretty much to issue certificates to end users. For example, if you were setting up a PKI for a company with offices in several countries, you could set up a separate, stand-alone, subordinate CA in each country. This would allow you to issue certificates to end users in each country without being able to cross-verify certificates issued in different countries.

Recovery Keys

Ordinarily, if you lose the key associated with a certificate, you're hosed— it's like losing the combination to that government-approved safe in your office. While a safecracker might be able to get in (assuming you could find and hire one), the odds aren't good. The risk of permanent data loss has scared lots of potential customers away from encryption, so Microsoft has provided a solution in the form of *recovery keys*. The idea behind recovery keys is much like the one behind those little magnetic boxes you use to stash house and car keys in case you lose yours. In the event that the key used to encrypt a piece of data (on an EFS volume, e-mail message, or wherever else) is lost, the recovery key can be used to decrypt the data. Signing keys aren't recoverable, so no one can surreptitiously pretend to be you by recovering your key.

Windows 2000 allows you to define a recovery policy that specifies who may recover data and under what conditions. Users who have recovery authority are called *recovery agents*, and they use special certificates and keys to enable recovery.

Recovery vs. Escrow

Don't confuse key recovery with key escrow. In key escrow, some third party holds a copy of your encryption keys. In some escrow schemes, this third party is a government agency like the National Security Agency or the Treasury Department; in others, it's an industry organization like the American Bar Association or the American Banking Association. If recovery is like those magnetic key holders, escrow is like giving the local police department a copy of your key. A simple way to remember this difference is that recovery lets *you* recover *your* keys, while escrow lets *someone else* recover *your* keys. Windows 2000 doesn't implement key escrow.

Installing MS Certificate Server

The actual process of installing and configuring MCS is pretty straightforward, especially when you compare it with the gyrations required to set up the equivalent service under Windows NT. However, some prior planning is necessary to avoid making the wrong configuration choices at installation—MCS doesn't allow you to change some of its settings once it's installed.

Four Questions to Answer

Before you proceed to install a CA anywhere on your network, you must know the answer to four questions that the setup program's going to ask you as part of the setup process:

- What type of CA are you installing: enterprise or stand-alone? You can't install an enterprise CA unless you've already set up and tested Active Directory.

- What role do you want the CA to play? At one point in the installation process, you pick between stand-alone and enterprise CAs, and after that point the installation options diverge.

- Do you want to use any CSPs other than the default Microsoft modules? If you install the optional (and North America–only) High Encryption Pack for Windows 2000, you can take advantage of CSPs that are cryptographically stronger than the ones included with Windows 2000.

- Do you want to allow end users to request certificates using the Web interface included with MCS? This interface makes it easier for users to get certificates, which may or may not be what you want to accomplish.

Doing the Installation Boogie

You install the Certificate Server using the Windows Components wizard; since it's just an ordinary system service, the system doesn't do anything out of the ordinary when you install it. When you run the wizard, you can install the CA service itself, the Web enrollment component, or both.

Microsoft *Exam* *Objective*	**Install and configure Certificate Authority (CA).**

Installing the CA

When you're ready to install the CA on a computer (after answering the questions listed earlier in the section, of course), here's what to do:

1. Open the Windows Components wizard by opening the Add/Remove Programs control panel (Start ➤ Settings ➤ Control Panel ➤ Add/ Remove Programs) and clicking the Add/Remove Windows Components icon. The wizard will open and list all the components it knows how to install or remove.

2. Select Certificate Services from the component list. You'll see a warning dialog box telling you that you can't change the name of the computer, or move it into or out of an AD domain, after installing the CA. If you want the machine you're installing on to function as an enterprise CA, make sure you promote it to a domain controller before continuing with the installation.

3. Click the Details… button and uncheck any component you don't want installed. For example, if you want to install only the Web enrollment components on a network kiosk, uncheck the CA options. Click OK when you're done, then click the Next button to move on to the next wizard step.

4. The CA Type Selection dialog box will appear, as shown in Figure 14.2. Here's where your premeditated decision about what type and role you want this CA to fulfill comes in handy. Notice the Advanced options check box—you'll need to check it if you want to change the CSPs this CA can use, if you want to reuse an existing key pair, or if you want to change the default hash algorithm. Click Next once you've filled out the page.

FIGURE 14.2 The CA Type Selection page of the Windows Component wizard

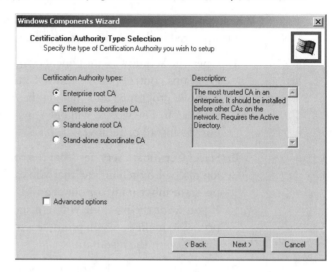

5. If you checked the Advanced Options check box, you'll see the Public and Private Key Pair Selection page (see Figure 14.3.) Apart from selecting the key pair you want to use, this dialog box allows you to choose the CSP, hash algorithm, and key length you want to use with its controls. By default, the Microsoft Base Cryptographic Provider is the standard CSP, though you may have others available depending on what hardware and software you have installed on your server.

FIGURE 14.3 The Public and Private Key Pair Selection page of the Windows Component wizard

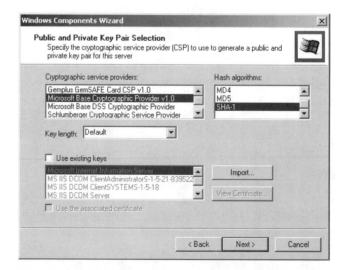

The fields in this dialog box do the following:

- The Cryptographic Service Providers list shows all the CSPs on your machine. Choose the one you want this CA to use. Be forewarned that if you choose a CSP that doesn't support the RSA algorithm suite (like, say, the Microsoft Base DSS CSP), your CA may not interoperate properly with CAs from other vendors.

- The Hash Algorithms list allows you to choose the hash algorithm you want to use for computing digital signatures. Don't use MD4. If you can avoid it, don't use MD5 either—both algorithms have known weaknesses. Instead, accept the default setting of SHA-1.

- The Key Length pull-down lets you select a key length if you're generating a key pair. You can take the default value of 1024 bits or you can go all the way up to 4096 bits if you need to, provided your CSP supports longer keys.

- The Use Existing Keys check box allows you to reuse an existing key pair for the CA's key, as long as it was generated with algorithms compatible with your selected CSP. As you choose different CSPs, you'll see that this check box (and the contents of the list below it) changes to reflect the keys you could potentially use.

- The Import... button lets you import certificates from a PFX/PKCS#12 file, and the View Certificate... button will show you the properties for the selected certificate.

- The Use The Associated Certificate check box lets you use an existing certificate if the key pair you've selected has one associated with it *and* if it's compatible with your chosen CSP.

Once you've set the options you want to use, click the Next button.

FIGURE 14.4 The CA Identifying Information page of the Windows Component wizard

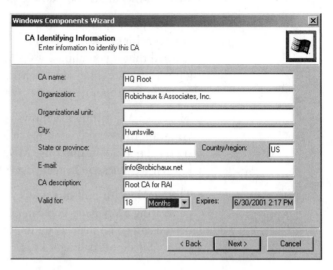

6. The CA Identifying Information page (see Figure 14.4) allows you to specify the information needed to uniquely identify this CA. You must specify a unique name for the CA itself, as well as an e-mail address where requests for the CA's services should go. You should also specify names for the organization that owns the CA and the organizational unit it's in; if you wish, you could specify information about its physical location, too. The Valid For: controls at the bottom of the dialog box allow you to set the validity interval for your CA's certificate. Click the Next button after you've filled in enough information to identify your CA.

You *cannot* change any of this identifying information once the CA is installed, because it's all encoded into the CA's certificate. Make sure the information you enter here is correct!

If you choose an organization name that includes special characters (like &, *, [,], and so on), the CA has to encode them with Unicode, because the X.509 standard for PKI certificates requires it. This may make some older (or broken!) applications unable to verify your CA certificate, so Setup will warn you and give you a chance to change the CA name before proceeding.

7. The CA stores its certificates in a database file, and you get to choose where that database lives on disk. Note that this database contains the CA's certificates, not the certificates it issues—those are published in Active Directory or wherever else you specify. The Data Storage Location page (shown in Figure 14.5) allows you to choose where on your server these database files reside. The Store Configuration Information In A Shared Folder check box allows you to force the CA to use a shared folder for storing the certificates it emits. This is handy if you're not using Active Directory or if you have clients that expect to get certificates only from a file on disk somewhere.

FIGURE 14.5 The Data Storage Location page of the Windows Component wizard

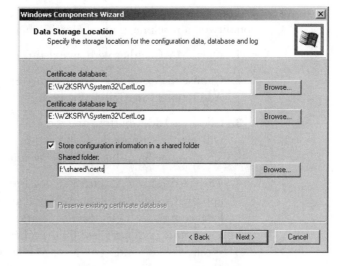

The Preserve Existing Certificate Database check box lets you reinstall the CA on top of an existing installation. For example, if you have a machine that you want to convert from stand-alone to enterprise mode, or if you need to reinstall to change the CA's name or Active Directory membership, checking this box tells Setup not to erase the old certificates.

Make sure whatever location you specify is on an NTFS disk volume and that it gets backed up regularly. If you lose a CA's certificates, you'll have to reissue all the certificates ever issued by that CA.

8. Once you're happy with the settings on all of the preceding pages, click the Next button. If you're currently using the Internet Information Service (IIS) WWW service, Setup will stop it for you so it can finish the installation. Once the setup is complete, you'll need to restart your machine. From then on, the CA service will automatically start whenever the server does.

Installing the Certificates and Certificate Authority Snap-Ins

Managing Microsoft Certificate Server involves using two different, but related, Microsoft Management Console (MMC) snap-ins: one for managing certificates and one for managing the CA itself. The process for installing the two snap-ins is identical, and you can usually keep them together in a single console file so that you can quickly manage all certificate-related functionality on a machine at once. Here's what to do:

1. Open MMC, either with an existing console file or a new one.

2. Choose the Console ➢ Add/Remove Snap-in... command to open the Add/Remove Snap-in dialog box.

3. Click the Add... button, and the Add Stand-Alone Snap-In dialog box will appear. Choose the Certification Authority item on the Available Stand-Alone Snap-Ins list, and then click the Add button.

4. The Certification Authority dialog box, shown in Figure 14.6, will appear. By default, this snap-in will always be used to manage the local computer. If you want to retarget the snap-in so that it manages some other computer, use the Another Computer radio button to specify the computer you want to manage. The Allow The Selected Computer To Be Changed When Launching From The Command Line check box enables you to change the snap-in's target at any time.

5. Click the Finish button, and you'll be back to the Add Stand-Alone Snap-In dialog box from step 3. This time, choose the Certificates snap-in instead of Certification Authority, then click the Add button.

6. The Certificates Snap-In dialog box will appear so that you can choose which set of certificates the snap-in will be used to manage. By default, the My User Account radio button is set, but you can also manage computer and service account certificates—just not with the same snap-in. Choose the certificate type you want to manage, then click the Finish button.

FIGURE 14.6 Use this dialog box to choose which CA you want to manage

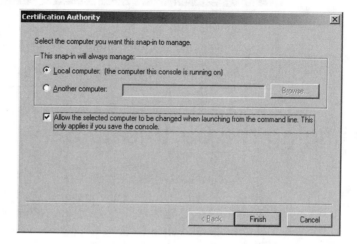

 To manage all three certificate types from a single MMC, just add three instances of the Certificates snap-in.

EXERCISE 14.1

Installing Microsoft Certificate Server (MCS)

Follow these steps to install MCS:

1. Choose Start ➢ Settings ➢ Control Panels ➢ Add/Remove Programs, and select the Add/Remove Windows Components button.

2. Select Certificate Services from the component list. When the warning dialog box appears, click OK.

3. When the CA Type Selection dialog box appears, choose the Enterprise Root CA button if your server is part of an Active Directory domain; if it's not, choose the Stand-Alone Root CA button. Click the Next button when you're done.

4. Fill in the fields in the CA Identifying Information page. Make sure to specify a unique name for the CA. Click the Next button when you're done.

EXERCISE 14.1 *(continued)*

5. When the Data Storage Location page appears, write down the database paths for future reference. Then click the Next button.

6. Complete the installation by clicking the Finish button.

Managing the Certificate Server

Once you've installed the Certificate Server and the CA snap-in, you're ready to configure and manage your CA. When you open the CA snap-in in the MMC, you'll see that it contains several items. The snap-in interface is shown in Figure 14.7; it looks very much like every other MMC snap-in. In the left half of the console window, you'll see one node for each CA running on the server you're managing.

FIGURE 14.7 The Certification Authority snap-in

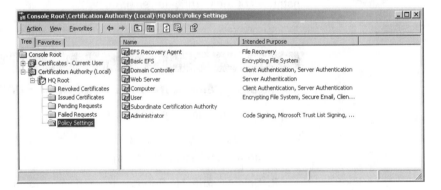

If you expand any one of those CA nodes, you'll see the following five folders below it:

- The Revoked Certificates folder holds all certificates that have been revoked by this CA. Once revoked, a certificate can't be unrevoked; it will stay on the CRL forever.

- The Issued Certificates folder lists the certificates that this CA has issued since its installation. Double-clicking a certificate shows its properties, and right-clicking a certificate allows you to revoke it.

- The Pending Requests folder lists the requests that are queued on the CA, waiting for you to approve or disapprove them. Enterprise CAs will never have any items in this list, but stand-alone CAs may display zero or more requests at any given time.

- The Failed Requests folder lists all the requests that failed *or* were rejected, including the CN, e-mail address, and submission date of the failed request.

- The Policy Settings folder shows the certificate templates that are available for use on this server. You may change the set of available templates by right-clicking the Policy Settings folder and using the New ➤ Certificate to Issue or Delete commands. Double-clicking a template shows you the certificate purposes available with that certificate, but there's no way to change the template directly.

Each folder actually expands into a list, and (following the standard MMC behavior) you can customize the list's columns and fields using the View submenu on the context menu. To do this, right-click the folder, then select the Choose Columns... and Customize commands until you have the list configured the way you want it. You can also define filters using the View ➤ Filter... command; for example, you could create a filter that showed only certificates that were due to expire after a particular date.

Controlling the CA Service

Since MCS is just another Windows 2000 service, you can configure it to start when you want to. The installer automatically configures the service to start when the system starts; for extra security, you can set it to start manually so that it can only issue certificates when you want it to.

As with every other Windows 2000 service, you can use the Services item in the Computer Management snap-in to start and stop the services, set recovery options for it when it stops, and change the account used to run it. You can also do most of these functions, plus some other useful ones, directly from the Certification Authority snap-in. When you right-click a CA, you gain access to several commands that simplify your day-to-day management tasks; the following primary commands appear under the All Tasks submenu of the Context menu you get when you right-click the CA.

Switching to a Different CA

The first command actually appears when you right-click the Certification Authority node, not an individual CA. The Retarget Certification Authority command lets you point the snap-in at a different CA; you may remember that during installation you have to specify which CA you want to manage, and this is how you change it. When you use this command, you'll be able to browse the network and change to any CA to which you have management rights.

Starting/Stopping the Service

In addition to starting and stopping the CA from the Services item in Computer Management or from the command line, you can use the Start Service and Stop Service commands from the context menu. These operations take effect immediately; you don't get a chance to change your mind or confirm your command.

Backing Up and Restoring CA Data

Doing a solid backup of the CA's data is a two-step process, and it involves two separate tools. While this seems more complicated than necessary, doing good backups is critical; if you lose the CA's certificates you won't be able to issue, renew, or revoke certificates for that CA's domain. Of course, backing up data is pointless unless you have the ability to restore it when you need to.

Backing Up the CA

The two-step process of backing up the CA is conceptually simple. First you use the Certification Authority Backup wizard to make a usable copy of the CA's data. Since the CA keeps its files open when it's running, you can't just copy the files unless you stop the service; however, the wizard can copy the needed data while the service is running. To begin this first step, right-click the CA and use the Backup CA... command. After an introductory wizard page, you'll see the Items to Back Up page (see Figure 14.8). Use it to specify what you want backed up.

FIGURE 14.8 Use this dialog box to choose which CA you want to manage.

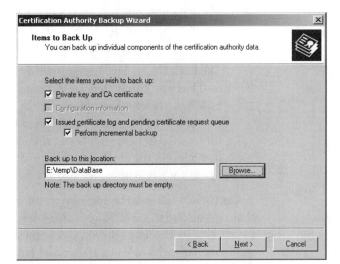

The following settings specify what should be backed up:

- The Private Key And CA Certificate setting specifies that you want to back up the CA's private key and the associated certificate. If you choose this option, the wizard will ask you for a password that it uses to encrypt the private key and certificate data and store it in a PKCS#12 file.

- The Configuration Information check box specifies that you want the CA's settings to be backed up, too. Servers that are part of Active Directory store their information in AD, so this check box will be disabled. If you're using a stand-alone CA and want its configuration saved, be sure to check this box.

- The CA keeps log files that record certificate issuance and revocation. It also keeps a queue of pending requests. If you want these backed up (and you should since losing the queue means end users will have to resubmit their requests, and losing the logs means you lose historical information about certificate issuance), check the Issued Certificate Log And Pending Certificate Request Queue (whew!) check box.

  If you choose to back up the log and queue files, you can further specify whether you want to back up the entire set of files at each backup (the default) or only those items that have changed since the previous backup (by checking the Perform Incremental Backup check box.)

Incremental backups reduce the amount of data required for your regular backups, but you must still do at least one non-incremental backup. We recommend doing incremental backups during the week, with full backups either at the week's beginning or its end.

- The Back Up To This Location field (and the associated Browse… button) lets you specify where you want the backed-up data to go. You must specify an empty directory; the wizard will put a file named `<caName>.p12` (containing the private key and certificate) and a directory named `DataBase` (which contains the actual logs, queues, and CA database) in the location you provide. You can't store multiple backups in the same directory without overwriting them.

Once you've chosen the appropriate settings, click the Next button. If you chose to back up the private key material, you'll be prompted to enter a password to secure the data on disk. Once you've done that (if necessary), you'll see a summary wizard page; clicking its Finish button will actually perform the backup.

Once you've used the CA Backup wizard to make a backup of your CA data, the second necessary step is to use Windows 2000 Backup (or another backup tool, like ARCserve or BackupExec) to back up your CA data to disk, tape, CD-R, or whatever you use for backup. Don't skip this step—all the CA Backup wizard does is make a clean copy of the CA's data on your local machine where it's no more protected than the original data was.

Restoring the CA

The Microsoft Word thesaurus lists "raze," "ruin," and "break" as antonyms for "restore." However, "restore" is really an antonym for "backup." A restore reverses the backup process, returning the target machine to its original backed-up state. Restoring CA data is thus the reverse process of the backup process: First you restore your backed-up CA data from its storage media using Windows 2000 Backup or whatever, then you use the Certification Authority Restore wizard with the Restore CA… command. The wizard allows you to restore whatever you've backed up, in any combination you choose. For example, you can restore just the queue; the queue and the logs; or the queue, the logs, and the key material.

There are some differences in the actual process, though. First, the CA service has to be stopped to use the Restore wizard; the wizard offers to do this for you. The meat of the wizard is the Items To Restore page (see Figure 14.9). Using the check boxes on this page, you specify what you want to restore; you must also use the Restore From This Location controls to tell the wizard where to find the specific backup from which you want to restore.

FIGURE 14.9 Use this dialog box to choose what CA data you want to restore.

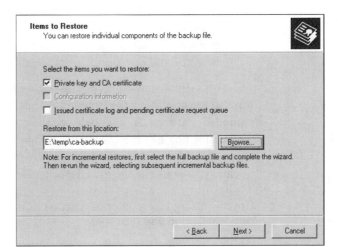

If you want to restore several incremental backups in a row—as you might need to if it's been awhile since your last full backup—you must first restore the correct full backup, then restore each of the incremental backups that match it, in the right order. To facilitate this process, you might want to name your CA backups with a code that indicates the date when the backup was made.

Renewing the CA Certificate

Like real-world credentials, certificates eventually expire. When you control the CA, you get to control the expiration interval for certificates it issues, which can be pretty handy. CA certificates aren't exempt from this process, so it's likely that you'll need to renew your CA certificates periodically. For subordinate CAs, renewal is accomplished by requesting a new certificate from the issuing CA, but root CAs get to renew their own certificates. There are two ways to accomplish this:

- The CA can take its existing keys and bind them to a new certificate. This is the most common option, since it allows you to keep reusing the existing keys for signature verification and signing. If you do this enough times, though, the CA's CRL can grow very large, and that slows performance of all your PKI components.

- The CA can generate a new key pair and use it to create a new certificate. This option is useful when you want or need to generate a new key (say, because you fear the old one has been compromised). In essence, this is equivalent to creating a brand-new CA since there's a new key and certificate.

To begin the renewal process, just right-click the CA whose certificate you want to use and select the Renew CA Certificate... command. You'll be reminded that the CA must be stopped to renew the certificate, then you'll see a dialog box like the one shown in Figure 14.10. You use this dialog box to specify whether or not you want to create a new key pair for the new certificate; you can't change the CSP or key length, though.

FIGURE 14.10 Use this dialog box to choose whether or not you want to rekey a CA certificate when you renew it.

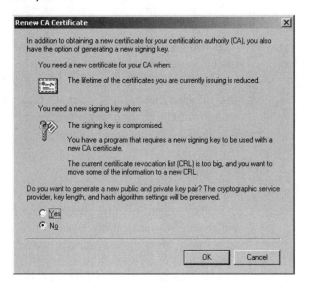

Configuring the CA

CAs have a number of configurable properties that control how they behave. Most of these settings have reasonable default values, but there are times when you might need to change them. All of the CA's properties, including its policy and exit module settings, are available through the Properties dialog box that appears when you select a CA and use the Properties command (either from the Action menu or the Context menu).

Microsoft
Exam
Objective

Install and configure Certificate Authority (CA).

Setting General Properties

The first thing you'll see in the CA Properties dialog box is the General tab, shown in Figure 14.11. Most of the information here is strictly for reference—although the tab shows you the name and description for the CA, along with the CSP and hash algorithm in use, you can't change them. You can view the CA certificate's details with the View Certificate button.

FIGURE 14.11   The General tab of the CA Properties dialog box

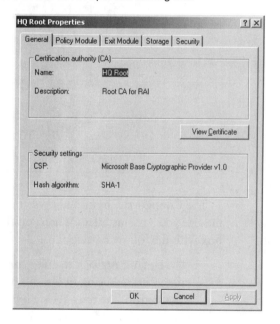

Setting Policy Module Properties

The Policy Module tab is definitely more interesting than the General tab, if only because it has controls you can adjust. As seen in Figure 14.12, this tab shows you which policy module is active, and it lets you configure the current module or change to another one altogether. The selected policy module will almost always be the Enterprise And Stand-Alone Policy module that Microsoft supplies with Windows 2000 (unless you've written your own or bought a replacement from a third party). In that case, use the Select... button to pick a new policy module from the list of those registered with the system.

FIGURE 14.12   The Policy Module tab of the CA Properties dialog box

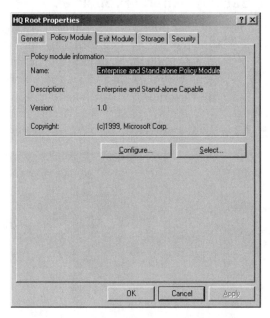

The Configure... button allows you to set options for whichever policy module you have installed. When you click it, you get a Configuration dialog box with the following two tabs:

- The Default Action tab gives you control over how incoming requests are processed using two radio buttons. The Always Issue The Certificate button (the only choice for enterprise CAs) tells the CA to immediately process the request, while the Set The Certificate Request Status To Pending tells the CA to mark the request as "pending" and stuff it in a queue until you approve or reject it.

- The X.509 Extensions tab (see Figure 14.13) allows you to tailor two lists of locations: one for where CRLs are published (known as *CRL Distribution Points*, or *CDPs*) and one that specifies where users can get the CA's certificate (known as *Authority Information Access Points*, or *AIAs* for short). The lists of CDPs and AIAs are encoded as part of the CA certificate, so any client can look at the certificate and figure out which CDPs and AIAs exist for it to use. By default, MCS will use HTTP and LDAP CDPs and AIAs, but there are also file system–based URLs. You can use the Add AIA... and the Add CDP... buttons to specify additional CDPs or AIAs. You can specify literally any URL, but it doesn't make sense to specify a URL unless you plan to actually serve CRLs or CA certificates from it.

FIGURE 14.13 The X.509 Extensions tab of the Policy Module Properties dialog box

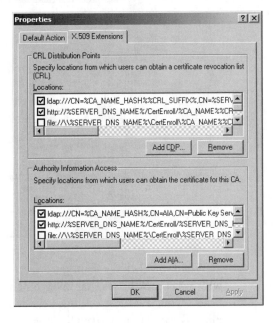

 If you change any of the X.509 extension values by using this tab, you'll have to stop and restart the CA before the changes will take effect. This requirement holds for most changes to the CA.

Setting Exit Module Properties

The Exit Module tab (see Figure 14.14) is very similar to the Policy Module tab; it shows you which exit modules you've currently configured to work with your CA. A CA can use only one policy module at a time, but it may use several exit modules, which are executed in a series. For example, you could use the Microsoft policy module to publish newly issued certificates to Active Directory and the file system, then use your own module to publish certificates on a Web page or in an Exchange public folder.

FIGURE 14.14 The Exit Module Properties dialog box

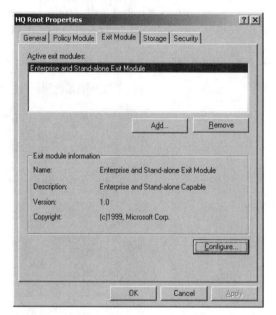

When you click the Configure… button, you'll see a Properties dialog box with two check boxes that give you control over where certificates are published. Your available options here depend on whether or not your CA computer is part of an Active Directory domain:

- The Allow Certificates To Be Published In The Active Directory check box will be marked by default on servers that participate in an AD domain. To allow the exit module to load certificates into AD when it's present, check this box.

- The Allow Certificates To Be Published To The File System check box lets you specify that you want new certificates stored in the shared folder you specified when you installed the CA.

At this point, you may be wondering where CRLs are published, since there's no explicit way for you to specify their disposition. By default, the CA always puts newly generated CRLs in %systemroot%\system32\ certserv\certenroll. Each CRL gets a name that starts with the letter "c" and includes the date it was generated (in YYMMDD format). If you generate multiple CRLs on one day, the CA adds a suffix number. For example, c000214.crl is the only CRL published on 14 February 2000, while c0007115.crl is the fifth CRL published on 11 July 2000. The CRLs will be available to LDAP and HTTP clients (according to the CDPs you specified), and you can take the generated files and publish them wherever you like.

Viewing Storage Properties

The Storage tab shows the paths where the CA is keeping its configuration and certificate database files. You can't change these values after the CA is installed, but it might be useful to have a way to double-check the file locations in case you need them, and this is the quickest way to do so. There *is* one thing you can change here: If your CA is a stand-alone CA running on a computer with Active Directory access, checking the Active Directory check box will move the CA's configuration information into the directory.

Setting Security Properties

Like practically everything else in Windows 2000, MCS servers can be assigned their own set of permissions that control who can see and change the information the CA owns. Table 14.3 shows the twelve permission settings that you can apply to the CA; each permission allows someone who holds it to do something specific with the CA. Right out of the box, the following four groups have permissions to use the CA:

- The Administrators group has the Manage, Enroll, and Read Configuration rights. Even though Manage enables the other permissions, you can turn it off if you want to allow administrators to enroll users without giving them permission to manage the CA itself.

- The Authenticated Users group has Enroll and Read Configuration permission.

- The Domain Admins and Enterprise Admins groups have Manage, Enroll, and Read Configuration permissions.

TABLE 14.3 CA Permissions That May Be Assigned to Users and Groups

Permission	What Holders Can Do
Manage	Change anything on the CA. Granting or denying this permission grants or revokes all the other permissions.

TABLE 14.3 CA Permissions That May Be Assigned to Users and Groups *(continued)*

Permission	What Holders Can Do
Enroll	Request new certificates for users or computers.
Read	Read certificates only from the database.
Write configuration	Save CA configuration changes and make them permanent.
Read configuration	Read CA configuration data; this implies Read Control permission, too.
Read control	Read control information for the CA.
Delete	Remove objects from the CA database.
Modify permissions	Change permissions on the CA and its objects.
Modify owner	Change ownership of the CA objects.
Revoke certificate	Revoke a user, computer, or CA certificate.
Approve certificate	Approve or reject a certificate request whose status is "pending."
Read database	Read certificate information from the CA database.

Configuring Certificate Templates

Part of configuring the CA is telling it which certificate templates can be used and who can use them. When someone requests a certificate from your CA (as described in the "Requesting New Certificates" section later in this chapter), they can request that the CA use any of the templates you've made available, and the issued certificate will be filled out according to the rules in the template. By adding and removing templates, and by setting permissions on the templates that are installed, you get control over what people can do.

Assigning Permissions to Templates

You set permissions on the CA itself using the CA Properties dialog box, but to set permissions on the certificate templates you have to leave the familiar environment of the Certification Authority snap-in. The Active Directory Sites and Services snap-in is where you actually adjust permissions for enterprise-wide services, including the use of certificate templates and other PKI components.

To set permissions, do the following:

1. Open the Active Directory Sites and Services snap-in (you can install it, if necessary, using the instructions from the "Installing the Certificates and Certificate Authority Snap-Ins" section earlier in this chapter).

2. Right-click the Sites node, then choose the View ➤ Show Services Node command.

3. Expand the Services node until you see the Certificate Templates node, and expand it, too. This will fill the right half of the MMC window with a list of installed templates.

4. Right-click the template whose permissions you want to set, then choose the Properties command. When the Properties dialog box appears, switch to the Security tab.

5. Adjust the permissions to suit your needs. To keep users from using the template to request new certificates, make sure that you deny the appropriate groups the Enroll permission.

Enabling Automatic Enrollment

Users aren't the only ones who have certificates; Windows 2000 computers have them, too. Normally, you'd have to manually issue certificates for new computers as they join your AD domain, but this is a pain. Instead, you can use automatic enrollment to have the CA automatically generate a new certificate for each computer that joins the domain. To do this, you have to adjust a setting in the Group Policy Object (GPO) for your domain. Here's what to do to adjust this setting:

1. Open the Group Policy snap-in and use it to select the GPO for which you want to turn on automatic enrollment.

2. Open the GPO's Computer Configuration node, then open the Windows Settings, Security Settings, and Public Key Policies nodes beneath it. This exposes four subfolders beneath the Public Key Policies node.

3. Right-click the Automatic Certificate Request Settings folder under the Public Key Policies node, then use the New ≻ Automatic Certificate Request... command. This starts the Automatic Certificate Request wizard.

4. Click Next to get past the wizard's introductory page. When page 2 appears, it will list all the types of certificates that can be automatically issued to computers. Normally, you'll use the basic Computer type, but separate types exist for domain controllers and devices that participate in IPSec. Select the template type you want to use, then click the Next button.

5. Page 3 of the wizard lists all the CAs available in the AD domain. Choose the one that you want to issue certificates for newly added computers, then click the Next button.

6. When the summary page of the wizard appears review your choices, then click the Finish button to actually create the request.

Once you've completed these steps, the new request will appear as an item in the Automatic Certificate Request Settings folder; you can edit or remove it later by selecting it and using the commands in the Action menu.

EXERCISE 14.2

Configuring Microsoft Certificate Server (MCS)

Follow these steps to configure MCS:

1. Open the Certification Authority snap-in from an MMC console session.

2. Right-click the CA you want to manage, then select the Properties command from the Context menu. The Properties dialog box will appear.

3. Click the Exit Module tab. When the Exit Module tab appears, click the Configure... button.

4. Make sure that both the Allow Certificates To Be Published In The Active Directory check box and the Allow Certificates To Be Published To The File System check box are checked, then click the OK button.

5. Click the OK button on the Exit Module tab to close the Properties dialog box.

Configuring Stand-Alone CAs

Although the code that runs them is identical, stand-alone and enterprise CAs have a few differences, which you've already read about. To pass the Microsoft exams, you have to understand how these differences are exposed in the CA management tasks. There are two primary things you need to know how to do, both of which pertain to handling incoming certificate requests.

Enterprise CAs always process incoming requests automatically; by default, though, stand-alone CAs tag inbound requests as "pending" and dump them in the Pending Requests folder under the CA's node in the Certification Authority snap-in. Once queued, the requests will sit there until you either approve or reject them.

Microsoft
✓ ***Exam***
Objective

Issue certificates.

Setting the Default Action for New Requests

If you don't want requests to automatically be marked as "pending," you can change the arrival behavior by adjusting the controls on the Default Action tab, which you get to by clicking the Configure button in the Policy Module tab of the CA Properties dialog box (see Figure 14.12 earlier in this chapter). Once you make this change, newly arrived requests will be treated in accordance with your instructions, but you'll still need to approve or reject any previously queued requests.

Handling Pending Requests

The process of approving or rejecting a pending request couldn't be easier. Navigate to the Pending Requests folder and select it; when you do, all pending requests will appear on the right side of the snap-in window. Right-click the request you want to approve or reject, and you'll see commands for either action.

Configuring Revocation and Trust

Issuing certificates is necessary if you want to use a PKI, but it's not the only thing you have to do. To get ongoing use and security out of your PKI, you have to decide which certificates and issuers you trust, and you need to be able to revoke certificates once their useful life span is over. You do these things by using two separate mechanisms:

- The Certificate Trust List (CTL) for a domain holds the set of root CAs whose certificates you trust. You can designate CTLs for groups, users, or an entire domain. If a CA's certificate isn't on the CTL, its trustworthiness depends on how you've configured your clients (either explicitly or through a GPO) to behave when presented with an untrusted certificate.

- The revocation function adds the targeted certificate to the CA's certificate revocation list (CRL), and a new CRL is published. Clients are required to check the CRL before using a certificate; if the certificate appears on the CRL, clients may not use it. This mechanism is very similar to the authorization mechanism stores use to verify credit cards.

Trusting Other CAs

The Trusted Root Certification Authorities folder under the Public Key Policies node in the Group Policy snap-in contains a list of root CAs that you trust. Note that this isn't the same as a CTL (more on this in the next section); it's just a list of CAs that individual sites, domains, or organizational units may or may not trust. Since the set of trusted CAs for an Active Directory object is defined as part of the GPO for that object, you can designate exactly which Active Directory objects trust which CAs. For example, you could set up one GPO for your marketing department that allows them to trust external CAs and another for the engineering team that allows them only to trust internal CAs.

Once you've added the foreign CA certificate to your local certificate store, you've instructed your clients to trust any certificate issued by that CA as much as they trust certificates issued by their own CA. This is a useful capability, since it allows you to trust CAs operated by other organizations without requiring that they share a common root. Since Windows 2000 Active Directory forests allow you to do pretty much the same thing with domains, the combination of the two features allows you to selectively trust business partners, suppliers, or other "outside-the-fence" entities that need access to some, but not all, of your network resources.

You can modify the Trusted Root Certification Authorities list in three ways: You can add new CA root certificates to it by importing them, you can remove a certificate from it, and you can change the purposes for which the foreign CA is trusted. You do all three of these things from the Public Key Policies node in the Group Policy snap-in. Then do the following:

- To import a new root CA certificate and add it to the trust list, right-click the Trusted Root Certification Authorities folder and use the All Tasks ➤ Import… command. Tell the Certificate Import wizard how to find the new certificate; it will then load the certificate into the store and add it to the trust list.

- To remove a certificate from the folder, right-click it and choose the Delete command. You'll see a confirmation dialog box that warns you of the consequences of removing the certificate.

- To edit the list of purposes that a CA's certificates may be used for, right-click the CA's entry in the Trusted Root Certification Authority folder and open its Properties dialog box. By default, all purposes are enabled for newly added certificates, but you can control how these purposes are used by choosing either the Disable All Purposes For This Certificate radio button or the Enable Only The Following Purposes radio button. Figure 14.15 pulled.

This list of trusted root CAs is distributed by the GPO, which means that it is automatically available to all members of the group. Don't confuse this list with the CTL!

Managing the CTL

The Trusted Root Certification Authorities list shows which foreign CAs you trust at all. The CTL shows that you trust how those CA's certificates will be used. Normally, you use CTLs to designate trust when your enterprise doesn't have its own CAs. If you do have your own CAs, you'd use the Trusted Root Certification Authorities list to establish the trust list.

When you add a foreign CA to your CTL, you're actually generating a new, digitally signed list that is stored in Active Directory and distributed throughout the domain. You manage CTLs with the Enterprise Trust folder under the Public Key Policies component in the Group Policy snap-in; while this may seem odd, it does makes sense because the CTL is stored in Active Directory.

You can do two things with CTLs from the Group Policy snap-in: import a CTL from another machine, or create a new one. Both actions are available by right-clicking the Enterprise Trust folder. Then use All Actions ➤ Import… to use the Import Certificate wizard (covered in more detail in the "Importing, Exporting, and Finding Certificates" section later in this chapter), or use New ➤ Certificate Trust List… to create a new CTL.

FIGURE 14.15 The CTL Purpose page of the CTL wizard

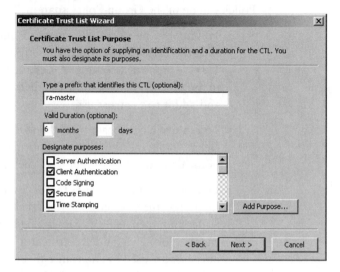

Creating a New CTL

When creating a new CTL, here's how the process works:

1. Use the New ➤ Certificate Trust List command to start the Certificate Trust List wizard. Click the Next button, and you'll see the page shown in Figure 14.15.

2. If you want to identify this CTL, enter a prefix for it in the provided field.

3. If you want the CTL to be valid for a fixed period, enter its life span in the Valid Duration fields.

4. If you want to restrict the purposes for which the certificate can be used, check the appropriate boxes in the Designate Purposes list. By default, none of these purposes is specified; you must check at least one purpose to create the CTL.

5. Click the Next button and the Certificates In The CTL page will appear (see Figure 14.16). The Current CTL Certificates list shows you which certificates are on the CTL. A newly created CTL will be blank until you add some certificates by using the Add From Store and Add From File buttons. Click the Next button once you're done.

6. Next, the Signature Certificate page will appear. You use this page to designate which certificate will sign the CTL. The Select From Store… and the Select From File… buttons will allow you to riffle through your certificate stash until you find a certificate that's marked for use in CTL signing (look for the purpose marked "Microsoft trust list signing"). Click the Next button once you've identified the certificate you want to use.

7. On the next page, you may choose to have the CTL marked with a secure timestamp, which guarantees the authenticity and integrity of the date and time recorded in the CTL. However, you must have access to, and the URL of, a secure timestamp service.

8. The wizard's final page allows you to enter a friendly name and description for the CTL; these items are displayed in the Group Policy snap-in whenever the CTL itself is shown in a list.

As you might expect, once you've completed the wizard you get the usual summary page; clicking the Finish button will create the CTL and store it in Active Directory.

FIGURE 14.16   This page shows which CA certificates are contained in the CTL.

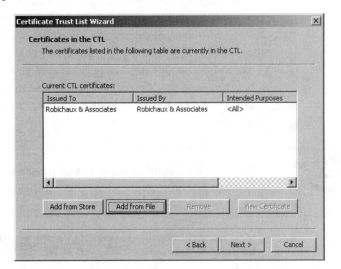

Managing Revocation

Certificate revocation is not something to be done lightly, because there's no way to unrevoke a certificate; once revoked, it stays revoked forever. Sometimes, though, it's necessary. For example, you typically need to revoke certificates issued to employees when they leave your organization or when they no longer need the particular certificate type you issued them. Whenever you have some reason to think that a private key may have been compromised, you'll naturally want to revoke the associated certificate as soon as possible.

Microsoft
Exam
Objective

Revoke certificates.

Revoking Certificates

You can revoke any certificate issued by the CA you're managing; you cannot revoke certificates issued by other CAs since you don't have the ability to sign a new CRL for them. To revoke one of the certificates you've issued, open the Issued Certificates folder in the Certification Authority snap-in, then right-click the certificate and pick the All Tasks ➤ Revoke Certificate... command. You'll have the opportunity to choose a reason code for the revocation (the default is "unspecified," but you can also mark a certificate revoked for a specific reason, like a change of the user's affiliation or cessation of operations). Once you click OK, the certificate is *immediately* revoked.

Don't revoke a certificate unless you're sure you don't need it anymore! Your best bet is to first create a new test certificate, then revoke it.

EXERCISE 14.3

Revoking a Certificate

Follow these steps to revoke a certificate:

1. Open the Certification Authority snap-in from an MMC console session.

EXERCISE 14.3 *(continued)*

2. Open the Issued Certificates folder, and then select the certificate you want to revoke.

3. Right-click the certificate and choose the All Tasks ➢ Revoke Certificate... command.

4. Select a reason code for the revocation, and then click the OK button.

Publishing CRLs

The CRL is just a signed list of certificate serial numbers. When you revoke a certificate, it's immediately added to the CRL, which is then resigned by the CA. However, the CRL isn't republished at that instant. The CA will automatically publish an updated CRL according to its schedule.

"Schedule?" you ask. "What schedule?" When you right-click the Revoked Certificates folder in the Certification Authority snap-in, you can open the folder's Properties dialog box. The only thing in that dialog box is a group of controls labeled Publication. You can use these controls to adjust the publication interval for CRLs to anywhere from 1 hour to 9999 years (the default is 1 week). Microsoft helpfully included some code that tells you when the next scheduled update will take place, so you can judge when that's going to happen.

If you need to manually publish a CRL, you can do so by right-clicking the Revoked Certificates item in the CA snap-in and using the All Tasks ➢ Publish command. The snap-in asks you to confirm that you want to overwrite the existing CRL; if you agree, the CA will publish the CRL to the set of CDPs that you've defined.

Clients still have to pick up the CRL from the CDPs, and that can take some time. Be aware that the time elapsed between your finger leaving the Publish command and the actual arrival of the new CRL on client machines may vary.

Changing CRL Distribution Points

Certificate requests normally include information that tells the CA where to publish (or distribute) the certificate when it's done. However, since CRLs are solely a function of the CA there's no external source for defining CDPs. You do that yourself with the X.509 Extensions tab of the Policy Module Properties dialog box.

Managing Certificates

Apart from the intricacies of managing your CA, you also need to be able to manage certificates for your account—including those issued to you. Windows 2000 implements a database of certificates, or a *certificate store*, for each user and computer account. This database contains end user and CA certificates and CRLs. (The certificates themselves may be stored in the local computer's Registry, in Active Directory, or in a database file, but they all appear as a single, seamless store.)

The Certificates snap-in allows you to manage the certificate store associated with your account, with a service account, or with a local computer. The snap-in also allows you to import and export certificates, request new certificates, renew existing certificates, and change various certificate properties. This particular snap-in is intended for use by end users and administrators; some of what it can do is duplicated in Internet Explorer 4.0 and later.

Using the Certificates Snap-In

Once you install the Certificates snap-in using the procedure described in the "Installing the Certificates and Certificate Authority Snap-Ins" section earlier in this chapter, you can begin managing certificates in the store you associated with the snap-in when you installed it. For example, if you install the snap-in to manage your certificates you'll see it listed as "Certificates – Current User" in the MMC. The snap-in works the same way no matter whose certificate store you're managing, but (depending on the account you use) you may not have permission to do everything described in this section.

When you open the snap-in, you'll see a number of folders including the following:

- The Personal folder contains a subfolder named Certificates, which in turn contains certificates that belong to you (both those issued to you and those you've imported from elsewhere).

- The Trusted Root Certification Authorities folder also contains a Certificates subfolder; it lists the roots you trust. Whether or not you can modify the contents of this list depends on the settings in the GPOs that apply to your account.

- The Enterprise Trust folder contains one folder, labeled Certificate Trust List. Your GPO determines its contents, as it's loaded with whatever CTLs the GPO administrators have defined for you.

- The Intermediate Certification Authorities folder contains separate Certificates and Certificate evocation List folders. CA certificates and CRLs from CAs other than your own end up here.

By selecting the certificate you want to work with, you gain access to several interesting commands—to find out what they are and what they do, keep reading.

Viewing and Changing Certificate Properties

The most common task you'll perform in the Certificates snap-in is probably viewing, and maybe even changing, properties for a particular certificate. Since the certificate is a big blob of attribute data signed by the CA, you would be right on the mark if you guessed that there are lots of interesting properties in each certificate. Viewing them and changing what you can change are two separate tasks:

- To see the certificate's properties, including the full path back to the top of the hierarchy and the certificate's attributes, double-click it or use the Open command on the Context menu.

- To change the purposes the certificate may be used for, use the Properties command from the Actions or Context menus.

This split in behavior seems a little confusing—after all, it would make more sense to view all of the certificate's properties with the Properties command. It makes more sense when you recall that the certificate's attributes are vouched for by the CA, so there's no way for you to change them without invalidating the CA's signature.

The General Tab

The General tab of the Certificate Information dialog box appears in Figure 14.17. It summarizes what purposes the certificate can be used for by listing each purpose as a plainly-worded bullet point. In addition, it shows the name of the holder, the name of the issuer, and the validity period for the certificate. There are a couple of interesting fillips to this page, too: At the bottom of the display area, you'll see a lock-and-key icon, along with a text message, if you have the private key that matches the certificate. The Issuer Statement button at the very bottom of the dialog box area allows you to view any message encoded into the certificate by the issuer.

These statements, often called certification practices statements (CPSs), normally set forth the terms and conditions under which the CA will issue certificates. Most big commercial CAs (like Verisign and GTE) include CPSs in their certificates, and they can make interesting reading if you don't mind wading through lots of legalese.

FIGURE 14.17 The General tab gives you a plain-language explanation of how this certificate can be used.

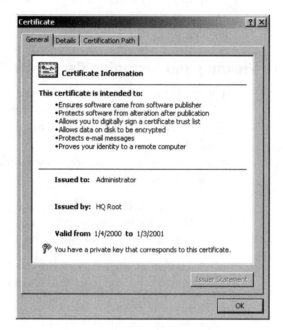

The Details Tab

The Details tab contains the meat of the certificate. Since each certificate attribute is a combination of an attribute name and a value, the centerpiece of this tab is a list of the attribute names and values. You can view the full contents of any field by selecting it; in Figure 14.18 you can see the full canonical name of the CA that issued the certificate.

FIGURE 14.18 The Details tab shows you the certificate's innards.

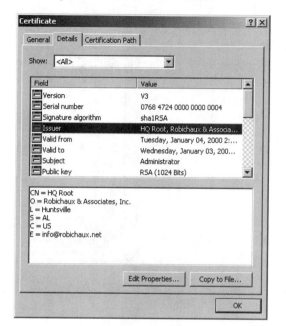

You can use the Show pull-down menu to control which attributes are displayed. By default, all of them are shown, but you can limit the display by asking to see only required extensions, all extensions, or old-style X.509 version 1 attributes.

The Certification Path Tab

Every certificate will be part of some kind of certificate hierarchy, even if it's a self-signed root certificate. It's often useful to view the full hierarchy for a certificate so you can see its exact provenance—much like you'd want to see the pedigree on an allegedly purebred puppy before taking it home. The Certification Path tab shows you the complete ancestry of the selected certificate. The tab does something else, too: It warns you when one, or possibly more, of the ancestors of the current certificate isn't trusted. If you look closely at Figure 14.19, you can see that it's displaying the certification path for a CA root certificate that isn't trusted; the Certificate Status field at the bottom of the tab explains exactly what's going on.

FIGURE 14.19 The Certification Path tab shows you the full hierarchy path for this certificate.

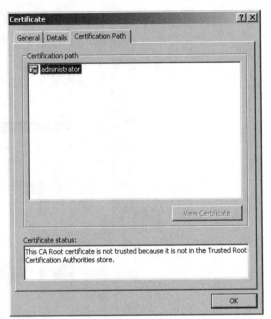

When you select a CA that's above you in the hierarchy, the View Certificate button in the dialog box becomes active. Clicking it displays a separate Certificate Information dialog box for the selected certificate.

Changing Certificate Purposes

If you use the Properties command on a certificate, you'll see a dialog box very similar to the one in Figure 14.20. By choosing the appropriate radio button, you can change what specific tasks this certificate can be used for:

- The Enable All Purposes For This Certificate button is set by default. When it's on, the certificate can be used for any purpose that's allowed by its issuer. That restriction exists because the issuer has control over which purpose flags are encoded into the certificate, so it's not possible for an end user to use a certificate for any purpose not provided for by the issuer.

- The Disable All Purposes For This Certificate button essentially shuts off the certificate, preventing its use for anything at all, without revoking or deleting it. This is a useful way to temporarily disable a certificate.

- The Enable Only The Following Purposes check box, in conjunction with the list box below it, allows you to mix and match only the purposes for which you want the certificate to be used. The note above the list box is telling you that the listed purposes will be drawn from the purpose flags encoded into the certificate.

FIGURE 14.20 The certificate's Properties dialog box allows you to edit the list of purposes for which it can be used.

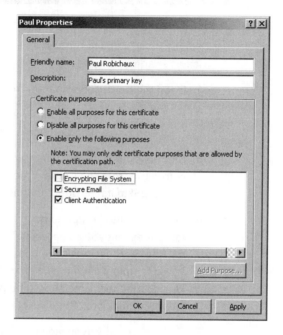

Requesting New Certificates

Requesting a certificate is simple, since you normally request one only for yourself (unless you're an enrollment agent, which is outside the scope of this book). When you right-click the Personal folder, or its Certificates subfolder, you'll notice that the All Tasks submenu has an additional command: Request New Certificate. When you choose that particular command, you're actually starting the Certificate Request wizard, which you complete by doing the following exercise.

Microsoft ✓ *Exam* *Objective*

Create certificates.

EXERCISE 14.4

Requesting a Certificate

Follow these steps to request a new certificate from within the Certificates snap-in:

1. Open the Certificates snap-in from an MMC console session.

2. Right-click the Personal folder and choose All Tasks ➢ Request New Certificate. The Certificate Request wizard will appear.

3. Right-click the CA you want to manage, then select the Properties command from the Context menu. The Properties dialog will appear. Skip its introductory page by clicking the Next button.

4. The Certificate Template page appears, listing all of the available templates that you can access. The contents of this list will depend on what permissions have been set for templates in your domain. Pick a template from the list. If you want to specify that the private key for this certificate should be protected, click the Advanced Options check box. Click the Next button when you're done.

5. If you checked Advanced Options in the Certificate Templates page, the next thing you'll see is the Cryptographic Service Provider page, which lists all of the available CSPs. If you want to use a particular CSP to request this certificate, choose it from the list. More likely, you'll want to check the Enable Strong Private Key Protection check box, which forces the OS to alert you any time an application attempts to use your private key. Click Next once you've made the appropriate changes.

6. If you checked Advanced Options, the next page you'll see allows you to choose the CA and computer to which your request will be sent. You can change them if you like; click Next when you're done.

7. The Certificate Friendly Name and Description page lets you supply a friendly, human-readable name and description for the certificate. These data won't be encoded into the certificate, but they will be stored with it so you can edit them later if necessary.

8. The Wizard Summary dialog box appears. Click Finish to send the request to your CA.

What happens next depends on your CA. If it's set to automatically process requests, then you'll (almost) immediately get either an error dialog box indicating that the request failed for some reason or a dialog box offering to automatically install the certificate in the store for you. If you're using a stand-alone CA that's set to mark requests as pending, you'll have to come back later and check the status of the request.

Using the Web Enrollment Agent

If you chose to install the web enrollment component of the CA, your CA can also issue certificates to web clients via a web-based interface—assuming, of course, that your clients are all using Internet Explorer for Windows. By default, the CA pages are at `http://ca-name/certsrv/`, where `ca-name` is the name of the CA in question. When you load that page, you see a welcome page that gives you three choices:

- The Retrieve The CA Certificate Or Certificate Revocation List button takes you to a set of pages from which you can download the current CRL, the CA's certificate, or the CA's entire certification chain.

- The Request A Certificate button leads you through a series of pages very similar to the ones in the snap-in's certificate wizard. One interesting difference is that you can use the Web interface to feed the CA a PKCS#10-format certificate request generated by another application; you can also take a private key that's already on a smartcard and request a certificate using that key pair.

- The Check On A Pending Certificate button looks up any pending requests and tells you whether they've been approved or not.

EXERCISE 14.5

Issuing Certificates

Follow these steps to issue a test certificate:

1. Install the CA and Web components, using the instructions in Exercise 14.1.

2. Open a Web browser and load the CA enrollment page (http://*yourServerName*/certsrv). If you're using Windows 2000, the browser will identify you to the CA. If not, you'll have to log on to the domain; the browser will prompt for credentials.

3. When the Microsoft Certificate Services page appears, select the Request A Certificate radio button, then click the Next button.

4. In the Choose Request Type page, select the User Certificate Request radio button, then click the Next button.

5. A summary page will appear telling you that the CA has all the information it needs. Click the Submit button to submit your request.

6. If you have automatic certificate approval turned on, you'll see a page titled Certificate Issued with a link reading Install This Certificate. Click it and your new certificate will be downloaded and installed; if your CA requires approval, you'll have to go back and manually approve the request.

Rekeying an Existing Certificate

If you need to, you can request that your existing certificate be reissued, either with the same key or a new one. You might want to do this if you lose the private key, but not if you suspect it's been compromised (in that case, the right thing to do is to revoke the old certificate). If you want to rekey your existing certificate, do so by right-clicking the target certificate and choosing either the All Tasks ➤ Request Certificate with New Key... command or the All Tasks ➤ Request Certificate with Same Key... command. Whichever one you pick will take you through the Certificate Request wizard again; the difference is that internally the wizard remembers that you want to change the key pair bound to the certificate, not issue an entirely new one.

Renewing a Certificate

Just as when you rekey a certificate, you can renew a certificate two ways—by keeping the existing key pair or by requesting a new one. When you rekey, the certificate attributes stay the same, but the key pair may change. When you renew, some certificate attributes change. Microsoft includes a Certificate Renewal wizard that you can get to by right-clicking a certificate and using the All Tasks ➢ Renew Certificate with Same Key… and All Tasks ➢ Renew Certificate with New Key… commands. In either case, the wizard starts off by asking you to choose whether you want to use your CA's default settings or buck the trend by setting your own. While you might think the dialog box's text about "settings" and "values" applies to the expiration interval, it doesn't—it's really just a pair of radio buttons that act like the Advanced Options check box in the Certificate Request wizard. If you choose the No, I Want To Provide My Own Settings radio button, you'll get to pick a CSP and a CA, just like you do when Advanced Options is checked.

Importing, Exporting, and Finding Certificates

Your certificates can be added to your store when you request them, but it's frequently desirable to move certificates in and out of your own personal store. For example, let's say one of your users needs to exchange encrypted e-mail with a business partner. Neither you nor the business partner wants to cross-certify your CAs, so the easiest way to make the communications happen is to have your user export their certificate and send it to the other party, and vice versa.

Importing a Certificate

Importing certificates is the best way to move your certificates from some other computer or program into the Windows 2000 PKI. For example, if you have a Verisign certificate that you've been using with Netscape Navigator on your home PC, you can export it and then import it onto your laptop so you can use it with Internet Explorer.

The Certificates snap-in can import certificates in several different formats. In general, the hardest part of using the Import Certificate wizard is remembering where on the disk you put the file—the wizard takes care of all the details for you. To start the wizard, right-click a Certificate Storage folder and choose the All Tasks ➢ Import command from the Context menu. When the wizard starts, you'll need to do the following steps:

1. Skip the introductory page by clicking its Next button.

2. Provide the full path and file name of the certificate file that you want to import, then click the Next button. You can import certificates in three formats:

    - PKCS#12 (PFX or P12) files are used to store certificates with their associated private keys. Outlook, Outlook Express, and Netscape's tools all produce PKCS#12 files when you export a certificate, as do many third-party PKI components.

    - PKCS#7 (P7B, P7C, or CRT) files are used to store certificates without keys. A PKCS#7 file can contain an entire certificate chain (including CA certificates) or just a certificate—the application that creates the file gets to decide what goes in it. Almost every PKI component that runs on Windows can produce PKCS#7 files.

    - Microsoft's own SST format, which is sparsely used.

3. The next wizard page allows you to choose the store in which you want to put the certificate. You have two choices:

    - Choose the Automatically Select The Certificate Store Based On The Type Of Certificate radio button to let the snap-in determine the proper store for the certificate based on its type, issuer, and owner information. This is probably the easiest choice for ordinary use, especially since PKCS#12 and PKCS#7 files can contain multiple certificates.

    - Choose the Place All Certificates In The Following Store radio button, and then use the Browse... button to locate the store you want to use. If you're sure where the certificate goes, this is the better choice (in fact, the snap-in sets this as the default choice if you select a certificate folder before you use the Import command).

    Once you've chosen the destination for the certificate, click the Next button.

4. The wizard displays a summary page. Click Finish to actually import the certificate. You'll get a dialog box indicating whether the import attempt succeeded or not.

Exporting Your Certificates

You may find it necessary to export a certificate from your store so that you can import it someplace else. In a welcome display of flexibility, the Certificates snap-in can export certificates and private keys in a wide variety of formats. To export a certificate, you right-click it and use the All Tasks ➤ Export... command to fire up the Certificate Export wizard. After dismissing the obligatory wizard introduction page, here's how the process works:

1. If you're exporting a certificate for which you have a corresponding private key, you'll see a page asking you whether you want to export the private key or just the certificate. If you created your certificate with the Enable Strong Private Key Protection check box set, the Yes, Export The Private Key radio button will be grayed out since you can't export protected private keys.

2. Next, the Export File Format page appears so that you can choose the format for the exported certificate. If you're only exporting a certificate, your choices are:

    -   Plain binary X.509 format (labeled as "DER encoded binary X.509 [.CER]"). This format is just a bunch of binary data, so it's well suited for copying around on the network, onto removable disks, and so on. Most programs can accept CER files in this format, so this is a pretty portable choice.

    -   X.509 format, encoded using the base-64 encoding system. Base-64 encoding is used for moving binary data around in e-mail messages; in addition, some PKI components expect to see base-64 certificates only.

    -   PKCS#7 binary format (P7B). This is the format used by most e-mail security tools, and it can contain many certificates in a single file—something that the CER files can't do. The Include All Certificates In The Certification Chain, If Possible check box causes the exporter to include as many of the intermediate and root CA certificates as possible in the output file, which makes it possible to deliver a complete end-to-end certificate chain to someone in a P7B file.

    If you're exporting a certificate with a private key, you get only one choice—PKCS#12 format (in the form of a PFX file)—because the PKCS#12 standard defines a secure way to encrypt a private key and store it along with the certificate. When you use PKCS#12 format, there are three check boxes you can use to control what else goes in the PFX file:

    -   The Include All Certificates In The Certification Path If Possible option puts as much of the certificate chain as possible in the PFX file.

- The Enable Strong Protection option turns on strong protection for the exported private key. A protected private key can't be exported, and the operating system will notify you whenever an application requests access to the key. This only works if you have Windows NT 4.0 SP4 or later, or Windows 2000, both with Internet Explorer 5.0 or later.

- The Delete The Private Key If The Export Is Successful option removes the private key from your local store. Use this option when you want to permanently move a key pair someplace else while leaving the certificate in place for future use.

3. If you're exporting a PFX file, you'll be prompted to enter and confirm a password.

4. Check the confirmation page to double-check what the wizard is about to do, and then click the Finish button when you're done. The certificate will be exported, and you'll receive notice of the operation's success or failure.

Removing EFS Recovery Keys

Earlier in the chapter, you learned about key recovery and how EFS uses it to protect you from losing data if someone encrypts data but then isn't around to decrypt it. Given the need to guarantee recovery, you might well wonder why there's a section on removing EFS recovery keys in this chapter. The answer, of course, is that doing so is an exam objective—but why? Microsoft decided that the best way to restrict access to EFS is to turn it off altogether when there are no recovery agents defined.

Microsoft ✓ *Exam Objective*   **Remove the Encrypting File System (EFS) recovery keys.**

By default, the administrator is designated as the recovery agent for a computer the first time they log on to that particular machine. You are free to tweak recovery settings by designating additional recovery agents and modifying the applicable GPOs to regulate who can initiate recovery. For the Windows 2000 network infrastructure exam, the important trick to know is that deleting all of the EFS recovery keys will turn off EFS in that scope. For example, removing all of the EFS recovery keys on a local machine will turn off recovery on that local machine, but it won't affect any recovery policies imposed by higher-level GPOs.

If you want to turn off EFS, simply follow the steps outlined in Exercise 14.6.

EXERCISE 14.6

Removing the EFS Recovery Keys

To remove the EFS recovery keys, follow these steps:

1. Open an MMC window and add the Group Policy snap-in if it's not already present. (To disable EFS on the local machine, add a GPO for the local computer; to disable it for a domain or other unit, use the appropriate GPO.)

2. Open the Public Key Policies node (it's under Computer Configuration ➢ Security Settings in the GPO).

3. Right-click the Encrypted Data Recovery Agents folder and choose the Delete Policy command. When asked to confirm the command, click the Yes button.

Summary

In this chapter, you learned:

- What a certificate authority is, what it does, and how Microsoft's CA works

- How to install and configure the certificate server included with Windows 2000

- How to issue and revoke certificates

Key Terms

Before you take the exam, be sure you're familiar with the following terms:

Authority Information Access point (AIA)

Certificate authority (CA)

Certificate hierarchy

Certificate revocation list (CRL)

Certificate store

Certificate trust list (CTL)

CRL distribution point (CDP)

Digital certificates

Encryption

Exit module

Policy module

Private key

Public key

Public-key encryption

Recovery agent

Recovery key

Root certificate authority

Secret-key encryption

Signing

Review Questions

1. Janelle suffered a disk failure and lost her private key. She wants to continue to use her existing certificate. This requires which of the following?

   A. Her certificate must be revoked.

   B. Her certificate must be reissued.

   C. Her certificate must be rekeyed.

   D. Her certificate must be renewed.

2. End users can request new certificates in which of the following ways? (Choose two.)

   A. Completing the web enrollment page (if it's installed)

   B. Using the Certification Authority snap-in

   C. Using the Certificates snap-in on a domain controller

   D. Using the Certificates snap-in on their local machines

3. The certificate templates supplied with Windows 2000 _____.

   A. May not be edited

   B. May be edited with the tools in the Windows 2000 Resource Kit

   C. May be edited with the Certificates snap-in

   D. May be edited with the Certification Authority snap-in

4. When can you change the CSPs used by a CA?

   A. Only during installation

   B. After installation, by using the Sites and Services snap-in

   C. For each certificate request

   D. Never

5. Dave wants to restrict who can request certificates for users. What does he need to do to accomplish this?

   A. He needs to remove the Enroll permission from the Authenticated Users group.

   B. He needs to remove the Enroll permission from the Administrators group.

   C. He needs to remove the Issue Certificate permission from the Administrators group.

   D. He needs to remove the Enroll and Manage permissions from any groups he doesn't want to be able to issue certificates.

6. Thomas installed a CA on a Windows 2000 member server. He now wants to join an Active Directory domain. What effect will this have on the CA installation?

   A. It will have no effect.

   B. The CA will need to be removed and reinstalled.

   C. The CA will need to have its certificate reissued.

   D. The parent CA will need to be reinstalled.

7. Automatic enrollment allows you to do which of the following?

   A. Automatically create certificates for all user accounts in a domain

   B. Automatically issue certificates to users as their accounts are added

   C. Automatically issue certificates to computers as they join an Active Directory domain

   D. Automatically issue certificates for any object that doesn't already have one

8. Ann has set up a stand-alone subordinate CA for her users. Users started requesting certificates as soon as the CA was activated, but no user has received a certificate. What is the most likely problem?

    A. The CA is misconfigured.

    B. User requests have been going to the wrong CA.

    C. The certificates have been issued and published, but not yet returned to the users.

    D. The requests are marked as pending, so they're sitting in a queue for approval.

9. Adding a CA to the CTL means which of the following?

    A. You explicitly trust certificates issued by that CA.

    B. You explicitly trust only that CA.

    C. You explicitly do not trust that CA.

    D. You explicitly do not trust certificates issued by that CA.

10. Dolan revoked a user's certificate because she left the company. She came back. What's the best way to reintegrate the user into Dolan's PKI?

    A. Issue her a new certificate

    B. Rekey her old certificate

    C. Manually remove her old certificate from the CRL

    D. Regenerate a new CRL

11. Conrad needs to restrict certain user accounts so that they can request only User certificates. To do this, he must use the _____ snap-in to _____.

    A. Active Directory Sites and Services; deny the users Enroll permission on everything except the User template

    B. Active Directory Users and Computers; deny the users Enroll permission on everything except the User template

    C. Certificates; remove the users' certificates

    D. Certification Authority; turn off enrollment for those users

12. The exit module settings control which of the following?

    A. Where newly issued certificates are published

    B. Where CRLs are published

    C. Where newly issued certificates are stored

    D. How often CRLs are generated

13. A stand-alone CA cannot issue certificates for which of the following purposes?

    A. EFS recovery

    B. Smartcard logon

    C. E-mail signatures

    D. E-mail encryption

14. What is the primary difference between a root CA and a subordinate CA?

    A. The root usually issues certificates only to subordinate CAs; the subordinates usually issue certificates to users and computers.

    B. The root must be an enterprise CA; the subordinate must be a stand-alone.

    C. The root must be part of an Active Directory domain; the subordinates may or may not be.

    D. The root must be physically secure, while the subordinates don't have to be.

15. On a stand-alone CA, you can control whether certificate requests are automatically approved or marked as pending. How do you do this?

    A. By modifying the setting on the Default Actions tab of the policy module's Configuration dialog box

    B. By modifying the setting in the Policy Module Properties dialog box

    C. By modifying the setting on the Default Actions tab of the exit module's Configuration dialog box

    D. By switching the CA type from stand-alone to enterprise

16. Which of the following is *not* a true statement about enterprise certificate authorities?

   A. They require Active Directory.

   B. They can use certificate types and templates.

   C. They always reject or approve certificate requests.

   D. They can mark certificate requests as pending for later action.

17. Encryption provides _____.

   A. Confidentiality only

   B. Confidentiality and authentication

   C. Authentication only

18. To support recovery, EFS must do which of the following?

   A. Leave the secret key unprotected

   B. Encrypt the secret key to the owner only

   C. Encrypt the secret key to both the owner and all recovery agents

   D. Encrypt the secret key to the recovery agents only

19. Which snap-in do you use to manage EFS capability?

   A. The Group Policy snap-in

   B. The EFS snap-in

   C. The Certificates snap-in

   D. The Certificate Authorities snap-in

20. To remove EFS capability, you must do which of the following?

   A. Disable the Administrator certificate

   B. Revoke the Administrator certificate

   C. Remove the Administrator as a member of the Recovery Agents group

   D. Delete the Encrypted Data Recovery Agents folder from the appropriate group policy object

Answers to Review Questions

1. C. Rekeying causes the CA to re-sign the existing certificate after its key material has been regenerated.

2. A, D. End users shouldn't have permission to log on to a DC or to use the CA snap-in.

3. A. You can't edit the templates, though you can control access to them.

4. A. When you install the CA, you can select a set of CSPs to use.

5. D. Enroll permission allows a user to issue certificates. By default, the Authenticated Users group has this permission, as do all of the Administrators groups. To restrict access, you have to remove this permission from all groups, and then grant it only to the users you want to have it.

6. B. You can't rename a computer or join or leave a domain once the CA is installed.

7. C. Automatic enrollment causes the group policy mechanism to issue certificates to computers as they're added to a domain. There's no corresponding function for users.

8. D. Stand-alone CAs can mark requests as "pending," in which case the requests will be enqueued until the administrator approves or rejects them.

9. A. Adding a CA to the CTL essentially brings the foreign CA "inside" your own CA network; your clients will trust certificates issued by the foreign CA as though one of your own CAs had issued them.

10. A. Once the certificate is revoked, it can't be unrevoked, even by removing its serial number from the CRL. The only way to get the user back into the PKI is to issue her a new certificate.

11. A. To restrict which templates a user can use, set permissions for those users in the Active Directory Sites and Services snap-in.

12. A. The exit module settings allow you to specify where newly issued certificates will be published: either in AD or in the file system.

13. B. Only an enterprise CA may issue a certificate for use with smart-card logon.

14. A. Root and stand-alone CAs are very similar in most respects. The primary difference is that the root CA normally issues certificates only to subordinate CAs, not to users or computers.

15. A. You can switch a stand-alone CA between these two modes by altering the settings on the Default Actions tab, which you get to from the policy module's Properties dialog box by pressing the Configure button.

16. D. An enterprise CA must always approve or reject a request, based on the requestor's security group membership.

17. A. Encryption provides confidentiality only; you need to use signing (with or without encryption) if you want authentication.

18. C. The secret key unique to each EFS item has to be encrypted to the owner so she can read it. To support recovery, it must also be encrypted to each recovery agent.

19. A. The Group Policy snap-in controls who's in the data recovery agents group, which controls who can, and cannot, act as a recovery agent.

20. D. To turn off EFS altogether, you have to remove the Encrypted Data Recovery Agents folder, which removes all recovery agents.

Appendix A

Practice Exam

1. What is the standard framework used for describing and comparing different network systems?

   A. The OSI reference model

   B. A network protocol

   C. TCP/IP

   D. A network service

2. Which of the following services is provided as part of the application layer of the OSI reference model? Choose all that apply.

   A. Routing

   B. Web server

   C. File transfer

   D. Guaranteed data delivery

3. Which of the following protocols can be routed? Choose all that apply.

   A. IP

   B. IPX

   C. AppleTalk

   D. NetBEUI

4. What is the function of the presentation layer of the OSI reference model?

   A. Establishes communication between machines

   B. Provides network protocols

   C. Translates data from the network to the application

   D. Provides an interface to the user

5. Which protocol would you use to automatically assign IP addresses to clients?

   A. DNS

   B. WINS

   C. TCP/IP

   D. DHCP

6. Which of the following are required when administering Active Directory? Choose all that apply.

   A. DNS

   B. WINS

   C. TCP/IP

   D. DHCP

7. A lease request is a component of which of the following protocols?

   A. DNS

   B. WINS

   C. TCP/IP

   D. DHCP

8. What specifies which server is authoritative for a specific domain?

   A. An SOV record

   B. An SOS record

   C. An SRV record

   D. An SOA record

9. When is a cost, or metric, used?

   A. During authentication

   B. When routing

   C. When establishing a dial-up connection

   D. When establishing a VPN connection

10. OSPF routers use a link state map in place of what?

   A. A route list

   B. A routing table

   C. A network neighborhood

   D. A route database

11. Which of the following is *not* a PPP authentication method?

   A. NTLM

   B. PAP

   C. MS-CHAP

   D. CHAP

12. Which of the following is updated when the routing topology changes?

   A. Static routes

   B. Dead routes

   C. Dynamic routes

   D. Active routes

13. What is *nslookup* used for?

   A. To verify that basic network connectivity exists between two machines

   B. To see local IP addresses and subnet masks

   C. To query a WINS server for address information

   D. To query a DNS server for address information

14. What is a default gateway address used for?

   A. To send packets to another machine on the same subnet

   B. To route packets outside of a local network

   C. To dynamically obtain an IP address from a DHCP server

   D. To resolve DNS name queries

15. What is the *ping* tool used for?

   A. To verify that basic network connectivity exists between two machines

   B. To see local IP addresses and subnet masks

   C. To query a WINS server for address information

   D. To query a DNS server for address information

16. Which of the following statements is true if you have multiple network adapters in one computer?

   A. You cannot use DHCP.

   B. If you change any settings for one adapter, you must change the settings for all of the adapters.

   C. You must specify the protocols and addresses for each of the adapters individually.

   D. Every installed protocol is bound to each of the adapters.

17. Which of the following is a way to assign multiple logical subnet addresses to DHCP clients on a single physical network?

   A. Subscope

   B. Superscope

   C. Scope

   D. Multiscope

18. You want to deactivate a scope without disrupting the current leases contained in that scope. What should you do?

   A. Deactivate the scope without taking any further action.

   B. It cannot be done.

   C. Assign a new superscope.

   D. Assign a new multicast scope.

19. How many superscopes can a single DHCP server support?

    A. 1

    B. 10

    C. 100

    D. 1000

20. Which of the following steps must you take when using a DHCP scope? Choose all that apply.

    A. Apply

    B. Create

    C. Authorize

    D. Activate

21. What are primary and secondary zones used for? Choose all that apply.

    A. Minimizing total network impact

    B. Minimizing network traffic when zones are updated

    C. Fault tolerance

    D. Storing copies of the zone files on multiple servers

22. What will happen if DNS root server hints are not configured or updated?

    A. The server will be able to answer simple queries, but not recursive queries.

    B. The server will be able to answer recursive queries, but not simple queries.

    C. The server will not be able to answer simple or recursive queries.

    D. The server will not be able to support dynamic updates.

23. What will happen if the name server database contains a large number of stale records? Choose all that apply.

 A. Scavenging will not be as effective.

 B. Space will be wasted.

 C. A server might use a stale resource record to answer a query.

 D. DNS name resolution will slow down.

24. When can you configure pull replication to run? Choose all that apply.

 A. At service startup

 B. When triggered

 C. At service shutdown

 D. At intervals

25. At what level must you maintain a WINS server?

 A. Network

 B. Domain

 C. Subnet

 D. Subdomain

26. Where can you configure how often the WINS server replicates its database?

 A. General tab of the Replication Partner Properties dialog box

 B. Pull Partners tab of the Replication Partner Properties dialog box

 C. Push Partners tab of the Replication Partner Properties dialog box

 D. Advanced tab of the Replication Partner Properties dialog box

27. What is the best way to fix a corrupt WINS database?

 A. Delete the database and rebuild it from the replication partners

 B. Run a consistency check on the database

 C. Reinstall the WINS service

 D. Reboot all of the WINS clients

28. What is a linked collection of individual networks commonly known as?

   A. Intranetwork

   B. Intranet

   C. Internet

   D. Internetwork

29. Which of the following is manually generated and stays in the routing table until removed?

   A. Dynamic route

   B. Static route

   C. OSPF route

   D. Default route

30. Which of the following modes can a RIP router operate in? Choose all that apply.

   A. Periodic update

   B. Triggered update

   C. Manual-static

   D. Auto-static

31. What is a demand-dial interface used for?

   A. Connecting to a router via a modem

   B. Connecting remote and LAN routers

   C. Configuring a router from a touch-tone phone

   D. Configuring a router from a serial interface

32. What is the DHCP relay agent used for?

   A. Provides DHCP servers with RRAS functionality

   B. Provides RRAS servers with DHCP functionality

   C. Allows DHCP broadcasts to bridge routers

   D. Stores a DHCP scope in a router

33. Which of the following authentication method(s) supports certificates?

  A. EAP with the EAP-TLS type

  B. EAP with any EAP type

  C. MS-CHAP v2

  D. MS-CHAP v3

34. Which of the following can be configured using a remote access policy? Choose all that apply.

  A. Encryption requirements

  B. The users that have dial-in access

  C. CHAP

  D. DHCP relay agent

35. What must you do in order to enable the use of CHAP with RRAS? Choose all that apply.

  A. Enable CHAP as a supported authentication protocol

  B. Modify the group policy for all users who need to use CHAP

  C. Reset or change the password of all users who need to use CHAP

  D. Enable reversible password encryption for all users

36. Which of the following VPN-related protocols are included with Windows 2000? Choose all that apply.

  A. PPLP

  B. GTP

  C. L2TP

  D. PPTP

37. What are the main purposes of virtual private networking? Choose all that apply.

    A. Provides network connections to computers that do not have any network hardware

    B. Allows remote users to access the corporate LAN

    C. Links networks at different physical locations

    D. Provides dial-in access to the network

38. Which of the following must be available on a VPN server? Choose all that apply.

    A. Public network interface

    B. Private network interface

    C. DHCP

    D. IPSec

39. Which of the following does PPTP support? Choose all that apply.

    A. Machine authentication

    B. Complete end-to-end encryption

    C. User authentication

    D. Data link encryption

40. Which of the following authentication methods can be used with IPSec? Choose all that apply.

    A. NTLM authentication

    B. Kerberos

    C. Certificates

    D. Pre-shared keys

41. How many IP filter lists can you assign to a single policy rule?

    A. 1

    B. 2

    C. 3

    D. Any number

42. Which tool can you use to verify whether IPSec is in use?

    A. *Ipsecmon*

    B. *Tracert*

    C. The IP Security Properties dialog box

    D. *Ipconfig*

43. On which of the following can a filter specify a match? Choose all that apply.

    A. Source address

    B. Destination address

    C. Source port

    D. Destination port

44. Which settings have priority when assigning IP addresses?

    A. DHCP-assigned settings

    B. Manually assigned settings

    C. DHCP or manual settings; whichever was assigned first

    D. Neither; the client will not receive an IP address

45. Which of the following commands releases an existing DHCP lease?

    A. *Ping /release*

    B. *Ipconfig /end*

    C. *Ipconfig /release*

    D. *Ipconfig /stop*

46. Which of the following allows a network of computers to share a single computer's Internet connection?

  A. ICS

  B. ICCS

  C. DNS

  D. IC

47. Which operating systems can run the NAT component? Choose all that apply.

  A. Windows 2000 Professional

  B. Windows 2000 Server

  C. Windows 2000 Advanced Server

  D. Windows 2000 Datacenter Server

48. How many NAT interfaces should you have on each adapter?

  A. 1

  B. 2

  C. 3

  D. One for each network

49. Which of the following cannot be used to exchange data with Internet addresses?

  A. Public address

  B. Private address

  C. Masked addresses

  D. IP address

50. Which of the following is a guaranteed unique hardware address for an Ethernet device?

  A. DNS name

  B. TCP/IP address

  C. MAC address

  D. IP address

Answers to Practice Exam

1. A. The OSI reference model is a framework used for describing and comparing different network systems. See Chapter 1 for more information.

2. B, C. A Web server and file-transfer functions are handled at the application layer of the OSI reference model. See Chapter 1 for more information.

3. A, B, C. The IP portion of TCP/IP and the IPX portion of IPX/SPX protocols are routable. AppleTalk is routable as well. NetBEUI is not a routable protocol. See Chapter 1 for more information.

4. C. The presentation layer of the OSI reference model translates data from the network to the application that is requesting the data. See Chapter 1 for more information.

5. D. DHCP dynamically assigns IP addresses to clients. See Chapter 2 for more information.

6. A, C. Active Directory requires DNS and TCP/IP. See Chapter 2 for more information.

7. D. The DHCP negotiation process consists of a lease request, a lease offer, and a lease acknowledgment. See Chapter 2 for more information.

8. D. A Start of Authority (SOA) record specifies which server is author-itative for a particular domain. See Chapter 2 for more information.

9. B. The cost, or metric, is used by the router to determine the best route. See Chapter 3 for more information.

10. B. OSPF uses the more efficient link state map instead of a traditional router's routing table. See Chapter 3 for more information.

11. A. NTLM is not a PPP authentication method. See Chapter 3 for more information.

12. C. Dynamic routes discover the best route, even after the routing topology changes. See Chapter 3 for more information.

13. D. Windows 2000 provides the *nslookup* tool to query DNS servers. See Chapter 4 for more information.

14. B. You need to specify a default gateway if you want the computer to be able to send packets to a gateway for routing. See Chapter 4 for more information.

15. A. The *ping* tool is used to verify basic connectivity by sending a packet to the specified address and waiting for a reply. See Chapter 4 for more information.

16. C. Each network adapter is treated individually and must use its own IP address and network protocols. Each adapter can use a static IP address or receive one dynamically from a DHCP server. See Chapter 4 for more information.

17. B. A superscope is a way to assign a consistent group of options to multiple scopes. See Chapter 5 for more information.

18. A. Deactivating a scope has no effect on the client until it needs to renew the lease. To renew a lease, the client will need to find another server. See Chapter 5 for more information.

19. A. A server supports only one superscope. See Chapter 5 for more information.

20. B, C, D. You need to create, authorize, and activate a scope before it can be used. See Chapter 5 for more information.

21. C, D. By configuring primary and secondary zones, multiple servers will have copies of the zone files. This improves fault tolerance. See Chapter 6 for more information.

22. A. When a DNS server processes a recursive query and a query cannot be resolved from local zone files, the query must be escalated to a root DNS server. Each standards-based implementation of DNS includes a cache file (or root server hints) that contains entries for root servers of the Internet domains. See Chapter 6 for more information.

23. B, C, D. Scavenging will help eliminate any stale records. See Chapter 6 for more information.

24. A, B, D. The WINS service allows you to trigger pull replication at service startup, when a trigger arrives, and at specified intervals. See Chapter 7 for more information.

25. C. Each subnet must have its own WINS server in order to resolve names. See Chapter 7 for more information.

26. C. Push partners send change notifications, so this property is set in the Push Partners tab. See Chapter 7 for more information.

27. A. The easiest way to fix a corrupt WINS database is to delete the database and let the replication partners fill in the data for you. See Chapter 7 for more information.

28. D. The term *internetwork* refers to a group of networks linked in some way. The Internet is the best-known internetwork, but there are many others. See Chapter 8 for more information.

29. B. Static routes stay in the routing table until you remove them; they're not dynamic in any way. See Chapter 8 for more information.

30. A, D. RIP routers support both periodic (or timed) updates and a mode in which updated entries are sent around as they arrive (auto-static). See Chapter 8 for more information.

31. B. Demand-dial interfaces are used to connect routers at remote sites to the corporate LAN. See Chapter 8 for more information.

32. C. The DHCP relay agent allows DHCP broadcasts to bridge routers. See Chapter 9 for more information.

33. A. EAP requires you to use the EAP-TLS type for any kind of certificate-based authentication. EAP-TLS is the only authentication method that supports certificates. See Chapter 9 for more information.

34. A, B. You can create a policy that allows the specified users to connect, then set its profile to allow or disallow unencrypted calls. See Chapter 9 for more information.

35. A, C, D. CHAP must be enabled before it can be used with RRAS. CHAP requires that passwords be stored with reversible encryption, and each user who wants to use CHAP must reset or change their passwords. See Chapter 9 for more information.

36. C, D. PPTP and L2TP are the two VPN-related protocols included with Windows 2000. See Chapter 10 for more information.

37. B, C. VPNs allow users to access the corporate LAN through public networks such as the Internet, and they can be used to link networks at different physical locations. See Chapter 10 for more information.

38. A, B. The VPN server needs to have access to both the private network and the public network in order to properly support VPN services. See Chapter 10 for more information.

39. C, D. PPTP supports user authentication and data link encryption. See Chapter 10 for more information.

40. B, C, D. Kerberos, certificates, and pre-shared keys can all be used with IPSec. See Chapter 11 for more information.

41. A. You can assign only one filter list to a policy rule, but you can define many rules in a policy. See Chapter 11 for more information.

42. A. *Ipsecmon* is the only tool listed that can be used to monitor IPSec. See Chapter 11 for more information.

43. A, B, C, D. A filter can specify a match based on a source or destination address and a source or destination port. See Chapter 11 for more information.

44. B. Manually configured settings override DHCP settings. See Chapter 12 for more information.

45. C. *Ipconfig /release* releases an existing DHCP lease. See Chapter 12 for more information.

46. A. ICS stands for Internet Connection Sharing. See Chapter 13 for more information.

47. B, C, D. NAT runs on the Windows 2000 Server family. See Chapter 13 for more information.

48. A. NAT depends on having one interface for each of the two adapters (public and private) so it can transfer traffic between them. See Chapter 13 for more information.

49. B. Internet hosts are not allowed to exchange data with addresses that fall in the private range. See Chapter 13 for more information.

50. C. The MAC address is a unique hardware-specific ID that is used at the data link layer. Any Ethernet device will have a MAC address, even if it's not using TCP/IP. See Chapter 1 for more information.

Glossary

A

access control entry (ACE)   An item used by the operating system to determine resource access. Each access control list (ACL) has an associated ACE that lists the permissions that have been granted or denied to the users and groups listed in the ACL.

access control list (ACL)   An item used by the operating system to determine resource access. Each object (such as a folder, network share, or printer) in Windows 2000 has an ACL. The ACL lists the security identifiers (SIDs) contained by objects. Only those identified in the list as having the appropriate permission can activate the services of that object.

access token   An object containing the security identifier (SID) of a running process. A process started by another process inherits the starting process's access token. The access token is checked against each object's access control list (ACL) to determine whether or not appropriate permissions are granted to perform any requested service.

account lockout policy   A Windows 2000 policy used to specify how many invalid logon attempts should be tolerated before a user account is locked out. Account lockout policies are set through account policies.

account policies   Windows 2000 policies used to determine password and logon requirements. Account policies are set through the Microsoft Management Console (MMC) Local Computer Policy snap-in.

ACE   See *access control entry.*

ACL   See *access control list.*

Active Directory   A directory service available with the Windows 2000 Server platform. Active Directory stores information about network resources in a central database and makes this information available to users that have a single user account (called a domain user account or Active Directory user account) on the network.

Active Directory user account   A user account that is stored in the Windows 2000 Server Active Directory's central database. An Active Directory user account provides a user with permissioned access to all network resources. Also called a domain user account.

adapter   Any hardware device that allows communications to occur through physically dissimilar systems. This term usually refers to peripheral cards that are permanently mounted inside computers and provide an interface from the computer's bus to another medium such as a hard disk or a network.

Address pool   The range of IP addresses that the DHCP server can actually assign.

Addressing component   A portion of the Internet Connection Sharing or Network Address Translation services that assigns IP addresses to clients; takes the place of a DHCP server.

Administrator account   A Windows 2000 special account that has the ultimate set of security permissions and can assign any permission to any user or group.

Administrators group   A Windows 2000 built-in group that consists of Administrator accounts.

AH   See *Authentication header*.

AIA   See *Authority information access point*.

alert   A system-monitoring feature that is generated when a specific counter exceeds or falls below a specified value. Through the Performance Logs and Alerts utility, administrators can configure alerts so that a message is sent, a program is run, or a more detailed log file is generated.

Anonymous Logon group   A Windows 2000 special group that includes users who access the computer through anonymous logons. Anonymous logons occur when users gain access through special accounts, such as the IUSR_ computername and TsInternetUser user accounts.

application layer   The seventh (top) layer of the Open Systems Interconnection (OSI) model that interfaces with application programs by providing high-level network services based on lower-level network layers.

Application log   A log that tracks events that are related to applications that are running on the computer. The Application log can be viewed in the Event Viewer utility.

Area   A contiguous group of network resources that contains one or more physical subnets.

Area border router   A special OSPF router that connects adjacent areas.

Area router   An OSPF router that is restricted to routing traffic between machines inside a single area.

audit policy   A Windows 2000 policy that tracks the success or failure of specified security events. Audit policies are set through Local Computer Policy.

Authenticated Users group   A Windows 2000 special group that includes users who access the Windows 2000 operating system through a valid username and password.

authentication   The process required to log on to a computer locally. Authentication requires a valid username and a password that exists in the local accounts database. An access token will be created if the information presented matches the account in the database.

Authentication header (AH)   Used to digitally sign the entire contents of each packet.

Authority information access point (AIA) A list of locations where users can get the CA's certificate and authentication information.

Auto-static update mode   RIP update mode in which the RIP router only broadcasts the contents of its routing table when a peer router asks for it (see also *periodic update mode*).

B

backbone   Connects all OSPF areas allowing any router in the AS (area) to connect to any other AS; this can be accomplished with tunnels.

binding   The process of linking together software components, such as network protocols and network adapters.

Border routing   The passing of packets from one internetwork to another.

C

CA   See *Certificate authority.*

CDP   See *CRL distribution point.*

Certificate authority (CA)   A server that controls the issuance and use of digital certificates for users and computers in some group.

Certificate hierarchy   A "stack" of CAs. Each CA has a "parent" in the hierarchy that has issued the "child" its CA certificate. Eventually, this works up to a root CA, which has no parent.

Certificate revocation list (CRL)   A list of certificates that have been revoked for some reason, such as expiration. Each CA builds and maintains its own CRL.

Certificate store   Certificate storage that holds foreign CA certificates; this allows the clients to trust any certificate in the store without requiring a common root.

Certificate trust list (CTL)   A certificate list that lets PKI administrators tell PKI clients to trust certificates issues by a particular set of CAs. The CTL information is stored in Active Directory.

Certificates   The codes exchanged to allow for encrypted information interchange. Each party has its own certificate identifying (uniquely) the party sending or receiving information.

Challenge Handshake Authentication Protocol (CHAP)   Remote access authentication protocol that uses encrypted challenge and response messages instead of sending passwords and user names in plain text.

CHAP   See *Challenge Handshake Authentication Protocol.*

CIPHER   A command-line utility that can be used to encrypt files on NTFS volumes.

cipher text   Encrypted data. Encryption is the process of translating data into code that is not easily accessible. Once data has been encrypted, a user must have a password or key to decrypt the data. Unencrypted data is known as plain text.

Computer Management   A consolidated tool for performing common Windows 2000 management tasks. The interface is organized into three main areas of management: System Tools, Storage, and Services and Applications.

computer name   A NetBIOS name used to uniquely identify a computer on the network. A computer name can be from 1 to 15 characters in length.

connectionless service   A type of connection service that does not establish a session (path) before transmission. This type of communication is fast, but it is not very reliable.

connection-oriented service   A type of connection service in which a connection (a path) is established and acknowledgments are sent. This type of communication is reliable but has a high overhead.

connection-specific DNS suffix   The DNS suffix is added to resolver requests on a particular connection. Allows the proper lookup of an unqualified name.

Convergence time   The time it takes a change from any RIP router to propagate to all other routers in the internetwork.

counter   A performance-measuring tool used to track specific information regarding a system resource, called a performance object. All Windows 2000 system resources are tracked as performance objects, such as Cache, Memory, Paging File, Process, and Processor. Each performance object has an associated set of counters. Counters are set through the System Monitor utility.

CRC   See *Cyclic Redundancy Check*.

CRL   See *Certificate revocation list*.

CRL distribution point   List of locations where CRLs are published for client or server access.

CTL   See *certificate trust list*.

Cyclic Redundancy Check (CRC)   Helps the network determine whether or not a packet has been damaged in transmission.

D

data encryption   See *encryption*.

data link layer   In the Open Systems Interconnection (OSI) model, the layer that provides the digital interconnection of network devices and the software that directly operates these devices, such as network adapters.

Database verification   Allows you to adjust the interval at which the consistency and integrity of a WINS or DHCP database is verified.

default gateway   A TCP/IP configuration option that specifies the gateway (router's address) that will be used if the destination address is outside of the local network.

Default response rule   IP filtering rule that governs what the IP filtering stack does when no other more explicit filter rule applies.

Default route   The route packets take when there is no explicit route; if a router encounters a packet bound for some remote network whose route cannot be resolved in the routing table, it takes the default route.

Delegated domain   The name of the domain for which you want to delegate authority to another DNS server.

Demand-dial interface   A network interface that routes packets over a connection that's established only when there is traffic to pass over it. These interfaces are usually built with dial-up connections.

Demand-dial routing Allows the use of an impermanent connection, like an analog modem or ISDN, to imitate a dedicated Internet connection.

device driver Software that allows a specific piece of hardware to communicate with the Windows 2000 operating system.

DHCP *See* Dynamic Host Configuration Protocol.

DHCP authorization The process of enabling a DHCP server to lease addresses by registering the server in Active Directory.

DHCP discover message Message broadcast by a DHCP client that's looking for a nearby DHCP server; the discover message contains the hardware MAC address and NetBIOS name of the client, which the server can use to direct the request.

DHCP integration Feature that allows you to pass out addresses to DHCP clients while still maintaining the integrity of your DNS services.

DHCP lease request Request sent by a DHCP client for assignment of an IP address (and related parameters) from a DHCP server.

DHCP relay agent To enable DHCP on a multisegment network, you can use a DHCP relay agent or proxy to forward requests.

DHCP server A server configured to provide DHCP clients with all of their IP configuration information automatically.

DHCPACK An acknowledgment message sent by the DHCP server to the client after the server marks the selected IP address as leased.

DHCPNACK A negative acknowledgment sent by the DHCP server to the client. This generally occurs when the client is attempting to renew a lease for its old IP address after it has been reassigned.

Dialing rules Allow you to tell Dial-Up Networking what country and region you're in so that it knows to add the appropriate long-distance codes, area codes, and calling card numbers when it's dialing.

Dialup group A Windows 2000 special group that includes users who log on to the network from a dial-up connection.

Dial-Up Networking (DUN) A service that allows remote users to dial into the network or the Internet (such as through a telephone or an ISDN connection).

directory replication The process of copying a directory structure from an export computer to an import computer(s). Any time changes are made to the export computer, the import computer(s) is automatically updated with the changes.

Disk Management A Windows 2000 graphical tool for managing disks and volumes.

DNS *See Domain Name Service.*

DNS server A server that uses DNS to resolve domain or host names to IP addresses.

domain   In Microsoft networks, an arrangement of client and server computers referenced by a specific name that shares a single security permissions database. On the Internet, a domain is a named collection of hosts and subdomains, registered with a unique name by the InterNIC.

domain name   The textual identifier of a specific Internet host. Domain names are in the form of server organization type (`www.microsoft.com`) and are resolved to Internet addresses by DNS servers.

domain name server   An Internet host dedicated to the function of translating fully qualified domain names into IP addresses.

Domain Name Service (DNS)   The TCP/IP network service that translates textual Internet network addresses into numerical Internet network addresses.

DUN   See *Dial-Up Networking.*

Dynamic DNS   Allows Windows 2000 clients to update host information in the DNS database files automatically.

Dynamic Host Configuration Protocol (DHCP)   A method of automatically assigning IP addresses to client computers on a network.

Dynamic routing   Can discover its surroundings by finding and communicating with other nearby routers.

E

EAP   See *Extensible Authentication Protocol.*

EAP type   Authentication scheme supported in EAP.

EFS   See *Encrypting File System.*

Encapsulating Security Payload (ESP)
Used to encrypt the entire payload of an IPSec packet, rendering it undecipherable by anyone other than the intended recipient. It provides confidentiality only.

Encapsulation   A process where the client takes a packet with some kind of "forbidden" content, wraps it inside an IP datagram, and sends it to the server.

Encrypting File System (EFS)   The Windows 2000 technology used to store encrypted files on NTFS partitions. Encrypted files add an extra layer of security to the file system.

encryption   The process of translating data into code that is not easily accessible to increase security. Once data has been encrypted, a user must have a password or key to decrypt the data.

End-to-end mode   When you use IPSec to encrypt or authenticate connections between two machines, network traffic is protected before it leaves the originating machine, and it remains secured until the receiving machine gets it and decrypts it.

ESP   See *Encapsulating Security Payload*.

Ethernet   The most popular data link layer standard for local area networking. Ethernet implements the Carrier Sense Multiple Access with Collision Detection (CSMA/CD) method of arbitrating multiple computer access to the same network. This standard supports the use of Ethernet over any type of media, including wireless broadcast. Standard Ethernet operates as 10Mbps. Fast Ethernet operates at 100Mbps.

Event Viewer   A Windows 2000 utility that tracks information about the computer's hardware and software, as well as security events. This information is stored in three log files: the Application log, the Security log, and the System log.

Everyone group   A Windows 2000 special group that includes anyone who could possibly access the computer. The Everyone group includes all of the users (including Guests) who have been defined on the computer.

Exclusion   Any IP addresses within the scope range that you *never* want the DHCP server to automatically assign.

Exit module   Contains the rules that specify where and how a newly issued certificate is published.

Extensible Authentication Protocol   A protocol that allows third parties to write modules that implement new authentication methods and retrofit them to fielded servers.

Extinction   In reference to WINS, the Extinction interval (four days by default) controls how long a released WINS record will remain marked as "released" before it's marked as "extinct." The extinction timeout, set to six days by default, controls how long an extinct record may remain in the database before it's removed.

F

Failure Audit event   An Event Viewer event that indicates the occurrence of an event that has been audited for failure, such a failed logon when someone presents an invalid username and/or password.

fault tolerance   Any method that prevents system failure by tolerating single faults, usually accomplished through hardware redundancy.

File Transfer Protocol (FTP)   A simple Internet protocol that transfers complete files from an FTP server to a client running the FTP client. FTP provides a simple, no-overhead method of transferring files between computers but cannot perform browsing functions. Users must know the URL of the FTP server to which they wish to attach.

Filter action   Dictates which action should be taken when a security filter match occurs.

Filter list   Groups of individual filters that allow you to easily build rules that enforce complicated behavior, then distribute those rules throughout your network as necessary.

Forward lookup zone   A name-to-address database that helps computers translate DNS names into IP addresses and provides information about available resources.

frame A data structure that network hardware devices use to transmit data between computers. Frames consist of the addresses of the sending and receiving computers, size information, and a checksum. Frames are envelopes around packets of data that allow the packets to be addressed to specific computers on a shared media network.

frame type An option that specifies how data is packaged for transmission over the network. This option must be configured to run the NWLink IPX/SPX/NetBIOS Compatible Transport protocol on a Windows 2000 computer. By default, the frame type is set to Auto Detect, which will attempt to automatically choose a compatible frame type for the network.

FTP See *File Transfer Protocol.*

G

groups Security entities to which users can be assigned membership for the purpose of applying the broad set of group permissions to the user. By managing permissions for groups and assigning users to groups, rather than assigning permissions to users, administrators can more easily manage security.

Guest account A Windows 2000 user account created to provide a mechanism to allow users to access the computer even if they do not have a unique username and password. This account normally has very limited privileges on the computer. This account is disabled by default.

Guests group A Windows 2000 built-in group that has limited access to the computer. This group can access only specific areas. Most administrators do not allow Guest account access because it poses a potential security risk.

H

Host record Associates a host's name to its IP addresses. Also known as an address or A record.

Host route Provides a route to a single system; normally used when you want to direct traffic to remote networks through a particular machine.

HTTP See *Hypertext Transfer Protocol.*

Hypertext Markup Language (HTML) A textual data format that identifies sections of a document such as headers, lists, hypertext links, and so on. HTML is the data format used on the World Wide Web for the publication of Web pages.

Hypertext Transfer Protocol (HTTP) An Internet protocol that transfers HTML documents over the Internet and responds to context changes that happen when a user clicks a hyperlink.

I

Iasparse A utility (included in the Windows 2000 Resource Kit) that will digest an RRAS log, in IAS or database formats, and then produce a readable summary.

ICMP See *Internet Control Messaging Protocol.*

ICS See *Internet Connection Sharing.*

IEEE See *Institute of Electrical and Electronic Engineers.*

IIS See *Internet Information Services.*

Inbound port mapping Controls where requests from outside your network should be routed.

Information event An Event Viewer event that informs you that a specific action has occurred, such as when a system shuts down or starts.

inherited permissions Parent folder permissions that are applied to (or inherited by) files and subfolders of the parent folder. In Windows 2000 Professional, the default is for parent folder permissions to be applied to any files or subfolders in that folder.

initial user account The account that uses the name of the registered user and is created only if the computer is installed as a member of a workgroup (not into the Active Directory). By default, the initial user is a member of the Administrators group.

Institute of Electrical and Electronic Engineers (IEEE) A professional organization that defines standards related to networks, communications, and other areas.

Integrated Services Digital Network (ISDN) A direct, digital, dial-up connection that operates at 64KB per channel over regular twisted-pair cable. ISDN provides twice the data rate of the fastest modems per channel. Up to 24 channels can be multiplexed over two twisted pairs.

Interactive group A Windows 2000 special group that includes all the users who use the computer's resources locally.

interactive logon A logon when the user logs on from the computer where the user account is stored on the computer's local database. Also called a local logon.

interactive user A user who physically logs on to the computer where the user account resides (rather than over the network).

internal network number An identification for NetWare file servers. An internal network number is also used if the network is running File and Print Services for NetWare or is using IPX routing. This option must be configured to run the NWLink IPX/SPX/NetBIOS Compatible Transport protocol on a Windows 2000 computer. Normally, the internal network number should be left at its default setting.

internal routing Term that refers to the process of moving packets around on your own internetwork.

Internet Connection Sharing (ICS) A Windows 2000 feature that allows a small network to be connected to the Internet through a single connection. The computer that dials into the Internet provides network address translation, addressing, and name resolution services for all of the computers on the network. Through Internet connection sharing, the other computers on the network can access Internet resources and use Internet applications, such as Internet Explorer and Outlook Express.

Internet Control Messaging Protocol (ICMP) Protocol designed to pass control and status information between TCP/IP devices.

Internet Explorer A World Wide Web browser produced by Microsoft and included with Windows 9*x*, Windows NT 4, and now Windows 2000.

Internet Information Services (IIS) Software that serves Internet higher-level protocols like HTTP and FTP to clients using Web browsers. The IIS software that is installed on a Windows 2000 Server computer is a fully functional Web server and is designed to support heavy Internet usage.

Internet Protocol (IP) The network layer protocol upon which the Internet is based. IP provides a simple connectionless packet exchange. Other protocols such as TCP use IP to perform their connection-oriented (or guaranteed delivery) services.

Internet Service Provider (ISP) A company that provides dial-up connections to the Internet.

Internet Services Manager A Windows 2000 utility used to configure the protocols that are used by Internet Information Services (IIS) and Personal Web Services (PWS).

internetwork A logical collection of several physically connected networks made up of multiple network segments that are connected with some device, such as a router. Each network segment is assigned a network address. Network layer protocols build routing tables that are used to route packets through the network in the most efficient manner. The Internet is the best-known internetwork.

InterNIC The agency that is responsible for assigning IP addresses.

intranet A privately owned network based on the TCP/IP protocol suite.

IP See *Internet Protocol*.

IP address A four-byte number that uniquely identifies a computer on an IP internetwork. InterNIC assigns the first bytes of Internet IP addresses and administers them in hierarchies. Huge organizations like the government or top-level ISPs have class A addresses, large organizations and most ISPs have class B addresses, and small companies have class C addresses. In a class A address, InterNIC assigns the first byte, and the owning organization assigns the remaining three bytes. In a class B address, InterNIC or the higher-level ISP assigns the first two bytes, and the organization assigns the remaining two bytes. In a class C address, InterNIC or the higher-level ISP assigns the first three bytes, and the organization assigns the remaining byte. Organizations not attached to the Internet are free to assign IP addresses as they please.

IP datagram The structure that enables a client and server to transfer other types of network traffic. (The data is wrapped inside an IP datagram.)

ipconfig A command used to display the computer's IP configuration.

***ipconfig* tool** Command-line tool provided by Windows 2000 used to configure, and to see the configuration of, TCP/IP interfaces on your local machine.

IPSec See *IP Security Extensions*.

IPSec client   The computer that attempts to establish a connection to another machine. See also *IPSec server*.

IPSec Policy Agent   A service running on a Windows 2000 machine that connects to an Active Directory server and fetches the IPSec policy and then passes it to the IPSec code.

IPSec server   The target of an IPSec client's attempts.

IPSec tunnel   See *tunnel mode*.

IP Security Extensions (IPSec)   A process that makes it possible to transfer sensitive information to other hosts across the Internet without fear of compromise. IPSec provides authentication and encryption for transmitted data.

ISDN   See *Integrated Services Digital Network*.

ISP   See *Internet Service Provider*.

K

Kerberos   A standard mechanism for authenticating a user or system.

L

L2TP   See *Layer 2 Tunneling Protocol*.

layer   Part of the OSI model, for which there are defined roles during data communication.

Layer 2 Tunneling Protocol   A generic tunneling protocol that allows encapsulation of one network protocol's data within another protocol. Used in conjunction with IPSec to enable VPN access to Windows 2000 networks.

Lease   The offer of service provided by a DHCP server to a client upon successful negotiation.

LLC sublayer   See *Logical Link Control sublayer*.

LMHOSTS file   A file that consists of computer name–to–IP address mappings. Used in name resolution if the broadcast doesn't generate a useful answer.

Local Computer Policy   A Microsoft Management Console (MMC) snap-in used to implement account policies.

Local group   A group that is stored on the local computer's accounts database. These are the groups that administrators can add users to and manage directly on a Windows 2000 Professional computer.

Local Group Policy   A Microsoft Management Console (MMC) snap-in used to implement local group policies, which include computer configuration policies and user configuration policies.

local logon   A logon when the user logs on from the computer where the user account is stored on the computer's local database. Also called an interactive logon.

local policies   Policies that allow administrators to control what a user can do after logging on. Local policies include audit policies, security option policies, and user rights policies. These policies are set through Local Computer Policy.

local security   Security that governs a local or interactive user's ability to access locally stored files. Local security can be set through NTFS permissions.

local user account   A user account stored locally in the user accounts database of a computer that is running Windows 2000 Professional.

local user profile   A profile created the first time a user logs on, stored in the Documents and Settings folder. The default user profile folder's name matches the user's logon name. This folder contains a file called NTUSER.DAT and subfolders with directory links to the user's Desktop items.

Local Users and Groups   A utility that is used to create and manage local user and group accounts on Windows 2000 Professional computers and Windows 2000 member servers.

locale settings   Settings for regional items, including numbers, currency, time, date, and input locales.

Logical Link Control (LLC) sublayer   A sublayer in the data link layer of the Open Systems Interconnection (OSI) model. The LLC sublayer defines flow control.

logical port   A port that connects a device directly to the network. Logical ports are used with printers by installing a network card in the printer. Logical ports are also used to offer VPN services to remote callers.

M

MAC (media access control) address   The physical address that identifies a computer. Ethernet and Token Ring cards have the MAC address assigned through a chip on the network adapter card.

MAC sublayer   A user profile created by an administrator and saved with a special extension (.man) so that the user cannot modify the profile in any way. Mandatory profiles can be assigned to a single user or a group of users. See also *Media Access Control (MAC) sublayer*.

Machine certificates   Digital certificates issued to machines instead of people.

MADCAP   See *Multicast Address Dynamic Client Allocation Protocol*.

Media Access Control (MAC) sublayer   A sublayer in the data link layer of the Open Systems Interconnection (OSI) model. The MAC sublayer is used for physical addressing.

member server   A Windows 2000 server that has been installed as a non-domain controller. This allows the server to operate as a file, print, and application server without the overhead of account administration.

Metric   Cost information used to calculate the most efficient route for packets to take.

Microsoft CHAP (MS-CHAP)   A protocol that Microsoft created, compatible with CHAP, with capabilities of working with various members of the Windows family of operating systems.

Microsoft Management Console (MMC) The Windows 2000 console framework for management applications. The MMC provides a common environment for snap-ins.

Mirrored   A mirrored filter rule creates two separate rules with opposite effects. For example, an inbound filter rule allowing traffic from any address to TCP port 80 will, when mirrored, create a rule allowing traffic to any address on TCP port 80.

MMC   See *Microsoft Management Console*.

modem   Modulator/demodulator. A device used to create an analog signal suitable for transmission over telephone lines from a digital data stream. Modern modems also include a command set for negotiating connections and data rates with remote modems and for setting their default behavior.

MS-CHAP   See *Microsoft CHAP*.

Multicast Address Dynamic Client Allocation Protocol (MADCAP)   A protocol that issues leases for multicast addresses only.

Multicast routing   This occurs when one machine sends to an entire network.

Multicast scope   Range in which multicast addresses may be assigned.

Multihoming   Adding multiple IP addresses on a single physical network connection.

Multiprotocol routing   Allows a Windows 2000 computer to accept packets from other computers on its local network, sort out the correct destination for each, and route them accordingly.

N

Name renewal   Request sent by the client to notify the primary WINS server that it wants to continue using its registered name so that the server will reset the time-to-live (TTL).

Name resolution component   The component that acts as a DNS server for other machines on the local network; this works as a "proxy" for DNS.

Name server   A server that can give an authoritative answer to queries about its domain.

NAT   See *Network Address Translation*.

NAT editor   A component responsible for changing data in the protocols it supports.

NAT interface   Network interface that supports Network Address Translation services for LAN clients.

Native mode   Active Directory mode in which you can use remote access policies to apply and enforce consistent policies to all users in a site, domain, or organizational unit. It allows the use of universal groups and the nesting of global groups.

NBMA   See *non-broadcast multiple access*.

NDIS   See *Network Driver Interface Specification*.

NetBEUI   See *NetBIOS Extended User Interface*.

NetBIOS   See *Network Basic Input/Output System*.

NetBIOS Extended User Interface (NetBEUI)   A simple network layer transport protocol developed to support NetBIOS installations. NetBEUI is not routable, and so it is not appropriate for larger networks. NetBEUI is the fastest transport protocol available for Windows 2000.

NetWare   A popular network operating system developed by Novell in the early 1980s. NetWare is a cooperative, multitasking, highly optimized, dedicated-server network operating system that has client support for most major operating systems. Recent versions of NetWare include graphical client tools for management from client stations. At one time, NetWare accounted for more than 70 percent of the network operating system market.

network adapter   The hardware used to connect computers (or other devices) to the network. Network adapters function at the physical layer and the network layer of the Open System Interconnection (OSI) model.

Network Address Translation (NAT)   A service that allows multiple LAN clients to share a single public IP address and Internet connection by translating and modifying packets to reflect the correct addressing information.

Network Basic Input/Output System (NetBIOS)   A client/server IPC service developed by IBM in the early 1980s. NetBIOS presents a relatively primitive mechanism for communication in client/server applications, but its widespread acceptance and availability across most operating systems makes it a logical choice for simple network applications. Many of the network IPC mechanisms in Windows 2000 are implemented over NetBIOS.

Network binding   Links a protocol to an adapter so that the adapter can carry traffic using that protocol.

Network Driver Interface Specification (NDIS)   A driver interface developed by Microsoft to bind multiple protocols to one card or the same protocol to multiple cards.

Network group   A Windows 2000 special group that includes the users who access a computer's resources over a network connection.

network layer   The layer of the Open System Interconnection (OSI) model that creates a communication path between two computers via routed packets. Transport protocols implement both the network layer and the transport layer of the OSI stack. For example, IP is a network layer service.

Network naming   Three services (DNS, DHCP, and WINS) that provide network name and address information to applications that request it.

Non-broadcast multiple access   A single router that can talk to multiple peers without using a broadcast.

nslookup   A tool that allows one to query a DNS server to see what information it holds for a host record.

NWLINK IPX/SPX/NetBIOS Compatible Transport   Microsoft's implementation of the Novell IPX/SPX protocol stack.

O

Open Shortest Path First   A protocol designed for use on large or very large networks; it's more efficient than most routing protocols but harder to set up and administer. The routes are calculated so that the shortest path (e.g., the one with the lowest cost) is used first.

Open Systems Interconnection (OSI) model   A reference model for network component interoperability developed by the International Standards Organization (ISO) to promote cross-vendor compatibility of hardware and software network systems. The OSI model splits the process of networking into seven distinct services, or layers. Each layer uses the services of the layer below to provide its service to the layer above.

OSI model   See *Open Systems Interconnection model.*

OSPF   See *Open Shortest Path First.*

Owner-version mapping table   It keeps track of which WINS server owns (or holds) a particular registration, along with the highest version ID received from that server.

P

Packet   Small chunks of data that are constructed, modified, and disassembled by network protocols at various levels of the OSI model. Each packet consists of three parts: a header, data, and a trailer.

PAP   See *Password Authentication Protocol.*

Passthrough action   A security filter action, this "Permit" action tells the IPSec filter to take no action. It neither accepts nor rejects the connection based on security rules, meaning that it adds zero security. It allows traffic to pass without modification.

Password Authentication Protocol   The simplest and least secure authentication protocol; it transmits all authentication information in clear text, which makes it vulnerable to snooping.

password policies   Windows 2000 policies used to enforce security requirements on the computer. Password policies are set on a per-computer basis, and they cannot be configured for specific users. Password policies are set through account policies.

Payload   The data to be transmitted to the remote computer.

Peer filters   Filters that give you control over which neighboring routers your router will listen to; use the RRAS snap-in to configure peer filters and route filters.

Performance Logs and Alerts   A Windows 2000 utility used to log performance-related data and generate alerts based on performance-related data.

Periodic update mode   RIP update mode in which routing table updates are automatically sent to all other RIP routers on the internetwork. See also *auto-static update mode.*

permissions   Security constructs used to regulate access to resources by username or group affiliation. Permissions can be assigned by administrators to allow any level of access, such as read-only, read/write, or delete, by controlling the ability of users to initiate object services. Security is implemented by checking the user's security identifier (SID) against each object's access control list (ACL).

physical layer The first (bottom) layer of the Open Systems Interconnection (OSI) model, which represents the cables, connectors, and connection ports of a network. The physical layer contains the passive physical components required to create a network.

ping A command used to send an Internet Control Message Protocol (ICMP) echo request and echo reply to verify that a remote computer is available.

Pointer record (PTR) Associates an IP address to a host name.

Point-to-Point Protocol (PPP) Enables any two computers to establish a TCP/IP connection over a dial-up modem connection, direct serial cable connection, an infrared connection, or any other type of serial connection.

Point-to-Point Tunneling Protocol (PPTP) A Microsoft-specific VPN protocol that encapsulates IP, IPX, or NetBEUI information inside IP packets, hiding data from onlookers.

Poison-reverse processing An option that, when enabled, specifies that routes learned from a network are rebroadcast to the network with a metric of 16, a special value that tells other routers that the route is unreachable. This also prevents routing loops while still keeping the routing tables up to date.

Policies General controls that enhance the security of an operating environment. In Windows 2000, policies affect restrictions on password use and rights assignments, and determine which events will be recorded in the Security log.

Policy module The module that contains information about how the CA handles an incoming request.

PPP See *Point-to-Point Protocol*.

PPTP See *Point-to-Point Tunneling Protocol*.

presentation layer The layer of the Open Systems Interconnection (OSI) model that converts and translates (if necessary) information between the session layer and application layer.

Primary DNS server A primary DNS server is the "owner" of the zone files defined in its database. The primary DNS server has authority to make changes to the zone files it owns.

Primary DNS suffix Automatically appended upon DNS requests if the Append Primary And Connection Specific DNS Suffixes radio button is selected on the DNS tab of the Advanced TCP/IP Settings dialog box.

Private addresses These addresses cannot receive traffic from, or send traffic to, the Internet. In every other respect, though, they're just ordinary IP addresses. The idea behind private addresses is that you can use them to configure a network that's not connected to the Internet. If you wish to connect these machines to the Internet, you can use NAT to translate between public and private addresses.

Private key A key that must be held only by its owner and should never be publicly disclosed; also called a secret key.

protocol An established rule of communication adhered to by the parties operating under it. Protocols provide a context in which to interpret communicated information. Computer protocols are rules used by communicating devices and software services to format data in a way that all participants understand.

Protocol stack A group of protocols that implements an entire communication process. TCP/IP is an example of a protocol stack.

PTR See *Pointer record.*

Public key See *public-key encryption.*

Public-key encryption An encryption technique that uses private-public key pairs. Each actor has a public and a private key. Public keys are shared between the two parties and are used to sign and encrypt data. This encrypted data can be decrypted only by using a private key.

Pull partner Pulls data from another server.

Pull replication trigger A request for new data that works by sending a record number and asking for any records that are newer.

Push partner Pushes data to another server.

Push replication trigger Signals the receiving server to request the changed data.

Push/pull partnership A partnership in which one server pulls while the other pushes. Often used when you want to pair up servers in even groups across a high-speed LAN connection.

R

RADIUS See *Remote Authentication for Dial-In User Service.*

RAS See *Remote Access Service.*

Recovery agent Users that have recovery authority. These users can recover encrypted files when the original key material is unavailable. See also *recovery key.*

Recovery key A key that allows encrypted data to be unencrypted without the original key.

Registry A database of settings required and maintained by Windows 2000 and its components. The Registry contains all of the configuration information used by the computer. It is stored as a hierarchical structure and is made up of keys, subkeys, and value entries.

Remote access policies Like group policies, remote access policies allow the administrator to control whether users can get access or not. Unlike group policies, remote access policies are available only in native Windows 2000 domains.

Remote access profiles Allows an administrator to determine who can actually use dial-up capabilities. Remote access profiles work on individual accounts, whereas remote access policies work on groups of users.

Remote Access Service (RAS) A service that allows network connections to be established over a modem connection, an Integrated Services Digital Network (ISDN) connection, or a null-modem cable. The computer initiating the connection is called the RAS client; the answering computer is called the RAS server.

Remote Authentication for Dial-In User Service A common authentication scheme, used by (for example) ISPs using non-Microsoft systems.

Replication partners Two servers that replicate data back and forth.

Requests for Comments (RFCs) The set of standards defining the Internet protocols as determined by the Internet Engineering Task Force and available in the public domain on the Internet. RFCs define the functions and services provided by each of the many Internet protocols. Compliance with the RFCs guarantees cross-vendor compatibility.

Reservation An IP to MAC mapping that allows a DHCP server to always give the same IP address to a DHCP client.

Reserve lookup zone A database that helps computers translate IP addresses into DNS names.

Resolver DNS client computer that makes requests to a server; these requests ask the server to resolve a client DNS name into the corresponding IP address, or vice versa.

Resource records Contains information about some resource on the network. There are several types of resource records.

RFC See *Request For Comments*.

RIP See *Routing Information Protocol*.

Root certificate authority The top-level CA, which signs its own certificate, asserting that it is root.

Route filters Filters that allow you to pick and choose which networks you want to admit knowing and for which you want to accept announcements.

router A network layer device that moves packets between networks. Routers provide internetwork connectivity.

Routing and Remote Access Service (RRAS) Windows 2000 component that provides multiprotocol routing and dial-up access.

Routing Information Protocol An IP routing protocol that allows routers to interchange information about the presence and capabilities of other routers on the network. (See also *OSPF*).

Routing table Table of information maintained by an IP router. Each entry in the table contains a destination network ID, gateway address, and metric.

RRAS See *Routing and Remote Access Service*.

S

SA See *Security Association*.

SAP See *Service Access Points*.

Scope Contiguous range of addresses.

Secondary DNS server Pulls DNS information from the specified master server. Secondary DNS servers receive a read-only copy of zone files. The secondary DNS server can resolve queries from this read-only copy, but cannot make changes or updates.

Secret-key encryption An encryption technique that works with keys that are shared between two parties, but are unknown to an external party. The keys are exchanged via a secure channel. See also public-key encryption.

security The measures taken to secure a system against accidental or intentional loss, usually in the form of accountability procedures and use restriction, for example through NTFS permissions and share permissions.

Security Association (SA) Provides all the information needed for two computers to communicate securely. It contains a policy agreement that controls which algorithms and key lengths the two machines will use, plus the actual security keys used to securely exchange information.

Security identifier (SID) A unique code that identifies a specific user or group to the Windows 2000 security system. SIDs contain a complete set of permissions for that user or group.

Security log A log that tracks events that are related to Windows 2000 auditing. The Security log can be viewed through the Event Viewer utility.

Security method A pre-specified encryption algorithm with a negotiated key length and key lifetime.

security option policies Policies used to configure security for the computer. Security option policies apply to computers rather than to users or groups. These policies are set through Local Computer Policy.

Service Access Points (SAP) Provided by the LLC sublayer so that other computers can transfer information through this sublayer to the upper OSI layers.

Service record (SRV) Links the location of a service such as a domain controller with information about how to contact the service. It provides seven items of information: service name,

a transport protocol, the domain name for which the service is offered, the priority, the weight, port number on which the service is offered, and the DNS name of the server which offers the service.

session layer The layer of the Open Systems Interconnection (OSI) model dedicated to maintaining a bi-directional communication connection between two computers. The session layer uses the services of the transport layer to provide this service.

SID See *security identifier*.

Signing One of the two fundamental operations associated with public-key cryptography (the other is encryption). Signing proves the origin and authenticity of some piece of data.

Simple Mail Transfer Protocol (SMTP) An Internet protocol for transferring mail between Internet hosts. SMTP is often used to upload mail directly from the client to an intermediate host, but can only be used to receive mail by computers constantly connected to the Internet.

SMTP See *Simple Mail Transfer Protocol*.

snap-in An administrative tool developed by Microsoft or a third-party vendor that can be added to the Microsoft Management Console (MMC) in Windows 2000.

Special group A group used by the system, in which membership is automatic if certain criteria are met. Administrators cannot manage special groups.

Special Ports tab Lists the port mappings you have in effect; you can add, edit, and remove them using buttons at the bottom of the tab.

Split-horizon processing   A processing and loop detection option that disallows a RIP router from rebroadcasting to that network.

SRV   See *service record*.

Static route   A specification of where packets bound for certain networks should go.

Static routing   Doesn't make any attempt to discover other routers or systems on the networks.

subdomain   Branches of a network.

subnet mask   A number mathematically applied to IP addresses to determine which IP addresses are a part of the same subnetwork as the computer applying the subnet mask.

Success Audit event   An Event Viewer entry that indicates the occurrence of an event that has been audited for success, such as a successful logon.

Superscope   Allows you to group two or more scopes together even though they're actually separate.

System log   A log that tracks events that relate to the Windows 2000 operating system. The System log can be viewed through the Event Viewer utility.

System Monitor   A Windows 2000 utility used to monitor real-time system activity or view data from a log file.

system policies   Policies used to control what a user can do and the user's environment. System policies can be applied to all users or all computers, or to a specific user, group, or computer. System policies work by overwriting current settings in the Registry with the system policy settings. System policies are created through the System Policy Editor; they only apply to Windows NT, Windows 95, and Windows 98 machines.

T

TCP   See *Transmission Control Protocol/ Internet Protocol*.

TCP/IP   See *Transmission Control Protocol/ Internet Protocol*.

TCP/IP port   A logical port, used when a printer is attached to the network by installing a network card in the printer. Configuring a TCP/IP port requires the IP address of the network printer to connect to.

tracert   A tool used to map out the path that the packets are taking as they flow to a remote system.

Transmission Control Protocol (TCP)   A transport layer protocol that implements guaranteed packet delivery using the IP protocol.

Transmission Control Protocol/Internet Protocol (TCP/IP)   A suite of Internet protocols upon which the global Internet is based. TCP/IP is a general term that can refer either to the TCP and IP protocols used together or to the complete set of Internet protocols. TCP/IP is the default protocol for Windows 2000.

transport layer   The Open Systems Interconnection (OSI) model layer responsible for the guaranteed serial delivery of packets between two computers over an internetwork. TCP is the transport layer protocol in TCP/IP.

Transport mode   Another name for the end-to-end mode, in which IPSec is used to encrypt before data is sent and decrypted at the other end, while the data is protected during transport (obviously).

transport protocol   A service that delivers discreet packets of information between any two computers in a network. Higher-level, connection-oriented services are built on transport protocols.

Tunnel   A private, virtual circuit between a client and a server using the Internet as a transportation medium.

Tunnel endpoint   The systems at the end of a two-way IPSec tunnel.

Tunnel mode   The use of IPSec to secure traffic that's being passed over someone else's wire.

U

UDP   See *User Datagram Protocol.*

Unicast routing   One machine sends directly to one destination address.

Unicast scope   DHCP scope used to assign unicast (point-to-point) addresses. Compare with *MADCAP.*

User Datagram Protocol   A connectionless Internet transport protocol included in the TCP/IP protocol standard.

user profile   A profile that stores a user's Desktop configuration. A user profile can contain a user's Desktop arrangement, program items, personal program groups, network and printer connections, screen colors, mouse settings, and other personal preferences. Administrators can create mandatory profiles, which cannot be changed by the users, and roaming profiles, which users can access from any computer they log on to.

user rights policies   Policies that control the rights that users and groups have to accomplish network tasks. User rights policies are set through Local Computer Policy.

Users group   A Windows 2000 built-in group that includes end users who should have very limited system access. After a clean installation of Windows 2000 Professional, the default settings for this group prohibit users from compromising the operating system or program files. By default, all users who have been created on the computer, except Guest, are members of the Users group.

V

Version iD   An internal record used to identify which server in a replication partnership has the more recent version of a registration.

virtual private network (VPN)   A private network that uses links across private or public networks (such as the Internet). When data is sent over the remote link, it is encapsulated, encrypted, and requires authentication services.

VPN   See *virtual private network.*

W

Warning event   An Event Viewer event that indicates that you should be concerned with the event. The event may not be critical in nature, but it is significant and may be indicative of future errors.

Windows Internet Name Service (WINS)   A network service for Microsoft networks that provides Windows computers with Internet numbers for specified NetBIOS computer names, facilitating browsing and intercommunication over TCP/IP networks.

WINS   See *Windows Internet Name Service*.

WINS name registration   A request sent by the client to the designated WINS server to register its name and IP address.

WINS name release   A request sent by the client to relinquish ownership of its name.

WINS server   The server that runs WINS and is used to resolve NetBIOS names to IP addresses.

Z

Zone transfer   Copies information from a primary DNS server to a secondary DNS server.

Zones   Subtree of the DNS database that is considered a single unit.

Index

Note to the Reader: Page numbers in **bold** indicate the principal discussion of a topic or the definition of a term. Page numbers in *italic* indicate illustrations.

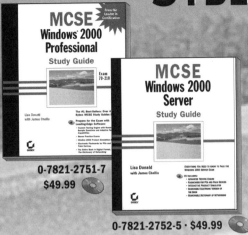

MCSE: Windows 2000 Network Infrastructure Administration Study Guide

Exam 70-216: Objectives

SYBEX